IQ and Human Intelligence

IQ and Human Intelligence

N. J. Mackintosh

Department of Experimental Psychology,
University of Cambridge

OXFORD NEW YORK TOKYO
OXFORD UNIVERSITY PRESS
1998

Oxford University Press, Great Clarendon Street, Oxford OX2 6DP

Oxford New York

Athens Auckland Bangkok Bogota Bombay Buenos Aires Calcutta
Cape Town Chennai Dar es Salaam Delhi Florence Hong Kong Istanbul
Karachi Kuala Lumpur Madrid Melbourne Mexico City Mumbai
Nairobi Paris São Paolo Singapore Taipei Tokyo Toronto Warsaw

and associated companies in
Berlin Ibadan

Oxford is a trade mark of Oxford University Press

Published in the United States
by Oxford University Press, Inc., New York

A catalogue record for this book is available from the British Library

Library of Congress Cataloging in Publication Data
Mackintosh, N. J. (Nicholas John), 1935–
IQ and human intelligence/N. J. Mackintosh.
Includes bibliographical references and index.
1. Intellect. 2. Intelligence levels. 3. Intelligence tests.
I. Title.
BF431.M358   1998
153.9–dc21   98-18010   CIP

ISBN 0 19 852368 8 (Hbk)
0 19 852367 X (Pbk)

Typeset by Joshua Associates Ltd., Oxford
Printed in Great Britain by
Redwood Books Ltd., Trowbridge, Wilts

Preface

I am not the first animal learning theorist to write a book about human intelligence and IQ testing. Nor, in all probability, will I be the last. I do not believe that such trespassing across academic boundaries needs apology or defence: perhaps psychology would be the better if we all attempted to understand, and occasionally write about, topics that lay outside our own narrow specialism. Nor shall I bore the reader with an account of my motives in doing so—except to say that I have not written this book out of a burning desire to advance any political or social thesis. Of course, as the reader will discover, I have a number of strongly held views on the topics covered in this book, and I have not attempted to hide them. It is sometimes thought that a textbook should strive to be balanced and impartial, and that impartiality requires the writer to present every possible side to every question, without presuming to judge their merits. Although this book is intended to serve as a suitable text for advanced undergraduates or graduates, I have not followed this path. Here, indeed, is my first strongly held conviction: such a policy guarantees boring and bland books, which usually insult their readers' intelligence. The history of IQ testing has been controversial, generating a large number of acrimonious disputes. I can see no point in simply presenting all sides of all these disputes, without attempting to judge the relative merits of different positions. Good textbooks should pass judgement—having presented enough evidence to allow readers to disagree with that judgement if their reading of the evidence goes another way.

I should, perhaps, admit at the outset to a second conviction that has grown stronger during the course of writing this book. The study of individual differences in intelligence seems to me an interesting and important branch of psychology, and there is much to admire in the work of numerous people who have done research on this question. I hope that interest and admiration will be apparent. But at the same time, I believe that much arrant nonsense has been written about the measurement of human intelligence, and not only about some of the political and social implications thought to follow from such measurement. Once again, I have not attempted to hide my views. Some readers may therefore find some of my judgements unduly harsh. My hope is that I may challenge them into thinking harder about some of their own preconceptions—even if they conclude that they are right and I am wrong.

Finally, it is a pleasure to acknowledge the help I have been fortunate enough to receive during the course of writing this book. Robert Sternberg read an earlier draft of some half-dozen chapters. His kind remarks provided much-needed encouragement for me to complete a project that had already dragged on too long. His more critical comments caused the project to drag on even longer by persuading me that much revision was still needed. I have no doubt that the result is a much better, although still sadly imperfect book, and I am very grateful for his advice—even if I did not *always* take it. Duncan Mackintosh produced most of the figures in a very professional manner, and Ian Cannell the remainder. My thanks to both of them. Sheila Bennett and Felicity Fildes provided invaluable assistance with the references, and Felicity Fildes heroically typed and retyped what must have seemed a never-ending series of revisions produced by a dithering author unable to make up his mind. Without her loyal help, the book would never have been completed. Last, but in this case very far from least, I am truly grateful to my wife for her forbearance.

Cambridge   N.J.M.
December 1997

Contents

Contents

1 *The early development and uses of IQ tests*

Introduction

Textbooks on the psychology of perception or memory, or on developmental or social psychology, usually imply that the facts that they describe and the theories that explain those facts are well-nigh universal. We know, of course, that there are exceptions to any general psychological laws: some people are born colour blind; others lose their memory; dyslexic children experience specific difficulties in learning to read; different people react differently to social pressures. Any good textbook will take due note of these differences, if only because exceptions often provide unique insight into the normal case. But the emphasis remains firmly on that normal case, on what is common to all of us, not on what distinguishes one person from another.

For better or worse, the psychology of intelligence is not quite like that. For much of its history, the focus has been on differences between people, on what it means for one person to be more intelligent than another, and on how such differences might have arisen. Until the recent development of cognitive psychology, indeed, this focus on individual differences quite overshadowed any attempt to study the general nature of human intelligence, what people share in common rather than what sets them apart. One reason, no doubt, is that this is a central part of the meaning of the word. The *Oxford English dictionary* gives as the second meaning of 'intelligence':

> Understanding as a quality admitting of degree; *spec.* superior understanding; quickness of mental apprehension, sagacity.

and similarly of 'intelligent':

> Having a high degree or full measure of understanding; quick to understand; knowing, sensible, sagacious.

Our everyday use of these and related terms is firmly comparative and evaluative. When we exclaim: 'What a clever idea', or 'That was a stupid thing to do', we are contrasting this idea or that action with others. And when we say that Mary is a clever girl or that Johnny is a stupid boy, we are comparing them, one favourably and the other not, with their fellows. We believe that children and adults vary in their intelligence, even if we might be hard pressed to specify precisely what we really mean when we say this, let alone how we might set about measuring these supposed differences in intelligence. That became the task of science.

It might seem that the proper place for science to start is by providing a proper, scientific definition of intelligence. Is it not a common practice for textbooks of learning, memory, attention, or whatever, to begin with a definition of these terms? Should not a textbook on intelligence begin in the same way? The short answer is, no. 'What is intelligence?' may seem a simple question, admitting of a straightforward answer. It is not, and does not.

For a start, to pose the question in this form may imply that there is a single process or faculty, which we can label 'intelligence' and distinguish from other human faculties, such as learning, memory, etc. But is there? We use terms such as intelligent, unintelligent, clever, or stupid, to describe some of the things that people, or sometimes other animals or even machines, can do. For example: the pianist played that piece with great insight and intelligence; the footballer committed a really stupid foul; computers are not really intelligent, they are just programmed to follow instructions; what a clever baby she was to find the hidden toy; it was stupid of me to say that to John in front of Mary; chimpanzees are more intelligent than monkeys, because they can use tactical deception to manipulate other members of their group.

We have no difficulty understanding any of these statements. But is it really plausible to suppose that they are all referring to a single process or faculty (or lack thereof)? Is the intelligence displayed by a performance of a piece of music the same as the intelligence so obviously lacking in a tactless remark made in casual conversation? Is the baby who finds the hidden toy exercising the same faculty as the chimpanzee who pretends not to notice the hidden food? Are computers and some football players unintelligent in the same way? The answer to all these questions might be yes; indeed some psychologists seem to have thought so, for they have insisted that 'intelligence' is a single, very general process entering into all that we do or say. But even if this turns out to be true, it is surely not true by definition. We shall discover whether this is a plausible idea only by further enquiry, and we should wait upon that enquiry before making dogmatic pronouncements.

The point is this. We have, no doubt, a rough and ready idea of what we mean by 'intelligence' and other cognate terms. The objective of scientific enquiry is to advance beyond this primitive, common-sense understanding (what is often termed 'folk psychology') to a more securely grounded set of scientific theories, based on empirical evidence and capable of ordering the world in possibly new and illuminating ways. We shall not achieve this goal by insisting on a rigorous, precise definition of terms at the outset. New definitions are the end product of scientific enquiry, not its starting point. To see this, consider some of the definitions offered by various psychologists. Intelligence has been described variously as:

Box 1.1 Is intelligence a good thing? The case of Odysseus

Homer's *Iliad* and *Odyssey*, the earliest examples of European literature, prove that the concept of intelligence has been around for a long time. Odysseus, the hero of the *Odyssey*, although playing only a small role in the *Iliad*, is quite different from the other heroes: he is portrayed as intelligent. The contest between Odysseus and Ajax at the funeral games at the close of the *Iliad* is a classic contest between brains and brawn. And the more conventional heroes, such as Ajax and Achilles, do not really approve of someone who is so willing to resort to stratagem to gain his ends. But it was Odysseus's stratagem of the Trojan horse that finally won the war for the Greeks. In the *Odyssey*, he fools the Cyclops, Polyphemos, by a trick that only an intellectually challenged giant would fall for. He tells Polyphemos that his name is Nobody. When, later, the blinded Polyphemos calls out for help to his fellow Cyclopes, and they ask him who is troubling him, he shouts back 'Nobody'. The other Cyclopes retort that if nobody is troubling him, his trouble must come from the gods and there is nothing he can do but pray.

In addition to the standard epithets applied to all the heroes—handsome, lordly, god-like, and so on—Homer describes Odysseus as resourceful, clever, wily-minded, full of wiles, of great intelligence, quick-witted, and so on. Although there are hints that Odysseus is occasionally a bit too devious and, in the *Iliad* at least, perhaps not as manly as some of the other heroes, it is hard to believe that Homer does not admire him, and prefer his resourcefulness and subtlety to some of the more conventional heroic virtues. But later Greek writers, followed by Virgil in the *Aeneid*, portrayed Odysseus with notably less sympathy. Rather than subtle, resourceful, and intelligent, he is described as shifty, unscrupulous, smooth speaking, unprincipled, cowardly, and a typical, despicable politician (see Stanford and Luce, 1974).

Of several morals one might draw from this tale, one is worth bearing in mind throughout this book: intelligence is not synonymous with virtue. Ranking people by their IQ score is not the same as awarding them badges for varying degrees of merit. Some people are too clever by half, or too clever for their own, or anyone else's, good. Honesty and integrity are more valuable, and may be more effective, than unprincipled sophistry. These banal platitudes really ought not to need saying, but much writing about IQ tests, especially that from IQ testers themselves, has often appeared to imply that IQ and general worth are one and the same thing. They are not.

---

general mental efficiency (Burt, 1949); innate general cognitive ability (Burt, 1955);

the aggregate or global capacity of the individual to act purposefully, to think rationally, and to deal effectively with his environment (Wechsler, 1944);

a quintessentially high-level skill at the summit of a hierarchy of intellectual skills (Butcher, 1968);

a general reasoning capacity useful in problem-solving tasks of all kinds (Kline, 1991);

the mental capacity of emitting contextually appropriate behavior at those regions in the experiential continuum that involve response to novelty or automatization of information processing as a function of metacomponents, performance components, and knowledge-acquisition components (Sternberg, 1985).

We may understand these definitions—although perhaps not all. We may agree with some, or disagree with others. But are they really of any great practical value? Are they necessary to direct the course of scientific enquiry? Are they even helpful? The answer to all these questions is: probably not. All we need to start our enquiry is a rough and ready understanding of the area we wish to study—preferably sufficient to allow us to draw some tentative boundaries round it, so that our enquiry is confined, at least in the first instance, to some topics to the exclusion of others. It is not, in fact, very difficult to achieve some measure of consensus here. Sternberg *et al.* (1981) asked two groups of people, one consisting of psychologists whose main research was in the area of human intelligence, the other non-psychologists, to say how characteristic of an intelligent person certain courses of action or patterns of behaviour were. The replies of the two groups were not identical, but they were remarkably similar, and converged on three important aspects of intelligence: problem-solving ability, verbal intelligence, and practical intelligence or social competence.

It is necessary to acknowledge the limitations of this sort of consensus, and the tentative nature of any initial decisions that might flow from it. Further enquiry may suggest, for example, that we have drawn some boundaries in the wrong place. And different investigators may still disagree sharply with one another about some of these initial decisions. Thus in contrast to those psychologists, such as Spearman (1927), who have argued for the unitary nature of a single process of general intelligence, others (e.g. Thurstone, 1938) have insisted that there is a multiplicity of different intelligences. While some have stressed abstract reasoning ability as the core of human intelligence, others, such as Gardner (1993), wish to talk in addition about musical intelligence, social or personal intelligence, and bodily, kinaesthetic intelligence.

Some more or less arbitrary decisions must probably be taken at the outset. Thus I shall not, in this book, have much to say about social or musical intelligence, and nothing at all about bodily intelligence. My reasons for this omission will certainly not convince everyone—and may turn out to be wrong-headed. For what it is worth, however, one can argue that what Gardner terms musical intelligence is more normally described as musical ability, talent, or creativity. Of course, people differ widely in musical talent, and we may eventually find that the study of such talent is illuminated by, and itself helps to illuminate, our understanding of other aspects of human intelligence. This, too, will depend on the outcome of our enquiry. Be this as it may, I shall start, conservatively, by following historical tradition, and confine myself in the first instance to those aspects of human intelligence that first became the object of scientific enquiry.

From the outset, the main goal of the scientific study of human intelligence was measurement rather than abstract theory construction. Operationalism implied that only if we could measure it, could we claim to have any understanding of intelligence, and measurement meant measuring differences between people. The result was the development of intelligence or IQ tests—heralded by some as one of psychology's proudest achievements (Herrnstein, 1973), denounced by others as instruments of oppression against the poor (Kamin, 1974). What cannot be disputed is that, historically at least, IQ tests have represented psychology's main contribution to the study of human intelligence, and in particular to the study of individual differences in intelligence.

As a result of the way in which they developed, which we shall shortly describe, psychologists found themselves with a variety of test batteries, described as measures of intelligence or IQ tests, without knowing precisely what it was that these tests were measuring. To this day, critics of the tests have used this as a stick to beat them with (e.g. Block and Dworkin, 1976; Richardson, 1991). But for reasons implied by what has been said so far, the criticism is largely misplaced. Eventually, of course, the scientific measurement of intelligence must be based on an adequate scientific theory of human intelligence, and such a theory will bring in its train a number of new definitions. But at the outset of our enquiry, the important questions to ask are not whether we know what intelligence really is, or whether IQ tests succeed in measuring it. On the contrary:

> The important point is not whether what we measure can appropriately be labelled 'intelligence', but whether we have discovered something worth measuring. (Miles, 1957, p. 159)

In this context, of course, something worth measuring must be something to do with the concept of intelligence as we normally understand it, but we do not need to know precisely what in advance. That is something we shall discover by further investigation. And, as we shall see, although IQ tests are undoubtedly far from perfect and were originally constructed on the basis of a mixture of common sense and relatively crude psychological theory (critically aided by trial and error), these much reviled instruments do seem to satisfy at least some of the criteria we should expect to see satisfied by any adequate measure of anything we should want to call intelligence. For example:

1. A person's score on an IQ test does not vary capriciously from day to day with changes in mood, etc. Indeed, after the age of 5 or 6, people's IQ scores remain *relatively* stable for much of the rest of their life. This is at least consistent with the notion of intelligence as a relatively enduring trait—rather than something that fluctuates from day to day or even year to year.

2. At least some IQ tests require one to solve precisely the sort of abstract reasoning problems that seem central to many conceptions of the nature of intelligence. (In another survey of expert opinion, Snyderman and Rothman (1988) found that 'abstract thinking or reasoning' was named by 99 per cent of their respondents as an important element of intelligence.)

3. Those who believe that intelligence can be manifest in a wide variety of ways can take comfort from the fact that other IQ tests are, on the face of it, quite different; some, for example, asking for definitions of the meanings of words, phrases or proverbs, others requiring one to solve problems of mental arithmetic, detect hidden patterns, or perform certain routine tasks rapidly and accurately. In spite of the diversity of content, however,

all tests *tend* to agree with one another, in the sense that people who do well at one will tend to do well on others, and those who do poorly on one will tend to do poorly on others. This is consistent with the notion that they are all measuring, if not a single process of 'general intelligence', at least a number of more or less closely related processes.

4. Finally, IQ tests succeed in predicting some other aspects of human behaviour in a way that one would expect of a measure of intelligence. Children with high test scores, for example, tend to do better at school than those with lower test scores. Up to university level, indeed, educational attainment is moderately well predicted by IQ.

It should go without saying that this very brief and glib account of some of the apparent virtues of IQ tests will need to be expanded, and seriously qualified, in later chapters. It was intended simply to illustrate the argument that a start can be made to the task of trying to measure intelligence without getting bogged down in interminable wrangling about definitions. It was not intended as a definitive summary, still less to imply that we can be confident that IQ tests are perfect measures of human intelligence. They are emphatically not perfect. Some of the most widely used test batteries consist of a pretty motley assortment of tests chosen for no good theoretical reason. All IQ tests quite certainly fail to capture some important aspects of human intelligence. Neither of these assertions should come as a surprise, nor should they be a cause for despair. Trial and error combined with advances in theoretical understanding should serve to improve imperfect test batteries. If we can understand what IQ tests fail to measure, as well as what they do measure, our map of human intelligence and its variation will surely be more nearly complete.

The remainder of this chapter, then, will describe the way in which IQ tests first developed, because an understanding of that development is necessary for a proper understanding of the tests; and will conclude with a brief digression on some of the uses to which tests were first put. Chapter 2 describes the later development of modern IQ tests, discusses the theories of intelligence underlying that development, and reviews evidence of the reliability and validity of the tests—that is to say how well they satisfy some of the criteria listed above. Given that the tests can lay at least some claim to measuring some of the variation in intelligence we see around us, it becomes important to understand how that variation arises (Chapter 3), how it is influenced by the environment (Chapter 4), and how far different groups in modern societies may differ in average IQ (Chapter 5).

But it is then important to turn seriously to the question of trying to understand what the tests do measure, and how far they succeed in measuring important aspects of human intelligence (Chapters 6–10). Traditionally, the psychometricians who developed IQ tests sought to answer these questions by using the statistical technique of factor analysis to explore the relationship between different types of test, in the belief that this would shed light on the structure of intelligence (Chapter 6). But factor analysis alone cannot answer questions about the nature of the psychological processes underlying performance on IQ tests, and psychometricians have made less progress than they might in understanding these processes—as will become apparent in Chapter 7. One reason for this is that they have resolutely paid little or no attention to the data and theories of modern cognitive psychology—just as cognitive psychologists have paid scant regard to the task of understanding individual differences in intelligence. Chapters 8 and 9 recount some of the preliminary attempts now being made to rectify this sorry state of affairs.

Finally, Chapter 10 addresses the question whether IQ tests measure differences in 'intelligence' outside the psychological laboratory. How far do they predict how intelligently people behave in the real world, how well they succeed at solving life's problems, how eminent they become? Is the ability to solve particular practical problems the result of general intelligence or of local expertise, which is simply the product of prolonged practice? Are there other cognitive abilities, besides those measured by IQ tests, that are equally important determinants of everyday skills and expertise? Psychometricians have usually wanted to make large claims for their tests, and have vigorously dismissed such a suggestion. But that is largely because they have been concerned to extol the practical value of their tests—by proving that they measure everything of importance. From a *psychologist's* point of view, however, IQ tests would have been shown to measure 'something worth measuring' (in Miles's phrase) if they had identified a circumscribed set of psychological processes and operations that enter into at least some aspects of intelligent behaviour. If there are other, independent, cognitive abilities, not measured by IQ tests, so be it.

Let us begin, then, at the beginning, with some history.

The origins of IQ testing

Galton

The two most important figures in the early history of IQ testing are the Englishman, Francis Galton, and the Frenchman, Alfred Binet. Galton was a cousin of Charles Darwin, and the origins of some of his ideas on intelligence can be found in Darwin's theory of evolution by natural selection. Two of the basic premises of that theory are that there is variation among members of any species, and that this variation is inherited, differences between parents in one generation being transmitted to their offspring in the next. If we take these ideas seriously, they suggest the possibility that there may be inherited differences among people in such an important characteristic as mental ability or intelligence. In *Hereditary genius* (1869), Galton set out to prove this conclusion. The book greatly impressed Darwin himself, who wrote:

I do not think I have ever in my life read anything more interesting and original . . . You have made a convert of an opponent . . . for I have always maintained that, excepting fools, men do not differ in intellect, only in zeal and hard work. (Galton, 1908, p. 290)

Galton's first task was to establish that people do differ in intellect. He did this partly by assertion:

I have no patience with the hypothesis . . . that babies are born pretty much alike, and that the sole agencies in creating differences between boy and boy, and man and man, are steady application and moral effort. It is in the most unqualified manner that I object to pretensions of natural equality. The experiences of the nursery, the school, the University, and of professional careers, are a chain of proofs to the contrary. (Galton, 1869, p. 12)

He argued that the results of public examinations confirmed this conclusion. Even among the highly selected undergraduates of Cambridge University, for example, there was an enormous range in the number of marks awarded in the honour examinations in mathematics, from less than 250 to over 7500 in one particular two-year period. As a first step towards showing that this wide range of marks arose from variations in natural ability, he established that these scores (like other physical measurements) were normally distributed, the majority of candidates obtaining scores close to the average, with a regular and predictable decline in the proportion obtaining scores further away from the average.

The main part of *Hereditary genius*, however, was devoted to establishing the hereditary basis of these differences in ability. His argument was simple: eminence runs in families. For example, of the 286 judges appointed to the English bench between 1660 and 1865, 109 had one or more relatives who were also eminent. This proportion was even higher (24 out of 30) among those who were appointed Lord Chancellor. Moreover, close relatives were much more likely to be eminent than more distant relatives: 36 per cent of the sons of these judges were eminent, but only 9.5 per cent of their grandsons and 1.5 per cent of their great-grandsons. Similar analyses of distinguished statesmen, military commanders, and men of science, as well as of poets, painters, and musicians, gave similar results. There were, of course, important differences, and Galton did not suppose that success in all walks of life depended solely on a single faculty of general intelligence. For example, successful military commanders, he noted, were often very small men. Rather than the now popular suggestion that explains this by reference to the inferiority complex that small stature supposedly confers, Galton proposed a rather simpler notion, that a necessary precondition for promotion to supreme command is that one should survive numerous battles:

There is a principle of natural selection in an enemy's bullets which bears more heavily against large than against small men. Large men are more likely to be hit. I calculate that the chance of a man being accidentally shot is as the square root of the product of his height multiplied into his weight. (Galton, 1869, p. 136)

Galton was fully aware of the obvious objection to his conclusion that genius or outstanding ability is inherited. If the son of a successful judge is himself successful, this might be only because 'he was promoted by jobbery, and jobbed when he was promoted; he inherited family influence, not natural intellectual gifts' (Galton, 1869, p. 64). The test of this proposition was to find 'two large classes of men, with equal social advantages, in one of which they have high hereditary gifts, while in the other they have not' (Galton, 1869, p. 37). His ingenious idea was to compare the sons of eminent men with the adopted sons (often nephews) of popes and other dignitaries of the Catholic Church. Without providing much hard evidence, and acknowledging that he had 'not worked up the kinships of the Italians with any especial care', he concluded that these adopted sons were much less likely to achieve eminence than were the natural sons of other eminent men: 'The social helps are the same, but hereditary gifts are wanting' (Galton, 1869, p. 38).

The relative importance of nature and nurture (the phrase was his) continued to preoccupy Galton in his later writings. In *Inquiries into human faculty and its development* (1883), he discussed the similarities and differences between twins. He knew that it was important to distinguish between identical (monozygotic or MZ) and fraternal (dizygotic or DZ) twins, although he did not use modern terminology and lacked modern techniques for determining zygosity.

> The word 'twins' is a vague expression, which covers two very dissimilar events—the one corresponding to the progeny of animals that usually bear more than one at a birth, each of the progeny devolved from a separate ovum, while the other event is due to the development of two germinal spots in the same ovum . . . The consequences of this is that I find a curious discontinuity in my results. (Galton, 1883, p. 156)

He collected from correspondents numerous examples of close similarities between the latter group of twins, who had looked and behaved alike from birth and, equally important, of differences between the former group. Identical twins seemed to be astonishingly alike not only in physical appearance but also in character, temperament, tastes and dispositions—and even in their associations of ideas. Where differences were found, they were usually said to have arisen when one of the twins suffered a serious illness or accident, which permanently altered their life. Galton acknowledged that identical twins had experienced similar nurture, and this might well explain their similarities. Here was the importance of the differences between fraternal twins (such as Esau and Jacob). He cites one correspondent:

> They have had *exactly the same nurture* from their birth up to the present time; they are both perfectly healthy and strong, yet they are otherwise as dissimilar as two boys could be, physically, mentally, and in their emotional nature. (Galton, 1883, p. 170)

Galton was not content to rely on correspondents for anecdotal evidence of this nature. He wanted to *measure* differences in mental ability. The culmination of his endeavours was the Anthropometric Laboratory, set up at the International Health Exhibition in London in 1884, where for a fee of 3d. visitors could undertake tests of their

Keenness of Sight and of Hearing; Colour Sense; Judgement of Eye; Breathing Power; Reaction Time; Strength of Pull and of Squeeze; Force of Blow; Span of Arms; Height, both standing and sitting; and Weight. (Galton, 1908, p. 245)

The basis of most of these tests had been laid in the *Inquiries into human faculty*, where Galton argued why they (or at least some of them) should be regarded as measures of intelligence.

The only information that reaches us concerning outward events appears to pass through the avenue of our senses; and the more perceptive the senses are of difference, the larger is the field upon which our judgement and intelligence can act . . . The discriminative faculty of idiots is curiously low; they hardly distinguish between heat and cold, and their sense of pain is so obtuse that some of the more idiotic seem hardly to know what it is . . . During a visit to Earlswood Asylum I saw . . . a boy with the scar of a severe wound on his wrist; the story being that he had first burned himself slightly by accident, and, liking the keenness of the new sensation, he took the next opportunity of repeating the experience, but, idiot-like, he overdid it. (Galton, 1883, p. 19)

It is easy to disparage many of Galton's ideas. His arguments for the relative importance of nature over nurture would convince few environmentalists today. It is even easier to object to the evidence of insensitivity and prejudice in his writings. He had no doubts about the intellectual inferiority of savages, and most readers will already have detected a certain element of male chauvinism even from the few extracts I have quoted. They would not be mistaken. Galton had no doubt of the general intellectual inferiority of women, and one reason he advanced for his belief that fineness of sensory discrimination was a mark of intelligence would convince only the most confident of male chauvinists today:

At first, owing to my confusing the quality of which I am speaking with that of nervous irritability, I fancied that women of delicate nerves . . . would have acute powers of discrimination. But this I found not to be the case . . . I found as a rule that men have more delicate powers of discrimination than women, and the business experience of life seems to confirm this view. The tuners of pianofortes are men, and so I understand are the tasters of tea and wine, the sorters of wool, and the like. These latter occupations are well salaried, because it is of the first moment to the merchant that he should be rightly advised on the real value of what he is about to purchase or to sell. If the sensitivity of women were superior to that of men, the self-interest of merchants would lead to their being always employed. (Galton, 1883, p. 20)

Finally, as we shall see, the measures of intellectual ability which Galton proposed were soon discredited. But the list of his achievements remains remarkable, and it is a mark of his stature that, for better or worse, they have continued to influence IQ testing to this day.

Cattell

Galton's idea that intellectual ability could be assessed by measures of sensory acuity, reaction time, and the like was taken up by James McKeen Cattell (not to be confused with a more modern psychometrician, Raymond Cattell, whom we shall meet in due course). Although American, Cattell had studied in Wundt's laboratory in Leipzig, and spent some time in Cambridge, before returning to the USA. In 1890, he published a provisional list of 10 'mental tests' (the phrase was his), designed to measure individual differences in fundamental mental processes. The tests included measures of two-point tactile threshold, just noticeable difference for weights, judgement of temporal intervals, reaction time, and letter span.

It is not at all obvious that this heterogeneous collection of tests could provide any measure of anything we should want to call intelligence. It seems more likely that they were chosen simply because the techniques required were already available. These were the standard experimental paradigms of nineteenth-century experimental psychology, and whatever it was that they were measuring, at least they were measuring it accurately. But as Galton noted in a comment on Cattell's article:

> One of the most important objects of measurement . . . is to obtain a general knowledge of the capacities of a man by sinking shafts, as it were, at a few critical points. In order to ascertain the best points for the purpose, the sets of measures should be compared with an independent estimate of the man's powers. We may thus learn which of the measures are the most instructive. (Cattell, 1890, p. 380)

The need for some independent validation seems obvious enough now, but it took another 10 years or so before anyone acted upon it. When they did, it signalled the end of this approach. Wissler (1901), employing the new technique of correlation perfected by Karl Pearson from Galton's original ideas, compared the scores obtained by undergraduates at Columbia University on Cattell's tests with their college grades. His first finding was that there was essentially no correlation between any of Cattell's mental tests: in other words, a student good at one was not necessarily good at any of the others. The implication was that if one of the tests was actually measuring intelligence, none of the others could be. However, Wissler's second finding was even worse, for it implied that none of the tests was measuring intelligence: although a student's grades on one course tended to correlate quite well with his grades on others, none of them correlated with his scores on Cattell's tests. The implication was that college grades and Cattell's tests could not *both* be measuring intellectual ability. The prejudices of the university teacher outweighed those of the research psychologist. The generally accepted conclusion was that Cattell's mental tests, whatever else they might be measuring, did not succeed in measuring intelligence.

Both Galton and Cattell based their choice of test on psychological theory, Galton on the associationism of classical British empiricist philosophy, Cattell on the new experimental psychology pioneered in Wundt's laboratory. Whatever one may think of the particular theories they espoused, the reliance on theory does have something to commend it. If we are trying to devise a test that will measure a particular trait or characteristic, it may help if we have a psychological theory of the defining features of such a trait, so that our test will map onto them. The problem is that we must have some way of verifying the success of our enterprise; if we are trying to devise a test of intelligence, we must have some independent criterion of intelligence with which our test can agree. Wissler's results seemed to show that Cattell's mental tests failed on this score. No doubt there are many attributes of the successful university student, but intelligence is surely one of them. If Cattell's tests failed to predict university students' grades, it seemed unlikely that they were succeeding in measuring intelligence.

Binet

It is one thing to say that any test of intelligence must agree with some independent criterion of intelligence. It is another thing to find a suitable criterion. After all, if we already knew who was intelligent and who was not, why should we need a new test to prove it? One of Alfred Binet's major achievements was that he showed a way out of this apparent dilemma. Binet had been charged, by the French Ministry of Public Instruction, with the task of finding a quick and reliable method of identifying any child who 'because of the state of his intelligence, was unable to profit, in a normal manner, from the instruction given in ordinary schools' (Binet and Simon, 1905a, p. 163; here and elsewhere, my translation). Such children were to be assigned to special classes (the equivalent of what were later to be called in Britain ESN classes—for the educationally sub-normal). The intention was certainly benign, but as Binet and Simon (1905a, p. 164) noted: 'It will never be a good sign to have been a member of a special school. At the least, we must ensure that those who do not merit it, are spared the record.'

Rather than base his tests on philosophical theory or esoteric laboratory experiments, Binet took a more pragmatic approach. To say that he had no theory of intelligence would be misleading. But that theory owed more to common sense than to the experimental psychology of his day. He spent some time discussing what he meant by the term 'intelligence', but his discussions were more inclined to stress what intelligence was not rather than what it was. This is not necessarily a bad idea: an important part of specifying the nature of a somewhat indeterminate concept, as I have already argued, is to limit its boundaries by drawing distinctions. Binet drew a firm distinction between intelligence and scholastic knowledge:

> Our purpose is to evaluate a child's level of intelligence. It should be understood that this means separating natural intelligence from instruction. It is his intelligence alone that we seek to

measure, by disregarding as far as possible the degree of instruction which the child has enjoyed. (Binet and Simon, 1905*b*, p. 196)

But although he thought of intelligence as pervading much of mental life, he also wanted to distinguish it from sensation, perception, attention, and memory. Bearing Cattell's tests in mind, that was quite a radical suggestion and seems eminently reasonable. But what of a positive definition? The one passage where Binet comes closest to providing such an account is:

> It seems to us that there is a fundamental faculty in intelligence, any alteration or lack of which is of the utmost importance for practical life. This is judgement, otherwise known as common sense, practical sense, initiative, the ability to adapt oneself to circumstance. To judge well, to comprehend well, to reason well, these are the essential ingredients of intelligence. (Binet and Simon, 1905*b*, pp. 196–197)

Reasoning is mentioned, but hardly emphasized. The stress is rather on practicality, common sense, the ability to cope with the world. Thus it is not surprising that Binet's tests measured everyday practical knowledge and skills; they required children to point to various parts of their body; to name objects seen in a picture; to give definitions; to repeat a series of digits or a complete sentence; to copy a diamond; to say what is the difference between paper and cardboard, or a fly and a butterfly; to find as many rhymes as possible in a minute for a word such as '*obeissance*' (remember, this was in French); to tell the time from a clock and to say what the time would be if the positions of the minute and hour hands were reversed; and to fold a sheet of paper over, cut a shape out of the folded edge, and say what shape would appear when the sheet was unfolded (a task which can be made harder by increasing the number of initial folds).

At least some of these tasks seem more plausible candidates as measures of a young child's intelligence regardless of one's precise definition of intelligence, than did most of Cattell's. But Binet's most important contribution to the development of intelligence tests was the simple insight that, since he was dealing with young children, he could use their *age* as an independent criterion of intellectual competence. By and large, as children grow older, so they become capable of solving more demanding problems. His measure of intelligence, therefore, amounted to discovering whether a child was advanced or backward for his age, and what that required was a measure of what was normal for any given age. He thus developed a series of test items ranged according to the age at which the majority of children in his sample were capable of solving them. This constituted his 'measuring scale of intelligence': 'A scale composed of a series of tests of increasing difficulty, starting from the lowest intellectual level that can be observed, and ending at the level of average, normal intelligence' (Binet and Simon, 1905*b*, p. 194).

By giving their tests to samples of normal children of various ages, Binet and Simon found out which set of tests could be solved by the majority of 4-year-olds, 6-year-olds, 8-year-olds, etc. The further requirement was that relatively few 4-year-olds, but essentially all 8-year-olds, should be able to solve the 6-year-old tests, and similarly for the tests for other age groups. The process of test construction was one of continuing experimentation and refinement. To take one example: the task of copying a square drawn on a sheet of paper by the examiner appears as an item in the 4-year-old test, because the majority of 4-year-olds, and essentially all older children, could do it. But it turned out that the task of copying a diamond was significantly harder, and it appears as part of the 6-year-old test. The final set of tests (Binet and Simon, 1911), published in the year in which Binet died, consisted of five tests for each year from age 3 to age 10 (except the 4-year-test which still had only four items), together with some further tests for 12- and 15-year-olds and adults.

The tests were used to assign a child a 'mental age': a child who passed the 6-year-old, but failed the 7-year-old test, had a mental age of 6. The concept of mental age is still sometimes used, most usually in the context of mental retardation or handicap, but, as we shall see, it has been replaced by the concept of mental quotient, intelligence quotient, or IQ. Nevertheless, Binet's procedure still marks an important change from the ideas of Galton and Cattell. Their tests gave an absolute measure of mental performance (thresholds measured in intensity units, reaction times measured in milliseconds or whatever). Binet replaced this with a *relative* or *normative* measure of intelligence: a mental age of 6 was simply the average score obtained by normal 6-year-old children. A 6-year-old child with a mental age of 6 was average; a 5-year-old with a mental age of 6 was advanced; but a 10-year-old with a mental age of 6 was backward or retarded.

The Binet scales, as they were known, formed the basis of modern IQ tests, just as mental age formed the basis for IQ scores. Translated and expanded by Lewis Terman in America and by Cyril Burt in England, they became the norm against which later tests were judged. Although Galton was the first to try to measure individual differences in intelligence, it was Binet who appeared to have succeeded. He owed his success in part to his empirical, pragmatic approach, but also to his robust, common-sense attitude to psychological theory, which allowed him to ignore the limitations both of associationist philosophy and of the techniques of the new experimental psychology then available. He differed from his predecessors (and from many of his successors) in other ways also. He did not, for example, believe that his tests were necessarily measuring innate ability.

> Our purpose is, when a child is brought to us, to measure his intellectual capacities in order to ascertain whether he is normal or retarded. We need, therefore, to study his condition at the time and that only. We have no need to concern ourselves either with his past history or with his future; consequently we shall neglect his aetiology, and we shall make no attempt to distinguish between acquired and congenital idiocy; . . . we do not seek to establish or prepare a prognosis, and we leave unanswered the question whether his retardation is curable, or even improvable. We limit ourselves to ascertaining the truth about his present mental state. (Binet and Simon, 1905*b*, p. 191)

The Stanford–Binet and army tests

Most of the next steps in the development of modern IQ tests were taken in America, largely by three men, Henry Goddard, Lewis Terman, and Robert Yerkes. Henry Goddard was director of the research laboratory at the Vineland Training School in New Jersey, an institution for the retarded, a position that involved him in the assessment of their intellectual status. He came across Binet and Simon's papers of 1905 on a visit to Brussels in the spring of 1908, but thought little of them. When, the following year, he read their 1908 paper, the first to produce a systematic series of tests graded by year, his initial impressions were still quite unfavourable. As he wrote some years later, 'Probably no critic of the scale has reacted against it more positively than I did at that first reading. It seemed impossible to grade intelligence in that way. It was too easy, too simple' (Goddard, 1916, p. 5). When he eventually decided to give it a try, however, 'our use of the scale was a surprise and a gratification. It met our needs. A classification of our children based on the Scale agreed with the Institution experience' (Goddard, 1916, p. 5).

Goddard became an enthusiastic advocate of Binet's scale, translating and distributing 22 000 copies of a condensed version of the 1908 paper, together with 88 000 record blanks (Goddard, 1916). The real breakthrough, however, was the work of Lewis Terman, who produced the Stanford revision of the 1911 Binet–Simon scale, generally known as the Stanford–Binet test (Terman, 1916; Burt's translation and adaptation of the Binet scales was not published for another 5 years (Burt, 1921)). Although based on Binet's 1908 and 1911 scales, the Stanford–Binet was a virtually new IQ test. Forty completely new items were added, which allowed Terman to drop some of Binet's less satisfactory items and to bring up to six the number of items comprising the test at each age. The standardization procedures, although still defective by modern standards, marked an enormous advance on those of Binet. Whereas Binet had tried out his tests on no more than 50 children specified by their teachers as of normal intelligence, Terman tested approximately 1000 children aged 4 to 14. They were sampled by taking all children of the appropriate ages from schools situated in communities of average social status. Terman thus obtained much more accurate information than had Binet on the true level of difficulty of the items making up the various tests, and found that it was necessary to relocate to a different age the majority of the items actually retained from the Binet–Simon scales.

Finally, although still employing Binet's method of scoring in terms of mental age, Terman also borrowed the idea of the intelligence quotient or IQ which had earlier been proposed by Stern (1912). The definition of IQ was:

$$(\text{mental age} \div \text{chronological age}) \times 100. \qquad (1.1)$$

On a properly standardized test, therefore, a child of average intelligence would necessarily have an IQ of 100, while a 6-year-old child with a mental age of 8 would have an IQ of 133, and so on. As Terman wrote some years later:

I knew that my revision of Binet's tests was superior to others then available, but I did not foresee the vogue it was to have and imagined that it would probably be displaced by something much better within a few years. (Terman, 1932, p. 324)

In fact, Terman's tests became the standard against which all later IQ tests were judged: the proof that a new test was indeed a good measure of intelligence was, in part, that its results agreed with those obtained by the Stanford–Binet test. It was not replaced for more than 20 years, and then, at first, only by a revised version (Terman and Merrill, 1937) and subsequently by various versions of the Wechsler tests (Wechsler, 1944, 1958). But in its fourth edition, the Stanford–Binet remains one of the standard tests of intelligence to this day.

Box 1.2 The Stanford–Binet test

The Stanford–Binet consisted of a series of 10 tests, each appropriate for children of one age between the ages of 3 and 14 years. Each test consisted of six different items. The 4-year-old and 9-year-old tests were as follows:

Four-year-old test:
1. Say which of two horizontal lines is longer.
2. Find the shape that matches a target shape.
3. Count four pennies.
4. Copy a square.
5. Answer questions such as: What must you do when you are sleepy?
6. Digit span of 4.

Nine-year-old test:
1. Dates: What day of the week is it today? What year?
2. Arrange five weights from heaviest to lightest.
3. Mental arithmetic.
4. Backward digit span of 4.
5. Generate a sentence containing three particular words.
6. Find rhymes.

The Stanford–Binet and Wechsler tests are individual IQ tests, administered by an examiner to a single person at a time. The examiner needs to be trained in the correct procedures for administering and scoring the tests, and scoring often calls for potentially arbitrary decisions about the adequacy of particular answers. What, for example, counts as a satisfactory definition of the word 'revenge'? According to Terman's manual, 'You kill a person if he does something to you' is all right, but 'To hate someone who has done you wrong' is not. The tests abound with items calling for similar judgments. This may be sufficient for many purposes, but it would clearly be impractical if we wished to obtain IQ scores from a large number of people in a short space of time. To do this, what is needed is a group test, i.e. one administered by a single examiner simultaneously to many testees; the format needs to be that of a multiple-choice questionnaire, since the answers will then consist in the selection of one of several alternatives and can be scored automatically. The first such group tests were introduced in the USA shortly after the publication of Terman's Stanford–Binet test. They were devised by a group of psychologists, including both Goddard and Terman and led by Robert Yerkes, and were designed for use by the US army. Yerkes believed that the army's need to select, and train for various occupations, the large number of new recruits produced by America's entry into the First World War, provided an opportunity for the new science of psychology to prove its worth. He and his colleagues produced two tests, the alpha and beta tests, which became the prototype for many subsequent group tests. The alpha test included such items as verbal analogies, series completions, and synonyms and antonyms, that have since become familiar. The beta test was designed specifically for illiterates. Subjects were required, for example, to fill in the missing part from an incomplete picture of a supposedly familiar object, a pig without a tail, or a revolver without a trigger; they had to perform simple series completion problems, a visual search task where they had to decide whether two sets of digits were identical or different, and a recoding task where they had to match the digits 0–9 to 10 different patterns. All the problems were strictly timed, and in several cases, such as these last two, the test was largely one of performing a simple task as quickly as possible. Several items in the beta test were incorporated into subsequent 'non-verbal' or 'performance' tests (see Chapter 2).

The army tests, although of questionable value in helping America's war effort, brought about a transformation in the public's attitude to mental tests: After the war, Yerkes received hundreds of requests for copies of his tests (which had remained a classified secret in wartime), and, supported by a grant from the Rockefeller Foundation, published a new National Intelligence Test in 1919, which sold over half a million copies in a year. The tests were used in primary and secondary schools, and soon by some universities as an entrance requirement, as well as by business firms. But in Yerkes's eyes at least, the major value of the army tests lay in the huge body of information about the nation's intelligence that had been provided by a programme that had tested approximately 1 750 000 young American men in a little more than a year. Yerkes was not the only person to draw a number of startling social implications from these supposedly authoritative data.

Uses and abuses of IQ tests

Galton, as we have seen, had no doubt that nature was far more important than nurture in determining intellectual ability, and, typical of the society and class into which he was born, was similarly confident that the races of mankind were far from equally endowed with such ability. Binet, on the other hand, although acknowledging the possibility that there were natural differences in ability between young children, explicitly denied that his tests were intended to measure this native endowment. But Goddard, Terman, and Yerkes had few such qualms. Goddard found that Binet's tests served to identify not only 'idiots' and 'imbeciles' (severely retarded or handicapped in more modern terminology, those with an IQ below about 50), but also the 'feeble-minded' or 'morons' (mildly retarded or handicapped, those with an IQ between about 50 and 75). In his book *Feeble-mindedness: Its causes and consequences* (1914), Goddard adopted the technique of Galton's *Hereditary genius* to prove that feeble-mindedness was hereditary: it ran in families. Indeed, by Goddard's calculations, it was more hereditary than were more severe forms of retardation. He estimated that some 85 per cent of the feeble-minded cases that he had studied, but only 50 per cent of the most severely retarded, were of hereditary origin. We may quibble about these precise estimates, but Goddard's general conclusion was by no means unreasonable, and foreshadowed the distinction, drawn by Lewis (1933) and many others since, between pathological, severe retardation and subcultural or familial, mild retardation. Both genetic and environmental factors contribute to both, but the causes of pathological retardation, if genetic, are often harmful single genes or aberrant chromosomes and, if environmental, often particular physical hazards before, during, or after birth. Mild retardation, it is commonly assumed, is due to polygenic inheritance or general family environment. In other words, it is more likely to run in families (see Clarke *et al.*, 1985, where this simplified picture is duly complicated).

Terman was equally convinced that the feeble-mindedness identified by intelligence tests was permanent and therefore hereditary (e.g. Terman, 1916, p. 6); while Yerkes roundly asserted that the army alpha and beta tests

> were originally intended, and are now definitely known, to measure native intellectual ability. (Yoakum and Yerkes, 1920, p. 27)

The evidence for these beliefs was patently weak or non-existent, and they must be taken to reflect, in part, preconceived opinion. Scientists are popularly supposed to be influenced by facts rather than by preconceived opinion, but it would be surprising if they were wholly immune to the prejudices that affect others. Binet himself did not doubt that there were biological causes of individual differences in intelligence, and had indeed spent some years studying differences in skull size and their relationship to intelligence (Binet, 1900). Where he was exceptional was in his declared agnosticism: as we have seen, he regarded his tests as measures of current intellectual performance without commitment as to the origins of the differences they measured. The prevailing opinion, however, was that expressed by Goddard, Terman, and Yerkes in the USA, and by Spearman (1927) and Burt (1912) in Britain: intelligence, like most other human characteristics, was affected more by nature than by nurture, and differences in intelligence could now be measured by means of IQ tests.

Several later critics have argued that the hereditarian beliefs shared by these early pioneers of IQ testing, reinforced by the prestige accorded their new, scientific tests, had sinister and malign influences on public policy (see, for example, Kamin, 1974; Evans and Waites, 1981; Rose *et al.*, 1984; Gould, 1997). It is worth pausing briefly to examine some of these arguments, for they have formed a small, but significant part of the case against IQ tests. In Britain, it has been suggested, IQ testers and their tests were instrumental in establishing a divisive and elitist system of secondary education. In the United States, they were involved in legislation to control immigration and forcibly sterilize the less desirable elements of society. Thus:

> The testing movement was clearly linked, in the United States, to the passage, beginning in 1907, of compulsory sterilization laws aimed at genetically inferior 'degenerates' . . . [And] the army IQ data figured prominently in the public and congressional debates over the Immigration Act of 1924. That overtly racist act established as a feature of American immigration policy a system of 'national origin quotas'. The purpose of the quotas was explicitly to debar, as much as possible, the genetically inferior peoples of Southern and Eastern Europe, while encouraging 'Nordic' immigration from Northern and Western Europe. (Rose *et al.* 1984, pp. 87–88)

As we shall see, a substantial body of legislation was indeed passed in the USA to control immigration and provide for sterilization. We may now deplore much of that legislation (although no modern state permits immigration on the scale of the American experience between 1880 and 1914). The question at issue, however, is whether the IQ testing movement should be implicated in the passage of this legislation. There is at least some reason to believe that the critics' charge both overestimates the influence of psychologists on social policy, and underestimates the pervasive influence of eugenic thought in the USA at the beginning of the twentieth century. The term 'eugenics' was coined by Galton to refer to

> the science of improving stock . . . which . . . takes cognisance of all influences that tend . . . to give the more suitable races or strains of blood a better chance of prevailing speedily over the less suitable than they otherwise would have had. (Galton, 1883, p. 17)

In a common misinterpretation of Darwinian theory, it was widely believed that it was no longer the fittest, but the least fit, who were surviving and multiplying (a misinterpretation because the definition of 'fittest' in Darwinian theory is precisely those who survive and multiply). Organized charity and improved public health, it was said, were allowing the poor and perhaps even the feeble-minded to survive in ever greater numbers (left alone, nature would have eliminated most of them), while the more prudent and prosperous classes, on whom the future of civilization depended, were limiting their families and hence failing to reproduce themselves. In the USA these fears were fuelled by the rapidity of social change. In the 10 years preceding the First World War, some 10 million immigrants entered the country, crowding into the large industrial cities of the east coast and mid-west, forming a new, and perhaps dangerously radical, urban proletariat, and undercutting the wages of established workers. It was time for society to act.

Curbing feeble-mindedness

Goddard and Terman were quite clear about the action that had to be taken:

> It is clear from the data already presented that feeble-mindedness is hereditary in a large percentage of the cases, and that it is transmitted in accordance with the Mendelian formula . . . If both parents are feeble-minded all the children will be feeble-minded. It is obvious that such matings should not be allowed. (Goddard, 1914, pp. 560–561)

Where only one parent was feeble-minded, the position was more complex, since the immediate offspring might appear normal, but feeble-mindedness would appear in subsequent generations. The conclusion was inescapable: 'No feeble-minded person should ever be allowed to marry or to become a parent. It is obvious that if this rule is to be carried out the intelligent part of society must enforce it' (Goddard, 1914, p. 565). Terman believed that one of the main uses of IQ tests was to identify the feeble-minded so that they could be brought

> under the surveillance and protection of society. This will ultimately result in curtailing the reproduction of feeble-mindedness and in the elimination of an enormous amount of crime, pauperism, and industrial inefficiency. (Terman, 1916, pp. 6–7)

In the last analysis, the only way to curtail this reproduction was by sterilization.

It is one thing to show, however, that some early proponents of IQ tests advocated the sterilization of the feeble-minded. It is another to establish that they or their tests had any great effect on public attitudes, policy, or legislation. For it is, in fact, quite clear that there had been public pressure for eugenic measures long before Goddard and Terman brought Binet's tests to America, that these measures were to be directed not only against the mentally retarded, and that the pressure for them had often been successful (Kevles, 1985). Beginning with Connecticut in 1896 and Indiana in 1905, some 30 states had, by 1914, enacted new restrictive marriage laws, or amended old ones. The Indiana law forbade the marriage not only of the mentally retarded but also of habitual drunkards and anyone with a transmissible disease. Sterilization was also advocated and practised. The superintendent of a training school for the feeble-minded in Elwyn, Pennsylvania had, with parental permission, started castrating some of the inmates in 1889. Dr Harry Sharp, the medical superintendent at the Indiana State Reformatory at Jeffersonville, pioneered the sterilization of criminals by vasectomy, and, by 1907 when Indiana passed the first compulsory sterilization law, had already performed vasectomies on more than 465 inmates. Within the next 10 years, 15 more states passed similar laws. But once again they were not directed particularly against the mentally retarded. Their net included epileptics, the insane, drug addicts, sexual offenders, and other criminals. It is hard to believe that the new IQ testing movement had very much to do with any of this.

However, although it is difficult to sustain the argument that the IQ testing movement

Box 1.3 The rise and fall of eugenics

In 1927, the US Supreme Court, in the case of *Buck* v. *Bell*, ruled in favour of a new statute from the state of Virginia. The particular case concerned a 17-year-old woman, Carrie Buck, who, shortly before being committed to the Virginia Colony for Epileptics and Feebleminded, had given birth to an illegitimate daughter. Carrie's mother was also an inmate of the colony, and had a mental age of less than 8 on the Stanford–Binet test. Carrie's own mental age was 9. Although her daughter was still less than 1 year old, she was given an infant test and said to be below normal. In the words of Justice Oliver Wendell Holmes, who wrote the Supreme Court's opinion: 'The principle that sustains compulsory vaccination is broad enough to cover cutting the Fallopian tubes . . . Three generations of imbeciles are enough' (Gould, 1986).

The USA was not, of course, the only country where compulsory sterilization was widely advocated and sometimes practised. Eugenic ideas were common throughout Europe during the early part of the twentieth century. They found their most notorious champions in Nazi Germany, but long before Hitler came to power German psychiatrists and others were seriously debating the question what was to be done about the incurable, long-term inmates of asylums for epileptics, the insane, and the seriously retarded. There were many advocates of compulsory sterilization, and some who talked of even more extreme measures (Burleigh, 1994). It was left, however, to Hitler's government to put these ideas into serious practice. One of the first acts to be passed by the new government in 1933 was a Eugenic Sterilization Law, under whose auspices well over 300 000 people were compulsorily sterilized by 1939 (Kevles, 1985). The outbreak of war, and the perceived need to concentrate the state's resources on those who would benefit the state most, led to a new, more drastic policy of compulsory 'euthanasia'. Between 1939 and 1945, some 200 000 men, women, and young children were killed—by starvation, lethal injection, gas, or shooting (Burleigh, 1994). Most, but not all, of the victims had been inmates of asylums for the disabled, mentally ill, or severely retarded. This last group seems to have been a small minority and, for what it is worth, those who planned and executed this policy of deliberate murder showed scant interest in the results of IQ tests.

If the case of Carrie Buck marked a high point in the public esteem accorded to eugenic ideas, the evidence from Germany of what could happen when people took those ideas to what they saw as their logical conclusion marked the end, at least for the time being, of the eugenic ideal.

was responsible for the initial passage of such legislation, there is no doubt at all that IQ tests were later used to justify sterilization in cases of mental retardation. Many of the earlier state laws were declared unconstitutional by the courts, but many survived, and the total number of states with such laws on their statute books eventually rose to 30. By 1928 nearly 9000 people had been subject to compulsory sterilization and by 1964 over 60 000 (Robitscher, 1973; Kevles, 1985). Although all these laws provided a variety of different grounds for sterilization ('pauperism', which had always been popular with earlier eugenicists, became even more popular in the depression of the 1930s), mental retardation accounted for nearly half the total number of victims.

Control of immigration

Some of the early American IQ testers also argued vigorously for the control of immigration. Goddard (1917) administered Binet tests to newly arrived immigrants at New York and discovered that an astonishingly high proportion tested at what he termed the feeble-minded level or below. But by far the most important information was provided by Yerkes's army data. They showed enormous differences between men of different national origins. When results were collapsed across both alpha and beta tests and scores translated to a letter grade, some 20 per cent of those of English origin, 15 per cent of Scottish, and 10 per cent of Dutch or German origin scored A or B, the two highest grades; but less than 1 per cent of Italians or Poles were in these grades. Conversely, less than 15 per cent of the British, Dutch, or German, but over 60 per cent of the Italians and Poles scored D. The new immigration from southern and eastern Europe was leading to an inexorable decline in the national intelligence. As Carl Brigham wrote in *A study of American intelligence* (1923), based on the army data: 'The decline in intelligence is due to two factors, the change in the races migrating to this country, and to the additional factor of the sending of lower and lower representatives of each race' (Brigham, 1923, p. 178). What was to be done? 'The steps that should be taken to preserve or increase our present intellectual capacity must of course be dictated by science and not by political expediency. Immigration should not only be restrictive but highly selective' (Brigham, 1923, p. 210).

Brigham got his wish. The following year saw the passage of an Immigration Act of 1924 which established national quotas and, more to the point, based those quotas on the incidence of each national group in the 1890 census. No one was in any doubt why 1890 was chosen as the base year: it marked the beginning of the new immigration from southern and eastern Europe, and thus kept the number of new immigrants from these countries to a minimum. Gould (1997) and Kamin (1974) appear to see a simple case of cause and effect: IQ tests, and their interpretation at the hands of racist psychologists, were responsible for the passage of this act. Once again, however, the story is more complex than those who enjoy conspiracy theories of history would like (Samelson, 1975, 1979; Snyderman and Herrnstein, 1983).

We can begin with a simple point. In spite of Gould's and Kamin's suggestion that the congressional debates leading to the passage of the 1924 Act continually invoked the army data, the facts are rather different. The Act itself makes no mention of IQ tests of any sort at all; the 600-page record of congressional debates leading to the passage of the Act contains *one* exchange on the subject of the army data; the committee hearings contain the record of three occasions (all carefully cited by Kamin, 1974) on which the army data were mentioned; the committee's report to congress contains no mention of these occasions. No psychologist was called to give testimony before the committee (Snyderman and Herrnstein, 1983).

This may dispose of one specific claim, but still leaves open the question whether the testing movement in general, and the army data in particular, exerted a more subtle influence. In fact, IQ tests entered the debate on immigration very late in the day. Legal restrictions on immigration dated back at least to 1882, when an act barred the immigration of lunatics and idiots; an act of 1903 barred epileptics and the insane; and one of 1907 barred imbeciles and feeble-minded. This was not enough to satisfy those who professed to believe that native American stock (a term which in those days meant white, Anglo-Saxon, northern European stock) was being diluted by the new wave of immigrants from southern and eastern Europe. But their objections were economic, political, and social, rather than intellectual. American values were being destroyed by radicals and Bolsheviks, who were disrupting society and would never be assimilated. It was the inability of the 'melting pot' to cope with such a mass of people of such different background, and the consequent threat to national unity and homogeneity, that worried most of the proponents of restriction. The army data were certainly mentioned, and provided additional ammunition for those whose minds were already made up, but Yerkes himself believed that IQ tests should be used on an *individual* basis to screen out intellectually inferior immigrants. This impractical suggestion commended itself neither to politicians anxious for a simple solution nor to racists anxious to preserve America's Nordic heritage (Samelson, 1975, 1979). Samelson's conclusion seems more reasonable than Gould's or Kamin's:

> the eventual passage of the 'racist' immigration law of 1924 was not crucially affected by the contributions of Yerkes or other psychologists. (Samelson, 1979, p. 135)

Selection for secondary education

The final example of the supposedly dire uses to which IQ tests have been put is in selection for secondary education in England. According to Kamin:

> The IQ test played an even more central role in England, where it formed the basis for the selective education system introduced after the Second World War. On the strength of Cyril Burt's enthusiastic argument that a test given to a child at the age of 11 could measure its 'innate intelligence,' it was decided to use the results of tests administered to 11-year-olds to 'stream' children into one of three separate—and far from equal—school systems. (Kamin, 1981, p. 94; see also Gould, 1997, p. 323 for the identical claim)

It is certainly true that IQ tests played a part in the 11+ exam, and that after 1944 the results of this exam were used to determine the type of secondary school which a child would attend. But a somewhat longer historical perspective may help to correct the impression given by this quotation (Evans and Waites, 1981; Sutherland, 1984). The point is simple: selection for secondary education in England long antedated any use of IQ tests for such purposes. Before 1900, the state's provision for public education in England consisted of free elementary schooling up to the age of 12. Secondary schools were fee-paying, with only a handful of scholarships or bursaries. By 1918, the school-leaving age had been raised to 14, and the principle established that there should be a certain proportion of free places in secondary schools, but there continued to be huge differences from one part of the country to another both in the number of free places and in the procedures used to select children for them. In many cases parental wishes did the job of selection: there was in effect no competition. Where there was, it was done by the headmaster interviewing the parents, with or without their child, or by elementary school teachers' assessments, or by some sort of examination, usually of English or mathematics.

It was on this somewhat chaotic scene that IQ tests first appeared. The central government slowly attempted to impose some uniformity both of provision and of selection. The Department of Education received advice from educational psychologists, notably Godfrey Thomson (much more important on the national scene than Cyril Burt), who argued that IQ tests could provide a more uniform and fairer method of selection. The advice was at least occasionally heeded. By 1945, when the 1944 Education Act had decreed that all children should go on to secondary school and the question was therefore which kind of school they should attend, most schools did actually rely, at least in part, on some kind of IQ test at 11+.

IQ tests were thus not used to *establish* a system of selective secondary education. That system was already in effect. One could, if one wished (and psychologists such as Cyril Burt certainly did so wish), use the results of IQ tests to justify such a system. But that was not the reason why, as late as 1939, only 15 per cent of English children were educated in grant-aided secondary schools. Given that the English system was already highly selective, it is hardly unreasonable to have some sympathy for Thomson's argument that the selection procedure should be efficient and fair. Thomson argued from the very outset, and produced evidence in support of his argument, that IQ tests would succeed in identifying children from deprived backgrounds, or living in remote rural areas, who would otherwise be denied secondary education (Thomson, 1921). Subsequent evidence amply confirmed Thomson's arguments (Vernon, 1957). The classic study was by Floud and Halsey (1957) in Hertfordshire. When the local education authority dropped IQ tests from its 11+ exams, there was an immediate and significant decrease in the proportion of children from working-class families entering grammar schools, and a comparable increase in the proportion of children from professional families. There is equally little doubt that scores on IQ tests predict children's subsequent educational attainments (see Chapter 2), and that, when added to the results of conventional tests of English and arithmetic, they significantly improved the accuracy with which 11+ tests predicted secondary school attainments (Vernon, 1957).

It is not my purpose to attack or defend the varying systems of secondary education prevailing in England at different times since 1900—only to defend IQ tests and their proponents from the charge of *imposing* an unjust system of selection for secondary education. Opponents of selection can, of course, argue that IQ tests did have a malign influence: the selective system might conceivably have collapsed earlier from its own perceived injustices had it not been thought to be legitimized by the apparent objectivity of IQ tests as measures of innate ability. But it is worth pausing to question whether the results of any IQ test, even when interpreted by the most extreme hereditarian, really could legitimize a selective system of education. Intelligence might be innate, and measurable with perfect accuracy at the age of 11, but why would it follow that children with different levels of innate ability should be educated in different schools, or that some should not be educated at all? Historically, education was confined to a small percentage of the population because it was thought to be an expensive luxury, irrelevant to most people's lives: what is the point, according to this elitist argument, of teaching a peasant how to read or write? We now regard this as unworthy, and in most industrialized societies education up to a certain age is compulsory. But how shall everyone be educated? The argument for selection and segregation was largely an educational one: more able children would benefit from a more intensive and academic education which could only be provided in a selective school. But that is an empirical question and one not particularly well supported by research. And even if it were true, it is also relevant to ask whether less able children benefit from segregation. If they do not, then one has to weigh the educational costs and benefits of segregation. It is also easy to see that other considerations are relevant. For example, is segregation socially divisive? The truth is surely that the decision to operate a selective or segregated system of education at any level, up to and including universities, is for the most part a political, social, and educational one. It is largely, if not wholly, independent of the question whether children differ in IQ, whether these differences are permanent, and whether they are genetic in origin.

IQ tests have not always been benign in their influence, and, as we shall see, can certainly be criticized on other grounds. Many IQ testers have held social and political views that, although relatively commonplace at the time, are widely regarded as repugnant today; and they have sought support for those views in the results of their tests. But there is no point in propagating or perpetuating myths: neither the tests nor the testers were as powerful as has sometimes been made out. Several of the critics who have sought to saddle them with responsibility for reprehensible social policy have been less interested in historical truth, and more concerned to believe anything bad both of the tests and of those who constructed them.

Summary

It is commonly assumed that we must begin any psychological enquiry with a clear and precise definition of the object of our enquiry; and since IQ testers have failed to provide such a definition of the 'intelligence' which their tests purport to measure, they have failed at the first hurdle. But good definitions are the end product of scientific investigation, not its starting point. Provided that we have a rough and ready idea of what we are trying to study, we can proceed by trial and error. So it has been with the development of IQ tests: initial attempts by Galton and Cattell to measure intelligence by tests of sensory discrimination or reaction time were abandoned when it seemed that they failed to agree with an obvious external criterion of intelligence—students' college grades. On the assumption that children become intellectually more competent as they grow older, Binet used young children's age as an external criterion of intelligence and developed a series of tests based on this simple premise: an intelligence test for 6-year-olds should contain a series of items which the majority of 6-year-olds, but fewer 4-year-olds and virtually all 8-year-olds, could answer correctly. Further refinement and empirical trial and error, based on a standardization sample of some 1000 children between the ages of 4 and 14, resulted in Terman's Stanford–Binet test, which for a long time served as the benchmark against which other IQ tests were measured.

Is the Stanford–Binet test a good measure of intelligence? Once again, we should not seek to answer that question immediately. But it can be shown that scores on this and other IQ tests do roughly what we would expect a measure of intelligence to do (a point documented more thoroughly in Chapter 2). A less strictly scientific question is whether IQ tests have served good or evil purposes—a common charge being that, from their inception, they were used as instruments of oppression against the poor and disadvantaged. The men who devised and developed early IQ tests were, no doubt, subject to many of the prejudices of their time, and today we find some of their views repugnant. But because these views were so widely held, it is unsurprising that they informed social policy at the time, and there is rather little evidence that these policies were much affected by IQ testers themselves or their tests.

2   *Psychometric theories of intelligence*

Introduction

Although the initial development of IQ tests probably owed more to empirical trial and error than to profound psychological theorizing, early IQ testers, like those who followed them, did hold theoretical views about the nature of the intelligence that their tests were supposedly measuring. We saw that Binet himself tried his hand at defining intelligence—even if largely by exclusion. One of the other most influential figures in the early history of IQ testing was Charles Spearman. He did not himself devise new tests: his influence rested entirely on his development of a precursor of modern factor analysis, which he used to advance a theory of the structure of human intelligence as measured by IQ tests.

Some modern cognitive psychologists, such as Gardner (1993) and Sternberg (1985, 1990), have developed theories of intelligence that seek to go 'beyond IQ' (the title of Sternberg's book published in 1985). While accepting the importance of the IQ testing movement and of the factor analytic approach initiated by Spearman, Sternberg argues that neither IQ tests nor the type of laboratory paradigm used by most experimental cognitive psychologists can capture all that we implicitly understand by the concept of intelligence. He is surely right—if only because that concept is so fuzzy round the edges. But rather than take up his argument at this point, I shall follow the strategy outlined in the preceding chapter of first trying to understand what it is that IQ tests succeed in measuring, and only then addressing the wider question of what they fail to measure (Chapter 10).

Gardner (1993) has gone further than Sternberg in arguing that, at best, IQ tests measure only a sub-set of the multiple intelligences he believes he has identified. To the extent that his musical, bodily kinaesthetic, and personal–social intelligences are indeed independent of IQ, they too do not need to be discussed at this point. But there is a further reason for questioning their relevance to our immediate concerns. As Sternberg (1990) and Brody (1992) have argued, Gardner's criteria for identifying an 'intelligence' would surely allow the inclusion of a far wider range of intelligences than he has proposed. Virtually any specific skill or cognitive operation could probably qualify. Thus two of Gardner's criteria are that an intelligence should depend upon some identifiable brain structures, and that there should be wide individual differences between skilled and less skilled exponents. As Brody notes, the ability to recognize faces meets these and Gardner's other criteria at least as well as some of his other intelligences. One might equally add episodic memory (Parkin, 1997) or the ability to learn foreign languages (Ellis, 1994).

The present chapter, then, discusses the psychometric theories of intelligence that informed the subsequent development of IQ tests after the pioneering work outlined in Chapter 1.

The variety of IQ tests: one intelligence or many?

Whether or not IQ tests served a malign purpose from the outset, what cannot be disputed is that the 1920s and 1930s saw, especially in the USA, a great expansion in their use. One consequence of this popularity was a proliferation of rival tests, as psychologists and publishers hastened to exploit a seemingly ever-expanding market. By 1935, Buros started publishing a yearbook, listing all mental tests (a term covering much more than IQ tests). Later editions appeared less frequently, but with more detail and evaluation of the tests. The eighth edition, published in 1978, included details of some 100 tests described as measures of intelligence or ability.

There is no need to describe all, or even many, of these tests in any detail. But it is worth discussing two of the more important, the Wechsler Scales and Raven's Matrices, partly because they have been among the most widely used, but also because they differ very sharply from one another and thus give some idea of the diversity of tests and test batteries described as measures of IQ.

The Wechsler tests: WAIS and WISC

Although the Stanford–Binet test has been revised several times, most recently in 1986, it has been overtaken in popularity. The most widely used individual IQ tests today are the Wechsler tests, first published in 1939 as the Wechsler–Bellevue Scale. Binet's original tests, as we saw, were designed for use with young children, and although Terman's original standardization sample included children up to the age of 14, and also some 400 older teenagers and adults, he readily acknowledged that this older sample was far from representative of the population as a whole, and the next revision of the Stanford–Binet did not include adults at all. The Stanford–Binet thus provided imperfect adult norms, and did not even pretend to provide norms for adults of different ages. The Wechsler–Bellevue test, designed for and standardized on a sample of some 1500 adults (as well as some children), thus filled an important gap in the market. In 1955, it was revised as the Wechsler Adult Intelligence Scale (WAIS), with a standardization sample of over 2000 people, aged 16–75, for by now Wechsler had also developed a version of the test suitable for children aged 5–16, the Wechsler Intelligence Scale for Children (WISC). Both have since been revised, as WAIS-R and WISC-R (and more recently, WISC III).

Both the Stanford–Binet and Wechsler tests are individual tests, administered by a single examiner to a single examinee. David Wechsler, however, introduced two major methodological changes. Following Binet's original model, the Stanford–Binet test consisted of a number of different sub-tests, which were grouped by age. Thus a typical 6-year-old child would take a set of half-a-dozen sub-tests designed for 6-year-olds, while a 10-year-old child would take a quite different set of sub-tests (although, of course, any child could be given more than one set of sub-tests). This was a reflection of Binet's original concept of mental age, which was still used in the original Stanford–Binet test.

Wechsler's first innovation was to devise a single set of sub-tests, suitable for all ages, with each sub-test ranging from easy to difficult items. The sub-tests used in the WISC used almost exactly the same format as those from the earlier Weschler–Bellevue test and later WAIS, and although incorporating many easier items than those used in the adult tests, still spanned a wide range of difficulty so that a single test was deemed suitable for children ranging in age from 5 to 16.

Wechsler's second innovation was the concept of the 'deviation IQ'. In the Stanford–Binet test, as we saw (equation 1.1), IQ was defined as:

$$\text{(mental age/chronological age)} \times 100.$$

But this formula makes any sort of sense only when applied to children whose mental age, i.e. ability to answer items in an IQ test, is continuing to increase as they grow older. As Terman discovered when testing his adult sample, mental age does not continue to grow indefinitely—that is to say, his adult sample did not obtain appreciably higher test scores than his sample of high-school students. Strict application of the IQ formula above, therefore, would have meant that the average 32-year-old had an IQ half that of the average 16-year-old. To avoid this absurdity, Terman had to resort to another: he assigned all adults a chronological age of 16.

Although the First World War army tests had, of course, been designed to assess adult intelligence, it was sufficient, for the purpose to which the tests were put, to rely on absolute test scores, or even a crude division of such scores into one of four categories, A–D. But when Wechsler introduced the first individual adult IQ test, he needed a new method for assigning IQ scores. His solution was to define IQ not in terms of mental and chronological age, but in terms of an individual's actual score on a test (the number of items correctly answered) relative to the expected average score obtained by people of the same age. The formula was:

$$\text{(actual test score/expected score)} \times 100. \tag{2.1}$$

Thus to measure the IQ of a 30-year-old individual, what Wechsler needed was a representative (standardization) sample of 30-year-olds: he could then ascertain their average test score (number of items correctly answered), and compare the individual's score to this average. And so on, for every other age group. Thus Wechsler's standardization sample was carefully stratified by age as well as by other standard demographic characteristics (sex, social class, region of the country), and divided into age groups spanning 5–10 year ranges.

A test score equal to the average of one's age group defined an IQ of 100. But how does one convert test scores above or below this mean into IQ scores? Deviations from the mean of a set of scores are measured by calculating the standard deviation of that set of scores. If the scores are distributed approximately normally, as is shown in Fig. 2.1, roughly 68 per cent will fall within ±1 standard deviation of the mean, 95 per cent within ±2 standard deviations, and so on. We calculate the standard deviation of test scores for our sample of 30-year-olds (20 in the illustrative example of Fig. 2.1) and convert these scores into IQs by adopting the wholly arbitrary convention that the standard deviation of IQ is 15 points. Thus a test score of 100, one standard deviation above the mean of 80, translates into an IQ of 115; a score of 40, two standard deviations below the mean, translates into an IQ of 70. And so on.

Thus an IQ score on the WAIS (a deviation IQ) is simply a reflection of an individual's relative standing with respect to others of the same age. It is not an absolute score. In the jargon of psychological measurement theory, IQ is an ordinal scale, where we are simply rank-ordering people. There is no absolute zero for IQ, as there is for height or weight, and someone with an IQ of 150 is not twice as intelligent as another with an IQ of 75, in the

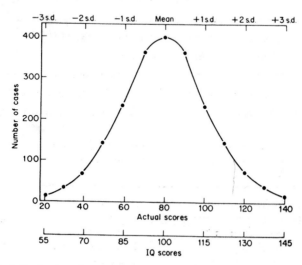

Fig. 2.1 Hypothetical distribution of scores on an IQ test. The mean of this distribution is 80, which thus defines an IQ score of 100 for this sample of individuals. The standard deviation (s.d.) of the scores is 20—that is to say, a score of 60 is 1 standard deviation below the mean of 80; by adopting the convention that the standard deviation of IQ is 15, a score of 60 translates into an IQ of 85 (100 − 15).

sense that someone 6 feet (1.8 m) tall is twice as tall as someone of 3 feet (0.9 m). It is not even appropriate to claim that the 10-point difference between IQ scores of 110 and 100 is the same as the 10-point difference between IQs of 160 and 150 (although some psychometricians, such as Jensen (1980) have disputed this last point, seeking to argue that IQ is an interval scale—where equal intervals signify equal differences). To say that someone has an IQ of 130 is simply to say that their test score lies within the top 2.5 per cent of a representative sample of people of the same age. In this respect, IQ scores are following the path set by Galton in the nineteenth century. Galton did not seek to measure ability or eminence on any absolute scale, but simply in terms of individuals' rank order in the population—whether they were in the top 1, 5, or 25 per cent.

Content of the Wechsler tests

In its present form, the WAIS-R consists of 11 sub-tests, each comprising a number of different items. The sub-tests are shown in Table 2.1, divided, as is conventional, into six 'verbal' and five 'performance' tests. The nature of this distinction may not be immediately obvious: a vocabulary test may reasonably be described as verbal, but why should a test of mental arithmetic or of digit span be so described? The distinction rests, in the last analysis, on the results of factor analysis: scores on the verbal tests tend to correlate more highly with one another than they do with scores on the performance tests, which in turn tend to correlate more highly with one another than they do with scores on the verbal tests: this is illustrated in Table 2.2, where the argument from factor analysis is briefly explained. But the origin of the two types of test can be traced back to the army alpha and beta tests (verbal and non-verbal or performance respectively); indeed several of the Wechsler performance tests are directly derived from the army beta tests.

The nature of the items in each of the 11 sub-tests is illustrated in Box 2.1. Readers more familiar with IQ tests that require the solution of analogies, odd-one-out, or series completion problems may find the content of the Wechsler tests mildly surprising. There is

Table 2.1 Sub-tests comprising the Wechsler Adult Intelligence Scale (WAIS) and Wechsler Intelligence Scale for Children (WISC)

Verbal	Performance
Information	Picture completion
Vocabulary	Picture arrangement
Comprehension	Block design
Arithmetic	Object assembly
Similarities	Digit symbol
Digit span	

relatively little of this sort of problem solving or reasoning required here: the information, vocabulary, and comprehension tests seem to be tests of knowledge rather than problem-solving ability; other sub-tests place a premium on rapid execution of a straightforward task that everyone could get right given the time (digit symbol); while yet others seem simply to require an eye for detail (picture completion). The only explanation given by Wechsler for this absence of reasoning problems is the cryptic, and, as we shall see later, wholly false assertion that items demanding abstract reasoning are sometimes very poor measures of intelligence (Wechsler, 1958). But one other salient characteristic of the test as a whole, the remarkable diversity of the various sub-tests, was quite deliberate policy.

This policy was based partly on the belief that particular types of test might favour or penalize particular people or even groups of people. Diversity of content was thus one way of ensuring that the test as a whole was fair. More generally, Wechsler argued, rather as Binet had earlier, that a person's intelligence could be manifest in a variety of different ways, and the wider the range of sub-tests, and items within sub-tests, the greater the chance that the test as a whole would provide a well-rounded view of that person's intelligence. But he stopped well short of the view espoused by Thurstone (1938), or Gardner (1993), which holds that intelligence should be conceptualized as a set of half-a-dozen or more quite independent faculties. In the dispute between Thurstone and Spearman (1927), who argued that there was a single general factor of intelligence, g, common to all tests, Wechsler wanted it both ways. On the one hand: 'while intelligence may manifest itself in a variety of ways, one must assume that there is some communality or basic similarity between those forms of behavior which one identifies as intelligent' (Wechsler, 1958, p. 5).On the other hand, he insisted that 'other salient factors besides g enter into measures of intelligence . . . [and] that the entity or quantity which we are able to measure by intelligence tests is not a simple quantity. Certainly, it is not something which can be expressed by one single factor alone' (Wechsler, 1958, pp. 12, 14).

Be this as it may, Wechsler tacitly accepted a central implication of Spearman's position: although the items and sub-tests included were deliberately chosen to be as diverse as possible, they simultaneously had to satisfy a further essential criterion: they should all correlate with one another. This may seem an unnecessary restriction, but further reflection suggests that it is quite a natural one to impose. If one is setting out on the business of constructing an intelligence test, it is almost inevitable that one will adopt it. To see why, it is only necessary to recall the results of Wissler's experiment described in Chapter 1. Wissler (1901) found that the various mental tests devised by Cattell did not correlate with one another, and drew the conclusion that they could not all be adequate measures of intelligence: if one was, then the others, which did not agree with it, could not be. Once we believe that we have found one test that measures intelligence, it seems only reasonable to insist that further tests should tend to agree with it. But however reasonable, such a strategy comes close to endorsing Spearman's key assumption that intelligence is a unitary process. It certainly guarantees that factor analysis will yield the strong general factor, g, which

Box 2.1 The Wechsler tests

The six verbal tests may be characterized briefly as follows (the examples given are illustrative only; they are not the same as actual questions in the test):

Information is a general knowledge quiz, with a careful mixture of questions covering science, religion, politics, geography, literature, etc.

Vocabulary asks for definitions of the meanings of words, such as interrupt, ambivalent, or sonorous.

Comprehension asks the meaning of various sayings or proverbs, or what is the appropriate thing to do in certain situations, or such 'good-citizen' questions as: why is it important to vote in a general election?

Arithmetic sets problems in mental arithmetic: if two men dig a hole in 1.5 hours, how long would it take six men to dig the same hole?

Similarities ask in what ways two things are alike, for example, a hammer and a screwdriver, or avarice and gluttony.

Digit span requires the examinee to repeat a series of digits, e.g. 7, 1, 6, 9, 3, read out by the examiner. In a second, harder part of the test, the task is to repeat the series in reverse order; thus 2, 8, 5, 4 would become 4, 5, 8, 2.

The performance tests are:

1. *Picture completion* shows line drawings of more or less familiar objects or scenes, from which one important part is missing—exactly as in the army beta test.
2. *Picture arrangement*: each item consists of a number of pictures on separate cards which, when arranged in the correct order, tell a simple story.
3. *Block design* gives the examinee nine coloured cubes, each with two red, two white, and two diagonally red and white faces. The task is to arrange them so as to form certain patterns, and bonus points are earned for rapid answers.
4. *Object assembly* is a series of simple jigsaw puzzles, once again timed.
5. *Digit symbol* is the only pencil and paper test. The test sheet displays, at the top, the digits 1–9, in order, beneath each of which is a particular symbol, a square, an inverted T, an oblique line etc. Having studied this briefly, the examinee's task is to fill in the appropriate symbol in the blank space below each of 90 more digits presented in random order (with instructions *not* to go through the list filling in all the symbols for 1, then all those for 2, but rather to fill in each item in the random order in which they are printed). Only a short time is allowed, and one's score is simply the number of items correctly filled in within this time limit.

Spearman regarded as evidence for his view—but that is a story to which we shall return in Chapter 6.

Whether or not one insists that all parts of an IQ test should correlate positively with all other parts, a second sensible principle of test construction is that no two sub-tests should correlate absolutely perfectly with one another. If they do, they must be giving the same answers, and one of them is redundant. Thus the correlation matrix for most test batteries looks something like that for the WAIS-R, shown in Table 2.2: the intercorrelations between each pair of tests are all positive, ranging from a low of 0.33 to a high of 0.81. A further feature of Table 2.2 is that, although there are exceptions, there is some tendency for the verbal tests to correlate more highly with one another than with any of the performance tests, and a similar (albeit weaker) tendency for the performance tests to correlate more with one another than they do with the verbal tests. Even clearer is the fact that each verbal test correlates more highly with the total score on the remaining verbal tests than with the total performance score, while the performance tests tend to correlate better with the performance total than with the verbal total. It is this fact that justifies the division of the test as a whole into verbal and performance halves. It also carries a further, important implication. If a strong positive correlation between two or more tests is consistent with the assumption that they both, in part, measure the same underlying trait or process, there is an even clearer implication that if two tests do *not* correlate with one another, they cannot be measuring the same thing. Thus the *relatively* low correlations between verbal and performance halves of the WAIS suggest that it cannot be measuring only a single process of general intelligence, but that a distinction can and should be drawn between 'verbal' and 'non-verbal' IQ. More on this later.

The fact that all sub-tests of the WAIS correlate positively with one another is, of course, a consequence of the decision to include in the test battery only those sub-tests that satisfy this criterion. In that sense, it is unsurprising and might even be thought to be without empirical implication. But it is, surely, somewhat surprising that tests of such diverse content should be able to satisfy such a criterion. Why should it be the case that people with a large vocabulary and fund of general knowledge should also be good at arranging coloured blocks to make particular patterns, or quick at filling in the appropriate symbol below each of a series of

Table 2.2 Intercorrelations between scores on sub-tests of WAIS (from the standardization sample of the WAIS-R)

	Info.	Vocab.	Comp.	Arith.	Sim.	Digit span	Pic. comp.	Pic. arr.	Block design	Object. assem	Digit symbol
Information	–										
Vocabulary	0.81	–									
Comprehension	0.68	0.74	–								
Arithmetic	0.61	0.63	0.57	–							
Similarities	0.66	0.72	0.68	0.56	–						
Digit span	0.46	0.52	0.45	0.56	0.45	–					
Picture completion	0.52	0.55	0.52	0.48	0.54	0.37	–				
Picture arrangement	0.50	0.51	0.48	0.46	0.50	0.37	0.51	–			
Block design	0.50	0.52	0.48	0.56	0.51	0.43	0.54	0.47	–		
Object assembly	0.39	0.41	0.40	0.42	0.43	0.33	0.52	0.40	0.63	–	
Digit symbol	0.44	0.47	0.44	0.45	0.46	0.42	0.42	0.39	0.47	0.38	–
Verbal score	0.79	0.85	0.76	0.70	0.74	0.57	0.61	0.57	0.61	0.49	0.54
Performance score	0.62	0.65	0.61	0.62	0.64	0.50	0.65	0.56	0.70	0.62	0.52

digits? There is no a priori reason why this should have been so, and in this sense it is an empirical discovery that such a wide variety of tests should satisfy such a criterion. And it is an empirical discovery of considerable importance, for it serves to reinforce the test constructors' claim that their tests are probably not doing too bad a job at measuring something that we could call intelligence. But why that should be so will be answered more convincingly after consideration of some quite different tests.

Raven's Matrices

According to Spearman (1927), the most important ingredient of general intelligence was the ability to see relationships between objects, events, or ideas, and to draw inferences from those relationships (he phrased this differently, see Chapter 6; but for the moment we can stick to normal English). To this he later added the further criterion that intelligence involved the ability to think in abstract rather than in particular, concrete terms (Chapter 7). Spearman's argument implied, it seemed to Penrose and Raven (1936), that a good measure of general intelligence would be a series of analogical reasoning or series completion tests. A simple analogy is:

cat is to purr, as dog is to bark.

More generally, analogies can be represented as:

A is to A' as B is to B'.

Their solution requires one to see the relationship between A and A', and whether it is the same as the relationship between B and B'—this latter part of the problem often requiring one also to see the relationship between A and B. A simple series completion task is: B, C, B, C, D, C, D, E, what letter comes next? This particular example can also be conceptualized as requiring the solver to see the relationships between letters within groups (here groups of three), the relationships between each group of three, and thus the appropriate third letter in the third group.

Penfield and Raven also took seriously Spearman's notion that intelligence involved the ability to handle abstract terms. Thus the results of their cogitations were test items of the form shown in Fig. 2.2. The main box contains a 3 × 3 matrix of diagrams with the third diagram in the third row missing. The examinee's task is to select, from the alternatives on offer below, the item that will complete the third row. The test was later published as the Standard Progressive Matrices (Raven, 1938), and has since been slightly revised. There are two other versions of the test, the Coloured Progressive Matrices for young children, and the Advanced Progressive Matrices for university students and other adults of relatively high IQ. I shall usually refer to them all, indifferently, as Raven's Matrices. All three versions of the test consist of a number of items (up to 60) like that illustrated in Fig. 2.2, covering a fairly wide range of difficulty. In the Advanced test, the items increase in difficulty as one progresses through the test; the Standard test is divided into five blocks of 12 items, each block embodying slightly different rules, and beginning with easier and ending with harder items within each block.

The contrast between the Raven and Wechsler tests could hardly be greater. Raven's Matrices is a paper-and-pencil, multiple-choice test, which can be administered at the same time to an indefinitely large group of people. It is carefully constructed to start with extremely simple and straightforward items, which everyone can understand, and get right, with the absolute minimum of instructions (the Advanced Matrices begins with a set of practice items). One of its perceived virtues, therefore, has been that it can be used with populations, such as the deaf or those whose first language is not the same as that of the examiner, who might find it difficult to follow all the examiner's instructions and questions during the administration of the WAIS or WISC. Deaf children, indeed, obtain scores on Raven's Matrices well within the normal range, in spite of a Wechsler verbal IQ significantly below normal (Conrad, 1979).

In addition to these differences in the way the tests are administered, the contents of Raven's Matrices seem to have virtually nothing in common with the Wechsler tests. Yet the correlations observed between Raven's and Wechsler scores in the general population are typically of the order of 0.40 to 0.75 (Burke, 1958, 1985; Court and Raven, 1995). What is the explanation of this highly significant correlation? A final difference between the two tests, already noted above, is that Raven's Matrices were explicitly designed to provide a direct measure of those cognitive processes theoretically supposed to underlie general intelligence.

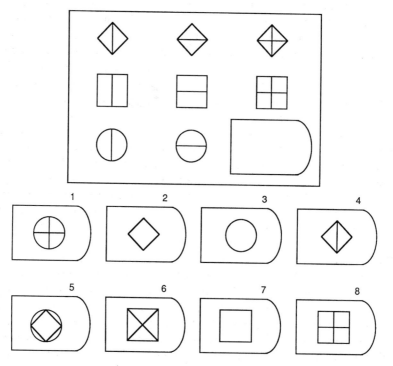

Fig. 2.2 Illustration of the type of item appearing in Raven's Matrices. The task is to select, from the alternatives below, the diagram which best completes the 3 × 3 matrix above.

By contrast with Wechsler's approach, which deliberately sought diversity of content as a way of ensuring that he did not miss any of the ways in which intelligence might be manifest, Penrose and Raven equally deliberately concentrated on one particular class of test, which they believed would measure abstract reasoning ability and nothing else. The most optimistic interpretation of the correlation between the two tests, therefore, is that Spearman was right. Abstract analogical reasoning ability is the central process underlying general intelligence or *g*, and Raven's Matrices provide a direct measure of this ability. But, indirectly, the Wechsler tests also measure this same general factor, since all parts of the test correlate with one another, and the only reason why IQ tests, or sub-tests, intercorrelate in this way, is because they all measure, to a greater or lesser extent, one and the same general factor.

For the time being, it is not necessary to evaluate this argument—or even fully to understand it. We shall take it up again in Chapter 6. For present purposes, we need only acknowledge that two quite different IQ tests, constructed on different principles, administered in different ways, and containing entirely different kinds of items, still

---

Box 2.2 Verbal and non-verbal IQ and the Wechsler tests

As we saw above, the distinction between the verbal and performance halves of the Wechsler tests also points to the difference between verbal and non-verbal measures of IQ. Paradoxically, however, the WAIS and WISC provide notably less clear evidence of the distinction than do other tests. One indication of this, perhaps already noted by sufficiently sceptical readers from their perusal of Table 2.2, is that the pattern of intercorrelations between the various sub-tests of the WAIS is hardly consistent enough to justify any sharp distinction. *That* would require that all verbal sub-tests correlated more highly with one another than with any performance sub-test, while the performance sub-tests in turn correlated more highly with one another than with any verbal sub-test. As was acknowledged above, there is at best only a modest tendency in this direction. Another indication of this point is that scores on the verbal half of the WAIS or WISC show much the same correlation with scores on Raven's Matrices as do scores on the performance half of the test. In Burke's (1985) study, the former correlation was 0.61, the latter no more than 0.63, and this seems to be typical of other studies (Court and Raven, 1995). If there really is a distinction between measures of verbal and of non-verbal IQ, and if we accept, as we surely must, that Raven's Matrices measure the latter rather than the former, the necessary conclusion is that the two halves of the Wechsler tests do *not* map on to this distinction very clearly.

The criteria employed, implicitly or explicitly, in selecting items or sub-tests to include in test batteries such as the Stanford–Binet, WAIS, or WISC, may have resulted in excellent tests for many of the purposes for which they were intended. The tests probably do give an adequate overall or global measure of a person's intellectual abilities. But, as many commentators have noted (e.g. Carroll, 1993), and as we shall document in due course, they do not necessarily measure the full range of people's different abilities or skills, and they certainly do not provide a theoretically well-grounded list of what such a range of abilities might encompass. That was not what they had been designed to do.

correlate surprisingly highly with one another. This is a sufficiently important observation in its own right. The intercorrelation between the various sub-tests of the WAIS or WISC, as we saw above, can in one sense be attributed to the criteria adopted for the inclusion of items in the test. But that argument cannot seriously apply here. There is no evidence that Penrose and Raven tinkered around with the items that eventually contributed to the Matrices until they had found ones that correlated with existing IQ tests such as the Stanford–Binet. Nor, of course, did Wechsler select items for his tests on the basis of their agreement with Raven's Matrices. The correlation between such diverse tests, therefore, is of some theoretical significance, and poses a challenge to critics who argue that IQ tests completely fail to measure anything they would want to call intelligence. The challenge can be spelled out thus: if no existing IQ test measures intelligence, then it ought to be possible to devise some other test or tests that did. And these new tests would, necessarily, show zero correlations with any existing IQ test, since the claim is that existing tests, unlike the new ones, fail to measure intelligence. But given the diversity of tests that do correlate quite substantially with one another, this challenge begins to look a serious one: it seems difficult to find a test, with any sort of face validity as a measure of intelligence, that will not correlate with existing IQ tests.

The variety of tests expands to include measures of specific abilities

The publication of Raven's Matrices prompted a number of similar group tests of non-verbal reasoning, among them Cattell's tests, which he explicitly and confidently described as a 'culture-fair' intelligence test (Cattell, 1940). Cattell's argument, which was accepted by many others, was that tests such as the Stanford–Binet or Wechsler tests could not give a fair picture of the intelligence of children from different backgrounds, because they asked questions about the meanings of English words or for evidence of specifically cultural knowledge that would simply not be equally available to all. By contrast, his tests used abstract and diagrammatic material that would be equally familiar or unfamiliar to all, and the tasks required, the solution of series completion tests, odd-one-out problems, as well as analogies and matrices, were testing skills that were not explicitly taught in school.

The idea that non-verbal tests were culturally fairer than verbal tests had its origin in the First World War army tests (alpha and beta). As we shall see, like many other long-cherished beliefs about IQ tests, it contains no more than a small grain of truth (Chapter 5). That is another matter. What is evident, however, and of more immediate concern, is that there does seem to be some sort of distinction between 'verbal' and 'non-verbal' IQ tests. In representative samples of the population, performance on a paradigmatic test of non-verbal reasoning, such as Raven's Matrices, correlates more highly with performance on other non-verbal tests than with scores on verbal tests (for a review of early evidence, see Burke,

1958). In a subsequent study of some 3000 adults, Burke (1985) reported a correlation of 0.68 between Raven's scores and performance on the Shipley abstract reasoning test, but one of only 0.48 between Raven's and the Shipley vocabulary test. Several other studies have confirmed that the correlation between Raven's Matrices and various vocabulary tests is of the order 0.40 to 0.50 (Court and Raven, 1995: many of these studies have employed the Mill-Hill vocabulary test, specifically designed by Raven to complement the measure of abstract, non-verbal reasoning provided by his Matrices). But correlations between Raven's scores and other non-verbal reasoning tests, including Cattell's tests, have usually been of the order 0.60 to 0.85 (Court and Raven, 1995).

Although Spearman's main contribution to the theory of IQ was his concept of g or general intelligence, his influence can still be detected in these developments. His argument that there is a single, fundamental process of general intelligence which permeates all intellectual activities, and determines performance on any test properly described as a measure of intelligence, provided a simple and satisfying explanation of the finding of positive correlations between a wide variety of different tests. His further argument that the more diverse the set of sub-tests included in a test battery, the better that battery would measure general intelligence, because idiosyncrasies in particular sub-tests would cancel each other out, provided the justification for the construction of test batteries such as the WAIS and WISC. But at the same time, the very simplicity of Spearman's hypothesis, and its apparent eminent testability, encouraged some IQ testers to look for evidence that would contradict it. What they were searching for was evidence of the existence of more specialized sets of abilities. Thurstone and his followers were the most prominent champions of the view that human intelligence is better conceived as a set of quite independent faculties or relatively specialized abilities. But although they repeatedly contrasted their position with that of Spearman and his followers, sometimes referred to as the 'London school', it was in fact members of that 'school' who were among the first to challenge Spearman's hypothesis. Burt (1917) argued that some tests revealed evidence of a more specialized set of verbal abilities, in addition to Spearman's general intelligence, while other British psychologists were identifying a set of specifically visuo-spatial abilities (El Koussy, 1935; Smith, 1964). As in other cases, the basis of such claims was that certain tests tended to correlate more highly with each other than with other tests. Examples of the type of test used to identify a set of visuo-spatial abilities are shown in Fig. 2.3.

Although there are some similarities between these spatial tests and tests of abstract or non-verbal reasoning, such as Raven's Matrices, it turns out that they are not necessarily measuring the same set of abilities. Scores on Raven's Matrices show no higher correlation with scores on tests such as those shown in Fig. 2.3 than they do with specifically verbal tests, such as measures of vocabulary (Court and Raven, 1995). Non-verbal tests themselves, therefore, need further sub-division, into what we could call tests of general abstract reasoning, and other tests of more specifically visuo-spatial skills. The distinction between verbal, non-verbal reasoning and spatial IQ is by now accepted by virtually all

Target   Comparison

(a)

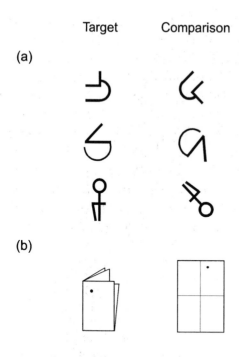

(b)

Fig. 2.3 Examples of spatial IQ tests. In (a), the subject's task is to decide whether the figure on the right, if rotated, is the same as, or a mirror-image of, the figure on the left. In (b), the task is to mark where the holes would appear in the sheet of paper when it is unfolded. More examples of spatial IQ tests are shown in Fig. 8.2.

writers on the subject (see Carroll, 1993). Even Gardner (1993) follows common practice by labelling three of his six intelligences linguistic, logical-mathematical, and spatial. Gardner also follows Thurstone (1938) in insisting that these three intelligences are all quite unrelated, but on the face of it the results of correlational analyses suggest that this is untrue.

Thurstone himself believed that human intelligence consisted of some half-dozen specific abilities, and attempted to devise tests that measured each of these abilities, as far as possible independently of the others. The result was a series of tests of seven 'primary mental abilities'. In addition to tests of spatial ability and induction or general reasoning, he proposed two verbal tests, verbal comprehension and word fluency (how many words beginning with the letter F can you think of in 1 minute?), and a separate mental arithmetic test. The final two primary mental abilities were associative memory, which tested simple rote learning, and perceptual speed, measured, for example, by requiring one to check all the Ps in a list of letters of the alphabet. We shall come across both these last two in subsequent chapters. The actual tests constructed by Thurstone have been widely criticized on technical grounds, and are no longer in general use. A more comprehensive battery of tests, based on similar theoretical principles, and described as a 'kit of reference tests' has been published in the USA by the Educational Testing Service (Ekstrom *et al.*, 1976), but a more widely used set of rather similar tests is the Differential Aptitude Test (DAT), originally published in 1947, most recently revised in 1990.

It is not necessary to prolong this discussion of different kinds of test. To list and discuss all possible IQ tests would take for ever, and serve no useful purpose. Enough has been said to show that IQ tests are diverse, and that some of them appear, on the face of it, to measure a number of rather different skills and abilities—although it is always important to remember that people who are good (or bad) at one kind of test will, more often than not, also be good (or bad) at others. This last point provides sufficient justification for accepting an overall score on a diverse test battery, such as the Wechsler or Stanford–Binet tests, as a measure of someone's 'IQ', and for believing that IQ, so measured, is worth exploring further, to see what it is related to and what it predicts, how it develops over the lifespan, how it is affected by genetic or environmental factors, and so on. Those who cannot wait for a more detailed discussion of the structure of different human abilities and their interrelationships may proceed directly to Chapter 6. The remainder of this chapter will discuss two further criteria that guided the construction of modern IQ tests.

What do IQ tests measure? Test validity

Early validity studies

However high the correlation between scores on one IQ test and scores on all others, such a pattern of intercorrelations alone would never be sufficient to prove that any of the tests was measuring anything we should want to call intelligence. For all we know, they might all be measuring, perhaps very successfully, some quite different human characteristic. For an IQ test to qualify as a measure of intelligence, the test constructor must establish its *validity*, i.e. measure the extent to which its results agree with some external, independent criterion of intelligence. But what shall we use? Two external criteria that have been traditionally accepted by most psychometricians were both first used by Galton (1869). He argued that eminence and achievement provided one criterion of intelligence: successful generals, judges, politicians, men of affairs, were presumably more intelligent than those less successful at these professions, let alone than those who failed to acquire such positions in the first place. And he also used performance at public examinations, specifically at the University of Cambridge and in the civil service, as a second criterion of intelligence. Educational and occupational attainment have been the most popular external validators of IQ tests ever since.

It was, indeed, their failure to correlate with one index of educational attainment, college grades, that proved the downfall of Cattell's original mental tests (Wissler, 1901; see Chapter 1). Binet himself, however, showed scant regard for the importance of these external validators, and his somewhat cavalier attitude was also adopted by many other pioneers of IQ tests. As we saw in Chapter 1, it was Binet's insight that, in the case of young children, age provided an independent criterion of intelligence, that provided him with the handle he needed to validate his original set of tests.

Age alone could hardly provide the only external criterion of intelligence: as we have just noted, it soon became apparent that it ceased to work after the age of 16 or so. And even below that age, it is not sufficient: children grow in height and weight as they grow older, but no one has suggested substituting a ruler or pair of scales for an IQ test. But although Binet noted, for example, that his tests succeeded in identifying children classified as feeble-minded (mildly or moderately retarded), he immediately went on to insist that the tests did this job rather better than current medical practice:

> the typical doctor, when he is confronted with a retarded child, does not examine him by listing, interpreting and classifying each of the symptoms the child presents; he is content to rely on a subjective, global impression, and to make his diagnosis by instinct. (Binet and Simon, 1905*a*, p. 168)

As for schoolteachers, Binet argued, they were often prepared to classify as subnormal children who were simply ignorant or troublesome. Why, then, should one suppose that one has validated an IQ test by establishing its agreement with such an unreliable criterion? As we shall see, this turns out to be a critical issue for most attempts to validate IQ.

Binet also noted that his test results agreed with one indicator of scholastic ability: children with above-average test scores were more likely to be a year or more ahead in school, while those whose mental age was lower than their chronological age were more likely to be a year or more behind at school (Binet, 1911). But although acknowledging the significance of this finding, it did nothing to qualify his insistence that intelligence and scholastic aptitude were *not* the same. He was even more dismissive of schoolteachers' assessments of their pupils' intelligence. When he asked teachers how they undertook such assessment, many of their replies seemed to him to be pointless and merely verbose, while others confused knowledge (usually simply the ability to remember what the teacher had told them) with judgement or intelligence. In effect, Binet had sufficient confidence in the validity of his own methods for devising tests that he hardly seems to have felt the need for much external evidence of their validity.

In his introduction to the Stanford–Binet tests, Terman dwelt at much greater length on the question of his tests' validity. But the impression he gives is that of a salesman eager to extol his wares, rather than of a scientist soberly evaluating the evidence. He begins by arguing that most people have greatly underestimated the extent to which children (and adults) differ in natural intelligence, with the result that on the one hand they do not appreciate the true magnitude of the burden imposed on society by the large number of feeble-minded people, and on the other that they fail to recognize how many exceptionally intelligent children receive an education that does no justice to their abilities. Properly used, intelligence tests will more than pay for themselves.

> Not only in the case of retarded or exceptionally bright children, but with many others also, intelligence tests can aid in correctly placing the child in school . . . The hour of time required for the test is a small matter in comparison with the loss of a school term [resulting from incorrect placement] . . . The time is probably not far distant when intelligence tests will [also] become a

recognized and widely used instrument for determining vocational fitness . . . Any business employing as many as five hundred or a thousand workers . . . could save in this way several times the salary of a well-trained psychologist. (Terman, 1916, pp. 16–18)

Terman agreed with Binet that teachers cannot be trusted to assess their pupils' intelligence with any degree of accuracy, and provided examples of discrepancies between test scores and teachers' assessments that invariably illustrated the accuracy of the former and the egregious error of the latter. But how did he know that his test scores were right? With little sense of embarrassment, he happily validated the test scores of his standardization sample by reporting 'a fairly close agreement' (Terman, 1916, p. 73) between IQ scores and teachers' grading of their pupils' school work on a five-point scale from very superior to very inferior. The correlation was in fact only 0.45. Even then he was not content to accept the teachers' gradings as themselves valid, but argued that most discrepancies were caused by teachers' failure to take their pupils' chronological age into account (superior work by a child a year older than the rest of her class would be entirely consistent with an average, or even below average, IQ score). The only other correlation he reported as evidence of the validity of his test was one of 0.48 between IQ and teachers' ratings of intelligence. Here too, whenever there was disagreement, 'the fault was plainly on the part of the teacher' (Terman, 1916, p. 75).

A similar confidence marked the work of those who sold IQ testing to the US Army in the First World War. The tests were given to some 1.75 million recruits, but although their test scores sometimes affected the jobs they were assigned to (frequently being used for selection for officer training, for example), little or no evidence was ever presented to establish that those scores provided a valid indicator of anyone's ability to undertake any military job, or their success at it. This is not really very surprising. The world of adult work does not provide such a convenient testing ground for the validation of IQ tests as does the school classroom. Schoolchildren are routinely assessed by their teachers; they are required to take exams; they can be given other tests of attainment as part of the school system's evaluation of their progress and its own efficiency. There is little difficulty in comparing the results of all these evaluations with those of an IQ test. But what constitutes success in a given job, and how is any assessment of that success to be obtained? Certainly when he came to develop his individual IQ tests for adults, Wechsler had little evidence to which he could point to establish the validity of his tests. He noted that adolescents' scores on his test correlated highly (0.82) with their scores on the Stanford–Binet test, and also, moderately well, with teachers' ratings of their intelligence. In the case of adults, he noted that his tests discriminated well between those classified as retarded and those not so stigmatized. For the rest, he simply acknowledged the problem:

How do we know that our tests are 'good' measures of intelligence? The only honest reply we can make is that our own experience has shown them to be so. If this seems to be a very tenuous answer we need only remind the reader that it has been practical experience which has given (or denied) final validity to every other intelligence test. Regrettable as it may seem, empirical judgments, here as elsewhere, play the rôle of ultimate arbiter. (Wechsler, 1944, pp. 127–128)

Regrettable—but certainly honest! In later editions, Wechsler was able to rely on evidence of a correlation between IQ scores and adult occupational status. However, one of his main arguments for the value of his tests remained the distinctly dubious claim that the *pattern* of scores people obtained on individual sub-tests provided a uniquely valuable clinical insight into their psychological strengths and weaknesses. In this case, at least, his judgment was less than perfectly reliable. As we have seen, the distinction between verbal and performance scores on the WAIS and WISC, although surely a real one, is rather less clear or precise than that between other verbal and non-verbal tests, while other test batteries also provide a somewhat more securely based distinction between these and other component abilities (such as spatial ability or perceptual speed).

IQ and educational attainment

This brief excursion back into the early history of IQ testing should not be taken to imply that there are no external criteria to which one can point as validators of IQ. There is, in fact, no shadow of doubt that IQ scores correlate moderately well with Galton's two criteria of intelligence, educational and occupational achievement. Since IQ tests were first developed for use in schools, it is not surprising that their validity has been most extensively studied by measuring their correlation with various indices of educational attainment. One type of study has examined the relationship between IQ scores and specific, formal tests of reading or mathematics. Others have relied on more general measures of educational attainment, such as public exams (in Britain) or school grades (in the USA). Yet others have reported correlations between IQ and whether students complete high school or obtain university degrees: a variant on this last type of measure is simply the total number of years of education. And an important subsidiary question addressed by some studies is whether IQ at one age predicts educational attainment at a later age.

Correlations between IQ scores and formal tests of reading, mathematics, or other subjects, and between IQ and school exam performance or grades, range between 0.40 and 0.70 (Vernon, 1947; Lavin, 1965; Jensen, 1980; Brody, 1992). In both cases the higher correlations are usually found with younger children, and they decline as the students progress through school, college, or university. This decline is usually attributed to increasing restriction of range, since those of lower IQ and educational attainment are likely to drop out from older samples, leaving a more restricted range of scores in those samples. But no one seems to have undertaken the longitudinal study that would test the truth of this assumption: we do not, in other words, know whether the selected sample of those who stay in school beyond the age of 16 or 17 would have shown an equally low correlation between IQ and educational attainment when tested at age 8 or 10.

There is also a significant correlation (of about 0.60) between IQ and total number of years of education (e.g. Jencks, 1972; McCall, 1977), and thus between IQ and educational qualifications. In the USA, for example, there is a 10–15 point difference in average IQ between those who graduate from high school and those who drop out before graduating, and a similar difference between high-school graduates and those who go on to obtain a college or university degree (Herrnstein and Murray, 1994). According to Herrnstein and Murray, indeed, the size of these differences has increased throughout the twentieth century.

If our sole purpose was to provide an external criterion against which to validate IQ tests, we could perhaps rest content at this point. There can be no reasonable doubt that IQ scores do not just record people's ability to answer the arbitrary questions posed by IQ testers; they say something about how long people stay in the educational system, and the qualifications they obtain, as well as their performance on standard measures of educational attainment. But it is reasonable to want to go further—to ask for an explanation of these correlations. Why should there be such pervasive correlations between IQ and educational attainment?

A sceptical answer might be that the correlations were built into the tests: IQ tests were constructed precisely with the requirement that their scores should correlate with educational attainment, and therefore included items that simply measured educational attainment. This is a common criticism (e.g. Block and Dworkin, 1976; Evans and Waites, 1981), part of which has a certain plausibility when one thinks of such items as the arithmetic sub-tests of the WISC and Stanford–Binet test. But it will hardly do as a sufficient explanation. Binet's dismissive attitude towards teachers' judgments should make it clear that he did not go about the business of test construction by carefully selecting items that would agree with them. Nor is there any reason to suspect that Raven's Matrices were carefully constructed with this end in mind. In the end, the argument has no more force than that which dismisses the overall positive correlation between a wide variety of different IQ tests as an artefactual consequence of the decision of test constructors to produce tests that did agree with one another. Even if this were true (and it is at best an exaggeration), it would not explain *why* such diverse tests correlate with one another—nor, in the present case, *why* performance on, say, Raven's Matrices should correlate with performance on school exams or tests of reading and arithmetic.

Although we shall need to return to the question at later points in this book, it is worth establishing two points now. First, the correlation between IQ and educational attainment is not just a correlation between two concurrent measures: IQ scores at one age predict educational attainment at a later age. The IQ scores of kindergarten children predict their performance on tests of reading 2 or 3 years later (Horn and Packard, 1985). In Britain, the correlation between 11-year-old IQ scores and later educational attainment, including performance on school examinations at age 16, is about 0.50 (Vernon, 1947; Mackintosh and Mascie-Taylor, 1986). American longitudinal studies have shown that as early as the age of 7 or 11, IQ correlates between 0.40 and 0.50 with total years of education (Jencks, 1972; McCall, 1977).

The second, even more important point, is that the correlation between IQ and educational attainment cannot be explained away by arguing that it is simply a consequence of the fact that both are a by-product of some other, more important factor. A perennial problem in social science, which we shall come across repeatedly, is that of disentangling the real causal links between a host of different factors when they are all correlated with one another. In the present instance, we know that IQ is correlated with educational attainment, but we also know both are correlated with family background. One could argue, therefore, that the IQ–attainment correlation is a by-product: middle-class parents endow their children with a high IQ (whether genetically or by providing a suitable early environment); they also, but independently, teach them to read at an early age, provide them with books and encyclopaedias, place an emphasis on school attainment, supervise their homework, send their children to good schools, and can afford to keep them there beyond the minimum school-leaving age. And so on. So the correlation between children's IQ scores and their educational attainment does not reflect a direct causal link from one to the other, but only the fact that both are determined by the children's family background or social class (socio-economic status, or SES, in sociological jargon).

The argument is a popular one, and may contain some truth. But it cannot be the whole story—because the correlation between family background, however measured, and educational attainment, however measured, is not nearly as high as many people suppose. Different studies have reported widely differing estimates of the strength of this relationship, but the most systematic analysis of, mostly American, data suggest that the correlation is no more than 0.20–0.30 (White, 1982). If that is true, it cannot possibly account for the correlation between children's IQ scores and their educational attainment, which, as we have seen, is typically of the order 0.40–0.70. Moreover, even among brothers and sisters living in the same family, there is a correlation of about 0.30 between IQ and educational attainment (Jencks, 1972).

Statistical analysis confirms this conclusion. There are various statistical techniques, ranging from partial correlation, through full-scale regression analysis, to path analysis, which can be used to separate out the true interrelationships between a variety of intercorrelated variables. Jencks (1972) used path analysis to estimate that children's own IQ scores are twice as important as their family background in determining their educational attainment. Herrnstein and Murray (1994) used regression analysis to support the same conclusion. They showed that when parental SES is held constant, IQ scores are still strongly related to two measures of educational attainment—obtaining a high-school diploma and a university degree. But when IQ is held constant, the relationship between parental SES and these educational achievements is quite modest. Their results are shown in Fig. 2.4. They also present evidence to suggest that the relative importance of IQ and family background has changed during the course of the twentieth century: entrance to, say,

Harvard, Yale, or Princeton in the USA, or to Oxford or Cambridge in England, is now more dependent on prior educational attainment (and, it seems probable, on IQ), and less on family background, than it was in the first half of the twentieth century. The correlation between IQ and educational attainment cannot (nowadays at least) seriously be attributed solely to the advantages of a middle-class family background.

It seems fair to conclude that a variety of measures of educational achievement provide reasonable grounds for accepting that IQ scores measure something other than the ability to answer questions on IQ tests, and that this something is related to success in one sphere of activity where 'intelligence' has traditionally been thought to be relevant.

IQ and occupation

The optimistic interpretation of the studies reviewed in the preceding section is that IQ scores successfully measure academic intelligence. Many critics have been willing to accept this, but immediately gone on to argue that this is *all* they measure (Neisser, 1976): IQ tests, they suggest, miss out on everyday, practical abilities—those needed for success in the real world outside the school classroom or university ivory tower. It is here that Galton's second criterion of intelligence—worldly distinction or eminence—needs to be considered. How well do IQ scores predict whether people will succeed after they leave full-time education?

More prosaic, and jargon-ridden, than Galton, IQ testers have sought to validate their tests by showing that they predict socio-economic status or income, and the ability to perform a job effectively. They have argued that IQ scores correlate with three rather

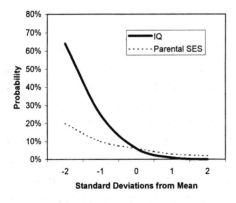
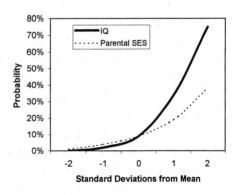

Fig. 2.4 Relationship between IQ, parental SES, and two measures of educational attainment. In both figures, the solid line represents the relationship between IQ and attainment when SES is held constant, and the dotted line the relationship between SES and attainment when IQ is held constant. It is evident that people's own IQ scores are more important than their family background. (Data from Herrnstein and Murray, 1994.)

Table 2.3 Average IQ and range of scores in various occupations (from Harrell and Harrell, 1945)

Occupation	Mean IQ	IQ range
Accountant	128	94–157
Lawyer	128	96–157
Teacher	123	76–155
Clerk-typist	117	80–147
Machinist	110	38–153
Butcher	103	42–147
Carpenter	102	42–147
Labourer	96	26–145
Truck driver	96	16–149
Farmer	93	24–147

different aspects of occupational achievement: the status of a person's job; the income they earn; and the efficiency with which they perform their job. I shall take up each of these in turn.

Occupational status

There is reasonably general agreement that some jobs confer higher status and prestige than others. Table 2.3 lists a range of different occupations: although readers may quibble with the precise rank ordering shown there, most would probably agree that the job of lawyer or other professional has a higher status than that of shop assistant, truck driver, or farm labourer. Different classificatory schemes assign jobs to anywhere between 5 and 12 status bands, the details of which need not concern us. Table 2.3 gives sufficient idea of what is meant by the concept of 'occupational status'. Studies of adult job-holders, both in Britain and the USA, have consistently reported a significant correlation, of the order of 0.50–0.60 between their IQ scores and the status of their jobs. (See Harrell and Harrell (1945) and Vernon (1947) for early studies and reviews; Jencks (1972), Brody (1992), and Herrnstein and Murray (1994) provide more recent evidence.) In one important longitudinal study, McCall (1977) showed that the IQ scores of children as young as 8 years old correlated over 0.40 with the status of their adult jobs when they were 40.

One aspect of this correlation has been widely seen as particularly significant. It is shown in Table 2.3, which presents a selection of data from a large-scale study of the IQ scores of American servicemen in the Second World War, who had previously been engaged in different civilian occupations (Harrell and Harrell, 1945). The important point to note in this table is not just that lawyers have a higher average IQ than typists, who in turn have a higher average IQ than butchers, carpenters, labourers, or truck drivers. The interesting observation is that the variation in IQ within each occupation *increases* as the average IQ decreases; this is because, as the final column shows, people with high IQ can be found in all jobs, but those with lower IQ only in the lower status jobs. Harrell and Harrell assumed that this evidently meant that

> a certain minimum of intelligence is required for any one of many occupations and a man must have that much intelligence in order to function in that job. (Harrell and Harrell, 1945, p. 239)

And Jensen has endorsed their conclusion, arguing that:

> a certain threshold level of intelligence is a necessary but not a sufficient condition for success in most occupations: a diminishing percentage of the population is intellectually capable of satisfactory performance in occupations the higher the occupation (Jensen, 1980, p. 344).

Other commentators (e.g. Herrnstein and Murray, 1994) have also accepted this inference. But it surely requires further justification. It is one thing to show that, as a matter of fact, few lawyers or doctors have an IQ below 100. It is another thing to assert that no one with an IQ below 100 is intellectually capable of performing the job of lawyer or doctor.

What, then, is the explanation of the correlation between IQ and occupational status? As we saw for the case of educational attainment, so here, a popular explanation has been that both are a by-product of the social class into which one is born. Middle-class parents not only endow their children with a high IQ, they also pass on their high-status jobs. There is, it hardly needs saying, a significant correlation between one's parents' social class and one's own eventual occupation: children born into middle-class families are indeed more likely to end up in middle-class jobs than the children of unskilled or unemployed parents. But most studies suggest that this correlation is no more than about 0.35 (e.g. Jencks, 1972). If that is so, then just as with the case of educational achievement, so here, parental status cannot possibly be the *sole* cause of the higher correlation (of between 0.50 and 0.60) between a person's own IQ and the status of their occupation. Even at age 8, IQ seems to be a better predictor of later occupational status than is parental social class.

Although we shall need to return later to the relationship between IQ and social class (in Chapters 4 and 5), it seems reasonable to insist that people's adult occupational status is not simply inherited from their parents' status. The relationship between childhood IQ and later, adult status, cannot be explained away in this fashion. But that still does not mean that there is a simple, direct causal link from one to the other. In fact there is good evidence that the link is largely via education. We have seen that IQ is well correlated with educational attainment and qualifications; not surprisingly, adult occupational status is also predicted by educational qualifications, if only because many jobs require formal educational credentials. Thus it is plausible to suppose that one reason why people with higher IQs obtain higher-status jobs is because they obtain superior educational qualifications. Table 2.4 shows the correlations between occupational status and both IQ and education in two American studies; in both cases, educational level predicts occupational status slightly better than does IQ. But it is also possible to compute the partial correlation between occupation and each of these variables when the other is held constant. The results, also shown in Table 2.4, reveal that even when IQ is held constant, educational level still predicts occupational status pretty well: in a group of people with the same IQ those with superior qualifications will still obtain superior jobs. But, particularly in the Bajema study, when education is held constant, the partial correlation between IQ and occupation, although still significant, is quite small: in a group with the same educational qualifications, variation in IQ has a relatively small effect on occupational status.

Another way of representing these relationships is by the technique of path analysis. The results of one such analysis (Jencks, 1972) imply that although both IQ and years of education are associated with occupational status, IQ exerts most of its influence by its effect on level of education. The remaining (or direct) effect of IQ on occupation is small—no more than 0.10.

These figures have been seized upon as proof that IQ *per se* is entirely unimportant as a determinant of occupational status (Bowles and Gintis, 1976; Evans and Waites, 1981; Ceci, 1990). But this inference is no more justified than that which saw the correlation between IQ and status as proof that no one with a low IQ is intellectually up to the demands of a high-status job. In the first place, the effect of IQ is still significant even when all other variables in these analyses have been allowed for. Secondly, however, it is important to see just what partial correlations or path analyses can show. Let us accept that the most important single factor determining whether one becomes, say, a lawyer or a doctor, is the possession of the appropriate educational qualifications (a medical or a law degree, for example). The fact of the matter is that only those with above average IQs will obtain such qualifications: IQ may not have much further impact because it has already done its work by being a necessary ingredient of the acquisition of the relevant educational qualifications. Only if one could obtain a medical degree regardless of one's IQ would it be reasonable to conclude that IQ scores had no bearing on occupational status. Unless the correlation between IQ scores and educational attainment can be explained away as a consequence of other causal factors, it seems more reasonable to accept that IQ scores do indeed have an important bearing on people's job prospects, even if much of their effect is mediated through educational qualifications.

Income

But none of this is sufficient to establish the conclusion drawn by Jensen (1980) or Herrnstein and Murray (1994) from data such as those shown in Table 2.3—that no one

Table 2.4 Relationship between IQ, education, and occupational status

| | | (Bajema, 1968) | | (Waller, 1971) | |
		IQ	Education	IQ	Education
Correlation with	Raw	0.46	0.58	0.50	0.52
occupational status	Partial	0.15	0.42	0.21	0.27

with an IQ below, say, 100 is intellectually capable of holding down the job of a lawyer, doctor, or accountant. The fact that few doctors have an IQ below 100 can be explained by saying that you need a high IQ to get into medical school. What is required to prove that the abilities measured by the tests are actually relevant to the demands of the job, is some evidence that IQ scores predict which doctors will be successful. But what independent measure of success might we use? One obvious answer is some rating or evaluation of actual performance, and we shall turn to this in a moment. But a rather simpler measure is worth considering first—income. One could, of course, argue that income is simply another measure of occupational status: are not lawyers and doctors paid more than secretaries, nurses, or lorry drivers? No doubt. But, as university professors are the first to point out, the pay associated with certain jobs is not always commensurate with their importance or social prestige. Some relatively prestigious jobs (teachers) are no better, and often a great deal worse, paid than other less prestigious ones. Status and income are correlated (if they were not we could hardly have come up with the concept of socio-economic status), but the correlation is far from perfect; in American data, analysed by Jencks, the correlation is only 0.40 (Jencks, 1972).

Thus income does provide a partially independent measure of occupational success, and it turns out that its association with IQ is rather different from that between status and IQ. In the first place, the overall correlation between IQ and income is notably smaller than that between IQ and occupational status—0.30 as opposed to 0.60 according to Jencks (1972). Once again, of course, these correlations cannot be taken at face value; income is also correlated with other correlates of IQ such as schooling, parental income, parental status, and we have the usual problem of attempting to disentangle the true causal pathway. According to Bowles and Gintis (1976), when these other factors are taken into account there is *no* residual effect of IQ *per se*. Although their conclusion has been cited frequently, their results seem to be quite atypical. Jenck's analysis suggests a more complicated and interesting story.

> The relationship between IQ test scores and income is . . . quite different from the relationship between test scores and occupational status. On the one hand, men with high test scores are more likely to enter high status occupations than to have high incomes, on the other hand the effect of test scores on income seems to be more genuine than their effect on status in that more of it persists after we control family background and [educational] credentials. (Jencks, 1972, p. 22)

This is because, according to his analysis, educational credentials actually have little or no direct effect on income at all: entrepreneurs educated in the university of life make a great deal more money than university professors with PhDs. That conclusion may also be too strong—or at least out of date. Herrnstein and Murray (1994, Chapter 4) argue that more recent data suggest that both educational level and IQ are *independently* associated with income.

One of the problems in the analysis of IQ and income is that the relationship varies with age—being substantially lower in a sample of 25- to 30-year-olds than in a group of people aged 50–60 (Duncan *et al.*, 1972). When one stops to think about it, this is only to be expected: neither graduate students nor junior doctors are very well paid, and it is not until we are dealing with people over the age of 35 or so that these, and the numerous other cases where a relatively high IQ and prolonged education are initially associated with low income, have disappeared from the analysis. Thus it is not entirely surprising that Ceci (1990), in an analysis of some 2000 30-year-olds, should find no relationship between IQ and income once social class and schooling were controlled for. He also found that the effect of parents' social class on their children's income was significantly greater among those of lower IQ than those of higher IQ. But this seems not at all surprising: it merely inclines one to believe that the less intelligent need the benefit of parental background while the more intelligent can rely on their own resources. Neither of Ceci's observations can justify his conclusion that 'the relationship between IQ and adult income is illusory' (p. 66). On balance, the evidence implies that there is a small, but significant, relationship between the two.

Occupational performance

But do IQ scores predict how efficiently people perform their jobs? This seems the critical question. No one can seriously doubt that income and status are influenced by all manner of educational and social advantages. But if IQ tests measure a set of intellectual or cognitive skills of general significance, they should predict the skill and efficiency which people bring to their job. Moreover, to the extent that some jobs (those of high status) require greater intellectual proficiency, the relationship between IQ and efficiency should be more apparent in some jobs than in others.

That there is a significant relationship between IQ and various measures of job performance is now indisputable, and there is good evidence that the magnitude of the relationship varies with the demands of the job. Although earlier studies implied that the relationship varied widely and seemingly haphazardly from one study to another (Ghiselli, 1966), meta-analysis of this early work, together with one or two large-scale recent studies, has brought more order onto the scene and yielded a reasonably consistent picture: IQ scores do predict how well people are judged to be performing their job, and the correlation between IQ scores and ratings of proficiency are generally rather higher for jobs of higher status than for those of lower status (Hunter and Hunter, 1984; Hunter, 1986; Hartigan and Wigdor, 1989; for reviews, see Jensen, 1980; Ree and Earles, 1992; Herrnstein and Murray, 1994).

What remains a matter of considerable dispute is the magnitude of the relationship between IQ and proficiency. Hunter and Hunter (1984) report correlations that have been adjusted or 'corrected' to take account of the unreliability of the measures being correlated and the restriction in the range of test scores of those in the running for different types of job. The correlations they report range from 0.25 to 0.60 for different jobs. Hartigan and

Wigdor (1989), analysing similar data sets, apply fewer, more conservative corrections and report correlations in the range 0.15 to 0.30. There is no need to argue here the merits and pitfalls of such statistical manipulations. Although they can be justified for certain purposes, it is usually more sensible to err on the side of caution. In this case, caution implies that IQ scores are not very good predictors of the efficiency with which people perform their jobs.

The fact remains, however, that even correlations of 0.15–0.30, although modest, are significant when the sample is large enough—and for what it is worth, not without economic consequence. Regardless of their absolute magnitude, a more informative picture of the validity of IQ scores is provided by comparing them with some other possible predictors of job performance. If you are an employer screening applicants for a job, what information should you rely on to choose between them? Hunter and Hunter's (1984) analyses establish that IQ scores are a better predictor than any of the following: biographical data, references, educational level, college grades, or interviews. How well someone will perform a job may depend on so many factors—some of them idiosyncratic or not easily measured—that prediction will always be imperfect. The fact remains that IQ predicts performance rather better than these other indices, and IQ is not just a surrogate for years of education or college grades, both of which show notably lower correlation with performance.

In the large majority of these studies the criterion of successful job performance has been a supervisor's rating. This has led some critics to suggest that all we are seeing is a tendency for supervisors to base their judgments on irrelevant, but IQ-related aspects of their supervisees' behaviour, with higher ratings going to those who are well spoken, well behaved, etc. In other words, it is such factors as family background and level of education that are actually predicting the ratings being given. No doubt supervisors' ratings are not the perfect objective evaluation one would like, but the argument fails for two reasons. First, as we have just seen, IQ provides a better predictor of rated performance than any other single factor, including biographical information and educational level: it is difficult to believe that supervisors are more likely to be swayed by employees' unknown IQ scores than by readily ascertainable information about their past life and education. Secondly, and more important, there is good evidence that objective measures of work samples correlate even more highly with IQ scores than do supervisors' ratings. Jensen (1980, p. 350) has analysed partial correlations (with education and years of experience held constant) between IQ and actual performance of particular duties falling within the remit of the job. He reports correlations ranging from 0.32 to 0.38, compared to correlations of only 0.11–0.26 between IQ and supervisors' ratings.

Conclusions

Although the point is still disputed, there can be no serious doubt that IQ scores do correlate with a variety of indices of educational and occupational attainment. A part of this

Box 2.3 Does IQ measure cognitive components of success?

Scores on IQ tests predict both educational and occupational success, but very far from perfectly. Although one would only expect a moderate correlation between a measure of intelligence and a measure of achievement, since actual achievement must depend on other factors, an alternative interpretation is possible. Perhaps IQ tests simply measure some of these other factors that contribute to, say, educational attainment, and quite fail to measure the cognitive or intellectual components of such attainment. Perhaps they simply measure 'test-taking skills', or docility, or lack of anxiety, or ambition, or whatever.

This is the sort of logical possibility beloved of armchair critics or philosophers (e.g. Block and Dworkin, 1976). But is it plausible? Two lines of evidence suggest that it is not. First, if all that IQ tests measure is one's ability or willingness to concentrate and put effort into solving a set of quite difficult problems, then people with high IQ scores should do better than people of low IQ at any sort of moderately difficult test. Although IQ scores do indeed correlate with performance on a lot of other tasks, many of these correlations are quite low. Correlations between IQ and forward digit span, choice reaction time to visual stimuli, or rote memory for nonsense syllables are all less than 0.30 (Chapters 7–9), but all these tasks require effort and concentration, and all can be made as difficult as the experimenter chooses, without affecting, to any serious extent, their correlation with IQ. If IQ simply measures test-taking skills, why are these correlations not a great deal higher?

Secondly, if IQ scores measure only the non-cognitive components of educational attainment, such as personality or temperament, one would expect measures of temperament to correlate more strongly with IQ than with educational attainment. This is the reverse of the truth. For example, Petrill and Thompson (1993) gave IQ and achievement tests to 163 children, together with a measure of some half-dozen aspects of temperament—emotionality, attentiveness, sociability, etc. Achievement and IQ correlated 0.46; achievement correlated with temperament 0.25, but the correlation between IQ and temperament was only 0.14. Partial correlations were even more revealing: the partial correlation between achievement and temperament, holding IQ constant, was still 0.21; but the partial correlation between IQ and temperament, holding achievement constant, was only 0.02. The plausible interpretation is that the shared variance between IQ and achievement is primarily cognitive, and that the reason why IQ correlates only moderately with achievement is because achievement also depends on temperament, but IQ does not.

relationship can be attributed to a variety of other, correlated factors; indeed, some studies have suggested that family background is even more important than IQ in determining occupational status or income (e.g. Bowles and Gintis, 1976; Jencks, 1979). The balance of the evidence, however, suggests that IQ is at least as important as these other factors, and very few studies have succeeded in discounting the significant, independent contribution of IQ. When all other factors are taken into account, IQ remains one source of variation in school achievement, occupation status, income, and the efficiency with which people actually perform their jobs.

The contribution of IQ is not large, but it is probably real. Although some persistent critics have stressed how small this contribution actually is, it is worth concluding by insisting that the demonstration of a *moderate* correlation between IQ scores and these other indices of success is the best result IQ testers could have asked for. If correlations between IQ and other measures had turned out to be zero (or negative!), there would surely have been reason to question whether IQ tests could possibly be measuring anything we normally understand by the term 'intelligence'. Paradoxically, however, too high a correlation between IQ and measures of educational or occupational success would have been equally problematic. For the fact of the matter is that these other measures are themselves surely quite imperfect and unreliable indices of intelligence. Not only are teachers' assessments, as Binet and Terman argued, unreliable; more importantly, no one could seriously suppose that intelligence was the sole determinant of such success: hard work, ambition, and good fortune are surely just as necessary. A test that purports to measure intelligence rather than industry and determination, therefore, should not correlate too highly with such an imperfect criterion.

It cannot be emphasized too strongly that, at the end of the day, we do not have any perfect, independent criterion of intelligence—if only because we are not quite clear what 'intelligence' might be. All we have is a variety of different indices, many of them (those relying on people's judgments) probably very unreliable, and most of them contaminated by other factors that we surely wish to distinguish from intelligence. In the absence of a perfect criterion, the quest for external validity can take us only so far, and it is a mistake to suppose that we shall, or could, achieve much more than we have: IQ scores do show modest correlations with various indices of educational and occupational achievement. Binet, Terman, and Wechsler were, perhaps, right not to lay too much stress on whether their tests agreed with other criteria (beyond age). As I have already argued, the question whether IQ tests are good measures of intelligence is not a simple one—and possibly not even a sensible one to ask. It will certainly not be answered solely by looking at evidence of external validity, and it is time to turn to one final criterion which a satisfactory measure of intelligence ought to satisfy.

What do IQ tests measure? Test reliability and the stability of IQ

Reliability

This final criterion is that of reliability. In the technical jargon of test theory, the validity of a test refers to the extent to which the test measures that which it purports to measure. The reliability of a test is an index of the extent to which it measures *anything*, or more precisely of the extent to which a score on that test reflects anything other than chance. On a perfectly reliable test, if the same person could be tested again under exactly the same conditions, they would obtain exactly the same score; on an unreliable test, by contrast, their scores both being largely a matter of chance, would be unrelated to one another. It will be obvious that reliability is a prerequisite for validity: an unreliable test cannot claim to be a valid measure of anything.

The reliability of IQ tests is measured in a variety of ways. 'Split-half' reliability simply involves comparing individuals' scores on, say, odd and even items in the test. Other measures rely on testing people on separate occasions—either on alternate forms of the test (the first revision of the Stanford–Binet test provided alternate forms for measuring IQ on separate occasions), or on the original form again. This last measure, referred to as 'test–retest' reliability, requires, of course, some minimum interval between the two occasions. The higher the reliability of the test, the higher the correlation between the two scores people obtain. The reliability of individual tests such as the Stanford–Binet or Wechsler tests is, by any reckoning, satisfactory, with reliability coefficients of about 0.95. Multiple-choice group tests generally have slightly lower reliabilities, partly because they are shorter and partly because guesswork can always play a part. A multiple-choice vocabulary test requires one to choose between half a dozen alternatives as the correct definition of each word, but the Stanford–Binet and Wechsler vocabulary tests require one to offer one's own definition. Even the sketchiest knowledge, quite insufficient to solve this latter task, may allow one to rule out some of the alternatives in the multiple-choice test and thus affect one's chances of guessing correctly. Nevertheless, most multiple-choice IQ tests, such as the DAT or Raven's Matrices, have reliabilities in the range 0.85–0.90 (Jensen, 1980; Court and Raven, 1995— although they report occasional studies of Raven's Matrices with reliabilities as low as 0.75).

When we assess the test–retest reliability of a particular IQ test by giving it to the same group of people on more than one occasion, we must obviously allow some minimum interval between first and second tests. Where that interval is, say, a year or more, we are in effect asking a slightly different question, namely, what is the long-term stability of an IQ score? We are inclined to believe that intelligence is a relatively stable characteristic of any individual. Although acknowledging that someone may feel sharper on some occasions than others, or feel slow, stupid, and unable to concentrate when suffering from a bad cold or hangover, we do not expect their intelligence to fluctuate wildly from one day to another. And although we believe that children may develop at different rates, with some being precocious and others late developers, we should still be surprised if there were *no* relationship between a child's level of intelligence at age 10, and their adult intelligence some 10–20 years later. If IQ tests purport to measure intelligence, therefore, your IQ score today should correlate reasonably well with your IQ score not only tomorrow, but also next year or in 10 years time. Contrast this with a test of mood, which might be a perfectly reliable and valid measure, but still give entirely different answers on different occasions— because your mood can change from day to day.

Numerous studies have demonstrated high correlations between scores on the same IQ test taken on two separate occasions up to a year or two apart (Bloom, 1964; Jensen, 1980).

For the Stanford–Binet and Wechsler tests, one-year test–retest correlations average about 0.90. More interesting are the results of a long-term longitudinal study that followed up children from the age of 2–3 until age 40. This allows one to see how stable IQ scores remain over very much longer intervals. Figure 2.5 plots the correlation between IQ at each age, separately for males and females, from infancy to adolescence, with IQ at age 40. The results suggest two main conclusions. First, after the age of 6–10, IQ scores remain relatively stable: the correlation between IQ at age 40 is over 0.70. This is surely evidence of considerable long-term stability, and thus consistent with our expectations of a measure of intelligence. Secondly, however, it is clear that the correlations of less than 0.50 between IQ scores taken before the age of 4 or 5 and later, adult IQ are distinctly unimpressive, and an IQ test given at age 2 tells one almost nothing about later IQ.

What is the explanation of this failure of very early IQ scores to predict later IQ? Those who believe in the overriding importance of the environment as a determinant of IQ will not be surprised that it should require several years of experience before a child's intelligence is sufficiently established to be measured with any reliability. One could even argue that variations in experience in the first year or two of life are not necessarily predictive of the critical variations that will shape IQ later. Moreover, since IQ tests simply measure whether one child is advanced for her age, or another is lagging behind, very young children's scores at any given moment in time will depend on whether they have just mastered a particular accomplishment (pointing to their nose or toes, counting up to four) or whether they are just about to. Minor variations in developmental spurts and lags may have a disproportionate effect on early test scores.

Another possibility is that the accomplishments measured by IQ tests at age 2–3 are simply unrelated to those measured later. This is clearly true of most tests designed for even younger infants. Scores on the best known of these, Bayley's scales (Bayley, 1969), show near-zero correlation with IQ scores at age 6–10. Bayley's scales measure such physical skills as sitting or standing, grasping or looking for objects, and there is no a priori reason why the age at which such skills are mastered should predict the later acquisition of the knowledge and skills measured by standard IQ tests.

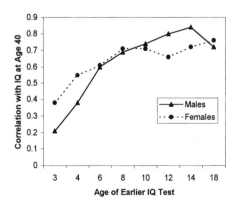

Fig. 2.5 The long-term stability of IQ scores in males and females. The ordinate of the figure shows the value of the correlation between earlier IQ and IQ at age 40, and the abscissa shows the age at which the earlier IQ score was measured. (Data from a study by Honzik, reported by McCall, 1977.)

There is, however, one striking and important exception to this general failure to find early predictors of later IQ. The correlation between measures of habituation to a novel stimulus taken in the first year of life and IQ scores at age 5–7 is in the range 0.40–0.50 (see reviews by Bornstein and Sigman, 1986; McCall and Carriger, 1993), and some later studies have reported correlations of the same value between infant habituation and IQ scores out to age 10–12 (Rose and Feldman, 1995). Interestingly enough, there is some suggestion that these correlations are higher when habituation is measured at age 3–7 months rather than at 1 year (McCall and Carriger, 1993; Rose and Feldman, 1995).

When presented with a novel visual stimulus, infants direct their gaze towards it, and will fixate it for a certain length of time. Repeated presentation of the same stimulus will result in a decrease in the duration of such fixation—but at this point, replacement of the original stimulus with a new one will restore gazing and fixation. There are various measures of such habituation and dishabituation that can be taken: the total length of time the infant fixates the stimulus over a given series of trials; the number of trials needed to produce a given reduction in the duration of fixation; the extent to which fixation is restored by substitution of a novel stimulus; or finally, in a choice test, the proportion of time spent looking at a novel stimulus rather than one seen before. This last test is usually described as a measure of recognition memory. McCall and Carriger (1993) concluded that there was little evidence to suggest that any one of these measures yielded reliably or substantially higher correlations with later IQ than any other.

Although a churlish critic might complain that a correlation of 0.40–0.50 is not dramatically high, it is certainly higher than those found between any other measure of infants' behaviour and their IQ score up to 10 years later. Indeed, one reason why the correlation is not even higher may well be that measures of infant habituation are themselves relatively unreliable, and it is a general tenet of test theory that an unreliable test cannot reliably predict performance on any other test. Since the correlation between habituation scores taken on two separate occasions is itself no more than about 0.50, that they should correlate nearly as well with IQ scores taken years later is surely rather impressive—especially since, on the face of it, the two measures seem to have rather little in common. What is the explanation of such a correlation?

Some answers to that question are easier than others, and some of the harder ones will have to be postponed. At this juncture only a few points need to be made. First, a correlation between later IQ and any measure of an infant's behaviour in the first 6–9 months of life tends to argue against the sort of environmentalist position sketched above, which suggested that a child's IQ is a product of years of intellectual stimulation and cannot be measured before those years have been experienced. It is not, of course, necessary to jump to the conclusion that IQ is a fixed, innate property of the brain, in some mysterious way directly measured by rate of habituation, for it is always possible to point to an even earlier environment (perhaps even *in utero*) as a determinant of test performance. Consistent with this, there is evidence that infant habituation scores also predict later IQ for pre-term babies and others identified as at risk from perinatal complications (McCall and Carriger, 1993).

The point of departure for this discussion was the issue of the long-term stability of IQ scores. The question posed by these results, however, is rather different: measures of habituation, dishabituation, and recognition memory are hardly conventional IQ tests (even if, sensibly enough, the most recent version of Bayley's developmental scales now include such measures; Bayley, 1993). So the puzzle is to see what they could possibly have in common with conventional IQ tests that would explain the relatively strong correlation between the two over periods of up to 10 years. But the puzzle is not just an idle, intellectual curiosity, for if we knew the answer we should surely have taken an important step to ascertaining what it is that conventional IQ tests are measuring.

The problem, however, is that tests of habituation, dishabituation, and recognition memory themselves presumably measure a variety of different psychological processes, any one of which could be responsible for their correlation with IQ. Rapidity of habituation presumably depends, among other things, on the efficiency and rapidity with which the infant nervous system stores a representation of the repeated stimulus, for in the absence of any such representation of past occurrences all stimuli will always remain equally novel. Dishabituation to a novel stimulus, or preference for the novel stimulus in a test of recognition memory, requires that the stored representation of the familiar stimulus be sufficiently precise that it is discriminated from the novel stimulus. Those who have sought to reduce IQ to the efficiency of sensory registration or basic information processing in the nervous system have been quick to emphasize these aspects of the habituation task (Chapter 7). But although some such processes must surely be involved in habituation and recognition memory, it does not follow that *variations* in such processes are responsible for variations in speed of habituation or magnitude of dishabituation, let alone for their correlation with IQ. The processes of sensory registration and storing of accurate representations of stimuli might be equally rapid and efficient in all infants, and differences in rate of habituation might have much more to do with the efficiency of mechanisms for inhibiting the initial fixation response (McCall and Carriger, 1993). Such a possibility would be consistent with some neurobiological evidence that points to the maturation of the nervous system, and particularly of the frontal cortex, as one mechanism subserving the development of the ability to inhibit prepotent responses (Johnson and Morton, 1991; Russell, 1996). Other, rather vaguer possibilities are equally plausible or implausible (Chapter 3). At present there are few grounds for choosing between any of them. But it is not being naively optimistic to suppose that further understanding of the causes of differences in rate of habituation and dishabituation will surely help to illuminate the nature of the processes being measured by IQ tests.

Stability of IQ scores over the lifespan

A final question about the long-term stability of IQ scores remains to be acknowledged. If a person's IQ did not remain relatively constant over intervals of weeks, months, or even a few years, we should seriously question whether IQ tests measure anything we should want to call intelligence—since our concept of intelligence implies that it will not fluctuate wildly from one moment to another. So the relative stability of IQ between the ages of, say, 10 and 40 is consistent with our preconception of how a measure of intelligence should behave. But what do we expect to happen as people grow even older—at age 60 or 80? Will their intelligence increase, decrease, or stay the same? One point of view, popular with the old, is that old age brings increasing maturity and wisdom, and provides a greater store of knowledge on which to base one's sounder judgments. Another, more popular with the young, is that it brings increasing rigidity and inflexibility, that people slow down as they grow older—and intelligence is partly a matter of being quick on the uptake. It seems, then, that the results of IQ tests over the lifespan might be quite informative: it is not that test scores *must* stay constant if IQ is to count as a good measure of intelligence. We do not actually know what to expect.

The first IQ test to provide any serious information on this issue was the Wechsler–Bellevue (the precursor of the WAIS), since Wechsler's original standardization sample included adults stratified by age, as well as some younger children. Wechsler's results, shown in Fig. 2.6a, seemed to answer the question unambiguously. Absolute test scores, on both the verbal and performance halves of the test, first increased as children grew up, but eventually started to decline, so that by the age of 50–60 people were obtaining scores no higher than those of 10–12-year-old children. This decline, moreover, was more pronounced, and started at an earlier age, on the performance than on the verbal scales. Figure 2.6b shows comparable data for adults aged 20–70 in the latest standardization sample of the WAIS-R. The results are broadly similar: here, performance on the verbal scales improves up to age 40 before declining, while scores on the performance scales decline steadily from age 20 on, and by age 70 are less than 75 per cent of the scores obtained at age 20. This is not a trivial effect.

Such a pattern of results could be seen as suggesting that the preconceptions of both old and young contain a grain of truth. For what is the explanation of the difference between the verbal and performance scales? A plausible answer is that verbal sub-tests, which ask questions about the meaning of words and general knowledge, largely measure accumulated experience or wisdom, while the performance sub-tests require one to solve novel puzzles or problems, often giving bonus marks for rapid answers, and thus measure speed, flexibility, and related aspects of intelligence which do indeed start declining from a relatively early age. Both old and young can thus take comfort from the data—by valuing more highly those aspects of the tests at which they excel.

It is, perhaps, this apparent confirmation of prior expectation that explains why the

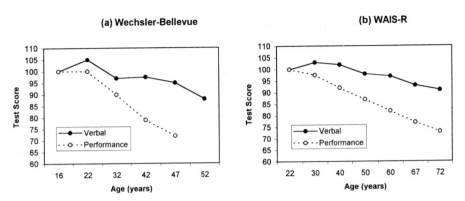

Fig. 2.6 Performance on the Weschsler tests as a function of age. The data are from the standardization samples of (a) the original Wechsler–Bellevue test, and (b) the WAIS-R. In both cases, the actual test scores of each age group are expressed as a percentage of the test scores of the youngest age group.

results shown in Fig. 2.6 were so long accepted, at face value, as a true picture of the changes that occur in IQ test scores with age. But, although there is no reason to question the accuracy of these data, they seriously misrepresent what actually happens to people's test scores as they grow older. How can that be? The answer is because the data are *cross-sectional*, and thus confound two quite different things. They were all collected in a given year—those for the WAIS-R in (let us say) 1980—from people ranging in age from (let us say) 20 to 80. This difference in age is thus confounded with a difference in the year in which they were born. That is so obvious that it may be hard to see how it could matter. But it does. We are assuming that the 80-year-olds obtain lower test scores in 1980 than the 20-year-olds because test performance declines as people grow older. But it is possible that people born in 1900 *always* had lower test scores than those born in 1960, and would have obtained just as low a score if tested, at age 20, in 1920. And, as a matter of fact, it is now clear that this is largely true. Surprisingly enough, performance on standard IQ tests has been improving from one generation to the next ever since IQ tests were first invented, and this improvement has been very much more marked on non-verbal or performance tests than on verbal tests (Chapter 4).

Since there is now incontrovertible evidence that this is true, it would seem to follow that the only way to ascertain what happens to IQ test scores as people grow older is to undertake a *longitudinal* study, in which a single group of people is followed up, given IQ tests at 5–10 year intervals from the age of 20 to the age of 80. Since such a study would take 60 years to complete, it has not yet been done, and probably never will be. But longitudinal studies spanning 20 years have been conducted, and by starting off with different cohorts, aged 20, 30, 40, and 50 at the beginning of the study, they have succeeded in providing a comprehensive picture of the changes that occur in test scores from age 20 to 70. Figure 2.7 compares the longitudinal and cross-sectional data from the Seattle Longitudinal Study (Schaie and Hertzog, 1983; Schaie, 1990, 1996). It is evident

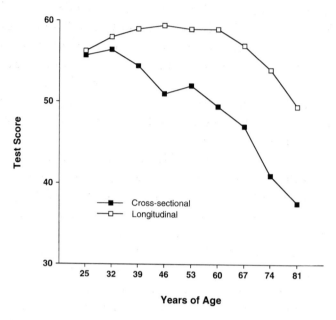

Fig. 2.7 Longitudinal and cross-sectional data illustrating different patterns of changes in IQ test scores with age (from Schaie, 1990).

that cross-sectional and longitudinal data give quite different pictures. As in Fig. 2.6, cross-sectional data imply a sharp decline in test scores, starting at a remarkably early age. But the longitudinal data suggest that test scores can continue to increase at least until age 50, hold up reasonably well up to the age of 60–65, and only then start to decline seriously. There is some reason to believe that even this decline is not necessarily general, being confined to those about to die within the next 5 years. Since that will be true of a much higher proportion of 70-year-olds than of 60-year-olds, average test score is lower at the later age.

If the pattern of results seen in Fig. 2.6 seemed consistent with certain preconceptions about the distinction between verbal and non-verbal IQ, one based on accumulated knowledge, the other on speed of novel problem solving, the discovery that this pattern is an artefact of cross-sectional data suggests that this intuitive distinction may be mistaken. That there is some distinction between verbal ability and non-verbal reasoning should not be doubted. But the nature of that distinction may not be quite what some people have imagined. We shall return to this point in Chapter 9.

Summary

After Binet's and Terman's pioneering work, the subsequent development of modern IQ tests was marked by a proliferation of different tests as psychometricians sought an answer to the question whether intelligence was best conceptualized as a single general process or a multiplicity of different abilities and skills. Some tests, such as the Wechsler Scales, followed the Stanford–Binet tests in including a wide variety of different types of item, partly on the pragmatic intuition that different types of item might favour or penalize different people. The only fair test, therefore, would be one that ensured a careful balance between items favouring one person and those favouring another. On theoretical grounds, Spearman also believed that the more diverse the items in a test battery, the better it would measure the general factor, *g*, common to all IQ tests.

It soon became apparent, however, that different types of test were measuring rather different aspects of intelligence: a general consensus agreed that a distinction could be drawn at least between verbal IQ, non-verbal reasoning, and spatial IQ. According to Thurstone, a finer set of distinctions could be drawn between at least half a dozen 'primary mental abilities' (that included verbal, reasoning, and spatial IQ), but the fact remains that in the population as a whole, people who obtain high scores on one kind of test *tend*, on average, to obtain high scores on most others. At the very least, this perhaps allows one to talk sensibly of some people being generally more intelligent than others, and to use an overall IQ score as a useful summary. Further understanding of the inter-relationships between different types of test requires the techniques of factor analysis, which will be taken up in Chapter 6.

But how did IQ testers know that any of their tests were measuring anything we should want to call intelligence? An examination of the writings of Binet, Terman, and Wechsler reveals a remarkable confidence, based on relatively little by way of empirical evidence. Both Binet and Terman could show some modest agreement between children's test scores and teachers' assessment of their intelligence or school performance, but both argued that such assessments were themselves neither reliable nor valid indices of intelligence. Working with adults, Wechsler had virtually no external criterion of intelligence against which to validate his tests. Subsequent empirical research has, however, confirmed that IQ test scores correlate moderately well, in the range 0.40–0.70, with a variety of indices of educational attainment, about 0.50 with measures of occupational status, and more modestly (mostly in the range 0.15–0.40) with other indices of occupational performance, such as income earned or supervisors' ratings of effectiveness. In most of these cases the correlations are predictive: thus children's IQ scores at age 10 correlate at about 0.40 with their final level of education and their occupational status at age 40. Nor can these correlations be wholly explained away by saying that both IQ and educational or occupational status are a by-product of parental socio-economic status.

Scores on IQ tests are also reliable and relatively stable over quite long spans of time. By the age of 7 or 8 childhood IQ predicts adult IQ very well. Standard IQ tests given at age 2–4 do not predict later IQ at all well, but one measure taken in the first year of life, rate of habituation to a novel stimulus, correlates with 10-year-old IQ at about 0.50. It has long been thought that although the test performance of adults remains reasonably stable between the ages of 18 and 40, it then declines quite sharply—especially on tests of non-verbal IQ. It turns out that this is largely, although not entirely, an artefact of cross-sectional studies. Longitudinal research suggests that IQ test performance holds up pretty well until 5–10 years before death.

3   *The heritability of IQ*

The meaning of heritability

Darwinian theory implies that members of any population will vary in many characteristics and that much of this variation is inherited. Francis Galton's insight, as we have seen, was to suggest that this general truth applied to human intelligence. By the beginning of the twentieth century, this was an idea whose time had come. With the honourable exception of Alfred Binet, the pioneers of IQ testing had no doubt that their tests measured a genetically determined biological reality, innate intellectual capacity, which varied widely in the general population. Their confidence was hardly based on hard scientific evidence, for there really was no such evidence. Galton (1869) and Goddard (1914) had attempted to show that genius and feeble-mindedness ran in families. Burt (1912) and Terman (1916) had shown that children's IQ scores were related to their parents' social status. But without further information, these observations are as consistent with an environmental, as with a genetic, explanation of variations in intelligence. It was not until the 1920s and 1930s that any serious data on the heritability of IQ became available. And it is important to note that the question addressed by such data was neither whether intelligence is inborn, nor whether IQ tests measure innate ability. It was (and is) whether IQ scores have significant heritability. What does this mean?

Heritability is a term from population genetics. It refers to the proportion of the total variation in a given characteristic in a given population that can be attributed to genetic differences between members of that population. Variation not attributable to genetic differences is caused by differences in the environment experienced by members of the population. This is, as we shall see shortly, an oversimplification, but it will do for the moment. The heritability of a particular characteristic is not immutable, but is a statistic true for a given population at a given time, dependent on the genetic variability of that population and on the degree of variation its members experience in relevant aspects of the environment, (where 'relevant' means those features of the environment that affect the characteristic in question). Where such environmental differences are large, heritability will be low; at the other extreme, in the limiting case where there are no such differences, heritability will be 1.0.

Box 3.1 Sharing genes

It is perhaps worth noting that all humans share virtually all their genes with all other humans. Indeed, the current orthodoxy is that we share more than 97 per cent of our genes with the common chimpanzee (*Pan troglodytes*) and perhaps even more with the bonobo or pygmy chimpanzee (*Pan paniscus*). So when behaviour geneticists talk of members of the same family sharing, say, half their genes, and unrelated individuals sharing none, they are talking of only the 1 or 2 per cent of genes that are not shared by *all* humans. Put another way, as Jones (1996) entertainingly does, there is no such thing as two wholly unrelated human beings: we are all, distantly, related to one another. For example, two recent British prime ministers, John Major and Margaret Thatcher, turn out to be fifth cousins once removed, both being descended from an eighteenth century Lincolnshire farmer, John Crust.

Members of the same nuclear family are more closely related, and therefore share more genes in common. The common assumption is that DZ twins and other brothers and sisters share 50 per cent of their genes (i.e. of those not common to all of us). Token acknowledgement is usually made that the phenomenon of assortative mating (husbands and wives do not choose one another at random) means that this is an underestimate (p. 88). But few behaviour geneticists are willing to allow that the vagaries of human behaviour may mean that not all biological siblings are actually that. The definition of biological siblings is: children who share the same biological mother and father, but can we be sure that two siblings actually do so? Maternity is usually quite readily ascertained, although the ancient Roman practice of substitution—the secret substitution of another healthy infant for one stillborn or very sickly in order to ensure a family heir, illustrates one pitfall. But paternity is another matter. According to one British study, blood group tests of some 250 firstborn babies, their mothers and putative fathers, in a maternity hospital in south-east England, revealed that at least 30 per cent of the fathers could not actually have been the true fathers (Phillip, 1973). Other studies have suggested this to be a bit of an overestimate—but the true figure is probably not trivial (Edwards, 1957).

It is worth bearing in mind that the panoply of biometrical analysis and quantitative modelling deployed by some behaviour geneticists rests on this rather frail foundation: reproduction is an aspect of human behaviour where what is socially acceptable and what actually happens are not always the same thing—and people go to great trouble to conceal the discrepancies between the two.

There is no answer, therefore, to the question what is *the* heritability of IQ. It may differ in different societies, or in the same society at different times. Since some people profess to see sinister consequences in the possibility that the heritability of IQ might be quite high, and impute sinister motives to those who claim that it is, it is worth suggesting that the heritability of IQ may well have increased in Western societies in the past 100 years or so, and that this is a consequence of some modest improvements in the conditions of those societies. Other things equal, in a society where the heritability of IQ is low, this must be because that society permits significant differences in those environmental circumstances that affect IQ. These circumstances must surely include access to formal education, and probably include many other things that we now take for granted as universal rights—adequate nutrition, reasonable health care, etc. In a society where many children are severely malnourished and live in grossly overcrowded slums, ravaged by infectious diseases; where relatively few children receive any formal education at all, and even fewer remain in school after the age of 12; there can be little doubt that differences in IQ scores will be partly a result of these environmental differences. Any moves towards equality of health care or of educational opportunity, however imperfect, will probably reduce the total variance of IQ in the population, but increase the proportion of that variance attributable to genetic differences between members of that population. In other words, the changes in this direction that have occurred in most industrialized countries in the past 150 years have probably been associated with an increase in the heritability of IQ. And any future increases in such equality of opportunity will presumably increase the heritability of IQ further. A low heritability for IQ could be regarded as a mark of an unjust society.

Those who worry about the heritability of IQ often confuse heritability and immutability. A genetic effect, they believe, is fixed for all time, but an effect due to the environment can easily be modified, for we can always change the environment. This requires a remarkable confidence in the possibility of social engineering: if it turned out that the single most important cause of differences in children's IQ scores was the way that their parents interacted with them in their first 2–3 years of life, would it really be so easy to eliminate this difference? More important, however, is the fact that heritable is not the same as immutable. To say that a particular characteristic has high heritability is to say that it is not greatly affected by *existing* environmental differences experienced in that population. It says nothing about the consequences of new environmental manipulations. Height is a characteristic with very high heritability (probably greater than 0.90 in most populations), but the average height of Europeans and North Americans increased by over 5 cm between 1920 and 1970 (Van Wieringen, 1978)—presumably due to improvements in nutrition and a decrease in various diseases.

A hypothetical example from the realm of IQ testing may drive the point home. Although hypothetical, some of its premises are certainly true; even if others are not, the example remains instructive. The first observation (which is unquestionably true, see Chapter 5) is that the average IQ of American blacks is some 15 points lower than that of whites. The second (which is almost certainly true, although it has been questioned; see Chapter 4) is that high concentrations of lead in the body are associated with low IQ. The third (for which there is some evidence; see Mahaffey *et al.*, 1982) is that the average concentration of lead is higher in American blacks than in whites, even when attempts are made to allow for differences in income and neighbourhood. The hypothesis (for which, as far as I am aware, there is no evidence whatsoever) is that a genetic difference between blacks and whites causes the former to absorb a higher proportion of lead from the atmosphere. Given the truth of the premises, the hypothesis would constitute a genetic explanation for part of the difference between the average IQ scores of American blacks and whites. But the moral of the story, of course, is that the explanation would imply no inevitability about this difference. It could be eliminated by a relatively modest environmental intervention, a reduction in the level of lead in the atmosphere. Genetically caused differences may be every bit as malleable as those due to environmental variation.

Having perhaps cleared away some misunderstandings about the meaning of heritability, we can start to consider how it may be estimated. As should by now be clear, that is a matter of partitioning variance. The broad heritability of a particular phenotypic characteristic in a given population is the proportion of variance in that characteristic attributable to genetic differences between members of that population, the remainder being attributable to environmental factors. But broad heritability may be further divided into additive and non-additive sources of genetic variation (see below, p. 88). Similarly, it is customary to divide environmental sources of variation into two components: between-family or common environment (CE) and within-family or special environment (SE). The former refers to the effects of environmental factors that members of the same family share in common, but which may differ between families; the standard examples are social class, income, and neighbourhood. The latter refers to the different experiences of different members of the same family; parents do not, after all, treat all their children alike, and those children will pursue their own interests and make their own friends outside the family, will often have different teachers, and may even go to different schools. Finally, behaviour genetic analyses have generally recognized the possibility of two other sources of variation that involve both genes and environment: covariation and interaction. Covariation refers, in general terms, to the possibility that there might be a correlation between genes for, say, high or low IQ and environments conducing towards high or low IQ. Thus the children of parents of high IQ might inherit genes for high IQ from those parents, and also be brought up in a family environment favourable for the development of high IQ. The importance of different forms of covariation should not be underestimated, and we shall return to this issue later (p. 95).

The second possibility is that of an interaction between genes and environment. It is necessary to understand what is meant here, for some critics of behaviour genetics have implied that such interactions make nonsense of any attempt to estimate heritabilities. According to one version of the critic's argument, all human characteristics are a product of an interaction between genes and environment during the course of development, and attempting to estimate the independent contribution of the two is like asking whether the area of a field is due more to its length or its breadth. This argument simply reflects a misunderstanding of what estimates of heritability are all about. To repeat: they are attempts to partition variance, i.e. to understand the sources of differences between members of a population, *not* an attempt to ascertain how much any individual's particular characteristics are due to his genes or his environment. Of course, we are all a product of both, but the question that is being asked is why we resemble, or differ from, one another. It makes perfectly good sense to ask, of a particular set of different sized fields, whether the difference in their areas is due more to the differences in their length or to the differences in their breadth.

The only sense in which gene–environment interaction does raise an important issue for the estimate of heritability is this: it is possible that particular genetic variations might have different phenotypic effects in different environments. Thus it might be the case that genotypes that resulted in a high IQ in one environment had no effect on IQ in another, or even had a deleterious effect on IQ in a third. The children of high-IQ parents might develop a higher IQ than those of low-IQ parents only if both sets of children were brought up in a 'high-IQ' environment. If brought up in a 'low-IQ' environment, the two groups of children might not differ in IQ at all—or the difference might even reverse. The problem is, in principle, a real one; indeed, in certain extreme cases, such interactions probably do occur. If they were both brought up in serious deprivation—severely malnourished, provided with no intellectual stimulation whatsoever, kept out of school, etc.—it does indeed seem probable that two such groups of children would not differ greatly in IQ. In practice, however, over the normal range of environments found in Western industrialized societies, there is little or no evidence to suggest that such dramatic interactions do occur for IQ, and at least some to suggest that they do not (see p. 148). It may be rash to say that the possibility of such interactions can be safely ignored, but in the absence of more concrete evidence of their importance, little will be gained by anxious worrying.

The measurement of heritability

The relative importance of genetic and environmental sources of variation in producing differences in any characteristic may be estimated by ascertaining the extent to which variation in that characteristic is associated with genetic variation in the population and how far with environmental variation. In other animals or plants, geneticists are free to conduct controlled experiments: they can measure the extent to which a particular characteristic responds to selective breeding, or they can rear animals in controlled environments. We cannot perform such experiments on people. We can study only what natural circumstances provide, and for the most part those circumstances inevitably confound environmental and genetic sources of variation. In order to estimate heritability, we need to measure the extent to which increases in either genetic relatedness, or in environmental similarity, are associated with increasing resemblance of the character in question. In most human societies, however, people who are genetically related, i.e. members of the same family, tend to share similar environments. The fact that members of the same family also tend to resemble one another in IQ does not allow us to disentangle the genetic and environmental sources of this resemblance.

Nevertheless, we must start by measuring resemblance. We do this by calculating correlations, not, as in Chapter 2, between the same person's scores on different tests or on the same test at different times, but between different people's scores on the same (or similar) tests. Thus we can calculate correlations between the IQ scores of parents and their children, of brothers and sisters, or of identical (monozygotic or MZ) twins. For many of these calculations, the appropriate statistic is the intra-class correlation, the formula of which is given as:

$$(V_b - V_w)/(V_b + V_w) \tag{3.1}$$

If, for example, we are dealing with 50 pairs of MZ twins all given an IQ test, then V_b is the variation between the scores of the 50 pairs of twins, and V_w is the variation between one twin and the other within each pair. If MZ twins resemble each other perfectly in IQ, the variation within each pair is zero, and the correlation is 1.0. If the variation within pairs is as great as that between pairs, the correlation is zero. The correlation thus measures the extent of resemblance between one twin and the other within each pair, and therefore, it is to be presumed, the extent to which their IQ scores have been determined by common influences. Exactly the same line of reasoning applies to any other pairings—of parents and their children, of brothers and sisters, or of unrelated people.

Table 3.1, derived from Bouchard and McGue (1981), summarizes the results of a large number of studies, published before 1981, that have reported correlations between various family members and also between unrelated individuals. But how will these data help to resolve the issue? It is evident that parents and their children, or brothers and sisters, resemble one another in IQ (the correlations are about 0.40–0.50) very much more than unrelated people. But this is equally consistent with a genetic and with an environmental account. Nature and society, however, have given the human behaviour geneticist two kinds of natural experiment that may go some way towards answering their questions; nature has provided twins, and society the practice of adoption. MZ twins are genetically identical, but fraternal or dizygotic (DZ) twins are genetically no more similar than any other pair of siblings, in principle sharing only 50 per cent of their genes. It is clear from Table 3.1 that MZ twins resemble one another in IQ substantially more than DZ twins. On the face of it, this implies a significant genetic effect. The practice of adoption means both that some biologically unrelated people live together in the same family (adoptive parents and their adopted children; two or more adopted children), and equally that some biologically related people live apart (two siblings or twins adopted into different families; adopted children and their true biological parents). From Table 3.1, it can be seen that in all cases, kin living together in the same family resemble one another in IQ more closely than those living apart. On the face of it, this implies a significant effect of family environment on IQ, a conclusion also suggested by the observation that biologically unrelated people who live in the same family show *some* resemblance in IQ. Conversely, the finding that biologically related people living apart also show some resemblance in IQ (the most striking, but unsurprisingly also the rarest example of this being MZ twins brought up apart) suggests a significant genetic effect.

Table 3.1 Kinship correlations for IQ (from Bouchard and McGue, 1981)

Kinship	Living together	Living apart
MZ twins	0.86	0.72
DZ twins	0.60	–
Siblings	0.47	0.24
Parent–child	0.42	0.22
Adoptive parent–adopted child	0.19	–
Unrelated children	(a)0.34	–
	(b)0.29	

The two correlations for unrelated children living together refer (a) to two adopted children in the same adoptive family, and (b) to an adopted child and a biological child of the adoptive family.

The implication, then, of the results illustrated in Table 3.1 is that variations in IQ in the general population are caused by both genetic and environmental variation in the population. That conclusion is almost certainly true. It will, however, require rather more detailed analysis of the various types of study summarized there in order to establish it securely.

Analysis of kinship correlations

MZ and DZ twins

The classic twin method of estimating heritability was first suggested by Galton. It remains popular to this day, and not only in studies of IQ. The comparison of MZ and DZ twins probably provides the largest single source of evidence for the heritability of many, if not most, human characteristics. The studies summarized in Table 3.1 establish that MZ twins resemble one another in IQ substantially more than DZ twins, whether they have been brought up together or apart (although we shall defer consideration of separated twins until the next section). A more recent meta-analysis of twin studies conducted between 1967 and 1985 produced very similar results: a weighted mean correlation of 0.81 for MZ twins and of 0.59 for DZ twins (McCartney *et al.*, 1990). Is this good evidence for the heritability of IQ?

On the face of it, that conclusion must depend on the assumption that the greater resemblance of MZ twins is due to their genetic identity rather than to any greater similarity in the environments they experience. The results shown in Table 3.1 suggest that DZ twins resemble one another in IQ somewhat more closely than other brothers and sisters. One interpretation of that observation is that twins share more environmental experiences than siblings of different ages. Might it not be possible that MZ twins experience even more

---

Box 3.2 The variety of natural experiments

Virtually all behaviour genetic studies of human characteristics have relied on two natural experiments provided by nature and society, twins and adoption, and I discuss only these in this chapter. Other times and other societies have provided other kinds of natural experiment, and our own time provides at least one other kind of natural experiment, which behaviour geneticists have been slow to exploit.

Beginning in the thirteenth century, many large European cities started to open foundling hospitals, that is to say charitable institutions expressly designed to look after infants and young children abandoned by their parents (Boswell, 1988). Within 50 years of its opening in 1455, the Innocenti Hospital in Florence was receiving 900 abandoned children a year. By the eighteenth century, French records suggest that some 15–30 per cent of *all* newborn children in most large French cities were abandoned to these foundling hospitals. Jean Jacques Rousseau famously abandoned all five of his children to such hospitals. Add to this the widespread practice in urban middle-class families of farming out their newborn infants to rural wet nurses for the first year of their life (Schama, 1989), and the eighteenth-century French social scientist was provided with endless possibilities for natural experiments.

Foundling hospitals or orphanages survived into the twentieth century, and one early British study (Lawrence, 1931) did ask an obvious question: given that a group of children living in an orphanage are all exposed to a rather similar environment, does this reduce the variability in their IQ scores as an environmental hypothesis might predict? Lawrence found only a small reduction in variability, and her results have often been cited as evidence of the limited effect of the environment. Kamin (1981), a staunch environmentalist, has pointed out that the children in one of these orphanages, although separated from their mothers at 6 months, spent the next 5 years in foster homes before going to live in the orphanage's own premises. He suggested that differences in these foster homes might have been sufficient to produce differences in the children's IQ scores, but omitted to mention that the foster homes were all 'cottage homes in the country', and that the foster parents were 'usually agricultural labourers of the better type' (Lawrence, 1931, p. 4). This must represent a rather drastic reduction in the variability to be found in early twentieth-century English society.

Behaviour geneticists have taken little advantage of the new opportunities for natural experiments offered in Britain and the USA by rising rates of divorce and remarriage. Many families today contain half-brothers and -sisters sharing only one biological parent, and stepbrothers and stepsisters sharing none. Many of these children will have lived together, and with a step-parent, for much of their life. At the same time, the children of divorced parents may live with one and never see the other. And, although rarer and still more recent, such developments as artificial insemination and the donation of eggs, mean that some children of ordinary nuclear families are no longer genetically related to both their parents.

---

similar environments than DZ twins? It is not only possible; it is relatively well established (e.g. Loehlin and Nichols, 1976). MZ twins are more likely to dress alike, play together, share the same teacher, sleep in the same room, and be treated alike by others than are DZ twins. This is hardly surprising: genetic identity will normally produce marked physical similarity, and perhaps also similarities in character and temperament; it would be surprising if these did not lead to their spending more time together and being treated more alike. However, the question remains whether these differences are relevant to any differences in IQ: it is one thing to show that MZ twins are treated more alike; it is quite another to prove that this is the *cause* of the greater resemblance of their IQ scores. Loehlin and Nichols themselves argued that it was not, since they could find no evidence that MZ twins who shared more similar experiences resembled one another in IQ more than those who did not. Even if this were true (and Kamin (1981) provides one counter-example in Loehlin and Nichols's own data), it would not necessarily justify Loehlin and Nichols's conclusion. If all MZ twins share more experiences in common than all DZ twins, then this difference *between* the two groups of twins might still be responsible for the difference between them in similarity of IQ, even though the rather small range of variation in similarity of experience *within* each group was not associated with variation in resemblance for IQ.

There are, in fact, two lines of evidence to suggest that variations in the similarity of DZ twins' experiences is associated with variation in their resemblance for IQ. First, DZ twins of the same sex tend to resemble one another slightly more than those of opposite sex: Bouchard and McGue (1981) reported that the average correlation in IQ for the same-sex twin pairs is 0.62, while that for opposite-sex pairs is 0.57. The difference is small, but presumably reflects the fact that twins of the same sex share more interests in common than those of opposite sex. Secondly, there is some evidence that, as they grow older, DZ (unlike MZ) twins, come to resemble one another less and less (McCartney *et al.* 1990; McGue *et al.*, 1993). McCartney *et al.* calculated a correlation of −0.25 between DZ twins' age and their correlation for IQ (as opposed to one of +0.15 for MZ twins). In a longitudinal study, Wilson (1983) reported that at age 9 the IQ correlations for MZ and DZ twins were 0.83 and 0.65, but that 6 years later these correlations were 0.88 and 0.54, respectively. We shall see below that DZ twins are not the only family members whose resemblance in IQ may decrease as they grow older. The most plausible interpretation of this change is in terms of a decrease in the importance of shared family environment (CE) and an increase in the importance of special environment (SE) as children grow older, spend more time outside the home, and pursue their own interests. The fact that this does not seem to happen for MZ twins implies that they maintain their similarity precisely because they continue to spend time together or share similar interests.

All of this suggests that some of the difference between MZ and DZ twins may be attributable to differences in the similarity of their experiences. But it does not mean that environmental differences are solely responsible for the greater resemblance of MZ twins, still less that the *only* reason why MZ twins resemble one another so closely in IQ is because they share such similar experiences. The fact is that the correlation between the IQ scores of MZ twins sometimes approaches the limits of the reliability of the tests. To assert that this is *entirely* because they have been treated identically is to ignore the fact that there are numerous respects in which MZ twins differ from one another quite markedly. In

McCartney *et al.*'s review (1990), for example, the average correlation for eight measures of personality was no more than 0.50 (see also Bouchard *et al.*, 1990); and the concordance of MZ twins for schizophrenia is also no more than 50 per cent (Gottesman, 1991). If differences in their experience of life have been sufficient to produce differences such as these between two twins, why have they not also resulted in differences in measured IQ? The argument may not convince the determined sceptic, but it is, at least, suggestive: their genetic identity is probably one reason why MZ twins have such similar IQ scores. Indeed, as I shall argue below (p. 95), it is also probably part of the reason why they share such similar environments. That is to say, MZ twins spend time together and are treated alike because they share similar interests, etc., and one reason why they do that is because they are genetically identical. We are, in fact, dealing with a case of gene–environment covariation. Nevertheless it is time to turn to the supposedly decisive evidence for the heritability of IQ—that from studies of MZ twins brought up apart.

Separated MZ twins

> If I had any desire to lead a life of indolent ease, I would wish to be an identical twin, separated at birth from my brother and raised in a different social class. We could hire ourselves out to a host of social scientists and practically name our fee. For we would be exceedingly rare representatives of the only really adequate natural experiment for separating genetic from environmental effects in humans—genetically identical individuals raised in disparate environments. (Gould, 1997, p. 264)

It is not hard to see why behaviour geneticists have been so enamoured of separated MZ twins. Provided that they have been truly separated, it would seem that the only explanation of any resemblance between them, in IQ or any other characteristic, must be their identical genotypes.

As Gould notes, separated MZ twins are exceedingly rare. Table 3.2 gives the summary results of five published studies of such twins, excluding that published by Burt (1966). The grand total in these five studies is only 162 pairs. Whether or not Burt's data were actually fraudulent, as has been suggested, they contain so many errors, inconsistencies, and anomalies that they cannot be relied on (Box 3.3). One of the more striking of Burt's claims was that all his twins had been separated before 6 months of age and that there was no correlation between the social circumstances of the families in which they had been brought up. Of none of the remaining studies is this true. The three earlier studies provided case histories which make it clear that many of the twins were separated only in a somewhat Pickwickian sense. In 27 of Shields's pairs, for example, one twin was brought up by the mother and the other by a relative, usually a maternal aunt or grandmother. A majority of the twins in the studies of Newman *et al.* and Juel-Nielsen were also both brought up by relatives. In all three of these earlier studies, no more than about half the

Box 3.3 The strange case of Cyril Burt

Cyril Burt died, aged 88, in 1971, widely honoured as the foremost British educational psychologist and psychometrician of his generation, whose contributions to the early development of factor analysis we have already come across. Among his many empirical contributions, he had published a series of papers reporting the results of what appeared to be an ongoing study of kinship correlations for IQ—the most notable feature of which was data on a sample of separated MZ twins. Starting with a brief mention of 15 pairs of such twins in 1943, he published three updates in the 1950s, with 21, 'over 30', and 42 pairs, culminating in a final paper published in 1966 when the sample of such twins had grown to 53 pairs—at that time, and still, the largest study ever published (Burt, 1966). His data were relied on extensively by Jensen (1969) as the best evidence for the heritability of IQ. On the face of it, indeed, they appeared to be: according to Burt, all 53 pairs had been separated before they were 6 months old; there was no correlation between the social circumstances of their adoptive families; and these family backgrounds spanned the full range to be expected in the general population.

Within a few years of his death, Burt's reputation as an empirical scientist had been destroyed. Kamin (1974) found so many anomalies in his data, combined with such inadequate reporting of critical procedural details, that he concluded that 'the numbers left behind by Professor Burt are simply not worthy of our current scientific attention'. His official biography (Hearnshaw, 1979), indeed, concluded that much of his later research, not only that on the twins, was fraudulent, and the data simply fabricated.

Whether or not the twin data were fabricated, they cannot be relied upon, for one simple reason. The relevant table of correlations for various IQ and other measures for the twins and other kinship categories in the 1966 paper contains 66 correlation coefficients, all given to three decimal places. Nearly half of them are *identical* to those published in earlier papers in the series, even though all the sample sizes (not only those for the twins) had changed over time. One or two correlations might, by chance, have remained the same. Thirty could not have, and it must be assumed that Burt had simply copied down a lot of the old numbers. But with the evidence of this sort of carelessness, how can we then believe either these old numbers or the 30 or so new ones?

Many critics took the invariant correlations to be evidence of fraud; if that is true, Burt was not only a fraud, he was a spectacularly stupid one. And Hearnshaw's charges of deliberate fraud have been disputed by Joynson (1989) and Fletcher (1991), whose defence has been accepted by many—rather depressingly usually by those of a hereditarian point of view (e.g. Herrnstein and Murray, 1994). The invariant correlations, it should be clear, are quite insufficient to prove fraud, but there is other evidence that points rather more conclusively to fabrication, not only in the twin data but also in some of Burt's other later papers (Mackintosh, 1995). In the case of the separated MZ twins, for example, Burt eventually responded to requests for his raw data with a set of IQ scores for all 106 twins—although in his diary he records that he spent a week *calculating* these data (what on earth was there to calculate?). These scores do, indeed, yield the correlation coefficient reported in the 1966 paper, but there are numerous other inconsistencies between these individual scores and other aspects of the data reported not only in that paper but also in earlier papers in the series. A plausible interpretation is that some (or all?) of the individual scores he eventually produced were simply invented to produce the desired correlation, but that they could not simultaneously agree with all the other summary statistics published earlier.

Leaving aside the question of how far Burt's data were actually fabricated, an issue of rather wider import is why they were treated with such respect for so long. It did not take a particularly careful inspection to see that they were inadequately reported and riddled with error. It is tempting to see evidence of a hereditarian conspiracy, or at least of a reprehensible readiness to accept, at face value, data that conformed to the reader's prior expectations. We shall come across comparable instances of others only too happy to believe inadequate data that support environmentalist positions. But it is worth adding that the scientific enterprise is also based on trust; by and large, we are reluctant to believe that scientists fabricate their data.

Table 3.2 Correlations between separated MZ twins

Stud	Number of pairs	Mean correlation
Newman *et al.* (1937)	19	0.71
Shields (1962)	37–38	0.75
Juel-Nielson (1980)	12	0.69
Bouchard *et al.* (1990)	42–48	0.75
Pedersen *et al.* (1992)	45	0.78

All studies gave more than one IQ test to each twin, and sometimes not all twins took all tests. The correlation shown is the average for the various tests, except in the Pedersen *et al.* study, where it is for the general factor extracted from a number of different tests.

twins had been separated before the age of 6 months, and about three-quarters of them were reunited, for shorter or longer periods, at some point in their childhood. None of this should come as any great surprise. The real world does not arrange perfect experiments for the benefit of social scientists. Mothers of identical twins do not obligingly send one twin off to an adoption agency; if, for any reason, they cannot look after both, they ask a friend or relative to look after one. An adoption agency receiving two MZ twins may try to keep them together. And in the rare cases where real separation occurs, the twins may not even know of each other's existence, let alone be simultaneously available for study.

How far, then, is the resemblance in IQ of these supposedly separated MZ twins to be attributed to the similarities in their environments? The data from the 70-odd pairs of twins in the three earlier studies have been subject to prolonged and (depending on one's point of view) painstaking or nit-picking analysis—first by Kamin (1974), and later by Taylor (1980) and Farber (1981). These critics have been able to persuade themselves that there was no good reason to accept a genetic explanation of the twins' resemblance, but they have persuaded few other commentators. Those who want to examine some of the arguments and counter-arguments surrounding these earlier studies are referred to the Appendix to this chapter (A.1, p. 98). Of the two more recent studies, that by Bouchard *et al.* (1990) provides the more detailed analysis of the circumstances surrounding the twins' separation, degree of contact, and similarity of circumstances, and I shall concentrate on it. Table 3.3 provides the relevant information. It can be seen that although these twins were, on average,

Table 3.3 Details of the Minnesota Study of separated MZ twins (from Bouchard *et al.* 1990)

(a) Measures of separation

Measure	Mean	SD
Age at separation (months)	5.1	8.5
Total amount of contact before testing (months)	9.2	19.2
Age at testing (years)	41.0	12.0

(b) Correlations between separation and differences in WAIS IQ

Measure	Correlation
Age at separation	0.06
Time apart to first reunion	0.08
Total amount of contact	−0.14
Percent of life spent apart	0.17

(c) Correlations between family backgrounds and twins' IQ scores

Background measure	Correlation between twins' families	Correlation with twins' IQ
Father's education	0.13	0.10
Mother's education	0.41	0.00
Father's SES	0.27	0.17
Material possessions	0.40	0.28
Scientific/cultural	0.15	−0.09
Cultural	−0.08	−0.28

separated before the age of 6 months, and had spent only a small part of their lives in contact with one another before participating in the study, when their average age was over 40 years (in these respects being better separated than the twins of earlier studies), there was still substantial variation in their degree of separation. But Table 3.3b shows that this variation was not closely related to variation in their resemblance for IQ. Twins separated earlier, for example, were slightly *more* alike in IQ than those separated later, and none of the correlations shown in Table 3.3b is significant. Table 3.3c shows that, as in the earlier studies, the twins were not brought up in wholly uncorrelated home environments. In at least some potentially relevant respects, such as father's occupation, mother's education, material possessions in the home, there were significant correlations between their family backgrounds. But, as can also be seen in Table 3.3c, there is actually no evidence that these aspects of the home environment had substantial effects on the twins' IQ scores. The only two variables where there was evidence both of a correlation between the twins' homes and of an effect of this variable on their IQ scores were father's occupation and the material possessions in the home. Since these two variables will themselves have certainly been correlated, they cannot have contributed independently to the separated twins' resemblance for IQ, and it is quite evident that most of that resemblance remains unexplained by the factors enumerated in Table 3.3. Another possibility is that the resemblance is partly explained by a shared prenatal environment (see Devlin *et al.* (1997) for one suggestion to this effect). Although it is impossible to rule out a contribution from such a factor, the available evidence suggests that the impact of prenatal environment, even on young children's IQ scores, is very small (Chapter 4). Moreover, there is also good evidence that differences in their prenatal environment can cause differences in the IQ scores of MZ twins (Bouchard *et al.*, 1990): sharing the same womb at the same time does not guarantee that MZ twins experience an identical prenatal environment. Bouchard *et al.* conclude that the IQ correlation between their separated MZ twins is essentially all attributable to their shared genotypes. That may be too strong a conclusion, but it is surely nearer the truth than an extreme environmentalist position.

It would be surprising if the IQ scores of separated MZ twins were wholly unaffected by similarities or differences in their life experiences. It follows, therefore, that in so far as many of the twins in these five studies experienced somewhat similar environments, the observed correlations in their IQ scores may overestimate the heritability of IQ. That seems plausible enough, even if Bouchard *et al.*'s analyses suggest that the overestimate may not be very great. Is it really plausible, however, to suggest that these studies of separate MZ twins are consistent with a zero heritability for IQ? Writing about the earlier studies, Kamin has pointed to the 'glaring tendency' for the environments of so-called separated twins to be highly correlated:

> This tendency, no less than identical genes, might easily be responsible for the observed resemblance in IQs. We cannot guess what the IQ correlation would be if, in a science fiction experiment, we separated pairs of identical twins at birth and scattered them *at random* across the full range of available environments. It could conceivably be zero. (Kamin, 1981, p. 113)

It is true that MZ twins have not been taken at birth and scattered at random across available environments; so it must also be true that we do not know exactly what the correlation between the IQ scores of such twins would be. But is it conceivable that it would be zero? To suppose that it might be is to say that similarity of environment provides a complete explanation of the correlations reported in Table 3.2. But even if every pair of twins had been brought up in related families, which closely resembled one another in social, cultural, and economic circumstances, and even if all pairs of twins had met one another while growing up, it is difficult to see how they could have experienced *more* similar environments than children growing up in the same family. But the kinship studies summarized in Table 2.1 suggested that the IQ correlation between two unrelated children brought up in the same adoptive family is no more than 0.34, and several more recent studies suggest that it may be even lower than this (see p. 84 below). Even brothers and sisters living in the same family show a correlation of less than 0.50, and DZ twins one of only 0.60.

To attribute correlations of approximately 0.70 or more to the shared environment of children living in different families, when children living in the same family correlate substantially less, requires a remarkable act of faith—even greater than that required to suppose that the correlations reported for separated MZ twins provide a direct, uncontaminated estimate of the heritability of IQ in the population as a whole. The only sensible conclusion is that, in spite of their inevitable imperfections, these studies of separated MZ twins strongly suggest that the heritability of IQ is significantly greater than zero. But those imperfections should not be forgotten. The twins were usually not separated at birth, and were certainly not assigned to a random selection of homes spanning the variety of homes to be found in the general population. As Bouchard *et al.* (1990) note, very few of the twins in any of the published studies were brought up in serious poverty or by illiterate parents, and none have had an IQ in the retarded range. This alone means that their results cannot be extrapolated to the general population. But perhaps the most obvious problem is that the studies are *small*. Some 160 pairs of numbers, collected over 50-odd years in a number of different countries, do not provide a very secure basis from which to extrapolate to the population (what population?) as a whole.

Adoption studies

MZ twins comprise about 0.33% of live births, and the proportion of such twins brought up apart must be a minute fraction of the total. What other data for estimating heritability may lack in elegance, they must surely make up for in sheer abundance. In principle, any group of adopted children provides several ways of disentangling genetic and environmental causes of variation in IQ, and adopted children are, at least by comparison with separated MZ twins, plentiful—even if they have become rather less plentiful in most Western countries in the past 25 years or so.

Adoptive families have been used in at least three kinds of design. First, one can compare the magnitude of correlations between various family members (parents and children, one child and another) observed in adoptive families with those observed in 'biological' families (i.e. those where the children are the biological sons and daughters of both parents). If these correlations are higher between members of biological families, this may be because they share both genes and family environment, whereas members of adoptive families share only the same family environment. Secondly, one can ask whether the correlations observed in adoptive families are significantly greater than zero. If they are, this suggests that shared family environment does contribute to similarities in IQ. Finally, some studies have asked whether the IQ scores of adopted children resemble those of their true biological parents (with whom they have never lived) more or less than those of their adoptive parents (with whom they share no genes). In practice, of course, it has often been possible for a single study to address all of these questions at once, but it will be simpler to discuss them separately, and in the order just given.

Adoptive and biological family correlations compared

The studies summarized in Table 3.1 suggested that the correlation between children and their parents in ordinary, biological families is about twice as large as that between adopted children and their adoptive parents (0.42 v. 0.19). On the face of it, this implies a significant effect of shared genes, but there are some reasons to question this implication. A comparison of correlations in adoptive and biological families will yield an estimate of the role of shared genes only if there are no other differences between the two kinds of family. But a moment's reflection suggests that there will be many other differences. Adoption agencies do not hand over children to anyone who asks: would-be adoptive parents are carefully screened, often to rule out the very poor or the feckless, and certainly to exclude alcoholics, drug addicts, criminals, and so on. The environments provided by adoptive families, it seems likely, are of higher average standard, and less variable, than those to be found in the population at large. To the extent that this is true, adopted children will not be exposed to those environments potentially responsible for low IQ, and we should expect to see less variability in their IQ scores. But correlation coefficients are extremely sensitive to this sort of restriction of range. From the formula for the intra-class correlation (equation 3.1), it is obvious that the smaller the variance between pairs, the smaller the numerator and the lower the correlation. It should come as no surprise, therefore, if we find only a low correlation between adopted children's IQ scores and their adoptive parents' IQ or any other measure of their adoptive homes. The fact that it is lower than that observed in biological families may be entirely artefactual, unless the biological families have also been similarly selected, i.e. carefully matched to the adoptive families both for their average value of relevant environmental variables, and (just as important) for their variability.

Three American studies, two conducted more than 50 years ago, have attempted to address this question by comparing a group of adoptive families with a group of biological families matched as far as possible for at least some obvious environmental variables (e.g. parental IQ, education, social class, neighbourhood. etc.). The results are shown in Table 3.4. The correlations in the more recent Scarr and Weinberg study are somewhat lower than those in the two older studies, but otherwise the three agree quite well; as in the more heterogeneous collection of studies summarized in Table 3.1, the correlations are at least twice as high in biological as in adoptive families.

If we could be assured that the two types of family had been perfectly matched for all relevant environmental variables, these three studies would provide strong additional evidence for the heritability of IQ. All three studies made a serious attempt to match the two

Table 3.4 Parent–child IQ correlations in adoptive and matched biological families

	Burks (1928)		Leahy (1935)		Scarr and Weinberg (1978)	
	Adoptive	Biological	Adoptive	Biological	Adoptive	Biological
Mother	0.19	0.45	0.20	0.51	0.09	0.41
Father	0.07	0.45	0.15	0.51	0.16	0.40

groups of families, and although some differences remained, it is difficult to sustain the argument that these differences are sufficient to explain their results (but see the Appendix to this chapter (A.2, p. 100), for a discussion of Kamin's attempt to do just this). One might still insist, of course, that since we do not know what the relevant environmental variables are (i.e. those that actually affect children's IQ scores), the matching process may have allowed critical differences to remain. Adoptive parents may, after all, be more committed to parenthood; they might take more (or less) interest in their children's development than biological parents. As Kamin (1974, 1981) has argued, a better design would be to find a group of adoptive families which also have some biological children of their own. We could then compare the correlation between adoptive parents and adopted children with that between parents and their biological children in one and the same group of families. The results of several such studies are shown in Table 3.5. As Kamin would expect, the differences between adoptive and biological correlations are now rather smaller than those observed in Table 3.4, and this is because the biological correlations in these adoptive families are rather lower than those observed in other biological families. However, all correlations between parents and their biological offspring are higher than those between parents and their adopted offspring, and some of the differences are quite substantial.

Taken together, the data shown in Tables 3.4 and 3.5 suggest that the heritability of IQ is greater than zero, but there is one discordant observation. In the Texas adoption project (Horn *et al.*, 1979; Table 3.5), the correlation between adoptive mothers and their adopted children is essentially no different from that between this group of mothers and their own biological children. (In general, it is worth noting, the mother–child correlations in adoptive families are rather higher than the father–child correlations—the only exception is the Scarr

Table 3.5 Parent–child IQ correlations in adoptive families some of whom have their own biological children

	Leahy (1935)		Scarr and Weinberg (1978)		Horn *et al.* (1979)	
	Adoptive	Biological	Adoptive	Biological	Adoptive	Biological
Mother	–	–	0.23	0.35	0.19	0.23
Father	–	–	0.15	0.39	0.17	0.42
Mid-parent	0.18	0.36	0.25	0.51	–	–

and Weinberg study in Table 3.4; this is not particularly surprising in a society where mothers are more likely to be responsible for looking after children than are fathers.) This particular comparison in the Texas study would be consistent with a zero heritability for IQ. However, even this support for an environmentalist position is rather transient. Ten years after their original study, Loehlin *et al.* (1989) were able to trace some 250 of the original adopted children (now aged between 13 and 25) and some 90 of the biological children of their adoptive parents. Table 3.6 shows the correlations between these parents and their adopted and biological children, both at the time of the original study and 10 years later. It is evident that while the correlations between biological relatives remained more or less constant over this 10-year interval, those between the adopted children and their adoptive parents all decreased.

Table 3.6 also shows the correlations between different children living in the same family—between two adopted children, an adopted child and a biological child, and, in a small number of cases, between two biological children of the same family. The pattern of these correlations is rather similar to that observed between parents and children. At the time of the original study, the correlation between two biologically related children (0.27) was not *very* much higher than those between two unrelated children living in the same family (0.20 and 0.11). Ten years later, however, these latter correlations were negligible (one was actually negative), while the correlation between biologically related children had barely changed. The implication of the entire pattern of results seen in Table 3.6 seems quite clear. Members of biological families continue to resemble one another in IQ as the children grow older; but, since members of adoptive families do not, the resemblance between biological parents and their children, or between brothers and sisters, is not easily attributed

Table 3.6 Parent–child and child–child IQ correlations in the Texas Adoption Study (from Loehlin *et al.*, 1989)

(a) Parent–children

	Initial study	10-year follow-up
Adoptive mother–own child	0.04	0.14
Adoptive father–own child	0.29	0.32
Adoptive mother–adopted child	0.13	0.05
Adoptive father–adopted child	0.19	0.10

(b) Between children

	Initial study	10-year follow-up
Two biological children in same family	0.27	0.24
Two adopted children in same family	0.11	−0.09
Adopted–biological in same family	0.20	0.05

solely to their shared family environment. It must surely be partly attributed to their shared genes.

Environmental effects of adoptive families

Those studies of which the results are shown in Tables 3.4, 3.5, and 3.6 have also, of course, addressed this second question: any resemblance in IQ between unrelated members of adoptive families suggests that IQ is also partly affected by shared family environment. In Tables 3.4 and 3.5, correlations between adopted children and their adoptive parents ranged from 0.07 to 0.23; the average correlation reported in Table 3.1 was 0.19, and the value of the correlation between two unrelated children living in the same family was either 0.34 or 0.29. However, by now it should come as no surprise to learn that there are problems in accepting these figures as true estimates of the influence of family environment.

First, to the extent that adoptive families are not fully representative of the entire population, this restriction of range will reduce the size of any correlation between members of such families, and hence underestimate the role of family environment.

Secondly, however, the phenomenon of 'selective placement' may result in *overestimation* of the importance of family environment. Adoption agencies not only screen potential adoptive parents, they may also attempt to match the child to the home, placing children whose natural parents were well educated with well-educated adoptive parents, and those of poorer natural parents into poorer adoptive homes. To the extent that such selective placement occurs, the correlation between adoptive parents' and adopted children's IQ scores might, in principle, be partly genetic—a consequence of placing children, who had inherited a high IQ from their natural parents, with adoptive parents who also happened to have a high IQ. It is often possible, of course, to obtain some estimate of the magnitude of selective placement effects by looking at the correlations between aspects of the children's natural and adoptive parents or homes, and in none of the studies shown in Tables 3.4, 3.5, and 3.6 were these effects very large. But they were usually not negligible, and the possibility remains that selective placement has contributed to the resemblance between adopted children and their adoptive parents in these studies.

Since these two methodological problems act in opposite directions, one to overestimate and the other to underestimate the contribution of family environment, it is tempting to wash one's hands of them, to suggest that they probably cancel each other out and can therefore be safely ignored. A more cautious attitude would acknowledge that these adoption studies will never give an accurate estimate of the contribution of shared family environment to resemblances in IQ. There is a further reason to accept this, for there is probably no single value for this contribution. There is reason to suspect that the magnitude of correlations between adopted children and their adoptive parents, or between one adopted child and another living in the same family, may depend on the age of the child. In the Texas adoption study, shown in Table 3.6, both sets of correlations decreased between the initial study and the 10-year follow-up: indeed at this second test, none of the adoptive correlations was significantly different from zero. The only other longitudinal study to have followed up adopted children until they were teenagers is that of Scarr *et al.* (1993). They found no such reduction in the correlation between adopted children's and their adoptive parents' IQ scores—indeed the correlation between adopted child's and adoptive mid-parents' IQ actually rose from 0.22 to 0.27; and there was only a small reduction, from 0.31 to 0.19, in the correlation between two unrelated children living in the same adoptive family. However, two other adoption studies have reported IQ correlations near zero in adoptive families when the children were teenagers. Scarr and Weinberg (1978) reported a correlation of −0.03 between the IQ scores of adolescent adopted children living in the same family; while Teasdale and Owen (1984) reported a correlation of 0.02 between a sample of 18-year-old Danish adopted sons and their adoptive fathers. The implication is that the effect of family environment on IQ scores may be quite small by the time children leave home.

Do adopted children continue to resemble their biological parents?

The final question addressed by some adoption studies is whether adopted children's IQ scores resemble those of their own biological parents—even though they have never lived with them. According to Table 3.1, the average correlation here is 0.22. By the same logic as was used for studies of separated twins, such resemblance suggests a genetic influence on IQ.

Once again, however, we must consider the problem of selective placement, which here, as in the case of separated twins, may result in an overestimate of heritability: adopted children may resemble their true biological parents, not because they share the same genes, but because they have been placed in adoptive homes carefully selected to provide the same sort of environment as would have been provided by their biological parents. It will come as no surprise to learn that Kamin (1974, 1981) has argued that selective placement is sufficient to explain why adopted children resemble their biological parents (see Appendix A.3, p. 101).

The argument does not accord very happily with his earlier claim that adoptive homes provide such a restricted range of environments that it is impossible to see any substantial correlation between adopted children's IQ scores and those of their adoptive parents, since it is precisely this latter correlation (or something related to it) that is supposed to be the cause of the children's resemblance to their biological parents. More to the point, however, his argument requires that adopted children should resemble their adoptive parents *at least* as closely as their true, biological parents. But several studies that have made the direct comparison have shown that they do not.

Table 3.7 shows the results of three American studies—from Minnesota, Colorado, and Texas. The Colorado data are from the most recent report, when the children were 7 years old: at earlier ages, both biological and adoptive correlations were small, and fluctuated from year to year. This is quite consistent with an earlier study by Skodak and Skeels

(1949), who reported that as their adopted children grew older, so their IQ scores increasingly came to correlate with the educational level of their biological mothers but not with that of their adoptive mothers. At age 13, the two correlations were 0.32 and 0.02. The Texas study has, of course, followed some children to an even greater age: while the resemblance of this sub-group of children's IQ scores to those of their adoptive mothers declined from 0.13 to 0.05, their resemblance to the scores of their true, biological mothers increased from 0.23 to 0.26. The only reasonable conclusion is that the resemblance between adopted children and their biological parents cannot sensibly be attributed solely to selective placement. It implies unambiguously that the heritability of IQ is greater than zero.

Quantitative estimates of heritability

It may seem to have taken an inordinately long time to establish a relatively banal conclusion—that the heritability of IQ is greater than zero. But for many people that conclusion is anything but banal. At one time, for example, Kamin completely rejected it, insisting that

> there exist no data which should lead a prudent man to accept the hypothesis that IQ test scores are in any degree heritable. (Kamin, 1974, p. 1)

He has argued, moreover, that those who accept any such conclusion do so only because it suits their social and political prejudices to do so. Thus it has seemed worth documenting that, however imperfect the data may be, however much the product of necessarily ambiguous, natural experiments rather than of carefully controlled experimentation, they no longer permit a reasonable person to accept that the heritability of IQ is zero.

In fact, the evidence reviewed in this chapter does suggest one or two more surprising conclusions—for example, that the influence of family environment on IQ may decline as children grow older, and that much of the environmentally caused variation in IQ may be attributed to differences in the experiences of members of the same family. These conclusions, if true, represent a significant departure from earlier conventional wisdom.

Table 3.7 Correlations between adopted children's IQ and characteristics of their biological and adoptive parents

	Minnesota (Scarr and Weinberg, 1983)		Colorado (Phillips and Fulker, 1989)	Texas (Loehlin *et al.*, 1989) Mother's IQ	
	Mother's education	Father's education	Mother's IQ	Initial study	10-year follow-up
Biological	0.28	0.43	0.37	0.23	0.26
Adoptive	0.09	0.11	−0.05	0.13	0.05

Nevertheless, the claim that the heritability of IQ is greater than zero hardly amounts to a very precise estimate of that heritability. How are such estimates arrived at? How, in particular, have authors such as Eysenck (1979), Jensen (1981), or Lynn (1996*a*) so confidently asserted that the heritability of IQ is approximately 70–80 per cent?

Quantitative estimates of heritability require quantitative models. Quantitative modelling, however, requires the modeller to start making a number of assumptions, some plausible enough, others notably less plausible. To illustrate: we know that resemblances in IQ between parents and their children can be attributed to the factors (affecting IQ) that they share in common—a shared family environment and a certain genetic resemblance. In this case, they are inevitably confounded. But if we compared this correlation with that between adoptive parents and their adopted children, or that between parents and their children sent away for adoption, *and if we made certain simplifying assumptions*, we should be able to obtain estimates of the importance of these genetic and environmental sources of resemblance. Table 3.8 illustrates the procedure. As in Table 3.1, we have a list of various kinships—MZ twins brought up together or apart, parents and their children, adoptive parents and their adopted children, etc. But what we need now is a set of assumptions specifying the factors they share in common. The column labelled 'simple model' makes the simplest possible set of assumptions: first, that MZ twins are genetically identical, while DZ twins, other siblings, and parents and their children all share 50 per cent of their genes, and unrelated individuals share no genes; and, secondly, that people living in the same family all share exactly the same common family environment, while those who do not, share no common environment.

Armed with these assumptions, we can now estimate the contributions of genetics and environment to similarities in IQ. For example, while the resemblance of MZ twins brought

Table 3.8 A simple model for estimating heritability

Kinship	Simple model	Observed correlations (Bouchard and McGue, 1981)	Estimates	
			G	CE
MZ (t)	G + CE	0.86		
MZ (a)	G	0.72	0.72	
DZ (t)	0.5G + CE	0.60		
Sib (t)	0.5G + CE	0.47		
Sib (a)	0.5G	0.24	0.48	
Parent–Child (t)	0.5G + CE	0.42		
Parent–Child (a)	0.5G	0.22	0.44	
Adoptive parent–adopted child (t)	CE	0.19		0.19
Unrelated children (t)	CE	0.32		0.32

MZ, MZ twins; DZ, DZ twins; Sib, siblings; (t), brought up together; (a), living apart.
G, contribution of genetic variance; CE, contribution of common (family) environment.

up together reflects the contribution of shared genes and shared environment, the resemblance of MZ twins brought up apart reflects only that of their shared genes—and therefore provides a direct estimate of the magnitude of that contribution. Equally, however, the resemblance between parents and the children they have given up for adoption is also due only to their shared genes; but in this case, since they only share 50 per cent of their genes, the full genetic contribution is estimated by doubling the value of the correlation. Other, indirect estimates of heritability can be achieved by *comparing* the correlations between different kinship categories: the difference between the correlations between parents and children in biological and in adoptive families is due to the difference between sharing 50 per cent and 0 per cent of genes, and can again be doubled to give an estimate of heritability. In a similar way, estimates of the contribution of common family environment can also be achieved either directly or indirectly: the correlation between adoptive parents and their adopted children, or that between two unrelated children living in the same family, provides a direct measure of common environment; while a comparison between MZ twins, or siblings, brought up together and apart provides an indirect measure.

On the face of it, however, many of the assumptions made in this simple model are demonstrably false. Let us list only the most obvious, some of which I have already noted in passing:

1. The model assumes that all members of a family share the same common environment, to exactly the same degree. But MZ twins may well share more experiences in common than DZ twins, who in turn may share more common experiences than siblings of different ages. And can it really make sense to suppose that parents and their children experience the same similarity in family environment as do brothers and sisters growing up together? Presumably, much of the effect of family environment must be on young children; there is no reason to expect that the environment parents themselves experienced as young children is the same as that in which they bring up their own children. All these differences in shared environment may well help to explain why, as can be seen in Table 3.8, MZ twins resemble one another more than DZ twins, who resemble one another more than other siblings, who in turn resemble one another more than children resemble their parents.

2. There is no allowance for the possibility that adoptive families may not provide a completely representative cross-section of the population, nor for the phenomenon of selective placement. As we have seen, the former implies that correlations from adoptive families may underestimate the true contribution of variations in common family environment. The latter, on the other hand, may sometimes result in an overestimate of the heritability of IQ, as when resemblances between, say, twins brought up apart are attributed solely to their shared genes. But it may also result in an overestimate of the role of family environment, as when one ignores the possibility that adopted children may resemble their adoptive parents because those parents may resemble their true biological parents.

3. The genetic assumptions of the model are no more plausible. In the first place, they ignore the well-documented phenomenon of assortative mating—the tendency for husbands and wives to resemble one another in various ways (e.g. education, social class, and height). Bouchard and McGue (1981) report a weighted mean correlation between husbands and wives in IQ of 0.33—not so very much less than the correlation between parents and their children. The assumption that DZ twins and other siblings share no more than 50 per cent of their genes is based on the fact that children receive a random 50 per cent of each parent's genes, and on the assumption that there is no correlation between their two parents' genes. But if there is assortative mating for IQ, and if IQ is partly heritable, that assumption is false. Sometimes this will result in an overestimation of heritability, at other times in an underestimation. Thus if siblings share more than half their genes, then a doubling of the correlation between siblings brought up apart will overestimate heritability. On the other hand, if DZ twins share more than half their genes, the difference between DZ and MZ twin correlations reflects a difference of less than 50 per cent genetic similarity, and the model will be underestimating heritability.

4. Finally, the model also makes no allowance for the distinction between additive and non-additive genetic variance, and thus ignores the distinction between narrow and broad heritability—the former being that due to additive effects only, the latter being that due to both additive and non-additive effects. Non-additive genetic effects are those due to dominance and epistasis, the former referring to the different phenotypic effects of two alleles of the same gene, the latter to the possibility that phenotypic effects are a consequence of particular combinations of genes at different loci. The effect of this would be that even if siblings share, say, 50 per cent of their genes, they might display much lower concordance for a phenotypic character that depended on particular combinations of genes. Since MZ twins, of course, share all their genes, they will necessarily show concordance for such characters. To the extent that such non-additive effects are important, DZ twin and sibling correlations will underestimate broad heritability.

What, then, is the point of attempts to estimate the precise heritability of IQ if they rely on a model that appears to be based on some quite untrue assumptions? It is possible, of course, that such appearances are deceptive. Perhaps the assumptions are less important than we had supposed. But how could we prove this? Some behaviour geneticists have sought to do so by proving that the model works—because it gives reliable and consistent answers. As we have seen, a whole variety of different kinship correlations may be used to yield estimates of the heritability of IQ, some directly, others indirectly by comparisons between two correlations. According to Eysenck, they all yield much the same estimate: 'the agreement . . . is truly striking . . . The overall consistency . . . has been remarkable . . . This remarkable consistency' (Eysenck, 1979, pp. 113–115). And later, he claims that the simple model with an estimate of heritability of 69 per cent and of the effect of common environment of 18 per cent 'explains 98% of the variation in the kinship correlations, a better fit for any model being difficult to imagine' (Eysenck, 1979, pp. 113–116). If so many different comparisons all yield virtually the same estimate for heritability, the argument runs, we have every right to accept that estimate as valid. The apparently arbitrary assumptions involved in one comparison are quite different from those underlying another, but since they make no difference to the final outcome, they must have been either less arbitrary or less important than they seemed. If there were errors in one comparison, they have been cancelled out by the opposite errors in another. Convergence between many lines of possibly imperfect evidence somehow removes their imperfections.

The trouble with this argument is that, as can been seen in Table 3.8, its premise is simply not true. For example, if the correlation between the IQ scores of MZ twins brought up apart is 0.72, then, according to the simple model, that is the heritability of IQ. But the correlations between siblings brought up apart and between parents and their children sent away for adoption are 0.24 and 0.22; since the model assumes that both reflect 0.5G, they yield estimates of heritability of 0.48 and 0.44. Yet other, indirect estimates of heritability, not shown in Table 3.8, can be provided by comparing different correlations. The classic twin method for estimating heritability involves comparing the resemblance of MZ and of DZ twins. The MZ correlation of 0.86 is due to G + CE; the DZ correlation of 0.60 is due to 0.5G + CE. So the difference between the two correlations (0.86 − 0.60 = 0.26) represents the effect of 0.5G, and can be doubled to yield an estimate of heritability of 0.52. In the same way, the correlation of 0.47 between siblings brought up together is due to 0.5G + CE, while that of 0.32 between two unrelated children brought up together is due solely to CE. Again the difference represents the effects of 0.5G and can be doubled to yield an estimate of heritability of 0.30. Where now is this remarkable consistency converging on an estimate of 0.69? The answer is that Eysenck was using rather different values for the various kinship correlations, largely derived from an earlier summary put together by Erlenmeyer-Kimling and Jarvik (1963), which included a number of early studies rightly excluded by Bouchard and McGue (1981), who also, of course, included a large number of later studies. Thus Eysenck used values of 0.34 and 0.32 for the correlations between siblings and parents and their children living apart, which give estimates of heritability of 0.68 and 0.64, respectively, and relied on a single, very old study to give a correlation of only 0.53 for DZ twins which, when subtracted from a correlation for MZ twins of 0.87 yielded a heritability estimate of 0.68. Relatively small changes in many of these correlations result in disproportionately large changes in estimates of heritability.

Bouchard and McGue's summary of kinship correlations, shown in Table 3.1, is probably more reliable than that of Erlenmeyer-Kimling and Jarvik. But how reliable is it? For example, they give a value of 0.32 for the correlation of unrelated children living together. As we have seen, the studies published since their survey have reported values as low as −0.09, with a median close to zero. These numbers cause havoc. They supposedly provide a direct estimate of the variance attributable to common family environment, thus suggesting that it is negligible, and, when subtracted from the correlation for siblings living together, yield an estimate of heritability of over 0.80.

It hardly seems necessary to belabour the point further. No one seriously wishes to defend all the assumptions of the simple model: the problems they generate suggest the need for more complex and more realistic models. Chipuer *et al.* (1990) have provided one such model. As can be seen in Table 3.9, it marks several advances over the simple model:

1. It acknowledges the distinction between additive and non-additive genetic variance, assuming that although MZ twins are identical in both respects, the value for additive genetic effects for DZ twins and other siblings is 0.5, but that for non-additive effects only 0.25.

2. On the environmental side, it assumes that twins share more similar experiences than other siblings, who in turn share more similar experiences with one another than they do with their parents. But the model makes no allowance for selective placement, nor for the possibility of restriction of range in adoptive family environments.

3. Although not shown in Table 3.9, this model acknowledges the possible importance of assortative mating, and thus allows that the values for shared sources of genetic resemblance in all relatives except MZ twins may be too low. The problem here is that even if we had a perfect estimate of the extent of assortative mating for IQ, that would only be an estimate of the phenotypic correlation between husbands and wives. What we need to know is the correlation between their genotypes for IQ, and to estimate that we need to know the heritability of IQ.

Chipuer *et al.* (1990) fitted their model to a slightly updated version of the Bouchard and McGue summary shown in Table 3.1. The best estimates for the various parameters of their model are also shown in Table 3.9. Broad heritability (the contribution of additive and non-additive genetic variance) is only 51 per cent; the shared environment of twins is more powerful than that of other siblings or of parents and their children; and in these last two cases, the effects of shared environment are smaller than those of unique, unshared environment. Although the model provides a reasonable fit to the data, there are still some notable discrepancies. For example, it predicts that the correlation between MZ twins brought up apart should be only 0.51, and the estimate of the effects of common environment (provided by subtracting the MZ-apart from the MZ-together correlation) is only 0.14, rather than 0.35. Related to this, as Plomin and Loehlin (1989) had also noted, there is a substantial discrepancy between direct estimates of heritability, such as those provided by twins or other relatives brought up apart, and indirect estimates, which depend on comparisons between different kinship correlations.

This conflict between the estimates of heritability derivable from different data sets

Table 3.9 A more realistic model for estimating heritability (from Chipuer *et al.*, 1990)

(a) Contribution of genetic and environmental factors to resemblances of various kinships

Kinship	Sources of resemblance
MZ (t)	G (a) + G (n) + E (t)
MZ (a)	G (a) + G (n)
DZ (t)	0.5G (a) + 0.25G (n) + E (t)
Sib (t)	0.5G (a) + 0.25G (n) + E (s)
Sib (a)	0.5G (a) + 0.25G (n)
Parent–child (t)	0.5G (a) + E (p–c)
Parent–child (a)	0.5G (a)
Adoptive parent–adopted child (t)	E (p–c)
Unrelated children (t)	E (s)

(b) Percentage of variance accounted for by different factors

Factor		% Variance
G (a)	(Additive genetic variance)	0.32
G (n)	(Non-additive genetic variance)	0.19
E (t)	(Family environment shared by twins)	0.35
E (s)	(Family environment shared by siblings)	0.22
E (p–c)	(Family environment shared by parent and child)	0.20
	(Unique environment unshared by twins)	0.14
	(Unique environment unshared by siblings)	0.27
	(Unique environment unshared by parent and child)	0.29

throws into sharp relief the central problem plaguing these exercises in modelling. This is not so much the difficulty of accepting that the weighted mean from a large number of studies of variable quality, performed at different times, on different populations, with different IQ tests, provides the best possible estimate of the 'true' correlation for any particular kinship. It is more that there is no reason whatsoever to believe that there should be a single 'true' value for any of these correlations. As we noted at the beginning of this chapter, heritability is a population statistic, and there is no reason to believe that an estimate obtained for one population at one time will be true for that population at other times or for other populations at any time. Although of distinctly variable quality, there is some evidence that kinship correlations for IQ, and heritability estimates based on them, do vary in this sort of way. In Hawaii, De Fries *et al.* (1979) found that correlations between parents and their children were higher in white than in Japanese families, while correlations between siblings were higher in the Japanese families. Sundet *et al.* (1988) reported correlations for seven cohorts of Norwegian MZ and DZ twins born between 1931 and 1960. Although the MZ correlations varied only between 0.79 and 0.88, those for DZ twins varied from 0.34 to 0.58. Taken at face value, these numbers imply that the heritability of IQ in Norway has fluctuated, in a pretty haphazard manner, between 0.30 and 0.85 over this period. That seems distinctly implausible, and it is perhaps more sensible to remember that the twin method of calculating heritability is sensitive to quite small variations in the values of MZ and DZ correlations (since it involves doubling the difference between them), and that correlations based on small samples have a substantial probable error associated with them. Brody (1992) discusses a number of other studies that imply similarly large variations in heritability, which should probably be treated with similar caution.

A perhaps more surprising possibility, which has been endorsed by many behaviour geneticists, to the point where it is accepted as orthodoxy, is that the heritability of IQ might increase as children grow older (e.g. Brody, 1992; McGue *et al.*, 1993; Lynn, 1996*a*; Bouchard, 1997; Jensen, 1997). One piece of evidence adduced in support of this suggestion is that correlations between adoptive parents and their adopted children, like those between two unrelated children living together, seem to be lower in older than in younger children (see Table 3.6, p. 82, and other studies cited there). This certainly suggests that the influence of family environment may decrease as children grow older, but the natural interpretation is surely to say that other, unique environmental factors take over from family environment as sources of influence on IQ, as children start spending more of their time outside the home. The only reason for arguing that heritability increases, on the basis of the Texas adoption data, is that none of the correlations between biological relatives in these adoptive families (parents and their own children, two biological siblings) decreased as the children grew older. On the assumption that part of the earlier correlation between these biological relatives was due to the influence of family environment rather than common genes, it seems to follow that the genetic influence must have increased to compensate for the decline in the family environment effect . This can be no more than suggestive. It is also a rather strange line of reasoning to employ here, since behaviour geneticists have, elsewhere, been equally happy to point to a decrease in the correlation between some biologically related children as they grow older as evidence of an increase in heritability (McGue *et al.*, 1993). As we have already seen (p. 73), the correlation between DZ twins decreases as the twins grow older, while that between MZ twins does not. Since the difference between MZ and DZ correlations is standardly thought to provide a simple estimate of heritability, an increase in the magnitude of this difference as twins grow older implies an increase in heritability. Once again, the argument does not seem particularly convincing. An alternative explanation, already alluded to (p. 73) is that MZ twins continue to share common interests and experiences long after DZ twins, like other siblings, have begun to grow apart.

There is one final argument. The assumption that heritability increases from childhood to adulthood may explain the discrepancy between estimates of heritability based on adoption studies and that based on separated MZ twins. The model of Chipuer *et al.*, illustrated in Table 3.9, estimated broad heritability at about 50 per cent. The majority of the data on which that model is based come from adoption studies of relatively young children. The one finding that is strikingly discordant with the model is that the correlation for MZ twins reared apart is over 0.70. The simple behaviour geneticist's assumption is that this provides a direct estimate of the heritability of IQ. But the large majority of these twins have been tested as adults.

There are, of course, reasons for suggesting that the MZ-apart correlation may be an overestimate of heritability (p. 79). At the very least, it should be acknowledged that the discrepancy between this correlation and the estimate of heritability derived from adoption studies provides only indirect evidence for the hypothesis that heritability increases as children grow older. Before this hypothesis really does become established orthodoxy, it ought to be tested directly. The direct test is to see whether correlations between biological relatives, who have lived apart, increase as they grow older. There is no evidence that this is true. In the Texas adoption study, the correlation between adopted children and their biological mothers was 0.23, when they were first tested and 0.26, 10 years later—hardly a dramatic increase. And not all separated MZ twins have been tested as adults. The Newman *et al.* (1937) and Shields (1962) studies both provided individual case histories, which reveal that 12 of their pairs of twins were tested before the age of 20. The IQ correlation for this set of 12 pairs is 0.77—certainly no less than that for the entire sample. In other words, there is no evidence that younger separated MZ twins resemble one another any less than older twins. The hypothesis that the heritability of IQ increases as children grow older should be treated with some caution. For the present, it seems safer to conclude that the main change in influences on IQ as children grow older is that variations in family environment become less important, but variations in unique environment factors become more important.

Is the estimate of 0.50 for the broad heritability of IQ provided by Chipuer *et al.* (1990) more, or less, plausible than the figure of 0.70 proposed by Eysenck (1979)? Many commentators have favoured the former figure over the latter (e.g. Scarr and Carter-Salzman, 1982; Loehlin, 1989; Plomin, 1994). But others still opt for the higher figure (e.g. Lynn, 1996*a*). The more reasonable conclusion, however, is that the broad heritability of IQ in modern industrialized societies is probably somewhere between 0.30 and 0.75, and that neither the data nor the models justify much greater precision. The data are too variable, partly because they are necessarily imperfect, but partly because there probably is genuine variation from one age, time, and place to another. Many of the assumptions on which the models are based are demonstrably false, while others are, at best, implausible. Even if we had any reason to believe that they all cancelled out and could thus be ignored, because all estimates of heritability agreed so closely, it would be odd to accept as true assumptions known to be false. It is not difficult to discern one justification for doing so, which is only rarely made explicit: without some arbitrary, simplifying assumptions, it would be impossible to derive any estimate of heritability at all. The number of unknowns in any equation would soon exceed the number of data points to be predicted, and any model would be indeterminate. If true, however, that is no reason for accepting false assumptions; on the contrary, it seems rather a good reason for desisting from the attempt to provide a precise estimate of heritability.

The mechanism of heritability

Most early IQ testers described their tests as measures of inborn capacity or innate ability. However high the heritability of IQ turned out to be, that would remain a misleading claim. But it is difficult to rid ourselves of the belief that if the heritability of IQ is high, this means that some people are born with more efficient brains than others. There is, of course, some evidence for this in that certain cases of mental retardation, some genetically transmitted, others the result of chromosomal abnormalities and thus congenital, although often not heritable, are associated with errors of brain metabolism. The popular textbook example is phenylketonuria, an autosomal recessive trait, in which the normal hydroxylation of the amino acid phenylalanine to form tyrosine is blocked, with a consequent build-up of phenylalanine and the danger of permanent brain damage. Another, more recently discovered example is fragile X syndrome (Plomin, 1997).

But it is rash to generalize from such rare and abnormal cases. Although some of the variation in IQ scores between, say, 70 and 150 in North American and European populations is certainly attributable to genetic differences between members of those populations, it does not follow that it is a consequence of inherited differences in the efficiency of the brain as a processor of information. The route from genotype to IQ may be much more circuitous. To illustrate the argument, consider the following possible scenario. Each of two pairs of MZ twins is separated at birth, and the four infants are brought up in four quite unrelated families. But because the two twins within each pair are genetically identical, they resemble one another not only physically, but also in temperament. In one pair, both twins are restless, easily bored, and fractious; in the other, both are placid, undemanding, and sleep a lot. The two adoptive mothers of the first pair have to spend their time taking their babies out of their cots, talking to them, entertaining them, trying to find them something new to play with; while the two mothers of the second pair can relax, leaving their perfectly contented babies alone and undisturbed for long periods of time. These differences in stimulation in the first year of life have a cumulative effect on the cognitive development of the two pairs of twins: by the age of 10, the first pair both have IQs of about 120, the second pair about 95. Since separated MZ twins have ended up with similar IQ scores, we correctly conclude that IQ has high heritability. But the reason why their IQ scores are similar is because their genetically caused similarities in temperament resulted in their experiencing environments that had similar effects on their intellectual development.

The scenario is not altogether fanciful. We have already seen (Chapter 2) that the earliest reliable predictor of IQ scores in later childhood is the responsiveness of a 6-month-old infant to a habituation test. High IQ is associated with rapid habituation to a repetitive stimulus and strong dishabituation to a novel stimulus. In other words, a child with high IQ is likely to have been an easily bored infant. Moreover, there is now suggestive evidence that MZ twins may be treated alike even when they are brought up by separate adoptive parents. When asked, as adults, to rate their early home environment on a variety of dimensions, separated MZ twins' ratings of the emphasis placed on cultural and intellectual achievement had a correlation of 0.42 (Plomin *et al.*, 1988). Plomin (1994) has reviewed a wide variety of evidence (of admittedly variable quality) which suggests that biologically related children experience more similar environments than unrelated children, whether or not they have lived together. We are dealing here with the possibility of gene–environment covariation (Jensen, 1981; Scarr and McCartney, 1983; Plomin, 1994). Genetic relatedness causes environmental similarity, which feeds back to produce a resemblance in a phenotypic characteristic such as IQ. The effects could surely be cumulative. To follow up our hypothetical scenario of the easily bored and placid pairs of MZ twins: the initial impetus to rapid cognitive development provided by early stimulation might cause the first pair of twins to seek out, and to be offered, further intellectual stimulation as they grow older. Their adoptive parents might be more likely to read to them since they are more rewarding to read to, and later still, they would choose to read more themselves. At school, finding the work reasonably easy, and enjoyable, they become popular with their teachers, who give them more demanding work to do. And so on.

It is obvious that the argument could equally apply to children living in the same family. MZ twins brought up together may resemble one another as closely as they do because, within the family, they create for themselves environments that are much more similar than those experienced by their genetically less similar other siblings. On the other hand, two unrelated, adopted children living in the same adoptive family may initially show some resemblance to one another because their adoptive parents strive to treat them as fairly (and thus as equally) as possible. But as they grow older, their parents start responding to their (genetically based) differences in interests, temperament, and behaviour, thus reinforcing their initially small differences in IQ; by the time they are teenagers, they have created for themselves two different environments, sets of friends, and so on, and their IQ scores are driven yet further apart.

It is possible to distinguish between at least three types of gene–environment covariation—passive, reactive, and active (Plomin, 1994). Passive covariation occurs to the extent that parents of high or low IQ not only transmit genes for high or low IQ to their children, but also, simply as a consequence of their own IQ, provide either an intellectually stimulating or unstimulating family environment. Reactive covariation would be illustrated by the hypothetical scenario of the separated MZ twins: parents and others who interact with young children may respond to genetically influenced differences in their behaviour. Active covariation occurs to the extent that children, as they develop, actively seek out friends and situations that serve to reinforce their genetic differences: if a high-IQ child chooses to read more and more demanding books, chooses to spend more time on homework, and, against parental wishes, insists on staying on at school after the age of 16 and then going on to university, the environments she has sought out are precisely those likely to enhance her already high IQ.

The reader will have noticed, by now, that the examples of gene–environment covariation I have given have been largely hypothetical. This is no accident. However plausible these examples might seem, there is rather little direct evidence to prove that such covariation really does explain much of the variance in IQ. Much of the data relied upon by Plomin *et al.* (1988) and Plomin (1994) consist of adults' and older children's *recollections* of their early family environment. But separated MZ twins may give similar answers to questionnaires probing their recollections of the past, not because they really experienced similar treatment at the hands of their adoptive parents, but because a genetic similarity in temperament predisposes them to answer such questionnaires in a similar manner. Nor should one press too far the argument that MZ resemblances in IQ can be attributed to the similarity of the environments they experienced as a consequence of their genetically based similarities in temperament or personality. The fact of the matter is that MZ twins, whether brought up together or apart, resemble one another in IQ a great deal more than they resemble one another in personality (p. 74).

But the argument has been worth pursuing because it should reinforce two conclusions. First, in other than a minute number of cases of single gene effects, we simply do not know how genetic similarities and differences cause similarities and differences in IQ. Secondly, the distinction between genetics and environmental sources of variation in IQ is not a sharp or clear one. When brought up in the same family, MZ twins resemble one another in IQ significantly more than DZ twins. In an earlier section of this chapter, we discussed whether this is because they are genetically more similar or because they share more similar environments. But, as I hinted there, it turns out that the distinction between these two possibilities is not entirely clear-cut. MZ twins are, of course, genetically more similar to one another than DZ twins, but it is possible that the reason why they are more similar in IQ is because their genetic identity causes them to experience a more similar environment, and it is this closer similarity in environment that results in their resembling one another more in IQ. This possibility cannot be tested by separating the twins, since the genetic identity of MZ twins may continue to ensure that they experience more similar environments even if they are brought up in different families. Nor can it be tested by removing the possibilities of such gene–environment covariation by ensuring that all children are treated exactly alike. In such a science fiction society, there would be no environmental variation at all, and the heritability of IQ, as of any other characteristic, would necessarily be 1.0.

Summary

Heritability is a population statistic, referring to the proportion of the total variation in a given characteristic in a given population that can be ascribed to genetic differences between members of that population. Thus there is no reason to believe that there is a single number representing *the* heritability of IQ: it may vary from one population to another, or from one time to another in the same population.

Estimates of the heritability of IQ, or of any other human characteristic for any population, can be obtained only if we can disentangle genetic from environmental sources of variation in that characteristic. The existence of identical (MZ) twins, and the practice of adoption, provide the two most commonly used methods for estimating heritabilities. MZ twins, whether brought up together or apart, do resemble one another in IQ very closely; when brought up together, the correlation in their IQ scores approaches the reliability of the tests, and is notably higher than that for most other psychological measures. When children are adopted, the correlation between their IQ scores and those of their adoptive parents is usually less than that observed between children and their parents in ordinary biological families; at the same time, these adopted children continue to resemble their natural mothers in IQ—usually more than their adoptive mothers.

All this is consistent with the supposition that IQ has substantial heritability. But it should always be remembered that the natural experiments on which such a conclusion rests are inevitably imperfect. Although today we can surely reject the critic's claim that there exist no data sufficient to persuade a prudent man that IQ scores are in any degree heritable, we need to remember the confounds that plague most natural experiments and the problems that attend their interpretation. And we should also remember two other points: attempts to provide quantitative estimates of the heritability of IQ have serious problems explaining all features of the data; and we have next to no idea how genes actually affect the developing child's IQ. There is no good evidence that variations in later IQ are caused by variations in the efficiency of the neonatal brain (whatever that may mean), and it is just as plausible to suppose that genetic effects on IQ are mediated indirectly via the environment. Thus separated identical twins probably resemble one another in IQ *partly* because they continue to create similar environments for themselves in their separate adoptive homes.

Behaviour genetic studies also make it clear that environmental factors have a direct impact on children's IQ scores. People living in the same family generally show a greater resemblance in IQ than those living apart. But there is some evidence that this influence of family environment on IQ scores diminishes as children grow older, and some behaviour geneticists have argued that it has completely disappeared by the age of 18–20 years. There is thus some reason to believe that the most important environmental influences on IQ are those unique to each individual, i.e. those that cause brothers and sisters brought up together to differ in IQ.

Appendix

The heritability of IQ is an issue that has attracted a quite inordinate amount of polemical argument and counter-argument. Much of the argument has been *merely* polemical, amounting to little more than an attempt to discredit opponents' arguments by questioning their motives and credentials. But some of it has involved a detailed and, apparently, serious and meticulous analysis of the evidence. Some, but by no means all, of the critics' analyses have been convincing. For example, Kamin's analysis of Burt's studies, both those on MZ twins and others, revealed that his data, which had been widely regarded as the best evidence for the heritability of IQ, were totally worthless. That particular conclusion cannot possibly be disputed (Mackintosh, 1995). But this does not mean that one should accept Kamin's other arguments, directed against other studies. In this appendix, I advance reasons for disputing most of the critics' other detailed arguments.

A.1 Separated MZ twins

Kamin, Taylor, and Farber have sought to show that if the data are analysed sufficiently finely, very few twins were truly separated, and those who were resemble one another very much less than the majority who were not. For example, Kamin (1974, 1981) calculated that in 27 of Shields's 40 pairs of twins, the two twins were brought up by relatives; their IQs correlated 0.83. The correlation for the remaining 13 pairs, brought up in unrelated families, was 0.51. More systematically, Taylor (1980) classified the twins from all three studies as having been brought up in related or unrelated families, reunited or not during childhood, and experiencing similar or dissimilar environments. Only five of Shields's pairs satisfied three of these criteria for uncorrelated environments, and Taylor calculated the correlation of their IQ scores as only 0.24. He concluded:

> It seems reasonable to suggest that the IQ correlation characterising pairs of individuals with absolutely identical genes and absolutely uncorrelated environments would be extremely low. (Taylor, 1980, p. 100)

The argument may seem persuasive, but it is fraught with problems. An accurate estimate of the heritability of IQ would require a measure of the correlation in IQ scores of MZ twins brought up in *uncorrelated* environments; but that does not mean that all the environments should be completely different, let alone that they should have been specifically selected for their dissimilarity. If a set of twins had indeed been assigned at random to uncorrelated environments, one would expect, by chance, to find some of them in rather similar environments. Thus Kamin's 0.51 or Taylor's 0.24 could as well be underestimates as overestimates of the 'true' correlation. There is, however, a much more serious problem. The sure way to guarantee the truth of the adage that one can prove anything with statistics is to trawl through a set of data, performing numerous *post hoc* analyses on small sub-sets of the data, until one comes up with the desired conclusions. Conclusions so reached do not merit anyone else's attention unless they can be supported by some sort of independent analysis. Kamin's and Taylor's do not stand up well to this requirement, and one's confidence in them is not increased by evidence of biased reporting. Thus Kamin (Kamin, 1974; Rose *et al.*, 1984) has asserted that the correlation of 0.51 for the 13 pairs in Shields's study brought up in unrelated homes is still a serious overestimate since

> the most common pattern, even among pairs reared in unrelated families, was for the mother to raise one twin while the other was raised by close family friends. (Rose *et al.*, 1984, p. 107)

The facts are these: in 4 of the 13 pairs, one twin was brought up by a close relative (mother, father, or aunt) and the other by a friend; in the remaining nine cases, one and usually both twins were adopted by total strangers. Moreover, Shields himself, in a re-analysis of his own data, reported a correlation of .87 in 16 pairs of twins selected as experiencing the most similar environments, and one of 0.84 in 12 pairs experiencing the least similar environments (Shields, 1978).

Taylor's correlation of 0.24 was based on only five pairs of Shields's twins. But Taylor identified six other pairs satisfying his criteria of maximum separation (three in Newman *et al.* (1937) and three in Juel-Nielsen (1980)), although failing to report the correlation for all 11 pairs: it is, in fact, 0.67 (Bouchard, 1983). It is not that Taylor was reluctant to combine data from the three studies: most of his conclusions rest on just such a combination, ignoring some anomalous differences between them. For all three criteria of separation (brought up in unrelated families, in dissimilar environments, and not reunited), he claimed that the correlations from the three studies combined are invariably lower for the more separated twins, where they range from 0.46 to 0.56, than for the less separated, where they range from 0.75 to 0.86. But the effect of related families is confined to Shields's study: in the other two, twins brought up in unrelated families resembled one another slightly more (0.68 or 0.77 depending on which tests one relies on) than those brought up in related families (0.65 or 0.66). And although the overall effect of similarity of environment was present in all three studies, in Newman *et al.* (1937) and Juel-Nielsen (1965) it depended on which test scores were used. In both studies, the twins were given two IQ tests, Stanford–Binet and Otis in the former and Wechsler and Raven's in the latter. Taylor chose to analyse only the Stanford–Binet and Wechsler scores which, it is true, correlated more highly for twins experiencing similar environments than for those experiencing dissimilar environments (0.81 v. 0.54). For Otis and Raven's tests, however, these two correlations were 0.67 and 0.70 (Bouchard, 1983).

Like Kamin and Taylor, Farber also divided the twins into those she classified as more separated and those less separated. For all three studies, 39 pairs satisfied her criteria for being highly separated. She omitted, however, to report the IQ correlation for these 39 pairs. It is, in fact, 0.76 (Bouchard, 1997).

A.2 Matching of adoptive and biological families

The critical question is whether any study has succeeded in matching adoptive and biological families carefully enough that we should have confidence in any estimates of heritability based on a comparison between them. All three studies shown in Table 3.4 made some effort to find a suitable group of biological families, resembling the adoptive families in a number of respects. The most thorough and detailed attempt was made by Burks, in the oldest of the three, who provides information on the following factors: child's age and IQ; parents' age, IQ, education, occupation, and income; whether they owned their home, and what its value was; ratings for parental attitudes; economic and cultural rating of the home; extent of parental and other private instruction received by the child; number of people in the household. She was remarkably successful in matching the two groups of families, both in terms of average scores, and in terms of variability. The only differences she could find were that the adoptive parents were, on average, about 5 years older than the biological parents, had a higher average income, and were more likely to own their more valuable home; there were also more children in the biological families, and the supposedly matched biological children had an 8-point higher IQ. None of this is very surprising; adoptive parents are likely to have spent some time trying for children of their own before adopting, and the other parental differences would seem to follow from this. It would be surprising if adoptive families were not smaller than average; and the higher average IQ of the biological children follows from any genetic account, since these are all above-average families, and one might expect their children to have inherited genes for above-average IQ. In spite of his extravagant claims, it is difficult to accept Kamin's assertion that these differences might be sufficient to explain the low correlation between parents' and children's IQ scores in the adoptive homes (Kamin, 1974). He is not, it is true, content to rest with the differences acknowledged by Burks; from two tables summarizing the ratings of the two groups of homes for such factors as necessities, neatness, parental supervision, library, education, and artistic taste (a total of 10 sub-scores), he finds one case, the necessities score, where the variance is significantly less in adoptive than in biological homes, and concludes that

> this fact alone could account for the failure to find strong correlations between IQ of adopted children and measures of home environment. (Kamin, 1974, p. 119)

Neither Leahy (1935) nor Scarr and Weinberg (1978) provide as much detail as did Burks (1928), but the information on children's and parents' IQ and education, parental occupation and income suggest that both groups of families were reasonably well matched. A small difference in favour of adoptive parents on one IQ test in Leahy's study is matched by a small difference in favour of biological parents on the other. The biological parents are marginally better educated than are the adoptive parents in Scarr and Weinberg. The only other difference, noted by Leahy, is that the variance of adopted children's IQ scores was significantly less than that of biological children in her study. This, of course, is exactly what Kamin's argument would lead one to expect: the restriction in the range of environments found in adoptive families has resulted in a similar restriction in the range of the children's IQ scores.

The problem with Kamin's argument is that neither Burks (1928) nor Scarr and Weinberg (1978) found such a difference in the variance of children's IQ scores between their adoptive and biological families. In Scarr and Weinberg, the standard deviation of adopted children's IQ scores was 8.95, and of biological children 10.36. These are both much smaller than that to be expected in the population as a whole (15), but even though there is a tendency for the adopted children to be less variable, the difference is not significant. In Burks, the two standard deviations are (adopted children first) 15.09 and 15.13. These are the population norms, and clearly do not differ. Kamin attempts to deal with this as follows:

> Within the Burks study, however, the IQ variance for adopted children was inflated by the presence of a relatively large number of adopted children with *very* low IQ's—some as low as 40 and 50, entirely outside the range of the control children in her or in Leahy's study. (Kamin, 1974, p. 121).

This is nonsense. A total of 5 out of 214 adopted children had IQ scores lower than those of any control child, but since the mean IQ of the adopted children was 8 points lower than that of the controls, this is hardly surprising. The 'some as low as 40 and 50' amounts to two children with IQs between 40 and 54. Their exclusion does not materially affect the variance of the adopted children's scores.

A.3 Can selective placement explain why adoptive children continue to resemble their biological parents?

There is no doubt that significant selective placement has occurred in some adoption studies. A striking case in point is a study by Freeman *et al.* (1928), where there was a correlation of 0.34 between adopted children's IQ scores and ratings of their adoptive homes *before* the children had even set foot in those homes. Another way of measuring selective placement is by looking at the correlation between the test scores of adoptive parents and those of the biological mothers of their adopted children. In some recent studies, at least, these correlations have been relatively modest—e.g. 0.14 in the Texas adoption study (Horn *et al.* 1979). Kamin (1981) has used a different comparison as a measure of selective placement, namely, the extent to which the adopted child's true, biological mother resembled *other* children in the adoptive family (for example, biological children of the adoptive parents). Any such resemblance could not be genetically based, but could only reflect a correlation between the circumstances of the biological mother and the adoptive family. The relevant data for the Texas and Minnesota studies are shown in Table 3.10. Although greater than zero, these correlations are smaller than those between these biological mothers and their own, adopted-away children, and thus provide little reason to believe that the entire resemblance of the adopted children to their biological mothers can be explained by selective placement. Not satisfied with these numbers, Kamin looks for others. He notes that in the Minnesota study, although the mothers were all tested on the Stanford–Binet, only some of the children were—others were tested with the WISC. Claiming that 'the two tests can give substantially different results' (although in fact they correlate over 0.80), he recalculates the correlations on the smaller sample of children tested on Stanford–Binet. These are the numbers in brackets under Minnesota. He can now claim that here at least selective placement is, after all, sufficient. Turning to the Texas study, he finds yet another comparison—the correlation between the adopted child's biological mother and other *adopted* children in the adoptive family. Although smaller than the correlation with her own biological child, it is large enough to satisfy Kamin that selective placement was a significant problem here too. But the concern for the type of test, that had required the calculation of new correlations for the Minnesota data, has now been forgotten. The numbers shown in Table 3.10 are correlations between mothers' scores on the beta test and children's scores on the WISC. Data are equally available for mothers' WAIS scores, and these correlations are shown in brackets in Table 3.10. With these scores, it would be merely preposterous to argue that the correlation between a mother and her adopted-away biological child (0.32) is sufficiently explained by her correlation with other children in the adoptive family (0.11 or 0.07). The only reasonable conclusion is that adopted children do significantly resemble their biological parents, even when they have been separated from them from a very early age, and that this resemblance cannot be entirely due to selective placement.

Table 3.10 Kamin's evidence for selective placement in the Minnesota and Texas adoption studies

Correlation between adopted child's biological mother and:	Minnesota	Texas
Adopted child	0.32 (0.28)	0.31 (0.32)
Biological child of adoptive family	0.14 (0.33)	0.08 (0.11)
Other adopted child in adoptive family	– (–)	0.19 (0.07)

The numbers in parentheses for the Minnesota data are those calculated by Kamin for the smaller sample of children tested, like the mothers, on the Stanford–Binet test.
The numbers in parentheses for the Texas study are the correlations between the mothers' WAIS scores and the children's WISC scores.

4   *Environmental effects on IQ*

Introduction

Even the most ardent hereditarians have usually allowed that some of the variation in IQ in modern Western societies must be attributed to differences in the circumstances of people's lives. They are surely right, but it is important to clear up one possible confusion at the outset. No phenotypic character is produced by genetic instructions acting in an environmental void, and this is clearly true of performance on an IQ test. The knowledge and skills required to answer items in standard IQ tests could not possibly be an automatic consequence of a genetic blueprint, developing in the absence of any input from the environment: the normal cognitive and intellectual development of young children depends on their interaction with their environment. But this obvious truth says virtually nothing about the contribution of the environment to the actual variation in IQ observed in modern industrial societies.

The point can be illustrated by considering the occasional horrific cases of young children who are discovered, locked up in an attic where they have lived virtually all their lives, deprived of human contact (Clarke and Clarke, 1976; Curtiss, 1977). Of course, such an upbringing has a drastic effect on the children's IQ, even if, remarkably enough, these effects can be partially, if not wholly, reversed by prolonged and skilful education. But these cases are almost wholly irrelevant to the question that concerns us here. The fortunate fact is that very few children live locked up in attics. Normal cognitive development may well depend, as Piaget has argued, on the processes of assimilation and accommodation that occur as the child operates on, and is in turn operated on by, the environment. If essentially all children reap the benefits of this interaction, however, it will not contribute to variations in IQ. When we are discussing IQ, we are talking about the causes of differences between people, not about what is common to all: environmental factors responsible for differences in IQ must themselves vary widely in the general population.

There can, of course, be no serious doubt that differences in environmental experiences do contribute to variation in IQ. The kinship studies reviewed in Chapter 3 make it clear that the heritability of IQ is substantially less than 1.0, and all recent attempts to model kinship correlations, especially those involving children, have agreed that they are influenced both by family environment and by environmental effects unique to different members of the same family. The question at issue, then, is not whether there are environmental effects on IQ, but what those effects might be: what are the factors that influence IQ, and, perhaps even more important, how do they achieve their effect?

Secular changes in IQ

Since there is some difficulty in deciding on any rational order in which to list those environmental variables that might affect IQ, I shall start by considering the evidence that the average IQ test scores of the population of most industrialized countries have changed over the past two or three generations. One reason for doing so is that it illustrates nicely the point that it is possible to demonstrate powerful environmental effects on IQ without having the first idea what the critical environmental variables may be, let alone how they might be achieving their effect. But a simpler reason is that the data are surprising, demolish some long-cherished beliefs, and raise a number of other interesting issues on the way.

One of the social changes responsible for the rise of the eugenics movement at the beginning of the twentieth century was the adoption, initially by the educated middle classes, of some form of birth control. In mid-Victorian England, middle-class families contained, on average, about seven or eight children; by the early years of the twentieth century, the number had shrunk to fewer than three (Lynn, 1996a). But not all families were following this practice, and the implications of this fact were quickly seized upon. Here is Sidney Webb, writing in a Fabian tract, published in 1907:

> In Great Britain, at this moment, when half, or perhaps two thirds of all the married people are regulating their families, children are being freely born to the Irish Roman Catholics and the Polish, Russian, and German Jews, on the one hand, and the thriftless and irresponsible—largely the casual labourers and the other denizens of the one-roomed tenements of our great cities—on the other . . . This can hardly result in anything but national deterioration.

We may be surprised to find such remarks being expressed by a socialist, but fashions and sentiments change, and such attitudes were commonplace among progressive thinkers, both in England and America (Kevles, 1985). They were founded on at least one empirical fact: there was indeed a significant negative correlation between social class and family size. Illustrative data are shown in Table 4.1. For many eugenicists the problem seemed to be compounded by the phenomenon of social mobility. As the more able and energetic members of the labouring classes moved up the social scale, it was supposed, they adopted the manners and habits of the middle classes, including the practice of birth control, thus ensuring that it was only their less successful, more feckless brethren who were producing large families. The discovery of the correlation between social class and IQ seemed to complete the gloomy picture (Burt, 1912; Terman, 1916): if the lower social classes not only had larger families, but also a lower average IQ, than the middle classes, it seemed

Table 4.1 The relationship between social class and family size (from Lynn, 1996*a*)

	Socio-economic status						
	1	2	3	4	5	6	7
US Census, 1910 Total number of children born to women aged 45–50	3.0	3.5	3.2	4.3	4.5	4.9	5.2
British Census, 1911 Total number of children born to women aged 45–50	2.6	3.4	4.2	4.5	4.8		

likely that, in each generation, more children were being born to parents of low IQ than to those of high IQ. Since IQ was inherited, it followed that IQ must be declining in each generation, and the end of civilization as we know it could not long be averted.

A few voices spoke out against the doom and gloom. Gray (1936) noted that whatever might be the difference in average IQ between social classes, the large majority of children with high IQ were born to parents of low social class, and most of them were denied any opportunity for secondary education (a point, to his credit, also noted by Burt, 1943). Penrose (1948) pointed out that any correlation between children's IQ and the size of the family they were born into must ignore the case of those married couples who have no children and of those adults who do not even get married. Cattell (1937, p. 41) had acknowledged this, but believed, on inadequate evidence, that childlessness was more common among the more intelligent and therefore that the true picture was even worse than he had painted. Penrose argued that these calculations ignored adults with very low IQs, particularly the retarded, and subsequent studies seemed to bear out his argument.

A large-scale study carried out some years later in the state of Minnesota was thought at the time to have settled the issue. Higgins *et al.* (1962) found the usual negative correlation between children's IQ and family size: in their sample of 1016 families the correlation was −0.30. They also provided the first proper evidence on the relationship between *parental* IQ and number of children. In these same families, the correlations were −0.11 for mother's IQ and −0.08 for father's IQ. The substantially smaller size of these correlations (confirming Cattell's earlier observation), suggests that any correlation between children's IQ and family size will seriously distort the true relation between IQ and fertility. But when Higgins *et al.* turned their attention to these parents' unmarried brothers and sisters, they found that these parental correlations were masking the true picture: the higher reproductive rate of parents with lower IQs was balanced by a higher proportion of adults with lower IQs who never married or had children at all. Taking all adults into account, those with IQs above 100 had 2.3 children on average, while those with IQs below 100 had 2.2. The negative correlation between IQ and fertility seemed to have completely disappeared, a finding soon confirmed in two other studies (Bajema, 1963, 1968).

And there the matter rested for some 20 years. But by the 1980s, a new series of

Box 4.1 The fight for our national intelligence

In a book with this title, published in 1937, Raymond Cattell calculated that the available data indicated

> a decline of average IQ for town and country of about three points per generation . . . or one point per decade. If this were to continue for three hundred years half the population would be mentally defective. Since the changes which mark the rises and declines of history are certainly not as drastic as to require wholesale mental deficiency, the present rate of change must be one of the most galloping plunges to bankruptcy that has ever occurred. (Cattell, 1937, pp. 42–43.)

But what were the data used to establish such doom-laden conclusions? Lacking a direct comparison of the IQ scores of one generation with the next, Cattell, like others before and after him, resorted to arguments based on differences in fertility. But even this was not measured directly. Instead of demonstrating, in a representative sample of the population, a negative correlation between *adults'* IQ scores and the number of children they produced, Cattell was content to follow earlier IQ testers in demonstrating a negative correlation between *children's* IQ scores and the number of children in the family. But this correlation, by itself, is quite insufficient to prove the point. Let us suppose that the experience of living in a large family somehow depresses a child's IQ score. What follows? Nothing. Cattell's argument depended on the assumption that the reason why such children had low IQ scores was because they had inherited them from their parents. He assumed that it was low-IQ parents who chose to have large families, with the consequence that, in each generation, more children were born to parents of low IQ than to those of high IQ. Cattell did, indeed, seek to establish this point; he carried out a study of 100 families, in which he measured both parents' and children's IQ scores, finding a correlation of 0.73 between mid-parent and mid-child IQ. But in his haste to accept the desired conclusion, Cattell brushed aside two other aspects of his data. First, there was essentially no correlation between parents' IQ and the number of their children. Secondly, the children's IQ scores were *higher* than those of their parents. The first observation implies that the negative correlation between family size and children's IQ has little to do with differential fertility on the part of parents with high and low IQ. The second would seem to demolish his entire argument: if children have higher IQs than their parents, IQ must be rising from one generation to the next, rather than falling. Cattell tried to explain this finding away by noting that IQ tests then available were not well standardized for adults, and, as a consequence, test scores declined sharply with age. But even when he applied a correction for age, the average IQ of the parents was only 112.3, compared to 120.0 for the children. It says much for the power of a preconceived idea that Cattell could continue to believe that IQ must be declining by three points per generation, when his own data indicated an increase of some eight points.

American studies, with larger and generally more representative samples, seemed to confirm beyond reasonable doubt the existence of a modest negative correlation between IQ and fertility (Van Court and Bean, 1985; Vining, 1986, 1995; Retherford and Sewell, 1988; Herrnstein and Murray, 1994; for a summary, see Lynn, 1996*a*). Although the size of this negative relationship is certainly exaggerated by looking at the correlation between the number of children in a family and those children's IQ scores, and may be exaggerated by ignoring the childless, the overall relationship between IQ and fertility in the USA throughout most of the twentieth century has been slightly negative. (A partial explanation for the discrepancy between these studies and those of Higgins *et al.* and Bajema may be that their samples coincided with the baby boom immediately following the Second World War, when middle-class parents were indeed having large families—and when, in Van Court and Bean's study, the correlation between IQ and fertility was less negative than it had been earlier in the century and has been since.) The data for other countries are much more sparse and rather less reliable, but at least some European studies have also suggested that IQ is negatively related to fertility (see Lynn, 1996*a*).

That question may be reasonably well settled, but it is time to recall the original purpose of this whole discussion, which was to ascertain whether IQ test scores are or are not decreasing from one generation to the next. Although we might be able to answer this question by looking at the relationship between IQ and fertility, there are surely more direct ways. Cattell's data, it will be recalled, suggested that children had higher IQs than their parents; but a very much more reliable procedure would be to obtain IQ scores from two generations when they were both the same age, for example from a sample of 10-year-old children in 1950 and from another sample of 10-year-olds in 1980. In 1933 and 1947, the Scottish Council for Research in Education (1949) did more or less this, reporting the results of group IQ tests on virtually the entire population of 11-year-olds in the country in these 2 years. They found a significant increase, of some 2–3 IQ points, from the earlier to the later year, and their findings were soon confirmed by Cattell himself, who reported an increase of 1.28 IQ points in schoolchildren in Leicester between 1936 and 1949 (Cattell, 1950). In the USA, Tuddenham (1948) reported substantial increases in the test scores of men called up for military service in the Second World War by comparison with the First World War.

Subsequent research, documented and summarized by Flynn (1984, 1987*a*) has shown that, if anything, these studies underestimated the true rate of increase in test scores. It is now clear that average test scores have been increasing at a remarkable rate in most industrialized societies for the past 50–75 years or more. In France and the Netherlands, for example, where data are available for virtually the entire population of 18-year-old males (given IQ tests on call-up for military service), scores increased by some 20 to 25 points between 1950 and 1980. Relatively similar rates of gain have been recorded in several other European countries, Australia, and Canada. At least until 1960, even greater increases occurred in Japan, while Britain and the USA appear to have lagged behind somewhat, gaining no more than about three points per decade (Flynn, 1984; Lynn and Hampson, 1986*a*; Lynn *et al.*, 1988*a*). There is no reason to believe that the increases have come to a halt (e.g. Teasdale and Owen, 1989; Lynn and Pagliari, 1994).

A difference in the performance of groups of Dutch 18-year-olds in 1980 and 1950 will not say anything about changes in Dutch IQ unless we can be sure that the two groups of

18-year-olds are equally representative. If the two samples were drawn from different sections of the population, the difference in their scores would be uninterpretable. Since we are in fact dealing with virtually the entire male population in both cases, the problem does not arise—just as it did not in Cattell's and the Scottish studies, where the entire relevant population was studied. But few studies can hope to sample on such a generous scale, and where they cannot there must always be some question whether there has been some change in the constitution of the samples from one date to the other.

Fortunately, there is another technique which allows one to assess changes in IQ from smaller samples without too much concern for their representative nature. By definition, if we give a test standardized in 1995 to a large, representative sample of the population in 1995, they will obtain an average score of 100. Suppose that we also gave them a test standardized in 1950, and they obtained an average score of 120. We know that in 1950 a representative sample would have obtained a score of only 100 on this test, and we can therefore say that there must have been a 20-point increase in average IQ between the 1950 and 1995 samples. But we could draw much the same conclusion from smaller, less representative samples. If a group of 15-year-old children in 1995 obtains a score of 110 on a 1950 test, and of only 90 on a 1995 test, this is good evidence that the 1950 test is 20 points easier than the 1995 test, and our confidence in that conclusion would be increased if another, unrepresentative sample of children obtained a score of 110 on the 1995 test and one of 130 on the 1950 test. Using this technique and some two dozen comparisons of performance on earlier and later versions of the Stanford–Binet and Wechsler tests, Flynn (1984) calculated that there had been a steady increase in American IQ of some 15 points between 1930 and 1980.

So much, then, for Cattell's and others' dire predictions about national decline. Those who enjoy prophesying the end of civilization must look for some other cause. But the results collated and analysed by Flynn, Lynn and others have an importance that far transcends this disproof of some foolish and ill-substantiated fears. What has caused these remarkable increases in IQ test scores, and what do they mean? In principle, at least, the explanation might have been genetic. A consistent positive relation between IQ and fertility could have produced some increase in IQ from one generation to the next. But to have been responsible for the sorts of increases we are talking about, of 10 or more points per generation, the positive relation would have had to be astonishingly high, and the overwhelming weight of the evidence is that, in the USA at least, the relationship between IQ and fertility throughout this century has been predominantly negative. Differential fertility can only have been acting to decrease the magnitude of the increases in IQ from one generation to the next.

If the explanation is not genetic, it must be environmental. But what are the environmental changes that have produced such dramatic effects? Cattell (1950) himself attributed the small increases he observed in Leicester between 1937 and 1949 to an increase in 'test sophistication'. In the 1930s, IQ tests were new and few children had taken one before. By the late 1940s, they were a fact of school life. The explanation is plausible enough for this limited case, and might equally apply to Tuddenham's comparison of American army recruits in the First and Second World Wars; but it becomes frankly incredible when applied to the data as a whole. There must be a limit to the benefits to be derived from test sophistication; it is difficult to imagine that from 1920 to the present day, each generation of Americans has been more accustomed to IQ tests than its predecessor.

An explanation in terms of changes in social class seems no more plausible. It is true that children's IQ is correlated with the social class of their parents. It is also true that, over the past 75 years, there has been a substantial increase in all industrial societies in the proportion of the population engaged in middle-class occupations at the expense of those in working-class occupations (e.g. Heath, 1981). In principle, therefore, the gain in IQ may be due to a gain in social class. But Flynn's analysis of the Dutch data led him to the conclusion that the gain in social class can have accounted for *at best* no more than 30 per cent of the gain in IQ from 1950 to 1980, and that even 15 per cent would be a generous estimate.

There is a further problem for this explanation. The correlation between social class and IQ tends to be higher for tests of verbal IQ than for tests of non-verbal or performance IQ (see below). But, almost without exception, the increase in average IQ over the past 50 years has been very much more marked on non-verbal than on verbal tests. Flynn's global figures are of an increase of 5.9 points per decade on non-verbal IQ, compared to one of 3.7 points on verbal IQ (Flynn, 1987a). The largest gains have been recorded on Raven's Matrices—the archetypal test of non-verbal reasoning; and wherever the data are available, gains on the Wechsler tests have been more pronounced on the performance than on the verbal scales. In the USA, indeed, large increases in non-verbal test scores occurred at a time when there were significant *declines* in scores on the verbal Scholastic Aptitudes Test (a test used for college entrance). Gains in test scores that are more marked for tests less sensitive to differences in social class can hardly be attributed to changes in social class.

Similar arguments make it equally unlikely that the gains can simply be attributed to an increase in the average number of years that children spend in school. Tuddenham (1948) attributed the American gains between the First and Second World Wars to an increase in the amount of education, and it is certainly true that in most industrialized countries there has been an increase since 1920 in the average age at which children leave school and a similar increase in the proportion of the population attending college or university. But increases in test scores have been observed in children well below the school-leaving age—in Japan as young as six and in Canada in 9-year-olds. Moreover, educational level, like social class, tends to correlate more highly with verbal than with non-verbal IQ (Snow and Yalow, 1982), and this can only mean that other factors must contribute to the gains in test score.

It is still possible to argue, but now almost wholly speculatively, that these other factors are still educational. In at least some countries, the 40 years following the Second World War are commonly assumed to have witnessed substantial changes in educational theory and practice, with less emphasis on rote learning and more on learning by discovery and conceptual understanding. It is not difficult to imagine how this might have increased children's ability to solve the abstract puzzles and problems that go to make up non-verbal IQ tests, without any concomitant improvement in their vocabulary, arithmetic, or general knowledge.

Finally, there have also, of course, been some general improvements in public health and nutrition since the 1920s. In western Europe, these improvements must have been particularly marked in the years immediately following the Second World War, and in Japan they have been sufficient to produce an increase in average height of some 2–4 cm per generation (Van Wieringen, 1978). Health and nutrition may well affect IQ (see below), and these improvements may have been a contributory factor—a case most persuasively argued by Lynn (1990).

It is easy to speculate; it is notably less easy to prove that any of these factors are actually responsible for the observed changes in IQ test scores. None of these suggestions amounts to much more than a claim to have identified a correlated change in some other variable that might or might not be causally related to the changes in test scores. None has provided unambiguous evidence of causality. There is, of course, no particular reason to suppose that the same factors have operated in all countries at all times since the 1920s, let alone that a single factor will ever be identified as responsible. It seems much more likely that a wide variety of different factors has been responsible, each contributing a small increment, some more important at one time or place, some more important at others.

There are several messages in all this. The most general is surely plain. We know that IQ is affected by the environment, and there is no difficulty in finding environmental correlates of IQ. But it is quite another matter to establish that any particular environmental factor is actually responsible for variations in IQ, let alone to identify its mode of operation. A second, more specific, message is that it may be vain to look for a single, magical environmental ingredient that changes IQ by 10 or 20 points. It is at least as probable that there is a whole host of factors, each having some effect on IQ, but none of overriding importance. Finally, although of more tangential relevance to our immediate concern, it should not be necessary to labour the point that supposedly 'culture-fair,' non-verbal IQ tests must be regarded as susceptible to large (and unidentified) environmental and cultural influences.

Environmental correlations and environmental causes

It is, then, one thing to establish a correlation between IQ and some other factor, it is another thing to prove that variations in this factor are responsible for variations in IQ. Factors that correlate with children's IQ scores are two a penny. They include: parental IQ, education, social class, income, and criminal record; the neighbourhood in which they live, the number of other children in the family and whether they are older or younger; the child's own height, weight, head circumference, and degree of myopia. The problem is not to establish the existence of such relationships; it is to interpret them correctly. It is a truism of social science that a correlation between A and B may be necessary, but is certainly not sufficient, to prove that A causes B. It is equally possible that B should cause A, or that both A and B should be the consequence of a third variable, X.

Why, for example, should family size correlate with IQ? Does this mean that the experience of growing up with numerous brothers and sisters somehow depresses a child's IQ score—and if so, *how* does this come about? Or is the correlation merely masking some other causal relation? In this particular case, there does not seem any obvious way in which a child's IQ score should affect the number of children his parents might choose to have. But other correlations certainly invite such speculation. Children's IQ scores are correlated, for example, with various aspects of their parents' behaviour. But is this because the parents' behaviour affects the child's IQ, or because children with high IQ encourage their parents to interact with them, constantly asking questions and demanding stories, while those of low IQ are more boring and less demanding of intellectual stimulation? And it seems easy to see how the relationship between IQ and family size might be a consequence of the independent relationship between these two variables and a variety of other factors. Family size, as we have already seen, is also correlated with social class: there is some tendency for middle-class families to have fewer children than working-class families. Perhaps, therefore, family size has no effect on IQ at all, and the correlation between the two reflects only the fact that working-class children, who are more likely to come from larger families, have on average a lower IQ than middle-class children. The problem is not, of course, confined to the case of family size: it is obvious enough that many of the variables mentioned so far, such as parental social class, income, and educational level, are correlated with one another. If one of these variables correlates with IQ, therefore, it is hardly surprising that the others should also, but this makes it no easier to decide which, if any, is actually effective.

For we must certainly acknowledge the possibility that *none* of these factors actually affects IQ: their correlation with IQ might simply be a consequence of a hidden factor X, whose effects we have failed to take into account. It should come as no surprise to learn that one persistent suggestion has been that the explanation of many of these correlations is a genetic one. If IQ has substantial heritability, the correlation between parents' and children's IQ scores will be partly a consequence of their shared genes. To the extent that parents of lower IQ have more children than those of higher IQ, children living in larger families may simply inherit their lower IQ from their parents. Moreover, as documented in Chapter 2, IQ testers have long argued that their tests were measuring something with profound social consequences, in other words, that a high IQ was necessary for success not only in school but also in life. Social class differences in IQ, they thus argued, must rest in part on genetic differences between those capable of holding down demanding professional or managerial jobs and those capable only of unskilled employment. Whatever we may think of this argument, and of the motives of those who first advanced it in the absence of serious evidence, it should not simply be ignored, and cannot be rejected by fiat. As we already know, it is not easy to disentangle genetic from environmental causes of variation in IQ.

The general problem is this: there is a multiplicity of factors correlated with a child's IQ score, but many of these factors tend to be correlated with one another; some of them (parental genotype) are not directly measurable, while many of those that are, such as family income, can hardly be the immediate, proximal cause of the child's IQ (money does not *directly* buy a high IQ; at most it buys an expensive education or other things that do affect IQ). How are we to disentangle these correlated factors, and how are we ever to discover what environmental factors are actually affecting the child's IQ? Although neither will guarantee success, there are two possible answers, one statistical, the other experimental. It is not altogether impossible, at least in principle, to disentangle the effects of correlated variables. Although, for example, there may be a general tendency for family size to be correlated with social class, there is still wide variation in family size within any one social class, and by studying, for example, professional families with one, two or more children, it should be possible to determine whether family size is related to IQ independently of social class, or for that matter whether the effect of social class on IQ is independent of family size. The statistical techniques of partial correlation, regression analysis, and path analysis provide ways of assessing the contribution of one factor, while controlling for the contribution of other, measured factors which are correlated with the first. In practice, as we shall see, the arguments are complex and not always easily resolved.

The experimental answer is to manipulate a particular environmental factor and to observe whether there is any consequential change in IQ. In the case of secular changes in IQ test scores, one can do little more than point to other factors that have changed over the past 50–75 years, and which are thus correlated with the observed changes in test scores. But although there are obvious limits to the possibilities of social engineering, there are natural experiments which can occasionally be informative, and other cases where deliberate, quasi-experimental intervention has been employed in an attempt to raise IQ scores. Thus children given up for adoption have often been brought up by adoptive parents who are both richer and better educated than their true, biological parents. If it could be shown that such children also ended up with higher IQ scores than they would otherwise have achieved, this would suggest that family background does exert an environmental influence on IQ. Various forms of educational intervention have also been tried, ranging from relatively brief periods of pre-school education to the massive intervention of the Milwaukee and Abecedarian projects (see below). And finally, there have been explicit experimental manipulations of such specific factors as nutritional intake. With the exception of this last type of manipulation, most forms of intervention have been too global to have succeeded in pinpointing any specific environmental cause of variations in IQ—and this for sufficiently obvious reasons. In many cases, the main purpose of the intervention was not particularly to raise IQ scores at all: this is not, after all, the normal reason why children are given up for adoption. In others, where one goal was indeed to raise the IQ scores of a target group of children, as in many instances of compensatory education, this has been pursued as a practical goal, for the sake of the children in question, rather than for the benefit of the social scientist, who would have sought to identify which precise factor was responsible for changing IQ scores, by varying one at a time while holding all others constant.

It is time to move on to a survey of some of the empirical findings in this area. I shall start by considering studies that have sought to elucidate the relationship between family background (by which is usually meant parental social class) and children's IQ scores, by attempting to assess the extent to which it does reflect an environmental effect of the former on the latter. In other words, we shall be looking for evidence of *between-* family environmental effects on IQ. To the extent to which we find evidence of such an effect, we wish to identify its more specific, proximal causes. I shall consider in turn: physical environmental factors; demographic variables; aspects of parental behaviour; and finally education. All of these factors are, of course, of interest in their own right, and not only for the light they may shed on the relationship between family background or social class and IQ. They may be equally responsible for variations in IQ between members of the same family. As we have just seen in Chapter 3, environmental sources of variation in IQ operate just as much within families as between families, even if there has been depressingly little attempt to understand the source of such within-family effects. It is obvious enough that parents do not necessarily treat all their children alike—they may not even send them all to the same school. Some environmental influences on IQ may operate outside the family, as children make their own friends etc. It is important to get away from the standard sociological view that children's IQ scores are *just* a product of their parents' social class.

Social class and IQ

The correlation between children's IQ scores and the social class or socio-economic status (SES) of their parents was, as we have already seen, one of the earliest discoveries of IQ testers, and has been documented repeatedly since. Socio-economic status is an amalgam of at least two conceptually distinct, although correlated, factors—occupation and income (to which is sometimes added parental education). Income is, at least in principle, rather easily measured. Occupations can be classified, according to the Registrar General's classification, into five broad bands:

1. professional, senior managerial;
2. junior managerial;
3. clerical and skilled workers;
4. semi-skilled workers;
5. unskilled.

Class 3 is often divided into non-manual (clerical) and manual (skilled workers). And the entire five-point scale is sometimes divided at the same point into two broad categories—non-manual and manual. Equally, other workers have resorted to much finer distinctions, containing up to a dozen categories.

Different studies have reported a wide range of values for the correlation between parental income or occupation and children's IQ, but they have rarely been negative. Terman (1916) found a difference of some 16 IQ points between the average scores of children of social class 1 and those of social class 5, and more than 50 years later the British National Child Development Study (NCDS), a longitudinal survey of some 15 000 children born in a single week of 1958, found a difference of 17 points between the average IQ scores of these two extreme groups at age 11 (Mascie-Taylor, 1984). Similar differences were obtained from the standardization sample of the WISC-R (Kaufman and Doppelt, 1976). These seem (and are!) large differences, but they translate into relatively modest correlations. A meta-analysis by White (1982) of a substantial number of largely American studies estimated that the average correlation between parents' SES and their offsprings' IQ was 0.33. Bouchard and Segal (1985) calculated the weighted mean values from five very large studies, totalling some 20 000 children: IQ correlated 0.22 with parental income, and 0.28 with parental occupation. An upper-bound estimate of the correlation between children's IQ scores and their parents' SES is thus perhaps 0.30–0.35, with the correlation being rather higher for verbal IQ than for non-verbal IQ (Kaufman and Doppelt, 1976). This is far from trivial, but perhaps rather smaller than has been implied by those critics who see children's IQ scores as nothing more than a measure of their familiarity with white, middle-class culture.

Before embarking on the task of attempting to identify any of the specific environmental factors that may underlie this correlation, we must first address the question whether it is to be explained in environmental terms at all. Sociologically minded critics of IQ tests may be surprised at the modest size of the correlation between social class and IQ, but they have rarely questioned the direction of causality it implies: poverty and its associated physical, cultural, and educational disadvantages depress children's IQ scores. In contrast, many IQ testers have followed Burt and Terman in assuming that the correlation is largely, if not wholly, mediated genetically. Pointing, for example, to the low correlations in IQ between members of adoptive families as the children grow older, they have concluded that differences in family environment contribute little to variation in IQ scores (e.g. Scarr, 1997). Since parental SES is only one component of family environment, its contribution must be vanishingly small.

A reasonable case can be made against both these extreme positions. It will certainly be as well to acknowledge at the outset that differences in average IQ scores between children in different social classes may well be partly genetic in origin. The evidence for this conclusion is discussed in Chapter 5. But although this evidence implies that *part* of the correlation between parental SES and children's IQ scores may be attributed to genetic differences between the parents, it certainly does not mean that the entire relationship between SES and IQ should be explained in this way. On the contrary, it has seemed to many to be blindingly obvious that children suffering from extreme poverty, cultural deprivation, malnutrition, physical illness, or poor education will also obtain low IQ scores, and that their low IQ will be a consequence of these disadvantages. But however plausible such an interpretation may seem, it requires proof: we must establish that the factor in question is actually capable of influencing IQ scores, and the only way to do that is by controlled experiment or intervention.

Thus, if we wish to ascertain whether parental SES has any environmental impact on children's IQs, we must resort to an intervention study—in this case, of course, adoption. Are adopted children's IQ scores affected by the social class of their adoptive parents? In the absence of selective placement, any such correlation must be due to an environmental effect of social class on IQ. Several of the adoption studies reviewed in the preceding chapter also obtained data on social class and can thus provide a comparison of the correlations between parental SES and children's IQs in adoptive and 'biological' families (Burks, 1928; Leahy, 1935; the Minnesota study—Scarr and Weinberg, 1978; and the Texas study—Horn *et al.*, 1982). Their results are shown in Table 4.2. In general, there is some tendency for these correlations to be higher in biological than adoptive families (the two medians are 0.22 and 0.12), but except in Leahy's study, the differences are all small. For our present purposes, however, the important observation is that the correlations in the adoptive families are all positive. On the face of it, this is evidence of an environmental effect of family background on children's IQ scores. And this conclusion is greatly strengthened by the results of a French adoption study which showed that children adopted into high-status adoptive homes obtained IQ scores, at age 14, some 15 points higher than those of children adopted into low-status homes (Capron and Duyme, 1989).

Some queries still remain. First, the correlation between adoptive home SES and adopted children's IQ scores shown in Table 4.2 might be due to selective placement: children may have been placed in high-SES adoptive homes only if their true parents were well educated

Table 4.2 Correlations between family background and children's IQ scores in biological and adoptive families

		Burks (1928)	Leahy (1935)	Minnesota study—Scarr and Weinberg (1978)	Texas study —Horn *et al.* (1982)
Biological	SES	–	0.45	0.10	0.20
	Income	0.24	–	0.22	
Adoptive	SES	–	0.12	0.12	0.16
	Income	0.23	–	0.06	

and from a 'good' background; if so, their high IQ may have been inherited from their true parents rather than moulded by the experience of living in a 'good' home (this was not a problem in the study of Capron and Duyme, where the two groups of children were carefully matched for the social class of their biological mothers). There is in fact evidence of some selective placement (in the form of correlations between various characteristics of the adopted children's true and adoptive parents) in most of the American studies. But the effect was never very marked, and in Burks's study, at least, where the correlation between adopted children's IQs and adoptive family income was 0.23, the correlation between the SES of the true and adoptive fathers was −0.02. It is unlikely that selective placement is sufficient to account for the full magnitude of the correlations observed in adoptive families. The second possibility is that these modest correlations may become even more modest, indicating an increasingly negligible effect of family environment on IQ, as the children grow older. There is some evidence, it will be recalled, of a decline in the correlations for IQ between adopted children and other members of the adoptive families as the children grow older (Loehlin *et al.*, 1989; p. 82). It seems possible that there might be a similar decline in the correlation between the children's IQ and measures of their adoptive family background as they grow older. But there is rather little evidence to support this conjecture. The 'children' in the Minnesota study were adolescents, aged between 16 and 22 at the time of testing; the data for the Texas study shown in Table 4.2 were divided by Horn *et al.* (1982) into those for children aged 5–7 and those aged 8+: both correlations were 0.16. Moreover, in the 10-year follow-up of the Texas study (Loehlin *et al.* 1989), the correlation between children's IQ and adoptive parents' SES showed only a small decline from 0.14 to 0.11 (the difference in initial value being a consequence of the change in the sample available for the longitudinal follow-up).

There is, then, reason to accept that the correlation between adopted children's IQ scores and their adoptive parents' social status reflects a true environmental effect. Indeed, there is some reason to suppose that the size of these correlations may *under*estimate the environmental effect of parental SES on children's IQs. With the sole exception of Leahy's study, the correlations between IQ and SES in biological families in Table 4.2 are all rather less than the value of 0.30–0.35 which seems to be the best estimate of the correlation in the population as a whole. This is presumably because these biological families, chosen to match the adoptive families in these studies (in the Texas study, they were in fact adoptive families which also happened to have natural children of their own) are no more representative of the population as a whole than are adoptive families. We are back to the problem of restriction of range. If all adoptive parents are 'good' parents, all adopted children will benefit from a 'good' upbringing, and this restriction of range will lower any correlations between adopted children and their adoptive parents. Some adoptive parents may have working-class jobs, be relatively poor and ill-educated, but may nevertheless be 'better' and more committed parents than others in apparently similar circumstances.

There is one set of results that tends to reinforce this suspicion. Instead of looking at the correlation between family environment and children's IQ in adoptive families, we can examine the absolute level of adopted children's IQ scores, to see whether they are higher than they might have been had the children not been adopted. If adoptive parents provide an unusually good environment, their children's IQ scores should reflect this. In all the studies listed in Table 4.2, adopted children's IQ scores were indeed well above average, 107 in Burks (1928), 110 in Leahy (1935), 106 in Scarr and Weinberg (1978), and 111 in Horn *et al.* (1979). The problem is to know what their IQ might have been if they had not been adopted. One indication would be the IQ scores of their true parents, but the only study to provide any relevant data is that by Horn *et al.*, where IQ scores for some 75 per cent of the true mothers were available. Pooling the results of different tests, their average was 108, hardly lower than the average score of their children.

However, some other studies have provided more reason to believe that if adopted children's biological parents come from an impoverished background, the children's IQ scores may benefit from the experience of adoption. The Iowa adoption project of Skodak and Skeels (1949) took an initial group of 180 children, all removed from their natural mothers before they were 6 months old. At age 13 100 of the children were still available, and had a mean IQ of 107, compared to one of 86 for 63 of their natural mothers. Although IQ scores were not available for the biological fathers, those that could be traced were said to be below average in terms of education and occupation. This apparent difference of some 20 points between mothers' and children's IQ scores has suggested to many commentators a substantial benefit from adoption into 'superior' homes, but it is clear that 20 points is a serious overestimate of the true difference between mothers' and children's IQ scores. A careful analysis by Flynn (1993), taking into account the differences in the tests taken by the mothers and the children, and the difference in the time since these tests had been standardized, led him to suggest that the true difference was probably no more than 10–13 points. But this is still a substantial difference, and it is hard to see how it could be explained without also supposing that the children's adoptive environment had helped to raise their IQ scores. If this is granted, it implies a further important conclusion, for at the same time that adoptive parents were raising their adopted children's IQ scores, the *correlations* between the children's IQ scores and their adoptive mothers' and fathers' educational levels were small, only 0.04 and 0.06. The implication is that the environment provided by most, if not all, adoptive homes was sufficiently good to raise the children's IQ, but the differences between the best and worst homes in relevant environmental variables were of little importance.

A more powerful design for determining whether adoption raises IQ scores is that of a small French study, which traced 32 children abandoned by their working-class mothers at birth and brought up in middle-class adoptive homes. They were compared with 20 siblings (in fact, in virtually all cases half-siblings, with the same mother but a different father) who were brought up either by the mother or a close relative, or occasionally by a nurse, and thus remained in an impoverished environment (Dumaret and Stewart, 1985). The scores obtained by the two groups of children on verbal and non-verbal IQ tests (both group and individual) are shown in Table 4.3. The differences are somewhat smaller on the group test than on the WISC, and notably smaller on the non-verbal than on the verbal part of each test. But they are all substantial, and since there is no reason to suppose that there was any systematic difference between the two groups of natural fathers, the adopted children's superior IQ scores must surely be attributed to their superior environment. The fact that the difference between the two groups of children is about twice as large on verbal as on non-verbal tests is consistent with the general observation that social class differences in IQ are more pronounced on verbal tests (see above), and suggests that this is largely an environmental difference. It should be noted that the adopted children obtained scores some 8 points lower than those of a control group matched for social class and attending the same schools.

Table 4.3 IQ scores of children adopted into higher status homes and of their half-siblings brought up by their biological mothers (from Dumaret and Stewart, 1985)

	WISC		Group test	
	Verbal	Performance	Verbal	Non-verbal
Adopted	106	111	104	107
Not adopted	86	103	91	101

Adoption studies surely confirm, then, that *part* of the social class difference in IQ observed in natural families is environmental in origin. We may discount the extreme hereditarian hypothesis which would attribute the entire difference to the superior genes passed on to their children by middle-class parents. It is, however, important to acknowledge that there is much that these studies have not told us. They have not provided any precise estimate of the size of the environmental effect on IQ associated with social class, partly because the numbers differ from one study to another, but also because we have little idea how representative either the adoptive or the natural parents may be. It is not just adoptive parents who may be atypical of the population as a whole; parents of illegitimate children, whom they give up for adoption, are presumably equally unrepresentative of the general population. Worse than this, however, these studies have hardly begun to tell us what are the critical aspects of the environment provided by adoptive families that are beneficial for their children's IQ scores. They do not say much more than that some family environments are better for the developing child's IQ than are others. To get any further, we must turn to studies that have sought to delineate more specific environmental factors related to IQ.

Physical environment

Poverty may cause physical as well as intellectual or cultural deprivation, but some forms of physical deprivation may be responsible indirectly for intellectual loss. It is well established that life expectancy is correlated with social class, and although part of this correlation may be attributed to differences in the incidence of the diseases of middle and old age, part is due to differences in infant mortality. If children of working-class parents are more likely to die than those of middle-class parents, perhaps they are also more vulnerable to less lethal forms of physical damage, caused by disease, environmental pollution, or inadequate nutrition, which are still capable of impairing their intellectual development. Perhaps they are also more likely to suffer from prenatal and perinatal complications with similar long-term consequences. The classic expression of this last possibility is in Pasaminick and Knobloch's concept of the 'continuum of reproductive casualty,' summarized in the following four propositions (Pasamanick and Knobloch, 1966, p. 7):

1. Since prematurity and complications of pregnancy are associated with fetal and neonatal death, usually on the basis of injury to the brain, there must remain a fraction injured who do not die.

2. Depending upon the degree and location of the damage, the survivors may develop a series of disorders. These extend from cerebral palsy, epilepsy, and mental deficiency through all types of behavioral and learning disabilities which are a result of lesser degrees of damage sufficient to disorganize behavioral development and all thresholds to stress.

3. Further, these abnormalities of pregnancy are associated with certain life experiences, usually socioeconomically determined, and consequently

4. they themselves and their resulting neuropsychiatric disorders are found in greater aggregation in the lower (socioeconomic) strata of our society.

Prenatal environment

There is, indeed, ample evidence of an association between prenatal experience and children's subsequent IQ scores (see Jensen, 1997). The simplest summary measure of prenatal development is birth weight, and numerous studies have suggested that there is a significant correlation between birth weight and later IQ (Rutter *et al.*, 1970; Broman *et al.*, 1975; Mascie-Taylor, 1984; Breslau *et al.*, 1994). Although the correlation between birth weight and later IQ is distinctly modest (for example, only 0.07 in white children and 0.11 in black children in the study of Broman *et al.*), this overall correlation conceals a much larger effect at very low birth weights, below 2500 g, where there is a significant increase in the risk of relatively low IQ (Breslau *et al.*, 1994; Baumeister and Bacharach, 1996).

What is the meaning of this relationship? Part of the overall correlation between birth weight and IQ is due to the increased incidence of severe mental retardation in babies who are seriously below weight (Rutter *et al.* 1970). Their low weight may, of course, be symptomatic of other developmental abnormalities rather than the cause of the retardation. Similarly, although an effect measurable at birth must be, in some sense, attributable to prenatal experience, the causal chain may be quite indirect, via the later, post-natal environment. It seems often to be assumed implicitly that low birth weight reflects a physical effect on the growth of the embryonic brain; there can be little doubt that this is sometimes true, but there are other, more mundane possibilities: perhaps very small babies turn into sickly children, whose IQ scores suffer because they miss so much school.

Can we point to any more specific prenatal factors that might affect IQ? There is evidence that smoking by the mother is associated with low birth weight in the baby (Broman *et al.* 1975), and is also associated with a deficit in the child's IQ even after allowance has been made for this and other factors (Mascie-Taylor, 1984). But once again, it is important to acknowledge that we have no idea how this relation is produced, and other studies have failed to confirm the association between maternal smoking and children's IQ (Streissguth *et al.*, 1990). On the other hand, Streissguth *et al.* did find a correlation of −0.11 between pregnant mothers' alcohol intake and their children's IQ at age 4.

Even if these effects are real, we still do not really know how they are mediated—whether via an effect on the development of the embryonic brain, or through some correlated later experience in infancy or early childhood. And since, in the large majority of these studies, children's IQ scores were measured at an early age, we do not even know to what extent prenatal effects are transient or relatively permanent. A suggestive answer to this question, for the case of maternal nutrition during pregnancy, is provided by two quite different studies, one American, the other Dutch. In the former, Rush *et al.* (1980) randomly assigned a number of black pregnant women to one of three groups, one receiving a high-protein supplement to their diet, one receiving a high-calorie supplement, and the third, control group no supplement. Their 1-year-old infants were given a visual habituation test, and those whose mothers had received the protein supplement habituated significantly more rapidly and showed greater dishabituation than either of the other groups. Since habituation and dishabituation scores are reliably correlated with IQ at age 5–8 (p. 58), this seems to be convincing evidence of a significant effect of maternal diet during pregnancy on young children's IQ (at least in this particular population). But the Dutch famine study suggests equally convincingly that maternal malnutrition during pregnancy may have no long-term effects on the child's IQ. In the winter of 1944–45, the Germans imposed a transport embargo on the Netherlands, causing very severe food shortages in certain parts of the country for about 6 months. We have already had cause to be grateful for the Dutch practice of giving IQ tests to all 18- to 20-year-old men on call-up for military service. Stein *et al.* (1972) took advantage of this fact to analyse the test scores of men born during the relevant period in towns affected or unaffected by the famine. Although hospital records established that birth weights were lower in the affected towns, absolutely no effect on adult IQ scores could be detected.

What can we conclude? There can be no doubt that some differences in prenatal and perinatal environment are associated with young children's later IQ scores. In virtually all of the studies cited earlier, differences in birth weight were associated with differences in parental social class. They may thus contribute to the overall relationship between parental social class and children's IQ scores. And this possibility is strengthened by the observation, again reported in most of these studies, that the association between birth weight and IQ remains significant even when differences in social class have been allowed for by regression analysis. For what this implies is that the effect of birth weight on IQ is a genuine one, not simply a by-product of other determinants of childhood IQ correlated with social class. Indeed, since there is evidence that differences in birth weight between children in the same family are equally associated with differences in their IQ scores (e.g. Lynn, 1990), birth weight may be a cause of both between-family and within-family environmental effects on IQ. But two points must be stressed: first that we really have remarkably little idea *how* such pre- and perinatal environmental variables actually affect IQ, and secondly that their independent contribution to children's IQ scores is actually rather small (except in the rare cases of *very* low birth weight). Broman *et al.* (1975) measured some 130 pre- and post-natal biological variables: none even approached in magnitude the importance of maternal education and social class as a predictor of the child's IQ. Among white children, for example, the latter correlation was 0.42; the addition of all other statistically significant variables raised the correlation only to 0.47 (see also Baumeister and Bacharach, 1996).

Post-natal environment

A plausible extension of the concept of the 'continuum of reproductive casualty' suggests that both chronic ill-health during childhood, and certain specific diseases might affect young children's cognitive development. Diphtheria, whooping cough, and measles, for example, may all cause damage to the nervous system; and all are more common in lower income groups than among middle-class children—partly because, although vaccination confers substantial immunity, the proportion of infants vaccinated against these diseases is a function of social class (Davie *et al.*, 1972). If serious illness causes prolonged absence from school, which is certainly associated with a decline in IQ scores (see below), mild ill-health may surely lead both to occasional absences and to lapses of attention even when the child is in the classroom.

Evidence on the relationship between health and IQ is, necessarily, almost entirely correlational. However plausible such arguments may seem, therefore, it is difficult to design well-controlled experiments, let alone any form of intervention study, that would establish a causal effect of health on IQ. Perhaps in consequence of this, most of the best evidence on the effect of physical environmental factors on IQ have concentrated on two other variables—nutrition and pollution.

One apparently convincing instance of a post-natal nutritional effect on young children's IQ scores is that pre-term infants fed on their mothers' breast milk develop higher IQ scores than those given formula diets (Morely, 1996). There is also more general evidence that children's IQ scores are related to their nutritional status (Warren, 1973; Sigman *et al.*, 1989), but this observation alone is hardly very informative. Malnutrition is, after all, normally a consequence of serious poverty, and the discovery of a correlation between malnutrition and IQ leaves open the possibility that it is some other aspect of social deprivation and poverty that is the effective determinant of IQ, rather than nutrition *per se*.

Experiments with animals have established that severe protein deficiency, either in the mother before or during pregnancy, or of the young, can result in significantly lowered brain weight (Dobbing, 1968). Whether this is relevant to the human case may be open to question, but it is consistent with studies that have documented differences in brain weight (measured at autopsy) between children recorded as malnourished and those not (Brown, 1966; see Lynn (1990) for a review). Brain weight is not, of course, the same as IQ, but there is some evidence that severe malnutrition, to the point where the child is admitted to hospital, may be associated with lowered IQ, even when differences in social class and family background have been allowed for. Two studies, one in Jamaica (Hertzig *et al.*, 1972), the other in Mexico (Birch *et al.*, 1971), compared a group of children admitted to hospital for malnutrition with their less severely malnourished siblings. Both found a significant difference (4 points in the former, 11 in the latter) in favour of the better-nourished child. One can speculate that there must have been other environmental differences between the two sets of children, but it is also obvious that a family where one child is desperately malnourished is unlikely to provide a wholly satisfactory diet for other children in the family. These studies, therefore, may well underestimate the full extent to which malnutrition can affect IQ. On the other hand, they may be quite irrelevant to the causes of variations in IQ in advanced industrial societies. The diseases of marasmus and kwashiorkor, from which children in these studies were suffering, are hardly common in western Europe or North America. What is not known is the extent to which there is a relatively abrupt threshold, below which severe malnutrition can lower IQ, but above which variation in diet has little effect.

The effect of nutrition on IQ lends itself readily to an intervention study: do dietary supplements improve IQ scores? A small study by Benton and Roberts (1988) triggered a spate of experiments addressing this question. Benton and Roberts gave an experimental group of 30 Welsh schoolchildren a vitamin and mineral supplement every day for 8 months, while control groups received either no treatment or a placebo. At the end of this period, the experimental group had gained some 10 points on a non-verbal IQ test, while the control groups gained no more than 2–4 points. But subsequent replications have tended to muddy the waters. Some experiments have failed to find any significant effect of vitamin or mineral supplements at all (e.g. Crombie *et al.*, 1990); others have reported positive results—but only in certain groups of children, or only for certain non-verbal tests, or only at some levels of supplementation rather than others (e.g. Benton and Buts, 1990; Schoenthaler *et al.*, 1991). The debate has generated much heat but rather less light, and has been marked by many dogmatic assertions but little to be dogmatic about. Eysenck and Schoenthaler (1997) have provided a somewhat optimistic review, in which they note that even where the effects observed have not been statistically significant, they have usually been in the direction of superior performance on non-verbal IQ by treatment groups. Certainly, there have been enough positive results to raise the possibility that dietary supplements may affect non-verbal IQ in some children, but legitimate doubts will not be fully dispelled until specific predictions (who will benefit, on what test, from what sort of supplementation?) have been formulated and tested successfully.

It seems virtually certain that severe, chronic malnutrition, of the sort common to many developing countries, has deleterious effects on the IQ of the children in those countries (an effect of perhaps rather less importance than the number of children it kills). But there is less reason to suppose that this is a significant factor affecting IQ in most industrial societies. Here, environmental pollution may well be more important. The possibility that has been most widely canvassed is that atmospheric lead may be detrimental to IQ. Experiments on animals have established, just as they did in the case of severe malnutrition, that high concentrations of lead can damage the nervous system (Lansdown and Yule, 1986), but the levels in question will not be reached by breathing any amount of polluted air. As usual there is the problem that children who are exposed to pollution are likely to suffer from various other forms of social disadvantage. One American study showed, reasonably clearly, that children with higher levels of lead in their body (assessed from analysis of their shed teeth) obtained IQ scores some 4 points below those of a control group with lower levels (Needleman *et al.*, 1979, 1985). Although other American and English studies have found much less convincing evidence for such an effect, two other studies, one in Scotland, the other in Australia, seem to provide relatively unequivocal evidence (Fulton *et al.*, 1987; McMichael *et al.*, 1988). Each obtained data from some 500 children exposed to varying levels of lead pollution, either from lead plumbing in Edinburgh, or from proximity to a lead-smelting plant in Australia. In both cases, after controlling for parental social status, there was a monotonic decrease in the children's IQ scores with increasing concentrations of lead in their bodies.

In conclusion, there can be little doubt that IQ is affected both by physical and biological environment, but it is equally clear that the magnitude of these effects, within the range of environments found in western industrial societies, is small. In the Schoenthaler *et al.* (1991) study, for example, the three groups of children who received nutritional supplements, gained on average only 2.1 IQ points over the control group, and the largest gain was only 3.7 points. At the extremes, the effects of lead concentration may be considerably larger than this: McMichael *et al.* (1988) calculated that the highest level of concentration they studied depressed IQ by approximately 15 points. This is a substantial effect, but very few children are unfortunate enough to receive such a high concentration, and differences in exposure to lead are unlikely to contribute more than a minute fraction to the variability of IQ in the entire population of most industrialized societies.

Demography: family size and birth order

We have already seen that there is a correlation of about 0.30 between children's IQ scores and the number of other children in their family. But it remains for us to consider what the explanation of this relationship might be. Early eugenicists had little doubt that feckless and irresponsible parents, who refused to plan their families, passed on their defective genes, including genes for low IQ, to their numerous progeny, but they produced little evidence to support this supposition, and we now know that the correlation between IQ and fertility is significantly smaller than this (see above, p. 105).

The natural inference to draw, then, is that the remainder of the association between family size and children's IQ scores is environmental in origin. But what is the route via which family size has its effect? Is it merely a by-product of other correlated factors? As we have also seen, family size is correlated with social class. Does this mean that children from larger families have lower IQs simply because they are more likely to come from poorer background? Or do children from lower-class families obtain lower IQ scores because their families are larger? Will regression analysis help to provide the answer?

In another study of Dutch conscripts, Belmont and Marolla (1973) reported that the effect of family size on IQ still remained significant even when differences in social class had been taken into account. However, they divided their sample into only three classes, non-manual, manual, and farm-workers, and it seems possible that a finer, more conventional division by social class might give a different outcome, and data from the British NCDS, shown in Fig. 4.1a, tend to confirm this suggestion. When allowance was made for all other variables in the study that were correlated with IQ, there was no relationship between family size and IQ. The NCDS measured not only social class, divided into five, rather than three categories, but also a number of other social variables, such as type of neighbourhood, financial status, overcrowding, all of which were, not surprisingly, also related to family size. Other things equal, families with only one or two children are less likely to suffer from overcrowding than those of six or more. So it is certainly not surprising that once some of these other correlated variables are taken into account, the effect of family size disappears. This should not be taken as proving that overcrowding, say, is the critical variable: without further information, such regression analyses cannot always determine which of two correlated variables is causal and which, so to say, parasitic on the other. All that can be concluded from Fig. 4.1a is that there is no evidence here that family size *per se* is causally related to IQ; the evidence is consistent with the possibility that the correlation between the two is due to other associated differences between large and small families.

There is an important sense, however, in which this conclusion is seriously misleading. As

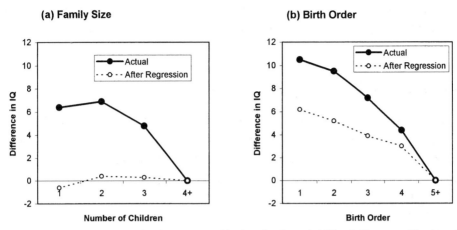

Fig. 4.1 The relationship between family size (a) and birth order (b) and children's IQ scores. The data shown are the difference in average IQ between children in small families and those in the largest families, or between first- and second- or third-born children and those born later. The solid lines show the actual differences observed; the dotted lines show the differences after regression analysis had removed the effects of other measured factors. (Data from Mascie-Taylor, 1984.)

can be seen in Fig. 4.1b, first- or second-born children tend to have higher IQs than third-, fourth- or fifth-born children—and this difference, which has been found in numerous other large data sets, such as Belmont and Marolla's (1973) study of Dutch conscripts, remains significant even after all other factors have been taken into account. The point is, of course, that birth order is not merely 'associated' with family size: if there is an effect of birth order on children's IQ scores, it necessarily follows that the average IQ of children in larger families will be lower than that of those in smaller families. Suppose that, on average, the second child in a family has an IQ 1 point lower than that of the first, the third an IQ 1 point lower than the second, and so on (this is very roughly the size of the effect shown in Fig. 4.1b); it necessarily follows that a family of six children will have a lower average IQ than one of two (2 points lower, to be precise), even though the first two children in the family of six obtained exactly the same IQ scores as the two children in the family of two.

At least part of the relationship between family size and IQ, then, must be interpreted as a consequence of the relationship between birth order and IQ, and our explanation of the former must depend on our explanation of the latter. Why should later-born children tend to have a lower IQ than those born earlier in the same family? It does not seem likely that the effect could be genetic. But since later-born children are likely to be born to older parents, and since there is evidence that the incidence of some conditions such as Down's syndrome increases with parental age, it is possible that chromosomal abnormalities contribute to the overall effect of birth order. It is certainly possible that prenatal and perinatal factors contribute. But the most widely promulgated theory, Zajonc's 'confluence model' attributes the effect to differences in post-natal family environment (Zajonc and Markus, 1975; Zajonc, 1983).

The central assumption underlying the model is that children's IQ scores will depend on the amount of time their parents spend with them. First-born children can receive their parents' undivided attention; by the time the third or fourth child is born, parents are too busy, too tired, or too bored to spend so much time with the child, whose IQ suffers accordingly. In order to account for the observation that only children have a rather lower IQ than first-born children in families of two or three (Fig 4.1a), Zajonc appeals to a second principle: that the opportunity to teach younger children also raises the IQ of older children in the family. This also helps to explain a second feature of some data on birth-order effects, that regardless of family size, the last-born child, who has never had the opportunity to teach younger siblings, shows a particularly large drop in IQ.

The theory makes intuitive sense, and is supported by one further observation, that twins have, on average, lower IQs than other children. In at least two large studies, the difference has been as large as 4–5 points (Husén, 1959; Record *et al.*, 1970). According to the theory, this would be because twins are particularly likely to form a close, intimate pair, spending more time in one another's company, and less in that of their parents, than other children. Record *et al.* reported an additional finding consistent with this interpretation: where one twin died in infancy, the survivor had an IQ barely distinguishable from normal, but, alas for the theory, Brackbill and Nichols (1982) failed to replicate this observation.

The confluence model has not lacked for critics (e.g. Jensen, 1997). Retherford and Sewell (1991) argued that it failed to predict the data from a large-scale study of Wisconsin high-school students. But some of their criticisms are not always well founded, and there can be little doubt that several very large studies have founded small but reliable effects of birth order on IQ (summarized by Zajonc *et al.*, 1991). One suspects, however, that the appeal of the confluence model has depended less on the intuitive plausibility of the assumption that parental interaction is beneficial for the growing child's IQ, and more on the fact that the theory can be expressed in a formal, and apparently rigorous, manner. In this format, the model states that the IQ of any child is a function of the average intellectual level of the entire family in which that child lives. Unlike IQ, 'intellectual level' is not corrected for age: it is assumed to be zero at birth, and only slowly to reach the average adult score of, say, 100. If we assume two average parents, the intellectual level of their family is 100 before the birth of their first child, and 67, (100 + 100 + 0)/3, immediately afterwards. If the first child has attained an intellectual level of 20 by the birth of the second child, this second birth will lower the family's level to 55, (100 + 100 + 20 + 0)/4. And so on. The average intellectual level of the entire family will be progressively lower with the addition of each successive child.

This all seems pleasingly rigorous, and the virtue of rigour is that it often permits the derivation of new predictions. Unfortunately, as here, the predictions are not always confirmed. One is that the effect of birth order should depend on the spacing between successive children: the greater the gap between children, the higher the intellectual level of older children when a new child is born, and the point can eventually be reached where the average intellectual level of the family is greater at the birth of a second or third child than it was at the birth of the first. There have been relatively few studies of this variable, but their results have not been very promising: neither Belmont *et al.* (1978) nor Brackbill and Nichols (1982), for example, found any evidence that spacing between children affected the magnitude of the birth-order effect.

The second prediction is that a child's IQ should be affected by the number of adults in the family, the intellectual level of the average one-parent family after the birth of the first child being only 50, compared to 67 for a two-parent family. While some studies have shown that children living in one-parent families have a rather lower IQ than others, even when other factors have been taken into account (Mackintosh and Mascie-Taylor, 1986), others have not (Brackbill and Nichols, 1982). Brackbill and Nichols, moreover, found no benefit from the presence of a third or fourth adult in the family.

There is, perhaps, a message here. A plausible psychological theory is not necessarily enhanced by the desire to give it spurious rigour. It makes sense to suppose that parents influence their children's IQ scores by the amount and quality of their interaction with them, that this depends on the number of other children already in the family, and that children who spend less time with their parents, either because the parents are too busy, or because, being twins, the children choose to spend their time together, may suffer a small depression in IQ as a consequence. But these intuitions are not necessarily well captured by the formal version of the confluence model. Many single parents may make special efforts to compensate for the absence of the other; some fathers might just as well be absent for all the time they spend with their children. In so far as the age gap between successive children affects their IQ, it is at least as likely to be because it affects the amount of time parents can spend interacting with younger children as because the greater the gap the higher the intellectual level of the older children. Family structure probably does affect children's IQ scores, but analysis of the way in which it does so would benefit more from careful observation and, possibly, experimental analysis than from the construction of simple-minded formal models.

Parental behaviour and family environment

The effect of birth order on IQ points to the unsurprising possibility that the amount of time parents spend with their children can have a modest but significant effect on those children's IQ scores. Perhaps qualitative differences in the way parents interact with their children also affect their IQ. Perhaps, indeed, such differences may help to explain some of the relationship between social class and IQ.

One of the more striking and important findings to emerge from analysis of the British NCDS data is shown in Fig. 4.2, which plots the raw, uncorrected differences in IQ between children in social classes 1 to 5, and the same data once all other factors measured in the study had been taken into account (just as in Fig. 4.1). It is evident that these other factors account for a significant part of the association between social class and IQ, but what is surely more remarkable is the size of the residual effect. Even after making allowance for differences in birth weight, family size, degree of financial hardship, overcrowding, type of accommodation, neighbourhood, etc., there is still a 10-point difference in average IQ between children whose fathers are in occupational classes 1 and 5. Since it still seems unlikely that a father's occupation could itself be a proximal cause of his children's IQ scores, we must look for other factors, not measured in the study but nevertheless correlated with parental occupation, to mediate the observed relationship. What might these factors be?

The NCDS was a large-scale survey, which obtained a mass of information on children's medical and educational history, but relied on readily obtainable information about their family background. It did not attempt to discover *how* children were brought up, how their parents interacted with them, and what their home life was like. If a middle-class upbringing is, in fact, beneficial for children's IQ scores, this is likely to be because they are encouraged to read or play educational games, and are talked to in a particular manner: the fact that they have a lot of money and live in a large house in an expensive neighbourhood may be much less important. Given that IQ tests measure vocabulary and general knowledge, require children to interpret pictures, do jigsaw puzzles and mental arithmetic, it seems plausible to suppose that it is the style of parent–child interaction that affects a child's IQ score, rather than the more material factors measured in large-scale social surveys.

It has, indeed, long been known that many other aspects of family background, even those as readily measured as the number of books owned and newspapers or magazines taken, can predict a child's IQ at least as accurately as parental occupation or income (e.g. Chapin, 1928). The classic American adoption studies of Burks (1928) and Leahy (1935) took a variety of measures of home environment, many of which showed substantial

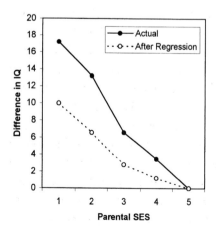

Fig. 4.2 The relationship between parental SES and children's IQ scores. As in Fig. 4.1, the data shown are the difference in average IQ between children of parents in social class 5 and those in other social classes, and the solid line represents the actual difference obtained, while the dotted line represents the difference after regression analysis has removed the effect of other correlated factors. (Data from Mascie-Taylor, 1984.)

correlations with children's IQ scores in their control (biological) families. In Burks's study, for example, while the correlation between parental income and child's IQ was only 0.24, two 'cultural' indices of the home correlated over 0.40 with the child's IQ. In Leahy's study, children's IQ correlated 0.37 with an economic index of the home, but over 0.50 with its cultural index and environmental status.

Both Burks and Leahy conducted extensive interviews to collect their data, and subsequent interview studies have confirmed and amplified their conclusions. In a study described by Bloom (1964), Wolf interviewed 60 mothers of 10-year-old children, obtaining information that he grouped under three main headings: emphasis on intellectual achievement, emphasis on language, and general provision for learning both inside and outside the home. He reported a multiple correlation of 0.76 between these factors and the child's IQ. In a study of some 200 Canadian boys, Marjoribanks (1972) interviewed their parents to obtain information both of their social status (education and occupation) and of their attitudes on such matters as emphasis on achievement, intellectual development and language. He found substantial differences between middle- and working-class parents not only in status but also in attitude. More important, he found that their children's scores on verbal, numerical, and non-verbal reasoning IQ tests all correlated more strongly with parental attitude than with parental status. Bradley *et al.* (1977) reported similar results in children as young as 3 years old: a multiple correlation of 0.77 between IQ and measures of the home environment that included provision of play materials, maternal involvement and responsivity, contrasting with one of only 0.56 between child's IQ and parental status (parental education and occupation). Two British studies with 11- and 12-year-olds have confirmed this picture. Fraser (1959) found a multiple correlation of 0.69 between a variety of indices of the home environment and the IQ scores of some 400 children in Aberdeen, while family income correlated only 0.35 with the children's IQ. Miller (1970) reported a correlation of 0.35 between parental occupation and the 11-plus scores of some 480 English children; correlations of about 0.60, however, were obtained with measures of intellectual aspirations, parental support, and children's autonomy.

The general pattern of findings in these studies is strikingly consistent, and the correlations reported with the developing child's IQ impressively high. But this does not mean that their interpretation is equally clear or unambiguous. However plausible it may be that parental involvement and attitudes, or the provision of appropriate toys, games, and books should be beneficial for a young child's IQ, the establishment of these correlations alone will never prove that one is a direct cause of the other. There are two obvious alternative possibilities. One is that any correlation between the behaviour of parents and the IQ of their children reflects the influence of children on their parents rather than that of parents on their children. Do parents raise their children's IQ scores by reading to them, or do clever children ask to be read to more than less clever ones? Do parents' expectations and pressures affect their children's test scores, or do children's IQs influence the expectations parents entertain for them? The second possibility is that parents influence their children's development at least as much by the genes they pass onto them as by their actual behaviour towards them. We have already considered this second possibility in our discussion of the correlation between parental status or social class and children's IQ. As in that case, so here, we should almost certainly concede that there is some genetic contribution to these correlations. Scarr (1997), for example, has shown that, if they ignore the possibility of such a genetic contribution, attempts to model the influence of parental attitudes and behaviour on their children's intellectual and academic attainments are remarkably unsuccessful. But although there seems to be an increasing consensus among behaviour geneticists that correlations between parental status, attitudes, and behaviour and their children's IQ scores can be almost entirely explained in terms of their shared genes (e.g. Scarr, 1992, 1997; Lynn, 1996a; Bouchard, 1997), the evidence for this strong position is less than overwhelming. For example, Longstreth *et al.* (1981) established, what is hardly surprising, that differences in these aspects of the home environment were correlated with the mother's IQ. More important, however, they claimed that when allowance was made for differences in maternal IQ, the effect of these other factors was no longer significant. If it was their mother's IQ score, rather than her attitudes and behaviour, that influenced the children's IQ, this seems plausibly attributed to genetic transmission. In fact, the correlation between home environment and child's IQ was only 0.32, which reduced to 0.18 after partialling out the effect of maternal IQ. It is true that, with this relatively small sample size, this latter correlation was not significant, but the effect of allowing for maternal IQ was not in fact very great. It seems unlikely that such an allowance would have been sufficient to abolish the effects of home environment seen in the other American and British studies reviewed above—where the correlation between home environment and child's IQ, often over 0.60, was substantially higher than that usually reported between mother's and child's IQ (usually 0.40–0.50, see Chapter 3).

The classic American adoption studies of Burks (1928) and Leahy (1935) provide direct evidence of an environmental contribution to these correlations. They reported correlations ranging from 0.12 to 0.25 (median, 0.19) between adopted children's IQ scores and various social and cultural ratings of their adoptive homes, as well as aspects of their adoptive parents' behaviour. These are relatively modest correlations but they are certainly not zero, and they are slightly larger than those between the children's IQ and their adoptive parents' economic status, occupation, or education. In the absence of alternative explanations, they suggest that children's IQ scores can be affected by their parents' cultural and educational attitudes and aspirations, and by their style of interaction. The behaviour geneticists' consensus should be viewed with some scepticism—although there remains a pressing need for more up-to-date data, especially longitudinal data which would assess whether parental attitudes continue to influence children's' IQ scores as they grow older.

Many parents will be inclined to suggest that the conclusion that parents can influence their children's IQ scores provides another example of academic psychology's 'discovery' of a blindingly obvious truth. No doubt. But wary readers should by now have learned to be suspicious of supposedly self-evident truths about the development of children's intelligence—especially when, as here, they are truths many adults *want* to believe. It would, after all, be depressing (at least for parents) if it turned out that parents' attitudes and behaviour had no effect on their children's IQ. But it is precisely where an opinion is not only commonly received but also devoutly to be wished that it should be viewed with suspicion. That is a truth which it will be worth bearing in mind in the next section.

Education and IQ

Scores on IQ tests are related to a wide variety of measures of educational attainment (Chapter 2). This is hardly surprising, since one of the main purposes of IQ tests was originally to predict children's performance in school, and educational achievements have always served as an external criterion against which IQ tests can be validated. The interpretation of a correlation between IQ and schooling, therefore, is likely to be particularly problematic: what would be required to show that it was the amount or quality of schooling that exerted a causal influence on IQ?

One well-established educational correlate of IQ is the number of years of formal education received. Such a correlation is obviously not sufficient to prove that each year of additional schooling will produce an increase in one's IQ score. Access to further education, after all, is often dependent on passing exams or the acquisition of the appropriate qualifications, and these will already be correlated with IQ. Sixteen-year-olds with low IQ scores will often choose to leave school as soon as they can; 18-year-olds may fail to obtain a place at university.

In an attempt to bypass this obvious confound, Harnqvist (1968) obtained IQ scores from a large sample of Swedish boys, first when they were 13 years old, and 5 years later when they were 18. This allowed him to take initial IQ into account and to go on to relate changes in IQ between 13 and 18 to differences in the amount and type of education received. He estimated that such differences could produce a difference in IQ at age 18 of up to 10 points. But although Harnqvist's procedure is ingenious and his results suggestive, they are not decisive. Even if they obtain exactly the same IQ score, after all, there must have been some other difference at age 13 between a boy who chooses a rigorous academic education, a second who chooses a less demanding one, and a third who opts to leave school at the first opportunity. Perhaps these other differences, in motivation, academic ambition, or intellectual interests, are largely responsible for the later differences in IQ?

One natural experiment that has seemed to promise a solution to this problem is to rely on the fact that most school systems admit children only at the beginning of the school term or year in which they reach a certain age. There can thus be a difference of up to a year in the age of children within any one class, but in many cases a very much smaller difference between the oldest children in one class and the youngest in the class above, although the latter will have enjoyed the benefit of a year's extra schooling. Ceci (1990, 1991) has reviewed a number of studies which have relied on this to measure the effects of schooling on IQ. A particularly clear example is a study by Cahan and Cohen (1989) of Israeli schoolchildren, some of whose results are shown in Fig. 4.3. As can be seen, for both tests shown here, there is a large increase in test scores from younger to older children within each class, but there is also a substantial and abrupt increase between the oldest children in one grade and the youngest in the grade above.

These results provide compelling evidence, from which teachers may take comfort, that schooling does influence young children's intellectual development. Figure 4.3 also suggests that the effect of schooling (measured by the increase from one grade to the next) was more pronounced on a verbal than on a figural test. This was in general true across the entire test battery Cahan and Cohen employed, but the effect was far from negligible even in the case of the figural, non-verbal tests. Moreover, a subsequent study of 10-year-old German schoolchildren found entirely comparable effects of an additional year of schooling on both verbal and non-verbal IQ scores (Stelzl *et al.*, 1995). Formal schooling not only teaches children to read, write, and do arithmetic (skills tested in many verbal IQ tests), but also imparts the skills to solve some of the reasoning tests that contribute to non-verbal IQ scores. We shall come across further evidence of this later (Chapter 5).

A different line of evidence provides converging support for the conclusion that schooling is good for your IQ. Children who, for one reason or another, are prevented from attending school suffer a decline in their IQ scores. In one American case from the 1960s, schools in a county in Virginia were closed for several years in protests against school integration. Local black children received no formal education at all and, compared to a control group, it has been calculated they suffered a decline in IQ of some 6 points for each year of school missed (Neisser, 1996). De Groot (1951) reported that children prevented from attending school in Holland during the Second World War had IQ scores depressed by about 5 points. Even

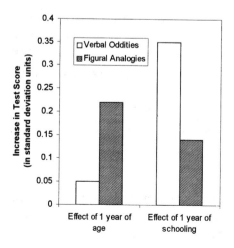

Fig. 4.3 The independent effects of young children's age and the length of time they have been in school on verbal and figural IQ scores (data from Cahan and Cohen, 1989).

earlier studies by Gaw (1925) and Gordon (1923) of gypsy and canal-boat children showed a similar effect. The children's peripatetic lifestyle meant that at best they moved from one school to another, but more often did not attend school at all. The older the children, the lower their IQ scores dropped.

We can accept that additional schooling is beneficial for children's IQ scores. But the practical significance of many of these findings should not be exaggerated. In general, the total number of years of schooling children receive will not depend on the accident of their date of birth. So the differences between children in different classes shown in Fig. 4.3 will, presumably, wash out by the end of their educational career. Moreover, it must be wrong to extrapolate from results such as these to assume that if the difference between 1 and 2 years' worth of schooling is so striking in 6- and 7-year-olds, there will be an equally striking difference between 8 and 9 years' worth of schooling in teenagers. The effect of a single additional year at school must surely decrease as the total number of years in school increases. But this rather obvious point does not seem to have been entirely assimilated by those who confidently assumed that 1 or 2 years of additional schooling before children started their normal school career would have a dramatic and permanent effect on their subsequent educational performance. That was the hope behind the policy of compensatory pre-school education, conceived as a noble social experiment, but an experiment which may have generated more academic controversy than practical good.

Compensatory education

'Compensatory education has been tried and it apparently has failed', Arthur Jensen announced in 1969. Project 'Head Start' had been initiated in the early 1960s, as part of President Johnson's war on poverty, in an attempt to break the cycle of poverty and deprivation which seemed to be transmitted from one generation to the next. Children growing up in poverty failed at school, remained poor, and thus passed on their own disadvantages to their children, who failed in their turn. Why did the ordinary school system not succeed in breaking this endless cycle? One answer was because children from advantaged backgrounds arrived in school with a head start provided by 5 years of middle-class home life. Thus for disadvantaged children, the ordinary school system started too late: such children were already doomed to failure when they first arrived at school. The Head Start programme would show the way out by getting to the children before they entered school and providing them with the basic skills they needed to succeed there. The further assumption was that early experience is critical: Bloom's conclusion was widely believed:

> The evidence so far available suggests that marked changes in the environment in the early years can produce greater changes in intelligence than will equally marked changes in the environment at later periods of development. (Bloom, 1964, p. 89)

Jensen's conclusion was fiercely denounced, particularly by those who objected to what they perceived to be Jensen's real message—that the reason why compensatory education had failed was because its recipients were mostly black. But at the time he was writing, there was little hard evidence that compensatory education programmes had any long-term beneficial effects. The critical question is whether the picture has changed since then. According to some commentators, at least, it has not (e.g. Spitz, 1986; Locurto, 1991*a*; Herrnstein and Murray, 1994): in spite of widespread hopes and loud claims to the contrary, they have argued, there remains little evidence that such programmes have much lasting impact. Even sympathetic reviewers (e.g. Zigler and Muenchow, 1992) no longer claim that Head Start programmes have any substantial long-term effects on IQ.

Many of the earlier programmes had been relatively brief, lasting only for 2 or 3 months in the summer before children enrolled in school. Few were planned in such a way as to allow a reliable evaluation of their effectiveness—for example with a matched, untreated control group. But even if attention was confined to the more reliable programmes, their effects were at best transitory, and most gains seemed to vanish within a year or two of the child's leaving the programme. The results of a meta-analysis of these studies are shown in Fig 4.4. By the end of the programme, it is clear, children in the treatment groups were performing substantially better than controls not only in terms of IQ (the difference is about 7–8 points), but also in 'readiness', a measure of use and understanding of language, and in school achievement. But, alas, these benefits were soon lost; after 2–3 years of normal schooling, there were no effects left (Locurto, 1991*a, b*).

Perhaps the programmes had been too short. The Consortium for Longitudinal Studies (Lazar and Darlington, 1982) analysed the results of 11 of the most thorough and extensive programmes, all of which met a variety of criteria. At least in terms of IQ, their results were much the same as before. The IQ data from one of the better known of these studies, the Perry Pre-school Project (Schweinhart and Weikart, 1980) are shown in Fig 4.5. They do not present a convincing case for any long-term effect: there were substantial gains for the treatment group, but they vanished within 3 or 4 years of the end of the programme, and in this respect the study was entirely representative of the other programmes included in the Consortium (Locurto, 1991*b*).

The earlier analysis of Head Start programmes (Fig. 4.4) raised the possibility that intervention might have longer-lasting effects on other measures than IQ. If true, this would be more than enough to justify them: in practical terms, it is surely more important that children should succeed in school than that they have their IQ scores raised by a few points. The Consortium studies provided some encouragement for this suggestion, but unfortunately these benefits were less readily demonstrated in possibly more important areas, such as actual tests of scholastic attainment. In the Perry Project, by the age of 12 or so, there was no difference between treatment and control groups on tests of either reading or mathematics. Although the project reported significant differences at age 14, only 77 per cent of the original sample was available for these tests, and there is reason to believe that

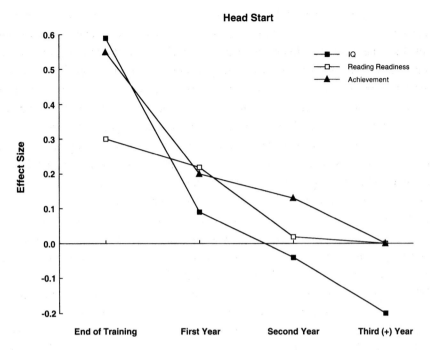

Fig. 4.4 The effect of Head Start programmes on children's IQ scores, general achievement, and 'reading readiness'. The data are shown in terms of 'effect size', or standard deviation units, where an effect size of 0.5 on IQ corresponds to 7.5 IQ points.

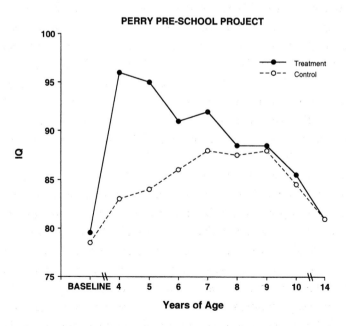

Fig. 4.5 Differences in IQ scores between treatment and control children in the Perry Pre-school Project. The treatment programme terminated when the children entered regular school at the age of 5–6 years.

there was greater loss of more disadvantaged children from the treatment than from the control group (Locurto, 1991*b*).

Apparently more reliable differences were reported for some other measures of 'social competence'. In the Perry Project, children in the treatment group were less likely to be classified as mentally retarded and spent less time in special education; they were more likely to graduate from high school and subsequently were more likely to be employed. On the face of it, these are important achievements. But legitimate doubts remain (see Locurto, 1991*b*). Only a small proportion of these measures actually showed a significant advantage for the treatment group. There was, for example, no difference between the groups in school grades or in the proportion of children required to repeat a grade; only 5 out of 37 measures of delinquent behaviour or of police records revealed significant differences; and in some cases, the treatment group did worse than the controls (e.g. in avoiding 'remedial' rather than 'special' education). The programme undoubtedly had some beneficial effects—as did other programmes in the Consortium. But it is not always obvious that the measures showing a beneficial effect of treatment were intrinsically more important or valid than those showing none.

What are we to make of this overall pattern of results? Although positive outcomes have frequently been seized upon with great enthusiasm, a more balanced assessment must be less optimistic. Several studies have indeed shown that the effects on tests of school attainment may outlast those on IQ, but there is little evidence that they are permanent. It is surely important that children from the treatment group in the Perry Project were more likely to graduate from high school, but even if we ignore the numerous measures which remained unaffected by this treatment programme, we must still ask whether the apparently successful measures reflected a change in the children themselves (either in their attainments, attitudes, or motivation) or rather a change in the school's attitude to them. It seems more than probable that the children's participation in a pre-school programme would have been well known to their schools, and not inconceivable that teachers and school administrators would then assume that such children were more competent, better able to cope, and deserving of more encouragement (Locurto, 1991*a*). One final result of the Consortium's analyses deserves comment. In spite of substantial differences between the 11 studies included in the analysis—differences in age at which treatment started, length of treatment, whether it was based in the home or in a school, and whether it involved the parents—there was no apparent difference in outcome. All programmes seemed equally effective—or ineffective, depending on one's point of view.

Undaunted, proponents of early intervention and compensatory education have argued that the programmes were still far too short. One or two years of part-time, pre-school education, it was argued, are hopelessly inadequate to counteract the cultural and material deprivation in which many children spend the first 5 years of their life. What is needed is full-time intervention from shortly after birth at least to the point where children enter the ordinary school system. Although it must be doubted whether intervention on this scale is a realistic, practical proposition for every child deemed to be at risk of growing up with a low IQ, two studies, the Milwaukee Project (Garber, 1988) and the Carolina Abecedarian Project (Ramey, 1992; Campbell and Ramey, 1994), have been mounted to see whether such a programme can achieve long-term effects.

Although they differed in a number of important respects, some of which seem more important in the minds of jealous authors than to a detached observer, they shared some common features. Both involved full-time day care, 5 days a week, all year long, from the time the children were a few months old to the time they entered the regular school system—and beyond. Both involved intensive training and education by a large staff of professional teachers and psychologists. And finally, both appear on the face of it to have achieved some long-term gains in the children's IQ scores. Figure 4.6 shows the IQ scores of treatment and control children in both projects, from the age of 1 year until well after the treatment had ended and the children were enrolled in normal schools. As can be seen, here for the first time there is evidence of some lasting effect. Although their test scores fluctuate, and tend to decline once the children leave the project and enter normal schools, children in the treatment groups maintain a significant advantage over those in the control groups (about 10 points in Milwaukee, about 5 points in Abecedarian) up to the age of 12 or 14. There seems good reason to believe that pre-school intervention, albeit on a heroic scale, can permanently enhance children's IQ scores.

Box 4.2 Miracle in Milwaukee

The Milwaukee Project was initiated in the 1960s. It was extraordinarily ambitious, not in terms of size, for there were only 20 children in each of the two groups (treatment and control), but in the scale of the intervention, which lasted from the time the children were only 3 months old and continued until they were 5 or 6 years old, involved individual or small-group tuition 5 days a week, 12 months a year, and included the mothers as well as the children. The tuition was provided by trained professionals and was expressly designed to stimulate the children's cognitive development. At a total cost of some US$14 million (Spitz, 1986), even if we accept the authors' own rather optimistic assessment of the magnitude of the gains, the cost of raising one child's IQ by one point must have been over US$30 000.

Throughout the 1970s, the project was hailed as proof that children at risk of mental retardation could be saved: intelligence was wholly malleable, and it was only lack of political will, aided by false psychological theory, that stood in the way of raising the IQ scores of black inner-city children by 25 points or more. Introductory psychology textbooks cited the study uncritically; the news media lauded it. What is so remarkable is that all this happened in the absence of any proper published report on the study, which did not become available until Garber's book in 1988 (for an account of this history, see Page and Grandon, 1981; Sommer and Sommer, 1983). Another, more spectacular, problem was that in 1981, Heber, the original director of the project, was sentenced to jail on charges of embezzlement (thus, perhaps, helping to explain the cost of the project as well as the delay in producing proper reports?).

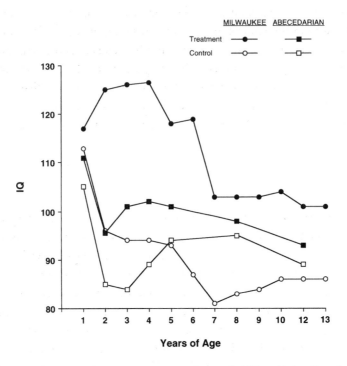

Fig. 4.6 Differences in IQ scores between treatment and control children in the Abecedarian and Milwaukee projects.

There remain some niggling worries. As can be seen in Fig. 4.6, the difference between treatment and control group children in the Abecedarian project was no greater at 12 years than it had been at age 1 or 2. This point has been seized upon by critics (Spitz, 1992, 1993) to argue that the two groups were not properly matched at the outset. In fact, this is a difficult charge either to prove or to disprove—since, as we have seen (Chapter 2), conventional IQ tests at the age of 1 or 2 years are wholly unreliable predictors of later IQ. Ramey (1992) has argued, not wholly unreasonably, that the two groups probably were quite well matched at the outset.

However, by a long way the most serious concern about the effectiveness of the Milwaukee project is that while the treatment seems to have enhanced children's IQ scores, that is *all* it has done. As we saw earlier, there was some evidence that intervention programmes might be more successful at the surely more important task of improving children's school performance than raising their IQ test scores. The Abecedarian project certainly succeeded in improving children's performance on various school tests as well as on IQ tests (Ramey, 1992). But the Milwaukee results are strikingly disappointing. In spite of the 10-point difference in their IQ scores, within a couple of years of their entering the normal school system, there was no difference between the treatment and control groups of children in any formal tests of scholastic attainment.

Indeed in some respects, the children in the treatment group were described as more troublesome than those in the control group. One possibility is that it does not pay for a black child from the inner city to be too clever. Another, equally depressing, possibility is that all that the Milwaukee project succeeded in doing was to teach children how to answer the questions in IQ tests—without having any effect on the 'intelligence' that is supposedly measured by such tests (Jensen, 1989; Locurto, 1991*b*). There is, after all, a finite set of questions that appear in children's IQ tests, and the answers to most of them can be learned.

Conclusions

Contemplating the large number of inconclusive studies reviewed in this chapter, and the relatively meagre amount of unequivocal information they have provided, it is all too easy to throw up one's hands in despair. It is true that there is much of which we remain ignorant, but despair is probably only a reaction to the disappointment of some wholly unrealistic expectations. Environmentalists have insisted, quite properly, that IQ is malleable, and have railed against the brutal pessimism of those who would assert that a 5-year-old with an IQ of 80, from an impoverished background, is doomed by virtue of that IQ score to second-class citizenship. But their rhetoric has often implied that it should be a simple matter to intervene and raise such a child's IQ, and that it is only a lack of political will that stands in the way of our doing so. Underlying that implication, of course, is a further set of assumptions: that we understand how the environment shapes the developing child's IQ, and that even if we do not have a fully articulated environmental theory of the development of IQ, we can at least point to a small number of general principles governing that development.

Nothing could be further from the truth. It should be clear by now that we have no theory of cognitive development that explains how different environments shape different children's different IQ scores. No general principles have emerged from the data reviewed in this chapter. Indeed, the most plausible conclusion suggested by these data is that there is no single environmental factor that has a magical and permanent effect on children's IQ scores. What the data imply is that there is a very large number of factors, each of which has no more than a small effect on IQ. In most modern societies, many of these factors happen to go together, such that a child benefiting (or losing out) from one will probably be fortunate (or unlucky) enough to benefit (or lose out) from another. But in terms of psychological mode of operation, they are probably quite independent: there are no grounds for believing that lead poisoning and loss of schooling depress a child's IQ for the same reason.

A list of the environmental factors that affect IQ contains relatively few surprises. From the data reviewed here, such a list would probably include: prenatal and perinatal factors; health and nutrition; amount and type of parental interaction; the experience of normal schooling. At the same time, however, the data do serve to dispel some myths and point to some conclusions that have not always been recognized. As I noted at the outset of this chapter, the most popular candidate for a single environmental determinant of IQ has been social class. There is, of course, a significant correlation between children's IQ scores and their parents' socio-economic status, but it is quite modest (0.30–0.35), and it is probable that *part* of the correlation reflects a genetic component (see Chapter 5). In so far as it does represent an effect of family environment on IQ, the evidence suggests that it is not so much the sociological or economic concomitants of social class that are important, but rather parental attitudes and aspirations. Several studies have shown that children's IQ scores are more strongly associated with 'cultural' than with economic measures of their home environment. Moreover, studies of adoptive families suggest that the characteristics of family environments that foster the development of IQ are not necessarily associated with social class at all. Even lower-class adoptive parents are capable of raising their adopted children's IQ scores. In Leahy's (1935) study, for example, children adopted by semi-skilled workers or 'day labourers' obtained IQ scores some 6–8 points higher than those of control children whose natural parents were in these occupational categories, and only 4–5 points below those of children adopted by professional or managerial parents.

There is a second message that reinforces and complements this first one. The effect of family environment on IQ cannot be of overriding importance, since members of the same family differ quite widely in IQ. The correlation between siblings for IQ is no more than about 0.40–0.50, and some 75 per cent of the variance in IQ in the population as a whole is to be found among members of the same family. As we saw in Chapter 3, behaviour genetic analyses suggest that by the age of 15 or so, within-family environmental differences are at least as important as differences between families in their impact on children's IQ scores. What are these environmental factors that cause members of the same family to differ in IQ? Just about the only unequivocally within-family effect we have identified so far is that first- and second-born children tend to obtain higher IQ scores than third-, fourth-, or fifth-born children. But even the most optimistic interpretation of the importance of birth order must admit that it can explain no more than a small fraction of the variance in IQ. So what are the other factors?

Parents do not, of course, treat all their children alike, and differences between siblings' IQ scores, therefore, could well be due to differences in parental treatment. One might argue, for example, that parents themselves change over time, not only in their attitudes and aspirations, but also in their own social status and income: people do, after all, sometimes get better jobs, or lose the job they once had. And some parents probably still have different aspirations for their sons and their daughters (many more probably used to). Is it not plausible to suppose that all these factors will contribute to differences between children in one and the same family? It may seem plausible, but such evidence as there is does not encourage this line of reasoning. Rodgers and Rowe (1985), for example, could detect no tendency for differences in IQ scores between siblings to be affected by the difference in age between them, by the number of other siblings intervening between them, or by whether they were the same sex. This last conclusion has been well documented by many larger studies (Bouchard and McGue, 1981).

Once again, we must acknowledge that differences in parental treatment, attitudes, and aspirations, even if correlated with differences in their children's IQ scores, may not be the cause of those differences. If parents have higher aspirations for one child than for another, this is just as likely to be in response to pre-existing differences between those children as to be their cause. To the extent that within-family differences in IQ are environmental in origin, they probably reflect a whole variety of chance, one-off events at least as much as any difference in parental attitude. Some of these effects may be prenatal or perinatal, while others may be related to the accident of ill-health (Jensen, 1997). In so far as they are due to the social environment, they may reflect a particular group of friends, or the good or ill fortune to be exposed to an inspiring or a boring teacher at school. And since siblings differ from one another in personality and temperament even more than they do in IQ (sibling correlations for most personality measures are less than 0.20, see Loehlin, 1992), it seems possible that such differences in temperament may lead them to pursue different paths that then impact back on their cognitive development. But at this point, it will be advisable to stop before the merely speculative nature of this analysis becomes too apparent.

One final point should be made in conclusion. One of the oldest beliefs in psychology is in the pre-eminent importance of early experience. It was reinforced by ethologists' studies of 'critical periods' in such phenomena as imprinting, and by the notion derived from developmental biology that the brain is particularly vulnerable at particular stages of its development. Such a belief, as we have seen, formed part of the philosophy underlying the Head Start programme. The fact of the matter is that there is remarkably little evidence that environmental factors have a greater impact on children's IQ scores at one age than at another. Early intervention will produce a transient increase in IQ, but the effect washes out unless the intervention is sustained (as it is when the child is adopted). Conversely, years of gross neglect can leave a child with an IQ below 50 (if it can be measured at all), but patient rehabilitation can restore the child to a fully normal level of intellectual functioning (Clarke and Clarke, 1976; Skuse, 1984). Perhaps early experience is critical only if it pushes the child down an environmental path from which it is difficult to escape.

Summary

Surprisingly enough, the best evidence of a sizeable environmental effect on IQ scores is the finding that in most industrialized countries, average test scores have increased by some 20 points or more over the past 75 years. The effect is both large and certainly environmental, but no one really knows what has caused it. The best bet is that it reflects the operation of a large number of factors, each of limited impact. That is probably just as true of environmental causes of differences in IQ within any one generation.

Numerous factors are correlated with differences in IQ: parental social class, prenatal behaviour and attitudes; prenatal and perinatal complications; nutrition and health; family size and birth order; amount of schooling. It is one thing to establish such correlations; it is another matter to interpret them correctly. Many of these factors are themselves intercorrelated, so that the magnitude of their own correlation with a child's IQ must overestimate the magnitude of their causal contribution. In many cases (e.g. parental attitude), the direction of causation may be from child's IQ to parent's behaviour, rather than vice versa. In many others (parental status, parental behaviour) there may be a genetic contribution to the correlation.

Although the behaviour geneticists' modern consensus appears to believe that differences in family background have virtually no impact on children's IQ scores after the age of 18 or so, the evidence for this view is less than overwhelming. Nevertheless, there is some reason to believe that most of the environmental sources of variation in IQ operate within families, to make brothers and sisters differ in IQ, rather than between families, to make them the same.

5   *Group differences*

Introduction

Of all the contentious issues thrown up by IQ testing, few have aroused more bad feeling and generated more shoddy argument than the suggestion that different groups may differ in average IQ. But from the earliest days of IQ testing such suggestions have been common. In his standardization of the original Stanford–Binet test, Terman, relying on school-teachers to classify children's social class into one of five categories, found a difference of some 14 points between the average IQ of children of 'very inferior' and those of 'very superior' social class. As we have seen in Chapter 4, a difference of approximately this magnitude has been more carefully documented in dozens of subsequent studies of social class and IQ in both North America and Europe. Thomson (1921) seems to have been the first to note that children living in towns tended to obtain higher IQ scores than those living in the country, and speculated that this might be partly because some of the more intelligent had migrated from country to town. The difference was also noted by Cattell (1937), and confirmed in the later standardization samples of the Stanford–Binet and Wechsler tests (Terman and Merrill, 1937; Seashore *et al.*, 1950). In the USA, at least, the size of this particular difference has declined sharply in recent years, and we shall not pay any further attention to it in this chapter (Kaufman and Doppelt, 1976; Reynolds *et al.*, 1987).

Perhaps the most notorious difference in average IQ scores has been that claimed to hold between different ethnic groups. First documented on a large scale in the US Army tests of the First World War, some at least of these differences, most notably that between blacks and whites in the United States, are clearly still with us today, and the controversy surrounding them has neither diminished nor apparently been resolved. The precise magnitude of the difference between blacks and whites in the USA, and whether it has stayed constant over time, are matters of some conjecture. But the evidence suggests that it was at one time of the order of 15–20 points (Shuey, 1958, 1966), and had not seriously diminished by the 1980s.

That different groups differ in average IQ cannot seriously be denied. The question at issue, about which there is ample room for argument, is the explanation of these differences. There is no reason to expect a single answer. The issues raised by social-class differences in

---

Box 5.1 A note on terminology

The 'correct' names for different racial, ethnic, or social groups have changed several times over the past 50 years. Any attempt to keep up with this ever-changing fashion seems doomed to failure, and I have not tried to do so in this chapter. So I usually refer to 'blacks' rather than use the more cumbersome terms 'African-Americans' or 'Afro-Caribbeans'—partly because I sometimes wish to refer equally to those living in the USA or in Britain. At other times, writing of British studies, I refer to them as West Indians or of West Indian origin, in the same way as I refer to Indians and Pakistanis, without thereby intending to imply that they are not all British citizens, most of whom were born in Britain. I have similarly talked of Chinese or Japanese Americans, rather than Orientals (let alone Mongoloids), and to American Indians, rather than to Native Americans.

Finally, I talk of 'sex differences' rather than 'gender differences'. The variable in question is biological sex, rather than socially perceived gender, even if the route by which it has any effect on IQ scores is social or cultural.

IQ are not necessarily the same as those raised by differences between ethnic groups. Differences between some ethnic groups may be due to quite different factors from those responsible for differences between others. And to round off the picture, we shall consider one final difference, that between the sexes, which raises issues different from either of these other two cases.

Social class

One reason why children from different social classes differ in their average IQ is, as we already have seen in Chapter 4, that they have been brought up in different circumstances. The evidence for this comes from demonstrations of significant increases in IQ when children are adopted into middle-class families, and of a significant correlation between the social class of adoptive families and the IQ scores of their adopted children. But we also encountered evidence which, on the face of it, implied that IQ differences between social classes might not be entirely environmental in origin. The correlation between parental circumstance and children's IQ scores is rather smaller in adoptive than in natural families. It is possible that restriction of range in adoptive families provides one explanation of this: adoptive families of lower occupational status may provide a better environment for developing their children's IQ than do ordinary families of apparently comparable status. But when all is said and done, one obvious interpretation of this finding is that in natural families genetic sources of resemblance are added to environmental.

Are there other reasons for supposing that social-class differences in IQ might be partly genetic in origin? On the face of it, it would seem that the answer will depend on one's estimate of the heritability of IQ in the population as a whole; if heritability is very high, then it surely follows that a large difference in average IQ between two groups within this population must be partly attributable to genetic differences between them. In the limiting case where heritability is 1.0 this must follow (although it does not follow, as we shall see below, for black–white differences, where we are dealing with separate populations). But even if the heritability for IQ were as high as 0.60–0.80, and differences between families accounted for only 20 per cent of the variation in IQ, then one standard deviation of such environmental differences between two groups would produce an approximately 6-point difference in their average IQ. Since it is hardly unreasonable to postulate a difference of two standard deviations in the average environmental circumstances of families in social classes 1 and 5, the difference of 15 or so points in their children's average IQ scores does not seem excessive for an exclusively environmental interpretation.

Abstract arguments of this nature are not going to settle the issue. We need concrete evidence. In fact, there are moderately persuasive reasons for supposing that the correlation between parental social class and child's IQ may be at least partly genetic in origin. The correlation between adults' social class and their IQ scores is about 0.50–0.60. But the correlation between the same adults' social class and their *children's* IQ scores is significantly lower—as we have seen, only about 0.30 (Chapter 4). This difference is illustrated in Fig. 5.1, which shows the average IQ scores of fathers in four different social classes and that of their sons. The difference in average IQ between fathers in the highest and lowest classes is over 30 points; the difference between their sons' IQ scores is less than 20.

One might suppose from results such as these that the average IQ difference between the social classes was fast disappearing. But this is not true: there is no good evidence that it is

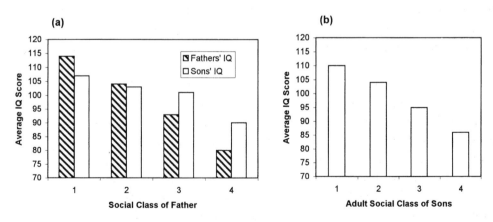

Fig. 5.1 Average IQ scores of fathers and their sons. (a) Fathers' and sons' IQ scores sorted according to the fathers' SES. Note that the difference in IQ between SES1 and SES4 is greater for the fathers than it is for their sons. (b) The IQ of these same sons sorted by their own, later-attained SES. Note that the differences in average IQ between the social classes have been restored to nearly the same as they were for their fathers. (Data from Waller, 1971.)

smaller today than it was 50 years ago. And in Waller's study shown in Fig. 5.1, the IQ scores of the sons, which correlated only about 0.30 with the social class of their fathers, correlated over 0.50 with their own, later social class as adults. This, too, is a general-enough finding (e.g. Jencks, 1972; McCall, 1977; Chapter 2). In other words, the social-class difference in IQ is, so to say, recreated in each generation.

It is recreated by social mobility. The social-class system of Western industrial societies is not a caste system. People are not necessarily ordained to remain in the social class to which they were born (the correlation between fathers' and sons' social class is only about 0.35), and there is direct evidence that one of the factors correlated with social mobility is IQ. Differences in social class between father and son are correlated with differences in their IQ scores; just as a son's eventual social class is not necessarily the same as that of his parents, so he may differ from his parents in IQ (the correlation between fathers' and sons' IQ scores is certainly no more than about 0.50). Studies in both the United States and Great Britain have shown that the direction of differences in social class tends to be the same as the direction of differences in IQ. Sons with higher IQs than their fathers are more likely to be upwardly socially mobile; those with lower IQs than their fathers are more likely to end up in a lower social class (Waller, 1971; Mascie-Taylor and Gibson, 1978). The British data are shown in Fig. 5.2.

There could be no correlation between social mobility and IQ without substantial variation in IQ with each social class. And so there is—especially when we are looking at children's IQ scores as a function of their parents' social class. In Waller's data, shown in Fig. 5.1, the variation in sons' IQ scores within each parental social class was only fractionally less than the variation in the population as a whole. Some sons of fathers in

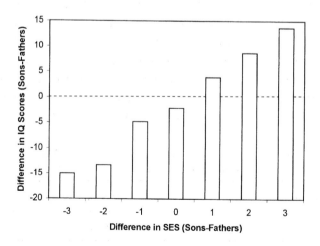

Fig. 5.2 The correlation between IQ and social mobility. The figure plots the difference in IQ between fathers and their sons as a function of the difference in their occupational status: sons with higher IQ than their fathers tend to end up in higher-status jobs. (Data from Mascie-Taylor and Gibson, 1978.)

class 1 had lower IQ scores than some of the sons whose fathers were in class 4. The former were likely to end up in a lower class, the latter in a higher one than their fathers. If social mobility is correlated with IQ in this way, it is difficult to resist the conclusion that such an effect is partly responsible for the maintenance of the correlation between IQ and social class in each generation, and therefore that the direction of causality is partly that IQ differences cause social-class differences rather than simply that social-class differences cause IQ differences. This may not be enough to prove that social-class differences in average IQ are partly genetic in origin, but it is clearly consistent with this possibility, and tends to undermine the alternative thesis that they are entirely a consequence of differences in family environment.

In the last analysis, however, the only way to find out whether there might be differences in average IQ genotype between social classes would be via an extremely improbable adoption study, where children were taken for adoption from two groups of parents, who were themselves selected as large representative samples of different social classes, and were then adopted by carefully matched families. A difference in the average IQ scores of the two groups of children would then suggest a genetic difference in IQ potential between the two groups of parents and, by implication, between the two social classes of which they were representative samples. Needless to say no such study has ever been done, but as we have seen in Chapter 4, there is, surprisingly enough, one very small French study which at least approximates to it. Searching through the agency records of children adopted before the age of 6 months, Capron and Duyme (1989) set out to find four groups of children, two groups born to biological parents of high social class, two to parents of low social class, with one of each group adopted into high-status adoptive homes and the other into low-status homes. The result is the 'perfect' 2 × 2 factorial design illustrated in Table 5.1, with status of biological and of adoptive parents as the two factors. Understandably enough, the most difficult cell to fill was that of children born to high-status parents but adopted into low-status homes, and there are only 8 children in this group as opposed to 10 in each of the others. The results shown in Table 5.1, however, suggest that the social class of both biological and of adoptive parents had significant and roughly equal effects on the children's IQ scores. The difference between children adopted into high-status and those adopted into low-status families provides an elegant demonstration of an environmental effect of social

Table 5.1 Adopted children's IQ scores as a function of the SES of their biological and adoptive parents (from Capron and Duyme, 1989)

Biological parents	Adoptive parents	
	High SES	Low SES
High SES	119.6	107.5
Low SES	103.6	92.4

class on children's IQ scores. But the difference between those born to high- and low-status biological parents provides, on the face of it, strong evidence of a genetic difference for IQ between the two groups of parents. Since there were no differences in birth weight between the two groups of children (i.e. no evidence of prenatal or perinatal environmental differences between the two groups), a genetic hypothesis is certainly the most plausible. It is also consistent with the earlier French adoption study where children of working-class mothers adopted into middle-class families obtained IQ scores some 8 points lower than those of a control group of middle-class children attending the same schools (Dumaret and Stewart, 1985).

For those who find this conclusion unwelcome or frightening, it is important to add one point. We are talking about differences in average IQ, but these averages conceal enormous variation within each group. As we have noted above, in Waller's study the variation in IQ score within each social class was not much less than the variation in the population as a whole. This has important implications. Suppose that an IQ score of, say, 120 or higher were a necessary qualification for entry to an elite university. Although a higher proportion of middle-class than of working-class children might obtain such an IQ score, the fact of the matter is that the total number of working-class children with such a score will be greater than the total number of middle-class children.

Ethnic groups

If the supposition that there might be some difference in average IQ between social classes brands one as politically reactionary, the suggestion of any such difference between ethnic or racial groups inevitably brands one as an unreconstructed racist. Many people, including some authors of textbooks on intelligence testing (e.g. Kline, 1991), find such suggestions so repugnant that they are unwilling to discuss the issue at all. Others are content with denunciation and condemnation, sometimes without taking much trouble to read that which they denounce. From the furore which followed publication of Jensen's paper in the *Harvard Educational Review* of 1969, or of Herrnstein and Murray's *The bell curve* in 1994, for example, one would hardly have guessed that only a small fraction of these works was devoted to the issue of black–white differences in IQ, and that neither claimed that we *knew* what the causes of these differences were.

It is not possible to review in detail the evidence bearing on all differences between various ethnic groups. The one that has attracted most attention has been that between blacks and whites in the United States. Without thereby implying that it is necessarily the most important, it will serve as the focus of the discussion that follows—although, where appropriate, other differences will also be addressed. There can be no serious doubt that North American blacks have an average IQ score some 15 points below that of whites. This difference showed up in the early US Army data, was repeatedly confirmed in subsequent studies between the wars (Shuey, 1966), and has been maintained after the Second World War (Loehlin *et al.*, 1975). The latest American standardizations of the Wechsler tests revealed that there was still a difference of some 15 points (Kaufman and Doppelt, 1976; Reynolds *et al.* 1987). Although there has been no comparably systematic analysis of the position in other countries, no doubt because no other Western industrial society contains such a long-established and substantial black minority, there can be little doubt that black children in Britain, the majority of West Indian origin, obtain IQ scores significantly below those of the white mean; the results of two national surveys (NCDS and CHES) of children aged 10 and 11, are shown in Table 5.2. The differences, particularly in the later study, are smaller than those typically reported in the USA and, as can be seen, that for the earlier study is inflated by the fact that some of the children had only recently immigrated. Those resident in Britain more than 4 years obtained IQ scores only 10–11 points below the white mean.

It is not easy to discuss data such as these rationally, for it would be naive to pretend that they have no social or political impact. In the United States they have been used to argue against the integration of school systems or the provision of compensatory education, in Britain to support bans on further immigration, and in both countries to argue that there is nothing to be done about black poverty or crime because they are both inexorable consequences of low black IQ. In the USA, for example, in 1959, black family income was still only 70 per cent that of whites, black adults were nearly four times as likely to be classified as living in poverty as whites, and also about four times as likely to be arrested (Herrnstein and Murray, 1994). But however suspect the motives of many of those who use these data, and however strongly one may deplore their political aims, it is questionable to suppose that much will be gained by pretending that the data do not exist or by refusing to discuss them at all. The trouble with such a response is that it seems to imply that the data really are of the utmost social and political consequence, and that those consequences are too terrible to contemplate. But why do we believe that? Of course, the results of IQ tests have been used by racists to support their doctrines; but it is absurd to suppose that they

Table 5.2 IQ scores of 10- and 11-year-old black and white children in Britain (from Mackintosh and Mascie-Taylor, 1986)

	NCDS (1969)		CHES (1980)	
	Verbal	Non-verbal	Verbal	Non-verbal
White	100.6	100.5	100.6	100.2
Blacks (4-)	83.7	81.0		
			92.0	96.5
Blacks (4+)	89.8	89.3		

(4-) = Children resident in Britain for less than 4 years at time of testing.
(4+) = Children resident in Britain for 4 or more years at time of testing.

need such data in order to justify their position. American and European prejudice and discrimination against Jews, Japanese, or Chinese can hardly rest on the claim (which would be wholly false) that these groups obtain low IQ scores. Conversely, we do not necessarily discriminate against identifiable groups, such as twins, whose average IQ scores are lower than that of the rest of the population. The difference in average IQ between blacks and whites is neither a necessary nor a sufficient condition for discriminating against blacks as a group, let alone against individual blacks who may well have IQ scores well above the white mean.

We should accept, then, without further ado that there is a difference in average IQ between blacks and white. But what is the explanation? On the face of it, there are three possibilities: genetics, environment, or bias in the tests. It has seemed obvious to many commentators that the real question at issue is the genetic one: if the difference were an artefact of the tests or could be explained in terms of certain environmental differences between black and white populations, would we be exercised by it? If bias in the tests were the culprit that would no doubt give us yet further reason to mistrust IQ tests or alternatively to try to devise better ones. If environmental factors could be shown to cause differences in IQ between blacks and whites, that might make us want to change society. The problem with the genetic explanation is that it seems final and immutable. But this argument is wholly fallacious. As Chapter 4 should have shown, it is one thing to establish that IQ scores are affected by the environment; it is another to pinpoint the precise factors responsible, let alone their mode of operation; and it is yet another matter to intervene in such a way as to influence test scores. And even if we did know how, it would not follow that the social engineering required would be socially acceptable. Conversely, genetic effects are not necessarily immutable—and are always expressed in a certain environmental context: change that context and the genetically caused effect may disappear (see Chapter 3).

Nevertheless, we may as well still start with the genetic hypothesis. Is it, in Jensen's words 'not unreasonable'? We should clear up two very general points at the outset. Human beings form a single interbreeding species and no serious geneticist or anthropologist today would subscribe to a view of genetically distinct 'races'. There is no single genetic marker common to all white groups and absent in blacks, or vice versa; all human genes are found in both groups. Some writers (e.g. Gould, 1986) have attempted to argue from this that there could not be genetic differences for IQ between blacks and whites. The argument seems curious, for it is clear enough that blacks and whites do, on average, differ in the distribution and frequency of certain genes, and the genetic hypothesis needs nothing more than an average difference in the distribution of the no doubt vast array of genes affecting IQ (Jones, 1996).

A second *a priori* argument, advanced by Lewontin (1975), seeks to establish that there is no connection between the heritability of IQ within populations and the cause of any difference in IQ between populations. When we are dealing with IQ differences between blacks and whites (unlike that between social classes) we are dealing, as far as heritability is concerned, with different populations where essentially all the data on heritability of IQ come from the white population. But however high the heritability of IQ among whites (or for that matter among blacks), it would still be entirely possible that the *difference* between blacks and whites was due to a difference in environment. The point is illustrated by a thought experiment. We take two handfuls of seed from a sack and plant them in different plots, one rich, the other poor in essential nutrients. Within each plot any difference between the plants is due to genetic variation within the original sack of seed, but assuming that the two handfuls of seed we drew were truly random samples, the entire difference between the plants in the two plots would be due to environmental differences between those plots. High heritability within populations or plots is entirely compatible with a purely environmental difference between populations plots. The logic is impeccable, but it is foolish to pretend that the argument carries no implication for explanations of the differences between blacks and whites in IQ. The thought experiment postulates a uniform environment within each plot combined with a substantial difference in environment between plots. Translated into our terms, the implication is that if heritability of IQ within black and white populations were very high, the difference between them in average IQ could be attributed to the environment only if there were some environmental factor or factors affecting IQ that varied *between* black and white populations, but not *within* either population. This is hardly an empty assertion; it says that we could not appeal to environmental factors that differ within either group (e.g. income, social class) in order to explain the differences between them. Although some writers have been happy to accept this conclusion, arguing, for example, that the experience of racial discrimination directly suppresses black IQ scores (rather than indirectly by depressing their social circumstances), we may be better off rejecting the premise on which it is based. The fact of the matter is that the heritability of IQ within the white populations of North America and Western Europe is not 1.0; there are numerous environmental circumstances that affect IQ, and some of them may have similar effects on the IQ scores of other ethnic groups.

Black—white differences: genetic evidence

Enough of arguments of principle. In this case, above all, they should be treated with grave suspicion. If it is easy enough to select data to suit one's prejudices, how much easier will it be to choose the arguments of principle which prove or disprove on *a priori* grounds that which one wished to conclude on other grounds? So are there any data that bear on the question? As we have just argued for the case of social class, it is a simple matter to imagine the critical experiment. Take a random sample of black and white children at birth and bring them up in carefully matched adoptive homes or other comparable environments and measure their IQ scores at age 10 or so. But it seems equally easy to see that this time the experiment really is impossible. Leaving aside the usual difficulties, common to any study designed to disentangle genetic from environmental sources of variation in IQ, here there is the added absurdity of imagining that it would ever be possible, in a racist society, for black and white children to experience comparable environments. In one version of the environmental hypothesis of black–white differences, it is precisely the experience of being black in a society permeated by white racism that is responsible for lowering black children's IQ scores. No doubt, well-meaning adoptive families can mitigate the harshness of society but they could never eliminate it. Thus the discovery of a significant difference between the IQ scores of black and white children in this hypothetical study would still not force one to accept the genetic hypothesis.

The argument seems sound enough, but says little for the courage of its proponents. For in fact they need not have erected such defences against unwelcome results. No study has achieved the ideal set out above, for no natural experiment ever could, but three have approximated it and, taken as a whole, their results provide little support for the genetic hypothesis. The results of the two earlier studies are shown in Table 5.3. In neither case is there any significant difference between the IQ scores of black, or mixed-race, and white children.

Table 5.3 IQ scores of black and white children brought up in comparable circumstances

	Eyferth (1961)	Tizard (1974)
Black	–	107—98—106
Black–white	96.5	106—99—110
White	97.2	103—99—101

The children in Eyferth's (1961) study were the illegitimate offspring of American (and some French) soldiers born to German women during the occupation of Germany after the Second World War, and brought up by these German mothers or by foster parents. The 181 black children were a representative sample drawn from the approximately 4000 such children for whom official records were available. The white children were matched to the black for location, school and mother's circumstances. What could not be ascertained was the status of the fathers, for in most cases their identity was simply not known. This is the most obvious imperfection in Eyferth's study, but is it sufficient to cast doubt on the conclusions suggested by his data?

Jensen himself has never discussed Eyferth's study in print, but Nichols, in a staunch defence of Jensen's position, briskly dismissed it as

so weak methodologically that it is of little consequence . . . The most serious methodological defect . . . is biased sampling. The black and white American fathers are not likely to be representative of the black and white American soldiers stationed in Germany; nor can the German girls mating with black soldiers be assumed to be equivalent to those mating with white soldiers (Nichols, 1987, p. 233).

In effect, what Nichols has to be claiming is that there are two reasons why Eyferth's data fail to reflect the 'true' difference between black and white IQ scores: first, the black fathers were of well above average IQ for black soldiers and/or that the white fathers were well below average; and secondly, that there was a substantial difference in IQ between the two groups of German mothers in favour of the mothers of black children. Both these suppositions are sheer surmise, and the second seems both intrinsically improbable, and contradicted by the available evidence. Eyferth went to substantial trouble to match the socio-economic circumstances of the two groups of mothers and the family circumstances of the two groups of children. The large majority of both groups of mothers were young, lower class, and often themselves illegitimate, and the circumstances in which both groups of children were raised were equally poor.

As Flynn (1980) has noted, there is no better reason to suppose that the black and white fathers were unrepresentative of the populations from which they were drawn. At least 80 per cent of young American soldiers dated German girls 'more or less frequently'; this included a high proportion of officers (virtually all white) as well as of other ranks; and a high proportion of black soldiers going absent without leave or contracting venereal diseases were of below (black) average IQ. None of this provides any support for Nichols's argument, which requires that the white fathers be below, and the black fathers above, the average IQ for their respective populations.

Curiously enough, Nichols ignores what is an unquestionable problem in Eyferth's study: the black soldiers in the US Army cannot have been a representative sample of the American black population. The American Army in the Second World War, as in the First World War, used IQ tests to screen all draftees, and since blacks obtain on average lower IQ scores than whites, such a procedure necessarily entails the rejection of a higher proportion of blacks than of whites. However, Flynn (1980) has calculated that when allowance has been made for this selection, at least 80 per cent of the usual IQ gap between American blacks and whites is left intact. Thus the trivially small difference between the IQ scores of the two groups of children suggests that there can be no great genetic difference between the two populations from which their fathers came—a conclusion more or less accepted by Herrnstein and Murray (1994).

The second study, by Tizard (1974), was of British children who had lived or were still living in residential nurseries (the majority that had left the nursery were now in adoptive homes). They were all given three separate tests. As can be seen, the white children tended to obtain rather lower scores than children with either one or two black parents. There are at least two problems with this study. First, the children were only 4–5 years old at the time of testing, and test scores at this age do not correlate particularly well with later IQ (Chapter

2). Secondly, although West Indian families in Britain are on average poorer, less middle class, and score higher on most indices of social disadvantage than whites (see below), in this sample there was no difference between the proportion of black and white fathers in semi-skilled and unskilled occupations. The black children, therefore, can hardly have been a representative sample of Britain's black population.

The results of a third study (the Minnesota trans-racial adoption study, Scarr and Weinberg, 1976; Weinberg *et al.* 1992) are shown in Table 5.4. This was an orthodox adoption study, similar in design to those we have come across before, and some aspects of its results have been discussed in earlier chapters. The unique feature of the study is that although the adoptive families were all comfortably off, white, and middle class, only a small proportion of the adopted children were white; the remainder had at least one black parent. A follow-up study, 10 years later (Weinberg *et al.* 1992), traced the majority of the children when they were in their late teens; these results are also shown in Table 5.4.

It is worth concentrating first on the initial data reported by Scarr and Weinberg. At that time, the average IQ of the adoptive parents was approximately 120 and that of their own natural children 117. As can be seen, no group of adopted children achieved average IQ scores of this level, but it is evident that there was no significant difference between the scores of white adopted children and those of mixed parentage. However, the average IQ of the children of two black parents, although well above the mean of the black population, was some 12–14 points below that of the other two groups. Here is the first piece of evidence consistent with a genetic hypothesis, but to complicate matters, there were several clear differences between the circumstances of the children with two black parents and those of the other two groups. The former had been adopted at a later age and had thus been in their adoptive homes a substantially shorter time than the other two groups (at the time of the original test, for 3.5 years, on average, as opposed to 5 or 8 years). Their biological mothers, unlike the biological parents of any other group, had received less education than was normal for the population from which they came, and their adoptive parents were also less well educated than those of the other two groups of children. In other words, the study falls far short of the ideal we imagined at the outset, and its results are inherently somewhat unambiguous. It is possible that the 12–14-point gap between the

Table 5.4 IQ scores of adopted children in the Minnesota trans-racial adoption study

	Scarr and Weinberg (1976)	Weinberg *et al.* (1992)	
		Initial	10-year follow-up
Black	96.8	95.4	89.4
Black-White	109.0	109.5	98.5
White	111.5	117.6	105.6

adopted children reflects a genetic difference, but it is easy to point to environmental factors that were not matched between the groups.

The most striking feature of the follow-up data shown in Table 5.4 is the apparent decline in the IQ scores of all three groups of adopted children. According to Weinberg *et al.*, this is largely a consequence of changes in test norms. As we have seen before, if people are tested with an old IQ test, their scores will be inflated. If they are retested at a later date with a new test, their IQ will appear to have declined. Thus little should be read into this apparent change. However, one of its consequences is that the children with two black parents now obtained scores not greatly different from what one would have expected of a random sample of black children brought up by their own parents in a state such as Minnesota. The implication is that the experience of adoption by a white middle-class family has not done very much to raise their IQ. Perhaps it is not surprising that those committed to a genetic hypothesis (e.g. Lynn, 1994*a*) should have concentrated on this particular feature of the results, and that other commentators (e.g. Herrnstein and Murray, 1994) should have argued that it suggests that the environmental impact of adoption must have been very small. But other features of the data should not be ignored: the largest apparent decline in IQ was in fact shown by the white adopted children. It is also important to note that the sub-set of these children available for the follow-up study was a biased sample: their mean IQ score was 117.6, as opposed to 111.5 for the initial, complete sample of white adopted children. Once allowance is made for this fact, then, as can be seen in Table 5.4, there is no good evidence in the 10-year follow-up of any difference in average IQ between white and mixed-race adopted children.

Weinberg *et al.* carried out a step-wise multiple regression analysis to see what factor or factors best predicted the follow-up IQ scores. When biological parents' race was entered into the analysis first, it accounted for 16 per cent of the variance in test scores, and measures of the adoptive homes and the children's adoptive experience accounted for only an additional 7 per cent of the variance. However, when these environmental measures were entered into the analysis first, they accounted for 17 per cent of the variance and biological parents' race accounted for only 6 per cent more. In other words, genetic and environmental sources of variance were almost completely confounded, and as far as the data themselves are concerned, there would seem to be no good reason for accepting one interpretation rather than the other.

It is hardly surprising that natural experiments should usually fall short of perfection; none of the studies shown in Tables 5.3 and 5.4 is an exception to this rule. So there can be no question of their settling the issue once and for all. Two of the three studies provide no support for a genetic hypothesis at all. The third contains data that are certainly consistent with a partly genetic hypothesis. If it would be rash to argue that they refute the genetic hypothesis, it would surely be absurd to argue that, taken as a whole, they support it. If we recall the cautionary note sounded at the outset of this discussion—that in a racist society it will never be possible to bring up black and white children in truly comparable environments, the results of these studies are surely consistent with the possibility that if environmental differences between blacks and whites could be miraculously eliminated, the two groups might well obtain approximately equivalent IQ scores.

Environmental causes of black–white differences

In the light of this conclusion it is hard to see what Jensen could mean when he says that

> the preponderance of the evidence is consistent with the hypothesis that genetic as well as environmental factors are the cause of white black IQ differences. (Jensen, 1981, p. 231)

What is this other evidence that supports a genetic hypothesis? In practice, Jensen and others have relied not so much on evidence that specifically favours a genetic hypothesis as on arguments and evidence that, in their judgement, rule out any alternative explanation. If the difference between blacks and whites in average IQ is not due to genetic differences, then it would seem that it must be due to environmental differences. The only other possibility is that it is not a real difference at all, being a mere artefact of biased tests. Jensen has considered both of these possibilities at length and concluded that they are simply not viable. Therefore the genetic hypothesis wins by default. I shall defer the discussion of bias to a later part of this chapter and consider here the arguments and evidence that seem to discount the possibility that environmental differences might be sufficient to explain the observed differences in test scores.

Jensen's general argument takes various forms. Of course, he acknowledges, the environmental circumstances of blacks and whites differ in many ways. But in some cases, differences in IQ remain even when these differences in circumstance are allowed for, and in others there is simply no evidence that such circumstances affect performance on IQ tests in the first place. The acid test of an environmental hypothesis, as we have seen in Chapter 4, is to manipulate the putative environmental factor and record a change in IQ. If differences in education are responsible for differences in IQ between blacks and whites, why has compensatory education so signally failed to have any lasting impact on black children's IQ scores and why, in spite of all the social engineering and legislation of the 1960s and early 1970s in the United States, was the black–white difference in IQ at least as great in 1980 as it was in 1940? Finally, if poverty and discrimination are the cause of low black IQ, why is it that other ethnic groups, suffering from even greater poverty, and just as much discrimination, nevertheless obtain significantly higher IQ scores?

These are serious arguments, many with at least some face validity, and should be taken seriously; but, with the honourable exception of Flynn (1980, 1987*b,c*), Jensen's critics have rather consistently ignored them. For example, they have suggested numerous possible environmental causes of black–white differences in IQ, but many of these suggestions testify more to a determination to find possible explanations than to a willingness to examine the evidence seriously. Jensen is quite right to dismiss many of these explanations as nonsense. Thus a popular suggestion is that black children perform poorly on IQ tests because they are poorly motivated, or too anxious, or have low self-esteem. All of these factors do show modest correlations with test scores, but there is little reason to believe that blacks suffer any serious disadvantage; they perform just as well as whites on tests of attention, rote learning or memory, letter checking, or simple reaction time, all of which are highly sensitive to the effects of motivational variables (Jensen, 1980, 1981). Similarly, there have been reports of modest correlations between test scores, educational attainment, and children's self-esteem. But the evidence that black children, either in Great Britain or in the USA, suffer from any serious lack of self-esteem is at best equivocal (Mackintosh and Mascie-Taylor, 1986), and even if it were better, it would not follow that we had identified the *cause* of their poor performance. Measures of self-esteem invite children to agree or disagree with such propositions as 'I'm not doing as well in school as I'd like to' or 'I often get discouraged at school'. It is hardly surprising that children who, for whatever reason, are actually doing badly at school should agree with such statements. But their agreement might be a consequence of their poor performance, rather than its cause.

The self-esteem hypothesis usually forms part of a wider argument about the effects of white society and attitudes on black performance. On one version of this argument, the main reason why white children obtain higher IQ scores than blacks is because both groups of children have typically been tested by white examiners. One or two studies have provided some support for this suggestion by showing that children perform better when tested by an examiner of their own ethnic group, but the effect has been at best small, and the majority of studies have found no such effect—or even one in the opposite direction (Jensen, 1980). A more general version of the argument says that black children perform badly on IQ tests because their teachers expect no better from them. There is certainly evidence that white teachers often have low expectations for black children (Mackintosh and Mascie-Taylor, 1986), but it is harder to prove that this affects those children's IQ scores (see Box 5.2).

Perhaps the problem is not so much that white attitudes towards blacks depress black children's IQ scores, but rather that white parents' attitudes towards their own children, and the way they interact with them, is conducive to the development of high IQ scores, while black children, brought up by black parents with different attitudes and styles of interaction, end up with lower IQ scores. Such an argument has sometimes been advanced by critics who believe that IQ tests are simply a reflection of white, middle-class values, and thus inherently biased against blacks. And it has also been denounced by those who see it as a racist attack on black families, who are thus labelled as pathological and blamed for their children's poor performance. Without entering into either of these disputes, we can ask whether the basic argument has any validity. What would constitute relevant evidence? The answer, presumably, is another improbable adoption study in which matched groups of children (both black and white) were brought up by either black or white adoptive families, who were also matched for educational and socio-economic status. Needless to say, no such

> ## Box 5.2 'Pygmalion in the classroom'
>
> The notion that IQ scores could be affected by teachers' expectations was popularized in a celebrated study *Pygmalion in the classroom* (Rosenthal and Jacobson, 1968), which purported to show that children's IQ scores would increase dramatically if their teachers were led to believe that a special test administered to all children in class had identified these particular children as 'late bloomers' due to show a marked spurt within the next year. Sure enough, a small number of the late bloomers did show a greater increase in IQ than control children. Although the study achieved widespread fame, it is hard to take it seriously. For one thing the IQ tests were administered by the teachers themselves rather than by a trained tester; thus a teacher who had been told that a particular child should show an increase in IQ over the year was at liberty to ensure that just such an increase occurred. And some of the IQ scores obtained, which ranged from 0 to over 200, must mean either that the test was not being administered properly or that it was an absurd one. More important, although several ingenious and better-controlled studies have established that a teacher's expectations can significantly affect a child's general performance at school, few have supported Rosenthal and Jacobson's claim that IQ scores can be so affected (Elashoff and Snow, 1971; Snow, 1995; but see Rosenthal (1994) for a spirited defence). According to Snow's most recent analysis, the median effect size (i.e. difference between experimental and control children) of 16 later studies is $0.025d$ (standard deviation units), i.e. 0.4 of an IQ point. It is possible, of course, that the *actual* attitudes held by teachers in schools have an adverse effect on black children's IQ scores even though it is impossible to demonstrate this in the contrived setting of a psychological experiment, but the fact remains that it is an act of faith to believe this.

study has been done, but there is one American adoption study that compared the IQ scores of black or mixed-race children adopted either by black or by white middle-class families (Moore, 1986). Those adopted by white families obtained IQ scores some 10–15 points higher than those adopted by black families.

This is a substantial difference, nearly as large as that found between blacks and whites in the general US population. On the face of it, the implication is that, for whatever reason, children brought up in black families are disadvantaged when it comes to taking an IQ test, and Moore's observations on the different ways in which the two groups of adoptive parents interacted with their children when they were attempting to solve a block-design problem from the WISC adds further support to this suggestion. But the study was not without its problems. There may have been differences between the biological parents of the two groups of children. Although the two groups of adoptive mothers were well matched for educational level, the fathers were less well matched, and there may, of course, have been other, unmeasured differences between the adoptive families. But when all is said and done, the study does point to a possible environmental cause of IQ differences between blacks and whites.

By far the most popular environmental explanation of such differences, however, has been that which appeals to socio-economic circumstances. In any Western country with a significant black minority, that minority is poorer and suffers from greater social hardship than the white majority. We know that IQ is correlated with socio-economic circumstances in the white population, and in the USA at least, where more plentiful data are available, similar (although slightly smaller) correlations are observed between IQ and socio-economic status in blacks (see Fig. 5.3). It seems to follow that part of the difference in average IQ between blacks and whites must be accounted for by this massive difference in their social circumstances. Jensen has prudently acknowledged that these differences may be relevant, but he has insisted that they can do no more than nibble at the edges of the IQ gap. His argument is based on one empirical assertion and one theoretical consideration. First, he has argued, blacks and whites matched for SES still differ by at least 12 IQ points; thus, *at best*, socio-economic circumstances could account for no more than 20 per cent of the black–white difference. Figure 5.3 shows that although IQ is correlated with social class in both blacks and whites, there is still a large difference between the two groups within each class: indeed the difference tends to increase as one moves from lower to higher classes.

This last point has been documented in a number of other studies (see Herrnstein and Murray, 1994)—and poses something of a problem to those who would attribute blacks' low average IQ to the poverty of inner-city ghettos. But there is less reason to accept Jensen's central claim that matching for SES reduces black–white differences by no more than 20 per cent. In addition to his own data shown in Fig. 5.3, Jensen has relied on a large number of earlier studies, dating back to the 1930s, summarized by Shuey (1966). But the attempts to match the socio-economic status in these earlier studies were often laughably inadequate and the only sensible strategy is to look at later data. In seven studies published in the United States between 1965 and 1975, summarized by Loehlin *et al.* (1975, Table 7.4), the average difference in IQ between black and white children of the same social class was in fact only 7.5 IQ points. In Herrnstein and Murray's (1994) sample, socio-economic status accounted for 37 per cent of the difference between black and white IQ scores.

When a wider range of social circumstance is taken into account, the difference may be

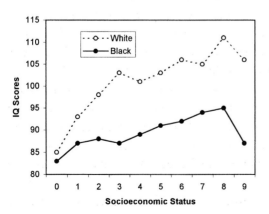

Fig. 5.3 Average IQ of blacks and whites as a function of social class (data from Jensen, 1981).

reduced even further. Mercer (1984) found that if differences in such factors as family size and structure and parental education were added to differences in parental occupation and income, they were sufficient to explain most of the differences in WISC scores in her sample of black, Hispanic, and white children. In two large British surveys, differences in IQ of 11 and 9 points between black and white children reduced to differences of 5.2 and 2.6 points respectively when the two groups of children were matched for a variety of social and family circumstances (Mackintosh and Mascie-Taylor, 1986). At the very least, it is surely not true to say that social and economic differences between blacks and whites *could not* be responsible for more than a trivial part of their difference in IQ.

But there is a further argument that can be advanced against the environmentalist here: a correlation between differences in social circumstances and differences in IQ is not sufficient to infer that the former causes the latter. To suppose this, is to commit what Jensen witheringly refers to as 'the sociologist's fallacy'. As we have already seen in this chapter, the correlation between socio-economic status and IQ is, in all probability, partly a genetic one, genes for high IQ causing high status rather than, or at least in addition to, favourable social circumstances causing high IQ. We can readily grant the truth of this general proposition. But it is not obvious that it will bear the weight Jensen places on it. In the present context, moreover, the argument implies a certain insensitivity to social reality, for it amounts to the assertion that blacks' low IQ scores are to blame for their low socio-economic status, rather than their low socio-economic status being responsible for their low IQ. But this is demonstrably false. In Great Britain, for example, there was ample evidence in the 1970s of discrimination against blacks in employment, such that a black youth needed significantly higher educational qualifications than a white to obtain the same job (Mackintosh and Mascie-Taylor, 1986). In the United States, Flynn (1987c) calculated from 1960 census figures that the average income and social status of blacks were very much worse than their IQ scores alone could ever have dictated. If we assume that blacks have an average IQ of 85, this figure is matched by the lowest 38 per cent of the white population. But this 38 per cent of the white population had an average family income and occupational status only half as far below the overall white mean as blacks. If parental income and occupation exerted any environmental effect on children's IQ scores at that time, then black children were suffering much more serious environmental disadvantage than whites of comparable IQ. So one should not reject this environmental explanation out of hand.

The implication of this environmental account is that any improvement in blacks' social and economic circumstances would ensure an improvement in their test scores. It is here that the environmentalists' position has been thought to be weakest: surely there have been massive changes in the socio-economic circumstances of blacks in the USA since 1920, but the black–white difference in average IQ has remained stubbornly fixed at about one standard deviation. There may indeed be a problem for an environmental explanation here, but the data need interpreting with some caution. It is not a simple matter to translate some of the earlier results, from the 1920s and 1930s, into modern test norms, and at least some of those earlier results suggest that the black–white difference was nearer 20 points than 15 at that time (Shuey, 1966). By 1970 or 1980, the difference was certainly no more than 15 points (see above). Moreover, as we have just seen, as recently as 1960 there was still a huge difference in the social circumstances and family income of American blacks and whites. But have there not been substantial changes since then? What have they done to close the IQ gap?

That there have been some improvements in the relative social circumstances of blacks in the USA over the past 30–40 years is certainly true. By the late 1980s, the discrepancy between black and white incomes was significantly reduced when they were matched for educational qualifications (Jencks, 1992); indeed, according to Herrnstein and Murray (1994) the discrepancy was virtually abolished when they matched for IQ. And there is good evidence that discrepancies in educational qualifications have greatly diminished, with a substantial decline in the proportion of blacks dropping out of high school—down from 28 per cent in 1970 to 15 per cent in 1988 (Jencks, 1992), and an equally substantial increase in the proportion attending university (Herrnstein and Murray, 1994).

Have these changes had any effect? They have certainly improved blacks' scores on many standard tests of educational attainment: according to Herrnstein and Murray (1994), the discrepancy between blacks' and whites' attainment in maths, science, and reading decreased by about 0.30 of a standard deviation between 1970 and 1990. But what of IQ? In the adult standardization sample of the WAIS-R, tested in 1981, the black–white difference was still 15 points. But this is hardly an appropriate measure of the impact of changes in educational and family circumstances that had started only 10–15 years earlier. At least some recent studies with children have suggested that the black–white difference may be decreasing slightly. Lynn (1996*b*), analysing data on children aged 6–17 years in the 1986 standardization of the Differential Ability Scale, found differences between blacks and whites ranging from 10.4 to 13.5 points. And Vincent (1991) has reported that differences on tests such as Ravens' Matrices or the Stanford–Binet may be no more than 7–12 points. If these findings prove reliable, they suggest a significant decrease in the black–white difference.

Set against this, one unwelcome possibility should be acknowledged (Flynn, 1992). As we saw in Chapter 4, for most of the twentieth century, there appears to have been a small negative correlation in the USA between IQ and fertility: by and large, adults of lower IQ have tended to have rather more children than those of higher IQ. The effect is not large, and has clearly been counteracted by others that have caused a steady rise in test scores. But there is some evidence that this 'dysgenic' tendency has been larger in some ethnic minorities, including blacks, than in whites (Flynn, 1992; Herrnstein and Murray, 1994; Lynn, 1996*a*). If that is true, it is likely to have worked against any factor tending to reduce the average black–white difference over time.

A common, and usually well merited, criticism of environmental hypotheses about IQ is that their proponents cannot identify the environmental variables presumed to affect IQ, let alone specify their mode of action. That is no doubt true in the present case also—although there is at least some evidence that differences in average IQ between blacks and whites are partly attributable to differences in social, economic, and educational circumstances, and partly, perhaps, to differences in the nature and pattern of parental and family interactions. But the fact that it is impossible to specify what are the environmental influences on IQ is not sufficient to prove that the only influences must be genetic ones. We know that within-family environmental differences have substantial impact on IQ, but have virtually no idea what they may be (Chapter 4). As Flynn (1987*a*,*b*) has argued, it is an undeniable fact that test scores increased substantially, probably by some 10–20 points, in virtually all industrialized societies in the 50 years immediately following the Second World War. Thus the test scores of US blacks in 1995 were much the same as those of US whites in 1945. Although we have no serious idea about which factors are responsible for these changes over time, there can be no doubt that they are environmental. By the same token, then, even if we cannot identify the environmental factors responsible for differences in IQ between blacks and whites, that is no reason for asserting that the difference *must* be partly genetic.

Other ethnic groups

Although the difference in IQ between blacks and whites in the USA has dominated discussion, it is not the only difference between ethnic groups in average IQ. In various reviews, Lynn (1978, 1991, 1997) has argued that there are significant differences between English, Scots, and Irish; between northern and southern Europeans; between Europeans and inhabitants of the Middle East or Indian subcontinent; between whites and blacks in Africa and whites and Aboriginals in Australia; and between Japanese and Chinese and everyone else. Within the USA, there are some differences between American Indians and those of European ancestry, and between the latter and those of Mexican, Puerto Rican, Japanese, or Chinese ancestry (Loehlin *et al.*, 1975).

Jensen has used some of these comparisons as further evidence that blacks' poor test scores cannot be attributed to their poor socio-economic circumstances:

> In a very large nation-wide survey [Coleman, 1966] it was found that on a composite of twelve SES and other environmental indices, the American Indian population ranks about as far below black standards as blacks rank below those of whites . . . But it turns out that Indians score *higher* than blacks on tests of intelligence and scholastic achievement. (Jensen, 1981, p. 217)

Coleman in fact found no difference in verbal IQ and only a small difference in non-verbal IQ between American Indians and northern, urban blacks: it was southern, rural blacks who pulled down the black mean. Moreover other studies, summarized by Lynn (1991), have provided little evidence of the difference Jensen claims. In 14 studies, the median overall IQ scores of American Indians was 88, with a verbal IQ of 79.5. The only notable difference from blacks was in tests of specifically visuo-spatial ability, where their score was 98.5.

British comparisons of children of West Indian, Indian, or Pakistani origin provide an independent test of the possibility that blacks obtain lower scores than other ethnic groups in spite of being less impoverished. In the NCDS data, in 1969, West Indian children obtained significantly lower IQ scores than either whites or Asians (not at that time differentiated into those of Indian or Pakistani origin). As can be seen in the top-left panel of Fig. 5.4, Asians and whites did not differ from one another. But, as can be seen in the lower left panel, this may be related to the fact that there was essentially no difference in the average social circumstances of whites and Asians, both of whom were better off than West Indian children. By 1980, however, there had been significant changes. The CHES data revealed that the most impoverished group was now those of Pakistani origin (and that all three ethnic minorities were now worse off than whites). But as the top right panel of Fig. 5.4 shows, the Pakistani children also obtained lower test scores than the West Indian—a difference that seems to have persisted through the 1980s (West *et al.*, 1992). Taken as a whole, the data shown in Fig. 5.4 imply a rather close relationship between a group's social circumstances and their IQ scores.

A rather longer historical view of the experience of other ethnic groups in the United States may also help to put the black–white difference in test scores in better perspective (Sowell, 1981; Flynn, 1992). At one time or another virtually every group of recent

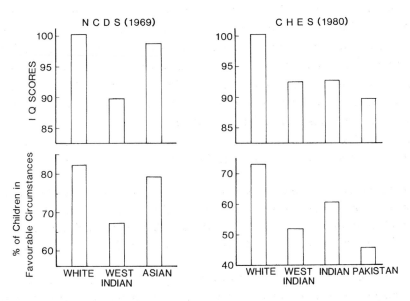

Fig. 5.4 Average IQ scores and social circumstances of different ethnic groups in Britain. The top two panels show the IQ scores of representative samples of white, Asian, and West Indian children in 1969, and of white, Indian, Pakistani, and West Indian children in 1980. The lower two panels show comparable data for the social circumstances of these groups of children. (Data from Mackintosh and Mascie-Taylor, 1986.)

immigrants has been found intellectually wanting. The First World War army data established that Italians, Poles, and Russians obtained test scores little better than those of blacks. And since at least half the immigrants from Poland and Russia were Jewish, these data were even said to 'disprove the popular belief that the Jew is highly intelligent' (Brigham, 1923, p. 190). Other studies in the 1920s, cited by Sowell (1978), reported average IQ scores below 90 for Slovaks, Greeks, Spanish, Portuguese, Slavs, Croatian, and Lithuanian immigrants. Irish and Italian immigrants remained most suspect. Although the peak rate of Irish immigration to the USA had been in the middle of the nineteenth century, the army test data revealed that the test scores of the Irish were below those of every other northern European group, and higher only than those of immigrants from southern and eastern Europe. Italian immigrants continued to be a cause for concern and gloom throughout the 1920s and 1930s. Even though the vast majority of Italian immigrants arrived before the First World War, Italian children in New York schools still obtained IQ scores well below the national average, and dropped out of school at an earlier age with fewer qualifications than other groups. Few commentators found this surprising: immigration from Italy had been overwhelmingly from the poor, rural south; it was only to be expected that the children of illiterate peasants should remain illiterate. Since they obtained poor scores not only on verbal, but also on non-verbal IQ tests, and since other non-English speaking immigrant groups obtained very much better scores on the latter type of test, a common interpretation was that they had inherited their parents' inferior mental capacities (see Sarason and Doris (1979) for an illuminating discussion).

In so far as the descendants of any of these groups can still be identified, by 1960–70 they were all obtaining IQ scores of at least 100 (Sowell, 1978). What seemed, to an earlier generation of commentators, to be immutable defects of innate character and intellect have blown away as though they had never been. It is a cautionary tale, worth bearing in mind when similar pronouncements are made about the intelligence of American blacks—some of whom were still living in strict segregation in the rural south as recently as the 1960s, while others continue to live in poor inner-city ghettos attending schools that are still, in effect, largely segregated.

Japanese and Chinese

In the past 25 years, a new group difference has threatened to displace that between blacks and whites as the main focus of attention and concern. Several commentators have argued that just as blacks lag behind whites, so do whites lag behind other ethnic groups— sometimes referred to as Mongoloids or east Asians (Lynn, 1991; Rushton, 1995). To be slightly more specific I shall talk of Chinese and Japanese, for whom most data are available. Vernon (1982) reviewed the earlier American studies, some dating back to the 1920s, of children of Japanese and Chinese origin, mostly resident in Hawaii and

California. He concluded that although such children had always scored lower than whites on verbal IQ tests, by 1980 this gap was no more than 2 or 3 points at most, and since their non-verbal IQ scores had always been some 10–12 points higher than their verbal scores, in the more recent studies they were now obtaining non-verbal scores of 110 or more, well above the white mean. That Japanese children outscored whites on non-verbal IQ seemed to be confirmed by an analysis of the Japanese standardization of the WISC-R (Lynn, 1982; Lynn and Hampson, 1986*b*). Here again there was a difference of some dozen points between the children's non-verbal and verbal IQ scores, the latter just below and the former apparently some 10 points above the white mean.

If Japanese or Chinese average no more than 1–3 points below whites on verbal IQ, but outscore them by 10 or more points on non-verbal IQ, their overall, full-scale IQ score must be significantly higher than that of whites. The gap was estimated by Lynn as about 5–6 points. This may be only a third of the gap between North American blacks and whites, but it is hardly trivial. And in the USA, at least, the actual achievements of citizens of Chinese and Japanese origin seemed to bear out these differences. Like other immigrant groups, of course, they initially suffered poverty and discrimination, exacerbated in the case of the Japanese from California by the outbreak of the Second World War, when they were deprived of much of their property and confined in prison camps (Sowell, 1981). Since then, however, they have rapidly become one of the most successful groups in American society, obtaining significantly higher educational qualifications and more prestigious jobs than whites. For example, the 1980 US census showed that 35 per cent of Asian adults had college degrees compared to only 17 per cent of whites, while 43 per cent of Chinese but only 27 per cent of white adults held professional, managerial, or technical jobs (Flynn, 1992). Nor was this only a recent phenomenon: Weyl (1969) analysed the 1960 census and showed that even then Chinese Americans were substantially over-represented in all professions except law.

Admission to higher education and success in obtaining professional or managerial jobs are correlated with IQ scores. It is hardly surprising then that above-average IQ should translate into above-average educational and occupational attainment. Indeed, Flynn (1992) calculated that the actual achievements of Chinese and Japanese in the United States were commensurate with average IQs of 120 and 110 respectively, relative to a putative white mean of 100. In other words, given the known relationship between IQ and achievement in the white population, a group of whites that matched Chinese in terms of actual achievement would have an average IQ of 120. This is a quite startling gap, much greater than has ever been suggested on the basis of IQ tests themselves. It therefore comes as even more of a surprise to find that Flynn's analysis of the actual IQ data led him to conclude that in all probability neither Japanese nor Chinese Americans have an overall average IQ any higher than that of whites.

How can this be? Flynn's conclusion seems to raise more questions than answers. In the first place, how can Vernon have believed that Chinese and Japanese obtained scores well above the white mean? Flynn's argument was that the studies that Vernon relied on were faulty on at least one or other of two counts. Where they provided direct comparison with whites, the samples were not adequately representative of their respective populations; and where they provided comparison against supposed white norms, those norms were seriously out of date. The latter, more important problem simply amounts to this: if test scores are steadily improving over time, then a group that obtains an apparent average IQ of 110 on a test standardized 30 years ago may not be above average at all. Flynn's analyses are generally convincing, and are, by and large, supported by the few studies that surveyed large representative samples of different ethnic groups at the same time. The largest single study is the Coleman Report, the results of which are summarized in Table 5.5. There is no evidence here that Chinese and Japanese obtain scores higher than the white mean, and since these results are based on sample sizes of 1000 at each of five ages, it is hard to see why their message should be rejected. In two of the five age groups, the Chinese/Japanese non-verbal score was below the white mean, and only at the youngest age level of all did the Chinese and Japanese children obtain substantially higher non-verbal scores than whites.

It is possible that the position has changed since the Coleman Report data were collected: the growing discrepancy since the 1960s between the educational and economic achievements of Chinese or Japanese and whites may have been accompanied by an increasing divergence between their children's IQ scores. Three later studies are consistent with this possibility. Stone (1992) and Lynn (1996*b*) analysed the 1988 and 1986 standardization data for the Differential Aptitudes Test and Differential Ability Scale, respectively, and reported that the Chinese and Asian samples obtained higher scores than whites on both non-verbal and spatial tests, the differences being of the order of 5 IQ points. Herrnstein and Murray (1994) reported a 3-point IQ difference in favour of Chinese, Japanese, and Koreans in their national sample. Unfortunately, although all these studies took representative cross-sections of the entire US population, for precisely that

Table 5.5 IQ scores of American children of Japanese or Chinese ancestry in the Coleman Report

Grade	Non-verbal	Verbal	Overall
1	104.1	97.0	100.5
3	97.6	93.9	95.7
6	95.5	93.6	94.6
9	101.2	95.8	98.5
12	100.2	96.7	98.5

The scores shown are set against white means of 100. According to Flynn (1992), the twelfth grade scores may underestimate true scores by 0.9 IQ points, since more whites than Chinese or Japanese left school before twelfth grade: in other words, the Chinese and Japanese twelfth grade students are a less selected sub-set of the population.

reason the numbers of people of Chinese, Japanese, or Korean ancestry were very small—less than 50 in each study. It would be somewhat rash to place more weight on these results than on those analysed by Flynn. In a substantially larger study, Jensen and Whang (1993) obtained scores on Raven's Matrices from 167 9–11-year-old children of Chinese origin in California, and 585 white children. They found an approximately 5-point difference in their IQ scores. If this sort of difference can be confirmed, it would suggest the possibility that the superior educational and occupational qualifications of earlier generations of Chinese Americans is being translated into superior IQ scores in their children.

What of the data from Chinese and Japanese children in Japan and China themselves? Flynn argued that here too there may be problems of unrepresentative sampling. Japanese standardization groups are not stratified by socio-economic status in the same way as in Western countries, but only in terms of such categories as government or private employee, or farm worker. Where smaller samples have been used, there are virtually insuperable difficulties in ensuring that they have been truly representative. But there is an even more serious problem in attempting to compare the IQ scores of people from different countries and cultures, especially on tests such as the Wechsler scales. How, for example, could one possibly establish that the translation of the Wechsler vocabulary sub-test into another language had resulted in a test of comparable difficulty? Even when there is no language difference between two populations, there are likely to be cultural differences. The point is easily illustrated by considering two countries as similar as the USA and Britain. The WAIS Information sub-test was modified for the British version of the test—questions about US presidents, for example, being changed into ones about British prime ministers. But the modifications were few and, quite obviously, wholly inadequate. Thus the original version of the WAIS contained the following item: 'Longfellow was a famous man; what was he?' Unsurprisingly, this turns out to be a harder question for a British than for an American audience. But what should the British translators of the WAIS have done? One obvious answer would be to have substituted a British poet for Longfellow. But who? Chaucer? Dunbar? Donne? Pope? Browning? Housman? The answer can only be found by trial and error. What is needed is a poet that is as well known to the British as Longfellow is to Americans. And what that in effect means is that the translators must demonstrate that the percentage of the British standardization sample that answers the question correctly is the same as the percentage of the American standardization sample who knew who Longfellow was. But now, when they have done this for every other item in the test, they will have guaranteed that British and Americans obtain identical IQ scores. And what will that have proved?

The comparison of average IQ scores of different nationalities is, at best, a hazardous enterprise, to be undertaken with caution and humility, and at worst, a nonsensical and mischievous waste of time. So, although Lynn (1991, 1997) has marshalled an apparently impressive array of studies suggesting that the average IQ of Japanese in Japan, and of Chinese in Singapore, Hong Kong, Taiwan, and mainland China, is a few points higher than that of British or Americans, we should not *necessarily* be convinced. Even Lynn acknowledges, when confronted with a verbal IQ score of over 120 in a study of Japanese children, that the vocabulary items may have been 'rendered too easy' for Japanese children. The conservative conclusion is that Flynn is probably right: there is no good reason to believe that Chinese or Japanese *seriously* outscore whites on general IQ tests. But even if he were wrong, and Lynn were correct in his assumption that their overall IQ is nearly 5 points above the white mean, we still have a problem on our hands. How are we to account for the actual achievement of Chinese and Japanese in the United States? If Chinese Americans obtain the educational qualifications and jobs commensurate with an average IQ of 120, but actually have an average IQ of only 100–105, how are we to explain the discrepancy? Perhaps the simplest answer is to remember that IQ is not the only predictor of educational or occupational attainment. Hard work, diligence, and ambition may be equally important ingredients of success. This not very surprising conclusion will need bearing in mind when we return, in Chapter 10, to the question of what IQ tests do and do not measure.

Finally, we should also consider why it is that Chinese and Japanese children typically obtain so much higher scores on non-verbal than on verbal IQ tests. At one time this can hardly have seemed surprising, given that children of Chinese or Japanese immigrants in the United States would have been living in homes where the first language was not English. But according to Vernon (1982), the discrepancy was just as great when the children spoke only English, and, where data were available, the correlation between children's verbal IQ and the amount of English spoken in the home was trivially small. Moreover, there is still a large discrepancy between verbal and non-verbal IQ scores obtained by Japanese children in Japan when tested on the Japanese translation of the WISC. Unless that translation has made the verbal scale notably harder than the performance scale (and what would count as evidence of that?), it seems more plausible to conclude that the difference is a genuine one. A better clue to one possible meaning of this discrepancy is provided by an analysis of Japanese children's scores on individual sub-tests of the WISC-R (Lynn and Hampson, 1986*b*). The data are shown in Fig. 5.5. Except on arithmetic and digit span the children obtained scores on all verbal sub-tests uniformly below than the white mean. This difference in arithmetic scores (which increased as the children grew older) seems most plausibly attributed to the greater emphasis placed in Japanese schools on formal mathematical teaching—an emphasis which has resulted in Japanese children far outscoring those of most Western countries on tests of mathematical attainment at age 16 or more (Vernon, 1982). The most striking feature of Fig. 5.5, however, is that the Japanese superiority on non-verbal tests was in large part due to a single sub-test, block design, where their score, if turned into an overall IQ, would give them an average IQ of over 125. The difference between Japanese and white children on the remaining non-verbal WISC tests amounted to no more than 2 or 3 points. The most plausible explanation for Japanese children's remarkable scores on block design is that it is the one sub-test in the WISC that taps a specifically spatial component of IQ. There is indeed good evidence that Japanese and

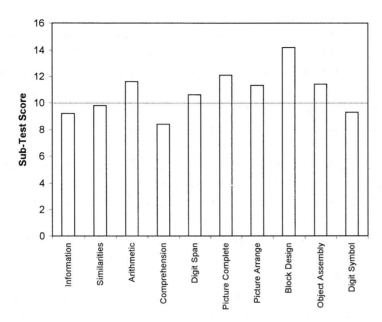

Fig. 5.5 Average scores on sub-tests of the WISC-R obtained by the Japanese standardization sample. The notional mean score of the American standardization sample on each sub-test is 10.0, with a standard deviation of 3.0. (Data from Lynn and Hampson, 1986*b*.)

Chinese children (as well as, perhaps, American Indians, see above, p. 163) obtain relatively high scores on spatial IQ tests (e.g. Lynn *et al.*, 1988*b*; Nagoshi and Johnson, 1987). To the extent that other non-verbal tests include spatial sub-tests or components, this may contribute to differences between Japanese or Chinese and other groups in non-verbal IQ.

The difference in spatial IQ scores, which certainly seems quite general, may or may not have a genetic component. There is really no good evidence to answer such a question one way or the other. There is certainly no evidence to suggest that any other differences in IQ scores between Chinese or Japanese and white Americans (which may well not be real anyway) are caused by genetic differences between these groups.

Test bias

The most popular reaction to the discovery of differences between ethnic groups in average test scores is to blame the tests. If blacks have a lower average IQ than whites, this can only be because IQ tests are biased against them—and not only against blacks, but also against any other group that obtains low scores.

> Social class and black-white differences were probably built in when the tests were constructed . . . The test questions often reflect the white middle-class academic milieu of their constructors rather than any culture free conception of human cognition. (Evans and Waites, 1981, p. 168)

This sounds quite reasonable: how could a comfortable, white professor of psychology pretend that he knows what constitutes intelligent behaviour in a black ghetto or village in Bangladesh? His conception of intelligence, and the tests he constructs to measure it, can only reflect his own parochial prejudices. Is it any wonder that other groups should be penalized when they are measured by these tests?

The argument seems even more plausible when one stops to look at some of the items that actually appear in IQ tests such as the Stanford–Binet or Wechsler tests. For example, the aesthetic comparison item from the Stanford–Binet test asks the child to say which of two drawings of faces is the prettier. Several critics (e.g. Karier, 1972; Block and Dworkin, 1976) have insisted that this item must discriminate against blacks and other ethnic groups since the correct answer is invariably the conventional middle-class white face, while the incorrect answer often has features popularly attributed to people from other groups. The comprehension sub-test of the WAIS and WISC has equally come in for criticism as a repository of white, middle-class values, with questions that ask one the meaning of various proverbs or what is the right or proper thing to do in certain everyday social circumstances.

However plausible they may seem, not all these arguments withstand serious scrutiny. For example, the standardization of the Stanford–Binet reveals that the aesthetic comparison item is the easiest in the whole test for black children, but only the third easiest for whites (Jensen, 1980, p. 5). Similar analyses of the actual performance of black and white children on various items in the WISC, widely thought to be particularly biased against blacks, have found no evidence that these items are any harder than others for blacks (Gutkin and Reynolds, 1981; McLoughlin and Koh, 1982). There is thus no evidence that these particular items are particularly biased against blacks.

Indeed, as can be seen in Fig. 5.6, the standardization data of the WISC-R make it plain that black children obtained, on average, lower scores than whites on *all* sub-tests. The black–white difference is larger on some sub-tests than on others, being particularly small on digit span and coding, but when one of the largest differences is on the block design test, it is hard to sustain the argument that it is items with transparently white, middle-class values that particularly discriminate against blacks.

As we saw in Chapters 1 and 2, non-verbal or performance tests (such as block design) had their origins in the US Army First World War beta tests, being specifically designed for those whose level of literacy appeared insufficient for the written, alpha tests. Subsequently, such tests were elaborated and expanded in a specific attempt to provide a supposedly fairer assessment of the intelligence of minority groups. Cattell, for example, explicitly described his tests of diagrammatic series completion, classification, and matrices, as a 'culture-fair' intelligence test (Cattell, 1940).

But now the finding that blacks perform just as badly on such 'culture-fair' tests has led some people to argue that their deficit must be real—by which they presumably mean, at least partly genetic in origin (Jensen, 1973; Nichols, 1987). It is important to see that this argument is no more valid than that which sought to dismiss the black–white difference as

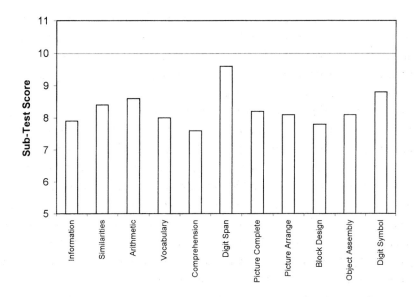

Fig. 5.6 Average scores on sub-tests of the WISC-R obtained by American blacks in the American standardization sample. A score of 10 is the mean sub-test score for the entire standardization sample. (Data from Gutkin and Reynolds, 1981.)

the product of a few, palpably 'unfair' items. Indeed it is based on much the same unstated assumption—that some items are unfair because they clearly reflect middle-class values, while others, which do not, must therefore be fair in the sense of providing an accurate assessment of anyone's inborn intelligence uncomplicated by differences in their social and cultural experiences. But it is quite false to suppose that just because tests like the block design (or Cattell's tests or Raven's Matrices) are non-verbal and embody no superficially middle-class values, they are providing a more direct measure of 'innate intelligence' than do verbal tests. There is, in fact, no evidence to show that the heritability of scores on Raven's Matrices or other supposedly culture-fair non-verbal tests is substantially higher than that of scores on the Wechsler verbal scale or Stanford–Binet test (see Chapter 9), and no reason to suppose that the ability to solve arbitrary abstract problems, such as those found in Raven's tests, is any less a learnt skill than the ability to do mental arithmetic or answer questions about the meanings of words. As we saw in Chapter 4, schooling may have just as profound an effect on non-verbal as on verbal IQ scores (Stelzl *et al.*, 1995). Consistent with this, as is shown in Table 5.6, studies of immigrant children in Britain have found dramatic increases in scores on these tests the longer the children have been resident and received their education in Britain.

Table 5.6 Indian children's non-verbal IQ scores as a function of length of residence in Britain (from Sharma, 1971)

	WISC performance	Raven's Matrices
Living in India	76	81
Less than 2 years in Britain	84	84
More than 6 years in Britain	99	104

All children were born in a single district of the Punjab in northern India.

Bias as underestimate of 'true' score

This discussion of test bias has rehearsed a number of popular arguments, but all too often those arguments have been based on little more than intuition or preconception and are not supported by the available evidence. Mere inspection of an item in an IQ test is not sufficient to prove that item biased against any particular group. But it is equally insufficient to prove the contrary. The discussion will make no progress until we stop to ask what it *means* to say that an IQ test is biased against a particular group. It may help if we start by showing what it does not, and cannot, mean. Taken as a whole, the evidence reviewed in the preceding section did not provide very strong support for the view that differences in IQ between, for example, blacks and whites are substantially genetic in origin. Let us suppose, for the sake of argument, that new evidence appeared which rendered this conclusion impregnable: a perfectly designed adoption study revealed identical average IQ scores for black and white children brought up in comparable circumstances, and everyone conceded that there is no difference in genetic potential between blacks and whites. Yet there would still be a large difference in measured IQ, for our new evidence would not cause the 10- to 15-point difference between American blacks and whites to vanish. Would this not now mean that there must be something wrong with the tests—that they must be biased against blacks?

It is very important to see just what is wrong with this argument. It contains an unstated premise, namely that IQ tests measure, and are supposed to measure, genetic potential. If this premise were actually true then there is no doubt that the conclusion would follow: if IQ tests revealed a difference when none existed, then they would be biased against blacks, for they have underestimated what they purport to measure. But the premise is false: IQ tests do not, and do not purport to, measure anybody's genotypic intelligence. If they did, there would be no question, for example, of trying to estimate the heritability of IQ scores: it would by definition be 1.0. An IQ test provides an estimate of a person's 'intelligence' only if that is understood to mean their actual intellectual accomplishments, knowledge, skills, and abilities, in other words, their phenotypic intelligence. We know that IQ scores are subject both to environmental and to genetic influence, and that it is quite possible, therefore, for two people or two groups to differ in phenotypic IQ even though their genetic potential for IQ is exactly the same. Blaming IQ tests for revealing large differences between various groups, as Vernon has remarked,

> is rather like blaming the weighing machine when it shows an undernourished child to be below normal weight. (Vernon, 1969, p. 70)

Of course a starved child will weigh less than a well-fed one, and there would be something seriously wrong with the weighing machine that failed to detect this difference; weighing machines are meant to measure what people weigh (phenotypic weight) not their genotype. If IQ benefits from environmental factor X and two groups differ in their exposure to factor X, then the group denied exposure will have a lower average IQ than the other. If it is true that black children are brought up in an environment unfavourable to the development of the knowledge, skills, and abilities measured by standard IQ tests then, of course, they will obtain relatively low IQ scores.

What then does it mean to talk about test bias? The proper meaning of bias is quite clear. A test that purports to measure a particular psychological character X is biased against a particular group if it systematically underestimates that group's true level of X. Since IQ tests purport to measure intelligence only in the sense of actual intellectual functioning, they are biased against blacks if they underestimate black people's true level of intellectual functioning—if, say, a black person with an IQ of 85 was in fact performing at the same intellectual level as a white person with an IQ of 100. In order to establish bias, therefore, we need to be able to ascertain the true level of intellectual functioning of the black population. But how shall we do that? It seems to require that we have an alternative, independent measure of intellectual functioning, against which we could compare our IQ tests. But what would that be?

The fact of the matter is, of course, that we have no such alternative measure of intelligence. If we did, the question whether IQ tests *really* measure intelligence would have been answered long ago—if indeed anyone had ever bothered to construct an IQ test. All that we have are various more or less imperfect indices of intellectual functioning—for example, the traditional criteria against which IQ tests have been validated, such as educational and occupational attainment. So all we can actually do is to ascertain whether IQ tests underestimate the level of intelligence or intellectual functioning implied by these other indices. The answer we get will be no better than these other indices themselves.

Evidence of bias?

Since IQ tests were originally designed to distinguish between those children capable of learning effectively in ordinary school classes and those who, for whatever reason, were unable to, performance in school or other assessments of educational attainment have always remained the principal external criterion for validating IQ tests. Thus, if the definition of bias

Table 5.7 Correlations between IQ scores and measures of educational attainment in various ethnic groups

| | American data (Reschly and Sabers, 1979) | | | | British data (Mackintosh and Mascie-Taylor, 1986) | | | |
	Whites	Blacks	Mexican American	American Indian	Whites	Blacks	Indian	Pakistani
Reading	0.59	0.64	0.55	0.45	0.74	0.75	0.77	0.75
Maths	0.55	0.52	0.52	0.41	0.74	0.72	0.72	0.74

in a test is systematic failure to predict a criterion performance, IQ tests will be deemed biased against blacks or other ethnic groups if they fail to predict how well they do at school.

Despite widespread belief to the contrary, however, there is ample evidence, both in Britain and the USA, that IQ tests predict educational attainment just about as well in ethnic minorities as in the white majority (Herrnstein and Murray, 1994; Jensen, 1980; Mackintosh and Mascie-Taylor, 1986). That IQ tests predict school attainment in whites is established by showing a correlation between the two. Similar correlations are found in blacks and other ethnic groups. Table 5.7 shows the results of two typical studies. The difference between the overall level of correlation in the two studies (presumably due to differences in the tests employed and perhaps in the ages of the children) is very much greater than any difference between groups within either study.

Table 5.7 makes it clear that, for minority groups as well as whites, a child with a higher IQ is likely to do better on tests of reading and maths than one with a lower IQ. But IQ scores might still systematically underestimate minority group children's attainments. A black child with an IQ of 100, for example, might do better at reading and maths than one with an IQ of 85—but he might also do better than a white child with an IQ of 100. The possibility can be tested by performing a regression analysis. Figure 5.7 plots the hypothetical scores of a group of white children on an IQ test and on some measure of school attainment. The line drawn through these points is the best-fitting straight regression line to the data, and allows us to predict, for example, that a child with an IQ score of, say, 85 will be likely to obtain a score of 25 on the attainment test, while one with an IQ of 115 would be likely to obtain a score of 45. We can now ask what would happen if we plotted black children's scores: would their best-fitting regression line fall on top of the white children's, or above or below it? Figure 5.7 shows two possible black regression lines, B1 above, and B2 below, the white regression line. According to B1, two black children with IQs of 85 and 115 are obtaining attainment scores of 30 and 50, i.e. better than those of white children of comparable IQ. With line B2, however, IQs of 85 and 115 are associated with attainment scores of only 20 and 40. If B1 is the appropriate regression line for blacks, their IQ scores do indeed *under*estimate their attainment scores; if B2 is the best-fitting line, IQ *over*estimates attainment; while if their regression line is not significantly different from line W, the IQ scores predict exactly the same attainment scores in blacks as in whites.

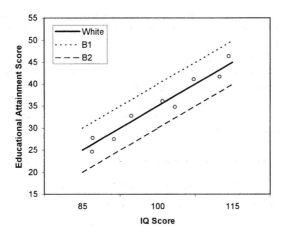

Fig. 5.7 Hypothetical scores obtained by a group of white children on an IQ test and on a measure of school attainment. Each individual child's scores are shown by a dot. The line, W, drawn through these points is the best-fitting regression line. Lines B1 and B2 are two hypothetical regression lines that might be obtained for a group of black children.

The results of a very large number of studies, mostly American but also some British, tell the same story: IQ scores do *not* systematically underestimate the educational attainments of blacks or most other ethnic minorities (Herrnstein and Murray, 1994; Jensen, 1980; Mackintosh and Mascie-Taylor, 1986). The only exception to this generalization is in the case of Americans of Chinese or Japanese ancestry (see above). In other words, the regression lines relating IQ and attainment tend to be very close. Where there is any discrepancy, it is in the direction of line B2 in Fig. 5.7: in other words, IQ scores are, if anything, slightly *over*estimating educational attainment. The largest single study, the American Coleman Report, provides some of the most convincing evidence: Jensen's analyses suggest that blacks' IQ scores, especially on non-verbal tests, tended to overestimate their scholastic attainment quite significantly (Jensen, 1980). A similar picture is provided by American data on the relationship between scholastic aptitude tests (SAT-V and SAT-M), which are used for college entrance exams, and subsequent performance in college. If college grade point average is used as the measure of attainment, it is predicted by SAT scores just about equally well for blacks and whites (Manning and Jackson, 1984). Where there is any difference, the typical finding (true in 18 of 22 comparisons reviewed by Linn, 1973) is that SAT tests slightly overestimate black students' subsequent grades.

There is equally little evidence that IQ tests underestimate blacks' performance on the other traditional criterion used to validate IQ—how well people do their job. IQ scores are used, more commonly in the USA than in Europe, to screen applicants for jobs and to determine job allocation and promotion. Several American studies have sought to justify this practice by examining the relationship between IQ test scores and performance on the job (Jensen, 1980; Hunter *et al.*, 1984; Hartigan and Wigdor, 1989; see Chapter 2). Over a wide variety of jobs, there is no evidence that test scores show lower correlations with various indices of job performance in blacks than in whites, and no evidence at all of any systematic underestimate of the performance of blacks. As with educational attainment, so with occupational proficiency: where there is any discrepancy, IQ scores *tend* to overestimate job performance (this was true in 60 of the 72 studies reviewed by Hartigan and Wigdor, 1989). It should be stressed that the criterion employed in these studies is usually some index of how well a particular job is being performed, not the status of the job itself. We have already seen that blacks have in the past often needed higher qualifications than whites in order to obtain a job in the first place.

It is of some practical importance to know that IQ scores predict both educational attainment and occupational performance just about as well for blacks as they do for whites—and certainly do not *under*estimate black people's proficiency in these areas. IQ tests are still used for purposes of selection in both cases, and if it turned out that they discriminated against black applicants by underestimating their performance, such use would clearly be unjustified. But the point from which we started was not the practical question of whether the use of IQ tests for selection is or is not fair; it was whether they are biased against blacks in the sense of underestimating their true level of intellectual functioning. There is an important sense in which this question remains unanswered. True, the data on educational and occupational attainment do not provide any positive evidence of bias against blacks. But it is, after all, entirely possible that educational attainment is just as serious an underestimate of blacks' true level of intellectual performance as are IQ tests themselves. This is hardly a fanciful suggestion: it is not difficult to think of reasons why black schoolchildren might not do as well at school as their abilities dictate. There is ample scope for discrimination and oppression to affect what children actually manage to achieve at school or students at university or college. As noted earlier (Box 5.2), subsequent attempts to replicate Rosenthal and Jacobson's *Pygmalion in the classroom* (1978) found no effect of teachers' opinions on children's IQ scores, but significant effects on other indices of school attainment (Elashoff and Snow, 1971; Snow, 1995). If teachers do indeed have a low opinion of the abilities of black children, they are more likely to depress their educational attainment than their IQ scores. It follows, therefore, that actual educational attainment might well be an even more biased measure of black children's intellectual competence than an IQ test.

Must we conclude, then, that the question is unanswerable—that we will never know whether IQ tests underestimate blacks' intellectual competence? Only if we accept that educational attainment and job performance are the only possible criteria against which to validate the tests. That seems unduly pessimistic. Consider one other use to which IQ tests have been put—the diagnosis of mental retardation or handicap (Ellis, 1979; Clarke *et al.*, 1985). According to the World Health Organization, an IQ of 50–70 (approximately) is indicative of mild retardation, 35–50 of moderate, 20–35 of severe, and below 20 of profound retardation. Earlier classifications added a category of borderline retardation in the IQ 70–85 range.

An IQ below 70 is 2 standard deviations below the mean of 100, and if IQ were normally distributed one would expect some 2.5 per cent of the population to fall into this category. But if US blacks have a mean IQ of 85, an IQ of 70 is only 1 standard deviation below the mean, and one could expect to see some 16 per cent falling into this category.

It is difficult to take seriously the suggestion that one in six US blacks could or should be classified as mildly retarded or worse. And in practice, an IQ score alone is not a sufficient criterion of retardation: the American Association on Mental Deficiency defines mental retardation as 'significantly sub-average general intellectual functioning existing concurrently with deficits in adaptive behavior' (see Meyers *et al.*, 1979). Various scales have been developed for the assessment of adaptive behaviour; although they differ in their emphasis, they usually include measures of language development and communication, some cognitive skills, such as telling the time or counting money, the ability to interact and co-operate with others in social settings, and the ability to look after oneself—feeding, dressing, etc. (Meyers *et al.*, 1979). The reliability of these scales is satisfactory, but, except where they include particular emphasis on language and communication, they rarely correlate more than 0.50 with IQ tests. Indeed, Mercer and Lewis (1978) reported a correlation of only 0.09 between IQ and performance on their Adaptive Behavior Inventory for Children.

On the face of it, many of the skills assessed by such scales seem more important than an IQ score in determining whether a person is able to live an independent life, outside any sort of institutional setting. In that sense, then, the scales have a certain face validity as an independent measure of intellectual retardation or competence. For our purposes, the critical observation is that the relationship between IQ and measures of adaptive behaviour differ in whites and at least some other ethnic groups. Mercer (1973) reported that if IQ alone was used as a criterion of retardation, 10 times as many blacks as whites would be classified as retarded; if adaptive behaviour measures were added to IQ, this difference completely vanished. In other words, blacks and whites with similar, low IQ scores differ in measures of adaptive behaviour, with blacks significantly superior to whites.

Here, then, for the first time is evidence that IQ tests *may* be biased against blacks. Certainly, from a practical point of view, this evidence suggests that IQ scores, taken alone, would seriously overestimate the proportion of blacks that should be diagnosed as mentally retarded, and that is an important enough implication in its own right. But it may seem only natural to take the next step, and say that we now have evidence that IQ scores underestimate blacks' true level of 'intelligence'. Before doing so, it is important to see what is implied by this step: it presupposes that adaptive behaviour scales provide a *better* measure of intelligence than do IQ tests. That may or may not be true: it would presumably depend on one's definition of intelligence. Rather than address that intractable issue head-on at this point, it may be wiser to try a smaller step: instead of insisting that the discrepancy between IQ scores and adaptive behaviour scales must prove that IQ tests underestimate blacks' true level of intelligence, let us simply accept that the discrepancy proves that the two must be measuring rather different things. In the long run, of course, if we could specify the nature of this difference, it would help to answer the more important, interesting, and tractable question: what do IQ tests measure? But there should also be a more immediate gain, in that it might help us to understand the reasons for the differences between blacks and whites on IQ tests.

Adaptive behaviour scales are intended to measure people's competence in a variety of everyday settings and tasks. We are not born with such competence; we presumably acquire much of it by learning. If black and white children of comparably low IQ differ in competence, this suggests that they may differ in how readily they can learn such simple tasks. Put another way, although blacks and whites may differ in average IQ, they may *not* differ in average ability to learn. In fact, there is good evidence that this is true. Laboratory measures of simple learning, e.g. paired-associate learning, show only modest correlations with IQ scores (e.g. Woodrow, 1940); and black and white children who differ in average IQ do not differ in speed of paired-associate learning—indeed, if anything, black children are often better at such a task (e.g. Hall and Kaye, 1980).

The implication is that differences between some ethnic groups may be confined to only certain aspects of intellectual functioning. The difference between Japanese or Chinese and whites seems to be most marked on one particular group of IQ tests, namely those measuring spatial ability. That between blacks and whites is wider than this, being seen in most types of IQ test, but is still restricted to IQ: there may be no differences in other aspects of intellectual functioning, which are not measured by IQ tests but which, in some respects at least, are of at least as much practical value. This conclusion is surely of both practical and theoretical importance and, one might have supposed, would be quite welcome to many critics of IQ tests, who have often insisted that the tests fail to measure important aspects of cognitive function. In fact, it has been widely dismissed—largely, one suspects, because a version of it is associated with the name of Arthur Jensen. Jensen (e.g. 1973) proposed a distinction between Level I and Level II abilities: blacks and whites, he suggested, differed only in Level II abilities, which are those measured by IQ tests. They do not necessarily differ in Level I abilities, which involve simple encoding, storage, and retrieval of sensory input. According to Jensen:

> Level I ability involves the accurate registration and recall of information without the need for elaboration, transformation, or other mental manipulation. It is most easily measured by *forward* digit span memory and serial rote learning of verbal material with minimal meaningful organization . . . Level II ability involves . . . reasoning, problem-solving, semantic generalization, conceptual categorization and the like. Level II is virtually the same as Spearman's construct of *g*. (Jensen, 1987*a*, p. 357)

Jensen has been insistent that this 'Levels Theory' is not a fully-fledged theory; it is little more than a simple empirical generalization from a simple set of observations. Blacks and whites do differ in their performance on most standard IQ tests. They do not differ in their performance on other cognitive tasks—most notably on paired-associate learning or forward digit span (Fig. 5.6, above, shows that the black–white difference on sub-tests of the WISC is smallest on the digit-span test. The Wechsler digit-span test includes both forward and backward span, and although there is some difference on backward span, there is none on forward span—see Jensen and Figueroa, 1975). From this he infers that there must be some distinction between the set of cognitive abilities measured by most IQ tests, and those tapped by such tasks as rote learning and simple digit span. The latter, presumably, include the ability to learn the tasks measured by adaptive behaviour scales. To the extent that the empirical data support the initial observations, and on the whole they do (reviewed by Vernon, 1981, 1987), the inference seems a reasonable one.

Jensen has, in fact, moved on from this theory, and now takes a slightly different, more general view, which he sometimes terms Spearman's hypothesis: that the black–white difference in IQ scores is a difference in the general factor (g) common to all IQ tests, and is therefore more pronounced on tests that correlate most strongly with this general factor (e.g. Jensen, 1985). That this is really just a development of the earlier hypothesis is suggested by the quotation above, where Jensen identifies Level II ability with Spearman's g. Although this claim, too, has been sternly criticized, Jensen has marshalled considerable empirical evidence to support it. At the least, it is better supported than the view of some critics (see above) that black–white differences are due to a few, patently biased items in the test. Although Jensen and others have sometimes implied that the validity of Spearman's hypothesis proves that black–white differences must be genetic in origin (an argument no doubt responsible for its rejection), this conclusion does not, even remotely, follow. Just because a test is a better measure of g, it does not follow that it is more heavily influenced by genetic factors. Many psychometricians, Jensen (1980, 1997) among them, have argued that Raven's Matrices provide one of the best measures of g. But scores on Raven's Matrices have probably been increasing faster over the past 50 years than scores on any other IQ test, and we know that these gains are environmental in origin (Chapter 4).

In this context, Spearman's hypothesis, if true, simply states that black–white differences are in *IQ*, not just in one or two special types of item or test, and that they are found in IQ more than in other skills. That seems to be probably true: some of the pain of that conclusion might be lessened if we could find out more about the limits of IQ, and one way of doing that will be to find out more about the nature of the other skills and abilities which yield no differences.

Conclusion

It is worth reiterating and elaborating one or two points that have been made, some implicitly, some explicitly, in this discussion of bias. To say that IQ tests are biased against a given group is to say that they underestimate, in that group, whatever it is that IQ tests purport to measure. We assume that IQ tests purport to measure intelligence, but since we are not clear what intelligence is, and have no independent measure of intelligence obviously better than IQ tests themselves, it will be foolishly optimistic to suppose that it is an easy matter to decide one way or another whether the tests are biased. If we find that IQ tests do *not* underestimate a given group's intelligence as that is indexed by some other, supposed criterion measure, we are not necessarily justified in absolving IQ tests of the charge of bias: our criterion may be equally biased. Thus the finding that IQ scores do not underestimate black students' educational achievements does not necessarily prove they are unbiased. But, by the same token, there can be no good reason to conclude that IQ tests *are* biased even if they do underestimate achievement by our criterion measure. Perhaps the criterion measure is really measuring something else. That is at least a possible interpretation of the difference between black and white scores on IQ and adaptive behaviour tests: perhaps adaptive behaviour depends on a learning process that is partly independent of IQ. An even clearer example to illustrate the argument here is provided by the case of Chinese-Americans. As we have seen, according to Flynn (1992) their educational and occupational attainments are commensurate with an average IQ some 20 points above the white mean. No one has suggested that their actual IQ scores are as high as this. So their IQ scores seriously underestimate their achievements on the two criteria most commonly used to validate IQ tests. Does this mean that IQ tests are biased against them, i.e. that they underestimate their true level of intelligence? That is a possible interpretation, but it requires one to accept that educational and occupational attainments are at least as good a measure of intelligence as IQ tests are. An alternative interpretation is that achievement at school, university or in a job depends not only on 'intelligence', but also on hard work, energy, ambition, etc. In other words our criterion measure is not just measuring intelligence, it is measuring many other things as well. The important point to remember is surely this: it is not a simple matter to decide whether an IQ test is biased. It requires the evaluation of alternative explanations and the balancing of probabilities, rather than confident, glib pronouncements.

   Finally, it is important to remember that most of the discussion of ethnic group differences in IQ has concerned different groups living either in Britain or the USA. Even these comparisons are fraught with problems: as numerous commentators have argued, many of these groups have probably created different sub-cultures, and probably differ in their access to the culture of the white majority. Differences in their test scores may, therefore, reflect differences in their values, attitudes, and beliefs. When we turn to comparisons between different nationalities, North American whites against Australian aboriginals or illiterate peasants in sub-Saharan Africa, these problems surely become insuperable. It is not just that, as I have already argued, we do not know how properly to translate a vocabulary or information test into a foreign language. We have no grounds for assuming that the modes of thought or reasoning that we take for granted as evidence of intelligence in Western industrial societies, will be the same as those to be found in an illiterate peasant society. The concept of intelligence is, in part, a social or cultural construct, as Sternberg (1985) among others has insisted. Mary Smith may be more intelligent than her brother John, but the way in which this difference manifests itself would probably be quite different if they lived in the Kalahari desert as hunter–gatherers, or were Amazonian Indians, rather than middle-class Americans.

Recall that Indian children still living in the Punjab obtained scores on Raven's Matrices some 20 points below those of other children originally from the same area, but who had been educated in Britain. Why? When the Soviet psychologist, Alexander Luria and his colleagues attempted to devise tests of reasoning suitable for illiterate peasants in central Asia, they were at pains to use material that would be concrete and familiar to their subjects rather than abstract and unfamiliar (Luria, 1976). It got them nowhere. As a test of syllogistic reasoning, they would present the following kind of problem:

> *In the far north, where it snows, the bears are white.*
>
> *Nova Zemblya is in the far north, and it is always snowy there.*
>
> *What colour are the bears in Nova Zemblya?*

The replies they received would be:

> *How should I know? I have never been to the north.*
>
> *Why are you asking me? You have travelled and I have not.*
>
> *So-and-so said the bears were white. But he is always lying.*

Does this prove the peasants were incapable of reasoning? Of course not. All these answers, although not those sought by the psychologists, contain evidence of implicit reasoning. You cannot believe liars; so-and-so is a liar; therefore even if he says the bears are white, they may not be. Someone who has travelled more widely is more likely to know the answer to questions about far-off lands; you have travelled more than me, so you are more likely than I am to know the answer to your question. Or: people usually only ask questions to which they do not already know the answer; so why are you asking me this silly question? It is not that these peasants could not reason; it is more that they do not understand the rules of these strange games the psychologists were trying to play.

Another example from Luria's work has also been documented by other psychologists working with other groups: in Western societies, as children grow older, so they become more likely to sort the world into taxonomic categories: given a knife, fork, spoon, orange, apple and banana, they sort the first three together as tools, the second three as fruit. So, presented with an 'odd-one-out' classification problem,

> *Hammer, saw, hatchet, log,*

they have no difficulty in saying that the log is the odd one out. Not so Luria's subjects. Typical responses were:

> *They all belong, you need the saw and hatchet to cut the wood, and the hammer to hammer it.*

Told that so-and-so had said the log did not belong, they replied:

He probably has plenty of firewood already. But we do not.

Rather than sort objects into taxonomic categories, they want to put together into one group a set of objects that can all be used to achieve something. Who is to say that one system of classification is more 'intelligent' than another? We happen to regard taxonomic categorization as, in some sense, more intelligent. Others do not. One African peasant said that the knife went with the orange because it cuts it, and that this was how a wise man would sort these objects. When asked how a fool would sort them, he promptly put all the utensils in one pile and all the fruit in another (Glick, 1975).

We need to remember that standard IQ tests were designed to measure the knowledge, intellectual skills, and cognitive abilities valued in Western industrial societies—especially by the educational systems of these societies. They may do a reasonable job of that. But there is no reason to assume that other cultures and societies share the same values. Administering such tests to people of other cultures may tell us whether they do or do not share the same values. But it will not necessarily tell us much about their 'intelligence' (Sternberg, 1985).

Sex differences

The equality of the sexes: fact or artefact?

> The one exception to the general rule that different groups or populations usually differ in average IQ is that both sexes have approximately the same average IQ on most tests. This is not, however, a true empirical finding but a consequence of the manner in which the tests were first constructed . . . the two sexes were *defined* to have equal intelligence rather than *discovered* to have equal intelligence. (Evans and Waites, 1981, p. 168)

This is a popular argument, endorsed by numerous commentators (e.g. Garcia, 1981; Rose *et al.*, 1984). But although it contains a small grain of truth, it is a serious misrepresentation of the history of IQ testing.

Like many men of his generation, Francis Galton had little doubt that men were more intelligent than women (see Gould (1997) for entertaining examples of nineteenth century male opinion of female intellect). But, to their credit, neither Burt nor Terman shared this prejudice. Both believed, moreover, that the question of any possible sex differences in intelligence was amenable to straightforward, empirical enquiry. Burt and Moore (1912) devised a wide variety of tests for measuring perceptual, motor, associative, and reasoning processes in various samples of schoolchildren of both sexes, and correlated the scores they obtained from their tests with assessments of the children's 'general intelligence' provided by their teachers. They found a variety of differences in their test results, some haphazardly favouring boys, others favouring girls, but most very much smaller than the differences measurable in various physical characteristics. The one consistent trend was a significant negative correlation between the size of the sex difference on a test and that test's correlation with teachers' assessments of general intelligence, leading Burt and Moore to conclude that 'The higher the process and the more complex the capacity, the smaller, on the whole, become the sex-differences' (Burt and Moore, 1912, p. 379).

That there was essentially no difference between the sexes in general intelligence was confirmed by Terman. Contrary to the implication of Evans and Waites's remarks cited above, it is quite clear that neither Terman, nor Binet before him, had given any thought at all to the question of possible sex differences in deciding what items to include or exclude from their tests. The result was, as Terman wrote in his introduction to the Stanford–Binet test, that he could use the scores of his standardization sample of approximately 1000 boys and girls, aged 4–16, to provide an empirical answer to the question.

> Many hundreds of articles and books of popular or quasi-scientific nature have been written on one aspect or another of this question of sex differences in intelligence; but all such theoretical discussions taken together are worth less than the results of one good experiment. Let us see what our 1,000 IQs have to offer towards a solution of the problem . . . When the IQ's of the boys and girls were treated separately there was found a small but fairly constant superiority of the girls up to the age of 13 years, at 14 however the curve for the girls dropped below that for boys . . . however the superiority of girls over boys is so slight . . . that for practical purposes it would seem negligible. (Terman, 1916, pp. 69–70)

Subsequently, the question of sex differences did receive some consideration during construction of new tests; in their introduction to the first revision of the Stanford–Binet, Terman and Merrill wrote: 'a few tests in the trial batteries which yielded largest sex differences were early eliminated as probably unfair' (Terman and Merrill, 1937, p. 34). And Wechsler, commenting on Terman and Merrill's procedure, merely reported 'we have done the same' (1944, p. 106). But the effect of this was not to abolish all sex differences in performance, and in the Wechsler–Bellevue test (the forerunner of the WAIS), as in the original Stanford–Binet, there remained a small difference in overall scores in favour of women, leading Wechsler to say "We have more than a 'sneaking suspicion' that the female of the species is not only more deadly but also more intelligent than the male" (Wechsler, 1944, pp. 107).

It should be clear, therefore, that IQ tests were not *designed* from the outset to yield equal scores for the two sexes. Terman thought he was making an empirical discovery in 1916 and, whatever the generality or validity of his conclusion, he was surely right. It seems probable that his original finding of essentially no difference between the two sexes had some influence on the subsequent practice of test construction, justifying the rejection of occasional items or sub-tests that seem to run counter to the general rule. The revised version of the Stanford–Binet, on the other hand, found a small but consistent difference in

favour of males—which Terman and Merrill attributed to problems with the standardization sample. But unless he and Wechsler were carefully concealing what they were up to,
their initial tests *discovered* that there were no more than trivial differences in overall IQ
between the sexes, and that such differences as there were favoured women.

Having set the historical record straight, it might seem that the obvious next step will be
to ask whether Terman's and Wechsler's original conclusions were correct. But that is easier
said than done. For there is a small grain of truth in the popular belief that the equality of
the sexes is a consequence of the way IQ tests are constructed. It is this: what both Terman
and Wechsler also found is that, although the overall difference between the sexes was
trivial, there were some items or sub-tests on which females did considerably better than

---

Box 5.3 Are men more intelligent than women because they have larger brains?

Although it has been strenuously denied, for example by Gould (1997), there is now quite
good evidence of a modest correlation between head circumference, cranial capacity or brain
size, and IQ. The data are reviewed in Chapter 7. Moreover, in spite of even more strenuous
denials, there is *moderately* good evidence that not only men and women, but also different
ethnic or racial groups differ in average brain size (Rushton and Ankney, 1996). There are, of
course, serious problems in making appropriate allowance for differences in body size between
different groups, since there is also a correlation between brain size and body size. A plausible
explanation of the finding that men have larger brains than women is that it is just a reflection
of the fact that they are, on average, taller and heavier. However, this is almost certainly not
sufficient to account for the sex difference in brain size (Ankney, 1992) and is also not going to
explain why whites have, on average, slightly larger brains than blacks.

Many of those who have accepted the evidence for these group differences in brain size,
have immediately assumed they prove that differences in average IQ between such groups are
both real and clearly genetic in origin (e.g. Lynn, 1994*b*, 1997; Rushton, 1995). No doubt this
explains why so many critics have been so anxious to dispute the evidence for differences in
brain size in the first place. The critics would have been better advised to question whether one
can make sensible inferences about differences in IQ between groups from evidence of
differences in their brain size plus evidence of a within-group correlation between brain size
and IQ. It is a rather simple matter to show that one cannot. According to Rushton (1992), the
average difference in cranial capacity, after allowance for age, stature, and weight, between
men and women in a sample of some 6000 US military personnel, was 110 cm^3. In the same
sample, the average difference in cranial capacity between whites and blacks was only 21 cm^3.
If this last difference is sufficient to produce a 15-point difference in average IQ between
whites and blacks, presumably the very much larger difference in brain size between men and
women should produce an even larger difference in their average IQ scores. Not even Lynn has
suggested that the sex difference in IQ is greater than the black–white difference. The only
way to escape this absurd conclusion is to acknowledge that one cannot extrapolate from
within-group correlations to between-group differences.

males, and others on which males consistently obtained higher scores than females. In the original Stanford–Binet and Wechsler tests, it so happened that the two more or less cancelled each other out to yield approximate overall equality, although there is absolutely no evidence to suggest that Terman or Wechsler deliberately juggled with the balance of items in their tests in order to achieve this desired state of affairs. But it now seems obvious that such juggling, i.e. a judicious choice of sub-tests to include in one's test battery, could yield this or any other outcome one wanted. But what would that prove? Not very much.

In what might seem to some as evidence of male conspiracy, indeed, later revisions of the Wechsler scales, the WISC-R and WAIS-R, have found clear evidence of significant overall male superiority (Jensen and Reynolds, 1983; Reynolds *et al.*, 1987). The differences in the original standardization samples for the two tests were small, 1.7 points for the WISC-R and 2.2 for the WAIS-R. But Lynn (1994*b*) has reviewed a number of other large-scale studies of the Wechsler tests which consistently found significant male superiority— amounting to about 3 points on the WAIS. There can be little doubt that the sex difference on these tests is reliable, i.e. statistically significant, and slightly larger for adults on the WAIS than for children on the WISC. But is it of any real significance? Or (as suggested above) is it that any such difference is likely to be nothing more than a consequence of the particular balance of items that now go to make up the Wechsler tests?

The first step towards answering this must be to look at the data from other general test batteries given to large, representative samples of the population. The results of some half-dozen other studies are shown in Table 5.8. Most of the differences are trivially small, although one is certainly not. More important, although some favour men, others favour women. There is no consistent pattern. Does this prove that the sex difference observed on the Wechsler tests can be ignored? Lynn (1994*b*) himself has argued that the Wechsler tests actually *under*estimate the true difference between the sexes—because they do not include the type of spatial and mechanical reasoning test at which males particularly excel (see below). It is, of course, true that, with the exception of block design, the Wechsler tests do not include measures of spatial ability, and that men obtain higher scores on such tests. But Lynn's conclusion does not necessarily follow: why might one not equally argue that the

Table 5.8 Sex differences on several general test batteries.

	Test				
	GATB	AFQT	ASVAB	Project Talent	British Ability Scales
Age	(18)	(18–23)	(18–23)	(16)	(14–17)
IQ difference between males and females	−7.9	+0.9	+5.5	−0.3	−0.03

+ means males obtain higher scores than females; − means females obtain higher scores.
GATB = General Aptitude Test Bttery; AFQT = Armed Forces Qualifying Test; ASVAB = Armed Services Vocational Aptitude Battery.

results could be biased towards female superiority by including more items at which they excel?

It seems more reasonable to insist that the question of whether the two sexes differ in overall IQ is uninteresting, because if by overall IQ we mean the average score obtained on a large diverse test battery, the answer given will depend on the test battery used. But that is not the same as saying the approximate equality of the sexes is an artefactual consequence of a deliberate decision to balance items favouring one sex with others favouring the other. On the contrary, the implication is a more interesting and important one, namely that the concept of 'overall IQ' may not always be a very useful one. In the present case, at least, the only sensible question we can ask is whether the sexes differ on particular kinds of IQ test or sub-test. The answer to this question is reasonably clear: they do. Males obtain higher scores than females on some kinds of test, females higher scores than males on others, and on yet others there seem to be no sex differences worth speaking of.

Both Terman and Wechsler found that males tended to outscore females on tests of mental arithmetic and spatial reasoning, while females outscored males on some verbal tests and on measures of perceptual speed. Some of these differences have been confirmed with other tests of these sorts of abilities. One clear example of this is provided by the Differential Aptitude Test (DAT) battery. The sex differences found in the most recent standardization sample for five of these tests are shown in Table 5.9a. As can be seen, females outscored males on the two verbal tests and on the speed test, while males outscored females on the two spatial tests. Moreover, the differences are not trivial, ranging from about 3 to over 13 IQ points. Table 5.9b shows similar data compiled by Hedges and Nowell (1995) from five recent, large-scale American surveys (which include the two databases used by Herrnstein and Murray (1994) and Lubinski and Humphreys (1990), whose overall IQ scores are presented in Table 5.8). Here, with the exception of mechanical

Table 5.9 Sex differences on tests of specific abilities (from Feingold, 1988; Hedges and Nowell, 1995)

(a) Differential Aptitudes Test

	Language	Spelling	Speed	Space relations	Mechanical reasoning
Sex difference	−0.45	−0.40	−0.34	+0.15	+0.76

(b) Various tests

	Reading comprehension	Vocabulary	Maths	Perceptual speed	Associative memory	Spatial ability	Mechanical reasoning
Median sex difference	−0.09	+0.02	+0.17	−0.23	−0.26	+0.19	+0.77

Differences are in *d*, standard deviation units, with + = male superiority and − = female superiority reasoning, the differences are rather smaller, but are still mostly significant.

There is, however, a second conclusion suggested by the literature: the sexes do *not* differ on other types of IQ test designed to measure a more general reasoning ability. The DAT has two such tests, abstract and verbal reasoning. The difference in the most recent standardization sample was 0.3 points on the verbal, and 0.6 points on the abstract reasoning test—both in favour of females (Feingold, 1988). Hedges and Nowell's (1995) survey yielded two studies of abstract reasoning, one finding a 0.6 point difference in favour of males, the other a 3.3 point difference in favour of females. One paradigm test of general non-verbal reasoning ability is, of course, Raven's Matrices. Large-scale studies of Raven's tests have yielded all possible outcomes, male superiority, female superiority, and no difference (Court, 1983). The most recent standardizations of the tests, in Britain and in Ireland, yielded no difference. If, as some IQ testers have argued (see Chapter 6 for further discussion), Raven's Matrices and other measures of non-verbal reasoning provide a good index of the general intelligence that IQ tests are trying to measure, the inference is plain: there are no great sex differences in general intelligence. And this conclusion is not dependent on a judicious selection of items designed to achieve overall balance between those favouring one sex and those favouring the other. There is no evidence of any such policy having dictated the construction of Raven's tests, or of the other reasoning tests cited above.

Differences in variability: myth or reality?

It is a commonplace observation that, throughout history, men have more often risen to positions of power and influence than women, and that more men than women have become famous for their achievements in art, music, literature, or science. Cultural attitudes, social expectations, and male power provide such an obvious explanation for these differences that it might seem perverse to look for any other. But IQ testers (mostly male) have not hesitated to do so. As Lynn (1994*b*) noted, even a small difference in mean IQ in favour of males would translate into a large difference in the proportion of males and females with an IQ over 140. But the explanation more commonly advanced to account for the existence of more eminent men than women has been to suggest that there is greater variability among males than among females. The implication is that even if there were no sex difference in average IQ there would be more males than females with an IQ over 140— and equally more males than females with an IQ below 70.

Studies of the prevalence of mental retardation have found little or no evidence for this latter suggestion (e.g. Rutter *et al.*, 1970; Reschly and Jipson, 1976): even though boys are more likely than girls to be classified as in need of remedial education, this is because they are more likely to display specific reading difficulties (Rutter *et al.*, 1970) rather than because of a higher incidence of IQs below 70. In the first serious attempt to measure the variability in IQ of boys and girls, Terman (1916) found no evidence of any difference. But once again his conclusion has been questioned by the data for the revised Wechsler scales, where the standard deviation for males (14.5 on the WISC-R and 15.3 on the WAIS-R) is some 5 per cent greater than for females (Jensen and Reynolds, 1983; Reynolds *et al.* 1987; see also Lynn, 1994*b*).

However, just as the Wechsler tests did not necessarily provide the last word on sex differences in average IQ, so their evidence of differences in variability has not always been substantiated by other tests. It is true that other general test batteries have often found more variation in males' than in females' scores, but the differences have been slight—less than 3 per cent in the study of Lubinski and Humphrey (1990), and less than 1 per cent in that of Herrnstein and Murray (1994). More specific tests of reasoning ability have found even less evidence of greater male variability. There is little evidence of such an effect in Raven's Matrices (Court, 1983), nor on the abstract and verbal reasoning tests of the DAT (Feingold, 1992). Hedges and Nowell (1995) reported slightly greater variability in males in two other studies of non-verbal reasoning, but the differences were small and not sufficient to produce an excess of males scoring above the 95 per cent percentile. Feingold (1992) also found no difference in variability on the verbal DAT tests: apart from spelling, the only tests to show greater male variability were spatial and mechanical reasoning and numerical ability; these latter differences were all substantiated in Hedges and Nowell's extensive survey.

Other spatial test batteries, however, have not always confirmed this difference (Stumpf and Eliot, 1995); indeed, some studies of mental rotation, a spatial task that yields a large difference in the average performance of the two sexes, have reported that females are more variable than males (Kail *et al.*, 1979). The one area where there is reliable and consistent evidence that males are more variable than females and where, as a consequence, there are more males than females with particularly high scores, is that of numerical reasoning and mathematics. For example, Lubinski and Humphreys (1990) in their study of some 100 000 American 16-year-olds, reported that boys not only obtained overall maths scores some 3 points higher than girls, they also had a standard deviation about 8 per cent greater. The data for this study were collected in 1960, and there is good evidence that the difference in *average* scores has decreased sharply since then—to the point where, if anything, girls may outscore boys (Hyde *et al.*, 1990). Nevertheless, Hyde *et al.* continued to find evidence of greater variability in males, with the consequence that there were more males than females in groups of above-average ability. As one instance of this, Benbow (1988) reported that in junior high-school students scoring above the mean for college entrants on the maths section of the Scholastic Aptitude Test, there were twice as many males as females, and in the top 5 per cent, this ratio increased to 12 to 1. Similar, albeit sometimes much smaller, differences were found in most ethnic groups.

Analysis of verbal and spatial abilities

If we define general intelligence as the average score on a diverse IQ test battery, the only answer to the question of whether there is a sex difference in general intelligence is that it depends on the test battery. That is such a trivial answer that it suggests that we should reject the premise on which the question rested, and define general intelligence instead as performance on tests of general reasoning, such as Raven's Matrices or the DAT reasoning tests (I return to this point in Chapter 6). On this definition, there appears to be no sex difference in general intelligence. But there are numerous sex differences on tests designed to measure more specific abilities and, not surprisingly, it is some of these differences that have attracted most attention. At a practical level, perhaps the most important is the preponderance of males among those of above average mathematical ability. But the major focus of theoretical concern has been the complementary differences in verbal and spatial abilities. By contrast, there has been virtually no attempt to understand the apparently reliable sex differences in perceptual speed.

Verbal ability

There has been a very large number of individual studies specifically examining performance on particular verbal and spatial tests; the problem is how to characterize the nature of the abilities in question, and how best to summarize the results of such a diverse array of studies. Maccoby and Jacklin (1974), for example, simply listed studies and their outcome. They found 33 studies of verbal abilities in adults and children over the age of 11. Of these 33, 12 found a significant difference favouring females, 19 found no significant difference, and 2 found males performing better than females. At first sight one is inclined to argue that this shows nothing but inconsistency, but that is too pessimistic. It can be calculated, for example, that even if there were a real difference of 0.5 standard deviations between females and males in verbal ability, then of 100 studies employing 30 of each sex, a majority (53 per cent) would find no significant difference. Conversely, if there really were no difference between males and females in verbal ability, then no more than 1 study in 20 (rather than 12 of 33) would spuriously find a difference significant at the 5 per cent level. A simple list of studies and their outcomes does not provide the information required. What is needed is a technique that *combines* the results of all relevant studies, with some explicit criteria for evaluating the reliability of individual studies and hence the weight that should be placed on their results. The techniques of meta-analysis, which assess effect size (in standard deviation units, or d) of all studies satisfying certain specified criteria, provide the most suitable way of summarizing their results.

Hyde and Linn (1988) conducted a meta-analysis of some 150 studies of verbal abilities. For studies published before 1973, and included in Maccoby and Jacklin's review, the effect size was $0.23d$ in favour of females (i.e. about 3.5 IQ points). For those published since then, however, the difference was less than half this, $0.10d$, or only 1.5 points on an IQ scale. This is a great deal smaller than the difference for the DAT verbal test shown in Table 5.9; indeed it seems hardly large enough to be of practical significance, and Hyde and Linn concluded that 'gender differences in verbal ability no longer exist'.

This may be a partial and misleading view, if only because it may blur distinctions between different measures of verbal ability. In the DAT data, while there were large differences in favour of females on two linguistic tests—spelling and verbal fluency—there was essentially no sex difference on the verbal reasoning test. Hyde and Linn (1988) noted that in the largest single study included in their survey, of close to 1 million students taking the verbal Scholastic Aptitude Test, males actually obtained slightly higher scores than females—and the WISC and WAIS verbal scales also yield evidence of male superiority. The most obvious interpretation of this pattern of results is, once again, that not all 'verbal' IQ tests are measuring the same thing (see Chapter 2 for earlier evidence that the Wechsler tests' division into verbal and performance scales does not map very well onto the distinction between verbal and non-verbal IQ implied by other tests). We shall return to the distinction between various verbal tests in Chapter 8. For the present, it will be prudent to view with a modicum of scepticism the suggestion that sex differences in verbal IQ have melted away. There is still evidence, for example, that young girls learn to talk sooner than boys, and have acquired a larger vocabulary by the age of 2 or 3 (e.g. Fenson *et al.*, 1994). Even if these early differences do not necessarily translate into later differences on all verbal IQ tests, they remain of some theoretical interest—if only for the light they may shed on the largest and most reliable sex difference in IQ, male superiority on tests of spatial ability.

Spatial ability

A meta-analysis of the studies published before 1973, and included in Maccoby and Jacklin's review, found an average difference of $0.45d$ in favour of males on tests of visuo-spatial ability (Hyde, 1981). But what seemed probably true for differences in verbal IQ is quite certainly true for spatial IQ: the size of the sex difference varies considerably across different kinds of test. For example, the DAT space relations test yielded a difference of only $0.15d$ in favour of males, but the mechanical reasoning test a difference of $0.76d$ (see Table 5.9). A factor analysis of the scores of males and females on a large battery of spatial tests confirmed that they could not all be measuring a unitary process of 'spatial ability' (Stumpf and Eliot, 1995). Although one determinant of the size of the sex difference on a particular test was how closely that test correlated with the central factor common to all the tests, this was not sufficient to account for the entire pattern of differences. The implication is that the tests were measuring more than one process and that the difference between the sexes was not uniform across the various processes.

This conclusion has been confirmed by the results of two subsequent meta-analyses of studies undertaken since Maccoby and Jacklin's review (Linn and Peterson, 1985; Voyer *et al.*, 1995). Both analyses implied that although men outscored women on all kinds of spatial test, the size of the sex difference varied from no more than 2 or 3 IQ points on some kinds of spatial tests to 10 or more points on others. An example of a test that yields a difference in this latter range is the Shepard—Metzler three-dimensional mental rotation task illustrated in Fig. 8.2 (p. 283; reviewed by Masters and Sanders, 1993). Unfortunately, research on sex differences has done remarkably little to elucidate the nature of the differences between various kinds of test, or the differences in the psychological operations they engage. Once again, this is a topic that must be deferred to a later discussion (see Chapter 8).

Be this as it may, the ubiquity of sex differences in a wide variety of spatial tests, together with the opposite difference that appears on some verbal tasks, has encouraged much speculative interpretation. It is obvious enough that boys and girls are treated differently—both by their parents and by the wider society. It is not difficult to see how such differences could eventually produce differences in specific abilities, and there has been no shortage of environmental explanations for such differences. But there has also been a proliferation of more or less 'biological' explanations. One line of reasoning (Lynn, 1994*b*) starts from the assumption that human evolution was closely bound up with hunting, and continues with the observation that in contemporary hunter—gatherer societies men do the hunting while women are engaged in the lower-status but more important task of gathering. It then assumes that hunting depends on spatial ability and concludes that a sex difference in spatial ability must have a biological origin.

The argument may have a certain plausibility, but hardly enough to force acceptance of its conclusion. Nevertheless, several more or less 'biological' explanations have been advanced. The most common suggestion is that there is a sex difference in the organization of the brain, and the most popular version of this idea is that there is a sex difference in lateralization. The initial impetus for this suggestion is the generally accepted fact that in the majority of the population language is predominantly a function of the left cerebral hemisphere and spatial perception a function of the right (e.g. McCarthy and Warrington, 1990). Since there is some reason to believe that females have an advantage over males in language, but that men outscore women on tests of spatial ability, it seems only natural to suppose that one difference must somehow be connected to the other. But how? That there is no compelling interpretation of the connection is evident from the fact that one explanation has suggested that the differences in ability arise because male brains are less lateralized than those of females (Buffery and Gray, 1972), while another suggests that it is because male brains are *more* lateralized (Levy, 1976).

The actual evidence on possible sex differences in lateralization is conflicting and confusing, and has led some commentators to conclude that there are none (e.g. Hahn, 1987). Consider only one problem: some studies have reported that women show greater involvement of the left hemisphere in the solution of visuo-spatial tasks than do men. But this might simply reflect the fact that women are more likely than men to employ verbal strategies to solve what are only ostensibly visuo-spatial problems (Chapter 8, p. 293). Nevertheless, if forced to choose between Levy's account and Buffery and Gray's, the

Box 5.4 Spatial ability and the sex-linked recessive gene hypothesis

One biological hypothesis that captured the imagination of even the most sceptical investigators was the sex-linked recessive gene hypothesis. The genetic difference between the sexes is confined to the sex chromosomes, with females having a pair of X chromosomes and males one X and one Y. It follows, therefore, that a character determined by a recessive gene on the X chromosome will be expressed in any male that carries the gene but in females only if they carry the gene on both chromosomes. If the frequency of the gene is 50 per cent, it follows that 50 per cent of males but only 25 per cent (0.5×0.5) of females will display the trait. Thus if high spatial ability is determined (in part) by a single recessive gene on the X chromosome, more men than women would show high spatial ability. The beauty of the hypothesis, however, was that it made some quite specific predictions about family resemblances. Sons receive their X chromosome from their mothers and their Y chromosome from their fathers; there should therefore be no correlation between fathers and sons for the trait, and a modest correlation between mothers and sons (only modest because the mother may be heterozygous, and although transmitting the critical recessive gene, may not display the trait herself). Daughters should also resemble their mothers, but less than sons do, since both mother and daughter may carry the gene without displaying the trait. Finally, daughters should resemble their fathers more than their mothers, since to display the trait they must have inherited the gene from both parents, and if the father transmitted it he certainly displayed the trait. Indeed, the father–daughter resemblance should be the same as that between mothers and sons. Thus the predicted resemblances are as shown in the top row of the following table, and the results of a study by Stafford (1961) on familial correlations for spatial IQ are shown in the next row. The agreement between data and theory is quite striking. What is so persuasive here is that the pattern of results makes little or no sense from an environmentalist point of view. The most plausible environmental hypothesis is that familial resemblances will depend on social learning within the family. It presumably, therefore, predicts that sons should resemble their fathers and possibly daughters their mothers. That the cross-sex correlation should be higher than the same-sex correlation, and that there should be no resemblance between fathers and sons at all, seems quite inexplicable.

Correlations for spatial IQ between different family members

	Mother–son	Father–daughter	Mother–daughter	Father–son
Predicted	Moderate	Moderate	Weak	Zero
Stafford (1961)	0.31	0.31	0.14	0.02
Composite (Boles, 1980)	0.27	0.31	0.31	0.25

Alas, as T. H. Huxley once remarked, there is no greater tragedy in science than the murder of a beautiful theory by ugly fact. Large-scale replications of Stafford's study, several with hundreds of subjects, have completely failed to confirm the critical pattern of familial resemblance. A summary of the larger studies yielded the correlations shown in the third row of the table.

majority of commentators have opted for Levy's: if there really are any sex differences, most of the evidence suggests that they are in the direction of greater degree of lateralization in males (McGlone, 1980; Bryden, 1982; Halpern, 1992). A particularly convincing observation, from a study employing magnetic resonance imaging, is that when people are asked to engage in a verbal task, female brains display more activity in both hemispheres than male brains (Shaywitz *et al.*, 1995). This, of course, immediately raises the next question: we must still ask why a greater degree of lateralization in males should mean that females are somewhat better at verbal, and males considerably better at spatial tasks. Levy's explanation is that the earlier development of language in girls than in boys results in linguistic functions spreading over into the right hemisphere, thus providing less capacity for visuo-spatial functions. This seems a somewhat simple-minded hypothesis, and in its simple form is not very well supported. For example, on the assumption that people who are left-handed are less likely to have language localized in the left hemisphere than those who are right-handed (McCarthy and Warrington, 1990), it seems to follow that left-handed people should be less proficient at spatial skills than the right-handed majority. The evidence for this supposition is distinctly equivocal: a few studies have found such a difference, the majority have not (Bishop, 1990).

There is *marginally* better evidence for a rather more complex effect of handedness on spatial ability: that it interacts with sex differences, and also with overall level of intelligence. The results of one study of left- and right-handed male and female university students on the DAT space relations test are shown in Fig. 5.8a (Harshman *et al.*, 1983). As can be seen, right-handed men obtained higher scores than left-handed men, but in women this difference was reversed. As a consequence, male superiority was observed only in right-handed people; in the left-handed minority, women actually outscored men. Harshman *et al.* were quick to acknowledge that this pattern of results has not always been observed. They suggested that it might be seen only in subjects of above-average ability, such as university students, and found evidence to support this suggestion in their re-analysis of two other studies. Neither had observed the interaction seen in Fig. 5.8, but when the subjects in each study were divided into those of above-average and those of below-average ability, in each case the above-average group yielded a pattern of results consistent with Harshman *et al.*'s own results. Figure 5.8 also shows the results of another study that yielded a similar interaction.

The results of the large number of studies that have examined the importance of lateralization as an explanation of sex differences are far from consistent, and have not convinced all sceptics (e.g. Bishop, 1990). Nor perhaps should they. There are many loose ends to the argument. As we have seen, spatial ability is not a simple, unitary concept. Nor, for that matter, is handedness (Bishop, 1990). Handedness is a distinctly imperfect index of lateralization, since the majority of left-handed people still have language predominantly represented in the left hemisphere. The evidence for sex differences in lateralization has not convinced everyone. And the concept of strict lateralization of function is one that has lost

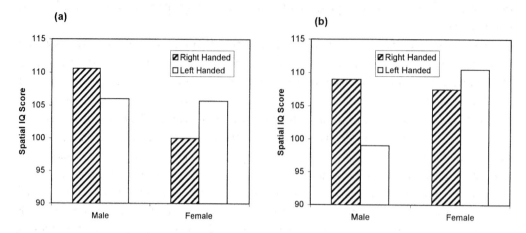

Fig. 5.8 The interaction between sex and handedness as determinants of performance on tests of spatial IQ (data in (a) from Harshman *et al.*, 1983; (b) from Gordon and Kravetz, 1991).

much of its appeal to neuropsychologists (Efron, 1990): to take one pertinent example, there is good evidence of left- as well as right-hemispheric involvement in spatial tasks in males as well as females (Mehta and Newcombe, 1991). Finally, although the results shown in Fig. 5.8, if reliable, no doubt imply that sex differences in spatial abilities are *somehow* bound up with sex differences in lateralization of function, there is no simple explanation of this interaction—let alone why it should be observed only in people of above-average ability. At the least, we should suspend judgement.

Since one of the major biological differences between the sexes lies in the relative concentrations of the 'female' hormones, oestrogen and progesterone, and the 'male' hormones or androgens, mostly notably testosterone, it is not surprising that another biological explanation of sex differences in cognition should appeal to differences in the relative concentrations of these hormones. And such an explanation is not, in principle, unreasonable, given that these hormonal differences do not just appear at puberty but start prenatally, and that there is ample evidence of hormonal effects on the brain.

Several lines of evidence provide some support for a hormonal hypothesis (Kimura and Hampson, 1992). Females with congenital adrenal hyperplasia, a condition resulting in abnormal prenatal androgen exposure, also obtained higher scores on several spatial tests than did a control group, but did not differ in their scores on Raven's Matrices (Resnick *et al.*, 1986). Conversely, women with Turner's syndrome, who experience a low level of androgens, tend to be poor at spatial tests (Hines, 1982), and other studies of more normal variations in androgen levels in both males and females have also reported an association between low androgen levels and poor spatial performance (Hier and Crowley, 1982; Shute *et al.*, 1983). However, just to show that here too the only rule is that there will always be exceptions to the rule, Jacklin *et al.* (1988) found that high levels of androgens in newborn girls predicted poorer than average performance on spatial tests 6 years later.

Even if the evidence were more consistent, the obvious question remains: how do hormonal differences achieve their effects on test performance? One possibility is that they affect the development of lateralization of function. According to Geschwind and Galaburda (1987), high levels of prenatal testosterone slow the development of the left hemisphere, and thus lead to right hemispheric dominance. Whatever the merits of Geschwind and Galaburda's theory, which attempts to explain a much wider range of sex differences than those in spatial ability, it is probably not a complete explanation of hormonal effects on cognitive abilities, for there is evidence that such effects can be very much more transitory, being observable indeed over the course of the female menstrual cycle. Hampson (1990) found that, at the mid-point of the cycle, characterized by high levels of oestrogen and progesterone, women obtained higher scores on verbal, but lower scores on spatial tests, than they did when menstruating.

Many people find it difficult to accept the idea that sex differences in cognitive abilities might somehow be 'biological', and prefer to point to differences in socialization, sex-role stereotyping, or similar processes. It is important to see that this is a largely false antithesis. For example, there is no particular reason to suppose that sex differences in lateralization of function, if real, are somehow immutable or hard-wired. According to Levy (1976), they originate in the way parents interact with their children: by talking more to baby girls than baby boys, parents encourage the development of verbal abilities in girls; this results in the spilling over of language functions into the right hemisphere; and the final result is less room for the development of spatial abilities. But why do parents talk to baby girls more than to boys? Perhaps because of a hormonal difference. There is good evidence that males are more aggressive than females, and that hormonal effects are partially responsible for this difference (Maccoby and Jacklin, 1974; Halpern, 1992). If aggression is associated with restlessness, then one reason why baby boys are talked to less than girls, is simply that they will not sit still long enough.

This is, of course, merely speculative. Is there any evidence of more direct environmental causes of, for example, sex differences in spatial ability? It is easy to point to differences in parental and societal attitudes and expectations, but here as elsewhere environmental correlates are not necessarily environmental causes. What would prove that they were? Several intervention studies have shown that spatial skills can be enhanced by specific instruction or education, and some have found that such instruction can reduce the size of the initial sex differences (Brinkmann, 1966; Connor *et al.*, 1977). But there have been failures: Thomas *et al.* (1973), for example, were surprisingly unsuccessful at teaching the principle of the water-level test to girls (Fig. 5.9). In reviewing this area of research, Baenninger and Newcombe (1989) concluded that such instruction was in general of as much, or as little, benefit to both sexes. Even if specific instruction were invariably successful, however, and even if it were invariably more successful with females than with

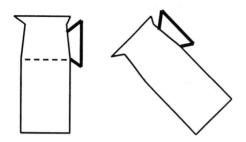

Fig. 5.9 The water-level test. The subject's task is to draw a line representing the surface of the water in the tilted jug. The correct answer is a horizontal line, not one bisecting the jug at right angles to its sides. Significantly more females than males fail to give the correct answer.

males, would it necessarily follow that differences in spatial ability could be attributed to differences in experience with spatial tasks? At the least, one would need evidence that these beneficial effects were relatively permanent, and that they generalized to other types of spatial test.

A second approach has been to ask whether sex differences in verbal or spatial abilities are universal, or whether they are confined to a few cultures. If they are not found in other societies, one might want to argue that they must be a product of particular cultural values. In most European countries the pattern of differences seems similar to that observed in Britain or the USA: for example, Stage (1988) found that among Swedish high-school students, males outperformed females on tests of quantitative ability and the interpretations of diagrams and maps, while females obtained higher scores on a vocabulary test. But these differences may not be universal—it will be recalled that sex differences in mathematical skills were not uniform in all ethnic groups in the USA (Benbow, 1988). Several commentators have implied that Eskimos show no sex differences in spatial abilities, and have suggested that this is because Eskimo women, like men, must be adept at navigating across Arctic wastes (Halpern, 1992). This is not particularly good anthropology and very much worse psychology, since the evidence on which it is based (a study by Berry, 1966) is performance on Raven's Matrices, which is not in fact a spatial test at all. One final piece of evidence comes from a comparison of sex differences in various ethnic groups in Great Britain, shown in Table 5.10. Although boys obtained slightly higher IQ scores than girls in all four ethnic groups, by far the largest difference was found in Pakistani children. Similarly, although boys obtained higher maths scores than girls in all four groups, only among Pakistani children did they also obtain higher scores on tests of reading. This is suggestive evidence that differences in cultural values (presumably Muslim attitudes towards the education of women?) can have an effect on attainment.

The best evidence in favour of an environmental account of sex differences in cognitive abilities comes from a relatively consistent pattern of findings that have hitherto been mentioned only in passing. Many sex differences in test performance have declined over the past 50 years. The meta-analyses of verbal and mathematical abilities undertaken by Hyde and Linn (1988) and Hyde *et al.* (1990) found that studies published after 1970 or so yielded smaller differences than those published before that date. And Voyer *et al.* (1995)

Table 5.10 Sex differences in IQ scores and educational attainment in 10-year-old British children from different ethnic groups (from Mackintosh and Mascie-Taylor, 1986)

Groups	IQ	Attainment	
		Maths	Reading
White	+0.05	+0.10	−0.15
West-Indian	+0.03	0.00	−0.12
Indian	+0.09	+0.19	−0.12
Pakistani	+0.23	+0.19	+0.16

Differences are in *d*, or standard deviation units, with + = male advantage, and − = female advantage.

established that on at least some spatial tests, such as embedded figures and the water-level test, there has been a significant decline in earlier sex differences. The restandardizations of the Differential Aptitude Tests between 1947 and 1980 (Feingold, 1988) have shown similar effects. Representative results are shown in Fig. 5.10. The consistent pattern is of rather little change in those tests where females obtained higher scores than males, but a consistent and substantial decline in male superiority on spatial tests, and the complete disappearance of male superiority on tests of abstract, verbal, and numerical reasoning.

It is difficult to attribute these changes to any change in the standardization samples. They can hardly reflect changes in, say, relative concentrations of male and female hormones. They must surely be environmental in origin. But as was the case with the secular increase in overall IQ, it is less easy to pinpoint any precise environmental factor, let alone

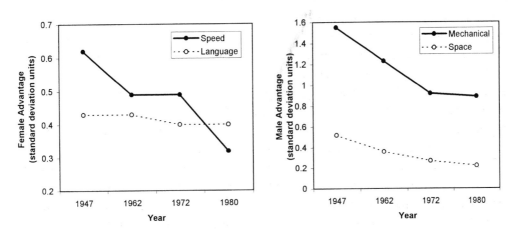

Fig. 5.10 The changing pattern of sex differences on different parts of the Differential Aptitude Test (data from Feingold, 1988).

elucidate the manner of its causal action. Most Western countries have surely seen substantial changes in society's attitudes to women since the 1940s, and it would be perverse to suggest that they have not contributed to the pattern of results seen in Fig. 5.10. But to what extent they have achieved their effects by changing parental behaviour, teachers' behaviour, sex-role stereotypes, or self-images may be hard to decide.

Perhaps it does not matter: what is important is that some unnecessary differences have disappeared. But not all: at least on the DAT tests, females' verbal superiority remained substantial; and the difference in favour of males on the mechanical reasoning test remained 10–12 points on an IQ scale. Moreover, other evidence suggests that there has been no decrease at all in the size of the sex difference on mental rotation tasks over the past 20 years or more (Masters and Sanders, 1993; Voyer *et al.* 1995). On the three-dimensional version of this task, the difference is still close to one standard deviation.

Of course, no one could seriously claim that there were no differences in the attitudes of parents and society towards the sexes when the children tested in the latest standardization of the DAT were growing up. It is possible that further changes in society will have yet further effects on the pattern of sex differences. But it would be going well beyond the available evidence to insist that a simple environmental explanation has been found sufficient. It is not easy to see why societal changes should have affected the sex difference on some spatial tests, but had no effect on others. And it does not seem very plausible to suppose that boys spend so much more time than girls pouring water out of jugs that experience alone will explain why about twice as many 10-year-old boys as girls pass the water-level test shown in Fig. 5.9. The only sensible conclusion is that we do not have a complete explanation of the causes of sex differences in various types of IQ test—and those who claim to know what the true cause is, are deceiving themselves.

Summary

Ever since their introduction, IQ tests have revealed differences in average test scores between various social and ethnic groups. Some at least of these differences are 'real', in the sense of being replicable and persistent, even if others, such as the differences between urban and rural populations in Britain and the USA, seem to have disappeared. The question is: what are the causes of such differences? There is no reason to expect a single answer for all cases.

Children's IQ scores are moderately correlated with their parents' social status. While some of this effect is probably an environmental effect of social class on IQ (Chapter 4), some is probably not. Children do not simply inherit their social class from their parents; they determine their own adult occupational status, and there is evidence that differences in status between parents and their children are associated with differences in their IQ scores: upwardly mobile children tend to have higher IQ scores than their parents. This suggests that social class differences in IQ are re-created in each generation, and that the association between the two is not just an effect of social status on IQ.

The most widely studied group difference in IQ is surely that between blacks and whites in the USA. The difference is usually described as one of 15 points, but it was probably greater than that at one time, and *may* be slightly smaller today. In spite of claims to the contrary, there is remarkably little evidence that the difference is genetic in origin. Some of the results of one American adoption study are consistent with a genetic interpretation, but other aspects of that study point just as strongly to an environmental interpretation, and two other studies of black and white children brought up in comparable circumstances, one German the other British, found no difference in their IQ scores. If the effect *is* an environmental one, it remains to be shown what the proximal environmental causes are.

There are other ethnic group differences in IQ scores. Chinese and Japanese seem to obtain higher scores than whites on spatial IQ tests, and *may* obtain higher scores on other non-verbal tests. There is no evidence to decide whether such differences are environmental or genetic in origin.

A popular argument is that differences between different groups are not due to real differences in intelligence, but merely reflect bias in the tests. The clearest sense of 'bias' is this: an IQ test is biased against a group if it underestimates their true level of 'intelligence'. From this, it should be clear that the only way to prove that an IQ test was or was not biased would be to compare its results with an independent, better measure of 'intelligence'. And what would that be? That said, it is important to acknowledge that confident pronouncements about the average intelligence of African peasants, based on the results of standard IQ tests, are foolish and dangerous: an IQ test can only purport to measure the intelligence of people with some common cultural background.

The two sexes do not, on the whole, seem to differ greatly in average IQ, and that conclusion is not simply an artefact of any deliberate policy by IQ testers to eliminate items that favour one sex or the other. But they do differ in certain components of IQ—the most salient of these differences being that men outscore women on most tests of spatial IQ. Both biological and environmental explanations of this difference have been advanced—but the distinction between the two is not as clear as many writers have implied.

6   *Factor analysis and the structure of human abilities*

Introduction

It is time to return to some of the themes first touched upon in Chapters 1 and 2. The issues reviewed in Chapters 3–5, genetic and environmental effects on IQ, and group differences, are traditional topics for discussion in any book on IQ tests and individual differences in intelligence. But they do not address what many commentators, reasonably enough, regard as the central questions. What do IQ tests measure? Do they measure intelligence? Is there any such thing as intelligence to measure? In Chapter 1, I argued that however central or fundamental these questions might seem, it would not be sensible to *start* our discussion of human intelligence and IQ tests by trying to answer them. They were better approached slowly and indirectly, for example by asking what we would expect to see from a successful measure of intelligence, and by then asking whether IQ tests did or did not satisfy any of these criteria. Chapter 2 considered some preliminary answers to some of these questions. Thus we do not believe that people suddenly become more or less intelligent overnight, and we therefore expect that a measure of intelligence should show reasonable long-term stability—as IQ test scores do. We believe that more intelligent children are likely to do better at school than less intelligent children, and that more intelligent adults are likely to be more successful in a variety of spheres than the less intelligent—although in both cases we also believe that other factors certainly play an equally important role. Thus we should expect to find *moderate* correlations between measures of intelligence and educational and occupational success—as we do for IQ scores. The fact that IQ scores are partly heritable is also consistent with some widely shared intuitions, for example that intelligence is not just the sum of what people have been taught, but also reflects how efficiently they learn from their experience. And many of the environmental factors that affect IQ, such as health, nutrition, schooling, parental interaction, are the sorts of factors we should expect to influence a growing child's cognitive or intellectual development. Finally, as was noted in Chapter 2, in spite of all doubts about, and criticisms of, existing IQ tests, the fact remains that a very wide variety of superficially quite different measures, that include general knowledge, vocabulary, mental arithmetic, manipulation of abstract patterns, analogies, and series completion tasks, all tend to agree with one another. Moreover, no critic has produced tests with higher face validity as measures of intelligence that did not agree with existing IQ tests.

So far, then, the evidence is weakly consistent with the proposition that IQ tests have succeeded in providing a moderately successful measure of at least some important aspects of human intelligence. But this is probably as far as this stealthy, indirect approach can take us. Its success must depend on there being at least some consensus about the nature of human intelligence—for example that it does not bounce up and down like a yo-yo. But on many issues there is no consensus at all. For example, to some people, starting with Francis Galton, it has seemed obvious that intelligence is a unitary trait, that some people have been endowed with greater all-round intellectual ability than others, and therefore that it should be possible to summarize these differences in a single IQ score. Others have attacked this unitarian view, either by insisting that human intelligence is far too subtle, complex, and various to be summed up by a single number (Medawar, 1982), or because they rebel against the possibility of any linear rank ordering of people, and wish to insist that although John may be cleverer than Mary in some respects, Mary will be cleverer than John in others (Gould, 1997). It is not difficult to see how these opposed beliefs might be influenced by people's social or political attitudes. Those who wish to believe that some people are generally more worthy than others, will adopt the unitarian view; those who wish to believe that everyone is worthy of equal respect, because everyone is equally talented in their own way, will insist that intelligence is not unitary.

The point is that if there is no consensual answer to the question of whether intelligence is better conceptualized as a single, general ability or as a loose confederacy of independent abilities, then the further question of whether IQ tests provide a good measure of human intelligence will hardly be answered by finding out whether they appear to be measuring a single underlying factor of general intelligence or a multiplicity of different intelligences. We have no alternative but to approach this last question with as open a mind as possible, and see what answers the data suggest. It would be foolish to pretend that this will be easy, for the history of attempts to decide whether IQ tests measure a single general ability or many independent ones is a history of acrimonious dispute, where strong preconceptions have only reluctantly, and fitfully, acknowledged the weight of empirical evidence. To this day, indeed, there are those, such as Gould (1997) and, in a more moderate way, Sternberg (1990), who will argue that no clear answer is suggested by the data, because the answer that emerges is entirely dependent on the method of analysis employed, and the method of analysis chosen is simply a consequence of one's theoretical preconception.

The factor analytic approach

From the first, the main approach taken by IQ testers to elucidating what they described as the structure of human abilities has been via factor analysis. Indeed, Charles Spearman's initial work, in which he outlined his 'two-factor' theory of intelligence, and identified the general factor of intelligence with general discriminative ability, was published the year before Binet's first tests appeared (Spearman, 1904). In other words, Spearman's theory was not based on any analysis of IQ scores as such: as a matter of fact the initial empirical base for Spearman's theory of general intelligence consisted simply of the school marks, and teachers' and fellow pupils' assessments, of a small handful of schoolchildren in a few English village schools.

But Spearman's ideas, however weak their empirical basis, were remarkably influential. For the next 25 years or so, he and his students attempted to develop better test batteries that would reveal more clearly the true nature of general intelligence. Even those British psychologists who disagreed with him worked on his agenda. Godfrey Thomson, although acknowledging the existence of Spearman's general factor, argued against his attempt to identify it with a single psychological process of general intelligence. Others, such as Burt and Garnett, developed techniques of multiple factor analysis which yielded evidence of 'group factors', i.e. more specific components of IQ, such as verbal or spatial ability, as well as Spearman's general factor (Blinkhorn, 1995). In the 1920s and 1930s, the centre of gravity of factorial research moved across the Atlantic. Lewis Thurstone (1931, 1938) independently (or at least without acknowledgement) developed techniques of multiple factor analysis which, in his hands, seemed able to eliminate Spearman's general factor altogether, while other American factorists, such as Guilford (1967), surpassed Thurstone in their zeal both to dispense with the general factor, and to multiply the number of independent group factors or special abilities.

There are times when it may seem to an outsider that some IQ testers have regarded factor analysis as an end in itself. In part, this may reflect the inability of the mathematically incompetent fully to understand some technically demanding methods. Those who want a detailed account of the techniques of factor analysis, with a full explanation of the meaning of eigenvalues and communalities, or the distinction between principal components and principal factor analysis, are referred elsewhere (e.g. Child (1990), for a clear and reasonably simple account; or Harman (1976), for a rather tougher one). And those who want a magisterial summary of the empirical results of 50 years or more factor analytic research will find it in Carroll (1993). In what follows, I shall attempt only to describe the logic of factor analysis, and only in sufficient detail to enable the reader to judge the validity of certain conclusions supposedly implied by the results of such analysis.

If the function of an IQ test is to assign an overall IQ score to each of a large number of people, in order to differentiate between them, the test constructor will want to examine the items that go to make up the test to see how well each one contributes to this central purpose. An item that gives a quite different result from all others in the test is merely contributing noise; one which gives exactly the same answer as another is merely redundant. In other words, the principles of test construction imply that one should reject items whose correlations with other items in the test are either too low or too high. What we want is a range of moderate correlations between all items in a test. And that, as we saw in Chapter 2, is what we find in most IQ tests.

What is true of individual items is equally true of sub-tests within test batteries such as the WAIS and WISC. And to the extent that a new test will be accepted only if it correlates with standard existing tests, such as the Stanford–Binet or Wechsler tests, and with the common validator of IQ tests, namely school achievement, it follows that entire tests all tend to correlate with one another. This is the so-called 'positive manifold', hailed by many as

> one of the most remarkable findings in all of psychology . . . that scores on all mental ability tests of every variety are positively intercorrelated in any representative sample of the general population. (Jensen, 1981, p. 52)

We should acknowledge that this positive manifold is partly a consequence of an implicit or explicit decision on the part of test constructors only to admit such tests as satisfy this criterion. But, as I argued in Chapter 2, this is not a sufficient explanation; there is no reason to suspect that the correlation between scores on Raven's Matrices and either the Stanford–Binet or Wechsler tests was built in to any of these tests by deliberate selection of items. Moreover, it is also an empirical discovery that it should be possible to include a remarkably diverse array of items, sub-tests, and whole tests that all correlate with one another.

For any given set of IQ tests or sub-tests, therefore, the correlation matrix of each test against every other test will consist of a series of positive numbers. The technique of factor analysis, properly understood, is simply a procedure for trying to simplify a large correlation matrix. Where we have a large number of different measures, whether they be scores on different IQ tests, performance on a variety of athletic events (100 yards, mile, high jump, javelin, marathon, etc.), or the lengths of various bones in the body (femur, tibia, metacarpal, etc.), each of which can be correlated with every other, the resulting correlation matrices will usually be too large and unwieldy to be readily comprehended. Factor analysis allows one to see whether patterns can be detected in the raw matrix which would suggest a simpler story. One might imagine, for example, that taller people had generally longer bones than shorter people and therefore that a factor analysis of bone length scores would reveal a single, general factor corresponding to height. On the other hand, although some people may be generally more athletic than others and thus better at all athletic events, one might equally expect to find people who were especially good or bad at, say, sprints or long-distance running, or field events, without thereby being out of the ordinary at others. Factor analysis will enable one to see whether there is any evidence for such clusters of ability in addition to, or rather than, any general athletic ability. This has been the goal of the factor analysis of IQ scores. Can we find evidence of an all-pervading factor of general intelligence running through performance on all possible IQ tests? Do we only see clusters of more specialized abilities—verbal, spatial, etc.? Do we see evidence of both?

General intelligence (g): *Spearman's two-factor theory*

Table 6.1 shows a hypothetical correlation matrix for a set of six hypothetical sub-tests of an IQ test battery. Although hypothetical (and, as we shall see shortly, much idealized), the matrix shares two features with real data. First, all the correlations are positive (the positive manifold); but, secondly, they vary considerably in magnitude, from 0.72 down to 0.20. Spearman believed that he had the explanation for both of these features. The reason, he supposed, why all tests of ability correlate with one another is because they all, to a greater or lesser extent, measure a single common ability or factor of general intelligence, g. The reason why they do not correlate perfectly is because each test also measures its own specific ability. Finally, Spearman argued, where two tests correlate highly this is because they both depend heavily on g; where they correlate less well this is because the relative importance of general and specific factors is weighted towards the latter.

Spearman's theory clearly provides one possible, perhaps even plausible, account of the facts, but Spearman believed that he had further proof of the correctness of his analysis. This came from:

> a curious observation made in the correlations calculated between measurements of different abilities . . . [which] were noticed to tend towards a peculiar arrangement which could be expressed in a definite mathematical formula . . . termed the tetrad equation. (Spearman, 1927, p. 73)

If $r_{1.2}$ stands for the observed correlation between tests 1 and 2 and so on, then Spearman's tetrad equation was as follows:

$$r_{1.2} \times r_{3.4} = r_{1.3} \times r_{2.4} \tag{6.1}$$

If we substitute the appropriate numbers from Table 6.1 into this equation (0.72×0.42

Table 6.1 Hypothetical correlation matrix for six tests yielding a single general factor

Tests	1	2	3	4	5	6
1	–					
2	0.72	–				
3	0.63	0.56	–			
4	0.54	0.48	0.42	–		
5	0.45	0.40	0.35	0.30	–	
6	0.36	0.32	0.28	0.24	0.20	–
Loading on g	0.90	0.80	0.70	0.60	0.50	0.40

= 0.63 × 0.48) we can see that the equation holds—as it will for any other two pairs of correlations in the table. Why should this be? For Spearman, the explanation was straightforward; the reason, the *only* reason, why tests 1 and 2 correlate is because both measure g. The observed correlation between the two tests is simply a product of each test's separate correlation with g:

$$r_{1.2} = r_{1.g} \times r_{2.g} \tag{6.2}$$

And since this is true of all other pairs of tests, we can rewrite equation 6.1 as follows:

$$r_{1.g} \times r_{2.g} \times r_{3.g} \times r_{4.g} = r_{1.g} \times r_{3.g} \times r_{2.g} \times r_{4.g} \tag{6.3}$$

which is obviously true. When the correlation matrix of a battery of tests forms a pattern, such as that seen in Table 6.1, to which the tetrad equation applies(recognizable from the fact that the tests can be arranged in such an order that the correlations decrease in size as one goes down or across the matrix), the explanation, said Spearman, is because the correlations between all tests are *entirely* due to each test's correlation with the single general factor, g.

The fundamental assumption of factor analysis is that expressed in equation 6.2 above: that the correlation between any two tests may be explained as a consequence of each test's correlation with, or 'loading on' a third, hypothetical measure or factor. The aim of factor analysis therefore is to find a 'solution' to an observed correlation matrix which explains the large number of observed intercorrelations between the various tests or measures in terms of a smaller number of underlying hypothetical factors. One problem, as we shall see, is that there will always be an indefinite number of possible solutions to any observed correlation matrix, and additional non-mathematical criteria will always be required to choose between alternative solutions. But sometimes the choice will seem relatively obvious. Our hypothetical correlation matrix of Table 6.1 yields one very obvious and straightforward solution: there is a single general factor responsible for the intercorrelations between these six tests, and the correlation of each test with this general factor is as shown in the bottom row of the table. Application of equation 6.2 will now show that this solution does indeed explain the entire matrix (which was, of course, so constructed that such a solution would be possible). So far so good. The solution seems so intuitively plausible that no one would wish to quarrel: we have explained the pattern of intercorrelations between the six tests by showing that every test correlates with, or measures, *one* general factor. And we have explained the difference in the size of correlations between different pairs of tests by noting that each test measures its own unique factor as well as the general factor, and the relative contribution of general and unique factors to scores on each test varies from one test to another. This is why Spearman's theory is properly called a two-factor theory.

Neither Spearman himself nor his followers were content to stop short at this mathematical solution. If we want a psychological explanation of the relationship between scores on different tests, we cannot rest content with a mathematical description that identifies one factor or, if necessary, several factors, underlying the pattern of observed correlations. We must seek to interpret those factors. It is essential, however, to keep clear the distinction between two quite separate questions. The first, empirical question, is whether the pattern of intercorrelations actually observed between different IQ tests does or does not allow one to adopt Spearman's solution of a single, general factor, plus a series of specific factors unique to each test. The second, theoretical question, is how we shall interpret the factorial solution or solutions most plausibly suggested by any observed pattern of intercorrelations.

Some of the criticisms advanced against Spearman's position have confused these two questions. For example, those who argue that there is no such thing as general intelligence, or that intelligence is too multi-faceted and complex an idea to be captured by a single number, often do not make it clear, perhaps even to themselves, which question they are addressing. Are they asserting that factor analysis of a battery of IQ tests will not, as a matter of fact, yield a large general factor? Or are they insisting that the observation of such a general factor does not necessarily imply the existence of a single underlying process of general intelligence? Both arguments are important, but they need to be addressed in turn. The first question, then, is whether Spearman's factorial solution provides a successful account of the observed pattern of correlations between IQ tests.

Thurstone's primary mental abilities

The correlation matrix of Table 6.1 yielded (because it was carefully constructed to do so) one very straightforward and natural solution: the correlations between all six tests were entirely accounted for by a single general factor. That is to say, if we insert the factor loadings of each test shown in Table 6.1 into equation 6.2, we should perfectly reproduce the observed correlation matrix. But suppose that no such factor could be found to account for the pattern of correlations in a real correlation matrix. This would be apparent when the extraction of the most general factor possible, i.e. that with the highest correlation with all tests, and which therefore accounted for as much of their pattern of intercorrelations as possible, still left a number of non-zero correlations between individual pairs of tests. A second factor would then have to be extracted to account for this residual pattern of correlations (and a third or fourth if significant residual correlations still remained). But now there is a decision to be made: how shall we select these factors?

Before proceeding further, it may help to outline an alternative, geometrical representation of the factorial structure of a battery of tests. Instead of expressing the results of factor analysis as a set of correlations between, or 'loadings' or 'saturations' of test scores on hypothetical factors, i.e. in numerical form, they can also, for those with more visual than numerical facility, be expressed geometrically. We can imagine (as Thurstone did) test scores as vectors of unit length with the correlation between any two tests being represented by the angle between their two vectors. If they are highly correlated, they will lie close together, and if uncorrelated, far apart. More exactly, the correlation is represented by the cosine of the angle between two vectors, since the cosine of $0° = 1.0$ (i.e. perfect correlation) and of $90° = 0$ (i.e. zero correlation). Figure 6.1a, for example, shows six different test scores all correlated with one another, i.e. with relatively small angles between them. If one draws the vertical axis labelled *g*, through this cluster it will represent in effect the principal factor of a factor analysis, i.e. the factor best correlated with all six tests.

One way to understand this is to realize that if we wished to summarize the overall performance of someone who had taken all six tests, the single number that would best do so, i.e. capture most of the information from the original tests, would be a point on the axis labelled *g*. Such a hypothetical score would allow one to predict the actual scores obtained on all six tests with considerable, although not perfect, accuracy. Further accuracy would be provided by placing a second axis, at right angles to the first. This would now allow us to distinguish, for example, between two people who obtained similar total scores on all six tests, but distributed differently between them. The one with higher scores on the right-hand group of tests would have a positive score on this second axis, the one with higher scores on the left-hand group would have a negative score on this axis.

In Figs 6.1b and c, we have introduced a small but possibly critical change; all six tests still subtend relatively small angles with one another, but they also form two apparently

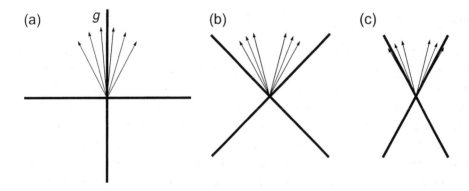

Fig. 6.1 Geometric representation of correlations between scores on six tests. Each test score is represented as a vector departing from the origin (the six arrows radiating out from the origin in each of (a), (b), and (c)). The correlation between each test is represented by the angles between the vectors, with small angles corresponding to high correlations. In (a), the vectors are equally spaced apart, but in (b) and (c), the six vectors form two distinct clusters. The natural factorial solution for (a) is thus to draw a first factor (labelled *g*) through the middle of the six vectors, and a second at right angles to the first. Although it would be perfectly possible to place two factors in the same place for the six vectors shown in (b) and (c), the alternative solution would be to place each of two factors as close as possible to one set of vectors. In (b), the constraint that the two factors be at right angles to one another means that they cannot be placed through the centre of each cluster. In (c), this constraint is relaxed and two oblique (i.e. correlated) factors are placed in the centre of each cluster. (This way of representing tests as vectors and their correlation as the angles between the vectors, although originally owing to Thurstone, is here taken from Gould, 1997.)

rather distinct clusters. It would obviously still be possible to draw a general axis through the middle of all six, and a second at right angles to it, as in Fig. 6.1a. Given these two clusters of test vectors, however, an equally obvious alternative solution would be to draw two new axes, one through each cluster, as shown in Figs 6.1b and c. The only distinction between these last two figures is that in Fig. 6.1b we have imposed the requirement that the two axes must be at right angles to one another, i.e. uncorrelated with one another; while in Fig. 6.1c we have allowed the two axes to be oblique—i.e. correlated with one another. In either case we should now be saying that the pattern of correlations between our six tests is best described by saying that three of the tests are measures of one factor and three of another. And this interpretation would seem all the more natural, of course, if we were told that the three left-hand tests were all to do with the meanings of words and phrases, while the three in the right-hand cluster were all diagrammatic, abstract problems. Note how the psychological interpretation of factorial solutions encourages the acceptance of one solution over another.

Thurstone (1938, 1947; Thurstone and Thurstone, 1941) argued that Spearman's factorial solution was based on a wholly false set of psychological assumptions. Thurstone's own preconception was that IQ tests measure a variety of independent 'faculties' and that the purpose of factor analysis was both to reveal these independent faculties and, if necessary, to guide the construction of better tests designed to be 'factorially pure' i.e. measures of one factor at a time. Given a matrix of intercorrelations between a dozen or more tests, the goal of factor analysis for Thurstone was not to find the general factor that accounted for as much as possible of the variation in scores on all tests, but rather a series of separate factors, one of which accounted for the intercorrelation between, say, tests 1, 2, and 3, a second for the intercorrelation between tests 4, 5, and 6, and so on (for example, the two factors in Figs 6.1b and 6.1c rather than a single factor drawn through the middle of all six vectors). If we return to the arithmetic representation of a correlation matrix, Thurstone's preconceptions would imply, in an ideal world, that the matrix should look like that shown in Table 6.2. Here there are relatively high correlations between each of tests 1, 2, and 3 on the one hand, and between each of tests 4, 5, and 6 on the other. But the correlations between each test in the first group and each test in the second are all zero. In practice, Thurstone's theory allowed that the correlations between different clusters of tests would not all be zero, or even necessarily close to zero, but it is worth postponing a discussion of that complication for a moment. Any such pattern is quite inconsistent with Spearman's hypothesis, for it would unambiguously contradict the law of tetrad differences: if we insert the relevant values for tests 1, 2, 5, and 6 of Table 6.2 into equation 6.1 it will be immediately apparent that the equality no longer holds. For Thurstone what this meant was that tests 1, 2, and 3 are measures of factor 1 while tests 4, 5, and 6 are measures of factor 2. Thurstone called the factors his analyses revealed 'primary mental abilities', and set about devising tests specifically to measure them (his PMA tests, briefly mentioned in Chapter 2). The 'fundamental idea of a primary mental ability' was that 'it behaves as a

Table 6.2 Hypothetical correlation matrix for six tests yielding two independent group factors

Tests	1	2	3	4	5	6
1	–					
2	0.72	–				
3	0.63	0.56	–			
4	0.00	0.00	0.00	–		
5	0.00	0.00	0.00	0.54	–	
6	0.00	0.00	0.00	0.45	0.30	–
Loadings						
on F1	0.90	0.80	0.70	0.00	0.00	0.00
on F2	0.00	0.00	0.00	0.90	0.60	0.50

functional unity that is strongly present in some tests and almost completely absent in many others' (Thurstone and Thurstone, 1941, p. 9). By 1941, Thurstone and Thurstone believed that they had securely identified six PMAs: numerical, verbal comprehension, word fluency, space, reasoning, and memory; and a possible seventh factor of perceptual speed.

The resolution? General and group factors

The contrast between Tables 6.1 and 6.2 seems so marked that a naive reader might be forgiven for wondering what the dispute is still all about. Surely it should have been settled by now: all we need to do is to look at the observed pattern of correlations between a large and representative battery of mental tests and see whether they correspond to the picture shown in Table 6.1 or to that of Table 6.2. In fact, we have already seen one example of the answer we get in Chapter 2, where Table 2.2 (p. 34) showed the correlation matrix for all sub-tests of the WAIS-R. Two more carefully selected examples are shown in Table 6.3: Table 6.3a also from six sub-tests of the WAIS-R, and Table 6.3b from six of Thurstone's own battery of 21 PMA tests. They tell more or less the same story: neither Table 6.1 nor Table 6.2 is correct, the reality lies somewhere between the two. Both in the WAIS and the PMA tests, all correlations between all tests are positive, as Spearman's hypothesis requires; but in both cases, as Thurstone's requires, there are clusters of high correlations, between each of tests 1–3 and each of tests 4–6, separated by lower correlations between all members of the first set and all members of the second.

It is still sometimes claimed that factor analysis of IQ tests is a wholly misguided enterprise since the results could never tell us anything: there is an indefinite number of possible factorial solutions to any particular correlation matrix. This last assertion may well be true, but it does not follow that factor analysis has told us nothing; the observed correlations between mental tests, as illustrated in Table 6.3, do in fact rule out certain factorial solutions, namely a simple application of either Spearman's or Thurstone's alone.

Table 6.3 Correlation matrices for six sub-tests of WAIS and for six PMA tests

(a) WAIS-R

	Info	Vocab	Comp	Block	Picture	Object
Information	–					
Vocabulary	0.82	–				
Comprehension	0.77	0.78	–			
Block Design	0.52	0.56	0.48	–		
Picture Completion	0.56	0.59	0.54	0.64	–	
Object Assembly	0.44	0.47	0.38	0.67	0.62	–

(b) PMA

	Flag	Figure	Card	Letter	Ped	Group
Flags	–					
Figures	0.64	–				
Cards	0.63	0.71	–			
Letter series	0.27	0.18	0.27	–		
Pedigrees	0.18	0.15	0.18	0.61	–	
Grouping	0.28	0.19	0.24	0.61	0.50	–

(a) From WAIS-R standardization sample, age group 65–69.
(b) From Thurstone and Thurstone (1941, Appendix Table 4).

Although both can take some comfort from the observed correlations—Spearman from the fact that they are all positive, Thurstone from the fact that there are clusters of high and of low correlations—the feature that gives comfort to one is precisely the feature that seems inconsistent with the other. Thurstone's solution seems to be contradicted by the fact that all correlations are positive, Spearman's by the existence of clusters.

The empirical question, therefore, turns out to have a perhaps somewhat equivocal answer. But that is hardly the same as no answer at all: on the face of it, we can reject both Spearman's and Thurstone's conclusions—although acknowledging that each has been able to describe certain features of the data. However, the rejection of scientific theory by scientific fact is never quite the simple, straightforward matter that the discoverer of the scientific fact would like to believe. For example, it is often possible to rescue a theory from embarrassing data by questioning the data. And so it has sometimes seemed here. There is a real problem in concluding that just because a particular battery of tests yields a correlation matrix incompatible with a particular factorial solution, we should reject that solution. Perhaps we should reject some of the tests instead. For Spearman, the problem with the correlation matrices of Table 6.3 is that there are some correlations that are too high, others too low. Perhaps the way to save the theory would be to argue that the occasional cluster of very high correlations arises simply because we have included two or more tests that measure the same unique factor. Spearman's account, it should be remembered, assumes that each test measures both a general factor common to all, and also its own unique factor. If a test battery has included several tests that are very similar, i.e. all measure the same unique factor, they will necessarily correlate more strongly with one another than with any other test in the battery, and we will appear to have an inadmissible Thurstonian primary mental ability. Might not it be possible to preserve the theory by dropping one or more of the redundant tests?

Although Spearman and his followers did initially pursue this line of reasoning, it was not for long. It soon became evident that clusters of high correlations could be observed between superficially rather different tests, and that it was not plausible to insist that all tests in such clusters were measuring a single, very specific, unique factor. By the 1920s, Spearman had acknowledged that the tetrad equation was sometimes contradicted, and that there was indeed good evidence of Burt's 'group factors' (corresponding roughly to Thurstone's primary mental abilities) in such areas as logical, mechanical and arithmetical reasoning (Spearman, 1927; in the second edition of this book, published 6 years later, he added a group factor of verbal comprehension).

In Thurstone's case, the solution is rather different, and requires acknowledging that I have seriously oversimplified his account. Thurstone knew perfectly well that the correlation matrix of a battery of IQ tests exhibited a positive manifold, i.e. that essentially all tests correlated positively with one another. His explanation was that existing tests were not 'factorially pure'. They did not just measure a single primary ability, but several different factors to varying extents. If tests 1, 2, and 3 correlate not only with one another, as they should, but also with tests 4, 5, and 6, this may be because tests 1, 2, and 3 do not measure only their own factor but also (albeit to a lesser extent) the factor common to tests 4, 5, and 6. In Table 6.3b, for example, tests 1, 2, and 3 are 'spatial' tests and tests 4, 5, and 6 are 'reasoning' tests, in the sense that tests 1–3 load most strongly onto the spatial factor and tests 4–6 onto the reasoning factor. But any test of reasoning may also correlate with the spatial factor because it fortuitously includes problems that require the manipulation of spatial relationships. Conversely, it may be difficult to devise measures of spatial ability that do not also make demands on reasoning ability.

Thurstone could argue, therefore, that the correlation matrix of actual test batteries would approximate more closely to the ideal shown in Table 6.2 if we could only devise better, i.e. factorially purer, tests. Indeed, this was precisely what he attempted to do, and the measure of his success is the difference between Tables 6.3a and 6.3b. Thurstone's tests, explicitly constructed and selected to measure his set of primary mental abilities, have produced a correlation matrix notably more like the Thurstonian ideal of Table 6.2 than do the Wechsler tests chosen on a quite different basis.

By what criterion, then, could one ever decide that Thurstone's account was correct or incorrect? Thurstone argued that the decisive disproof of Spearman's theory, and therefore the decisive evidence in favour of his own multiple factor theory, would be if it were possible to find a factorial solution to a correlation matrix that satisfied his principle of 'simple structure'. This required that each test in the battery should have high loadings on some factors (preferably on as few as possible), and zero loadings on some other factors (preferably on as many as possible).

How were such factors to be found? Thurstone's procedure for factor analysis involved 'rotating' his factors to approximate as closely as possible to simple structure. What this means may be more evident from the geometrical representation of test vectors in Fig. 6.1. The test vectors of Figs 6.1b and 6.1c *could* be analysed, as was that in Fig. 6.1a, by placing a first axis running vertically up through the middle of the six vectors, and a second axis orthogonal to the first. The first axis would, of course, represent Spearman's general factor g, on which all six tests loaded, and which therefore would not satisfy the requirements of simple structure. But, as in Fig. 6.1b, we could rotate these axes, so that one lay close to the three left-hand test vectors, and the second lay close to the right-hand cluster of three tests. We should now have two factors, on each of which some of the tests loaded strongly, while the remainder loaded only weakly.

The six test vectors of Fig. 6.1 showed a positive manifold, i.e. all correlated positively with one another. As a consequence of this, the two orthogonal axes of Fig. 6.1b lie outside their respective test clusters, whereas in Fig. 6.1c the two oblique axes run through the centre of their three tests, which are thus more strongly associated with them. In other words, where tests are all positively correlated, their factorial structure is more accurately represented, and one can achieve a closer approximation to simple structure, by allowing the factors to be correlated, as in Fig. 6.1c, rather than insisting that they be orthogonal, as in Fig. 6.1b. But this is critical, for where we have *factors* that are themselves all positively correlated, further factor analysis will yield a higher-order general factor that explains their intercorrelation.

Thurstone's earlier experimental work on his primary mental abilities was undertaken with undergraduates from the University of Chicago as subjects. With such a highly selected group of intelligent subjects, there was relatively little evidence of any general factor (see Box 6.1). But when Thurstone and Thurstone (1941) administered the PMA test battery to schoolchildren, they found that a general factor could readily be extracted from their test battery, after the extraction of the six or seven primary mental abilities, because these primary mental abilities all correlated with one another, and did so in a manner consistent with Spearman's law of tetrad differences. They concluded that

> if further studies of the primary mental abilities of children should reveal this general factor, it will sustain Spearman's contention that there exists a general intellective factor . . . Its interpretation here would be that . . . each of the primary factors can be regarded as a composite of an independent primary factor and a general factor which it shares with other primary factors. (Thurstone and Thurstone, 1941, pp. 26 and 38)

Something like this compromise solution has indeed seemed sensible to most, if by no means all, subsequent theorists (see Carroll, 1993). There is widespread agreement that

Box 6.1 General intelligence or general stupidity?

Spearman's general factor, g, arises because of the pervasive positive correlations between performance on virtually all different tests. The importance of this general factor (technically the proportion of variance in the correlation matrix accounted for by the first principal component of a principal components analysis) depends on the average value of these intercorrelations. In most IQ test batteries the first principal component accounts for over 50 per cent of the variance.

It turns out, however, that the importance of g depends on the population studied. Although both Binet and Spearman themselves had suspected that IQ tests were more informative about people of lower than of higher IQ (as far as Spearman was concerned, this meant that g was more important at lower levels of IQ), it is only recently that unequivocal evidence of this has become available. Using the standardization samples for the WAIS-R and WISC-R, Detterman and Daniel (1989) divided the samples into five IQ bands: below 78, 78–92 and so on up to above 122. For the WAIS-R, the average intercorrelation between all sub-tests ranged from a high of 0.56 for the lowest IQ band to a low of 0.26 in the highest band, and from 0.42 to 0.22 in the lowest and highest bands for the WISC-R sample. Lynn (1992) confirmed these findings for the Scottish standardization sample of the WISC-R.

The implication is that g is more important at lower levels of IQ. Although these findings need to be replicated with other test batteries (see Deary *et al.* (1996) for only partial confirmation in a study of intercorrelations between the DAT tests; but Legree *et al.* (1996) for rather more convincing data from the Armed Services battery), they certainly suggest that the overall positive manifold arises largely because people who perform badly on one IQ test tend to perform badly on others, rather than because people who do well on one do well on others. There is no general intelligence, only general lack of intelligence.

One practical implication, which will be worth bearing in mind in Chapters 7, 8, and 9, is that attempts to understand what it is that IQ tests measure, and certainly attempts to understand the nature of g, are less likely to be successful if they use university students as subjects. A population of relatively high IQ will not be able to tell one much about general lack of intelligence.

there is some sort of general factor—because virtually all mental tests, however diverse they appear on the surface, correlate significantly with one another. In other words, it does make sense to say that some people are generally more (or less) intelligent than others. Indeed, it may also be of some practical value to say so: in so far as IQ test scores predict how well people perform different kinds of job, the best predictor by far is the general factor (Schmidt *et al.*, 1992).

At the same time, however, because any correlation matrix of a large battery of mental tests will contain clusters of high and of low correlations, there must also be more specialized group factors—even if the number of such factors favoured by different theorists has varied from two or three to a hundred or more. The most conservative solution (Burt, 1949; Vernon, 1950) has settled for two, a verbal and a non-verbal or perceptual/mechanical factor. Others have insisted on distinguishing between at least four:

verbal, non-verbal reasoning, spatial, and perceptual speed; to which some would add Thurstone's memory, word fluency, and number to bring the total up to his seven primary mental abilities. Cattell (1971), employing a more sophisticated version of Thurstone's rotation to simple structure, has identified some 20–30 primary factors. But since these factors are all intercorrelated, further analysis yields a smaller number of second-order general factors. The most important of these are: Gc, or crystallized ability, corresponding roughly to verbal IQ, and Gf, or fluid ability, corresponding roughly to non-verbal reasoning. But three others have also been identified: Gv or spatial visualization, Gr or retrieval, and Gs or a speed factor (Horn, 1985; Carroll, 1993).

It is not only factorial or correlational evidence that points to the distinctions between some of these abilities or group factors. Several of the differences between various groups discussed in Chapter 5 were not differences in overall IQ, or any general factor; they were differences in these more specific abilities. Women obtain higher scores than men on tests of perceptual speed (Gs), at least as high scores on most verbal tests (Gc), but significantly lower scores on spatial tests (Gv). Similarly, Chinese and Japanese outscore North American whites on spatial, but not on verbal tests. This can only mean that these kinds of tests are measuring, in part, somewhat different sets of abilities. The distinction between verbal and spatial abilities is further documented by neuropsychological evidence of lateralization of function, and by genetic evidence, most strikingly by studies of individuals born with sex-chromosome abnormalities. Males with Klinefelter's syndrome (an extra X chromosome) show a specifically verbal deficit; by contrast, females with Turner's syndrome (a missing X chromosome) have a specific spatial deficit (Netley and Rovet, 1982; Rovet and Netley, 1982). That there is a distinction between a narrower set of spatial abilities (Gv) and a more general reasoning ability or non-verbal IQ (Gf) is suggested by the observation that although there is a substantial sex difference in the former there is none worth speaking of in the latter.

This confirmation from a relatively independent source provides gratifying evidence that psychometric or factorial theories of human intelligence do not operate in a complete vacuum. But lest we be carried away, we should acknowledge that the agreement between different theorists is far from universal. Gardner (1993), as we have seen (Chapter 2), has also proposed some half-a-dozen separate intelligences, only three of which, linguistic (verbal), logical-mathematical (non-verbal reasoning), and spatial, correspond to those favoured by most factorists (a fourth, musical intelligence, may be related to Carroll's auditory factor). Gardner has also argued that his intelligences are independent of one another. If by that, he means that there is no positive manifold, he is simply wrong. If he means that different intelligences engage different cognitive operations or processes, and are mediated by different structures in the brain, he may of course be right. We shall return to this distinction shortly.

The largest number of factors is the 120 proposed by Guilford (1967) and later expanded to 150 (Guilford, 1982). For Guilford, each 'factor' is defined by the execution of a particular kind of operation on a particular kind of product with a particular kind of content. There are five operations, six products, and four types of content, yielding (5 × 6 × 4) 120 factors. Although Guilford has claimed to be able to devise independent tests of most of these independent factors, his account has not commanded wide assent. The most devastating critique was provided by Horn and Knapp (1973), who showed that Guilford's factorial procedures, when applied to his test data, provided just as strong support for *randomly* generated factorial theories as they did for Guilford's own theory. Brody (1992) and Carroll (1993) provide more detailed, but not much more sympathetic, accounts of Guilford's theory.

The resolution: different factorial procedures converge on similar solutions

This apparent proliferation of somewhat different factorial theories has helped to reinforce the argument that, since there is an indefinite number of factorial solutions to any given correlation matrix, factor analysis alone will never be sufficient to decide between them. The conclusion is certainly true—but not for the reason stated. Factor analysis alone will never dictate any particular psychological interpretation of the nature of human intelligence. For that, we need psychological research and theory. Nor will further factor analytic studies serve to choose between alternative factorial solutions. That too will require psychological research and theory. But factor analysis remains a useful technique, both for summarizing a complex set of data (a 10 × 10 correlation matrix containing 100 numbers makes it difficult to see patterns that factor analysis can clearly reveal), and for suggesting hypotheses that can then be subject to psychological test. Moreover, and even more important, although there may be an indefinite number of factorial solutions to a given correlation matrix, the differences between them often turn out to be *relatively* minor, for in the end the data do in fact constrain the nature of the solutions possible. In what follows, I attempt to illustrate this by working through three different factorial solutions to a hypothetical correlation matrix. The data are hypothetical because hypothetical data often illustrate points of principle rather more clearly than the real world.

Table 6.4, then, gives a correlation matrix for six tests. Casual inspection shows that it is not going to yield either to Spearman's or to Thurstone's ideal solution. The high correlations within each pair of tests (1 and 2 , 3 and 4, and 5 and 6), separated by lower correlations between members of different pairs, will disconfirm Spearman's law of tetrad differences: there is clear evidence of distinct group factors here, and to make later exposition simpler, they are so labelled in Table 6.4. Tests 1 and 2 are verbal tests; tests 3 and 4 are tests of non-verbal reasoning; while tests 5 and 6 have been labelled as spatial. However, the overall positive manifold creates equal problems for Thurstone's analysis: no test meets his ideal by correlating well with one other test but hardly at all with the others.

Table 6.4 Hypothetical correlation matrix of six tests

Tests	Verbal		Reasoning		Spatial	
	1	2	3	4	5	6
Verbal						
1	–					
2	0.70	–				
Reasoning						
3	0.30	0.25	–			
4	0.30	0.25	0.70	–		
Spatial						
5	0.25	0.15	0.35	0.45	–	
6	0.20	0.20	0.30	0.40	0.70	–

How then are we to set about finding factorial solutions? Let us start with the approach suggested by Spearman's account. Even though the correlation matrix of Table 6.4 will not be explained by appeal to only a single general factor, we can start by finding that general factor, *g*, and then see how many additional factors we need to account for the residual variance not explained by *g*. The standard technique for doing this is known as a principal components analysis, in which each factor is chosen so as to explain the maximum possible amount of variance remaining in the data. Thus the first factor (*g*) is chosen to load as highly as possible on all tests; the second then explains as much as possible of the residual variance left behind by the first, and so on. Because each successive factor accounts for a progressively smaller proportion of the total variance in the matrix, later components will soon account for a trivially small proportion of variance. Since the purpose of factor analysis was to simplify, and we cannot allow more factors than there were tests in the original battery, some criterion will be used to determine when the procedure should stop and no more factors be extracted.

Table 6.5a shows the results of a principal components analysis of the correlation matrix of Table 6.4. Three factors have been extracted, each explaining a progressively smaller amount of variance. The first factor loads moderately on all tests although rather more on the reasoning tests 3 and 4 than on the remainder. Factor II accounts for the high correlation between the two verbal tests 1 and 2, and equally for the high correlation between the two spatial tests, but also shows that when you have made allowance for the overall positive manifold (i.e., extracted the general factor), performance on verbal tests is independent of performance on spatial tests (signified by the positive loadings of the former and negative loadings of the latter). Factor III is notably less important than Factors I and II, accounting for only just over 1% of the variance, so less regard should be had for its significance. But it accounts for the correlation between spatial tests independent of that between reasoning tests (and vice-versa).

Instead of selecting our factors in accordance with Spearman's criterion of the amount of variance they will explain, we could select them in accordance with Thurstone's, i.e. to approximate as closely as possible to the principle of simple structure. The standard procedure is first to perform a principal components analysis, in order to see how many factors can meaningfully be extracted, and then to rotate these factors so that they are close to some groups of tests but not to others (the reader is referred back to Fig. 6.1 for a graphical illustration of what this means). The effect of such rotation will be to reduce the proportion of variance in the correlation matrix explained by the first factor (i.e. to dethrone g), but to increase the proportion of variance explained by subsequent factors. A standard program for achieving this is termed 'varimax rotation', where the criterion is to maximize the variance of the loadings of tests on the factors. This will, of course, be achieved by finding factors with both high *and* low loadings—in effect rotating to simple structure. Varimax or orthogonal rotation gives the solution shown in Table 6.5b; the main difference from Table 6.5a, apart from the change in the proportion of variance explained by each factor, is that the first factor now loads more on the two reasoning tests 3 and 4 than on the remaining tests, while the second and third factors now do the work of the second factor of the principal components analysis, one accounting for the high correlation between the two verbal tests 1 and 2, and the other for the high correlation between the two spatial tests 5 and 6. The independence of these two factors accounts, of course, for the low correlation between verbal and spatial tests.

The orthogonal rotation shown in Table 6.5b fails to capture one salient feature of the correlation matrix of Table 6.4—the overall positive manifold. This is rectified by Table 6.5c, which shows an oblique rotation factor solution. The only difference from Table 6.5b (the same as that between Figs 6.1b and 6.1c) is that the factors are no longer required to satisfy the requirement of independence imposed in the original orthogonal rotation. The solution satisfies the same criterion as before, that of maximizing the number of high and

Table 6.5 Three alternative factorial solutions to the correlation matrix of Table 6.4

Tests	(a) Principal components analysis Factor loadings			(b) Orthogonal rotation Factor loadings			(c) Oblique rotation Factor loadings		
	I	II	III	I	II	III	I	II	III
Verbal									
1	0.53	0.70	0.16	0.17	0.90	0.12	0.03	0.90	0.02
2	0.46	0.75	0.18	0.11	0.92	0.07	−0.03	0.94	−0.02
Reasoning									
3	0.67	−0.08	−0.60	0.91	0.15	0.13	0.96	0.01	0.08
4	0.74	−0.16	−0.46	0.86	0.14	0.29	0.87	0.00	0.10
Spatial									
5	0.67	−0.43	0.40	0.24	0.09	0.88	0.06	−0.01	0.90
6	0.63	−0.41	0.49	0.15	0.11	0.91	−0.04	0.02	0.94

low loadings, but now without this added constraint. As can be seen, the results are similar to the solution of Table 6.5b, but significantly tidied up round the edges. The three factors have the same patterns of high and low loadings as in Table 6.5b, but the high loadings are somewhat higher and the low loadings significantly lower. Indeed, the three factors of Table 6.5c, unlike those of Table 6.5b, could now be said to approximate quite closely to Thurstone's ideal. Each test loads onto only one factor, or, put another way, each factor accounts for the performance of a different, non-overlapping sub-set of tests: the oblique rotation has identified three distinct factors, verbal, spatial, and reasoning. Remember, however, that this has been achieved by allowing the three factors themselves to correlate. In fact the reasoning factor correlates 0.31 with the verbal factor, and 0.42 with the spatial factor, while the verbal and spatial factors also correlate 0.22.

It is obvious, however, from inspection of Table 6.5 that the distinction between the three solutions is not as great as all that. In the original principal components analysis (Table 6.5a), the first factor loads onto all six tests, but substantially more onto the two reasoning tests than onto the rest, while the second and third factors account for the groupings of the two verbal tests and of the two spatial tests. In Table 6.5c the second and third factors do much the same work as in Table 6.5a, but factor I now loads only onto the two reasoning tests, not onto the verbal and spatial tests. The positive correlation between all six tests, which in the principal components analysis was accounted for by their all loading onto the first factor, is here explained by the correlation between the three factors. There is a final feature of Table 6.4 which deserves comment: the two reasoning tests 3 and 4 correlate both with the verbal and (more strongly) with the spatial tests. But the verbal and spatial tests scarcely correlate with one another at all. This, too, is represented both by the principal components analysis and by the oblique rotation, but in different ways. In the principal components analysis, the two reasoning tests have higher g loadings than do the verbal or spatial tests. In the oblique rotation analysis, this critical feature is represented by the pattern of the correlation between the three factors themselves: the reasoning factor I correlates more strongly with both the verbal and spatial factors than do these last two with one another.

There are, of course, differences between the three versions of Table 6.5, i.e. between different factorial solutions. And it is equally true that, in principle, one can generate an indefinite number of other 'solutions' to the correlation matrix of Table 6.4. But the actual matrix does still constrain the nature of the solution possible; all three versions of Table 6.5 acknowledge that the six tests form three clusters, with the second cluster being correlated with both the first and the third. The difference between the techniques of the principal components and oblique rotation solutions is whether the general factor is the first to be extracted, or whether it emerges, after group factors have been extracted, as the explanation of the correlation between them. In the principal components analysis, the general factor will not only explain a higher proportion of variance in the overall matrix, it will also, so to say, take over one of the group factors identified in the rotated solution. In Table 6.5a, the two reasoning tests 3 and 4 have higher loadings than the other tests only on factor I, i.e. on the general factor. There is no group factor, as there is in Table 6.5c, specifically for these two tests: it has been submerged into *g*.

The example we have worked through may have been hypothetical, but it was also carefully chosen to illustrate the differences between two different classes of factorial theory. According to the hierarchical theory of Vernon (1950) and Burt (1949), there is a general factor, *g*, plus two broad group factors, in Vernon's terminology *v:ed* or verbal/educational and *k:m* or spatial/mechanical. Vernon and Burt's procedure for factor analysing a correlation matrix corresponds to that shown in Table 6.5a: they first extract the general factor, then subsidiary group factors. Cattell (1971) also proposed a hierarchical theory, but his procedure corresponds to that shown in Table 6.5c, rotation to simple structure with oblique factors, followed by second-order analysis to extract more general factors, Gf, Gc, Gv, etc. (see p. 214).

What is the relationship between these two accounts of the structure of abilities? One reason why Cattell's model has more higher-order or broad group factors than the Vernon–Burt model is simply that Cattell has analysed a very much larger and more carefully chosen battery of tests. If, for example, a test battery contains only a single test that provides a good measure of speed, factor analysis will not yield a broad speed factor, since several tests must load onto a factor before it can be extracted (see Box 6.2). This probably explains why the Vernon–Burt model does not contain any group factors corresponding to Cattell's Gs and Gr. But apart from this, the differences between the models are relatively minor, and one model can in fact be readily translated into the other. To a first approximation, Cattell's Gf, Gc, and Gv correspond to Vernon's *g*, *v:ed*, and *k:m*.

The apparent difference between the models is largely a consequence of different techniques of factor analysis. The Vernon–Burt principal components analysis, as in Table 6.5a, extracts *g* first: since all tests tend to correlate with one another, they will all load onto this general factor, tests of reasoning more strongly than others. The residual intercorrelations between groups of more particularly verbal and spatial tests are accounted for by the verbal and spatial group factors, *v:ed* and *k:m*. In Cattell's model (as in Table 6.5c), these two group factors are labelled Gc and Gv respectively, but the general factor, *g*, has been split up between the group factor for the two reasoning tests 3 and 4, and the higher-order factor that accounts for the correlation between the three group factors. The group factor for tests 3 and 4 is, of course, Cattell's Gf. But it turns out that the higher-order factor also corresponds closely to Gf. Higher-order analysis of Cattell's correlated group factors reveals that they have quite different loadings on the higher-order factor: Gf has the highest loading, followed by Gc, with the other factors, Gv, Gs, etc. having distinctly weaker loadings. Indeed, although some commentators (e.g. Carroll, 1993) have questioned such a strong conclusion, Gustafsson (1988) has argued that the loading of Gf on the higher-order factor is essentially unity—i.e. that the two are effectively identical. If this is right, then Cattell's Gf corresponds almost exactly to Vernon's *g*.

Box 6.2 What you get out depends on what you put in

The factorial structure revealed by factor analysis of a battery of IQ tests will always depend on the nature of the tests in that battery. Given the pervasive positive manifold, factor analysis of a set of IQ tests will almost inevitably reveal a substantial general factor. But subsidiary group factors can only be revealed if more than one test loads onto them. Factor analysis of the Wechsler tests, for example, reveals at best only three subsidiary factors in addition to *g*: verbal, performance, and (usually) a small third factor which the arithmetic and digit-span sub-tests load onto. The verbal factor is similar to Cattell's Gc; but the performance factor, being based on a rather motley assortment of sub-tests is not particularly closely related to Cattell's Gf—nor to Gv or a spatial factor since block design and object assembly are the only two sub-tests with any substantial spatial component (see Fig 6.2). And, as can also be seen in Fig. 6.2, digit symbol is the only sub-test loading onto a factor of perceptual speed, so no such factor can appear from a factor analysis of the Wechsler tests.

A further problem that arises from factor analysis of relatively small test batteries is that the sensible identification of the factor becomes very difficult. Why should a factor that accounts for performance on arithmetic and digit span be labelled as 'freedom from distraction'? Why not 'number' or 'short-term memory'? Only when the inter-relations between these tests and several others have been clarified can one talk confidently of what it might be that they share in common.

One way of representing these relationships is illustrated in Fig. 6.2. This is a much simplified version of the results of an analysis presented by Snow *et al.* (1984), who used multi-dimensional scaling to represent the relationships between various tests. The distance between any two tests in the figure is inversely related to the similarity (i.e. correlation) between them, and the heavy lines drawn round clusters of tests represent the broad factors identified by more conventional factor analysis. As can be seen, tests of reasoning, such as Raven's Matrices or letter series are at the centre, defining the general factor or Gf, while verbal, spatial, memory, and perceptual speed tests form clusters round this central core—their proximity to the centre representing their loading on this general factor. Although employing rather different techniques, this analysis implies a very similar picture to that arising from Cattell's hierarchical model, and Gustafsson's identification of the general factor with Gf.

It would be misleading to suggest that there is perfect consensus between different factorists. Given the history of factor analysis, it is hardly surprising that there should remain substantial differences of emphasis, which proponents of rival approaches are sometimes happy to elevate to the status of fundamental differences of principle. But it would be equally wrong to think that factor analysis has totally failed to advance our understanding of the relationship between different types of IQ test, or to imply that no two factorists would ever agree on the best description of those relationships. For most purposes, it is immaterial whether there are 10, 25, 50, or 150 relatively narrow factors. To

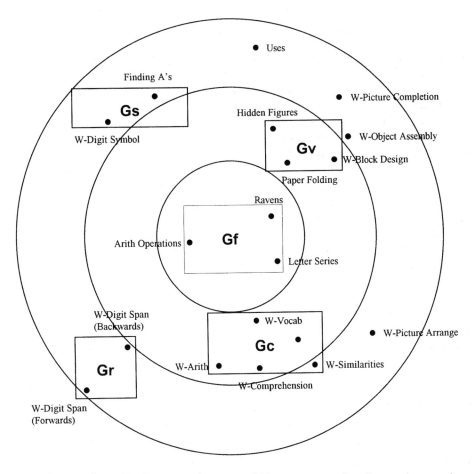

Fig. 6.2 The interrelationships between various types of IQ test represented as distances between the tests in two-dimensional space. Tests at the centre of the space are more closely related to all other tests than are those nearer the periphery. Solid lines are drawn round groups of tests defining some of Cattell's major factors, Gf, Gc, Gv, Gs. Tests labelled W are sub-tests of the WAIS. (Adapted from Snow *et al.*, 1984).

a large extent, the number that can be extracted depends on the size of one's test battery. It is more important to allow that it appears possible to distinguish between up to half a dozen or so broad factors (or groups of tests), one of which, *g* or perhaps Gf, is more central than the others to whatever it is that IQ tests measure, in that it correlates with a broader range of tests than the other factors do. These other factors certainly include a verbal/educational and a spatial/visualization factor, and probably also perceptual speed, fluency, and retrieval factors.

The interpretation of the general factor

Although different techniques of factor analysis converge on solutions that are recognizably similar to one another, differences between their solutions can still be discerned. The general factor extracted by a principal components analysis of an IQ test battery is that which is common to all tests in the battery. If we follow Cattell's method of analysis, and accept Gustafsson's interpretation of that analysis, the general factor is that common to tests of abstract reasoning, which happen to correlate rather strongly with most other kinds of IQ test. Which of these alternatives should we choose? Is there really any difference between them?

The answer to these questions will require consideration of evidence and arguments that go well beyond those of factor analysis. Indeed, they will form the substance of the following three chapters. But there remains one important point of disagreement between Spearman and Thurstone that we have not yet touched on, and the discussion of that disagreement will serve to introduce some of the psychological arguments, going beyond factor analysis, which will determine how we should interpret the general factor.

General intelligence as g

A large general factor, g, is revealed by a principal components analysis of any IQ test battery because, to a first approximation, scores on any one test correlate positively with scores on any other. The statistical importance of this general factor, i.e. the proportion of variance in the original correlation matrix it can account for, is simply a reflection of the overall magnitude of these positive correlations. But Spearman, of course, invested g with psychological importance as well. He had a rather low opinion of most IQ test batteries, which he thought were little better than a hodgepodge of arbitrarily and idiosyncratically chosen sub-tests. But this did not matter, since their very diversity meant that the various specific abilities each test measured cancelled each other out, leaving the general factor, g, to shine forth as the true measure of general intelligence.

Thurstone took strong issue with this particular argument, insisting that g could not possibly have any psychological validity, since the general factor extracted from one test battery was not necessarily the same as the general factor extracted from another battery (Thurstone, 1947). In principle, at least there can be no doubt that Thurstone's argument is correct. A principal components analysis of any set of intercorrelated tests will always yield a first principal component, or general factor that accounts for a significant proportion of the variance in those test scores. But this general factor *might* be quite different from that extracted from a different set of tests. Thurstone's illustration of his argument is shown in Fig. 6.3. The curved lines form a triangle on the surface of a sphere, and the small circles are the points where various test vectors, radiating out from the unseen centre of the sphere, intersect with its surface. The 12 tests shown in the left-hand figure yield as their general factor the g near the bottom right-hand corner of the triangle; the 12 different tests in the right-hand figure yield a quite different general factor. As an illustration of Thurstone's argument, consider the general factor extracted from the WAIS, which can only reflect the particular sub-tests that go to make it up. In one respect, at least, Spearman was right: they are, to put it bluntly, a fairly arbitrary set. As can be seen by referring back to Fig. 6.2, they provide a distinctly uneven sampling of the various factors identified in that figure—the majority being tests of Gc, with no test of Gf, only one of Gs, and perhaps two of Gv. This explains, as we have already seen, why the WAIS cannot yield a speed factor or a strong spatial factor. But it also seems probable that if some reasoning tests, several more speed tests, or several more spatial tests, were added to the WAIS, the centre of gravity of the new test battery (i.e. its general factor) would shift accordingly.

Spearman believed otherwise. His principle of 'the indifference of the indicator' implied that the precise contents of a set of tests was wholly unimportant: all that mattered were their g-loadings. In this he has been followed by modern theorists such as Jensen (1980), who has argued that the general factor extracted from one large and diverse test battery invariably turns out to be the same as that extracted from another. Given that *all* IQ tests tend to correlate with one another, it will indeed follow that different test batteries will tend to yield similar, i.e. correlated, general factors. The real question is: how similar? There is surprisingly little evidence: Jensen (1980), for example, cited only a single study, from 1935, to support his argument. A more recent study by Thorndike (1987) sought to approach the question from a slightly different angle, by measuring the loadings of a number of tests on the general factors extracted from six independent test batteries. The correlations between the g-loadings in one test battery and another ranged from 0.52 to 0.94. The latter figure suggests something close to identity, but at the low end of the range it is clear that the general factors of the different test batteries cannot be the same.

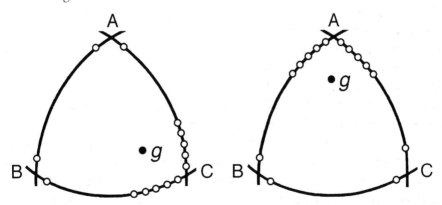

Fig. 6.3 Diagrammatic illustration of Thurstone's argument that the identity of g varies with the nature of the tests in a battery. The small circles represent the points on the surface of a sphere where 12 test vectors intersect the surface. The three points A, B, and C represent, according to Thurstone, three primary mental abilities or group factors. In the left-hand figure, the majority of the 12 tests happen to load on factor C; in the right-hand figure, the majority happen to load on A.

There is independent reason to question the identity of the general factors extracted from different test batteries. As we saw in Chapter 5, modern studies of the Wechsler tests have generally yielded a small but reliable sex difference, of the order of 2–3 points in overall IQ, in favour of males. Of course, this overall difference conceals a rather wide range of differences on the various sub-tests of the scale—some of which actually favour females. But it so happens that the sub-tests with the greatest male advantage tend to be those with the highest loadings on the general factor extracted from the total test. The consequence is that the sex difference on this general factor is even larger than that in overall IQ, with a male advantage of some 4 IQ points (Lynn, 1994*b*). But other test batteries, as we saw, typically yield much smaller overall differences in favour of males, and on others females come out ahead. There is no way that factor analysis of these other test batteries could give general factors on which males outscored females by 4 IQ points. Their general factors cannot therefore be the same as that derived from the Wechsler tests (Mackintosh, 1996).

Thurstone's conclusion was blunt:

> A general factor can always be found routinely for any set of positively correlated tests, and it means nothing more or less than the average of all the abilities called for by the battery as a whole. Consequently, it varies from one battery to another and has no fundamental psychological significance . . . As psychologists we cannot be interested in a general factor which is only the average of any random collection of tests. (Thurstone, 1940, p. 208)

Thurstone may have exaggerated the variation in *g* from one large and diverse test battery to another. But his point remains valid. To the extent that the general factor of one test battery differs from that of another, it seems perverse to set so much store by a general intelligence defined in this way.

But Spearman was perfectly clear that general intelligence or *g* was not to be defined solely by factor analysis. He saw that factor analysis was only the first step towards a theory of human intelligence: it may describe the pattern of interrelationships between a variety of different IQ tests, but that is not the same as revealing the structure of human abilities. Thus factor analysis of any IQ test battery will reveal a large general factor, *g*, because performance on one test correlates with performance on all others. But it does not explain *why* performance on all tests should correlate in this way. According to Spearman, the explanation is because performance on all tests in the battery depends, to a greater or lesser extent, on a single, psychological process. Spearman's thesis has been accepted by many later theorists. But it has also been vigorously disputed. According to one version of the critic's argument, Spearman's interpretation of the general factor amounted to

> the cardinal invalid inference that has plagued factor analysis ever since. He reified it as an 'entity' and tried to give it an unambiguous causal interpretation. He called it *g* or general intelligence, and imagined that he had identified a unitary quality underlying cognitive mental activity. (Gould, 1997, p. 281)

But Gould's argument is at best misleading, at worst plain false. Spearman's inference was invalid only if he believed that the existence of a general factor *necessarily* implied that there must be a single general process. That, as we shall see in due course, is certainly false. But a more sensible reconstruction of Spearman's argument is simply that he was advancing a possible explanation of the general factor. And that explanation is surely entirely plausible—for it is not absurd to suppose that the reason why performance on one test correlates with performance on another (or all others) is because both tests (or all tests) tap a single, common psychological process.

But what might this process be, and how shall we set about identifying it? Spearman's first answer was based on his factorial argument that performance on any given individual test was determined by two factors, one general, accounting for the correlation between this test and all others, the second unique, being specific to that particular test (Spearman, 1927). He argued that the specific factors could be regarded as the nuts and bolts of cognition, the particular processes needed for solution of a particular type of problem, while the general factor was the mental energy that powered these specific engines. It is not immediately obvious what to make of this suggestion, and perhaps even harder to see how it might be put to empirical test. But in a somewhat different guise, it has been resurrected by Anderson (1992), who has proposed a cognitive architecture of human intelligence consisting of a basic processing mechanism supplemented by a number of specific processors and modules. Variations in the speed and efficiency of the basic processing mechanism are responsible for variations in *g* or general intelligence, because they set limits to the performance of the specific processors which operate on particular types of information, such as verbal and propositional or visuo-spatial. Anderson's account shares much in common with an idea proposed by Brand and Deary (1982), Eysenck (1982, 1986), and Jensen (1982, 1987*b*), that the single psychological or neurological process underlying *g* is the speed and efficiency of information processing by the nervous system. Attempts to test this idea will form the main focus of Chapter 7: various laboratory tasks have been devised that supposedly provide a direct measure of such speed and efficiency of information processing, and the question at issue is whether performance on such tasks correlates with *g*.

General intelligence as reasoning ability

It is true that one possible, perhaps even plausible, explanation of the general factor is that performance on all types of IQ test depends on a single underlying psychological or neurological process. It is even possible that this single process can be conceptualized as the speed and efficiency with which the brain processes information. But it is a relatively simple matter to see that at least two other classes of explanation are equally possible. A general factor can be extracted from any IQ test battery because of the overall positive manifold: those who obtain high or low scores on one test are more likely than not to obtain high or low scores on others. But there is no compelling reason to suppose that a high correlation between performance on two different tests must mean that the two tests measure the same process: it is quite compatible with those two tests depending on wholly different psychological processes, skills or abilities—provided that possession of the skill required for test 1 happens, for whatever reason, to be correlated with possession of the skill required for test 2. Thus those who have a high verbal IQ, i.e. have a large vocabulary and a wide store of general knowledge, may, as a matter of fact, happen also to be good at solving the sort of mental rotation tasks that define spatial IQ. And the reason may be nothing more mysterious than the fact that an environment that encourages one ability may also be the sort of environment that encourages the other (Gould, 1997). As Gould has noted, one could even imagine a genetic cause of the correlation between psychologically distinct skills. To claim that different psychological processes underlie performance on two different tasks is to make a claim about the nature of the psychological theories needed to account for such performance. It says nothing about whether people who differ in terms of one set of processes will or will not differ in terms of the other.

There is a second, quite different, and for our purposes more interesting, possibility. Correlations between two or more tests may arise, not because each test depends, to a greater or lesser extent, on one single process, but because each test engages a sub-set of a very large number of elementary processes or operations, and there is bound to be some overlap between the processes tapped by one test and those tapped by another. The idea was first put forward by Thomson in Britain (1916, 1939) and by Thorndike (1925) and Hull (1928) in the United States. What they all had in mind was a classic associationist (nowadays we should call it connectionist) theory, which talked of bonds or connections between elementary or neural elements, or the like. Assume, for the sake of argument, a mind consisting of 1000 such elements. If two tasks each engage 500 of these elements, the chances are that 250 of them will be common to both tasks. But if half the elements operating in task 1 are the same as half the elements operating in task 2, the correlation between performance on the two tasks will be 0.5. In general, if P_1 and P_2 are the proportion of the total set of elements sampled by tasks 1 and 2, the correlation between performance on the two tasks will be $\sqrt{P_1 \times P_2}$. Tests that load strongly on g, on this account, are simply tests that sample a high proportion of the available elements, but it does not follow that any one set of elements is common to all tests that show positive correlations.

There is no need to resort to such an elementary theory of the mind. Thurstone relied on what amounts to the same argument to explain why two tests, that supposedly measured different primary mental abilities, correlated with one another. His argument, as we noted above, ran as follows: if a test of reasoning correlates with a spatial test, this could be either because part of the reasoning test incorporates spatial content, or because part of the spatial test requires non-spatial reasoning. The fact of the matter is that it may never be possible to devise factorially pure mental tests, i.e. tests that tap only a single primary mental ability.

Thomson's and Thurstone's versions of this explanation of *g* may be regarded as two ends of a continuum, Thomson appealing to a very large number of elementary units sampled by different tests, Thurstone to a much smaller number of very much higher-level abilities. Modern cognitive psychology would probably encourage a view somewhere between the two. Cognitive psychology postulates a variety of different processes or operations involved in the performance of cognitive tasks. At the perceptual level, these would include: sensory analysis, transformation of input, formation of representations, listing of attributes; beyond this initial sensory level, theorists will talk of the focusing or shifting of attention; the input must then be held in some sort of store—iconic memory, working memory, etc. before being elaborated on, combined with other information to solve a problem, or transferred to a longer-term memory; executive processes will determine the sequence of operations to be performed, choose between different strategies, or decide to shift from one strategy to another. And so on. Some or all of these processes are likely to be engaged by the task of answering different questions in IQ tests. The positive manifold might then arise because performance on different IQ tests depends on overlapping sub-sets of these processes. Some of the processes are, no doubt, more important than others, in the sense of entering into more tests than others, but there may be no single process, which we could label 'general intelligence', entering into all. An alternative possibility is that there might be many different cognitive processes entering into performance on all IQ tests. (This would mean that the general factor could not be reduced to a *single* common psychological process.)

This first idea is illustrated in Table 6.6; here there are six tests, divided into three groups, and given the same three labels, verbal, reasoning and spatial, as in Table 6.4. We have also postulated a number of different hypothetical processes (11 in all), tapped by the six tests. The tests within each pair share three processes in common with one another, but fewer processes in common with the other pairs of tests. Thus the two reasoning tests each share two processes in common with each of the verbal and spatial tests, but the two verbal and the two spatial tests share only one process in common. This pattern of shared processes would be sufficient to account for the pattern of intercorrelations between the six hypothetical tests shown in Table 6.4. The three pairs of tests form three clusters of high correlations, separated by lower correlations between pairs. Verbal and spatial tests correlate only weakly. The reasoning tests are central to the test battery in the sense that they correlate more strongly with both verbal and spatial tests than these latter two pairs do with one another. But notice that no process enters into performance on more than four of the six tests: in other words, there is no single process underlying performance on all.

The hypothesis that the general factor arises as a consequence of this overlap in the processes engaged by different IQ tests, it will be evident, sits quite comfortably with the view that general intelligence is best conceptualized as reasoning ability or Cattell's Gf. The centrality of measures of Gf is that they engage more processes shared by other tests than other tests share with one another.

Table 6.6 The general factor explained without appeal to a single underlying process common to all tests

Tests	Hypothetical processes										
	1	2	3	4	5	6	7	8	9	10	11
Verbal											
1	+	+	+	+							
2		+	+	+	+						
Reasoning											
3		+	+			+	+			+	
4			+	+		+	+				+
Spatial											
5		+				+			+		+
6				+		+			+	+	

A + sign means that performance on that test depends upon that hypothetical process.

It is worth noting that Spearman himself, in the same book in which he described *g* as the mental energy that fuelled the specific operations engaged by specific tests, also advanced a quite different psychological theory of general intelligence, in the form of his three 'noegenetic laws' (Spearman, 1927). He argued that general intelligence consisted of three processes (implying that it is not a single ability?): (1) the apprehension of one's own experience, (2) the eduction of relations, and (3) the eduction of correlates. When translated into less barbarous English, these last two, at least, have a certain face validity as an account of the set of intellectual operations involved in inductive or deductive reasoning and problem solving. Reasoning by analogy, after all, can be said to depend on perceiving (educing) relationships between terms, and then inferring the nature of the missing term that satisfies the same relationship (educing the correlate). A simple analogy, such as:

> *black is to white, as night is to ?*

is solved by seeing that black and white are opposites, and then working out what is the opposite of night.

Spearman's noegenetic laws, as we saw in Chapter 2, formed the theoretical basis for the construction of Raven's Matrices—a paradigmatic measure of reasoning ability or Gf. Whether or not Spearman's particular formulation is especially helpful, the view that general intelligence is best measured by tests such as Raven's Matrices, and that the overall positive manifold occurs because different IQ tests engage partially overlapping sets of psychological processes (with measures of Gf being particularly likely to engage processes in common with other tests) suggests a quite different strategy for further empirical and theoretical analysis. Rather than look for tasks that putatively measure the single process underlying *g*, and seeing whether performance on them correlates with measures of *g*, we should be trying to analyse the cognitive processes that contribute to performance on a variety of different IQ tests, and see whether one or more of these processes is implicated in more than one kind of test. Chapters 8 and 9 review attempts to pursue this strategy.

Summary

What do IQ tests measure? Test constructors claim that they measure individual differences in intelligence. But is there any such thing as intelligence to be measured? Psychometricians have used factor analysis as their first chosen method of attempting to answer this sort of question. Factor analysis, properly understood, is no more than a technique for trying to simplify, or see patterns in, large correlation matrices. If we administer a large test battery, say of 10 separate tests, to a sample of the population, we can calculate the correlation between each pair of tests, but the resulting matrix of 100 correlations will be far too unwieldy to make much sense. Factor analysis rests on the assumption that the reason why performance on two tests correlates is because these two tests are, partly, measuring the same thing. So our original 10 × 10 correlation matrix can be rendered more intelligible if we could show that it could be accounted for by postulating a much smaller number of hypothetical factors with which the 10 tests correlated to varying degrees.

In the limiting case, factor analysis may be able to show that the postulation of a single factor is sufficient to account for the entire pattern of correlations. Spearman believed that this was true for the correlation matrix of a battery of IQ tests, and labelled this single factor *g*. He thus claimed that IQ measured a single underlying process of general intelligence. Believing that human intelligence is better conceptualized as a set of largely independent faculties or cognitive abilities, Thurstone sought to dismiss Spearman's conclusion by showing that a different technique for factor analysis revealed evidence of clusters of tests which correlated quite strongly with one another, but less strongly with tests in other clusters.

Because Thurstone used rather different procedures for factor analysis (rotation to simple structure) from those employed by Spearman's followers (principal components analysis), it has often been argued that factor analysis will never reveal anything about the structure of human abilities. There is an indefinite number of mathematically equivalent factorial solutions to any correlation matrix, and the choice of one solution over another reflects no more than the factorists' theoretical prejudice. This claim ignores two important points. First, the actual pattern of intercorrelations observed between a large number of different IQ tests rules out both Spearman's and Thurstone's initially preferred solutions—and both men acknowledged this. Spearman's solution is ruled out because in any such matrix one does find clusters of tests that correlate more highly with one another than they do with tests in other clusters. Thurstone's solution is ruled out because of the overall positive manifold: correlations between different clusters of tests are all positive. But both Spearman and Thurstone could take comfort from that aspect of the data which contradicted the other's theoretical preconception. Thus there is a general factor common to all IQ tests, but there are also a number of more specific factors—usually labelled verbal, non-verbal reasoning, spatial, perceptual speed, etc., which are tapped by different groups of test.

Secondly, although different procedures for factor analysis will produce somewhat different factorial solutions for any correlation matrix, the nature of that matrix will determine what solutions are possible, and it is a rather simple matter to see the relationships between different solutions.

Factor analysis can do no more than describe the relationships between different IQ tests. This is not the same as uncovering the structure of human abilities. That will only be achieved by the development and testing of psychological theory. Thus the fact that a general factor can always be extracted from a battery of IQ tests does not mean that there is a single underlying cognitive process tapped by all IQ tests. It is equally possible that all IQ tests tap a large number of different processes, but that there is some overlap in the set of processes tapped by different groups of tests. Decision between these alternative possibilities will require experimental and theoretical analysis.

7   *The search for general intelligence: simple behavioural and neurological correlates of IQ*

Introduction

Factor analysis may suggest possible answers to the first questions that experimental psychologists should be asking about IQ and the nature of human intelligence. But it will never be sufficient to answer further questions. Thus even if we could all agree that factor analysis has revealed that there is a general factor, *g*, common to a very wide variety of apparently different IQ tests, it will not enable us to decide whether performance on each and every IQ test depends, to a greater or lesser extent, on a single process or ability, or whether different types of test tap a series of partially overlapping abilities, no one of which is involved in all tests. And if factor analysis cannot answer that question, it is obvious that it will be equally unable to answer the next set of questions: what is the nature of this single psychological process, or of this series of overlapping abilities? The present chapter reviews a series of research programmes that have taken as their starting point the hypothesis that *g* is a unitary process, and have sought to identify its nature. The following two chapters consider the alternative possibility.

It is clear that, to answer these questions, we need a psychological or biological theory of the nature of intelligence, and an experimental programme to test that theory. But what theory? And what programme of research? Let us take up these questions in reverse order. One popular strategy has been to look for correlations between IQ scores and some aspects of performance on some standard laboratory information-processing task. While this may seem, at first sight, a reasonable and profitable approach, a moment's reflection suggests that there is no *a priori* reason why it should greatly advance our understanding of the nature of IQ. Taken by itself, the discovery that scores on an IQ test correlate with performance on some particular laboratory task does little more than show that this task could well have been added to existing IQ tests. The Stanford–Binet test and the Wechsler scales already consist of a series of sub-tests, each of which satisfies the criterion that it correlates with performance on the remainder of the test. What is the point of adding yet another sub-test to the total scale? For example, one of the components of both Stanford–Binet and Wechsler tests is the digit-span task. But this has been a popular experimental paradigm for 50 years or more, so that we already know that IQ scores correlate with performance on one standard laboratory task. What has this discovery told us about the nature of IQ?

The question is worth posing, because in this particular case, a partial answer can be provided. But the answer is considerably more complicated than one might, naively, have supposed, and the provision of that answer would never have been possible without a reasonable theoretical understanding of the digit-span task. The naive explanation of the correlation between IQ and digit span is that IQ must involve, or depend on, short-term memory: perhaps a high IQ is synonymous with a large short-term memory capacity. There are two problems with this explanation. First, performance on digit-span tasks correlates rather poorly with other memory tasks (Martin, 1978; Miller and Vernon, 1992). Secondly, further analyses has revealed two rather distinct causes of differences in memory span: first, differences in the speed with which subjects are capable of articulating the items in the list; secondly, the development of various rehearsal strategies (see Chapter 8). Both of these differences are probably responsible for the correlation between digit span and IQ. The point is that understanding this correlation has depended on a detailed theoretical analysis of the processes underlying performance on the digit-span task, combined with a further analysis to show how one or more of these processes may be involved in performance on IQ tests.

This cautionary tale is intended as a preamble to a discussion of correlations between IQ and some other, apparently very simple, or basic, measures, including measures of the brain. The excitement generated by some of this research seems to have rested on two often unstated assumptions. First, these correlates of IQ are supposedly much simpler than IQ itself, and therefore *must* have advanced our understanding by allowing us to reduce something as mysterious and complex as an IQ score to something simple and therefore well understood. Secondly, some of these correlates, for example those involving measures of the brain, are frequently regarded as more fundamental or biological than an IQ score. It supposedly follows that the *cause* of the correlation is immediately obvious: differences in the brain are the direct cause of differences in IQ. It is all too easy to be carried away by this line of reasoning, but it needs to be resisted. The discovery of a correlation between IQ scores and some measure of the brain, or a new behavioural task, however simple it may seem, will not advance our understanding of the nature of IQ unless we have a theoretical explanation for these correlations. How does this measure of the brain relate to differences in IQ? What is the nature of the processes responsible for performance on that task, and why should they correlate with IQ?

One reason why so many investigators have looked for correlations between IQ scores and these apparently simple behavioural or neural measures, is because they have been committed to a belief in the unitary nature of g, and have assumed, with some reason, that any candidate for the role of unitary basis of g is likely to be some rather fundamental aspect of the 'efficiency' of the brain. On the face of it, after all, it is not easy to imagine what single process, measurable by performance on some simple laboratory task, could be of sufficient generality to contribute to performance on tests of general knowledge or vocabulary, mental arithmetic, digit span, mental rotation, letter cancelling and other measures of perceptual speed, the solution of Raven's Matrices, or letter-series problems, etc., etc. The problem seems a daunting one: the solution proposed is that the single process underlying g is not some complex set of cognitive operations; it is not to be construed as the possession of appropriate strategies for problem solving, for generating and testing hypotheses, inferring rules or abstracting generalizations. It is a basic property of the nervous system considered as an information-processing device. In one version of this hypothesis (Eysenck, 1982, 1986) the operation of the nervous system is said to involve the transmission of signals, encoded as a series of pulse trains. Decisions about the nature of a signal, and therefore of the appropriate response in a later part of the system, are taken by sampling over a series of such pulses. Errors of transmission will add noise and hence make it harder to reach a decision, and further sampling may be required before a sufficiently unambiguous message is received. Intelligence, then, is a function of the fidelity and speed of transmission of these signals. The 'intelligent' nervous system will respond accurately to incoming signals, and will therefore also be able to respond rapidly; the less intelligent will make errors and respond slowly. This is the biological substrate of the general factor common to all IQ tests. As we noted in the last chapter, a very similar account has been incorporated by Anderson (1992) into a modern version of Spearman's two-factor theory, according to which intelligence depends both on the speed and efficiency of a central basic processing mechanism and on particular specialized processors.

This necessarily crude and brief summary of Eysenck's and Anderson's theorizing will have served its purpose if it shows why we should expect to see a strong correlation between measured IQ and performance on certain, very simple tasks. Two particular behavioural tasks have been studied, inspection time and reaction time. In a typical inspection-time experiment, two vertical lines are flashed briefly on the screen and the subject's task is to report which is the longer. The difference in length is well above threshold, but the task is made difficult by reducing the duration of exposure to the point where errors occur. In a simple reaction-time experiment, subjects are instructed to press a key whenever a signal comes on: in choice reaction-time experiments, there are several alternative signals, only one of which is presented on a given trial, and the subject must press the appropriate key for that signal. Significant correlations have been reported between IQ scores and the duration of exposure necessary for accurate discrimination in inspection-time tasks, and the speed with which subjects respond in reaction-time tasks.

In addition to these simple behavioural correlates of IQ, there have been repeated attempts to find more 'biological' correlates of IQ, by taking measures of the size of the brain or functioning of the nervous system. One particularly active field of research has involved recording event-related potentials (ERPs) to brief auditory or visual stimuli. Some studies have reported remarkably high correlations between IQ and some measures of such ERPs. These last correlations suggested to Eysenck: 'that we have come quite close to the physiological measurement of the genotype underlying the phenotypic IQ tests results on which we have had to rely so far' (Eysenck, 1982, p. 6). But the correlations with the two simple behavioural tasks seemed to hold an equally important message, namely, 'the astonishing conclusion that the best tests of individual differences in cognitive ability are non-cognitive in nature!' (Eysenck, 1982, p. 9). The suggestion is that we can bypass the attempts of cognitive psychology to analyse the processes underlying thinking, reasoning, problem solving, etc., for we now know that the fundamental process underlying all these activities is simply the accurate and rapid transmission of information through the nervous system.

We should not be quite so readily carried away. The research to be reviewed in what follows has made some intriguing and potentially important discoveries, which certainly require explanation. But those discoveries have probably not lived up to some initial expectations. As yet, this research has still not uncovered either the biological or the psychological basis of *g*.

Neurological correlates of IQ

Bigger is better? Brain size and IQ

That there should be a correlation between IQ scores and *some* measures of the structure or functioning of the nervous system does not seem very surprising. Cognitive or intellectual activity is surely mediated by the brain, and differences in such activity are likely to be reflected in differences in the brain. It is rather more surprising that so many commentators should be so reluctant to acknowledge the possibility. One explanation is no doubt to be found in the crude biologizing of early generations of investigators, who did not hesitate to make confident pronouncements about differences in the average intelligence of different human groups as a function of differences in the size of their brains (see Gould (1997) for an entertaining, if not always perfectly accurate, history; Michael (1988) provides some corrections to Gould's account).

Human evolution has been marked by an approximately threefold increase in the size of the brain in the past 3 million years, from the 450 g brain of australopithecines to the 1200–1500 g brain of *Homo sapiens*. Yet the human brain is an extremely expensive organ: although comprising no more than 2–3 per cent of body weight, the brain consumes some

20 per cent of our metabolic energy. These two observations suggest that our brains have significant adaptive value, and the popular inference has always been that it is our brains that endow us with our superior intelligence. Even if that were all true, it would not automatically follow that larger brains were associated with higher IQ scores. But the evidence that they are is reasonably convincing.

Lacking any direct way of measuring the size or weight of the living brain, earlier investigators relied on less direct measures such as endocranial casts (from the dead) or, even less directly, circumference of the head (obtainable from the living). Van Valen (1974) and Rushton and Ankney (1996) have reviewed a number of studies of the relationship between head size (usually circumference) and IQ. Van Valen reported a weighted mean correlation of 0.27; Rushton and Ankney one of 0.21 from 17 studies of some 45 000 children, and one of 0.15 from 15 studies of over 6000 adults. No doubt some of these studies are more reliable than others: the earliest, at the beginning of the twentieth century, did not even have IQ measures available. But there are enough good, more recent studies, e.g. one of over 2000 Belgian 18-year-old males (Sausanne, 1979), or one of over 35 000 American 7-year-olds (Broman *et al.*, 1987) which have confirmed these values, to leave little doubt that the relationship is genuine.

It is still, of course, a rather modest one. But then the circumference of the head is only an imperfect measure of the size of the brain. The technologies of magnetic resonance imaging (MRI) and computer-aided tomography (CAT) allow more direct measures of the size of the brain *in vivo*. Since 1990, there have been five studies that have examined the relationship between such measures of brain size and IQ in normal adults: their weighted mean correlation is 0.38. Three other studies have reported similar correlations between brain size and measures of educational and occupational attainment (see Rushton and Ankney, 1996).

This is still not a particularly high correlation, but there can be no doubt of its reliability. The total number of subjects in the studies of brain size and IQ was over 200, and all five obtained remarkably uniform results, with correlations ranging from 0.35 to 0.43 (other studies, of clinical populations, have reported rather more variable and lower correlations— see Rushton and Ankney, 1996). But the interpretation of such an association is another matter. Even if we assume that larger brains somehow endow their owners with superior IQ, we should not have the first idea *how* they did so. It is tempting to suppose that all will be revealed when the association is narrowed down to some part or parts of the brain rather than others. No doubt that is one possible next step, but even if we knew that IQ is related to the size of, say, prefrontal cortex rather than cerebellum, we still should not understand why the size of prefrontal cortex was important. We should not even know whether differences in brain size were genetically determined or a consequence of differences in, say, early nutrition. And it would be equally plausible to suppose that an increase in the size of the brain occurred in response to the kinds of intellectually stimulating experience that foster cognitive development. There is, after all, evidence of just such an effect in other animals. Rats brought up in large cages, with numerous other rats and a variety of objects to play with, end up with larger brains than their equally well-nourished littermates reared in isolation in small, empty cages (Renner and Rosenzweig, 1987). At the end of the day, the establishment of a correlation between brain size and IQ has actually done rather little to advance our understanding of IQ—let alone of *g*.

Brain activity and IQ: EEGs and ERPs

If it was plausible to suppose that differences in the size of the brain might be associated with differences in IQ, it is surely inconceivable that there should be no relationship between IQ scores and *some* aspect of the functioning of the nervous system. The search for such relationships has been going on for much of the twentieth century, but it would be idle to pretend that it has been crowned with success. Indeed, if by success is meant any theoretical understanding of the ways in which neural mechanisms generate differences in IQ, the only reasonable conclusion is that progress has been minimal. One reason for this, no doubt, is that the problem is a difficult one: if neuroscientists cannot claim to understand the neural basis of learning and memory in the laboratory rat, how could they be expected to understand the neural basis of human intelligence? But the failure is also a reflection on the quality of the science. The fact of the matter is that significant progress has been made in research on event-related potentials (ERPs) and more specific issues in human cognitive psychology, for example, visual or spatial attention, the dynamics of information processing, language and memory, or motor control (Rugg and Coles, 1995). By comparison, most of the work on IQ has been, frankly, amateur. Too many investigators have conducted too many small studies, employing too many different procedures with too little thought of replication or building on earlier work. They have employed numerous different behavioural techniques and literally dozens of different measures of brain activity, often in one and the same study, in the hope of finding *one* that will correlate with IQ, without regard to the probability that 1 in 20 correlations will by chance be significant at the 0.05 level (i.e. a Type I error). Deary and Caryl (1993) have provided an informed and detailed account of the history of this research, which manages to be both critical and sympathetic. In what follows, I shall be a great deal more selective and rather less sympathetic.

Electrodes attached to the surface of the scalp can record the spontaneous activity of the brain as a series of voltage changes—no doubt the summed activity of many millions of neurones. This is the electroencephalograph or EEG record. The frequency of the EEG record changes when people are in different states, alert and engaged in mental activity, quiet, drowsy, asleep, dreaming, etc. The question at issue is whether there are differences in the EEG record, in the awake state, associated with differences in IQ. At least some studies have found higher-frequency resting records in people of higher IQ, and smaller changes in activity when they are required to perform a task such as mental arithmetic

(Giannitrapani, 1985). A rather plausible explanation of this latter result is that it is a consequence, rather than a cause, of higher IQ: the higher your IQ, the easier you will find any mental arithmetic problem, and the fewer resources you will need to devote to its solution. Finer analysis reveals that the results vary at different electrode sites, and with different frequency bands. Although this seems quite reasonable, the increase in the number of relationships studied inevitably increases the chances of Type I error.

Most recent work has relied on recording changes in activity to a particular stimulus or series of stimuli: these are event-related potentials (Rugg and Coles, 1995; in the present area of research they are still often called evoked potentials, and I shall sometimes use the term here). A typical procedure involves a subject sitting quietly in a dimly illuminated room listening to very brief tones, played through headphones, or waiting for brief flashes of light. Such stimuli cause changes in brain activity which can also be recorded by electrodes attached to the surface of the scalp. Because the minute changes in electrical potential in response to such signals are embedded in a background of continually fluctuating activity or noise, it is common to repeat the brief signal 50 or 100 times, once every few seconds, and to average the changes recorded over all 100 trials. These then constitute average evoked potentials (AEPs).

Jensen bluntly characterized early work on ERPs as:

> a thicket of seemingly inconsistent and confusing findings, confounded variables, methodological differences, statistically questionable conclusions, unbridled theoretical speculation, and, not surprisingly, considerable controversy (Jensen, 1980, p. 709).

The best known of this early work was that of Ertl and his colleagues, who claimed to show a high correlation between IQ and latency of the ERP to visual signals—high IQ being associated with shorter latencies to the first response (Ertl and Schafer, 1969). Figure 7.1 illustrates selected data from typical high-IQ subjects and from typical low-IQ subjects in Ertl's study. Inspection of these data suggested to Hendrickson and Hendrickson (1980) that the more striking difference between high- and low-IQ records was not the latency to the first peak or trough, but rather the overall complexity of the waveform—the number and amplitude of deviations from base-line in the first 250 to 500 ms following onset of the signal. They devised a measure which, perhaps inadvisedly, they referred to as 'string length of AEP'.

> In looking at the records, we noticed that as the waveforms of the low-IQ records became smoother, the circumference of the waveform envelope became shorter. If we thought of the waveform as a piece of string, and we went a standard length into the record, cut the string at that point, and pulled it straight the high-IQ people would have longer waveform strings than the low-IQ people. (A. E. Hendrickson, 1982, p. 195)

Subsequent studies reported a correlation of 0.72 between Wechsler IQ and AEP string length in a group of 219 schoolchildren (D. E. Hendrickson, 1982) and one of 0.53 between string length and scores on Raven's Matrices in a group of 33 undergraduates (Blinkhorn and Hendrickson, 1982).

Even the latter correlation is impressive enough, but both sets of results should be regarded with as much caution as earlier commentators urged for Ertl's data. The detailed account of the Hendricksons' procedures makes it clear that they worked hard to find measures that yielded such high correlations:

> When a reasonable sample of subjects' data had been processed in the way described above, the 'string' measure . . . was computed, and correlations were obtained between the string measure and the IQ measures. We were perplexed to find that the correlations were of the order of zero, or even in the 'wrong' direction. (D. E. Hendrickson, 1982, p. 201).

Undaunted, Hendrickson renewed her search, and eventually found a procedure that yielded the correlation of 0.72 cited above. Since this whole area of research must still be regarded as at an exploratory stage, it is perfectly legitimate to search around for a measure that results in more robust effects. But the next stage must be replication. No faith can be placed in effects obtained after prolonged search of this nature until they have been replicated in independent studies. Such prudence seems particularly justified when one reads of some of the procedures Hendrickson employed, which relied on 'visual inspection of the records, with rejection of those that were felt to show artefact of some kind . . . [And] if there were any records which seemed to be grossly distorted they were noted and subsequently eliminated' (D. E. Hendrickson, 1982, p. 201).

Deary and Caryl (1993) put a brave face on the history of these attempted replications. They make the important observation that Hendrickson's results were largely consistent with those of an earlier study employing what its authors called a 'map-wheel' measure of AEPs (Rhodes *et al.*, 1969). However, another contemporaneous study (Shagass *et al.*, 1981) found no relationship between IQ scores and string length of AEPs to a wide variety of different stimuli. Two subsequent small studies were marginally more encouraging. Haier *et al.* (1983) reported 12 correlations between different string-

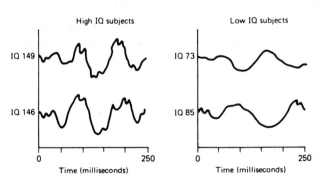

Fig. 7.1 Event-related potentials of four subjects, two high, two low IQ, in response to a brief visual stimulus (redrawn from Ertl and Schafer, 1969).

length measures and IQ: five were significantly positive. Stough, *et al.* (1990) reported a correlation of 0.43 between string length and scores on the WAIS in a sample of 20 university students—but, unlike Blinkhorn and Hendrickson (1982), no correlation with scores on Raven's Matrices.

Two further studies, however, should serve to dampen the hopes of the most determined optimist. In the largest single study of the relationship between ERPs and IQ, with a sample of 236 adults (mostly students), Vogel *et al.* (1987) reported correlations ranging from −0.087 to +0.035 between string length (and some other measures) of visual or auditory ERPs and a battery of IQ tests (including Raven's Matrices). Vogel *et al.* acknowledged that there were minor differences between their procedures and Hendrickson's, but regarded it as unlikely that they could have been decisive. Even this faint hope must be dashed by the results of a rather smaller study by Barrett and Eysenck (1992). They exhaustively and systematically attempted to examine the importance of the various procedural details recommended by the Hendricksons, and found correlations ranging from −0.20 to −0.44 between AEP string length and WAIS IQ scores. All eight correlations were negative, i.e. in the *opposite* direction to those reported by D. E. Hendrickson (1982), and four of the eight were significant.

What is to be made of this new 'thicket of seemingly inconsistent and confusing findings'? It is tempting to dismiss them out of hand and move on. But even the most sceptical critic might be hard pressed to dismiss, as mere chance, several studies reporting correlations of over 0.40 in one direction and others reporting correlations of comparable size in the opposite direction. Can they all just be random error? There are two other possibilities. The first is that there is indeed some measure of ERPs that is genuinely associated with differences in IQ, but string length is not that measure, although it is, somehow, an imperfect and unreliable reflection of it. Deary and Caryl (1993) have argued that the critical feature of ERPs that correlates with IQ might be the amplitude of certain components occurring between 100 and 200 ms after the onset of a stimulus—in particular the magnitude of the first major negative deflection at about 140 ms after stimulus onset (N140), or of the first major positive deflection at about 200 ms (P200), or the slope between the two (see Fig. 7.1). Both Haier *et al.* (1983) and Stough *et al.* (1990) observed effects generally consistent with this idea—although, confusingly enough, Stough *et al.* found no correlation between IQ and the actual measure preferred by Haier *et al.* And to add to the problem, a second study by Haier and his colleagues (Robinson *et al.*, 1984) was able to replicate the results of the first only after discarding nearly half the subjects. Another candidate for the critical feature of event-related potentials is their consistency from one trial to the next. Such consistency is likely to be reflected in the complexity of the waveform averaged over 50 or 100 trials, and D. E. Hendrickson (1982) did indeed observe a correlation of −0.72 between IQ and the trial-to-trial *variance* in each subject's evoked potential, i.e. a positive correlation between IQ and consistency of response. This result was confirmed by Barrett and Eysenck (1992), although with notably smaller correlations ranging from −0.37 to −0.45. Other studies, unfortunately, have not reported the relevant data, so it is far too soon to say whether this is a reliable finding.

The other possibility is that contradictory results are due to unsuspected differences in procedure. Given the difficulty of ensuring exact replication of recording techniques, this cannot easily be ruled out—although it is hard to see how minor differences could have such dramatic effects. More interestingly, Bates and Eysenck (1993a) and Bates *et al.* (1995) have argued that the critical difference is not in electrode placement or other aspects of ERP recording, but in the nature of the behavioural task presented to subjects. Specifically, they suggested that the correlation between IQ and string-length (or related) measures of ERPs will range from positive, through zero, to negative depending on whether subjects are able to ignore, or are required to attend to, the stimuli. The normal instructions to the subjects in these experiments are to sit quietly, doing nothing, while the stimuli are presented. This could clearly be construed as an instruction to ignore the stimuli, rather than to attend to them, although one can readily concede that subjects might differ in their interpretation of such instructions, and even that slight differences in their precise wording, or in the general atmosphere of the experiment, might tilt the majority of subjects one way or the other. Whether this is really sufficient to explain the variation in the results of different experiments is another matter. However, Bates *et al.* did find that when subjects were specifically required to attend to a series of tones, in order to discriminate their frequencies, high IQ was associated with low string-length measures, but when they were specifically instructed to ignore the tones, high IQ was associated with high string-length measures. In other words, instructions to attend to the stimuli produced a negative correlation between string length and IQ; instructions to ignore the stimuli produced a positive correlation (as in Hendrickson's initial experiment).

Several other studies have confirmed an association between ERP measures and IQ when subjects are required to attend to stimuli, as for example, in an inspection-time task. Bates and Eysenck (1993a) reported a negative relationship between IQ and string length, while Zhang *et al.* (1989) and Caryl (1994) took measures of the rise time of P200 or of the slope of the gradient from N140 to P200. Both these measures correlated significantly with performance on the inspection-time task (which itself correlates with IQ), and Caryl confirmed that his measure also correlated with IQ. Thus a number of studies have indeed shown a significant relationship between various ERP measures and IQ when subjects are specifically required to attend to briefly presented stimuli, but the nature of this relationship is the precise opposite of that discovered by the Hendricksons.

Why should high IQ be associated with small changes in ERPs to stimuli that subjects are required to attend to and discriminate? An obvious possibility, and the one advanced by Bates and Eysenck (1993a) and by Bates *et al.* (1995), is that when people are required to pay close attention to particular stimuli, in order to decide whether one is longer or louder or of a higher frequency than another, under conditions where such a discrimination is quite demanding, the lower their IQ the more effort and more resources they must devote to the task. The explanation is, of course, reminiscent of that offered to explain the negative correlation between IQ and changes in EEG when people are asked to solve problems in mental arithmetic (Giannitrapani, 1985).

But this leaves the other half of the supposed relationship between IQ and ERPs unexplained. When people are not specifically required to attend to a series of stimuli, why should the complexity, string length, or variance of their ERPs show any association with their IQ scores? The explanation offered by Bates *et al.* (1995) does not seem particularly convincing. Under circumstances such as these, they suggest, 'the levels of efficiency achieved by high-IQ subjects will leave them with surplus processing resources that they can (or perhaps must) distribute to additional stimuli or stimulus features' (Bates *et al.*, 1995, p. 32). This, then, is supposed to explain the original 'string length' correlations: high-IQ subjects have more resources to devote to stimuli, which they are actually free to ignore— and in some cases instructed to ignore. Even if such a suggestion made much theoretical sense, it is doubtful that it would really be sufficient to explain the diversity of results obtained from this paradigm. Although, as noted above, Bates *et al.* (1995) themselves observed a positive correlation between string length and IQ when subjects were specifically instructed to ignore stimuli, Zhang *et al.* (1989) found no relationship between their ERP measures and their subjects' previously established inspection-time scores after similar instructions. If there really is such a positive relationship, one can only conclude that it remains to be demonstrated, and is certainly not adequately understood. In the present state of our knowledge, it seems neither reliable nor particularly interesting. Indeed, according to Caryl (1994), the continued search to find and explain this distinctly elusive relationship has simply succeeded in diverting attention from the more promising problem of trying to understand the relationship between IQ and ERPs when people are actively engaged in attending to, and analysing, a series of stimuli. Its sole achievement, therefore, may have been to 'set back the understanding of mechanisms responsible for ERP/ability relationships by a decade' (Caryl, 1994, p. 43).

It is time to call a halt to this discussion. The most charitable conclusion is that research in this general area has thrown up one or two potentially important relationships between IQ and event-related potentials. Less charitably, it seems probable that an unknown number of these apparent relationships will turn out to be artefactual or unreplicable. And no one could seriously argue that such research has served to increase our theoretical understanding of the nature of IQ. The most obvious explanation of the apparently most reliable effect is that it is IQ that is responsible for differences in ERPs rather than vice versa; the higher your IQ the fewer resources you need to devote to the task of discriminating two difficult-to-discriminate stimuli. The one other reliable relationship that has been established is that there seems to be a correlation between brain size and IQ. But no one could seriously argue that this modest correlation has revealed the biological substrate of general intelligence, let alone proved that *g* is a unitary process. The fact is that we simply do not know why brain size correlates with IQ, and those who have laboured so hard to establish this relationship have explained neither why they attach so much importance to it, nor what its meaning might be. Let us move on to a discussion of supposedly simple behavioural correlates of IQ.

Behavioural measures of speed of information processing

Reaction time

We saw in Chapter 1 that the earliest attempts to measure differences in intelligence relied on the recently developed techniques of the new science of experimental psychology. Prominent among these was the reaction-time task, and Cattell's battery of mental tests included more than one measure of reaction time (Cattell, 1890). But when Wissler (1901) failed to find any relationship between reaction time or sensory thresholds and such apparent indices of intelligence as college grades, this approach was abandoned. The long-term consequence was that the development of modern IQ tests owed little to laboratory techniques, and everything to the work of Alfred Binet. However one judges the consequences of this, it is now clear that Wissler's results were somewhat misleading; his measures of reaction time, based on only a very small number of trials, were too unreliable, and his subject sample, undergraduates at Columbia University, too highly selected, to enable him to discover that there really is a small, but reliable relationship between IQ and reaction time (RT).

The first, systematic series of studies to establish beyond serious doubt that there is a correlation between IQ and RT (Roth, 1964) came from Erlangen, in what was then East Germany, and had relatively little impact on Western psychologists. Much of the more recent work has been conducted either by Jensen (1982, 1987b), or by others employing apparatus and procedures similar to his. The subject's task is to perform as rapidly as possible the appropriate response whenever a light comes on. Jensen's apparatus consists of a console containing a central 'home' button, above which is semicircular array of eight response buttons, each with a small light immediately above it. Subjects start each trial with their index finger on the 'home' button: when one of the lights is illuminated they must press the button below that light as rapidly as possible. Anticipatory movements off the 'home' button (i.e. before a light comes on) are not recorded, but prevent the occurrence of the next trial until the finger is replaced. This means that releasing the 'home' serves as a measure of RT or decision time, while the time taken to press the appropriate target button, after releasing the 'home' button, is usually described as movement time (MT). Although I shall talk only of RT below, in most, although not all, cases movement time shows similar relationships with IQ.

One of the most reliable results of RT research, first documented by Merkel (1885) but more usually described as Hick's law (Hick, 1952), is that RT increases as a function of the number of alternatives between which the subject has to choose. Hick's law states that RT is a linear function of the logarithm of the number of alternatives. Merkel's data demonstrating Hick's law are shown in Fig. 7.2. This serves to illustrate the various measures of RT that may be correlated with IQ. From a series of trials with varying numbers of alternatives the experimenter may take two direct measures:

(1) the overall mean RT, and
(2) the mean RT at each number of alternatives.

In addition, two derived measures may be taken:

(3) the intercept of the function shown in Fig. 7.2 (i.e. RT to a single light), and
(4) the slope of the function relating RT to number of alternatives.

Finally, and as we shall see most importantly, many investigators have reported a fifth measure:

(5) the variability of a subject's RT from trial to trial.

Jensen (1982) originally argued that IQ was related more strongly to choice RT or decision time than to simple RT, claiming that the correlation between IQ and RT increased in an orderly way with an increase in the number of alternatives. In terms of derived measures, therefore, IQ should correlate with the slope rather than with the intercept of the function relating RT to number of alternatives. He has subsequently, and correctly, retracted this suggestion, being content to argue that

> g is more highly correlated with a general factor common to all the Hick RT and MT variables than with any particular measure. (Jensen, 1987*b*, p. 168)

What is the evidence? Table 7.1a, from Jensen (1987*b*), gives the weighted mean correlation between IQ and four measures of RT, derived from 26 different studies with a

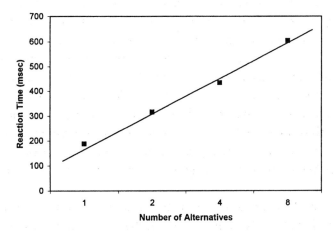

Fig. 7.2 Reaction time as a function of the number of alternatives (data from Merkel, 1885).

total of some 2000 subjects (not all of whom provide data for all four measures). The correlations are not large, but are all significant. Notice that they are negative: a high IQ is associated with a low RT. Notice also that the two highest are with overall mean RT and variability of RT, and that the correlation with the slope of the function relating RT to number of alternatives is only −0.12. Table 7.1b shows the correlation between IQ and mean RT for different numbers of alternatives ranging from one to eight (just over 1000 subjects provided data for this table). There is a regular, but very small, increase in the correlation as the number of alternatives increases from one to eight (from −0.18 to −0.23).

A correlation of −0.20 between RT and IQ may be significant, if based on a sufficiently large number of subjects, but it is hardly going to revolutionize our understanding of IQ. It is, after all, marginally smaller than the correlation between IQ and height, which Jensen and Sinha (1993) have estimated as 0.23. There are, however, other sources of data to confirm that there is a real relationship between the IQ and RT, and it may be that the results shown in Table 7.1 underestimate its true magnitude. The possibility of underestimate arises because many of the studies summarized in Table 7.1 employed university students, whose range of IQ scores is notably smaller than that of the population as a whole. Applying a correction for this restriction of range increases the correlation to −0.30. Such adjustments should, I believe, be viewed with considerable caution, but they may be justified here. In one of the largest single studies of the relationship between IQ and RT, employing subjects of approximately average IQ and with a normal range of IQs (they were 141 17-year-old high-school students with a mean IQ of 108 and a standard deviation of 15), Detterman (1987) found a correlation of −0.32 between IQ and RT.

The other reason for accepting that there is a genuine relationship between IQ test performance and RT in the population as a whole comes from developmental studies. Kail

Table 7.1 Correlations between IQ and measures of RT (from Jensen, 1987*b*)

(a)	Measures of RT			
	Mean	Intercept	Slope	Variance
Weighted mean correlation of 26 studies	−0.20	−0.12	−0.12	−0.21

(b)	Number of alternatives			
	1	2	4	8
Weighted mean correlation of 15 studies	−0.18	−0.19	−0.22	−0.23

(1991) has reviewed evidence from a wide variety of studies that have consistently shown a substantial decrease in RT between the ages of 4 and 14. Conversely, one of the best documented changes in performance on a variety of laboratory tasks as people grow older is an increase in RT (Salthouse, 1991; Rabbitt, 1993). Since IQ test performance improves as children grow older, and begins to decline after the age of 60 or so (see Chapter 2), here is evidence of correlated changes in RT and IQ.

Let us accept, then, that there is a correlation between IQ and RT of between −0.20 and −0.30. As we shall see, this is rather smaller than the correlation between IQ and inspection time, but it still needs to be explained. The first point to note is that, although one might naively have expected otherwise, there is no suggestion that the size of this correlation is affected by the use of timed or untimed IQ tests (Vernon *et al.*, 1985; Jensen, 1987*b*). This is important, for it implies that if RT is a measure of speed of processing, such mental speed enters into performance on all IQ tests, rather than just those tests that require rapid responding. For example, RT correlates as strongly with the Wechsler verbal scale as with the performance scale, although the latter includes several timed tests and the former none at all.

But is the RT task simply a measure of mental speed? The supposition that the correlation between IQ and RT proves that IQ is reducible to the speed and accuracy with which information is transmitted through the nervous system rests on the unstated assumption that RT provides a direct and uncomplicated measure of this transmission. This is a serious misconception; the RT paradigm has been studied by experimental psychologists for over a century, and a certain amount is now known about the determinants of RT performance. For example, it is well established that practice affects RT. Not only do RTs continue to decrease with practice over many thousands of trials, prolonged practice will also decrease the slope relating RT to the number of alternatives (Teichner and Krebs, 1974). In Jensen's studies of IQ and RT, the standard procedure, followed by most other experimenters, is to give a brief series of practice trials followed by 15 (occasionally 20 or 30) trials with each of four set sizes—one, two, four, and eight alternatives in ascending order. Jensen (1987*b*) has argued that there is actually no evidence of a practice effect within each set size, responding at the beginning of each set being as fast as at the end. But this does not rule out the possibility that there is a significant practice effect over all 60 trials; and if the size of the effect were related to IQ it might help to explain the overall correlation between IQ and speed of responding. More important, the routine confound between order of testing and number of alternatives means that any potential practice effects will have a greater effect on responding to eight alternatives than on responding to one. If subjects of high IQ learn faster than those of low IQ, this practice effect might explain why their superiority is more marked with greater numbers of alternatives. In other words, the (admittedly very small) correlation between IQ and the slope of RT as a function of number of alternatives may be an artefact. In confirmation of this, Widaman and Carlson (1989) found a correlation of −0.26 between IQ and slope of

RT when they tested subjects in the typical ascending order; but one of only −0.06 when they tested subjects in a random order; and one of +0.18 when they tested them in the reverse order, starting with eight alternatives and ending with one. Thus, when tested in ascending order, high-IQ subjects' greatest advantage was at eight alternatives, when tested in descending order their greatest advantage was at one alternative: IQ merely correlated more highly with performance towards the end of 60 trials than it did at the beginning, a result consistent with a simple practice effect.

A possible second key to understanding the cause of the relationship between IQ and RT is to note that IQ correlates as highly with a measure of the variability of RT as it does with mean RT (see Table 7.1*a*). In one sense, this is not entirely surprising, since the average correlation between mean and standard deviation of RT in Jensen's analysis is 0.71. But what is the explanation? One possibility would be to appeal to differences in concentration or sustained attention between people of high and low IQ: there is good evidence that measures of sustained attention correlate with performance on RT tasks (Carlson *et al.*, 1983). More detailed analysis of the RT task suggests further possibilities. The subject's instructions are to respond as rapidly as possible without making errors—of which there are two kinds, pressing the incorrect button and releasing the 'home' key before the start of a trial. There is an inevitable trade-off between speed and accuracy, and subjects need to titrate their own performance to find the fastest speed at which they can respond without making errors. Perhaps it is the precision of this titration process that distinguishes between subjects of high and low IQ. Brewer and Smith (1984), in an experiment with both normal and retarded subjects, found that both groups showed a steady increase in speed of responding over a series of errorless trials; eventually such a sequence was followed by an error, which in turn was followed by an immediate slowing down of responding. This increase in RTs following errors was much greater for the retarded group. Consistent with this, Larson and Alderton (1990) showed that the correlation between IQ and mean RT was significantly greater for each subject's slow responses than for their fast responses. They also reported a small but significant correlation (−0.17) between IQ and the magnitude of the increase in RT following errors. Rather surprisingly, however, they found that the overall correlation between IQ and variability of RT was not reduced when they partialled out differences in this increase in RT following errors. One problem of interpretation here is that the experimenter can only record when the subject actually makes an error. But subjects may also slow down after trials on which they thought that they might have made an error, but were lucky enough not to. However that may be, it is clear that the correlation between IQ and RT does not arise because people of high IQ are capable of responding more rapidly than those of lower IQ. It is because they make fewer slow responses. This hardly supports the idea that RT is simply a measure of the speed with which information is transmitted through the nervous system, let alone that differences in this speed are the cause of differences in *g*.

Inspection time

In a typical visual inspection time (IT) experiment, two vertical lines are briefly shown side by side on a screen, one substantially longer than another (Fig. 7.3). They are immediately followed by a mask which may, for example, be either a grid of vertical lines covering the entire screen, or two long vertical lines superimposed over the original lines. The subject's rather simple task is then to report whether the longer line was on the left or the right. Following a correct response, the exposure duration (more precisely, the interval between the initial onset of the lines and the occurrence of the mask) is shortened for the next trial, and so on, until the subject starts making errors, usually at exposures roughly between 50 and 150 ms. The briefest duration at which a subject is correct on a certain percentage of trials is usually taken as the measure of inspection time. Using this procedure, Nettelbeck and Lalley (1976) reported a correlation between IT and WAIS IQ of −0.70 in a sample of 10 subjects: high IQ was associated with short IT scores. The correlation with verbal IQ was only −0.32, but that with performance IQ an astonishing −0.92. Rather similar results were reported in a number of equally small studies from Edinburgh (Brand and Deary, 1982), and it seemed that inspection time correlated with at least some IQ measures as well as those measures did with themselves.

It rapidly became evident, however, that most of these early correlations had been inflated by the inclusion of a disproportionate number of retarded subjects in the relatively small samples. Subsequent studies, reviewed by Nettelbeck (1987) and Kranzler and Jensen (1989), have reported much more modest correlations, virtually never greater than −0.50, and in several studies not significantly different from zero. The results of Kranzler and Jensen's meta-analysis of studies undertaken up until 1988 are shown in Table 7.2. One feature of this analysis is consistent with Nettelbeck and Lally's original study: in adults at least, IT appears to correlate more strongly with non-verbal IQ (usually WAIS performance scale) than with verbal IQ (usually WAIS verbal scale) or general IQ (WAIS total IQ or Raven's Matrices). This observation may be of some significance, and I shall return to it later.

Kranzler and Jensen were able to increase the size of these correlations by excluding some studies (not always for very convincing reasons) and by correcting for supposed artefacts—unreliability of the measures and restriction in the range of IQ scores (as was the case for RT, many studies had employed undergraduates as subjects). This brought the average

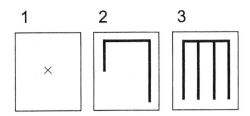

Fig. 7.3 The sequence of stimulus displays for a typical inspection-time experiment. In the interval between trials, the screen is blank; each trial consists in the brief presentation of the two vertical lines shown in the second panel, followed after a pre-determined interval by the masking stimulus shown in the final panel.

Table 7.2 Correlations between IQ and IT (from Kranzler and Jensen, 1989)

	IQ measure		
	Verbal	Non-verbal	General
Adults	−0.18	−0.45	−0.30
Children	−0.22	−0.23	−0.28

correlation to over −0.50 for non-verbal or general IQ and to about −0.40 for verbal IQ. But as Levy (1992) has noted, the methodology of most IT studies is not such as to justify this sort of manipulation, and unless these higher figures can be confirmed by large-scale studies with large, representative cross-sections of the population, it will be safer to rely on the actual correlations reported in Table 7.2. The largest, single study (just too late to be included in Kranzler and Jensen's review), with a sample of 343 naval recruits, reported a correlation of only −0.25 between IT and a composite IQ score derived from a US armed forces test and Raven's Matrices (Larson and Saccuzzo, 1989). On the other hand, several other reasonably large studies published after Kranzler and Jensen's review have reported correlations with at least some IQ measures ranging from −0.35 to −0.50 (Bates and Eysenck, 1993*b*; Chaiken, 1993; Deary, 1993).

There can be no doubt that there is a significant correlation between IT and IQ. The precise value of that correlation may be a matter of some dispute. It is certainly a great deal smaller than the figure of −0.80 or so suggested by some early studies. An upper-bound estimate of the unadjusted correlation would be no more than −0.50, and that with only some kinds of IQ test. But since a lower-bound estimate (at least for some kinds of IQ test) would have to be not much less than −0.25, we are left with a moderate, significant correlation, which is probably substantially higher than the correlation between RT and IQ. What is its explanation?

The IT task has a certain face validity as a measure of the speed and accuracy of transmission of information through the nervous system. According to the accumulator model of Vickers (1979), who developed the procedure, perceptual discriminations of this sort involve taking in information in a series of discrete samples: a decision is reached once sufficient information has been sampled or accumulated, and the time taken to reach such a decision will reflect both the accuracy with which one stage of the system produces different outputs for different inputs, and the reliability with which a later stage detects these differences in output. Vickers's model thus implies that IT is a direct measure of a fixed property of the nervous system—the speed and fidelity with which it responds to different sensory inputs.

Is this all? Does not performance on an IT task, like that on RT tasks, reflect a variety of other processes, any of which might be responsible for its association with IQ? There has been no shortage of alternative accounts. One of the earliest suggestions was that high-IQ subjects must develop strategies that enable them to solve the IT task more efficiently than others. There is good evidence that the presentation of the masking stimulus immediately after the two lines may produce an apparent movement effect, which can allow one to discriminate between the lines, and that subjects who use this cue will achieve significantly shorter IT scores than those who do not (Mackenzie and Bingham, 1985). But unfortunately for the argument, there is no difference in average IQ between those who do and those who do not report using this cue, and the correlation between IQ and IT is either not affected, or actually increased, by excluding subjects who report reliance on a strategy (Mackenzie and Bingham, 1985; Egan, 1994). It is clear that this particular strategy cannot explain the relationship between IT and IQ (see Deary and Stough, 1996).

A second possibility, however, is that differences in IT largely reflect differences in attention and vigilance. It seems reasonable to suppose that discriminating between two very briefly presented stimuli over a long series of trials must require sustained concentration on what is a relatively boring task, and one potential cause of longer ITs must be occasional lapses of concentration. Given the way IT is often measured, occasional errors, especially at longer stimulus durations, can have disproportionate effects on a subject's overall IT score. Brebner and Cooper, (1986) calculated that a single, additional error in several hundred trials, if it occurs at a long target duration, can increase measured IT by 17 per cent. It is simply not known how far this contributes to the correlation between IQ and IT. But several observations suggest that it may be important. In two large studies, Chaiken (1993) gave two separate IT tests in a single test session, separated by a series of other tests. In both experiments, performance on the second IT test, at the end of the session, was substantially worse than performance on the first. But, again in both experiments, the correlation between IT and IQ was substantially higher on the second test (-0.50 and -0.38) than it had been on the first (-0.35 and -0.27). A plausible explanation of the decline in IT performance from first to second test is that it represents a decline in vigilance during the course of a long, tiring session. If that is so, the increase in the correlation with IQ suggests that part of the IT–IQ correlation reflects a factor of vigilance or sustained attention. Bors and MacLeod (1996) gave subjects a single, long IT session, consisting of 600 trials with a fixed set of trial durations ranging from 40 to 140 ms. Although their subjects' IT scores averaged well under 100 ms, the accuracy of their performance correlated almost as strongly with IQ even at the longest duration of 140 ms. Low-IQ subjects must have been making errors at all durations.

It is also clear that performance on IT tasks, like that on RT tasks, improves with practice. Large practice effects are not usually observed during the course of a single session, presumably because they are masked by a decline in vigilance. But if trials are spread over several days, significant improvement has typically been found (e.g. Mackenzie and Bingham, 1985). Bors and MacLeod (1996) found that mean IT scores declined from over 80 to less than 70 ms over 3 days of practice. But even more important, the correlation between IQ and IT declined from -0.43 to -0.07 over the 3 days. That IT should improve with practice is not readily accommodated by the Vickers model. But Bors and MacLeod's results suggest that the IT–IQ correlation may depend on differences in the rate at which high- and low-IQ subjects show such improvement.

Interpretation of the correlations between IQ and RT or IT

There is no doubt that performance on two superficially rather simple laboratory tasks shows moderate correlations with IQ scores. What do these relationships mean? Have they shown that there is a single psychological process underlying *g*? Have they gone further and allowed us to identify that process with speed and accuracy of information processing? The answer is surely not.

The first problem is that the correlations between IQ and IT or RT are very much less impressive than initial enthusiasm led some proponents of this enterprise to claim. The correlation between IQ and IT is somewhere between −0.25 and −0.50. That between IQ and RT is only −0.20 to −0.30. Such correlations, especially those with IT, are far from trivial, and they may even be rather surprising, but they are hardly sufficient to justify the claim that either of these tasks provides a direct measure of the single, general process underlying IQ. It is one thing to say that one *component* of IQ scores is related to speed of processing, and that it correlates with performance on laboratory tasks that also stress speed and accuracy. That is hardly revolutionary. It is quite another thing to claim that the most important central ingredient common to all forms of intelligent behaviour is speed of information processing. That sounds as if it might be a revolutionary idea, even if it is not totally clear what it actually means. But it is not justified by the size of the correlations between IQ and IT or RT.

Secondly, if IT and RT tasks both measure a single factor of speed of information processing, they should clearly correlate rather strongly with one another. They do not. Indeed, performance on one IT task does not necessarily correlate particularly well with performance on others. In addition to the standard visual IT task reviewed above, there have also been studies of auditory and even tactile IT. In a typical auditory IT task, two brief tones are presented in rapid succession, followed by an auditory mask, and the subject's task is to decide whether the first or second tone was the higher frequency. Performance on such a task correlates with IQ—but sometimes, unlike visual IT, more highly with verbal than with non-verbal IQ (Irwin, 1984; Deary *et al.*, 1989). Perhaps not surprisingly, it also correlates moderately well with measures of pitch discrimination (Deary, 1994), but correlations between auditory and visual IT have ranged from 0.15 to 0.39 (Irwin, 1984; Nettelbeck *et al.*, 1986; Saccuzzo *et al.*, 1986; Langsford *et al.*, 1994). The implication must be that much of the variance in IT scores is modality specific and can hardly be related to any general process of intelligence. Deary (1994) was able to show that there was a speed component to auditory IT performance independent of pitch discrimination, that correlated significantly with IQ. It would be interesting to know whether this component represented the variance shared with visual IT.

In view of this, it is not surprising that numerous studies have reported only a small correlation between IT and RT (Nettelbeck and Kirby, 1983; Saccuzzo *et al.*, 1986; Larson *et al.*, 1988; Larson and Saccuzzo, 1989; Kranzler and Jensen, 1991). These correlations have ranged from zero to a maximum of 0.35, but the large majority, including those from the largest single study, with over 300 subjects (Larson and Saccuzzo, 1989) have been 0.20 or lower. It seems reasonable to conclude that, whatever may be the cause of the observed correlations between IQ and IT or RT, it is not because these two tasks provide equivalent measures of a single underlying process of speed of information processing that is the biological basis of *g* or general intelligence. To a large extent, they must be measuring different processes. Two other findings provide further confirmation of this. Bates and Eysenck (1993*b*) and Frearson *et al.* (1988) both found the usual values, mostly between −0.20 and −0.30, for correlations between IQ and various RT measures. However, they also gave their subjects a different RT task, which they termed 'odd man out' (OMO) RT. The apparatus for this test was the same, eight-light box, as that used for the standard RT task, but in OMO, three lights were illuminated on every trial, two relatively close together, one further apart. The subject's task was to respond to this third, odd man out, light. Performance on this problem correlated more highly with IQ than did ordinary RT and, unlike ordinary RT, correlated more highly with WAIS performance IQ and scores on Raven's Matrices than it did with verbal IQ (Frearson *et al.* 1988). Bates and Eysenck (1993*b*) showed that the reason for this was that OMO RT, unlike ordinary RT, shared features in common with IT. They found fairly typical values for the correlations between IQ and RT (−0.28) and between IQ and IT (−0.45), in spite of a correlation of only 0.06 between RT and IT. In other words, these two tasks predicted quite independent attributes of IQ. But the higher correlation between IQ and OMO RT arose because OMO RT correlated not only with ordinary RT (0.42), but also with IT (0.36). The clear implication is that the OMO task measured two relatively distinct processes, rapid or efficient sensory analysis and rapid or efficient decision making, both of which independently correlated with IQ.

Kranzler and Jensen (1991) also gave subjects a battery of different tests, including IT, standard RT, OMO RT, visual search, and memory search tasks. Although their detailed results differed in several respects from those of Frearson *et al.* (1988) and Bates and Eysenck (1993*b*), they performed a factor analysis of their subjects' scores on these tests and extracted four independent factors, each of which correlated with the general factor extracted from a battery of IQ tests. Although not all of these factors were readily identifiable, IT and RT loaded onto different factors and thus independently contributed to IQ. Kranzler and Jensen concluded that *g* cannot be considered to be a unitary psychological process.

There is, of course, a final problem that I have already discussed. The discovery of correlations between IQ and performance on other psychological tasks will advance our theoretical understanding of the nature of IQ only if these other tasks are themselves better understood than is IQ, and we have some theoretical account of the reason for the correlations. It is most doubtful if these conditions have been satisfied here. Much of this research has been premised on the assumption that IT and RT tasks are so simple (even so non-cognitive in nature) that they will yield up their secrets without any need for the theoretical and experimental analysis of cognitive psychology. This seems wholly unwarranted. Performance on both RT and IT tasks improves with practice and probably reflects, among other things, the ability to maintain vigilance or attention on a repetitive task. In the case of RT, analysis of changes in speed over trials and after errors suggests that subjects are attempting to titrate their performance so as to combine maximum speed with the fewest possible number of errors (or near errors?). At the very least, the fact that differences in IQ are associated with differences in *slow* RTs rather than differences in fast RTs suggests that the critical processes being measured in the RT paradigm are not simply speed of transmission. Since IQ may correlate with errors at long as well as short stimulus durations in the IT task, a similar conclusion may also hold here.

Correlations with *g* or with group factors?

The primary goal of the research reviewed thus far in this chapter was to identify the psychological or neurological basis of *g*, and in particular to test the hypothesis that the general factor common to all IQ tests arises because there is a single underlying process that enters into performance on all tests. By and large, this research has failed to provide overwhelming support for that hypothesis. No single measure has been found that accounts for a major part of the variance in IQ scores and, in so far as the processes involved in RT and IT tasks do contribute to variations in IQ, they seem to do so largely independently.

Inspection time revisited

The size of the correlation between RT and IQ is sufficiently small that no one could seriously argue that RT alone provides an explanation of *g*. But proponents of the IT paradigm, such as Anderson (1992) or Deary and Stough (1996), have frequently insisted that the size of the correlation between IT and IQ, optimistically said to be at least 0.50, means that if the IT task really did provide a direct measure of the speed and efficiency of a basic information-processing system, that system would have a fair claim to being the basis of *g*. I have already argued that measures of IT are probably *not* simply measures of speed of information processing. But there is a further, more serious problem with this claim: the correlation between IT and IQ does not seem to be a correlation with *g*.

In their meta-analysis of earlier IT studies, Kranzler and Jensen (1989) summarized the correlations between IT and three different measures of IQ (Table 7.2). In adults, IT correlated −0.18 with verbal IQ (usually the verbal scale of the WAIS), −0.45 with non-verbal IQ (usually the WAIS performance scale), and −0.30 with general IQ (usually WAIS total score, or Raven's Matrices). This difference between IT's correlation with the performance and verbal scales of the WAIS has been confirmed in other studies published since Kranzler and Jensen's review. In a sample of 87 adults, Deary (1993) reported a correlation of only −0.14 between IT and WAIS-R verbal IQ, but one of −0.35 between IT and WAIS-R performance IQ. Factor analysis of the WAIS makes it clear that the verbal scale loads more strongly onto the general factor than does the performance scale (Silverstein, 1982). So IT scores do not correlate particularly well with the general factor of the WAIS (nor, for that matter, particularly well with Raven's Matrices, a better measure of Gf than any part of the WAIS). This conclusion is reinforced by a more detailed examination of Deary's data. Table 7.3 shows the correlation between IT and performance on each of the sub-tests of the WAIS-R in his study, along with the *g*-loadings of each of these sub-tests taken from factor analysis of the WAIS-R (Silverstein, 1982). It is evident that there is a strong negative correlation between a sub-test's *g*-loading and its correlation with IT: the rank-order correlation is in fact −0.67.

Deary's results are very similar to those of an earlier study by Nettelbeck *et al.* (1986), who also found that IT correlated significantly only with the performance sub-tests of the WAIS, and that the highest correlation was with digit symbol. They are also very similar to those of a study by McGeorge *et al.* (1996), who employed a somewhat different visual IT task, tachistopic word recognition, which measured the shortest exposure duration at which subjects could correctly identify a certain proportion of a list of words presented one by one on the tachistoscope screen. Although the use of such verbal material might have been expected to increase correlations with verbal IQ, performance on this task correlated only −0.21 with scores on the WAIS-R verbal tests, but −0.47 with scores of the performance tests. Once again, the highest single correlation was with digit symbol.

Digit symbol is a timed test that simply requires the subject to fill in, as rapidly as possible, the appropriate symbol under a series of 90 digits. The most obvious interpretation

Table 7.3 Correlations between IT and WAIS-R sub-tests (from Deary, 1993)

Sub-test	Correlation with IT	Rank order	*g*-loading	Rank order
Information	0.17	7	0.82	2
Vocabulary	0.22	5	0.86	1
Arithmetic	0.15	8	0.78	5
Comprehension	0.18	6	0.80	4
Similarities	0.14	9	0.81	3
Picture completion	0.31	2	0.72	7
Block design	0.30	3	0.74	6
Object assembly	0.26	4	0.64	8.5
Digit symbol	0.33	1	0.64	8.5

of these findings, therefore, is that IT correlates most strongly with a perceptual speed factor in IQ (see Fig. 6.2 for evidence that digit symbol is a measure of perceptual speed). That implication is well supported by the results of other studies. In two large-scale experiments, with nearly 200 subjects in each, Chaiken (1994) found significant correlations, of about −0.40, between IT scores and performance on visual search tests, where subjects must find, as rapidly as possible, all instances of a particular target item embedded in a series of distractor items; while in another, much smaller, study Cooper *et al.* (1986) found no correlation between IT and tests of either crystallized or fluid intelligence, but did find a significant correlation between IT and measures of speed of closure and perceptual speed.

The conclusion seem inescapable: if performance on IT tasks shows a surprisingly strong correlation with IQ scores, this is not because IT provides a particularly good measure of the general factor common to all IQ tests, but is probably because it measures one particular component of IQ, namely perceptual speed. As we noted earlier, that does not seem such a surprising claim after all. The more general message is that it is not enough to show that performance on any laboratory task correlates with IQ. If we want to infer that this task taps any process underlying general intelligence, we need to ascertain what kinds of IQ test, or what components of IQ, the task relates to. In principle, that ought not to be very difficult. In practice, it has not always been done.

What causes a test to correlate with *g*?

With this sobering message behind us, let us return to our central question: how are we to discover the psychological substrate of *g* or general intelligence? We have looked for

---

Box 7.1 Why does inspection time correlate with IQ?

If, as I argue, differences in IT correlate not with any general factor common to all IQ tests, but largely with a perceptual speed factor, it would presumably follow that women, who tend to outscore men on measures of perceptual speed, should also outscore men on IT tasks. As far as I know, there is no evidence to answer this question.

An obvious possibility, which should be acknowledged, is that the IT task measures the accuracy (and rapidity?) of sensory registration. This might, of course, explain its correlation with perceptual speed, which is often measured by tests that require one to scan a list of letters or numbers, ticking off every appearance of a particular target item. But it also suggests another possibility—that the IT task may be the adult's or older child's version of the infant habituation test. In Chapter 2, we saw that the rapidity with which 6-month-old infants habituate to a novel stimulus predict their IQ scores 5 or 10 years later. Differences in speed of habituation may well depend on the accuracy (and rapidity?) of sensory registration. There is scope here for an interesting longitudinal study. Do infant habituation scores predict IT scores 10 or 20 years later? Do they predict perceptual speed scores better than other components of IQ?

correlations between simple information-processing tasks and IQ scores, on the assumption that only a process as basic and general as speed and accuracy of information processing could realistically be thought to contribute to performance on all manner of IQ tests. But we have not got very far. Perhaps we should take a more open-minded, empirical approach, and simply ask: what is the nature of those tasks that correlate with the general factor derived from an IQ test battery? And what is the nature of those laboratory tasks that do not? This second question, although it may seem paradoxical, is every bit as important as the first, for if we could get a theoretical handle on the difference or differences between tasks where performance does correlate with *g* and those where it does not, we should surely be in a better position to see what process or processes were responsible for a task's correlation with *g*, and should thereby have advanced our understanding of the basis of *g*.

Something like this strategy, applied to different sub-tests of IQ test batteries, was first proposed by Spearman himself as a way of elucidating the psychological nature of *g*. Spearman's two-factor theory implied that each sub-test of a test battery measures both *g* and its own unique factor. But, as he noted, some sub-tests are very much better measures of *g* than others: the sub-tests of the WAIS, for example, vary in their loadings on *g* from less than 0.65 to over 0.85 (see Table 7.3). If we wish to understand the nature of *g*, argued Spearman, we can do no better than examine the contents of tests that differ in their *g* loadings, to see if there is any consistent pattern underlying these differences (Spearman and Jones, 1950). Such an examination led Spearman and Jones to argue that, in addition to requiring the eduction of relations and correlates, tests with high *g* loadings were more abstract than those with low loadings: '*g* is essentially characterized by the combination of noegenesis with abstractness' (Spearman and Jones, 1950, p. 72). Spearman's strategy has been pursued by others. Jensen (1980, 1981), for example, has argued that

> if we arrange various tests, each composed of homogenous item types, in the order of their *g*-loadings, from highest to lowest, we notice that the *g* is related to the *complexity* of the cognitive activity demanded by the items . . . more generally, *g* seems to be involved in items that require mental manipulation of images, symbols, words, numbers, or concepts (Jensen, 1981, p. 59).

Plausible as this may sound, the level of analysis remains distressingly vague. Do we understand what we mean by saying that one item is more complex or more abstract than another? Ceci (1990) asked a group of eminent academics and writers to rate a number of items from the WAIS for their level of abstractness, and found little or no agreement between his different raters. The notion of complexity seems equally ill-defined, and thus equally unlikely to tell us what we want to know. For example, as Jensen has noted, forward digit span, where one simply has to repeat a series of digits, 3–1–7–4–9, read out by the examiner, has a lower *g*-loading than backward span, where one must repeat the digits backwards, 9–4–7–1–3. No doubt, backward span is a harder task than forward, but is it illuminating to say that it is more complex? It is surely not more abstract. And is the difference in complexity between the two tasks the same as the difference between, say, object assembly and vocabulary sub-tests of the WAIS, two other sub-tests that differ markedly in their g-loadings?

The problem with Spearman's and Jensen's suggestions is that they come perilously close to mere armchair speculation. What is needed, therefore, is not only a rather more refined level of theoretical analysis, but also some systematic empirical investigation, which might shed some light, for example, on the nature of the additional process or processes called for in the backward span task that accounts for its higher correlation with the general factor than the forward span task. Such a programme of research will need to involve the analysis not only of the various sub-tests that go to make up most IQ test batteries, but also of a variety of other laboratory tasks, where we may already have some idea of some of the processes or operations involved. Which laboratory tasks show high correlations with IQ, or better still with g, and which show lower correlations? What manipulations of a given task will increase the strength of its relation to, or dependence on, a general factor?

Such a programme might also help to answer the question whether g is dependent on a single, unitary psychological process or on a diverse and overlapping set of different processes. In the former case, there should be only one reason why tests increase their g-loading, and the difference between forward and backward span, for example, and that between object assembly and vocabulary, must both be caused by an increase in the demands placed on this one process. In the latter, we might expect to find a wide variety of different reasons why different tests vary in their g-loading.

Needless to say, the evidence available to settle the question is fragmentary rather than systematic, for few investigators have systematically set out to determine, for a wide variety of different tests, what is responsible for those tests' g-loadings. But a number of studies have begun to establish what changes to particular laboratory tasks will affect that task's correlation with people's IQ scores. As will become apparent, there does not appear to be any single common thread, but rather a number of independent reasons why some tasks correlate more strongly with IQ than others. On the face of it, this conclusion argues against the notion of a single process underlying g. But the problem is that most of these studies have been content to look for correlations with any IQ score, without much regard to the nature of the test battery employed, and even less to the question whether the correlation is with the general factor of that battery or not. An added complication is that g itself is not entirely stable (Chapter 6). Thus the discovery that one operation is responsible for increasing a test's loading on the general factor of the WAIS, while a different operation affects its correlation with scores on a series of measures of Gf, might mean little more than that the general factor underlying the two sets of IQ test is not the same.

However, the research we are about to review has yielded one important conclusion: while some operations do increase a task's correlation with IQ, others do not. Thus, although it might have been expected otherwise, difficulty *per se* does not seem to be a critical factor. There are plenty of ways of making various tasks more difficult, in the sense of increasing the number of errors people make on them, or slowing down their solution times, that have no effect whatsoever on their correlation with IQ.

Reaction time revisited

As we have seen, simple reaction time (RT) to a light shows a small but reliable correlation with IQ, of the order of −0.20 to −0.30. What changes to the task would increase the size of this correlation with IQ? Jensen (1982) originally supposed that one manipulation would be to increase the number of alternatives between which subjects must choose (a manipulation frequently described as one that increased the complexity of the task; Jensen, 1980). We have seen that, although RTs slow down with an increase in the number of alternatives, i.e. that the task certainly becomes more difficult, and no doubt in some sense more complex, there is at best only a trivially small increase in the size of the correlation between RT and IQ as one increases the number of alternatives.

There are, however, other manipulations that do succeed in increasing the correlation between RT and IQ. Indeed, there appear to be three rather different manipulations that have this effect. Two concern the nature of the stimuli to which subjects are required to respond, the third what else they are being asked to do at the same time.

We have already come across the first: while ordinary choice RT to two or more lights correlates less than −0.30 with IQ, OMO (odd man out) RT correlates over −0.40 with IQ (Frearson *et al.*, 1988; Bates and Eysenck, 1993*b*). Moreover, we also probably know the reason for this increase in the relationship to IQ. Performance on ordinary choice RT tasks is relatively independent of IT, but performance on OMO RT correlates quite well with IT. As a consequence of this, the high correlation between OMO RT and IQ is largely with the performance scale of the WAIS.

The second manipulation that increases the correlation between RT and IQ is to use letters, digits or, even better, words as the stimuli to which subjects are asked to respond. As in any RT task, the subject has to make a decision about the stimulus or stimuli occurring on each trial (which light came on; which light is furthest apart from the others) and then act on it. Here, the decision is about the lexical status of the stimuli. Figure 7.4 shows a variety of possible tasks; in each case the decision required is whether two simultaneously presented stimuli are the same or different. The tasks differ in the basis of this decision. In the two simplest versions, usually referred to as Posner's letter-matching tasks, the stimuli are letters of the alphabet. In the physical identity (PI) condition, 'same' means two physically identical letters, A–A, or a–a, while 'different' means an upper- and a lower-case letter, A–a. In letter name identity (NI) two As still count as the same, even if shown in different type face, A–a. The stimuli for the remaining tasks of Fig. 7.4 are words. Again, physical identity is a matter of whether two words are exactly the same, e.g. DEER–DEER. In the homonym identity condition, two words that merely sound alike are still to be judged the same, e.g. DEER–DEAR; while in categorical identity, two words from the same taxonomic category, e.g. DEER–ELK, count as the same, even if different in all other respects. People with higher IQ scores respond more rapidly than those with lower scores on all these tasks but, as can be seen in Fig. 7.4, these differences become greater as one progresses through the list. In other words, there is an increase in the correlation between RT and IQ. The subjects in these studies were all university students and thus of above average IQ. According to Hunt (1978), other populations take substantially longer to respond, and the *difference* between letter NI and letter PI tasks (no data seem available for the other cases) is greater than that shown in Fig. 7.4, ranging from 110 ms for young adults not at university, to 170 ms for adults over the age of 60, to over 300 ms for mildly retarded schoolchildren.

Some of these findings have been confirmed by Vernon and Jensen (1984) who reported actual correlations as well as differences in mean RT between groups differing in average IQ. They studied both vocational college students and university students: the former group showed correlations between RT and IQ ranging from zero, where the stimuli were lights, to about −0.35, for a synonym–antonym task (Fig. 7.5). Moreover, the size of the difference in RTs between the vocational and university students, who differed in mean IQ, mirrored the correlations shown in Fig. 7.5, and gave much the same values as the results shown in Fig. 7.4.

A proponent of *g* might argue that the two manipulations considered so far really amount to the same thing: any increase in the difficulty or complexity of the discrimination which subjects have to make in an RT task, whether it be a matter of deciding which of three lights

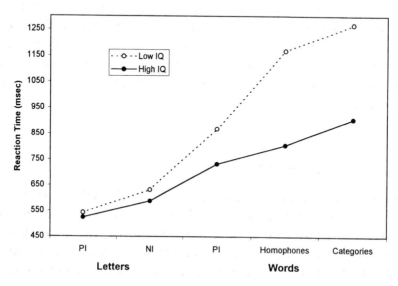

Fig. 7.4 Reaction times of students selected for high- or low-IQ scores on a variety of RT tasks. See text for further explanation. (Data from Hunt *et al.*, 1975; Goldberg *et al.*, 1977.)

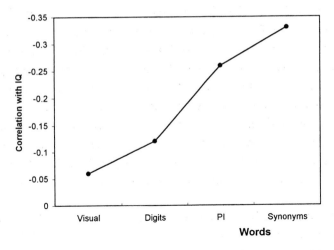

Fig. 7.5 Correlations between IQ and RT for a group of vocational college students on a variety of RT tasks. Visual RT was the standard choice RT task to lights; in the Digit task, a sequence of digits was displayed, followed after a gap by a probe digit, and subjects had to decide whether the probe had been in the list; Word PI was the same task as shown in Fig. 7.4; Synonyms required subjects to decide whether two words were synonyms or antonyms. (Data from Vernon and Jensen, 1984.)

is furthest apart, or whether DEER and DEAR are homonyms, will increase RT's g-loading. But there is good reason to question this. As we have seen, the change from the standard to the OMO RT task increases the correlation between RT and WAIS performance IQ, and it seems likely therefore, given OMO RT's high correlation with IT, that what we are seeing is an increase in RT's relationship to a perceptual speed component of IQ. The use of letters and words, instead of lights, in an RT task increases the correlation between RT and verbal IQ or Gc. Hunt's IQ measures were all exclusively measures of verbal IQ, and the test battery employed by Vernon and Jensen, the ASVAB, is predominantly a measure of Gc. If this is so, then rather than find operations that increase RT's g-loading, we have identified two distinct operations that increase the correlation between RT and two rather distinct IQ factors, Gc and Gs.

Concurrent and competing tasks

The third operation that increases the correlation between RT and IQ is to require subjects to perform another task at the same time. The digit RT task in Vernon and Jensen's (1984) study presented a series of digits followed, after a brief pause, by a probe digit, and the subject's task was to say whether the probe had or had not appeared in the initial list on that trial. In one condition of their study, after the initial list of digits, subjects were presented with one of the word identity tasks, and the probe digit was shown only after they had made their response to the words. Although the correlational data were rather inconsistent, this manipulation tended to increase the difference between the performance of university and vocational college students. An average difference of less than 100 ms on the digit task on its own was increased to nearly 200 ms when people were required to respond to the synonym–antonym task in the interval between presentation of the list of digits and the probe. A similar increase was found in the magnitude of the difference between the performance of subjects of higher and lower IQ on the word physical identity task when it was performed concurrently with the digit task rather than on its own. One interpretation of these data is that a third way of increasing the relationship between IQ and RT may be to require people to perform two tasks concurrently.

Several other lines of evidence concur in this suggestion: tasks which, performed in isolation, seem to make no demands on IQ, start to correlate significantly with IQ scores as soon as they must be performed together. A particularly clear instance of this is provided by a study of Roberts *et al.* (1988), who required students to sort playing cards as rapidly as possible, either by colour (red v. black, i.e. into two categories), or by suit (four categories), or by number (eight different numbers were used). The total time required to sort a pack constituted, in effect, a measure of 2-, 4- or 8-choice RT, while the task of simply sorting the pack into alternate piles provided a control measure of movement time. As can be seen in Table 7.4, except in this control condition, there was a modest correlation between speed of sorting and IQ (scores on Raven's Matrices). The correlation between IQ and 4-choice RT was rather higher than those typically observed in RT studies reviewed earlier, but the remaining data seem very similar, and there was clearly no systematic tendency for the correlations to increase with an increase in the number of alternatives. The important result, however, is that when people were required to perform another task at the same time (they had to listen to a list of words being read out to them, and report the semantic category of each), the correlations between card-sorting scores and IQ now averaged 0.65.

Spilsbury (1992) required people to perform a counting task. They were asked to listen to a series of sounds (a bell, a whistle, etc.) and, at the end of the list, to report the number of times each different sound had occurred. The task could be made harder by increasing the number of different types of sound that occurred from three to four, and lengthening the total list from six to twelve items. Although these manipulations led to a significant increase

Table 7.4 Correlations between IQ scores and card sorting when performed as a single task and when performed concurrently with a competing task (from Roberts *et al.*, 1988)

Sorting task	Single task	Competing task
Control condition	0.03	−0.07
2 Categories	−0.21	−0.65
4 Categories	--0.49	−0.71
8 Categories	−0.30	−0.59

in the number of errors, they did not increase the size of the correlation between performance on the task and people's IQ scores. But the requirement to perform the counting task at the same time as a second task (a computer-presented multiple-choice vocabulary test), which caused no greater an increase in errors, increased the correlation with IQ from 0.18 to 0.53. Here again is evidence that it is not difficulty *per se* that makes the efficient performance of a task dependent on IQ.

It is not necessary to ask people to perform concurrently two separate tasks from quite different domains in order to observe this increasing dependence on IQ. Single tasks that themselves can be construed as imposing such a requirement appear to correlate quite strongly with IQ scores. Consider again the difference between forward and backward digit span. Why does backward span correlate with the rest of the WAIS more strongly than forward span? Of course, backward span is more difficult, but that, we should accept by now, is not a sufficient explanation. A more plausible explanation, consistent with the data just reviewed, is that while both tasks require one to remember a list of digits, backward span requires one to perform a modestly complex operation on them, *vis* put them in reverse order, at the same time as holding them in memory, while forward span requires one only to register each new digit as it is presented.

A study by Vernon and Weese (1993) suggests that something like this may be the critical factor. They presented students with a list of 10 digits, and required them to give the sum of each successive pair as they appeared. Thus to the list:

1, 3, 6, 4, etc.,

the correct responses would be:

4 (1 + 3), 9 (3 + 6), 10 (6 + 4), etc.

The arithmetic operations required to produce the correct answer were extremely simple; presumably, the problem was the requirement to perform them at the same time as holding each new digit in memory, and performance correlated over 0.40 with IQ. Once again, difficulty *per se* was not the critical factor: an increase in presentation rate from 1 digit every 3 seconds to 1 digit a second increased errors from 6.5 per cent to 42 per cent, but only increased the correlation with IQ from 0.45 to 0.47.

Theoretical interpretation

Two secure conclusions can be drawn from the studies reviewed above. The first is that performance on a variety of relatively brief and, in at least some sense, rather simple laboratory tasks will show correlations with IQ scores of up to 0.50 or 0.65. This is substantially higher than the correlation between IQ and RT and rather higher than that between IQ and IT—in spite of the fact that the subjects of these experiments were usually college or university students with an equally restricted range of IQ scores as those participating in the IT and RT experiments. In some cases, indeed, direct comparison has established that the correlation between IQ and dual-task performance is twice as high as that between IQ and RT or IT (e.g. Larson and Saccuzzo, 1989; their experiment is described in more detail in Chapter 8).

Secondly, many of the studies reviewed above have shown that difficulty *per se* is not the critical determinant of a task's correlation with IQ. It is, of course, true that it takes longer to reach decisions about the meanings of words than about their physical appearance; equally, people often (but not always) make more errors when performing two tasks concurrently than on either alone. But there are all sorts of ways of making problems harder that have virtually no effect on their correlations with IQ. We have seen numerous examples of changes in procedure or task requirement that increased errors or slowed down reaction times without affecting a task's relationship with IQ. We thus have valuable evidence of discriminant validity: it is implausible to argue that where some change succeeds in increasing correlations with IQ, it is doing so simply because it makes a task harder.

But have we made any progress towards the goal of identifying a single cognitive process underlying *g*? The answer, yet again, is surely no. On the face of it, these studies suggest that there is no single change in task characteristics that affects that task's correlation with IQ. But this is hardly surprising, for there is reason to believe that the three operations we have identified so far cause increases in correlations with rather different aspects of IQ. As we have already seen, the change from standard to OMO RT probably increases the correlation between RT and Gs or perceptual speed. The change to lexical decision tasks increases the correlation between RT and Gc or verbal IQ. What about the addition of a concurrent competing task? The evidence is not entirely consistent. Thus in Vernon and Jensen's (1984) study, the addition of a competing task increased the difference in performance between groups differing in scores on a measure of Gc. But in most of the studies of Stankov and his colleagues on the relationship between IQ and dual-task performance, IQ was measured by tests of non-verbal reasoning or Gf. Fogarty and Stankov (1988) found that the change in correlation with IQ when two tasks were performed at once, rather than on their own, was more pronounced when IQ was measured by those sub-tests of the WAIS more plausibly thought of as measures of Gf (block design, picture arrangement, and completion) rather than with those sub-tests more plausibly thought of as measures of Gc (vocabulary, information, similarities, comprehension). More systematically, Spilsbury (1992) administered a wider variety of IQ tests, factor analysed to yield distinct Gc and Gf factors. Only Gf correlated with performance on her mental counting task, and interacted with the effect of introducing a second, competing task: Gc scores showed no such relationship.

It seems, therefore, that dual-task performance is probably more strongly associated with measures of Gf than of Gc. There is complementary evidence that performance on a variety of lexical decision tasks correlates more strongly with measures of Gc than of Gf. Thus

Lansman *et al.* (1982) gave a battery of IQ tests and various information-processing tasks to a group of 91 undergraduates. These included the Posner letter identification task used in Hunt's studies illustrated in Fig. 7.4 and Carpenter and Just's (1975) sentence-verification task, which requires one to say, as rapidly as possible, whether a given sentence provides a true or false description of a simple diagram (see Fig. 7.6 for a further description). Performance on both of these tasks, the sentence-verification task more than the letter identification task, showed moderate correlations with measures of Gc (vocabulary and information tests), but none at all with measures of Gf (letter series and matrices problems). A similar finding has been reported for another lexical task, a measure of the rapidity of retrieval from short-term memory devised by Sternberg (1975): subjects are given a list of digits or letters to remember, and then asked to decide whether a given probe item was or was not in the list presented on that trial. Reaction time is a monotonically increasing function of the number of items in the list—a finding taken to imply that people normally engage in a serial search of the list held in memory. Bowling and Mackenzie (1996) found that performance on this task correlated with measures of Gc but not with measures of Gf.

Lansman *et al.* (1982) included a third information-processing task in their study, the Shepard–Metzler mental rotation task, where one has to decide whether two three-dimensional block figures are or are not the same as one another when rotated into the same plane (see Fig. 8.2). Performance on this correlated strongly (0.78) with measures of Gv or spatial ability, a finding confirmed by McGue and Bouchard (1989). While this is hardly surprising, for a variety of mental rotation tasks form part of most spatial IQ test batteries, the more important finding of both studies was that performance on the Shepard–Metzler task showed negligible correlations with measures of Gc or Gf.

There is thus good evidence that performance on a number of different laboratory tasks correlates with performance on *different* aspects of IQ, and that different changes to different tasks can increase their correlations with these different components of IQ. A determined defender of the unitary nature of *g* might argue that none of this categorically disproves his hypothesis. He could insist that all we have done is identify some of the distinct psychological processes that underlie the distinct group factors whose existence he is perfectly happy to acknowledge. While that may be true, the fact remains that little or no evidence has been forthcoming of any laboratory task where performance correlates

Picture

Sentence   Star above Plus

Fig. 7.6 The sentence-verification task. The subject is shown a picture, here of a star and a plus sign, and a sentence that may, or may not, accurately describe the spatial relationship between the elements of the picture. Their RT to respond true or false is measured. (From Carpenter and Just, 1975.)

substantially with performance on *all* IQ tests, or of any single change that would significantly increase a task's correlation with *g*. In the light of this, it may be more sensible to pursue a different strategy. Since it has proved easy to find tasks that correlate with particular group factors or components of IQ, and equally easy to find operations that increase correlations with these more particular components, perhaps we should turn our attention to these specific factors themselves. A more intensive analysis of the processes involved in tests of Gc, Gv, and Gf, for example, may or may not turn up evidence for certain particular processes time and time again—perhaps even for one or two processes that appear to be involved in all types of IQ test. If so, then we shall have evidence that the general factor is indeed to be partly accounted for by one or more very general processes. But we should not prejudge the issue. It may be that all we shall find is evidence for a variety of independent but partially overlapping processes. Chapters 8 and 9 take up this challenge.

Summary

One possible explanation of the general factor that can be extracted from any IQ test battery is that performance on all manner of IQ tests depends upon a single underlying process of 'general intelligence'. But what might such a process be? Several authors have argued that it must be some aspect of the efficiency of the brain as an information-processing system, such as the speed and accuracy with which information is transmitted from one part of the system to another. They have sought to test this hypothesis by looking for correlations between IQ scores, or better still *g*, and various neural and simple behavioural measures.

It is surely unsurprising that IQ scores should correlate with some measures of the brain. They do. There is a modest correlation between IQ and the size of the brain—although what this means no one really knows. There are probably some correlations between brain activity, either EEG records or more specific event-related potentials (ERPs) and IQ. Many of these effects have proved hard to replicate; one that does seem real is that lower IQ is associated with larger changes in such activity when people become engaged in a particular task. That simply suggests that the higher one's IQ the less effort one has to expend to solve a particular problem.

Two simple behavioural measures, reaction time (RT) and inspection time (IT) have been found to correlate with IQ; the IQ–RT correlation is probably between −0.20 and −0.30 (higher IQ being associated with shorter RT); that between IT and IQ is higher, perhaps in the range −0.25 to −0.50. But neither the RT nor the IT tasks can be regarded as pure measures of speed of information processing; they are certainly not measuring the same thing; and the correlation between IT and IQ is not a correlation with *g*, but probably with the factor of perceptual speed.

The search for a single underlying process of general intelligence has not, as yet, met with much success. It turns out that there are other laboratory tasks that correlate with IQ scores—but usually with specific factors such as Gf, Gc, or Gv. And there is also evidence of particular operations that increase a task's correlation with IQ—but again, almost certainly with specific components of IQ. This suggests that an alternative strategy will be to see what cognitive processes or operations are engaged by specific IQ factors, and whether any of these processes or operations are common to more than one factor.

8 The search for cognitive operations underlying specific components of IQ: verbal and spatial abilities

Introduction

The task of identifying the cognitive processes underlying different aspects of overall IQ requires at the outset some decision as to the number of different aspects we are prepared to analyse. As we have seen in Chapter 6, most factor analysts are agreed on one broad distinction—that between crystallized and fluid intelligence, Gc and Gf. To these two broad factors, most would add further factors of spatial visualization (Gv) and perceptual speed (Gs), and many would add several more, for example, an immediate memory or short-term acquisition and retrieval factor (Cattell's Gm) and an auditory perception factor, which we could label Ga. Most modern factorists (see Carroll, 1993) have argued that further analysis will always be able to decompose these relatively broad factors into a much larger number of narrower, subsidiary or primary factors. Whether they are 'subsidiary' or 'primary' simply depends on the method of factor analysis employed: they are subsidiary if extracted, by a principal components analysis without rotation of axes, after more general factors have been extracted first; they are primary if extracted first by rotation to simple structure. That distinction need not concern us. Nor shall I be particularly concerned here with the very large number of such narrow factors that have been proposed. Carroll (1993) and Cattell (1971), for example, identify some 20–30; and even Vernon (1950), although a believer in a superordinate general factor, explicitly allowed that his *v:ed* factor, roughly the equivalent of Gc, was certainly divisible into more specifically verbal and numerical factors, and acknowledged that there were surely many more divisions that could be made. Although, in what follows, I shall occasionally acknowledge these further distinctions, the discussion of this and the following chapter will focus on the three main factors, Gc, Gv, and Gf. The perceptual speed factor, Gs, was discussed briefly in the preceding chapter.

The analysis of Gc, Gv, and Gf should be sufficient to test the viability of the strategy outlined at the end of the previous chapter. Our goal is to identify the major cognitive operations or processes implicated in these broad factors, to see how far they are unique to each or whether similar processes may be involved in all three. It can hardly be doubted that there will be some processes unique to each, but to the extent that there are processes common to them all, we may have identified the psychological basis or bases of general intelligence.

Crystallized ability (Gc)

In Cattell's theorizing, the factorial distinction between Gc and Gf is given psychological interpretation by saying that Gc is the product of Gf (Cattell, 1971): Gf is said to represent the biological potential for intelligence, which becomes manifest in Gc, as people acquire knowledge and experience, absorbing the culture in which they live and profiting, or not as the case may be, from the educational system their society provides. Typical measures of Gc are the vocabulary, information, comprehension, and arithmetic sub-tests of the WAIS and WISC. A common reaction to these tests, of course, is to say that they are *simply* measures of acquired knowledge, rather than of anything we should normally want to call ability or intelligence. The size of anyone's vocabulary, like their store of general knowledge, must depend on their past opportunity to have acquired the relevant information, and their ability or willingness to take advantage of that opportunity.

One version of this argument would attribute differences in Gc largely, if not entirely, to differences in family background and educational experience: children brought up in comfortable, middle-class homes, with a plentiful supply of books, serious newspapers, and magazines, daily listening to the informed and intelligent conversation of their well-educated parents, must surely acquire a larger vocabulary and fund of general knowledge than the impoverished inhabitant of an inner-city ghetto or an isolated rural community, where few adults received any education after the age of 16, and probably not too much before that age. Another version would appeal to the self-evident truth of the proposition that the teenager or adult who reads half a dozen books a week will surely acquire a larger vocabulary than one whose sole reading matter since leaving school is the back of a box of cornflakes, or the sports pages of a popular newspaper.

Both may contain an important grain of truth—but not necessarily much more. Although social-class differences in IQ are more pronounced for tests of verbal than of non-verbal IQ, i.e. Gc rather than Gf, family background is probably not the most important environmental determinant of children's IQ scores: differences between the experiences of children in one and the same family are every bit as important as differences between families (see Chapter 4). And while the avid bookworm will surely have a larger vocabulary than someone who never opens a book after leaving school, the chances are that they already differed in Gc from an early age, and that the difference in their tastes in reading matter is as much a consequence, as a cause, of their difference in measures of Gc.

Speed of lexical access

Nevertheless, it still seems plausible to suppose that differences in Gc must be largely a consequence of differences in past learning, or even past opportunity to learn, and are thus differences in current knowledge or expertise rather than in any natural ability. The argument has been advanced by several writers (e.g. Keil, 1984; Ceci, 1990), and extended to other measures of verbal IQ, including some of the elementary cognitive correlates of Gc discussed in the final section of Chapter 7. Why should differences in Gc be associated with differences in RT in Posner's letter- or word-matching paradigm, or in Sternberg's retrieval from short-term memory task, or in Carpenter and Just's sentence-verification problem? According to Ceci (1990), the answer is that all these laboratory tasks are measuring speed of access to stored representations of letters, words, sentences, etc. (hereafter, speed of 'lexical access'), and differences in lexical access simply reflect differences in the amount of practice people have had with related tasks, such as reading, and thus differences in the familiarity of the material used in these experiments. According to Brody (1992), performance on tasks such as these is probably influenced by the amount of formal schooling participants have received, and thus the correlation with measures of Gc may be a by-product of differences in schooling.

This last possibility does not seem particularly plausible, given that most of the studies reporting correlations between verbal IQ and speed of lexical access have employed university or college students as subjects, all of whom will have received an above-average amount of formal schooling. But there are other implications of Ceci's and Brody's general argument, which have fared little better in the face of empirical evidence. For example, one would expect to see differences in test performance disappearing if people were tested with material that was equally unfamiliar to all of them, such as a novel set of symbols or hieroglyphics with which they had all had equivalent experience. On the contrary, there is good experimental evidence that differences in Gc predict children's ability to learn a new, arbitrary vocabulary rather than simply reflecting past familiarity with the material. Gathercole and Baddeley (1990) asked two groups of 5-year-olds to learn new names for each of four toy animals. The names were either ordinary proper names, Simon, Michael etc., or nonsense names such as Tikal and Pemon. Children with higher scores on vocabulary and reading tests learned these new associations substantially faster than those with lower scores—even though the two groups were perfectly matched for scores on a measure of Gf—Raven's Matrices.

Jackson (1980) taught college students an artificial 'alphabet', in which arbitrary visual symbols were associated with nonsense syllables. By pairing two symbols with each nonsense syllable, he created two symbols with the same 'meaning', in a manner analogous to upper- and lower-case versions of the same letter of the alphabet. He still found a significant correlation between measures of reading skill and RT on this stimulus-matching task. By equating his participants' experience with the symbols, he had presumably made them equally familiar to every one. Moreover, the correlation he observed was between a quintessential measure of verbal ability and one involving access to the 'meaning' of arbitrary symbols or diagrams, rather than words or letter strings.

There is a final implication of Ceci's argument: if correlations between IQ scores and performance on the laboratory problems are based on their sharing a common *content*, they should be highly specific. Measures of vocabulary or reading proficiency would correlate with tasks requiring specifically lexical access, but not with similar problems employing numbers or diagrammatic symbols as their materials: performance on these latter problems would, presumably, show stronger correlations with numerical or diagrammatic IQ tests. There is little evidence to support this assumption.

In a study employing (for a welcome change) adults other than college students as subjects, Neubauer and Bucik (1996) found correlations in the range 0.30–0.50 between IQ scores and performance on the Posner stimulus-matching and Sternberg memory scanning tasks. They gave a variety of IQ tests, specifically designed to measure distinct verbal, numerical, and figural abilities. A more novel aspect of their experiment was that they employed three different versions of the Posner and Sternberg tasks, one employing letters, another numbers, and a third visual symbols. Thus for the Posner tasks, the first version used the usual letters of the alphabet (e.g. A, a, for the 'name' identity condition), the second used Arabic and Roman numerals (e.g. 5 and V), while the third used visual symbols for the two sexes (e.g. ♀ and ⚤ for females).

Correlations between performance on all six tasks were uniformly high, averaging well over 0.50. A principal components analysis thus revealed a strong general factor. More detailed inspection of the correlation matrix, however, revealed that the correlations between the three different versions (letters, numbers, symbols) of the same task were higher than those between the same version (e.g. letters) of the two different tasks. However, it was also possible to identify three factors corresponding to the verbal, numerical, and diagrammatic versions of the two tasks. But there was virtually no suggestion that these three factors were particularly strongly associated with verbal, numerical, and figural components of IQ scores. Table 8.1 shows the intercorrelations between the three IQ components and the verbal, numerical, and figural factor scores from the Posner and Sternberg tasks. Although there is some suggestion that figural IQ correlated particularly strongly with the figural factor, the main impression from Table 8.1 is that all these correlations are pretty uniform. Thus common content did not seem to be a particularly important determinant of correlations between performance on laboratory tasks and IQ tests, and Ceci's appeal to the familiarity of the content as an explanation of these correlations does not seem very persuasive.

Table 8.1 Correlations between verbal, numerical, and figural factor scores from Posner and Sternberg tasks and verbal, numerical, and figural IQ scores (from Neubauer and Bucik, 1996)

IQ score	Factor score		
	Verbal	Numerical	Figural
Verbal	0.52	0.44	0.43
Numerical	0.45	0.45	0.45
Figural	0.45	0.45	0.60

We should probably accept, then, that differences in Gc are associated with differences in speed of access to, and efficiency of processing and retrieval of, lexical, numerical, and symbolic material, even if we have as yet no good explanation of how this association arises. The reality, and generality, of the association, however, is further documented by analysis of the digit-span task—which forms part of the verbal scale of the Wechsler tests. We have already acknowledged that backward span correlates more strongly with the rest of the test than forward span, but why does forward span correlate with other verbal sub-tests at all? As we noted at the outset of Chapter 7, one might naively suppose that digit span is simply a measure of the capacity of some short-term memory store. Experimental analysis suggests, however, that one determinant of performance on any memory-span task is the speed with which the items can be processed or articulated.

Several lines of evidence support this conclusion. First, children who are bilingual in Welsh and English have a longer digit span in English than in Welsh, even if they regard themselves as more proficient in Welsh, because Welsh digits take longer to pronounce than English digits (Ellis and Hennelly, 1980). Similar effects have been reported for a variety of other languages, e.g. Spanish and English (Chincotta and Hoosain, 1995). Secondly, Baddeley *et al.* (1975) have shown that memory span for words is inversely related to the number of syllables in each word. The critical factor appears to be the rate at which items can be articulated or read. Baddeley *et al.* showed that span correlates 0.69 with the rate of reading words even when the number of syllables was equated. Thus a list made up of two-syllable words, such as BISHOP, WICKED, PEWTER, and PHALLIC would be more readily remembered than a list of words such as, COERCE, HARPOON, CYCLONE, and FRIDAY, which take longer to pronounce. Thirdly, memory span also, of course, increases as children grow older. Nicolson (1981) and Hulme *et al.* (1984) have shown that this improvement is partly attributable to an increase in speed of articulating or reading the items in the list. Children of different ages, but with the same reading rate, have the same span, and differences in span between different age groups can be eliminated by the use of words for one age group which are read at the same speed as the words used for the second age group. Although other factors are undoubtedly involved, and the picture is now more complicated than that suggested here (see, for example, Cowan, 1992; Brown and Hulme,

1995), something like speed of lexical access does appear to be implicated in performance on simple memory-span tasks, and presumably helps to explain why such tasks correlate with other measures of Gc.

Vocabulary learning

But even if one thread running through a variety of measures of Gc is speed of lexical and numerical access, and efficiency of processing such material, it does not seem likely that it can be the only cognitive process involved. All memory-span tasks must surely also measure some aspect or aspects of the efficiency of a short-term or working-memory system (a point we shall return to below). And it is a simple matter to show that such a central measure of verbal IQ as vocabulary size is not simply reducible to the efficiency of lexical access. At any given age, there is a correlation, of the order of 0.30–0.45, between vocabulary size and speed of performance on the Posner letter matching, Sternberg memory scanning, and Carpenter and Just sentence-verification tasks. But as soon as we turn to a comparison of different age groups, there is a striking dissociation between measures of vocabulary and of sentence-verification RT. Table 8.2 shows that across the age range 20–60, vocabulary size tends to increase, while performance on the sentence-verification task declines sharply, and ends up twice as slow at age 60 as it was at age 20 (the data shown here are cross-sectional; it may be doubted whether the decline would be quite as marked in longitudinal data, but that is irrelevant for the present argument).

If people's vocabulary increases as they grow older, one obvious explanation is that they have simply had a longer time to learn the meaning of a larger number of words. We are back to the suggestion that Gc is just a measure of one's opportunity to acquire a certain kind of information. Whether or not that is the whole story, it is worth stopping to ask the question: how do we learn the meanings of new words? As we have already noted, the critic's assumption is often that differences in acquired knowledge can be ascribed solely to differences in the opportunity to learn rather than to differences in the efficiency with which people take advantage of their opportunities. And the further, usually tacit, assumption is

Table 8.2 Vocabulary scores and performance on the sentence-verification task as a function of age (from Hunt, 1987)

	Age (years)			
	20	30	50	60
Vocabulary	78	98	92	100
Sentence verification	100	72	72	50

Scores are all set relative to the best performing group on each task, whose score is set to 100.

that the learning process involved is just a matter of rote (paired-associate) learning, and that people do not differ in their ability to learn by rote. There are two fallacies here. First, people do differ in their performance on laboratory paired-associate learning tasks, although the correlation between rote learning and IQ scores is probably no more than about 0.20 (Woodrow, 1940; see Chapter 5). Secondly, the simple rote-learning tasks studied in the laboratory may not provide a very good model of the processes involved in learning the meanings of new words in the real world. Young children do not acquire their vocabulary by paired-associate learning of each new word with a definition kindly provided by parent or teacher. The average child has a vocabulary of some 14 000 words by the age of 6 years; a rough calculation suggests that they must be learning a new word every waking hour. Ten years later, typical American high-school seniors have a vocabulary of some 40 000 words, and have learned about 3000 new words a year throughout their time at school (Ellis, 1994). No one can seriously suppose that they are explicitly taught, or explicitly look up in a dictionary, each of these words.

As several commentators have argued, it seems clear that we first acquire a vocabulary mostly by listening to what we hear people saying, and later by reading (Sternberg, 1985; Krashen, 1989; Ellis, 1994). In order to do this, we have to work out the meaning of new words from the contexts in which we hear them; in addition we rely on an analysis of the structure of a word, and sometimes on the known meaning of some of its parts. Acquiring a vocabulary depends on processes of inference and reasoning in the face of uncertainty. For example, what is the meaning of:

> *Antinomian*
>
> *Benedick*

or of the non-italicized word in the following sentence:

> *Many* thanes *and their followers joined Harold at Hastings, but they were not enough to save him from defeat.*

Familiarity with classical Greek, or with such obscure psychological jargon as 'nomothetical' or 'psychonomic', might allow one to guess that 'antinomian' has something to do with being against laws. While someone who has read Shakespeare's *As You Like It* might hazard the guess that a Benedick is a recently and reluctantly married man. Whole sentences can usually provide much stronger clues to the meaning of unfamiliar words. It requires only a passing acquaintance with English history to infer that thanes are some sort of Anglo-Saxon soldier. And the mention of their followers implies that they were men of some authority and power, albeit below that of a king, in Anglo-Saxon England.

It is often possible to work out the meaning of unfamiliar words and it seems plausible to suppose that this is how we acquired much of our vocabulary. No doubt, our ability to do so depends on our prior knowledge: someone who has never heard of the Battle of Hastings will find it difficult to work out what thanes are. But it also reflects our ability to bring

evidence to bear on the solution of a prob
and so on. Given all this, it becomes
measure of Gc. Experimental evidence
Powell (1983) gave American high
contained some extremely rare and
guess. For example:

> A middle-aged woman and a yc
> ready. The mother, Tanith, pee·
> long time since his last *ceilid*
> travels and adventures of th·
> touched his mother's arm ·

The students' task was r
accuracy and adequacy of then ·
similar experiment, Van Daalen-Kapteij·.
students a number of sentences to read, each con··
meaning they were asked to guess after reading a sentenc·.
IQ performed substantially more accurately on this task than tho··

There is also evidence of the converse of this—that in young children, a··
IQ correlates significantly with the ability to provide the appropriate word to fill a g·
sentence (Hunt, 1985). An example:

> *Aunt Jane was unhappy because the cat —— her canary.*

Working memory

A final ingredient of some, but perhaps not all, measures of Gc is that they impose some demands on some aspects of short-term memory. It is hard to believe that the only determinant of performance on memory-span tasks is one's familiarity with, or speed of articulating, the material to be retrieved. The Sternberg memory-retrieval task, which also correlates with some measures of Gc, similarly seems, on the face of it, to be a task imposing some demands on the efficiency of some short-term memory system. No doubt this is true—in part. But it is also a serious oversimplification. What we need, in order to understand the role of short-term memory in performance on tasks associated with measures of Gc, is a clearer theoretical understanding of what we mean by 'short-term memory'.

Baddeley and Hitch (1974; see also Baddeley, 1986) proposed a theory of 'working memory' which postulated, as shown in Fig. 8.1, a central executive together with two associated 'slave' systems, a phonological loop, and a visuo-spatial sketchpad. We shall return to this last system later; for present purposes, what we need to understand is the role of the central executive and the phonological loop. Let us start with the latter. The

...d into two components, a short-term phonological buffer
...phonological code; this information is assumed to decay very
...ed for a longer time by passing round the second component, a
...this rehearsal loop also acts to translate visually presented
...essary, into a phonological code.

..., ample introspective evidence for this subvocal rehearsal loop: when
...a list of words or sequence of digits, we repeat them to ourselves under
...here is also good experimental support—for example, the conclusion from
...iewed above that memory span for words or numbers is a function of the time
...ead or pronounce each item: if the loop is of fixed size, the number of items that
...hearsed in it will depend on how rapidly they can be articulated. Further evidence
...ided by experiments varying the phonological similarity of items in a memory-span
...and by others that have studied the effects of articulatory suppression (reviewed by
...ddeley, 1986; Gathercole and Baddeley, 1993). The former have shown that people
make more errors on a memory-span task if the items to be remembered sound alike (e.g.
the letters B, C, T, V) than if they do not (H, M, W, Z). This is not just because people get
confused when listening to a series of letters that sound alike, since the same effect is found
when items are presented visually, to be silently read by the subject. The implication is that
people translate them into a phonological code and the confusions arise during the course of
rehearsal. Experiments on articulatory suppression are designed to prevent use of the
phonological loop for rehearsal by occupying it with other material: asking someone to say
'the, the, the . . .' repeatedly while the items to be remembered are being visually presented,
severely disrupts memory span. A final source of evidence is provided by neuropsychology.
Patients have been found who have normal language and long-term memory, but an
immediate memory span of no more than two or three items. The important observation is
that this span is unaffected by those manipulations described above, such as word length,
phonological similarity, or articulatory suppression, that have such a profound effect in the
normal case.

There is good evidence, then, that the phonological loop is the system primarily involved

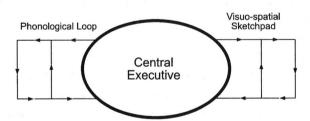

Fig. 8.1 A schematic representation of the Baddeley–Hitch model of the working-memory system. A central
executive processes and briefly stores information, but is aided in this task by two subsidiary buffer stores—one
for verbal, the other for visuo-spatial information.

in coping with the demands of the standard memory-span experiment. What else does it do? Gathercole and Baddeley (1993) have shown that one measure of the efficiency of the phonological loop, namely the ability to immediately recall a novel non-word heard for the first time, is a good predictor of vocabulary size in young children. For example, in their experiment, described above, where 5-year-old children learned new names for familiar toy animals (Gathercole and Baddeley, 1990), the two groups of children had actually been selected on the basis of their good or poor performance on this test of immediate phonological memory, rather than for differences in such traditional measures of verbal ability as vocabulary size or skill at reading.

The more interesting and important part of Baddeley and Hitch's model of working memory, however, if also the more mysterious and less well understood, is the central executive. Baddeley and Hitch argued that traditional theories of short-term memory in experimental psychology, based on experiments on memory span, completely ignored the way we actually use short-term memory in our daily lives. The digit-span task is a model of the way we temporarily memorize a telephone number that we have just looked up in the directory. But working memory did not evolve in anticipation of the invention of the telephone. The function of working memory is to hold some information in a temporary store while operating on new information that has just been presented. In order to solve many complex problems, we need to break them down into more manageable, smaller parts, work out the solution to one part, hold onto it while working out the solution to the next part, and so on, and finally combine all these part-solutions into an answer to the problem as a whole.

Even the act of reading or hearing a relatively simple pair of sentences may impose significant demands on working memory in this sense. Consider:

> *The problem you asked me to solve was easier for me than it would have been for John and Mary, since I had come across a similar one yesterday. But it would have been quite new for them.*

To understand these sentences requires one to remember early parts of the first sentence over an interval during which one was reading later parts, and the entire first sentence while reading the second. What, for example, is the referent of 'one' in the first sentence? What does 'it' (in both sentences) refer to? What does 'them' refer to?

Baddeley and Hitch's model assumes that verbal information can be held very briefly in the phonological buffer, and maintained there by passing round a subvocal rehearsal loop. But the theory also assumes that the central executive contains both a short-term memory system and an executive processor that operates on information and controls other activities. There is abundant evidence that it is this central executive that plays the more important role in language comprehension, and theorists such as Just and Carpenter (1992) use the term 'working memory' to refer only to this central system. The phonological loop does serve to maintain a brief verbatim record of a sentence—but we do not normally find ourselves subvocally rehearsing a previous sentence while reading the next one. The experimental manipulations that so affected performance on memory-span tasks, such as articulatory suppression and phonemic similarity, have rather less pronounced effects on comprehension (Gathercole and Baddeley, 1993), and neuropsychological patients with grossly impaired memory span are perfectly able to hold conversations, and to understand what they read (Martin, 1993). It is true that such patients show some difficulty with the correct parsing and understanding of some sentences, for example:

> *The cat that the dog chased was black.*

To understand that it is the cat, not the dog, that is said to be black, requires one to remember the precise wording, and hence structure of the sentence, and neurological damage to the phonological loop will indeed impair such precise recall. But it does not prevent such patients from understanding, and remembering, the content or meaning of what they hear. Sentences such as

> *The cat that the dog chased was a tabby.*

or

> *The cat that the bus ran over was black.*

are intelligible without one having to recall the precise word order and phrasing of the sentence when one gets to the end of it. Since dogs are not tabbies and buses are not often black, the last word of each must refer to the cat; understanding the sentence depends only on understanding the meaning of its constituent parts, and being able to recall the *meaning* of earlier parts when one gets to the end. Damage to the phonological loop does not interfere with this ability. One patient with a memory span of only 2–3 words, who was quite unable to provide a verbatim recall of sentences she had just heard, still had no difficulty in recalling their general meaning (Martin, 1993). Given the sentence:

> *Before calling her mother, the girl had a cup of tea.*

she paraphrased it as:

> *The girl drank some hot tea before she went to talk to her mother.*

All this is entirely consistent with what we already know from item analysis of IQ test batteries. As we saw in the Chapter 7, forward digit span correlates only moderately with the rest of the verbal scales of the WAIS, and other studies have found equally modest correlations between simple memory span and direct measures of verbal comprehension (e.g. Daneman and Carpenter, 1980). Thus in the population as a whole, performance on such memory-span tasks is not very strongly associated with measures of verbal ability, verbal comprehension, or Gc. And, again as we saw in Chapter 7, what is needed to increase digit span's correlation with other verbal IQ tests is to turn it into a backward span task, where the items must be held in memory while a more complex operation is performed on them. What is required to turn any immediate memory-span task into a better predictor of Gc is to turn it into a *working*-memory task, that imposes both processing and storage requirements.

There are various ways of turning a simple memory-span task into a working-memory task. Backward span requires one to reverse the order of the items before recalling them. Vernon and Weese (1993), again employing a digit-span task, required subjects to add neighbouring pairs of numbers together (see Chapter 7). Daneman and Carpenter (1980) devised a 'reading-span' task, specifically as an index of verbal comprehension and ability. Students were required to read aloud a series of sentences, visually presented one at a time, for example:

> *I went to the theatre last night for the first time in over a year, and met a friend I had not seen for ages.*

> *I wish summer were here so that we could sit out in the garden after supper.*

> *Darwin's theory of evolution by natural selection relied on an analogy with artificial breeding.*

> *In most societies, the majority of aggressive crimes have always been carried out by young males.*

They were then required to recall the last word of each sentence. This turns out to be a surprisingly difficult task, and few people can manage more than four or five sentences. In spite of the necessary restriction of range in these scores, Daneman and Carpenter reported a correlation of around 0.50 between various reading-span scores and students' scores on the Verbal Scholastic Aptitude Test, while Daneman and Green (1986) found a correlation of 0.57 between reading span and students' scores on a standard vocabulary test, and one of 0.69 between reading span and their ability to provide good definitions of very unusual words, such as *qualtagh*, from the context in which they appeared. Perhaps even more important, Daneman and Green found that the correlation of 0.61 between students' vocabulary scores and their ability to define words from their context was largely mediated by their reading-span scores. Their results are shown in Table 8.3. As can be seen, this correlation was reduced to an insignificant value when reading-span scores were taken into account. By contrast, the correlation between reading-span and word-definition scores remained substantial, and statistically significant, when vocabulary scores were taken into account. The implication is that we do indeed acquire a large vocabulary by being able to infer the meanings of new words from the context in which they occur, but that one reason why some people are better at this than others is because they have a more efficient verbal working memory.

There is even better evidence that the efficiency of this central executive working-memory system is implicated in the comprehension of connected prose (reviewed by Just and

Table 8.3 Correlations between reading span, vocabulary scores, and definitions of words from their context (from Daneman and Green, 1986)

	Correlation		Partial correlation	
	Vocabulary	Word definition		Word definition
Reading span	0.57	0.69	(Vocabulary partialled out)	0.53
Vocabulary	–	0.61	(Reading span partialled out)	0.33 (ns)

Carpenter, 1992). Daneman and Carpenter (1980) reported correlations in the range 0.70–0.85 between students' reading-span scores and their ability to answer factual questions about the contents of a passage of prose they had read, or to identify the referents of particular pronouns. As noted above, their ordinary immediate memory-span scores correlated significantly less strongly with any of these measures of comprehension. Other studies, both of university students (Cantor *et al.*, 1991) and of young children (Leather and Henry, 1994) have confirmed that reading span is a better predictor of comprehension and traditional measures of Gc than is immediate memory span. And although the two types of span measure are themselves correlated (for example, at 0.55 in Daneman and Carpenter's study), they appear to make independent contributions to comprehension and vocabulary scores. A factor analysis of scores on both immediate memory span and working-memory span in Cantor *et al.*'s study revealed two distinct factors, one for the immediate-span tasks, the other for the working-memory tasks. Both factors correlated significantly with the students' verbal SAT scores, even when the other had been controlled for, but the correlation was stronger for the working-memory factor.

There can be little doubt, then, that measures of reading span predict a variety of measures of verbal intelligence, such as vocabulary, comprehension, and verbal scholastic aptitude. It could be argued that it is hardly surprising that a test that requires people to read a series of sentences should correlate with other measures of reading comprehension. But this is not a sufficient explanation of the association. Daneman and Carpenter (1980) also developed a listening-span task, where the subject simply had to listen to a series of spoken sentences, answer questions about them (to ensure that they *were* listening) and then recall their last words. Listening span showed much the same correlation with verbal SAT and reading comprehension as did reading span. Daneman and Tardif (1987) developed a quite different word-span test. Each item consisted of four one-syllable words, for example,

end, barn, yard, owed,

and the processing task required subjects to join together two of the words to make a new one, whose syllable boundary did not coincide with the division between the two original words. In this case, endowed, rather than barnyard, is correct. The working-memory requirement was to recall the answer to each item at the end of the series. Scores on this task correlated 0.61 with a composite vocabulary and reading comprehension score. Even more convincingly, Daneman and Tardif also devised a number-span task, where each item consisted of three numbers, for example,

3, 7, 14,

and the requirement was to join (not add) two together to create a new number divisible by 3 (here, 714). Scores on the memory-span part of this task, which required subjects to recall the correct answer to each item at the end of the series, correlated 0.57 with the word-span test and 0.51 with composite vocabulary and comprehension scores.

That working-memory tasks with quite different materials and information-processing requirements should continue to correlate with verbal intelligence scores implies, as did earlier results on speed of lexical access (p. 269), that common content is not the underlying cause of correlations between IQ scores and various laboratory tasks. It is true that, in Daneman and Tardif's data and in other studies (e.g. Jurden, 1995), the correlations between measures of vocabulary or verbal comprehension and word span were rather higher than those with number-span scores, but that is hardly surprising. This pattern of results is, in fact, entirely consistent with factorial studies of human abilities: as we have seen, the higher-order factor, Gc, includes within it not only factors of verbal ability, reading comprehension, and general information, but also a factor of numerical facility (Carroll, 1993), and Vernon (1950) thought that his broad *v:ed* comprised distinguishable verbal and numerical factors. We should expect, therefore, that scores on verbal and numerical tasks should tap some overlapping processes. Of course, to the extent that both verbal and numerical factors can be extracted from large test batteries, they are partially distinct, but to the extent that they fall under the same broad Gc factor, they must also be related.

It seems intuitively plausible that working memory will indeed be one of those overlapping processes, for solving problems in mental arithmetic surely places some demands on working memory. If asked to add 377 and 84, most of us will solve this problem, as we were taught in school, by breaking it down into a series of sub-problems:

4 + 7 = 1 (carry 1)

8 + 7 + 1 = 6 (carry 1)

3 + 1 = 4

By holding the solution to each sub-problem in memory, we can come up with the answer, 461. Hitch (1978) has provided good evidence that this intuition is correct—at least for most of us; while Logie *et al.* (1994) have shown that performance on simple mental arithmetic tasks can be seriously disrupted by requiring people to perform concurrently another task that occupies the central executive memory store. The implication, then, is that

Table 8.4 Correlations between memory span, reading, vocabulary, and arithmetic tests in 7-year-old children (from Leather and Henry, 1994)

	Listen span	Count span	Vocabulary	Reading comprehension	Arithmetic
Listen span	–				
Count span	0.47	–			
Vocabulary	0.40	0.17	–		
Reading comprehension	0.61	0.36	0.48	–	
WISC Arithmetic	0.55	0.51	0.34	0.51	–

a measure of working-memory span would predict performance on mental arithmetic problems. But would all span tasks be equally strongly associated with mental arithmetic?

Leather and Henry (1994) gave 7-year-old schoolchildren two working-memory tasks: one involved listening to sentences and recalling their last words, the other required them to count the number of dots on each of a series of cards and recall the total number for each card. They also gave them a standard reading comprehension and vocabulary test and the arithmetic sub-test from the WISC. The correlations between performance on all these tests are shown in Table 8.4. It can be seen that the counting-span task predicted arithmetic performance rather better than it did vocabulary or reading, both of which were better predicted by the listening-span task. The two span tasks correlated quite well, and also predicted arithmetic scores equally well. However, subsequent regression analyses suggested that the counting-span task made no independent contribution to the prediction of reading scores, once listening-span scores had been taken into account, but that it *did* make an independent contribution to arithmetic scores.

Conclusion

Traditional measures of Gc, such as vocabulary and comprehension tests, a general knowledge quiz, or mental arithmetic problems, have seemed to many critics to prove that IQ tests do not measure differences in anything we would normally want to call intelligence. They appear to be measures of knowledge, not ability, and differences in performance on such tests, so the argument runs, can only be a consequence of differences in past opportunity to acquire the relevant information. Schools teach children to read and do arithmetic, so differences in schooling are bound to be reflected in these scores. The evidence reviewed above surely implies that, at the very least, this is an oversimplification. Differences in Gc are reasonably described as differences in verbal ability, because they partly reflect differences in the way people take advantage of their opportunities.

But what is verbal ability? According to Hunt:

Verbal ability is the result of a somewhat correlated set of skills. These skills depend upon a variety of more primitive psychological processes, including access to lexical memory, rapid consolidation of information into long-term memory, the possession of knowledge about how to process discourse in general, and the possession of knowledge about the topic of the discourse being comprehended. Some of these primitive processes can be thought of as properties of the brain . . . [but] other processes . . . are learned, and are highly culture dependent.

If the various verbal skills are distinct, why do psychometric analyses so consistently uncover a single dimension of verbal ability? It could be that all the primitive processes of language comprehension are derived from a single underlying brain process . . . [But] correlations between measures of different aspects of language comprehension could also be explained by interactions between them as they are developed. Being able to consolidate information into permanent memory rapidly would aid in the acquisition of lexical knowledge, and increasing one's vocabulary would increase one's ability to develop text and situation models, which could be used to increase lexical knowledge by defining new words in context. (Hunt, 1987, p. 388)

There are no prizes for guessing which explanation of the positive manifold I find more persuasive. But Hunt's account fails to mention one unifying process—working memory for verbal or numerical information. Not only are the correlations between measures of working memory and memories of Gc quite high, usually over 0.50 and sometimes as high as 0.60, but there is evidence that differences in working memory are responsible for the association between people's vocabulary scores and their ability to infer the meaning of unknown words from their context (Daneman and Green, 1986). Thus size of vocabulary is a good measure of verbal ability, because we do not acquire our vocabulary by rote memorization of dictionary definitions, but rather by a process of inferential reasoning that appears to be dependent on working memory.

Working-memory tasks, such as Daneman and Carpenter's reading span, require one simultaneously to process some information (read a sentence or answer some questions about it) and to hold some information in memory (the last word of the preceding sentence). What is the cause of the correlation between performance on such tasks and measures of verbal ability? We have already seen that changing the processing requirement from reading to listening and comprehending, or even performing simple numerical operations, does not greatly affect the strength of association. But it may still be differences in processing efficiency that are responsible for working memory's association with measures of Gc. Although the dependent variable in such span tasks is, for example, the number of words correctly recalled, the reason why some people do badly might be because they find the processing requirements more demanding, must therefore devote more resources to them, and thus have fewer resources to spare for the memory component of the task.

In fact, the evidence suggests otherwise. For example, Conway and Engle (1996) employed a word-span task in which each item in a list consisted of a simple mental arithmetic problem, followed by a word. Thus:

$(8 \div 4) + 2 = 4$?   *BIRD*

Subjects had to read out each problem, decide whether the answer provided was true or false, and read the single word. After three to six such items, they were required to write down, in the correct order, the words in that list. But the mental arithmetic problems had been carefully adjusted to suit each individual's mathematical ability as determined in a lengthy pre-test of similar types of item. In spite of this, word-span scores still correlated with scores on Verbal SAT between 0.50 and 0.60, and continued to do so even when allowance was made for individual differences in viewing time for each problem. Thus the correlation between working memory and verbal IQ is probably not a by-product of differences in the efficiency with which people perform the processing component of the task.

There is, of course, a final reason why this association between Gc and verbal or numerical working memory is of such significance. In the previous chapter, we saw that tasks which, when performed alone, showed only a weak association with IQ, might show a much stronger association when performed concurrently with another, competing task. The working-memory paradigms we have been considering in this chapter seem to be another instance of this. Simple memory-span tasks such as forward digit span correlate only moderately with IQ: it is when the task of remembering a list of digits or words has to be combined with another task that performance begins to correlate strongly with IQ. But the correlations we have been discussing here have been with measures of Gc. In the previous chapter, we noted that concurrent task performance seemed to correlate most strongly with measures of Gf. Does this imply that the efficiency of a central executive/working-memory system is a good candidate for the unitary psychological process underlying general intelligence or *g*?

Spatial ability (Gv)

We have already come across the notion of spatial ability, or Gv in Cattell's terminology (Chapter 2). Both factor analysis (Chapter 6) and the study of group differences (Chapter 5) made it clear that there is an identifiable sub-set of IQ tests which, even if they have overlapping features in common with numerous other types of test, can still be distinguished from those that measure either verbal or crystallized ability (Gc) on the one hand, or non-verbal reasoning or fluid ability (Gf) on the other.

A distinctive group of spatial tests was, in fact, the first to be reasonably securely identified by factor analytic techniques (Chapter 2) and, no doubt emboldened by this early success, factor analysts have continued their study of spatial ability by arguing that it is not unitary, but can be decomposed into a number of subsidiary abilities or skills (Guilford, 1967; Lohman, 1988; Carroll, 1993). The major factor, usually termed spatial visualization, is that defined by tasks such as three-dimensional mental rotation, paper folding, form board, or DAT space relations test (Fig. 8.2). A second group of tests, which require one to orientate oneself in a wider, spatial frame of reference, or visualize a scene from a different perspective, identifies a second factor, sometimes called spatial orientation. A typical test shows the view of the bow of a speed boat from the cockpit, and of the shoreline it is approaching. In a second picture, the boat has changed course slightly and the view of the shoreline has changed. The task is to state whether the boat has turned right or left, has rolled to the right or left, or has pitched up or down. Although the set of skills being tapped by a task such as this may be more closely related to what we mean, in everyday language, when we talk of someone as having a good sense of direction, and may be more relevant to the task of finding one's way round a novel environment or of reading a map, these skills have not been as extensively studied in the laboratory as those measured by tests of mental rotation, paper folding, etc., and in what follows I shall have little to say about them. One problem is that laboratory versions of such tests are necessarily done with paper and pencil, and the small scale of the drawings means that they can be just as readily solved by mentally rotating the scenes as by changing one's own imagined orientation. And at that point, as some commentators have noted (Carpenter and Just, 1986; Lohman, 1988), the distinction between spatial visualization and spatial orientation begins to break down. A third factor sometimes identified by factor analysis is defined by speeded tests of simple rotation—as in Thurstone's PMA test of mental rotation (see Fig. 2.3). Although some commentators have argued otherwise, it does seem quite plausible that the solution of the seriously difficult Shepard–Metzler three-dimensional rotation task, shown in Fig. 8.2, should call into play psychological processes rather different from those required to solve simpler rotation problems. I take this point up in another context below (p. 301).

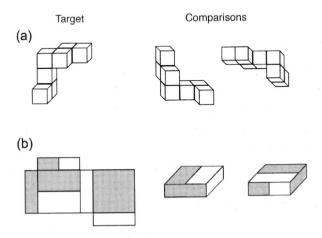

Fig. 8.2 Examples of spatial IQ tests. (a) The Shepard–Metzler mental rotation task: which of the figures on the right is the same as the target on the left? (b) The DAT space relations test. If you folded up the target stimulus to form a box, which of the alternatives would it match?

The psychometric starting point for the analysis of spatial ability will always involve grouping tests into sub-groups or clusters identified by factor analysis. But I shall not bother to pursue these finer distinctions here. My discussion will necessarily focus on the first broad group of tests, those loading on the spatial visualization factor, since they have received most attention. The most common description of these tests (e.g. Carpenter and Just, 1986; Lohman, 1988) is that they measure the ability to form or construct representations of relatively complex visual patterns, shapes or figures, representations that are sufficiently accurate, detailed, and durable that various operations can be performed on them, for example 'mental rotation' of the entire shape, decomposing it into its constituent parts, recombining those parts into a new pattern, or adding or deleting various components. This seems, on the face of it, a reasonable starting point. To solve an item from the DAT space relations test, for example, it appears necessary to start by constructing a representation of what the two-dimensional target pattern will look like when each of the folding operations has been performed. All of these operations must be combined to construct a complete three-dimensional representation, which must then be operated upon, for example by mentally rotating it, to bring it into the same orientation as the various alternatives on offer. A similar account seems equally plausibly applied to the Shepard–Metzler rotation task: the task of aligning the target shape with the alternatives on offer presumably involves the operation of rotation in more than one plane and, given the three-dimensional nature of the shapes, is perhaps sufficiently complex that many people will find it necessary to decompose the shape into some of its constituent parts or blocks before carrying out these rotations. If so, these components must then be recombined to reconstruct the complete figure in order to compare it with the alternatives.

The role of visual imagery

So far, perhaps, so good—although also perhaps not very far. The next step sometimes taken in the analysis of spatial ability is rather more contentious. It seems natural, to some people at least, to suppose that the mental representation of a complex three-dimensional figure must be a conscious visual image. There is no question but that some people report 'visualizing' the object they are constructing 'in the mind's eye', and then 'seeing' what it looks like when they have added or subtracted a part, rotated it into a new orientation, looked at it from behind, or whatever. There is equally no question but that people differ widely in the extent to which they report having visual imagery, and the vividness they ascribe to it. Here as elsewhere, Francis Galton was one of the first to attempt to collect relevant information. He asked people to imagine their breakfast table that morning, the food on their plate, the cups and jars on the table, etc. He found enormous variation in the replies he received: some claimed that their visual image of the scene was just as vivid as the original event; others said they had no visual image at all. Such results were, and often still are, greeted with a certain scepticism. What reliance should be placed on mere introspective reports? Is there any objective correlate of these differences? These are valid questions, but one suspects that some of the scepticism arises because each of us believes that we are typical: what is true for me must be true for you. Thus those who claim to have no difficulty visualizing trivial scenes from their everyday life, who 'see' numbers in an ordered spatial array, perhaps even coded by colour as well, find it hard to believe that there are others whose mental life is so impoverished that they have no internal TV screen to look at. And conversely.

But cognitive psychology cannot rely *solely* on such introspective reports. Is it possible to obtain independent, converging evidence for the reality of such imagery? Two lines of research have been thought to provide just such evidence. Shepard (Shepard and Metzler, 1971; Shephard, 1978) and Cooper (Cooper, 1975; Cooper & Podgory, 1976) have reported a series of studies of mental rotation which suggest that people do engage in a process reasonably described as rotating a mental representation of a target stimulus in much the same way that they might physically rotate the target itself if asked to do so. People's reaction times were recorded when they were required to decide whether two stimuli, one a standard, e.g. the letter R in upright orientation, the other a target rotated in one or other direction from the upright, were the same, or whether the target was the mirror-image of the standard (Я). Another version of the task is illustrated in Fig. 8.3. Here a target [R] is briefly displayed in an upright orientation, along with an arrow pointing, say, 135° clockwise. This display disappears to be replaced with a comparison stimulus in the orientation indicated by the arrow, and the task is again to say whether target and comparison stimuli are the same. Average reaction times were an increasing function of the angular discrepancy between comparison and target stimuli—suggesting that people were rotating a representation of the target at a given rate in order to align it with the comparison stimulus. Two further observations provided even more convincing evidence. If subjects were cued to expect that the target would be rotated clockwise from the comparison stimulus on a given trial, but in fact it was presented 90° anticlockwise from the comparison stimulus, their reaction times corresponded to a 270° rotation (i.e. the clockwise discrepancy) rather than to one of 90°. In other words, it was the mental trajectory traversed that determined reaction time rather than the actual angular difference between comparison and target. A further experiment provided crucial evidence of rotation of the

Target   **Comparison**

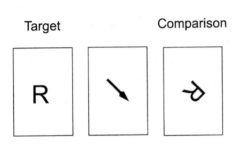

Fig. 8.3 A mental rotation test. The target display is shown first, followed by the comparison display. The subject's task is to say whether the comparison does or does not match the target.

representation of the target through *intermediate* orientations. On the assumption that mental rotation of a particular target occurs at a constant rate for any one subject, it is possible to predict for each subject the exact moment from the start of a trial when the orientation of their representation of the target should be, say, 30, 60 or 90 degrees from that at which the comparison stimulus was due to be shown. If, on probe trials, the comparison stimulus was instead shown at the precise orientation which, according to these calculations, their representation of the target had now reached, subjects' RTs were uniformly fast. But if the comparison stimulus was presented at a different orientation, RTs were longer, increasing linearly with increases in the magnitude of the discrepancy between the actual orientation of the comparison stimulus and the computed orientation of the representation of the target.

Kosslyn (1983) has reported a related set of experiments in which, for example, people were asked to study, and memorize, a map of a fictional island, containing a variety of features—a lake, a beach, a wood, a group of huts, etc. With the actual map then removed, they were asked to focus on one particular place on the island, and then to 'look for' a second place, pressing one response key when they found it, another if they failed to find it. Their RTs increased linearly with the distance between the two locations on the map. Further experiments suggested that this reflected the distance they had to scan across their mental representation of the map, rather than, say, simply the number of other locations intervening between the two in some 'list-like' representation of places on the map.

Reasonably objective indices of behaviour thus suggest that people operate on internal representations of external visual stimuli in much the same way that they would operate on the visual stimuli themselves. Since spatial IQ tests were defined as those that apparently require the construction, retention, and manipulation of such internal representations, we seem to have obtained good, independent evidence of the reality of such a set of processes, and it seems reasonable to infer that differences in spatial ability must be reflected in differences in the efficiency with which these operations are performed. Indeed, the reader will recall that spatial IQ scores are well predicted by the slope and intercept of RTs on the type of mental rotation task studied by Cooper and Shepard (Chapter 7, p. 263). But none of this is sufficient to establish that we should equate the internal representations of visual stimuli implied by Shepard and Cooper's or Kosslyn's experiments with conscious visual images. And it is certainly not sufficient to establish the stronger conclusion that we should identify differences in the efficiency with which people operate on these postulated internal representations, i.e. differences in spatial ability, with differences in the vividness of their reported visual imagery.

Differences in the reported vividness of visual imagery seem to be reliable. And they do predict other differences; for example, people reporting vivid visual imagery take longer than those not reporting vivid imagery to read a passage of descriptive prose, but not a passage of abstract prose (Denis, 1982; see Poltrock and Agnoli (1986) for other correlates of vividness of imagery). But the one thing that is *not* predicted by differences in vividness of imagery is spatial ability. The correlations between such measures of imagery and scores on spatial IQ tests hover round zero, and in spite of the fact that males routinely outscore females on most spatial IQ tests, they obtain lower scores on self-ratings of vividness of imagery (Poltrock and Agnoli, 1986). Many commentators have found this surprising. With the advantage of hindsight, it probably ought not to be. Performance on spatial IQ tests may indeed require the ability to construct, retain, and manipulate internal representations of external stimuli, but nothing in that definition of spatial ability says that these representations have to be visual images accessible to conscious introspection. There is equally little reason to believe that the representation of a target stimulus that subjects 'mentally rotate' in Shepard and Cooper's experiments is necessarily a *conscious* visual image. The brain constructs representations (in some sense of that term) of a whole variety of events of which we are not consciously aware—of the current position of our limbs and eyes, of the remembered size and weight of a familiar object which we pick up without being able to see it. Animal psychologists, these days at least, have no hesitation in talking of rats and pigeons having representations of the stimuli used in conditioning experiments, without thereby wishing to ascribe conscious experiences to their subjects. Mental imagery, as measured by self-report, refers only to those of our representations of the external world of which we happen to be consciously aware. The concept of a representation encompasses a much wider range of entities.

Moreover, although many people have talked of 'visuo-spatial' ability, or a 'visuo-spatial' sketchpad (Baddeley, 1986), as though 'visual' and 'spatial' were interchangeable terms, there are further, independent grounds for drawing a distinction between spatial and visual. For example, although many writers have divided the human brain into a left hemisphere devoted to linguistic, analytical, sequential processing, and a right hemisphere devoted to holistic, perceptual, visuo-spatial processing, there is unambiguous evidence that different regions of the primate brain subserve visual and spatial functions. The distinction drawn by Ungerleider and Mishkin (1982) between 'what' and 'where' aspects of visual function is based on a wealth of neuroanatomical and behavioural evidence from non-human primates. The 'what' system transmits information primarily to inferotemporal cortex and is involved in visual identification, or the learning of difficult visual pattern discriminations. Information about spatial location, the 'where' system, is primarily transmitted to parietal cortex, and lesions to these areas severely disrupt performance on spatial delayed matching, while leaving visual discrimination learning unscathed. From inferotemporal and parietal cortex, these two systems transmit information to prefrontal cortex—but again to different regions, one active when monkeys perform a spatial immediate memory task, the other when they are engaged in a similar task that requires them to remember the shape and colour of the stimulus that appeared at the outset of the trial (Wilson *et al.*, 1993).

Evidence from neuropsychological patients and PET scans of normal human volunteers confirm that this neuroanatomical distinction between spatial and non-spatial visual identification is not confined to non-human primates. Parietal and inferotemporal cortex are differentially activated when people are engaged in spatial and non-spatial visual tasks (Smith *et al.*, 1995), and patients have been observed who are seriously impaired on one kind of task, but not on the other (Farah *et al.*, 1988; Hanley *et al.*, 1991).

Psychometric and psychological evidence supports this distinction. Many IQ tests, such as Raven's Matrices or Cattell's tests employ purely visual, diagrammatic material. As we have seen, this does not make them tests of spatial IQ (Chapters 5 and 6). And laboratory studies of concurrent interference have confirmed the independence of visual and spatial information processing. Visual and spatial analogues of digit- or word-span tasks as measures of immediate memory have been devised by a number of psychologists. In a visual immediate memory task, people are required to remember the shape of geometrical patterns, or the precise shade of patches of colour briefly displayed on a computer screen. In an early version of a simple spatial span task, the experimenter shows the subject a 3 × 3 matrix of cubes, and touches half a dozen or so of them in turn. The subject's task is then to point, in the correct order, to those cubes touched by the experimenter. Modern versions of the task display a 3 × 3 matrix of blank squares on a computer screen; some of the squares are then filled, one at a time, with dots, and the subject's task is to remember the positions of these dots and the order in which they appeared. Performance on this spatial span task is not necessarily dependent on verbal recoding of the material, since articulatory suppression, which seriously disrupts performance on word- or digit-span tasks, has no more than a very small effect on retention (e.g. Smyth and Scholey, 1992). However, other distracters do prevent successful retention. Tresch *et al.* (1993) interpolated a 10-sec interval between presentation of a visual task (remembering a geometrical shape) or a spatial task (remembering the position of a dot) and the test of retention. They then filled this 10-sec interval with one or other of two distractor tasks, one requiring the discrimination of movement, the other discrimination of colour. Visual memory was disrupted by the interpolated colour discrimination, but not by the movement discrimination; spatial memory was disrupted by the movement discrimination but not by the colour discrimination. A similar dissociation between distractor tasks that disrupt retention of visual and spatial information has been reported by Logie and Marchetti (1991).

The implication of all these studies is that spatial visualization involves the ability to construct representations of the external world that preserve specifically *spatial* information about objects or scenes—what parts are to the left or right, or above or below others; how a complex object can be decomposed into its constituent parts, or reconstructed from those parts; how an object can be transformed or rotated, and how it would look from another perspective. This set of abilities is both broader and narrower than that involved in conscious visual imagery. A visual image of a patch of colour, or an object, or even of a visual scene, may not incorporate specifically spatial information at all. But conversely, there is no reason to suppose that spatial representations are necessarily visual at all (the blind can operate in a spatial world), let alone that they are conscious visual images. The possession of a rich mental life, full of vivid imagery is neither necessary nor sufficient to guarantee high spatial ability.

Spatial representations

What does it mean then, to talk of the construction, retention, and manipulation of accurate spatial representation of the world or objects in the world? Does such a notion really help to understand the concept of spatial ability—or is it yet another example of fancy redescription masquerading as explanation? Two rather different kinds of study may help to suggest a modestly optimistic answer.

Lohman (1988) devised a simple set of laboratory tasks designed to separate out some of these component operations and assess their contribution to spatial IQ. Trials on the task started with the brief presentation of a target shape on a computer monitor (Fig. 8.4); this was followed by instructions to perform certain operations on the shape, and finally by the presentation of a test shape. The subject's task was now to decide whether the test shape matched the target shape presented at the outset of the trial—once account had been taken of the operations performed on it. Fig. 8.4 illustrates a variety of types of trial. The first row depicts a simple shape matching task—no operations being required on the target. Two kinds of operation could be called for: addition of one or two further parts to the shape; or rotation through 90 or 180°. As illustrated in the final row, these could be combined.

The performance of students on these tasks was correlated with their scores on a variety of IQ tests, designed to give measures of, among other things, verbal IQ or Gc, perceptual speed, and spatial IQ or Gv. These correlations are shown in the right-hand three columns of Fig. 8.4. Both verbal and perceptual speed scores showed only modest correlations with performance on any version of the task, but spatial scores predicted performance rather well. Even the simple shape matching task correlated 0.21 with spatial IQ: when subjects were required to perform either the addition or the rotation operation on the shape, their performance correlated over 0.50 with spatial IQ scores, and the combination of both operations led to even higher correlations.

Since the target shapes were shown only briefly, the task required not only the establishment of a representation of the shape, but also its retention. When additional

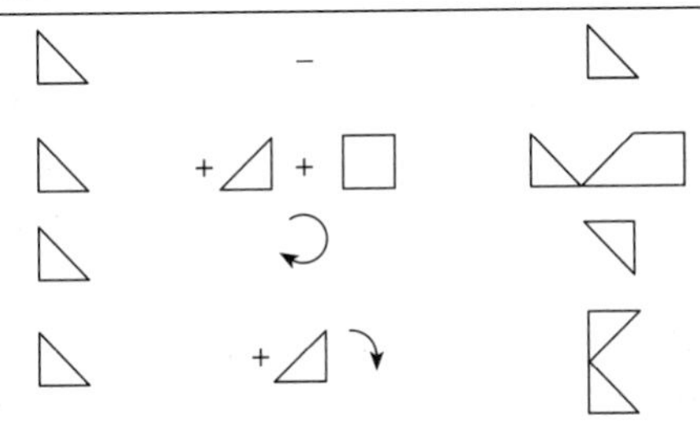

Task	Target Stimulus	Operations	Comparison Stimulus	Correlations		
				Gc	Gv	Gs
Simple Matching		–		0.03	0.21	–0.02
Add 2		$+\triangle+\square$		0.29	0.55	0.09
Rotate 180°				0.15	0.52	0.27
Add 1+ Rotate 90°		$+\triangle$		0.26	0.67	0.20

Fig. 8.4 Simple spatial addition and rotation tasks and their correlations with verbal, spatial, and speed components of IQ (from Lohman, 1988).

operations had to be performed on the target, the task required simultaneous retention and processing of spatial information—i.e. it became a working-memory task in the sense defined earlier. Thus Lohman's study is consistent with the idea that spatial IQ depends on the establishment and retention of representations that both preserve spatial information about an object and are sufficiently accurate and durable to allow various mental operations to be performed on them; the final implication, of course, is that one of the most important ingredients of spatial IQ is the ability both to store and process such spatial representations concurrently.

A study by Carpenter and Just (1986) provides some related insight into some of the differences between people of high and low spatial ability. They asked students to solve versions of the cube rotation task shown in Fig. 8.5, and both monitored their eye movements and fixations during the course of their solution, and asked them for immediate retrospective reports on how they had succeeded in solving each problem. Both sources of information suggested that subjects typically rotated one face of the cube at a time in order to bring pairs of matching letters into alignment. In Problem 1 of Fig. 8.5, for example, a 90° clockwise rotation of the target cube in the frontal place (i.e. the plane of the A surface), which produces the comparison cube, not only changes the orientation of the A, it also moves the position and changes the orientation of the C, and finally produces a hitherto unseen letter, D in the position formerly occupied by the C. Although a single rotation simultaneously produces all three changes, subjects typically operated on one change at a time. The greater the number of rotations required to solve a particular problem, the greater the difference in solution times between subjects of high and low spatial ability. One reason for this was that subjects of low ability were able to rotate each face of the cube only around the three axes parallel to the faces of the cube. Problem 2 illustrated in Fig. 8.5 requires two such rotations. But in principle it could be solved by a single rotation around an axis corresponding to a long diagonal of the cube. Subjects of high spatial ability reported doing just this. A second reason for the difference in the time taken to solve the more complex tasks was that subjects of low ability often had to go back and rotate a particular face of the cube a second or third time within a single trial. One interpretation of this would be that they were unable to remember the outcome of the rotation of the first face while rotating other faces. A similar difficulty was observed when a problem required two or more rotations, the first of which involved a particular letter disappearing to a 'hidden' side of the cube, only for it to need to re-appear after a second or third rotation. Subjects of low spatial ability made many more errors on these problems—presumably because they were unable to keep track of old information (the new orientation of a 'hidden' face) while simultaneously processing the information on the 'visible' faces. In Carpenter and Just's words: 'A general characterization . . . is that low spatial subjects have difficulty maintaining a spatial representation while performing transformations' (Carpenter and Just, 1986, p. 236).

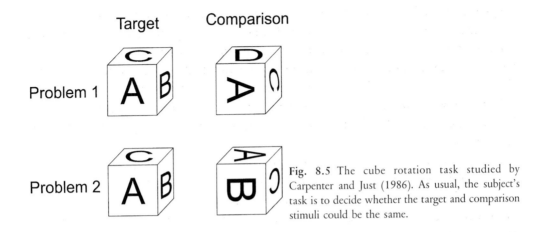

Fig. 8.5 The cube rotation task studied by Carpenter and Just (1986). As usual, the subject's task is to decide whether the target and comparison stimuli could be the same.

Spatial working memory

That conclusion should, by now, be sounding familiar, for what is implied is that performance on IQ-type tasks places demands on working memory, and variations in IQ scores are associated with variations in the efficiency or capacity of working memory. But is this the same working-memory system as that implicated in studies of verbal working memory and its relation to Gc?

Baddeley's model of the working-memory system, as we saw, postulated a central executive, plus two associated 'slave' systems, a phonological loop and a visuo-spatial sketchpad, which function as passive, buffer stores for, respectively, verbal and visuo-spatial information (Baddeley, 1986; Baddeley and Hitch, 1974). Although we have seen reason to question the unitary nature of the visuo-spatial store, and argued that there is an important distinction to be drawn between purely visual and strictly spatial information, this is a relatively minor modification. There is ample evidence, much of it reviewed above, that is consistent with Baddeley's general model. There is no question but that there is a distinction between verbal and either visual or spatial coding systems. There is virtually no correlation between performance on simple spatial span tasks, and on digit- or word-span tasks (e.g. Smyth and Scholey, 1996). Several experiments have shown that operations that interfere with performance on one kind of task have little or no effect on the other: articulatory suppression seriously interferes with digit span, but not with spatial span (Smyth and Scholey, 1992; see above), while tasks such as pointing to other targets interfere with spatial span but have no effect on digit span (Smyth and Scholey, 1994). Neuropsychological and brain imaging studies have confirmed the relative independence of verbal and spatial tasks (reviewed by Logie, 1995).

Equally important, however, there are several parallels between the operating characteristics of the phonological loop and the visual or spatial sketchpads. Just as phonological similarity makes it harder to remember a list of letters or words, so visual similarity can also interfere with the short-term retention of visually presented information (Logie, 1995). The phonological loop is not just a passive buffer store, but is involved in the active maintenance and rehearsal of acoustically coded information. There is similar evidence of a rehearsal process for visual or spatial information—especially where the latter involves movement (Smyth and Pendleton, 1989; Watkins *et al.*, 1984).

Nevertheless, the critical assumption of the Baddeley and Hitch model seems to be that most of the important cognitive functions of the working-memory system are performed by the central executive rather than by the peripheral, slave systems. The phonological loop plays *some* role in, for example, language comprehension and other verbal skills, but that role, as we saw, is quite limited. Performance on a task such as digit or word span, which clearly depends on the integrity and efficiency of the phonological loop, is not as strongly associated with verbal IQ as is the reading- or listening-span task, which requires one to process some other information while remembering a short list of words. The implication is that such working-memory tasks place demands on the central executive rather than the peripheral systems. Thus the question whether the working-memory system is the unitary psychological basis of a unitary factor of general intelligence seems to amount to the question whether there is a single central executive system responsible for performance on all kinds of working-memory task.

A number of studies have suggested that there is not. Jurden (1995) and Shah and Miyake (1996) have shown that verbal and spatial working-memory tasks are relatively independent of one another, and that while performance on a verbal working-memory task predicts verbal IQ it does not predict spatial IQ, while the reverse is true for performance on a spatial working-memory task. Shah and Miyake employed a verbal working-memory task, reading span, similar to Daneman and Carpenter's (see above). Their spatial working-memory task involved the presentation on each trial of a series of letters, for example the letter R, on a computer screen. Each letter was presented at a different orientation and the subject's task was to decide whether it was a normal R or a mirror-image Я. At the end of each trial, after up to five letters had been presented, a grid appeared on the screen and, by pressing the appropriate button, subjects had to indicate the direction in which the top of each letter in the series had been pointing. They were thus required to remember the orientation of a sequence of letters while simultaneously deciding whether each letter was normal or mirror-image.

Some 50 undergraduates performed these reading- and spatial-span tasks, as well as providing both spatial and verbal IQ scores (in the former case, a battery of four spatial tests; in the latter, scores on the verbal Scholastic Aptitude Test). Although there was a modest positive correlation, 0.23, between verbal and spatial working-memory scores, it was not statistically significant. The correlations between working-memory scores and IQ scores are shown in Table 8.5. As can be seen, while the reading-span score predicted verbal IQ, it did not predict spatial IQ and, conversely, spatial span predicted only spatial IQ.

Table 8.5 Correlations between verbal and spatial working memory and verbal and spatial IQ (from Shah and Miyake, 1996)

Working memory	IQ	
	Verbal	Spatial
Verbal	0.45	0.12
Spatial	0.07	0.66

Further experimental analysis supported the separability of verbal and spatial working memory and suggested that both the processing and the storage components of these tasks accounted for their association with verbal and spatial IQ. Within the constraints of this study, and particularly the subject population studied, there is little evidence of a unitary central executive or working-memory system underpinning general intelligence: verbal and spatial working-memory systems seem relatively independent.

Verbal and spatial strategies

It will be appropriate to conclude this section on spatial ability with a complication—but one which serves to reinforce the distinction between verbal and spatial ability. I have hitherto talked as though spatial IQ tests or laboratory tasks necessarily required the deployment of spatial abilities, and verbal IQ tests and laboratory tasks required people to make use of their verbal skills. No doubt this is what the psychometrician and experimental psychologist would like to believe. But the people who participate in their studies are not always so obliging. Different people can approach and solve the same problem in quite different ways. Problems such as the Shepard–Metzler mental rotation task, for example, are soluble by constructing an analogue mental representation (even a conscious visual image) of the target shape, and executing the appropriate set of spatial transformations on it, as theorists such as Cooper (1975), Kosslyn (1983), and Shepard (1978) have argued. But an alternative solution, proposed by Pylyshyn (1973), would be to form a *verbal* or propositional description of the target shape—that it consists of a central stem, four blocks high, with two legs at the top and bottom, one three, the other two blocks long, pointing in opposite directions. Such a verbal description will be quite sufficient to prove that at least some test stimuli could not possibly be the same as the target. In their study of the cube comparison task, Carpenter and Just (1986) described one subject who reported using a verbal description of the target cube—for example that the long side of the letter B was parallel to, and next to, the major axis of the letter A—in order to solve the problem.

Such introspective reports may not be sufficient to persuade a sceptical behaviourist that different people solve the same problem in different ways. But there is good experimental evidence to confirm this suggestion. A particularly convincing example is provided by analysis of the sentence-verification task, in which subjects are shown a picture—for example of a star above a circle, and have to decide whether a particular sentence, for example 'The star is above the circle', provides a true or false description of the picture (Fig. 7.6). Carpenter and Just (1975) proposed that people solve the problem by generating a verbal description of the picture, e.g. 'A star above a circle', and deciding whether this verbal description matches the sentence provided. If, as in the example given, the sentence is True Affirmative, the match is easily and immediately made. If the sentence provided is a False Affirmative ('The circle is above the star'), the decision will take a bit longer; but negative sentences, whether true or false ('The circle is not above the star' or 'The star is not above the circle') take even longer to match to the subject's own verbal description. Data from experiments such as this have shown that the behaviour of most subjects is well fit by this model: affirmative sentences are confirmed more rapidly than negative sentences; as we have seen, they also suggest that overall RTs correlate moderately with verbal IQ scores. Examination of individual data, however, usually reveals a sizeable minority of subjects who do not show this pattern of results: they do not respond more rapidly to affirmative than to negative sentences, but show instead a rather smaller difference in favour of true over false sentences; and their overall RTs do not correlate with verbal IQ (MacLeod *et al.*, 1978; Neubauer and Freudenthaler, 1994). That this is not just a matter of random noise in the data is strongly suggested by the observation that their RTs, unlike those of the majority of subjects, *are* well predicted by their spatial IQ scores. MacLeod *et al.*'s results are shown in Table 8.6.

Table 8.6 Partial correlations between verbal or spatial ability and mean sentence verification RT (from MacLeod *et al.*, 1978)

	Verbal ability (with spatial ability held constant)	Spatial ability (with verbal ability held constant)
Well-fit subjects (N = 43)	−0.44	−0.07
Poorly fit subjects (N = 16)	−0.05	−0.64

The implication, consistent with subjects' own reports of how they solve the problem, is that this minority do so by adopting a visuo-spatial strategy: rather than generating a verbal description of the picture, they generate a visuo-spatial representation of the sentence, which they can then match to the picture. Another demonstration that different people adopt different strategies to solve the same problem, in this case a transitive inference problem, is provided by Sternberg and Weil (1980). A simple transitive inference problem is:

Adam is taller than Benjamin

Benjamin is taller than Cain

Who is tallest?

The problem can be made harder by reversing the order of the premises, by using negative premises (Adam is not taller than Benjamin), and by using so-called 'unmarked' terms in the premises (Adam is shorter than Benjamin). One way of solving such transitive inference problems is surely linguistically: the information provided by the premises is coded in terms of underlying meaning or linguistic structure, the relationship between the two end terms, Adam and Cain, then inferred, and the question then answered. But another solution is visuo-spatial: one represents Adam, Benjamin and Cain in a spatial array, say from left (tall) to right (short) and then reads off the answer. These strategies lead to rather different predictions as to which problems will be harder or easier than others. From a detailed analysis of their subjects' performance on a whole series of problems, Sternberg and Weil concluded that the majority employed both verbal and spatial strategies, but some employed only verbal and others only spatial strategies. In those apparently employing verbal strategies, performance on the task correlated 0.76 with verbal IQ and only 0.29 with spatial IQ. In those apparently employing spatial strategies, however, the correlation with verbal IQ was 0.08 and with spatial IQ was 0.60.

The wider implications of these studies are of the utmost importance. One is that the argument between propositional theories of visuo-spatial representation, such as that proposed by Pylyshyn (1973, 1981), and analogue theories such as those of Kosslyn (1983) or Shepard (1978), may be misplaced. Both may be correct—for different individuals. A second, equally central to our concerns, is this: people surely differ in their aptitudes, skills, and abilities, but these differences in verbal or spatial abilities are only imperfectly assessed by the tests that psychologists have devised to measure them, since people also, perhaps partly as a consequence of these differences in ability, differ in the strategies they employ to solve various types of problem (in the study of MacLeod *et al.*, for example, a linguistic strategy was associated with a slightly higher average verbal IQ, and a spatial strategy with a significantly higher spatial IQ). But what this presumably means is that there may be no such thing as a pure test of, say, spatial ability, in the sense that everyone who attempts to solve the problem will do so in the same way—for example, by constructing a set of spatial representations which they then manipulate in certain ways. Some people will always try out other kinds of solution, converting the psychologist's 'spatial' test into one soluble by a verbal description of its terms. The implication for the theory of IQ testing is surely this: the positive manifold between scores on supposedly quite different kinds of IQ test may arise because, regardless of the name of the tests, many people bring the same strategies to bear on their solution, some translating all problems into a verbal code, others using visuo-spatial representations for all. This would be quite sufficient to produce an overall positive correlation between people's performance on verbal and spatial test batteries—even though verbal and visuo-spatial *strategies* tapped no common cognitive processes at all.

Summary

Measures of verbal ability or Gc include tests of vocabulary, general knowledge, verbal comprehension, mental arithmetic, and digit span. At least some of these seem to be tests of acquired knowledge, or of what children are explicitly taught at school, rather than tests of what we mean by intelligence. But there is good evidence that differences in verbal IQ are associated with differences in performance on a variety of simple laboratory tasks, which are not plausibly attributed to differences in the familiarity of the material used. Speed of lexical access in letter- or word-matching problems shows a modest correlation with verbal IQ, and the magnitude of these correlations is not greatly affected by the common content of IQ test and laboratory task.

The size of a person's vocabulary is a good measure of Gc, not because some people have had more opportunity to learn, by rote, the meaning of a larger number of words, but because people differ in their ability to infer the meanings of unfamiliar words from the context in which they appear. We learn the meanings of new words by a process of inferential reasoning. This ability seems to be closely associated with the efficiency of working memory, defined as a system that simultaneously operates on some information while holding other information in memory.

Tests of spatial ability or Gv require one to establish accurate representations of objects and scenes that preserve spatial information (what is above, below, left, or right of what else), and to maintain such representations in memory so that one can perform certain operations on them (add new parts, subtract old, rotate it, or 'view' it from a different perspective). The establishment of such representations may, or may not, involve conscious visual imagery: certainly there is essentially no correlation between measures of the vividness of visual imagery and scores on spatial IQ tests. But the execution of such spatial tasks clearly places demands on working memory.

One of the best-known models of working memory, that of Baddeley and Hitch (1974), postulates a central executive plus two associated buffer stores, one for phonological or verbal material, the other for visuo-spatial material. A seemingly attractive hypothesis, therefore, would be to say that the independence of these two buffer stores is what is responsible for the differences between Gc and Gv, while their common dependence on the central executive explains why Gc and Gv are related. Unfortunately for that argument, there is reason to believe that performance on working-memory tasks is more dependent on the central executive than on these peripheral buffers, but there is also good evidence for the partial independence of verbal and spatial working memory.

9 Fluid intelligence, reasoning, and problem solving

Introduction

The distinction between verbal and spatial abilities seems so obvious that it could hardly have come as a surprise to discover that there are numerous differences in the component processes involved in verbal and spatial tasks. Differences in the content of tests of Gc and of Gv should alone be sufficient to engage somewhat different operations (even if, as we have seen, people are often able to translate visuo-spatial content into a lexical code, or vice versa). It still remains possible, however, that there is another level at which identical operations must be performed on different types of content, and it is at this level that we should be looking for the cognitive basis of g or general intelligence. If that is so, examination of tests of non-verbal reasoning or Gf may help to reveal that basis, for there are grounds for believing that Gf is more closely linked to g (if not identical with it) than are Gc or Gv.

The study of reasoning, thinking, and problem solving has, rightly, occupied a central place in cognitive psychology, and the fruits of a large body of experimental research have been reviewed in a number of textbooks (Evans *et al.*, 1993; Garnham and Oakhill, 1994). It is certainly not possible to summarize all this work here, but fortunately it is also not necessary, for cognitive psychologists have paid scant attention to the central issue that concerns us: in what ways, and for what reasons, do people differ in their ability to reason effectively? However, here as elsewhere in these final chapters, where we are dealing with the cognitive processes responsible for performance on IQ tests, we cannot afford to ignore the theories and findings of cognitive psychology, and in what follows I shall attempt to interweave ideas from both psychometric and experimental research.

Cognitive psychologists, and philosophers, draw a sharp distinction between inductive and deductive reasoning—a distinction that is not always easily mapped onto the type of reasoning problems, such as analogies or series completion tasks, that appear in IQ tests. Inductive reasoning is said to involve the drawing of conclusions that go beyond the information given:

> *All swans I have encountered so far have been white; therefore the next swan I see will be white.*

In deductive reasoning, on the other hand, the conclusion is necessarily implied by, because contained in, the premises:

> *All swans are white.*

> *Therefore, if this bird is a swan, it must be white (and if it is black, it is not a swan).*

When the speaker visits Australia and first encounters a black swan, this will falsify the conclusion of the inductive argument, but not its premise (it will still be true that all the swans he had encountered up to that time had been white). But the first premise of the deductive argument will now be seen to have been false, and thus not to entail the conclusion.

It is not too difficult to see that reasoning by analogy in the real world involves going beyond the information given, i.e. drawing conclusions not necessarily implied by that information. If I argue that, since you have found the rest of this book boring, you will probably find this chapter tedious and boring, I am arguing by analogy. But I might be mistaken, for it might just be the case that this chapter contains the only information about intelligence and IQ testing in which you are interested. My premise would still be true, but my conclusion does not necessarily follow from it. Analogical reasoning is, therefore, a form of inductive reasoning—although that is not always obvious in the rather more cut and dried, self-contained problems that typically appear in an IQ test—where there is one, and only one, correct answer. For example, one, and only one, of the four alternatives in parentheses is the correct answer to an analogy of the form:

> *Hand is to glove as foot is to ?*   *(heel, toe, sock, hat).*

Similarly, if asked which alternative comes next in the following series, it seems clear that there is only one possible correct answer:

> *1, 3, 5, 7, ?*   *(8, 9, 15).*

But there is still no logical necessity about these answers. Indeed, given additional alternatives to choose from, such as shoe in the first case, or 11 in the second, it is no longer obvious what the correct answer would be (the number series might have been odd prime numbers rather than just all odd numbers). It is precisely a requirement of good multiple-choice IQ test items that there should be only one correct answer, and this can be achieved only by careful selection of the alternative answers provided. Consider the following 'odd one out' problem:

> *Moscow, London, Paris, Oslo, Toronto*

Which is the odd one out? Toronto because it is not a capital city? Or Paris because it is the only one without two 'o's? The point is that there are always alternative bases for classifying the terms in all these types of problem. The only way to force one classification rather than another is by restriction of the range of possible answers from which one is allowed to choose, and it is this trick that leads to the impression that there is one, and only one, necessarily correct answer to items in an IQ test, even when the reasoning involved is analogical and inductive rather than deductive.

Most of the problems in tests of fluid intelligence or abstract reasoning, then, are problems of inductive, rather than deductive reasoning, and I shall spend most of this chapter discussing inductive reasoning. But it will be worth briefly discussing deductive reasoning also—if only because people do differ markedly in their ability to solve some kinds of deductive reasoning tasks such as syllogisms, and our task is always one of trying to understand *why* people differ. I start with a relatively simple account of how people solve simple analogies, because a major goal of this particular account was to pinpoint the processes responsible for differences in performance.

Analyses of reasoning and problem solving

A componential model of analogical reasoning

Consider the simple, figural analogy illustrated in Fig. 9.1. The task is to choose, from the two alternatives on offer (D and D'), the one that correctly completes the analogy. The problem could also be presented with only a single D term, when the task would be to determine whether the analogy was true or false. A whole series of problems can be presented using the same basic figures, varying in the following attributes:

> *male-female; black or white hat; happy–sad; large–small.*

Sternberg (1977; 1985; Sternberg and Gardner, 1983) and Pellegrino (1986; Alderton *et al.*, 1985) and their colleagues have argued that the solution of such analogies involves the following components or sub-processes:

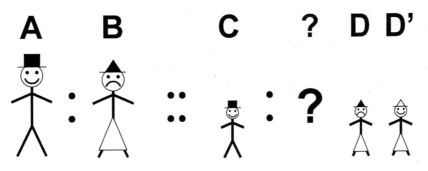

Fig. 9.1 A figural, 'schematic picture' analogy, of the type used by Sternberg and Rifkin (1979).

1. *Encoding* all the terms of the problem, A, B, C, and D (and D' if there are two alternative fourth terms to choose between). Encoding is to be understood as a matter of listing the attributes of each term. Thus the encoding of A in Fig. 9.1 would list the following attributes: large, happy, male, with black hat.
2. *Inferring* the relation between the A and B terms. This is a matter of listing the transformations that must be performed on A's attributes to turn A into B. In Fig. 9.1, this means transforming two attributes: happy to sad; male to female.
3. *Mapping* the relation between the A and C terms. This is exactly the same process as inference, as applied to the relationship between A and C (so here, the one transformation called for is: large to small).
4. *Applying* the A:B transformation to C. The inference process above listed two transformations from A to B: applying those transformations to C yields a sad, small, female with a black hat.
5. *Producing* the correct response. In several versions of the theory, this last step is itself decomposed into various component processes: the application stage generates a candidate fourth term of the analogy, which is then compared with the alternative(s) on offer, and in the case where the requirement is to choose between two alternatives, D and D', a process of justification may be invoked in the case where the application process generates a candidate that does not match either the D or D' on offer.

It is one thing to postulate a set of component processes such as these. But how are they measured? Because the problems presented in these studies, like that shown in Fig. 9.1, were all simple, and because it is possible to generate a large number of different problems all of the same general type, and using the same set of basic stimuli, Sternberg's and Pellegrino's basic measure of performance has been reaction time (RT), i.e. the time to produce a solution (errors were infrequent and only correct reaction times used). But how can this overall RT be broken down into the time taken up by these various component processes? Two techniques have been used. One is to present part of a problem in advance and to measure RT only after the remainder of that problem has been presented. The logic of the argument here is straightforward. Total solution time is presumably the sum of the times taken to: encode four terms; infer; map; apply; and produce a response. If the A and B terms are pre-exposed, then the subject will be able to encode two of the four terms, and map the A:B relation. His solution time when the final terms are presented will be shorter than his total solution time on other problems by the time it takes him to encode two terms and perform mapping. By similar logic, prior exposure to only one, or to three, of the four terms allows, by subtraction, a measure of the time taken up by other component processes. A second technique is to vary the distance between the various terms. For example, if A and B differ in only one attribute, then inference should take less time than if they differ in three attributes, and a measure of this difference in overall RT can be used to infer the time taken for each step of the inference (and application) component.

Sternberg's and Pellgrino's experimental techniques seem both simple and elegant, and have allowed them not only to obtain reliable measures of the time taken to execute various component process, but also to choose between alternative versions of this general model as providing the most accurate account of the data. As we shall see shortly, the model is also able to account for some differences in the way that people solve simple analogies, and can even predict differences in performance on other tests of reasoning. Moreover, the general model seems to make sense: that is to say, it does seem to summarize, and put together in a plausible package, the various operations that, one might suppose, must be performed by anyone solving analogical reasoning problems of this sort. The terms of the analogy must be encoded; the relationship between the A and B, and between the A and C terms must be worked out; and the A : B relationship must be applied to C. And so on.

But there surely remain some doubts, many of which, it should be acknowledged at the outset, have been raised by Sternberg himself. In his later theorizing (Sternberg, 1985, 1990), he regards the model we have just outlined as an account only of the 'performance components' of analogical reasoning. In addition to these more molecular operations, the later theory talks of 'metacomponents', whose function is to oversee the operations of the performance components.

> Metacomponents are higher order, executive processes used to plan what one is going to do, to monitor it while one is doing it, and to evaluate it after it is done. These metacomponents include (1) recognizing the existence of a problem, (2) deciding upon the nature of the problem confronting one, (3) selecting a set of lower order processes to solve the problem, (4) selecting a strategy into which to combine these components, (5) selecting a mental representation upon which the components and strategy can act, (6) allocating one's mental resources, (7) monitoring one's problem solving as it is happening, and (8) evaluating one's problem solving after it is done. (Sternberg, 1990, pp. 268–269)

Why is it necessary to appeal to this higher level of organization (as we shall do more than once in the remainder of this chapter)? One way of appreciating its importance is to ask the question: is it likely that analysis of the way people solve a series of simple analogies, like that shown in Fig. 9.1, will reveal all the cognitive operations involved in the solution of difficult analogies? Consider the problem of encoding the three or four terms of the analogy. What does this mean? According to the simple model, encoding is a matter of listing the attributes of each term. But which attributes? In problems of the sort illustrated in Fig. 9.1, this may not seem a serious issue. You just list them all: A is a large, happy man, with a black hat. But that, of course, is not quite true: A is also a black figure on a white background (rather than pink or purple); it is a stick figure with arms sticking out sideways; the hat is a square top hat; etc. etc. There is, of course, no need to list these attributes: they are not relevant to the solution of the analogy—because they, and a dozen others, are common to all the (male) terms. But this illustrates an important general principle: you cannot encode, i.e. list the relevant attributes of one term of an analogy, until you have taken note of the other terms in order to discover what the relevant attributes might be. One implication of this thought is that the successful problem solver may well be the one who encodes carefully, and therefore slowly, rather than rapidly. Consistent with this, in a developmental study of analogical reasoning, Sternberg and Rifkin (1979) found that after the age of 9 or 10, increases in age, although associated with a decrease in the time to execute inference and application components, were also associated with an increase in the time spent on encoding. In terms of Sternberg's later theorizing, this implies that older children differ from younger in the way they allocate resources to the problem, a difference which in this case was partly responsible for their superior performance.

But encoding may be an even more complex operation. One reason why some analogies are harder to solve than others, is because they make it difficult to discern what the relevant attributes of the various terms are. A favourite trick is to lead the solver down a garden path by suggesting the wrong attribute to encode, and that is done by providing an obvious relationship between two terms that happens to be the wrong one. Consider the following example from Sternberg (1977) (with apologies to American readers):

> *Washington is to 1 as Lincoln is to*   *(5, 10, 15?)*

Unless wholly ignorant of American history, no one will attempt to solve this analogy by listing all possible attributes of Washington and Lincoln. The fact that they are both US presidents is presumably the critical attribute they share in common, and it is presumably unnecessary to note (or is it?) that Washington is the capital of the US, or Lincoln the capital of Nebraska, that Washington is a state in the north-west of the US, or a town in the north of England where Nissan cars are manufactured, or that Lincoln is an English cathedral city, or the name of a type of car or type of biscuit.

The knowledge that Washington was the first president of the US adds to one's confidence. This is about American presidents, and non-Americans will complain that it is not a 'culture-fair' problem because its solution simply depends on knowing whether Lincoln was the fifth, tenth, or fifteenth American president. Maybe it is not *too* unfair, however, since some partial knowledge of American history and politics may be sufficient to suggest the correct answer. Washington would have served as president soon after independence (1776?); Lincoln was president during the civil war (1860?). American presidential terms are four years and only Franklin Roosevelt served more than two terms. So Lincoln could not have been the fifth president, and could hardly have been the tenth (unless we got our dates a bit wrong, or all his nine predecessors served two full terms). So the answer must surely be 15.

Actually Lincoln was the sixteenth president, and the correct answer is 5—because, although the problem is indeed about US presidents, the relevant connection between Washington and 1 is not that Washington was the first president of the US, but that his portrait appears on a $1 bill (and Lincoln's on a $5 bill). In other words, we have been misled into encoding the wrong attributes (1 should not be encoded as first) because an irrelevant attribute seemed to make such good sense. Encoding is not the routine, automatic process that is perhaps implied by the original, simple model, and the study of easy analogies, where the problem of encoding irrelevant attributes hardly arises, may not reveal all the processes engaged in the solution of more difficult problems. Although, as we shall see shortly, the original model, appealing only to performance components, can claim some success in predicting differences in performance on more difficult problems, the possibility must be acknowledged that prediction is not the same as explanation. It seems likely that a fuller understanding of human reasoning and problem solving will have to appeal to Sternberg's metacomponents.

A model for Raven's Matrices

If we wish to understand the processes underlying performance on difficult tests of abstract reasoning, or Gf, perhaps we should study those tasks directly. Raven's Matrices, in their various forms, are widely acknowledged to be a paradigm measure of Gf, and Carpenter *et al.* (1990) have both examined the performance of university students attempting to solve the Advanced Matrices set, and developed a general model that attempts to account for that performance. All items in the Advanced Matrices are of the same general format, as illustrated in Fig. 9.2, a 3×3 matrix with the third figure in the third row missing, and the task is to select from the alternatives on offer the figure that best completes this row.

How do people set about solving such problems? The basic components of Carpenter *et al.*'s model are as follows:

1. Description and coding of the figures.
2. Finding correspondences between figures by pairwise comparison.
3. Row-wise induction of a rule relating the figures in each row. The possible rules are:
   (a) Constant in a row.
   (b) Quantitative pairwise progression.
   (c) Distribution of three values.
   (d) Figure addition or subtraction.
   (e) Distribution of two values.
4. Store part-solutions in working memory while iterating the above processes on other parts of the problem.
5. A goal monitor plans overall strategy, setting up sequences of sub-goals, satisfying them in turn and moving onto the next appropriate step.
6. Selection of an answer.

The essence of the solution of Raven's problems is the induction of the rule governing the relationship between the figures in each row. Carpenter *et al.* identify five possible rules,

3(a) to (e) above, although other versions of some of these rules would be equally appropriate. Their application is illustrated in two of the problems shown in Fig. 9.2.

Problem 1 simultaneously illustrates rules (a)–(c):

(a) The inner lines are all vertical in Row 1, horizontal in Row 2, and oblique in Row 3.
(b) The number of these lines increases from 1 to 2 to 3 across each row.
(c) The lines are embedded in a circle, a square and a triangle.

Therefore the correct answer is number 1.

Problem 2 simultaneously illustrates rules (d) and (e):

(d) An x to the right of the vertical line in column 2 is subtracted from an x to the left of the vertical line in column 1.
(e) The half-square and half-diamond each appear twice and twice only in each row, with the third value being null.

The correct answer is 3.

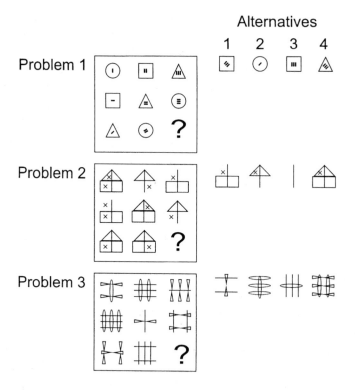

Fig. 9.2 Examples of the type of problem item appearing in Raven's Advanced Progressive Matrices. The matrix appears here on the left, together with four alternative solutions on the right. These are not real copies of original items for the RAPM: among other differences the originals always offer eight alternatives to choose from.

But it is important to note that Raven's Matrices are difficult, not just because some of these rules seem arbitrary, but because even when you have been told what the possible rules are, it is still not always easy to see how to apply the appropriate rule, or combination of rules, to particular cases. This difficulty is explicitly acknowledged by the model. Although it bears certain obvious resemblances to the simple componential model of analogical reasoning outlined above, at the same time there are certain important changes. For example, the model explicitly acknowledges that there is a critical interplay between components (1) and (2)—that the description or coding of the relevant attributes of the figures is a matter of searching for correspondences between them, and also explicitly acknowledges that the induction of the appropriate rule will be possible only if the figures have been coded properly to reveal the relevant correspondences between them. Consider, for example, the third problem shown in Fig. 9.2. Problem 3 actually depends on the application of rule (c)—each row should have three values of each of two types of figure. The problem is quite difficult, however, because most people's natural inclination is to suppose that the relevant attributes of the figures are their shapes—cigar, bow-tie, and straight lines. In fact, this is irrelevant: the relevant attributes are simply whether they are horizontally or vertically orientated. Each row has one instance of one, two and three vertical figures, and one instance of one, two and three horizontal figures, regardless of their shape.

The problem, in other words, is one of discovering what is the appropriate representation of the figures, that is to say, of seeing which attributes are relevant. And that, it seems probable, will be achieved only if one tries out alternative descriptions, to see whether they work, i.e. permit the induction of a rule, and if one is willing or able, if they do not work, to go back to the beginning and start again. It seems plausible enough to suppose that one of the hallmarks of the intelligent problem solver is precisely such a willingness to retrace one's steps when confronted with an impasse, the ability to question one's initial, obvious assumptions rather than persist with them in the face of evidence that something is wrong. All this is reminiscent of some of Sternberg's metacomponents. Carpenter *et al.*'s model certainly at least acknowledges some such idea, but whether it provides a convincing explanation of why and how people differ in this ability may be open to question.

In the same way, their model lists five rules which, between them, are indeed sufficient to solve essentially all items in Raven's Matrices. But where have the rules come from? Do not people differ in their ability to discover them, and are not such differences partly responsible for differences in test performance? Carpenter *et al.* acknowledge that they themselves have supplied the rules, so that the task for their model is to recognize which rules are appropriate for which items, rather than to work out all possible rules from scratch. Their justification is that all their subjects correctly and spontaneously identified four of the five rules, so that differences in test performance could not have been due to differences in the availability of those particular rules. Their model did indeed allow the possibility that the fifth rule (distribution of two—rule 3(e) above) might not be available to all subjects and that this would account for some differences in test performance (see below). One suspects, however, that had they studied less highly selected subjects than university students, they would have had to allow for the possibility that some of the other rules might equally be more readily discovered by some people than by others. Carroll cites an unpublished study by Tullos, which

> found that the primary source of individual differences on the Raven test seemed to be ability to apply rules of inference, along with lack of knowledge of certain types of rule frequently involved in Raven test items. (Carroll, 1993, p. 647)

Carpenter *et al.* acknowledge not only that rule 3(e) was harder for their subjects to induce than the first four, but also that rules 3(a)–(d) were not all equally easy: 3(a) and 3(b) were easier than 3(c) and 3(d). One plausible reason for this is that rules 3(a) and 3(b), constant in a row and quantitative pairwise progression, can be induced by comparing only neighbouring pairs of items in a row, first items 1 and 2, then items 2 or 3. Rules 3(c) and 3(d), distribution of three values and addition or subtraction, on the other hand, require the simultaneous comparison of all three items in a row.

All rules are discovered by comparing items in each row. The process involved is much the same as Sternberg's performance components of inference and mapping. Rules 3(a) and 3(b) simply describe the operations that must be applied to an attribute of one figure to transform it into the same attribute of the next figure in a row. Rules 3(c) and 3(d) describe the operations that must be performed on items 1 and 2 in each row in order to produce item 3.

Prediction of individual differences by componential theories

These two componential models, at least as we have considered them so far, are undoubtedly incomplete. But that does not make them worthless. Far from it. They are probably best understood as attempts to specify some of the processes or operations that may be involved in solving simple analogical reasoning problems or more difficult series completion tasks. Even if they do not explain the origins of these operations, or the processes that control their application, they constitute a necessary first step towards a complete account of inductive reasoning ability. And such models do shed light on the nature of some individual differences in problem-solving ability—or at least point to some of the operations that are carried out more efficaciously by some people than by others.

Proficiency in analogical reasoning, like performance on any type of IQ test, improves as children grow older. According to Piaget and Inhelder (1969), indeed, children are not capable of true analogical reasoning until they enter Piaget's 'formal operational' stage at the age of 11–12 years. But Goswami (1992) has argued persuasively that this is a serious underestimate of younger children's abilities. The reason why they fail to solve analogical reasoning problems is often simply because they do not understand the relationship between the A and B terms of the analogy. In Sternberg's terminology, they fail to execute the correct inference operation. Provided this relationship is one they *do* understand, children as young as 3 or 4 can solve analogies. Shown (in pictorial form) the following analogy:

> *Loaf of bread is to slice of bread as lemon is to ?*

Some 80 per cent of 4-year-olds selected a picture of a slice of lemon in preference to such alternatives as a slice of cake, a whole lemon, a yellow balloon, or two squeezed lemon halves. But many older children will fail an analogy, such as:

> *Pig is to boar as dog is to (wolf, cat, rat, turtle?)*

because they do not know either that a boar is a wild pig (a failure of inference) or that a wolf is a wild dog (a failure of application).

In a study specifically designed to test the componential approach, Sternberg and Rifkin (1979) showed that one developmental change in analogical reasoning ability is that children below the age of 10 do not readily understand the importance, and occasionally the necessity, of mapping the relationship between the A and C terms. Sternberg's experimental methodology allows him to measure the time taken for mapping by measuring the increase in overall solution time associated with an increase in the difference between the A and C terms. Referring back to Fig. 9.1, for example, only one transform must be applied to A to turn it into C (large to small). But if C's hat had been white, two transforms would have been necessary. With all else held constant, adults show an increase in solution time with such an increase in the distance from A to C. But children below the age of 10 did not.

Now most simple analogies can be solved without the need for mapping. For example:

> *Black is to white as night is to ?*

or

> *Glove is to hand as sock is to ?*

can be solved simply by applying the appropriate transform or relationship to the C term (opposite; worn on), without bothering about any possible relationship between the A and C terms. It really is not relevant that nights are usually dark or black, and the relationship of 'opposite' permits the construction of numerous analogies where there is no obvious relationship between the A and C terms at all. For example:

> *Black is to white as odd is to ?*

However, more difficult analogies are often those where the relationship between A and C terms does become important. The Washington–Lincoln analogy is not going to be solved by someone who does not realize they were both US presidents. Consider the analogy shown in Fig. 9.3. Its solution precisely requires one to map the elements of C onto those of A, i.e. to see that the three vertical lines in A correspond to the three small lines radiating out from a dot inside the square in C, and the four horizontal lines in A to the four-sided

A : B :: C : ?   D or D′

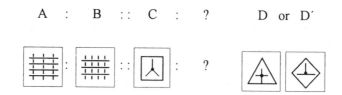

Fig. 9.3 Example of a figural analogy that requires one to map the relationship between the A (first) and C (third) terms. See text for further details.

figure of the square in C. Thus the A : B transform (three to four vertical lines; four to three horizontal lines) implies that D will have four lines radiating out from the dot inside a three-sided triangle. If mapping is an operation ill understood by younger children, it is unsurprising that they should be rather poor at solving certain kinds of analogy.

But well-educated adults are not always so good at mapping. Indeed, in somewhat more realistic settings than those provided by standard IQ tests, it is often a failure of mapping that is responsible for our failure to use an analogy to solve a problem. Consider the following classic problem (from Duncker, 1945):

> A patient has an inoperable stomach tumour. The tumour can be destroyed by radiation, but although weak radiation will not damage normal flesh, it will also not destroy the tumour. Radiation strong enough to destroy the tumour will also destroy normal flesh. How can the surgeon use radiation to treat the tumour?

Given no further clues, only about 10 per cent of university students solve this problem (Gick and Holyoak, 1980, 1983). Gick and Holyoak asked whether the provision of the solution to an analogous problem would increase their chances of success. One such analogous problem was this:

> A general is trying to capture a fortress that can be approached by a number of different roads, all of which have been mined. If he advances his entire army down one road they will set the mines off, but a small group will not. However, a small group will not be sufficient to capture the fortress. For that he needs his entire army. What is he to do?

The solution is simple: divide the army into small groups, all of whom advance down different roads and arrive at the fortress simultaneously. The analogous solution to the tumour problem is, of course, to use a number of independent sources of radiation that converge only on the tumour. But if they were just told about the general's problem, with no hint that it might help them to solve the surgeon's, only a minority of students saw the analogy (see also Keane, 1987). It was only when they were explicitly asked whether the story of the general might help to solve the tumour problem that a majority of people took the hint.

The failure to use the analogy can be described as a failure of mapping—that is a failure to see that we can translate the general into the surgeon, the fortress in the tumour, the roads converging onto the fortress into different routes from different sources of radiation onto the tumour, etc. But it is not obvious that describing this as a failure of mapping provides a principled explanation of it, let alone an explanation of why some people succeed and others do not. As Holyoak (1984) has argued, the simple componential model almost evades the issue, and one can see the role to be played here by some of the metacomponents of Sternberg's later theorizing, for example, deciding upon the nature of the problem confronting one, selecting a mental representation of the problem upon which strategies and performance components can operate, etc. But the first question we want to answer is: what is it about this problem that makes it so difficult? According to Holyoak and to Gentner (1989), it is because the surface differences between the two problems are so great; and it is the structural or relational similarities that must be detected in order to perform the mapping operation. Keane (1987) has shown that the greater the surface similarity between target and analogue problems, the more people will use the analogy to solve the target problem: an analogue problem about a general using rays to destroy a missile is much more helpful than one about a general storming a fortress.

For our purposes, what is missing from these experimental studies on the use of analogy in problem solving is any attempt to explain the individual differences they reveal. A significant minority of students see the analogy between the surgeon–tumour and general–fortress problems without any hint. Another minority fail to see the analogy even when given a hint. Given the general–missile problem, about half Keane's subjects saw the analogy and half did not. These differences can in principle be explained as differences in the ability to represent the terms of a problem in such a way that structural relations rather than surface features are emphasized. But we do not know whether these differences would be related to differences in IQ test scores (and if so, whether specifically to differences in Gf).

Sternberg has sought to test his model of performance components by seeing how well individual differences in the values of various parameters of the model predict individual differences in performance on standard tests of reasoning. Although I have questioned whether the speed with which people solve simple analogies necessarily tells us much about the ways in which they solve difficult ones, Sternberg and Gardner (1983) found highly significant correlations in a sample of Yale undergraduates between speed of solving simple pictorial, geometrical, and verbal analogies and performance on IQ tests. Even more important than this overall correlation, however, they were able to show that the highest correlation, of 0.70, was between a combined measure of inference, mapping, and application, and performance on tests of Gf. Other component scores showed lower correlations, and none of the component scores correlated significantly with measures of perceptual speed. In other words, the componential analysis has apparently succeeded in identifying a central rule-induction component which is the best predictor of IQ—and the component of IQ it predicts is Gf rather than (as might have happened given that the measure of performance on the analogy problems was reaction time) a speed component of

IQ. It is, as ever, important to remember that the mere occurrence of a correlation does not explain the basis for the correlation. The fact that students who were fast at solving simple analogies were also good at solving harder reasoning problems does not mean that they used the same cognitive operations for both: thus the occurrence of these correlations has not necessarily identified all the cognitive operations involved in performance on tests of Gf. But it may have made a start.

Carpenter *et al.* (1990) have also addressed the issue of individual differences in performance. They in fact developed two versions of their model, FAIRAVEN and BETTERAVEN; the former was able to solve 23 of the 34 items presented to it, a level of performance comparable to the median score of the group of university students tested; BETTERAVEN solved 32 of the 34 items, which corresponded to the performance of the best student tested. FAIRAVEN also predicted which items students would be able to solve and which items they would fail on: the correlation between model's and students' patterns of errors was 0.67.

There were three main differences between FAIRAVEN and BETTERAVEN: in other words, Carpenter *et al.* are claiming that there are three major sources of individual differences in performance (at this level of performance: the Advanced Matrices test is supposedly for use only with adolescents or adults of above-average ability, and Carpenter *et al.*'s subjects were university students). The first was that FAIRAVEN did not have rule 3(e) available—the distribution of two rule. Thus it was unable to solve any item that required the application of this rule. These items are indeed among the harder ones, and were not solved by low-scoring students. In this sense, the model is correct—although, as before, what one also wants to know is why this rule is harder than the others, and why some people are able to discover it for themselves while others are not.

The two further differences were that BETTERAVEN had a larger working-memory capacity, and it also had a 'goal planner', which was not part of the FAIRAVEN at all. The former, at least, should by now be a familiar enough suggestion. Taken together they do suggest some explanatory ideas worth pursuing.

Working memory

We have already seen that performance on both verbal and spatial IQ tests correlates with measures of verbal and spatial working memory. It would be surprising if measures of Gf were not also associated with performance on working-memory tasks. And some of the evidence reviewed in Chapter 7 strongly suggested that there must be such an association: we saw there that a task which, when performed in isolation, showed only a modest correlation with IQ, correlated more strongly with IQ when performed concurrently with another, competing task, and this increase in the strength of the association with IQ was often largely with measures of Gf (e.g. Spilsbury, 1992).

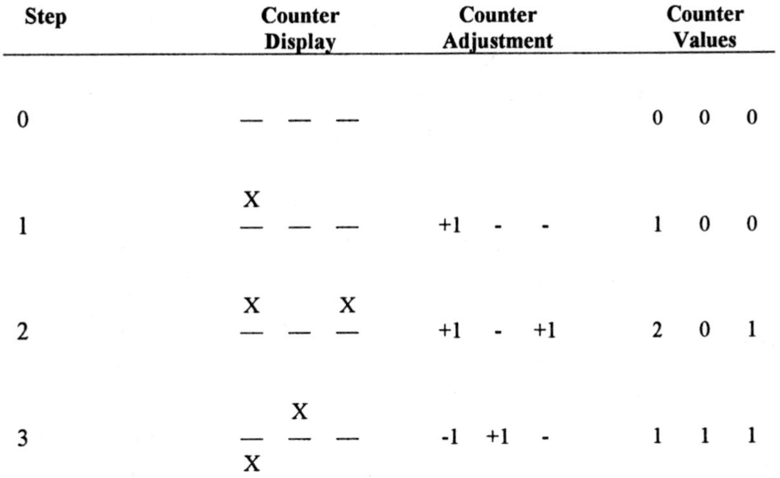

Step	Counter Display	Counter Adjustment	Counter Values
0	— — —		0 0 0
1	X — — —	+1 - -	1 0 0
2	X X — — —	+1 - +1	2 0 1
3	X — — — X	-1 +1 -	1 1 1

Fig. 9.4 Larson and Saccuzzo's 'mental counters' task. A computer screen displays, in succession, the sequence of stimuli shown. The subject's task is to keep a running track of the value of three 'counters', each corresponding to one of the three horizontal bars on the screen. The three counters start at zero: 1 is added to a counter whenever an x is shown above its bar; 1 is subtracted whenever an x appears below the bar. (From Larson and Saccuzzo, 1989.)

Several studies have indeed reported moderate to strong correlations between scores on tests of Gf and a variety of simple working-memory tasks. For example, Larson and Saccuzzo (1989) devised a 'mental counters' task, illustrated in Fig. 9.4. The three counters in the task were represented by three horizontal lines, appearing side by side on a computer screen. At the beginning of each trial, each counter was reset to zero. A trial consisted of a sequence of displays on the screen; in each display an x appeared above or below one of the horizontal lines. If the x appeared above a line, that meant that 1 was to be added to that counter; the appearance of an x below a line was the instruction to subtract 1. A trial consisted of five or seven successive displays, at the end of which the requirement was to report the cumulative total of all three counters. Performance on this task correlated 0.50 with scores on Raven's Matrices (although, as noted in Chapter 7, the correlation between Raven's scores and performance on simple RT and IT tasks in the same study was less than 0.20).

Kyllonen and Christal (1990) gave large groups of American airforce recruits various tasks involving simple operations with letters of the alphabet. In one, called alphabet recoding, the computer briefly displayed three letters, for example:

G, N, B

This was followed by an instruction, for example:

Add 2

To which the answer would be:

   I, P, D.

In another task, called ABC numerical assignment, they had to solve simple algebraic equations. They were shown three displays, for example:

   A = B + 2

   B = C − 4

   C = 6

The three displays would be followed by a request for the values of A and B. Although the program permitted unlimited time for the study of each display, only one display was shown at a time, and no backtracking was allowed. In two separate studies, with some 400 recruits in each, performance on the alphabet recoding task correlated up to 0.45 with scores on various reasoning tests, while the correlation between reasoning scores and the ABC task was as high as 0.58.

   Brody (1992) has argued that performance on Larson and Saccuzzo's and Kyllonen and Christal's tasks must depend on familiarity with alphanumeric symbols and proficiency at mental arithmetic, and that this may be why such performance correlated with IQ. The premise is no doubt true, but the conclusion does not necessarily follow. Brody's argument would lead one to expect correlations with measures of Gc rather than with measures of Gf. Moreover, the participants in all these experiments were military recruits who had completed high school and were of well above average IQ. It is hard to believe that if they had been asked to perform any one part of any of these tasks in isolation, their performance would have correlated substantially with any IQ score. They would all, have been able, surely, without error, to keep track of the value of a single counter in Larson and Saccuzzo's study, or just move two letters on from G in Kyllonen and Christal's alphabet recoding task. It seems more plausible to suppose that the reason why performance correlated so strongly with IQ was the requirement in one case to remember three letters of the alphabet, perform a simple operation on one and remember that outcome while performing the same operation on the next; or in the other case the need to keep track of the current value of each of three separate counters while performing a simple operation on the value of one.

   A study by Stankov and Crawford (1993) provides evidence consistent with this supposition. Their procedure is illustrated in Table 9.1. University students were shown three letters of the alphabet, but in this case, unlike Kyllonen and Christal's experiment, the letters remained on the screen along with the instructions. In the one-swap condition the instruction was to swap, say, the second and third letters; the two-swap instructions would then add the requirement to swap the (new) first and third letters; and so on up to three or four swaps. Correlations with measures of Gf (Raven's and a letter series test) ranged from zero in the one-swap condition, to 0.20 in two-swap, and 0.46 in the three- and four-swap conditions. Here, then, there seems to be unambiguous evidence that it is the requirement to

Table 9.1 Stankov and Crawford's swaps task (from Stankov and Crawford, 1993)

Condition	Start	Instructions	Answer
One swap	ABC	Swap 2 and 3	ACB
Two swaps	ABC	Swap 2 and 3; 1 and 3	BCA
Three swaps	ABC	Swap 2 and 3; 1 and 3; 1 and 2	CBA

hold the results of one operation in mind, while performing a further operation, that yields the substantial correlation with Gf.

Experimental evidence suggests that there is a genuine causal relationship underlying these correlations between measures of working memory and of reasoning ability. Reasoning problems that place greater demands on working memory are harder than those that place fewer demands, and manipulations to a reasoning task that increase these demands invariably impair performance. Much of this evidence comes from studies of deductive reasoning, in particular syllogistic reasoning, and a discussion of some of this evidence will also serve to broaden the scope of this review beyond the confines of inductive reasoning.

A standard syllogism consists of two premises, one relating A and B terms, the second relating B and C, and requires the solver to decide what relation, if any, might hold between A and C. Thus:

> *All Artists are Beekeepers*
>
> *All Beekeepers are Chemists*

From which it is possible, and easy, to draw the conclusion:

> *All Artists are Chemists*

Other syllogisms, however, are rather harder:

> *Some Artists are Beekeepers*
>
> *No Beekeepers are Chemists*

The valid conclusion is:

> *Some Artists are not Chemists*

Virtually everyone will produce the correct answer to the first problem, but only about two-thirds of students, in one study, got the right answer to the second (Dickstein, 1978). Why this difference? According to one influential account (Johnson-Laird, 1983; Johnson-Laird and Byrne, 1991), people first construct a mental model, or representation, of the state of affairs implied by each premise of a syllogism; in order to determine what conclusion follows from the premises, if any, they must combine these models in all possible ways to see what states of affairs could be true. Thus what makes a syllogism difficult is the number of possible ways of combining the representations of the premises—because as soon as there is more than one, we have to hold the implications of the first in working memory, while working out the implications of the second, in order to determine whether there is any conclusion compatible with both.

According to this account, the first syllogism above is easy, because there is only one way of combining the representations of the two premises. The first premise, that all artists are beekeepers, can be represented thus:

Artist - - - - - - - Beekeeper

Beekeeper

The artist and beekeeper connected by the dashes in the first line represent an artist who is a beekeeper. The second beekeeper on his own represents the fact that there may be beekeepers who are not artists. The second premise is similarly represented:

Beekeeper - - - - - - - - - Chemist

Chemist

And the two can be combined in only one way:

Artist - - - - - - - Beekeeper - - - - - - - - - Chemist

Beekeeper - - - - - - - - - Chemist

Chemist

From which it follows that all artists are chemists.

The first premise of the second syllogism, some artists are beekeepers, is represented thus:

Artist - - - - - - - - Beekeeper

Artist

Beekeeper

One artist is a beekeeper, but one is not and similarly there may also be a beekeeper who is not an artist. The second premise, no beekeepers are chemists, will be represented thus:

Beekeeper

Chemist

One way of combining these two representations would be:

Artist - - - - - - - - Beekeeper

Artist

Beekeeper

Chemist

From which it would follow that no artists are chemists. But there is a second, equally possible way of combining the two premises:

Artist - - - - - - - - Beekeeper

Artist - Chemist

Beekeeper

Chemist

From which it would follow that some artists are chemists. But this conclusion is incompatible with the first, and neither can therefore be valid. There is, however, a third possible conclusion compatible with both ways of combining the premises, namely that some artists are not chemists. The problem is difficult, according to Johnson-Laird's account, because it requires one to hold two distinct representations in working memory to see whether there is any single implication that follows from both.

Johnson-Laird's theory successfully explains other differences in difficulty between different forms of syllogism, again by appealing to constraints on working memory, but it may be more informative to provide somewhat more direct evidence that working memory load affects the difficulty of solving such problems. One simple way of varying the load on working memory is either to display the premises of a syllogism on a computer screen until subjects produce their answer, or to read them out loud once only, so that subjects must remember both premises while trying to work out their answer. This simple change of procedure has a significant impact on errors (Gilhooly *et al.*, 1993). Gilhooly *et al.* also investigated the effects of various interfering tasks on syllogistic reasoning. Subjects were allowed to read the premises of a syllogism from a computer display, but from the moment they started viewing them, until they had produced their answer, they had to perform one of three other tasks, in time with a metronome. One simply required them to repeat the digits 1–5 over and over again. The second required them to tap, in sequence, four targets on a board. The third required them to produce a random sequence of the digits 1–5 (e.g. 4 1 2 2 5 1 3, etc.). The three tasks were chosen on the assumption that each would occupy one component of Baddeley and Hitch's working-memory system. Simple repetition of a series of digits is articulatory suppression and supposedly occupies the phonological loop; the tapping task occupies the visuo-spatial sketchpad; while generating a random string of digits is assumed to occupy the central executive. Neither articulatory suppression nor tapping had any effect on the time subjects spent studying the premises, or on the accuracy of their solutions. But the random number task significantly increased both the time taken to study the premises and the number of errors people made.

It seems clear, then, that reasoning tasks do place demands on working memory, and therefore that the sizeable correlations observed between people's performance on a working memory task and measures of Gf represent a true causal contribution of one to the other. We have already seen, of course, that working memory is also implicated in performance on tests of both Gc and Gv. Does this mean that the efficiency of working memory is the cognitive basis of *g* or general intelligence? That natural inference seemed to be contradicted by the fact that verbal and spatial working memory were only weakly correlated, and that verbal working memory predicted only Gc scores and spatial working memory only Gv scores—at least in a population of university students. These observations naturally raise the question whether the working memory implicated in studies of non-verbal reasoning is independent of both visual and spatial working memory, whether it is identical with one or other—and if so which, or whether there is some sort of common core to all three systems. The short answer is that we do not know.

The working-memory tasks whose execution correlated with measures of Gf in the Kyllonen and Christal (1990), Larson and Saccuzzo (1989), and Stankov and Crawford (1993) studies involved individually very simple operations on letters of the alphabet or numbers. We do not even know whether performance on such tasks would or would not correlate with performance on reading-span or spatial-span working-memory tasks. We do know, it is true, that there are moderately high correlations between the various working-memory tasks that all correlate with Gf. Kyllonen and Christal (1990), for example, factor analysed subjects' scores both on their different working-memory tasks and on their different reasoning tests. They extracted a single working-memory factor and a single reasoning factor. The correlation between the two was about 0.80. The title of their paper seemed hardly to be an exaggeration: 'Reasoning ability is (little more than) working-memory capacity?!' But it has not gone unchallenged. In a re-analysis of their data, de Jong and Das Smaal (1995) were able to show that a two-factor solution for their working-memory tasks was more appropriate. Although the two factors were certainly correlated, tasks such as alphabet recoding loaded onto one, and various mental arithmetic tasks (including the ABC numerical assignment task) loaded onto the second. Unfortunately, however, we do not know which of these factors is the better predictor of Gf, or whether they would turn out to be equally associated with reasoning ability. There is some evidence that not all working-memory tasks are equally good predictors of Gf. When students were given a counting span task that required them to solve a series of mental arithmetic problems, remembering the answer to each, their scores correlated more strongly with their Raven's scores than did their reading span, a measure of verbal working memory (Jurden, 1995). But it is not known whether Raven's scores would also correlate with performance on a spatial working-memory task, and if so how strongly.

At present, the balance of evidence suggests that 'working memory' or Baddeley and Hitch's 'central executive' should not be thought of as a single, unitary system. At least among people of above-average IQ, there seems good evidence that one can distinguish between verbal, spatial, and counting working-memory tasks. But we should not forget that correlations between different IQ tests themselves are apparently weaker in people of above-average IQ than in those of below-average IQ. There is a pressing need for more experiments on working memory and their relationship to IQ with people of average or even below-average IQ, where it is entirely possible that stronger correlations between performance on these different tasks might be observed, permitting the conclusion that there may be some processes shared in common by all.

The central executive and executive control

There is another reason why experimental research with people of no more than average IQ is needed if we are ever to understand the cognitive processes underlying performance on IQ tests. Consider again the list of metacomponents in Sternberg's (1985) theory outlined above (p. 301). I suspect that some readers' immediate reaction to this list might have been to say that several of these metacomponents are trivial statements of the obvious. It goes without saying that one cannot solve a problem without recognizing the existence of a problem to be solved. Of course one must monitor what one is doing when trying to solve a problem, and then evaluate one's solution. No doubt the need for all this seems obvious enough to most readers of this book. But it is not necessarily obvious to everyone. Commenting on the retarded child's attempts to tackle any sort of problem, Binet noted particularly an absence of

> direction and persistence of thought, self-criticism and invention . . . The child is unreflective . . . he forgets what he is doing . . . lacks direction . . . He does not know that he does not understand. (Binet, 1911, pp. 118–122)

It was the failure to register the existence of a problem, monitor one's attempts to solve it, and evaluate whether it has been solved, that seemed to characterize retardate performance—which is perhaps why later research with the mentally retarded has made it clear that if they are provided with an explicit and detailed explanation of the nature of a problem and of the steps to be taken in its solution, their performance can approximate that of others (Belmont and Butterfield, 1977; Campione *et al.*, 1982). Even if failure to deploy such basic ingredients of problem solving only becomes obvious when one is dealing with special populations, it seems likely that there may be more variation in the normal population than is apparent when one studies university students.

Some of Sternberg's other metacomponents have found parallels in the theories of cognition advanced by experimental psychologists. Choice between alternative representations of a problem, the selection of an appropriate strategy for tackling it, the deployment and management of lower-order components and resources, are not dissimilar to some of the functions assigned to Baddeley's central executive (Baddeley, 1986, 1996) or by Norman and Shallice (1986) to their supervisory attentional system. The development of a central executive system which can switch attention, compare alternative representations, and plan, control, and monitor actions, has been seen by some as the critical mechanism underlying Piagetian cognitive development (e.g. Russell, 1996). And a failure of executive control has been seen as a central ingredient in mental retardation (Campione *et al.*, 1982). Finally, as we shall see, there is some evidence that such a system of executive control might be located in prefrontal cortex. But what do we mean by executive control?

In Carpenter *et al.*'s (1990) models of performance on Raven's Matrices, one of the differences between FAIRAVEN and BETTERAVEN was that the latter had a larger working-memory capacity, and a goal monitor. The function of the goal monitor was to decide the order in which sub-problems should be tackled, keep track of which sub-goals had been satisfied, and to modify the path being taken when a difficulty arose. Just as in Baddeley's account of the central executive, this planning and control function is intimately tied up with working memory: keeping track of one's progress in solving a Raven's problem must necessarily involve holding in memory, and being able to retrieve on demand, the results of earlier computations.

To provide a concrete illustration of what is meant here, consider a superficially quite different problem, the Tower of Hanoi problem illustrated in Fig. 9.5. The task is to move the three discs, A, B, and C, from their start position on peg 1 to their goal position on peg 3 in as few moves as possible, with the constraints that you are allowed to move only one disc at a time, and at no time to place a larger disc on a smaller one (C on top of B, or B on top of A). The minimum number of moves required is, in fact, $2^N - 1$, where N is the numbers of discs. The problem can be divided into a hierarchy of sub-goals, working back from the final goal (A,B,C on peg 3). To achieve that goal, you need to move disc C onto peg 3; to do that, you need to move discs A and B off peg 1, leaving peg 3 clear; to get discs A and B onto peg 2, therefore, you must first move disc A to peg 3, disc B to peg 2 and then disc A back to peg 2. And so on—as illustrated in Fig. 9.5. It is not difficult to see that the problem will become notably harder (and harder to explain!) as the number of discs increases to 4, 5, or 6. But wherein, precisely, lies the difficulty? The individual steps are always similar; the sub-goals are always the same—move the largest disc to peg 3, then the next largest, and so on. The difficulty comes at the initiation of the series of moves that will satisfy each sub-goal: which peg do you move the smallest disc to? It is not very difficult to work out that, for the 3-disc problem in Fig. 9.5, your first move must be disc A to peg 3. But what is the first move for a 4, 5, or 6 disc problem? And what is the appropriate next move of a 6-disc problem after you have achieved your first sub-goal of placing the largest disc (F) onto peg 3? The answer to these questions requires (unless you have succeeded in working out the rule) forward planning: since you always have to use the goal peg, 3, for intermediate stacking, you must work out how to start your sequence of moves in a way that will leave the goal peg free to take the largest remaining disc. Solution of the Tower of Hanoi problem requires working through a set of moves and keeping track of their consequences (in working memory) before committing yourself.

Having instructed university and college students in the structure of the Tower of Hanoi problem, and how it can be broken down into a series of sub-goals, Carpenter *et al.* (1990) gave them a series of 3- to 8-disc problems, correcting any errors immediately they occurred. Essentially all errors occurred on moves that initiated each new sub-goal, and the number of errors increased sharply with the number of moves required to complete that sub-goal, i.e. the depth of forward processing required. More to our present point, Carpenter *et al.* found a correlation of −0.77 between the number of errors made, and scores on Raven's Matrices. This correlation is not far short of the reliability of the Raven tests, and was obtained in a sample with a relatively restricted range of ability. It implies that, in spite of the marked difference in their surface characteristics, Raven's Matrices and the Tower of Hanoi problem may be tapping closely related underlying operations. A good characterization of those operations would plausibly look like this:

> Before embarking on an action sequence which is novel or complex, we usually spend some time thinking what we are about to do, how best to achieve the goal, in what order to perform the individual actions, and how much time and effort will need to be allocated to the task. Memory is involved in formulating such plans, holding the elements and sequence in mind while the plan is being assembled, evaluated, revised and implemented . . . [Then] the component actions are assembled in some form of output buffer and the memory system monitors the output of actions from the buffer to ensure that the plan is implemented correctly. (Cohen, 1989, pp. 17–18)

A variant of the Tower of Hanoi problem, the Tower of London, consists of three pegs,

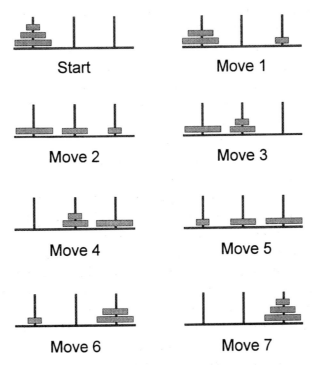

Fig. 9.5 The Tower of Hanoi problem. In the start position, O, three discs, A, B, and C, are on peg 1; the goal is to get them onto peg 3 (position 7), moving one disc at a time and never placing a larger disc on top of a smaller one. The correct sequence of moves is shown.

Box 9.1 The riddle of the frontal lobes

Prefrontal cortex comprises some 30 per cent of all cortical tissue in humans, but no more than 10 per cent in monkeys. Thus a sizeable fraction of the overall growth of the brain during the course of human evolution has been in prefrontal cortex. The implication is that this area must play a significant role in whatever makes us distinctively human. But what role? What are the functions of the frontal lobes? An obvious difference between us and other animals is our possession of language but, apart from Broca's area, there is little evidence of any specifically linguistic function in the frontal lobes. We also believe that we are more intelligent than other animals. Is prefrontal cortex implicated in intelligence?

Hebb and Penfield (1940) reported the case of a patient with intractable epilepsy who received complete bilateral ablation of prefrontal cortex. His preoperative IQ had been no more than 80. After the operation his IQ was normal. So far from depressing his IQ score, the removal of prefrontal cortex had enhanced it. Reviewing the evidence on the functions of the frontal lobes a quarter of a century later, Teuber (1964) concluded that they had nothing to do with the intelligence measured by IQ tests. The consensus view was that:

> Standard intelligence tests are especially *unsuitable* for revealing frontal impairments. The paradox has been accepted that frontal patients have impaired 'planning', 'problem-solving', etc., but preserved 'intelligence'. (Duncan *et al.*, 1995, p. 262)

It is odd that this paradox should have been accepted for so long, since Hebb himself saw quite early that frontal patients' IQ scores depended on the nature of the IQ test: they might obtain entirely normal scores on tests such as the Stanford–Binet, but were severely impaired on non-verbal tests (Hebb, 1949). This is exactly what Duncan and his colleagues have confirmed. In one of their studies, three frontal patients obtained IQ scores on the WAIS ranging from 126 to 130, but at the same time their scores on the Cattell culture-fair test were 108, 97, and 88 (Duncan *et al.*, 1995).

Neuropsychology must usually rely on damage to the brain arising from accident, injury, or disease. The most celebrated frontal patient, Phineas Gage, did indeed suffer an accidental injury: an explosion drove a large iron bar through his head. The story of this nineteenth-century American railroad worker, and his subsequent tribulations, is told by Damasio (1994). In the 10 years after the Second World War, however, the most common cause of damage to the frontal lobes was a deliberate neurosurgical operation. Following the lead of the Portugese neuropsychiatrist, Egas Moniz, who was awarded the Nobel prize for his pioneering work, American neurosurgeons performed prefrontal leucotomies or lobotomies on some 40 000 psychiatric patients during the 1940s and 1950s. The operation was a treatment of choice, or at least of last resort, for intractable anxiety, panic attacks, obsessive thoughts and compulsive behaviour, for schizophrenia, and for severe depression—in other words for virtually every known psychiatric disorder (Valenstein, 1973). There is no doubt that it was sometimes effective. One grateful patient exclaimed: 'Doctor, you have removed my worry centre'. And such patients often became more manageable, an outcome appreciated by many others, if not necessarily by the patients themselves. But other, less desirable effects were also observed—as they had been in the case of Phineas Gage. Patients might become emotionally labile, or show blunted affect; they would be tactless and rude and behave in other socially unacceptable ways; they would be irresponsible and make foolish decisions, or lethargic and refuse to make any decisions at all.

There is no doubt that, in the cognitive psychologist's laboratory, frontal patients show deficits in planning, decision making, goal monitoring, and other 'executive' functions. In the real world, on the other hand, many of their problems seem to be emotional and social (Damasio, 1994). It is still not clear whether the same underlying deficit manifests itself in different ways in different contexts, or whether we should accept that damage to prefrontal cortex disrupts a wide range of mental operations.

more complicated picture of the role of prefrontal cortex in working-memory tasks (reviewed by Owen, 1997). Although some studies have revealed different patterns of activation when people are engaged in verbal working-memory tasks (Petrides *et al.*, 1993), visual working-memory tasks (Smith *et al.*, 1995), and spatial working-memory tasks (Jonides *et al.*, 1993), others have suggested that the major distinctions may depend not on the modality of the stimuli being processed, but rather on the load imposed on working memory by the task requirements (Petrides, 1995; Owen, 1997). As Owen acknowledges, both these positions may turn out to be correct. The nature of the processing requirements may affect whether greater activation is found in dorsolateral rather than ventrolateral regions of prefrontal cortex; but there may be finer, modality-specific specializations within each region. The point is that no one could seriously suppose that prefrontal cortex subserves a single function, whether or not it is labelled general intelligence.

There is a further reason to remain somewhat sceptical. Appeals to a single general cognitive process underlying *g* (or even Gf) appear more persuasive, and certainly become harder to disprove, the more vaguely they are couched. To say that general intelligence depends on executive control, planning, and the allocation of resources, may have a certain air of plausibility. But what precisely do we mean when we say this, and what would count as disproof of such a hypothesis? Such ideas may mark a slight advance over the notion of general intelligence as mental energy or speed of information processing, dependent on the efficiency of the brain. But they still fall far short of a tightly specified theory of cognition. Consider again Sternberg's list of metacomponents (p. 301). The real problem with them is not that they are vacuous or incorrect. It is that they do not specify any precise set of cognitive operations. Planning, monitoring goals, and evaluating the consequences of alternative actions are all, presumably, ingredients of the sort of reasoning and problem-solving abilities that, it seems plausible to suppose, are measured by tests of Gf. To locate these operations, either in a physical place (the prefrontal cortex) or in a conceptual space (the central executive), does not really succeed in dispelling the worry that we have simply attached fine-sounding labels to processes we do not understand, or appealed to a homunculus to do our thinking for us. What are we to do? The best answer is: be alive to the danger.

The homunculus can be useful, given two provisos: (1) the continued recognition that it constitutes a way of labelling the problem, not an adequate explanation; (2) a continued attempt to understand the component processes that are necessary for executive control, gradually stripping away the various functions we previously attributed to our homunculus, until eventually it can be declared redundant. Whether we will then be left with a single co-ordinated system that serves multiple functions, a true executive, or a cluster of largely autonomous control processes— an executive committee—remains to be seen. (Baddeley, 1996, p. 26)

This task will require the combined efforts not only of psychometricians interested in individual differences in human intelligence, but also of cognitive psychologists and neuropsychologists.

The search for *g* concluded

Factor analysis implied that distinctions could be drawn between a number of different types of IQ test, for example, tests of verbal, spatial, and reasoning ability, as well as a few others such as tests of perceptual speed and memory retrieval. At the same time, the pattern of positive correlations between all these different tests suggested that they are not wholly independent. One possible explanation of this positive manifold is that all these different tests are measuring a single underlying cognitive process, which we can label general intelligence—until we know how to characterize it more precisely. Another is that each of these tests measures a wide variety of different processes, with some overlap between those measured by one kind of test and those measured by another.

Most psychometricians have probably inclined towards the first explanation. Cognitive psychologists are more likely to favour the second—because the standard approach of cognitive psychology has been to appeal to the operation of numerous modules or component processes to explain any complex behaviour. One component process that has seemed to be implicated in the solution to a wide variety of IQ tests is working memory— although one might be hard pressed to explain how the efficiency of any working-memory system contributes to performance on the sort of visual search test that measures perceptual speed. More detailed analysis, however, implies that working memory may itself be fractionated into partially independent systems specialized for different tasks.

The analysis of reasoning and measures of Gf has introduced us to more global cognitive concepts, such as planning and goal monitoring (Sternberg's metacomponents), that go beyond those discussed in the preceding chapter on verbal and spatial abilities. Is this evidence that cognitive psychology is forced to acknowledge some very general cognitive processes that might provide the basis of *g*? It is certainly plausible to suppose that operations such as these are central components of successful reasoning and problem solving, but are they equally critical ingredients in the wide variety of other tasks that comprise large IQ test batteries? Where, for example, is the need for forward planning in tests of perceptual speed? The question is worth raising because, for at least one other component of IQ, there is a surprising, positive answer. In his list of six or seven primary mental abilities, Thurstone (1938) had two verbal factors, verbal comprehension and word fluency. Carroll (1993) also recognizes this second factor. Tests of fluency typically require one to generate as many words as possible beginning with the letter F, or as many boys' names or animal names as one can in a minute. Although this may seem a rather trivial skill, it turns out to be another test remarkably sensitive to damage to frontal cortex (McCarthy and Warrington, 1990). Why should this be? The problem is not that such patients cannot remember any animal names: they perform quite adequately on cued recall or picture-naming tasks. We need to recognize that the task is an unusual one (we are not normally confronted with the need to generate animal names or words beginning with a given letter), and its solution therefore requires that one devise and execute an appropriate retrieval strategy, simultaneously monitoring the items produced by such a strategy to ensure both that they are appropriate and that they are not repetitious. Frontal patients, indeed, make both types of error (Baddeley, 1997). There is, therefore, an unsuspected role to be played by a central executive working-memory system in such a task, which may serve to explain why it is a measure of IQ.

There is, then, some reason to believe that the planning and monitoring functions attributed by cognitive psychologists and neuropsychologists to a central executive may constitute the basis of g or general intelligence. And one reason why the importance of such functions became more evident when we started analysing reasoning ability or Gf is that Gf is more central to IQ than are the other factors identified by factor analysis. All this may seem both plausible and moderately encouraging. But we should also recognize that no one has yet worked out, in any precise or formal way, what these functions are and how they are implemented.

Lest we get carried away, it may also be worth concluding this chapter on a more specific, but also more sceptical, note. What is the relationship between Gf and other components of IQ? Why, for example, should there be such a marked dissociation between the effects of damage to prefrontal cortex on measures of Gf and on measures of Gc? As we have seen, frontal patients may obtain normal, or even superior, scores on tests of Gc, at the same time as severely impaired scores on tests of Gf. The intuitively obvious answer is that Gf is the ability to solve novel problems, while tests of Gc measure the fruits of past problem solving—the knowledge and skills acquired before the patient's injury or operation. That may well be correct, but we should not necessarily generalize this argument to the normal case. It may seem that it would be only a short step to accepting the general theoretical position advanced by Cattell (1971), who has argued that fluid ability or Gf represents the biological substrate of intelligence, which is then 'invested' in the particular knowledge and skills taught by a particular culture to form crystallized ability or Gc. Cattell's argument suggests a number of testable implications, but few of them have received much empirical support:

1. A measure of inborn ability should have higher heritability than one of acquired knowledge. So tests of Gf should show higher heritability than tests of Gc. Moreover, in so

far as Gf is environmentally determined, it will be affected by aspects of the physical environment such as prenatal or perinatal environment or nutrition, rather than by social circumstances or education, which will be the factors influencing Gc.

2. Tests of Gf will be 'culture fair,' since the materials used in them are either equally unfamiliar or equally familiar to all who take the tests (either the abstract patterns or diagrams of Raven's Matrices or single letters or numbers in series completion tasks). Tests of Gc are tests of culturally acquired knowledge or information (words, general knowledge) specific to that culture, and will thus discriminate unfairly against any person or group unfamiliar with the culture of the test.

3. Finally, although all aspects of intellectual functioning may decline as people grow older, Gf, as a measure of the efficiency of the brain, will start declining from a very much earlier age than Gc, which is a measure of previously acquired knowledge.

All of these implications seem rather plausible, and they are indeed widely believed to be true. But the evidence for them is decidedly unimpressive.

1. There is little or no reason to believe that the heritability of Gf is substantially higher than that of Gc. Cattell himself has estimated the heritability of Gc as 0.73 and that of Gf as 0.77—not a very impressive difference (Cattell, 1971). Horn (1985), who rejects this aspect of Cattell's theorizing, has summarized a number of other studies that yield entirely comparable estimates for the heritability of Gc and Gf, and in some cases higher heritability for Gc. For example, in one twin study (Lochlin and Nichols, 1976), the correlations between MZ twins' scores on two verbal (Gc) tests were 0.82 and 0.84, while those for DZ twins were 0.61 and 0.60. On a test of inductive reasoning (Gf), the MZ correlation was only 0.70 and the DZ correlation 0.55. The standard formula for estimating heritability from twin studies (see Chapter 2) yields a heritability of over 0.40 for Gc and of only 0.30 for Gf.

The one aspect of the theory that finds very marginal support here is that improvement in nutrition may have a greater effect on non-verbal than on verbal IQ (Chapter 4). But the data on this issue remain distinctly controversial, and 'non-verbal IQ' has usually meant Wechsler performance scales, rather than good measures of Gf, such as Raven's Matrices.

2. Although it is true that some ethnic and social groups obtain lower scores on verbal than on non-verbal IQ tests, others do not (Chapter 5). Moreover one reason for this difference is that the non-verbal tests include tests of spatial ability which are measures of Gv, not of Gf: there is, in fact, much better evidence of group differences on tests of Gv than on tests of Gf. Finally, a few years of Western education can dramatically increase scores of ethnic minorities on such paradigmatic tests of Gf as Raven's Matrices (Chapter 5)

3. Finally, although there is some evidence that performance on tests of Gf may ⟨
decline from an earlier age than performance on measures of Gc, and although ⟨..
difference has been interpreted as evidence supporting Cattell's theory (e.g. Horn and
Donaldson, 1976), both the overall magnitude of the decline in IQ with age, and the
difference between different types of test are rather less marked than earlier, cross-sectional
studies once implied (see Chapter 2).

Longitudinal data tell a more complicated, and not always consistent, story. Figure 9.7
shows some of the data of a 14-year longitudinal study of a series of age cohorts, all of
whom were given several of the Thurstone PMA tests (Schaie and Hertzog, 1983). The two
most relevant tests, the results of which are shown in Fig. 9.7, are verbal meaning and
inductive reasoning, which may be regarded as measures of Gc and Gf, respectively. Both
tests show a significant decline in performance after the age of 60, but the differences
between the tests are relatively slight. A similar picture is suggested by a later, 28-year
longitudinal study, in which Schaie (1996) found a decline of $0.87d$ on a test of verbal
meaning between the ages of 53 and 81, and one of $0.82d$ on a test of inductive reasoning.
However, in a re-analysis of yet another of Schaie's data sets, Brody (1992) found evidence
of an earlier and more pronounced decline in performance on tests of inductive reasoning
than on tests of verbal meaning.

Longitudinal studies are not without problems of their own. It is not an easy matter to
keep track of a large group of people over a period of 10–30 years, and there is every reason
to believe that those who do remain available for study are a decreasingly representative
sample of the population, who have, for example, maintained above-average health, and are
more likely to be living independent lives (Brody, 1992). It is possible, therefore, that
longitudinal studies underestimate both the overall decline in intellectual abilities with old
age, and perhaps also the difference between changes in Gc and Gf—although it is less
obvious why this last possibility should be true. It does remain true that cross-sectional
studies routinely find no differences in scores on simple vocabulary tests between groups
aged 40 and 65, accompanied by large differences in their performance on tests of reasoning
(e.g. Rabbitt, 1993).

If it were really the case that tests of Gc simply required people to retrieve previously
learned information, while tests of Gf required them to solve novel problems, it might seem
only natural to expect that advancing years should witness a much earlier and sharper
decline in Gf. But the analysis of the cognitive components of Gc in Chapter 8 provided
rather little support for one part of the premise of this argument, and the evidence from
longitudinal studies provides little support for its conclusion. One implication is then that
this must be an oversimplification of the distinction between Gf and Gc.

A second implication, however, is that the effects of ageing on intellectual skills may also
be rather more complex than is sometimes supposed. There is no question but that IQ test
scores do decline in old age, but to attribute this decline to a decrease in the efficiency of the

brain is hardly illuminating. It seems at least as plausible to suppose that there might be a variety of different causes. One fairly obvious possibility is that changes in IQ are related to changes in mental speed (Salthouse, 1991). It is certainly true that older people have slower reaction times than younger people on almost any kind of task (Rabbitt, 1993), and equally clear that this translates into poorer performance on tests of perceptual speed (Schaie, 1996). But the claim that speed of information processing is the central psychological process underlying *g* or Gf is not well supported by the evidence (Chapter 7), and it is clear that these changes in speed are not sufficient to explain the decline in performance on tests of Gf. Salthouse (1993) has argued that one of the major difficulties that older people have with solving reasoning problems is a limitation on working memory—for example, in the ability to hold the results of one operation or calculation in mind while performing the next one needed to solve the problem. There is certainly no question but that older people perform poorly on tests of retrieval from short-term memory (Craik and Jennings, 1992).

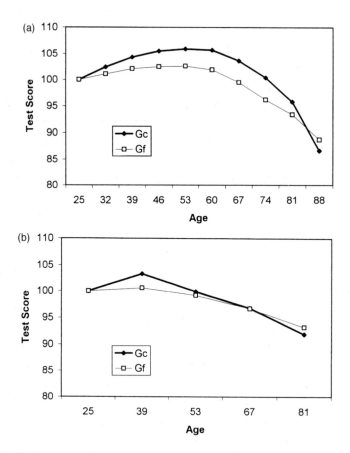

Fig. 9.7 Longitudinal data from the Seattle Longitudinal Study illustrating the change in scores on tests of Gc and Gf as people grow older ((a) from Schaie and Hertzog, 1983; (b) from Schaie, 1996).

Rabbitt (1993) obtained scores on Cattell's culture-fair test, a measure of Gf, as well as measures of performance on two tests of perceptual speed and two tests of immediate memory, from a large group of people ranging in age from 50 to 86. Factor analysis of these test results yielded distinct speed and memory factors, but age, which did of course correlate with Gf, was actually more strongly associated with the memory factor than with the speed factor. As we saw in Chapter 8, the efficiency of working memory seems just as important for measures of Gc (or Gv) as it is for Gf. Once again, then, there is little reason to accept the proposition that tests of Gf are measuring innate ability and tests of Gc only acquired knowledge or achievement.

Summary

Typical tests of non-verbal reasoning, Gf or fluid intelligence, are Raven's Matrices, Cattell's 'culture-fair' tests, or letter-series problems. These are all tests of analogical or inductive reasoning, rather than of deductive reasoning.

Attempts to understand the cognitive operations underlying performance on such tests have focused on psychological analyses of the nature of the problems they present, at least as much as on the search for correlates of performance on them. Thus componential analyses of analogical reasoning or Raven's Matrices have proposed that solving such problems requires such operations as coding of the items, and searching for the rules that describe the transformation of one item into another. A very simple componential model of analogical reasoning, although undoubtedly specifying many of the operations that must be performed in order to solve analogies, failed to acknowledge the interdependence of the various components. Thus coding of the relevant attributes of each term of an analogy will almost certainly be influenced by the detection of the relationships between the various terms—since those relationships define the relevant attributes. And failure to detect a relationship that will solve the analogy may suggest that one's initial coding was incorrect.

This interdependence of different components becomes more evident with more difficult problems such as those in Raven's Advanced Matrices. And the number of steps that must be worked through and combined in order to solve Raven's problems immediately suggests that one factor limiting performance on such tasks is the efficiency of working memory. Performance on simple working-memory tasks does indeed correlate well with performance on tests of Gf, and working memory is equally clearly implicated in deductive reasoning. But whether working memory can be fractionated into yet more component parts than the distinction between verbal and spatial memory seen in Chapter 8, remains unanswered.

When the solution to a reasoning problem requires a large number of steps, it seems plausible to suppose that 'metacomponents' of planning and goal monitoring enter into the picture. And performance on Raven's Matrices does correlate strongly with performance on at least one superficially very different task, the Tower of Hanoi problem, that also requires forward planning. Cognitive psychologists have invoked concepts such as a 'central executive' or 'supervisory attentional system' that perform such functions. And neuropsychologists have shown convincingly that damage to prefrontal cortex can seriously impair planning and executive control. Damage to prefrontal cortex also impairs performance on tests of Gf. But whether the central executive is the psychological basis of *g*—or whether it only seems so because it remains an ill-specified concept, also remains unanswered.

10 *Theories of intelligence*

Introduction

The data and theories reviewed in the last four chapters have begun to provide some tentative answers to one important question: what are the cognitive processes responsible for differences in IQ test performance? Factor analysis and experimental analysis agreed in suggesting that different types of IQ test, verbal, reasoning, spatial, perceptual speed, etc., tap at least some different processes. Factor analysis raised the possibility that, underlying these differences between various kinds of test, there might also be some process or processes common to all. All that can be said is that, to date, experimental analysis has failed to identify any such common process, at least with any degree of rigour or precision, and that it may be safer to assume that IQ tests measure a wide range of different cognitive processes, with only partial overlap between those measured by different types of test.

Some readers may still feel disappointed, perhaps even cheated, by these answers. The questions they really wanted answered were different. What is human intelligence? Do IQ tests really measure it? Even if they capture some limited aspects of intelligence, do they not miss out on many other, equally important aspects? One might have thought that the most appropriate way to answer these questions would be to engage in the sort of theoretical and experimental analysis reviewed in these last chapters. To the extent that successful performance on certain types of IQ test requires planning, goal monitoring, holding information in working memory, etc., it does not seem unreasonable to claim that such tests measure at least some of the important cognitive operations that underlie intelligent behaviour. But the IQ tester's traditional answers to these questions have been quite different. We reviewed them in Chapter 2: validity studies, so it is claimed, have established that IQ tests really do measure intelligence, because they predict a variety of other indices of intelligence, such as educational and occupational attainment. But is that response really sufficient? At best it seems banal; at worst, it misses the point. The observation of a correlation (of the order of 0.35) between US army recruits' IQ scores and their proficiency at making jelly rolls (Jensen, 1980) is hardly going to satisfy the critic who wonders about the nature of human intelligence and whether all its multifarious aspects can be summed up in a single IQ score.

It is worth reminding ourselves of a point made in Chapter 2: validity studies, which look for evidence that IQ scores correlate with other indices of intelligence, can never be of more than limited value. The fact is that we do not possess any perfect, independent criterion of intelligence, partly because we do not have any agreed definition of the nature of intelligence. There is no point, therefore, in insisting that IQ tests must correlate with something that does not exist. And it is equally pointless for the critic to insist that because the correlation between IQ and income or other measures of job performance is no more than 0.20–0.35 or so, IQ tests are clearly failing to measure all we mean by intelligence. An equally plausible interpretation of such modest correlations is that the reason why some people earn more, or are better at certain jobs than others, is not because they are more intelligent, but because they are more conscientious, industrious, ambitious, or glib (take your pick). As Chomsky has noted:

> One might speculate, rather plausibly, that wealth and power tend to accrue to those who are ruthless, cunning, avaricious, self seeking, lacking in sympathy and compassion, subservient to authority and willing to abandon principle for material gain, and so on. (Chomsky, 1972, p. 38)

The question whether IQ tests really measure intelligence is, of course, as much a question about the nature of intelligence as one about the nature of IQ tests. This chapter, therefore, is about theories of intelligence in this broader sense. We may as well acknowledge at the outset that different theorists have different implicit definitions of intelligence, and that these disagreements are not going to disappear overnight. Thus a writer such as Gardner (1993) uses the term to refer to competence in a variety of fields of human endeavour, many of which fairly clearly lie outside the scope of anything measured by an IQ test. Similarly, McClelland has repeatedly criticized IQ tests for their failure to predict real competence in such walks of life as business management (McClelland, 1973; see also Klemp and McClelland, 1986, discussed below). But these are grounds for criticizing IQ tests only if you accept one or other of two assumptions: either that the proper function of the tests is not to measure 'intelligence', whatever that may be, but rather to predict who will, and who will not, be successful in any walk of life; or that 'intelligence' is simply synonymous with every possible competence in every walk of life. Both these assumptions seem, at the least, open to question.

Many people would probably accept that if certain kinds of achievement depend on motivation, personality, or simple good fortune, it is hardly the function of a measure of intelligence to predict that achievement. The disagreement tends to become more heated when the processes responsible for the achievement turn out to be, in some sense of that term, cognitive in nature. But even then, one could argue, if these processes are indeed independent of IQ, the discovery of this fact is more profitably viewed as a scientific advance, rather than seen as another stick with which to beat IQ tests. We shall have advanced our understanding of the architecture of human cognition by discovering that there are several different sets of processes responsible for different kinds of achievement. In other words, the discovery of what IQ tests do not measure may well be even more instructive than the discovery of yet another modest correlate of IQ.

Let us start then, where we left off in Chapter 2, by considering how well IQ tests predict various kinds of achievement outside the psychologist's laboratory. I shall start with the issue of educational attainment because, although there can be no serious doubt that such attainment is moderately well predicted by the results of an IQ test, the interpretation of that prediction remains a matter of some dispute. Many psychometricians' implicit assumption has often been that IQ tests measure the underlying intellectual ability that is responsible for success at school, as well as for a wide variety of other practical achievements. But that assumption needs to be questioned.

Ability and achievement

IQ v. educational achievement

The correlation between IQ test scores and a number of different indices of educational attainment ranges from 0.40 to 0.70, and since IQ scores at one age predict educational attainment at a later age, it has been frequently assumed that this means that the ability measured by an IQ test is responsible for, or becomes manifest in, these measures of educational achievement (see Chapter 2). From which it is but a short step to arguing that we should draw a sharp distinction between inborn, native endowment and the knowledge and attainments acquired more or less successfully at school.

This distinction is, of course, enshrined in our everyday language and in our everyday assumptions about human psychology. But that is no guarantee of its reality. And even if it is a real distinction, the IQ tester's argument goes one step further—claiming that IQ tests measure this inborn ability while tests of educational attainment are measures of acquired knowledge. That is an even stronger claim, for which there is little evidence. The distinction between tests of attainment, aptitude, and ability is at best a blurred one (Anastasi, 1988). All any test can do is to measure a sample of a person's behaviour at a given point in time; regardless of the name of the test, that behaviour will reflect past learning, family background, and genetic endowment; it will also predict future behaviour. Even if we think we can draw a conceptual distinction between ability and attainment, it does not follow that we have tests that uniquely measure one of these to the exclusion of the other.

There is, of course, a distinction between what is directly taught in school—reading, writing, or (once upon a time) multiplication tables,—and what (some) children may learn while at school. But even this distinction is far less cut and dried than some have supposed. Schools aim to teach children to read, but children also learn to read by reading—whether at home or at school. At best, there may be a continuum of abilities or skills, some of which are relatively directly taught at school (reading, mathematics), while the ingredients of others are acquired with relatively little explicit instruction. By and large, schools do not explicitly teach children how to solve Raven's Matrices. But as we have seen, exposure to Western schooling has a major impact on children's scores on such a test (Chapters 4 and 5).

There is, of course, one obvious implication of the traditional IQ tester's assumptions: measures of educational attainment should have substantially lower heritability than IQ, but conversely should show a greater influence of family environment. Although both Eysenck (1979) and Jensen (1981) have claimed that this expectation is confirmed, that conclusion depends on a distinctly partial reading of the evidence. In fact, a large number of studies, whether they are of twins or of adopted children, have flatly contradicted it. At best, there are only marginal differences in the direction expected by the traditional assumption.

Twin studies compare the resemblance of MZ and DZ twins; a simple and crude estimate of the heritability of any trait is given by doubling the difference between MZ and DZ correlations; while the role of family environment is estimated as the difference between the heritability and the MZ correlation (see Chapter 3). For present purposes, it hardly matters whether the estimates so provided are reasonable or not; there are no obvious grounds for supposing that they are any less reasonable for educational attainment than for IQ. Table 10.1 summarizes the results of a number of surveys and twin studies. There are, unfortunately, rather few that simultaneously provide correlations for both IQ and attainment, but the large number of studies involved at least suggests that the values reported here for the various correlations cannot be far out, and their results are fully consistent with those studies that have provided direct comparisons. Table 10.1 also calculates the estimates of heritability and of shared and unique environments implied by these correlations. The main impression left by these numbers is surely that IQ and attainment have roughly similar heritability. There is, of course, more variability in the attainment data, but that is largely explained by the fact that the IQ data in the table are largely the averaged results of a large number of individual studies, while much of the educational data comes from individual studies. There are, indeed, a few cases where the heritability of attainment seems lower than that of IQ—but it is not difficult to find individual twin studies of IQ that give low heritability estimates (see Bouchard and McGue, 1981). Interestingly enough, where there are discrepancies between IQ and attainment they are to be found in the estimates of the contribution of unique environmental effects as much as in heritability or common environment.

The implication of these twin studies is that family environment exerts no greater an effect on attainment than on IQ. To a great extent, this is confirmed by the results of two of the American adoption studies reviewed in Chapters 3 and 4. For example, if family environment were more important for attainment than for IQ, then unrelated children living in the same adoptive family should resemble one another in attainment more than in IQ. The results, shown in Table 10.2, provide little evidence of this. It is not only IQ scores that show higher correlations between biologically related people than between members of

Table 10.1 MZ amd DZ correlations for IQ and educational achievement and resulting estimates of genetic and environmental effects

Study and measures	Correlations		Parameter estimates		
	MZ	DZ	G	CE	SE
(a) Loehlin and Nichols (1976)					
IQ	0.82	0.59	0.46	0.36	0.18
Achievement					
Language	0.81	0.58	0.46	0.35	0.19
Maths	0.78	0.59	0.38	0.40	0.22
Social Science	0.85	0.61	0.48	0.37	0.15
Natural Science	0.79	0.64	0.30	0.49	0.21
(b) Thompson *et al.* (1993)					
IQ	–	–	0.43	0.44	0.13
Achievement	–	–	0.53	0.37	0.10
(c) Bouchard and McGue (1981)					
IQ	0.86	0.60	0.52	0.34	0.14
(d) Husén (1959)					
Achievement					
Reading	0.72	0.57	0.30	0.42	0.28
Maths	0.81	0.48	0.66	0.15	0.19
(e) Husén (1960)					
Achievement					
Reading	0.89	0.62	0.54	0.35	0.11
Maths	0.87	0.52	0.70	0.17	0.13

G, CE, SE: estimates of heritability, common family environment, and unique environmental effects.

Table 10.2 Correlations for IQ and educational achievement between biological siblings and between unrelated children living in the same adoptive home

	Minnesota study (from Scarr and Weinberg, 1983)		Texas study (from Willerman *et al.* 1997)
	Biological siblings	Unrelated children	Unrelated children
IQ	0.35	−0.03	0.29
Achievement			
Reading	0.27	0.11	0.04
Maths	0.35	−0.11	0.09

adoptive families: much the same difference is found in the correlations for educational attainment.

The implication, that measures of educational attainment are hardly less heritable than are IQ scores, is both important and, surely, rather surprising. Whether or not we can draw a conceptual distinction between innate ability and acquired knowledge, it does not look as if anyone has yet devised a test which measures one or the other but not both. But the results of some of these studies have gone one step further along the road of diminishing the distinction between ability and attainment. For example, Thompson *et al.* (1991) observed that not only did MZ twins resemble one another in IQ more closely than DZ twins, they also showed higher correlations between IQ and attainment. The implication is that the relationship between IQ and attainment is itself, in part, genetically determined.

Eminence and genius

Chapter 2 reviewed traditional studies documenting some modest to moderate correlations between people's IQ scores and their occupational status and the proficiency they displayed in their job. One suggestive result from these studies was that IQ is more important in some jobs than others; the efficiency of a farm labourer may not be much affected by his IQ, but that of a business manager, accountant, or lawyer is. But does this relationship continue to hold at the very highest level? Is the difference between a good doctor or research scientist and a truly excellent one predicted by their IQ scores? If eminence and genius, as Galton supposed, are reflections of superior intelligence, is this superiority captured by an IQ score?

No one has supposed that genius is simply a matter of having an unusually high IQ score, but many writers have thought it probably important (surprisingly enough, even Gardner, 1997, accepts this), and some, such as Eysenck (1995), have argued that a high IQ is a necessary precondition of genius. How, one is inclined to wonder, could anyone know that? The study of genius poses an obvious problem. If we confine ourselves to those universally accepted as a genius, we shall end up with a rather small number of mostly historical figures—Julius Caesar, Leonardo, Newton, Dickens, Wagner (and so on). And how shall we decide whether they were intelligent—let alone would have obtained a high IQ score? If we want a larger, contemporary sample, we can select on the basis of success, distinction, and eminence—but these are hardly the same as genius.

There has been one heroic attempt to assign an IQ score to a large, historical group of geniuses (Cox, 1926). Cox selected some 300 men and women, living between 1450 and 1850, whose achievements, on the basis of the length of their entry in standard dictionaries of biography, could fairly be described as exceptional (royalty and aristocracy were expressly excluded). She attempted to assess their level of intelligence by examining such biographical information as she could obtain. Although she acknowledged that this was far from perfect and excluded a further 11 possible subjects (among them Rabelais and

Shakespeare) for lack of evidence, this did not stop her assigning two IQ scores (one, AI, when they were still young—age 17 or less; one, AII, as adults), and giving numerical estimates of the reliability of these scores.

There are, no doubt, some cases where sufficiently detailed information of a sufficient range of accomplishments is available that we can be confident that this person was pretty intelligent. Thus John Stuart Mill started learning Greek at the age of 3, was reading Plato when he was 7, having completed a history of Rome the year before, and started mathematics, physics, and chemistry the following year. Cox assessed his adolescent IQ at 190, with a reliability of 0.82. But for many of her subjects, Cox had no evidence worthy of the name. The main part of her biographical entry for Mozart, up to the age of 17, is given in Box 10.1.

Cox's assessment of Mozart's adolescent IQ was 150, with a reliability of 0.75. This will not do. To point to Mozart's extraordinary musical talent as evidence of his general intelligence is to beg the question. We already knew he was a musical genius. What we want to know is whether genius in one particular field of human endeavour necessarily depends on a high level of general intelligence, and whether that high level of intelligence would be reflected in a high IQ score. That Cox is willing to assess Mozart's IQ at 150 on the basis of the evidence shown in Box 10.1 can only cast doubt on the rest of her endeavour. Mozart may indeed have been very intelligent. Despite Peter Shaffer's portrayal of him in *Amadeus* as a scatological buffoon, one authority has characterized him as 'one of the most penetrating intellects of his age' (Till, 1992, p. xi). I have to say that a reading of Till's book did not convince me that he had provided any convincing evidence for this claim. But even if he were right, that would still not tell us whether Mozart would have obtained a high IQ score, and that is the critical point at issue. This must be equally true for any historical figure. Jane Austen and George Eliot were surely, in their very different ways, both unusually intelligent women. But we have no reasoned grounds for assigning them a specific IQ score. We must necessarily return to the contemporary scene, and settle for what we can discover about the relationship between IQ and more modest degrees of eminence or distinction. Two approaches to this question can be contrasted, one which selects people by IQ and then looks at evidence of their achievements, the other which takes the accomplishments first and then looks at IQ.

The most celebrated example of the former type of study is Terman's optimistically entitled 'Genetic study of genius'. Whatever its defects, and they are many, this massive longitudinal study had the virtue of trying to obtain a broad picture of the accomplishments of a group of individuals with high IQ scores. In a real sense, Terman set out to test Galton's hypothesis that intelligence is an essential ingredient of general eminence.

The study was initiated in 1921. Relying on teachers in various Californian schools to nominate the brightest children in their classes, Terman gave them a series of IQ tests that resulted in a selected group of some 1500 children, with an average age of 11, and an average IQ of 151 (virtually all with an IQ over 140). Terman belatedly acknowledged that relying on teachers to provide an initial screening was an unfortunate mistake: given

Box 10.1 Wolfgang Amadeus Mozart (1756–1791), a celebrated Austrian composer; AI IQ 150, AII IQ 155

I. Family standing

The Mozart family belonged originally to the artisan class. The grandfather was a bookbinder. The father, determined to rise out of the rank of his ancestors, studied law and also music; he became orchestral director in Salzburg and was the author of many musical compositions as well as a standard work on violin playing. The mother, a daughter of the steward of the convent of St. Gilgen, was a good woman, but in no way distinguished.

II. Development to age 17

1. Interests. From before his sixth year, Mozart's sole absorbing interest was in music, and even the games he played had some musical element. Whatever he did was done wholeheartedly, but apparently he had few interests unrelated to music, so absorbing was his art. Age of the age of 10, however, he constructed mentally an imaginary kingdom of children in which he was king. He had a map of it drawn by a servant, according to specifications which he drew up. At about the same time, he planned to compose an opera to be presented by the children of Salzburg. At the age of 11 he became skilful in card games and a good fencer. Before he was 16, he had felt the pleasures and pains of a first love.

2. Education. When Mozart was between 3 and 4, he was taught by his father to play the clavier; he learned minuets and other pieces, which he soon played 'with perfect correctness' and in exact time. At the age of 7 he began to receive instruction in singing by an Italian master, and at 14 he was studying and executing the most difficult counterpoint. Meanwhile his general education was not neglected. He studied arithmetic at the usual age, and evidences of a smattering of Latin appear in letters written at 13, while the correspondence of the following years shows that he had picked up some Italian in the course of his travels.

3. School standing and progress. (No specific record.)

4. Friends and associates. Mozart's associates were the musicians and the courtiers of Europe. Everyone like the agreeable and talented little fellow and made much of him. His sister was his comrade and confidante.

5. Reading. Mozart mentions reading the *Arabian Nights* in Italian when he was 14.

6. Production and achievement. At the age of 5 Mozart first felt the impulse to produce, and the little pieces he composed were written down by his father. Three works are recorded before the age of 6: a Minuet and Trio for Clavier (Op. 1), a Minuet (Op. 2), and an Allegro (Op. 3). These are not particularly original, but they exhibit the rounded simple melody always characteristic of their composer.

[There follows a further page of the young Mozart's musical accomplishments.]

plausible assumptions about the relative bias of teachers' assessments and IQ tests in favour of middle-class children, this procedure almost certainly resulted in the exclusion of a number of lower-class children with equally high test scores.

The main purpose of the study was to follow the later careers of these children: two final reports (Terman and Oden, 1959; Oden, 1968) give a detailed account of their adult accomplishments. Table 10.3 summarizes some of them. Although they do not include any Nobel prizes, by any reckoning they are impressive, and most commentators have been impressed:

> This single study remains the most convincing demonstration of how astonishingly well the one much criticised variable, measured intelligence, can predict level of achievement for decades. (Butcher, 1968, p. 270)

> It is very doubtful that the attempt to select children scoring in the top 1% of any other characteristic would be as predictive of future accomplishment. (Brody and Brody, 1976, p. 109)

But is it so doubtful? What reason do we have for believing that it was the children's IQ scores, rather than some other characteristics correlated with IQ, that predicted their later success? As several critics have noted (McClelland, 1973; Ceci, 1990), the vast majority of the children came from middle-class professional families (and those who did not were, as we shall see, significantly less successful). The fact that some 80–90 per cent of them (men and women) went to college, compared to less than 20 per cent of the population of California as a whole at that time, is neither here nor there. The proper comparison must be with a group of children from similar backgrounds. Given the large average difference between the IQ scores of members of the same family, the ideal control group would have been their brothers and sisters of lower IQ. Terman eventually recognized that a comparison with the general population was not particularly appropriate, and from 1947 on Terman and Oden compared their group of men with all college-educated men for such indices as income.

But the value of Terman's study does not lie in its demonstration (or failure to demonstrate) that a high IQ will guarantee riches—although in fact his sample did earn somewhat more than other college-educated men. What it may tell us is whether high IQ is

Table 10.3 Achievements of Terman's 700 men (from Oden, 1968)

Percentage in professional and managerial jobs	86.4%
Median income	$13 464
Members of National Academy of Science or American Philosophical Society	5
Appearing in *American men of science*	81
Appearing in *Dictionary of American scholars*	10
Appearing in American *Who's who*	46
Number of published books/monographs	200
Number of articles/papers	2500
Number of patents	350

associated with other more notable accomplishments than simply earning a lot of money. Certainly, Table 10.3 lists some impressive achievements. And it is not difficult to show that they cannot easily be attributed to family background alone. For example, in 1959, 70 men (10 per cent of the total) had entries in *American men of science*. Even the most generous estimates suggest that no more than 0.1 per cent of American men of comparable age appeared in this volume. In other words, Terman's men were 100 times as likely as the general population to achieve this distinction. Although their family backgrounds were above average, they were certainly not confined to the top 1 per cent.

Terman's study is undoubtedly consistent with the notion that a high IQ is associated with a broad range of accomplishments. But taken alone, it can be no more than suggestive. What is needed is the complementary approach: take more or less successful people—perhaps more or less eminent members of a particular profession, and see whether these differences in eminence or success are associated with differences in IQ. In fact, Terman's own study provides just this information. Terman and Oden (1947, 1959) divided their 700 or so men into the 150 most successful (called Group A) and the 150 least successful (Group C). The differences in various standard indicators of success were indeed substantial: for example, 90 per cent of Group A, but less than 40 per cent of Group C, had graduated from college; in 1940, 99 per cent of Group A were in professional or managerial jobs, compared to less than 20 per cent of Group C, and their income was over twice as high. Although there had been a difference in their initial IQ scores, the difference was small—a mean Stanford–Binet IQ of 155 for Group A and of 150 for Group C. The most notable difference was in their family backgrounds: 50 per cent of the A-group fathers had a college degree and in 1922, at the outset of the study, 38 per cent had professional jobs; the comparable figures for C-group fathers were 15 per cent and 18 per cent. The rather strong implication is that differences in family background had a greater impact on differences in Terman's subjects' achievements than did differences in their childhood IQ scores.

Two other studies have found equally little evidence that differences in achievement among groups of professionals are associated with differences in their IQ scores. Roe (1953) found no relationship between IQ and a variety of measures of eminence or success in a group of successful scientists. Similarly, MacKinnon (1962) found only a trivially small correlation of 0.11 between IQ and success (estimated by other experts) in a group of 185 successful architects. In one sense, perhaps, these negative results are hardly surprising. We are dealing here with highly selected people, *all* of whom are relatively successful and all of whom have relatively high IQs. None of the subjects in these two studies had an IQ below 105, and the average IQ of the two groups was about 130. But remember the proposition we are seeking to test: if above-average IQ is associated with above-average success, does it also follow that a *very* high IQ is associated with exceptional success? Although Terman's study has led some IQ testers to believe that the answer to this question is yes, that may be an optimistic reading of the evidence as a whole.

There is one plausible, but widely ignored, explanation for this, namely that, above a certain level, IQ scores simply cease to be reliable or valid. A precocious 8-year-old can obtain a high IQ on a standard test by scoring at the level of the average 12- or 14-year-old. But this does not apply for adults. The maximum score obtainable on the WAIS is an IQ of 150, and the difference between an IQ of 150 and one of 140 is a matter of a very small additional number of correct items (some carrying bonuses for speed). Where special tests have been constructed for groups of supposedly above-average intelligence, the construction of items is usually based on further extrapolation from already difficult items in existing tests. Here one can reasonably question the validity of the new test: by what criterion is one justified in concluding that such extrapolation poses sensible questions that succeed in measuring differences in the same sets of skills as are measured by normal tests? The answer is by no means obvious. For example, verbal IQ can be measured by a vocabulary test: you will obtain a high IQ score if you know the meaning of relatively obscure words, such as lapidary or ordnance. Does it follow that you are even more intelligent if you know that a killergang is something that crushes paper-pulp? Perhaps you just have a fund of esoteric and useless knowledge (or work in a paper mill). Just as there are not enough generally accepted geniuses in the world to undertake a proper study of intelligence and genius, so it has proved difficult to find enough people of very high intelligence to permit the standardization and validation of tests measuring IQ above 140.

Other predictors of occupational success

There may be good reason to question whether exceptional achievement is associated with exceptional IQ. But over the entire, normal range, there is no doubt that there is a significant, albeit modest, correlation between IQ and occupational success, typically in the range 0.15–0.35. As I have already suggested, one reason why these correlations are not higher is because personality and motivation are important determinants of such success, in addition to intelligence (Kline, 1993). The questions remains whether IQ scores capture all, or even most, of the relevant *cognitive* determinants.

There is by now quite good evidence that they do not. For example, according to Streufert and his colleagues, the mark of the really successful business manager or executive is 'cognitive complexity' (Streufert and Streufert, 1978; Streufert and Swezey, 1986). The two main ingredients of cognitive complexity are:

> differentiation (the number of dimensions that are relevant to an information processing effort), and *integration* (the relationships among these dimensions). [Cognitively complex managers] tend to hold more multiply determined (and consequently often more moderated) attitudes than do less complex individuals; they are more open to disconfirming information and tend to adjust their thinking accordingly. They engage in more effective information search. They tend to perceive co-workers, as well as opponents, more accurately and are effective in discerning those

persons' intents and strategies; they inter-relate decisions better, develop more appropriate strategies and are typically more flexible in their consideration of distant goals. They do not over- or under-plan. Their strategy development tends to proceed in step-wise fashion and they are open to feedback. In general, they are more effective managers. (Streufert and Swezey, 1986, p. 220)

In what they termed 'job competence assessment', Klemp and McClelland (1986) identified a number of outstanding managers in a variety of businesses ranging from industry, financial services, voluntary organizations, military hospitals, and colleges. To be classified as outstanding, the managers had to be nominated as such both by their peers and by senior executives, and to satisfy certain relatively objective criteria. They were then compared with 'average' performers who were nominated by no one and who failed to satisfy the performance criteria. Klemp and McClelland then conducted structured interviews focusing on a few 'key situations', and scored the transcripts of these interviews for the presence of various characteristics or 'competencies'. Many of these were concerned with motivation, personality, and social skills, but many were not. The 'intellectual competencies' identified as distinguishing outstanding from average managers in most, if not all, of the organizations studied are listed in Table 10.4.

Although presenting no details, Klemp and McClelland (1986) claim that scores on standard ability tests 'tend to be uncorrelated' both with actual proficiency in managerial jobs and with performance on simulated business problems used as part of their assessment programme. This may at first sight seem rather puzzling, for some of the skills listed in Table 10.4 bear more than a passing resemblance to some of the skills tested in standard IQ tests. The ability to see implications, consequences, and alternatives, to identify patterns or interpret a sequence of events, are all surely part of what is involved in solving the sort of deductive or inductive reasoning problems that measure Gf. Why then is there so little

Table 10.4 The intellectual competences of successful managers (from Klemp and McClelland, 1986)

Label	Indicators
Planning	Sees implications, consequences, alternatives or if-then relationships Analyses causal relationships Makes strategies, plans steps to reach a goal
Diagnostic information seeking	Pushes for concrete information in an ambiguous sitaution Uses questions to identify the specifics of a problem or other situation
Conceptualization/synthetic thinking	Understands how different parts, needs, or functions of the organization fit together Identifies patterns, interprets a series of events Identifies the most important issues in a complex situation Uses unusual analogies to understand or explain the essence of a situation

connection between the two types of problem? According to Klemp and McClelland, one critical difference is that items in IQ tests set well-defined problems: all the information necessary for solution is given, and there is only one permitted solution. But

> in real life problems are rarely so clear-cut: before figuring out a solution, one must first figure out the problem. Only then can one know what kind of information to seek out (it is not given) in order to solve it—and then choose a solution, usually from among several possible solutions. The process bears little relationship to the controlled one of an intelligence test . . . The major differences between outstanding and average managers in intellectual competence are that the former spend more time on the job exercising these capabilities than the latter and employ a greater repertoire of mental responses in doing so. In short, what we discovered is that the difference between capacity to act and disposition to act forms the distinction between average and outstanding senior managerial performance. (Klemp and McClelland, 1986, p. 31 and p. 48)

The charge that IQ tests set problems that are too cut and dried to find any parallel in the real world is not, of course, a new one: it is reminiscent of Neisser's argument that IQ tests measure academic not general intelligence (Neisser, 1976). And the contrast between being presented with a clearly defined puzzle plus six possible solutions to choose from, and the process of figuring out what the problem is in the first place so that one can then search for relevant information, is reminiscent of the distinction between solving analogies or series completion tasks in an IQ test and seeing that there is an analogy between two apparently disparate situations, so that one can use the known solution to one problem to suggest an analogous solution to the other. Recall that, when presented with Duncker's radiation problem, no more than a third of students saw that the story of a general dividing up his army to storm a fortress suggested an analogous solution (Gick and Holyoak, 1980, 1983). As soon as they were given a hint that the story of the general might be relevant, the majority, but still by no means all, now saw the connection. It is clear that people differ in their ability to see, and make use of, such analogies. Presumably these differences are also found outside the psychological laboratory. But it is at least open to question whether they are measured by standard IQ tests.

Can we get any further handle on what it is that IQ tests are failing to measure? A possible clue is provided by Roe's observation that the one feature distinguishing all the eminent scientists she studied was their enthusiasm for their work, which ensured that they spent a very high proportion of their time actively engaged in it (Roe, 1953). Perhaps the old saying about the relative importance of perspiration and inspiration in the creation of genius also contains a grain of truth. While this may sound simply like another motivational factor, it also suggests a quite different possibility—that those who are successful in any field of human endeavour are those who have learned a great deal about it.

General intelligence or domain-specific expertise?

Expertise at work: practical intelligence and tacit knowledge

That practice makes perfect, or at least improves things, is a familiar enough proposition. And no one would doubt it, when applied to most sports, the playing of a musical instrument, ballet dancing, or conjuring tricks. These are all activities where prolonged practice may be essential if you are ever to become seriously proficient. But it has not seemed so obvious that, in a more modest way, a similar truth may apply over a much wider range of activities: what distinguishes the more from the less successful in almost any sphere may be a difference in the amount of knowledge and expertise acquired about that activity. Successful businessmen simply know more about their business than less successful ones. Eminent architects spend more time thinking and reading about architecture. In any profession or occupation, success comes to those who find their work so absorbing that they devote most of their waking hours, at the expense of much else in their lives, to it. The expertise thus acquired is more important than an IQ test score. And this may be equally true for more mundane jobs (Box 10.2).

Is it possible to characterize more precisely the nature of this expertise? Following Neisser (1976) and Klemp and McClelland (1986), Sternberg *et al.* (1995) have drawn a distinction between academic and practical intelligence. We may use academic intelligence to solve problems that appear in IQ tests or the classroom, but we need practical intelligence to solve the everyday problems that arise in our work. In contrast to the cut and dried puzzles that characterize items in an IQ test,

> work problems often are (a) unformulated or in need of reformulation, (b) of personal interest, (c) lacking in information necessary for solution, (d) related to everyday experience, (e) poorly defined, (f) characterized by multiple 'correct' solutions, each with liabilities as well as assets, and (g) characterized by multiple methods for picking a problem solution (Sternberg *et al.* 1995, p. 913).

The solution of this type of problem requires practical intelligence, which depends on gradually acquired 'tacit knowledge' of the job. It is tacit knowledge that underlies expertise. The main defining characteristics of tacit knowledge are that it is procedural rather than declarative, informal and implicit rather than formal and explicit, and usually acquired without formal, explicit instruction. Tacit knowledge is reflected in your knowing what to do in a given situation (it is procedural knowledge), and getting on and doing it, without necessarily being able to articulate why you are doing it (i.e. without declarative knowledge), and without your having been explicitly instructed or taught what to do.

Are practical intelligence and tacit knowledge valid constructs? Sternberg and his colleagues (see also Wagner and Sternberg, 1986) have used various procedures, ranging from job analysis to interviews with acknowledged experts and others successful in their

Box 10.2 Making light work of shifting the milk

The traditional psychometrician's view is that the higher the status of the job, the greater the intellectual demands it makes: that is why you supposedly need an IQ over 100 to be a lawyer or accountant. An alternative view is that the more menial and boring the job, the more important it becomes to use your intelligence to cut corners and make your life easier. Skilled and experienced workers show considerable ingenuity in this. Thus Scribner (1986) describes a study of workers in a dairy in Baltimore. The job of an assembler was to respond to orders from drivers, for example, for:

10 quarts of wholemilk, 6 pints of skimmed milk, 4 pints of buttermilk

Analysis of their performance showed a striking economy of effort that invariably allowed the assemblers to fill each order with the least possible number of moves, given the materials at hand. The first part of this order, for 10 quarts of wholemilk, might be satisfied either by adding 4 to an already partially filled case of 6 or subtracting 2 from a case containing 12. If a case already contained 12 quarts of wholemilk and 4 pints of skimmed, the complete order would be filled by removing 2 quarts of wholemilk, adding 2 pints of skimmed and 4 of buttermilk. Newcomers, by contrast, responded literally to their instructions, and starting with an empty case would fill it up in the sequence specified by those instructions. Uninstructed practice was quite sufficient to turn a novice into a similarly skilled operator, but when better-educated, and presumably more intelligent, supervisors tried their hands at the job for the first time, they, too, were no better than novices.

It is equally important to use short cuts to reduce the need for mental effort. Scribner describes how the drivers solved problems calling for mental arithmetic. Their job included pricing their orders, but rather than operate with the company price list which gave prices per quart or per pint, skilled drivers simplified the problem by recasting it, where appropriate, as price per case. Thus if asked to work out the cost of 31 pints of chocolate milk at 42 cents a pint, they would not multiply 31×42, but calculated as follows: 1 case of chocolate milk, which contains 32 pints, costs $31.44 per case, minus 1 pint at 42 cents comes to $31.02. But given a paper-and-pencil arithmetic test, drivers whose accuracy on the job was well nigh perfect made numerous errors, even though the problems were formally identical.

chosen career, to generate a number of problem situations that might arise in any particular job or profession, along with an expert consensus on the most appropriate solutions to these problems. They then gave the problems to various groups of subjects, and scored their answers in terms of how well they agreed with the expert answers. In a number of studies, and with jobs ranging from business manager, through sales to academic psychology, they found that job experience and status predicted how closely subjects' solutions agreed with the experts'. For example, business managers produced 'better' solutions than business graduate students, who in turn produced better solutions than ordinary undergraduates, to problems of business management, and the same pattern of differences in solutions to problems of academic psychology was found between university professors of psychology, psychology graduate students, and undergraduates.

A carping critic might claim to be unsurprised by these findings. What would be surprising, one might argue, would be to find that business managers did *not* know more about business management than an undergraduate who has never worked in business. And there may be a certain element of circularity in these studies: it does not seem very surprising that the higher one's status in a given profession the more closely one's answers to the sorts of questions being posed will agree with those given by people of even higher status (the experts). But three further observations serve both to answer such criticism and to suggest that the concept of tacit knowledge is valid in its own right (Sternberg *et al.*, 1995). First, measures of tacit knowledge correlate not only with amount of experience in a given occupation, but also with various measures of competence and success. In one study, for example, business managers who were all participants in the same training programme, were required to work in small groups to solve a variety of practical problems. Evaluations of their performance correlated just over 0.60 with measures of their tacit knowledge. In another, correlations between tacit knowledge and salary or level of job, after controlling for age, education, and years of experience in the job, ranged from 0.35 to 0.40. Secondly, tacit knowledge predicts people's competence at their job independently of their IQ. In a number of different studies Sternberg and his colleagues have reported near-zero correlations between tacit knowledge and IQ scores. They have also shown that, although (as we already knew) IQ does predict job competence, the multiple correlation between competence and IQ plus tacit knowledge is significantly and substantially higher: the addition of a tacit knowledge score to an IQ score predicts an additional 30 per cent of the variance in measures of job competence. Finally, programmes of instruction designed to enhance tacit knowledge may improve people's performance. School curricula designed to impart some of the tacit knowledge useful at school have been reported to have a significant impact on schoolchildren's educational attainment.

The independence of IQ and domain-specific expertise

A successful business manager, and even a successful academic psychologist, must have a relatively wide range of skills. The tacit knowledge underlying success in such walks of life must include knowing how to manage one's time, set priorities, deal with other people—both those of higher and of lower status—and so on. Other jobs may make very much narrower, more specialized demands—but still ones that require a great deal of hard work to meet. According to Ericsson and Charness (1994), for example, by the age of 20, exceptional violinists will have put in some 10 000 hours of concentrated practice, and will continue to practice, 4 hours a day, 7 days a week, in order to maintain their exceptional status. Outside the realm of work, many people focus their energies on extraordinarily specific goals. People's hobbies are endlessly varied and, to those who do not share their enthusiasm, may seem to involve bizarre skills and a store of arcane knowledge of no general use whatsoever. But no one would dispute that the enthusiastic stamp collector, follower of baseball, local historian, amateur naturalist, or devotee of the novels of Agatha Christie, will all become experts in their chosen topic. We do not need to suppose that the general intelligence supposedly measured by an IQ test is an essential ingredient of all forms of expertise.

Or do we? At least some IQ testers have apparently wanted to argue that IQ can trump special interest. Thus Jensen (1981, p. 65) recounts his experience of interviewing a man with an IQ of 75 who claimed to be, and clearly was, particularly interested in baseball, but who had only a vague and inaccurate understanding of the rules of the game and could not even name any of the major league teams. When Jensen posed these same questions to a 'learned colleague' who disclaimed all knowledge of baseball and certainly all interest in it, the colleague had no difficulty in providing the correct answers. Jensen's anecdotal evidence notwithstanding, numerous studies have shown, on the contrary, that interest or expertise is often much more important than measured IQ in determining performance on various tests related to an area of interest. Walker (1987), indeed, has shown that the acquisition of new information about baseball contained in invented stories was more closely related to prior knowledge about baseball than to measured IQ. Similar observations have been made in many other areas. German schoolchildren who displayed a good knowledge of soccer were much better than their less knowledgeable fellows at detecting contradictions in, and making correct inferences from, a narrative about a game of soccer (Schneider *et al.*, 1990). These differences were reliable for children aged 8–14 years; they were stable over a year's longitudinal follow-up; and, most importantly, they were almost wholly independent of differences in IQ.

In a now classic study, De Groot (1965) showed that when expert and novice chess players were given a brief opportunity to view a chessboard containing some dozen or so pieces in positions reached after a game had been in progress for some moves, the experts were very much better than the novices at recalling the positions of all the pieces; but when the same pieces were placed at random on the board, their expertise was no longer of any avail: they could recall no more positions than the novices. Chase and Simon (1973) have expanded on De Groot's studies to provide a detailed account of chess expertise, and similar analyses have been made for other areas of human skills, such as bridge playing (Charness, 1989). In a nice twist to De Groot's original study, Chi (1978) showed that 10-year-old experts were substantially better than adult novices at recalling chess positions. We may reasonably assume that the experts' mental age, whatever their IQ, was well below that of the non-experts here: they were certainly significantly worse at traditional memory span (digits or letter) tasks than the adults. Skill at chess may seem rather like skill at playing a musical instrument in that no one would doubt that it depended on prolonged practice: indeed, most estimates suggest that it takes a good 10 years of practice before anyone can expect to attain the level of an international chess master (Ericsson and Charness, 1994). It may also require more in the way of general intelligence than does expert knowledge of baseball or soccer, even if expertise can outweigh measured intelligence in the realm of chess also.

There are numerous other activities in people's daily lives that appear to make demands on some of the skills and abilities that are supposedly measured by IQ tests, but, in spite of the apparent parallels between the everyday task and the IQ test, performance on one may bear no relation to performance on the other. Many people, for example, need to solve simple problems in mental arithmetic in their daily lives. Studies of poor, and poorly educated, Brazilian children, living in *favelas* or shanty towns, and supplementing the family income by selling fruit from stalls at street corners or in open markets, have shown that they have impressive mathematical skills (Carraher *et al.*, 1985). The children were first given a series of realistic problems: If one melon costs 35 cruzeiros (Cr$), how much must I pay for six melons? If I buy two coconuts at Cr$ 40 each, how much change will I get from Cr$ 500? From the problems answered correctly by each child, the experimenters constructed for that child a series of formally identical questions in standard arithmetic format: What is 6×35? What is $420 + 80$? The children now solved less than 40 per cent of the problems. These and other studies of performance on such Piagetian tasks as class inclusion and conservation make it clear that poor, uneducated children can solve problems when they are presented in a format or context with which they are familiar, but are likely to fail completely when presented with formal or abstract versions of exactly the same problems (reviewed by Ceci and Roazzi, 1994).

In a similar vein, Lave *et al.* (1984) observed that Californian shoppers at a supermarket performed complex feats of mental arithmetic in order to work out which item represented best value for money—at a time when supermarkets carefully refrained from printing unit prices. So which of three bags of rice is the one to buy, when one costs 47c for 1 lb, a second 99c for 32 oz, and a third $1.39 for 48 oz? The shoppers resorted to a variety of sensible strategies or heuristics to simplify their task. A decision between 20 oz at $1.79 or 24 oz at $1.89 would be made simpler by noting that you got 4 more ounces for only 10 more cents. But just as was the case with the young Brazilian street vendors, there was no correlation between the shoppers' skill in this real-life setting and their performance on formal tests of mental arithmetic.

Some jobs or daily activities place considerable demands on immediate memory. The barman or waiter who takes orders from a dozen customers at once needs to remember what was ordered and by whom. Bennett (1983) found that waitresses in a cocktail bar could regularly remember up to 20 different drink orders at a time—performance that was well beyond anything achieved by university students who had had no practice at the job. The plausible inference that the waitresses' achievements were indeed simply the result of prolonged practice is supported by the finding that deliberate, prolonged practice can improve anyone's performance on memory-span tasks, even in the arbitrary format in which they appear in the Wechsler and Stanford–Binet tests. Two years of practice allowed one subject, SF, to achieve a digit span (defined as the longest list length that he could recall without error on 50 per cent of trials) of 84, while 4.5 years was sufficient for a second subject, DD, to break through the 100 barrier to a digit span of 106 (Chase and Erikson, 1982; Staszewski, 1990). Neither SF nor DD are described as in any sense out of the ordinary, and their remarkable memory span for digits did not even translate into an unusually good memory span for letters or words.

Jensen (1990) provides another example of a discrepancy between overall IQ and performance on a second sub-test of the Wechsler and Stanford–Binet scales, mental arithmetic. An Indian woman, Mrs Shakuntala Devi, gives stage performances in which she provides the correct answers to questions such as 'What is the cube root of 61 629 875?' (the answer is 395), or 'What is the product of 7 686 369 774 870 and 2 465 099 745 779?' (the correct answer, is a 26-digit number which it is not worth repeating here). She does this, moreover, faster than anyone in the audience can extract that answer from their calculating machine. Jensen found that her performance on other IQ tests (apart from those calling for mental arithmetic) was entirely unexceptional.

There is ample evidence, indeed, that exceptional skill in one particular area or domain is quite consistent with abnormally *low* IQ. The term 'idiots savants' (now more usually just 'savants') has been applied to people of low IQ with one particular, highly developed skill. Such people are often classified as autistic (Hermelin and O'Connor, 1978; Howe, 1989; Gardner, 1993). A particular 14-year-old boy, studied by Howe and Smith (1988), had an IQ between 50 and 60, but was a calendar calculator who, entirely self-taught, had learnt the correct answers to any question of the form:

> What day of the week was or will be 28 January 1905, 3 July 1996, 10 August 2052?

Although capable of *very* simple mental arithmetic, he was quite unable to answer a question such as:

> What is 1981 minus 1963?

But he had no difficulty at all in providing the correct answer if the question were phrased:

> If born in 1963 how old will someone be in 1981?

He could even give the correct answer to:

> If someone was born in 1841 how old would he be in 2302?

Detailed analysis of his performance suggested that, among other things, he had a series of mental images of the possible calendars for any given month. Ignoring the problem of whether a month has 28, 29, 30, or 31 days, there are, after all, only seven different calendars because the only important difference is what day of the week the month starts on. Having also learnt which calendar corresponds to which month of each year it becomes a simple matter to 'read off' the answer to the sorts of questions that he was asked; and such a mental representation also made it easy for him to say which of the following was the odd month out—January 1971, February 1971, September 1972, June 1973, July 1974, August 1975, October 1976. He correctly answered February 1971 because that is the only one to start on a Monday (the rest all start on a Friday).

Is domain-specific expertise based on domain-specific modules?

What are the implications of these data for the theory of human intelligence? Some conclusions seem incontrovertible. Practice really can make perfect: with sufficient time at one's disposal, it requires only single-minded concentration to turn virtually anyone into a skilled practitioner at almost anything—be it memorizing strings of digits, performing feats of mental arithmetic, or calendar calculating, and perhaps even playing chess or the piano. In many of these cases, such expertise can be attained without anything special in the way of the intelligence measured by IQ tests, and in the case of savants, in spite of a very low IQ. Now to the extent that the skills involved in a particular form of expertise are rather specialized, and can reasonably be thought to make few demands on general cognitive resources, such local expertise hardly presents any insurmountable problem for the theory of general intelligence. Even such an arch-proponent of *g* as Spearman allowed that there was a whole host of specific skills tapped by individual IQ test items (see Chapter 6). But it is not obvious that this line of defence will always be so easy. Expertise in business management, for example, seemed to depend on a range of abilities which, although not well captured by IQ tests, were clearly cognitive in nature, of some generality, and could reasonably be labelled as instances of practical intelligence (Klemp and McClelland, 1986; Sternberg *et al.*, 1995).

The discovery of cognitive skills and abilities that appear to lie outside the scope of IQ tests is unquestionably important, for if there are some critical ingredients of human intelligence independent of those measured by IQ, their discovery and elucidation will contribute to a better, more complete theory of human intelligence. But some commentators have wanted to draw a much stronger conclusion. For them, the message of the research reviewed in the preceding sections is that there is no such thing as general intelligence: our intelligence is really no more than the sum of our knowledge and expertise in a variety of different domains, and is based on a series of domain-specific processing modules (Ceci, 1990; Hirschfeld and Gelman, 1994).

At first sight, this thesis may seem reminiscent of Thurstone's theory of primary mental abilities (Thurstone, 1938) or, even more clearly, of Gardner's theory of multiple intelligences (Gardner, 1993). What is being said is that, rather than a single general intelligence that enters into the solution of all kinds of problem, and to the acquisition of knowledge and skill in every possible field of human endeavour, the mind consists of a multiplicity of different modules specialized for solving problems in, and acquiring information about, a whole series of different domains—linguistic, numerical or spatial, the world of physical objects or of other people, and so on. These domains do indeed correspond quite closely to several of Gardner's multiple intelligences, and Gardner himself both acknowledges the relationship and relies on the data and arguments of 'domain theory' to support his thesis. Nevertheless, the origins of these domain theories do not lie in the study of individual differences in knowledge or expertise (just as Gardner's theory is not wholly based on such evidence). What domain theories were intended to explain was not the observation that, with sufficient practice, people can become expert in a particular area, but rather the fact that we are all expert at certain things, and become so without any apparent need for explicit instruction or dedicated practice. Essentially all human beings, for example, learn to speak their native language; they do so without being deliberately taught and, so the argument runs, in the face of an environmental input quite insufficient to specify the rules of the grammar they do in fact acquire. Domain theory can be traced to Chomsky's claim that, in order to explain this simple fact, human beings must be supposed to have an 'innate language acquisition device' (Chomsky, 1980; Pinker, 1994). The idea was extended by Fodor (1983), in his book *Modularity of mind*. Fodor postulated a number of different modules, for example for colour perception, shape perception, spatial relations, recognition of faces and of voices, and so on. Modules were, in effect, specialized processing systems, each dealing with a particular class of information. They were: 'domain-specific, innately specified, hard wired, autonomous . . . [and] associated with fixed neural architecture' (Fodor, 1983, pp. 36 and 98).

This is rather a far cry from the concept of domain-specific expertise, at playing a musical instrument or calendar calculating, gained by prolonged practice. Indeed, Fodor himself was clear that the concept of a domain-specific module applied only to the peripheral architecture of the human mind, that is, to systems dedicated to the processing of particular sources of information. Fodor's central cognitive system was not domain-specific: it was a general-purpose processor that could learn about, or solve problems in, any domain, that is to say, on any class of input. It seems clear, then, that there is nothing self-contradictory about a theory of human cognition that acknowledges that the mind may well contain a number of modules specialized for particular tasks (such as learning one's native language), but at the same time insists that it also contains a more general cognitive system that is not domain-specific. What grounds could there be for insisting that *all* cognition is domain-specific?

We have already come across one main line of evidence: people can solve problems when they are presented in one particular format, but cannot solve the formally identical problem when its format is changed (see Box 10.3 for another instance of this). A general-purpose cognitive system should not be affected by such superficial changes of format. In the examples we have considered so far, the difference between soluble and insoluble problems has been a matter of past experience: people can solve problems whose content and context

---

Box 10.3 Video games: baleful or benign?

Ten-year-old children were given the task of predicting the direction in which a shape on a computer screen would move (Ceci, 1990; Ceci and Roazzi, 1994). The shape would initially appear in the centre of the screen on each trial and after a short time move to another location on the screen, and the children were required to point to where they thought it would move on each trial. The underlying algorithm was simple enough if written down, but not easy to work out from observation. It might, for example, be:

Triangles move left; circles move right; squares move neither left nor right;

Dark shapes move up; light shapes move down;

Large shapes move a long distance; small shapes move a short distance.

After 750 trials, the children were barely above chance, and succeeded only to the extent of having memorized one or two specific instances, for example that a large, dark circle moved to the top right corner of the screen.

The task could be turned into a video game by changing some of the surface features without altering any of the underlying algorithms. Triangles, circles, and squares became birds, butterflies, and bees; sound effects were added; and rather than point to the place where they thought the stimulus would move, the children had to move a cursor resembling a butterfly net to capture the animal. Now the children all learned virtually perfectly within 400 trials. As Ceci and Roazzi note, the children's failure on the first version of the task is consistent with a large experimental literature which says that neither adults nor children are capable of complex, multi-causal reasoning; but any parent who takes a child to the local video arcade knows better.

---

are familiar to them; by dint of prolonged practice, for example, people can increase their memory span for digits by an order of magnitude, without having any effect on their memory span for words. According to many domain theorists, on the other hand, domain-specificity is a consequence of our evolutionary history: certain kinds of problem, in certain kinds of format, are naturally easy for us to solve because we have been programmed by natural selection to solve that kind of problem. According to Cosmides and Tooby, for example:

> There is no warrant for thinking that selection would have favored cognitive mechanisms that are well-engineered for solving classes of problems beyond those encountered by Pleistocene hunter–gatherers . . . [The] conditions encountered during hominid evolutionary history constituted a series of adaptive problems. These conditions selected for a set of cognitive mechanisms that were capable of solving the associated adaptive problems . . . [ranging] from solicitation of assistance from one's parents, to language acquisition, to modelling the spatial distribution of local objects, to coalition formation and co-operation, to the deduction of intentions on the basis of facial expressions, to avoiding incest, to allocating effort between activities, to the interpretation of threats, to mate selection, to object recognition. (Cosmides and Tooby, 1994, pp. 87–88)

I shall return to such adaptionist arguments later. For the moment, it seems worth noting that whatever problems confronted our hominid ancestors, they surely did not include memorizing strings of digits or playing chess. The domain-specific modules of this type of theory do not readily map onto the examples of domain-specific expertise we have considered so far. The only feature they share in common is their domain-specificity. But perhaps this is sufficient. For the question at issue is whether people are endowed with general-purpose problem-solving and reasoning abilities and skills, which they can bring to bear on any type of cognitive task, regardless of its content or the context in which they encounter it, or whether our cognitive abilities or skills are specialized for handling specific types of information and solving particular kinds of problem. For these purposes, it may not really matter whether the specializations are innate or acquired, the product of common evolutionary history or individual past experience.

Theories of domain-general intelligence are certainly not the preserve of Spearman and his followers, and the question at issue is not whether differences in general intelligence can be reduced to differences in a single, unitary process. A general-purpose cognitive system may well rely on a large number of independent component operations or processes. It may encompass a variety of processes that are not even measured by standard IQ tests. Indeed, I shall argue for precisely such a conclusion—that in addition to the general-purpose problem-solving skills measured by IQ tests, we are also endowed with a general-purpose associative learning system that is largely independent of IQ. So it is not only proponents of the concept of *g* or general intelligence who have proposed general-purpose cognitive systems. So have many cognitive psychologists and students of cognitive development. The trouble is that the most widely known theory of cognitive development, that of Piaget, has proposed a rather specific story about how, at least in adults, this general-purpose cognitive system operates. It does so by having internalized a mental logic. There are grounds for questioning a theory of mental logic, but these are not necessarily grounds for rejecting all general-purpose theories.

Is a general mental logic the only alternative to domain-specific reasoning modules?

In very general terms, a theory of mental logic postulates a general system which will operate on any information presented to it. Confronted with a specific instance of a particular class of problem, it translates it into its underlying formal terms; and having discerned this hidden structure, applies the appropriate solution—a solution which would be equally appropriate to any problem of this structure, regardless of the particular terms in which it was instantiated. In one form, such a theory implies that Raven's Matrices are a good test of general intelligence precisely because they are abstract and meaningless: devoid of particular social or cultural meaning, the items are pure tests of abstract problem-solving capacity.

According to some psychometricians, of course, such a capacity is inborn or innate, but this is a quite unnecessary gloss on the theory. Piaget's theory of cognitive development assumes a quite specific developmental sequence, dependent on interaction with the environment, but one which still leads to much the same end-state. For Piaget, the growing child passes through preoperational and concrete operational stages before ending up in the formal operational stage. Preoperational children have not yet acquired the structures that would allow them to reason about or operate on the world; they cannot draw inferences, cope with class relationships, or understand how objects can conserve their identity in the face of perceptual transformations. A concrete operational child has acquired such understanding and capacities—but only with respect to particular concrete cases. It is only the acquisition of formal operational reasoning that 'permits the handling of hypotheses and reasoning with regard to propositions removed from concrete and present observation' (Piaget and Inhelder, 1969, p. 131).

Thus to take a specific instance, Piaget reports a 4-year-old girl who knew that, if an apple or pear were cut in half, she would have two pieces of apple or two pieces of pear. But when asked how many pieces there would be if a melon were cut in half, she replied that it depended on how big the melon was. The ability to answer specific questions that fall within one's experience is no evidence that one's answers depend on the application of a general underlying rule; they may simply reflect specific (associative?) learning: when an apple is cut by a knife, two pieces of apple will appear. And even the generalization of this rule to melons may not guarantee its generalization to all concrete objects (people, for example), let alone the realization that all manner of things may be divided in half—space, power, etc.

Piaget assumed, however, that the end product of normal cognitive development, the attainment of the formal operational stage, did precisely endow the older child with a general mental logic that could be used for reasoning about anything—an assumption shared by a number of other cognitive psychologists (see Garnham and Oakhill, 1994). But, as Garnham and Oakhill point out, such theories must all face up to one critical finding. If intelligent problem solving is a matter of understanding the abstract logical form of a problem and then bringing one's mental logic to bear on its solution, one would surely expect that a problem presented in an abstract format would be easier to solve than one presented in a concrete format. However familiar the content of the problem, it would still be necessary to strip that content away to perceive the underlying logical structure. There is ample evidence that this expectation is false. It is not only young children who find familiar versions of a problem easier than an abstract version. Exactly the same holds for well-educated adults, including university students. The content of the premises of a simple syllogism are often critical. For example, from the premises:

All Artists are Beekeepers

Some Beekeepers are Chemists

Does it follow that:

> *Some Artists are Chemists?*

In fact, it does not, although the conclusion is commonly accepted. To see that it is erroneous, it is only necessary to provide a less abstract version of the syllogism:

> *All Frenchmen are gourmets*
>
> *Some gourmets are Italian*

The second premise reminds us that there are more gourmets than Frenchmen in the world, and therefore that anything said about gourmets may not necessarily be true of Frenchmen.

Still one of the more elegant demonstrations of the difficulty that many people have with a simple but abstract logical puzzle is Wason's four-card problem (Wason, 1968; see Garnham and Oakhill (1994) for a discussion of the research generated by this seemingly innocuous puzzle). Figure 10.1 shows four cards, two with letters, two with numbers; you are told that each card has a letter on one side and a number on the other and the problem is to decide which of the four cards must be turned over in order to test whether the following rule is being violated:

> *If a card has a vowel on one side it must have an odd number on the other.*

Not surprisingly virtually everyone sees that they must turn over the A and nobody wants to turn over the B. A sizeable number of students, up to 10%, want to turn over the 1— presumably to check that it really does have a vowel on the other side (although the rule says nothing about consonants *not* going with odd numbers, and would not therefore be violated whatever letter appeared on the other side). Even worse, however, only about 20% of students see that they *must* turn over the 2; if it does have a vowel on the other side the rule has, after all, been broken.

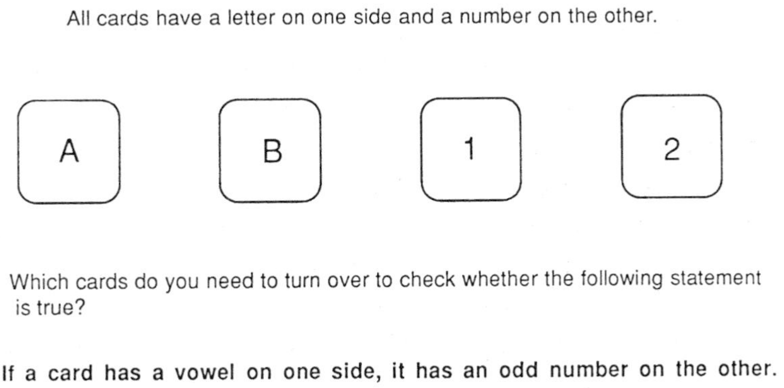

All cards have a letter on one side and a number on the other.

Which cards do you need to turn over to check whether the following statement is true?

If a card has a vowel on one side, it has an odd number on the other.

Fig. 10.1 Wason's four-card problem. You are shown the four cards above, together with the information that each has a letter on one side and a number on the other. Which cards do you need to turn over to check whether the rule is being violated? (From Wason, 1968.)

These are figures for British undergraduates. Graduate students and research scientists fare only a little better. But if the problem is presented in a realistic, concrete format the difficulty vanishes. One version is shown in Fig. 10.2. Imagine you are a postal worker sorting letters and your task is to ensure that they all have the correct postage; the rule is that sealed envelopes must have a first-class stamp, only unsealed letters can go second class (this was indeed the British post office's rule in force at the time of the experiment). Which envelopes need turning over to ensure that no one is trying to cheat the post office by putting a second class stamp on a sealed envelope? The answer is again the first and fourth envelopes: the first since a sealed envelope not having a first-class stamp would violate the rule; and the fourth because it has a second-class stamp and it is necessary to check that the envelope is not sealed.

Why is the second version so much easier than the first? If this were just another example of familiar content making a problem easier, the results would by now hardly be surprising, and would not merit extensive discussion. But there is reason to believe that it is not the *content*, so much as the nature of the logic, that makes the problem easy or hard. The abstract version of the problem presents an 'if . . . then' statement familiar to students of the propositional calculus:

> *If* p *then* q *(if a vowel, then an odd number).*

This statement is false, if and only if:

> p *is true, but* q *is false (there is a vowel, but the number is even).*

That is why, if you see an even number, you must check whether there is a vowel on the other side, since if there is, the statement is false.

But the version shown in Fig. 10.2 instantiates a different kind of logic—that concerned with rules, permissions and obligations (usually termed deontic logic): sealing an envelope obliges you to affix a first-class stamp. According to Cheng and Holyoak (1985), we are familiar in our everyday life with the logic of permission and obligation, and since we have no difficulty in bringing a 'permission schema' to bear on a problem, we also have no

If an envelope is sealed, it must have a 1st - class stamp.

Fig. 10.2 A more realistic version of Wason's problem. You are a postal worker sorting mail. Which envelopes must you turn over to check that sealed envelopes must have a 1st-class stamp? (The first envelope is sealed, the second unsealed).

difficulty in seeing when such obligations are potentially being violated. When Cheng and Holyoak asked their subjects to imagine that they were immigration officials at an international airport, checking arriving passengers to see whether they were entering the country or merely in transit, they had no difficulty in applying the rule: passengers entering the country (p) must have a certificate of inoculation for cholera (q), and virtually all turned over the not-q card.

Cheng and Holyoak's critical experiment demonstrated that even a wholly abstract version of a permission rule was solved by the majority of their subjects. They were asked to imagine that they were an authority checking whether people were obeying a regulation of the form:

> *If you are going to take action A, then you must first satisfy precondition P. In other words, in order to be permitted to do A, you must have fulfilled prerequisite P.*

The majority of subjects turned over the card stating that someone had not satisfied the prerequisite.

Cosmides (1989) has added a further twist to Cheng and Holyoak's idea, by suggesting that the critical feature of permission schemas is that they are about social contracts, costs, and benefits: if you wish to gain a particular benefit (send a sealed envelope which only the recipient will open; enter the country), then you must pay the cost (a first-class stamp, inoculation for cholera). And the reason why we find problems of this sort easy is because our evolutionary history involved learning to live in small co-operative groups, where there was a premium on detecting cheats. In other words, we possess an innate, domain-specific module for thinking about social contracts. The idea is intriguing, but does not easily apply to all permission rules. For example, Manktelow and Over (1990) found that people had no difficulty with the following 'if . . . then' rule:

> *If you are going to clean up spilt blood, you must wear rubber gloves.*

It is hard to believe that cleaning up spilt blood is a benefit for which one should be prepared to pay the price of putting on rubber gloves, or that you are cheating if you fail to do so.

Whatever the exact interpretation of those cases where people do solve 'if . . . then' problems, their failure when confronted with Wason's original, abstract version seems inconsistent with any theory that postulates a general mental logic. It is hard to believe that we first learn the abstract rules of the propositional calculus (let alone that they are somehow built into the human mind), and then learn to apply them to particular cases. If that were so, as I have already argued, one would presumably expect the abstract version of the problem to be easier than any concrete version. Is the only alternative to a general mental logic a domain-specific module, such as that proposed by Cosmides for detecting cheats? That particular suggestion does not seem particularly well supported, but there might, of course, be other innate predispositions which had the effect of making some versions of such problems easier than others. That remains an open question, but it is not one we need to answer. The evolutionary argument for a modular mind is an argument about universals—what is common to all people, not what distinguishes one from another, and finds its strongest support in the claim that only a specialized set of modules would have the power to achieve what every normal child succeeds in doing: seeing the world in three dimensions, recognizing faces, learning a native language, understanding kinship categories, interpreting other people's behaviour, etc.

Since our central concern is to understand why, and in what ways, people differ from one another in their cognitive abilities, we do not need to decide how far such universal competences are innate, or to what extent our expertise in particular domains is a product of dedicated, domain-specific modules. We can certainly accept that the ways in which people resemble one another are more plentiful and, for many purposes, more important than the ways in which they differ. It may even be, as Cosmides and Tooby (1994) argue, that many of these similarities are a reflection of past adaptations to selection pressures acting on our Pleistocene hunter–gatherer ancestors. But then again, it may not. The problem with such adaptationist arguments for the modularity of mind is that it is usually possible to construct adaptationist arguments for almost anything, including in this case one for general-purpose cognitive systems. Thus although the developing child ends up having acquired a lot of specific information in a variety of specific domains, for example, about other people, social relationships, plants, animals, inanimate objects, and so on, it is hardly necessary to suppose that distinct modules, each operating in accordance with its own unique rules, were responsible for each distinct category of knowledge. Our knowledge and expertise may be domain-specific, but we may have acquired much of it by some entirely general processes.

One of those processes may, of course, be the general intelligence measured by IQ tests. But, as I have already argued, there are probably others—including a general-purpose associative learning system. And it is a simple matter to construct an adaptationist argument for the existence of just such a system. Modern learning theory, based largely on the study of animal conditioning, postulates a general-purpose associative system which detects contingencies between events, or keeps track of statistical regularities in sequences of events in the environment. The system is well designed to allow animals to build up a picture of the causal structure of their world (Box 10.4), and it is general precisely because causal laws are rather general ones. By and large, causes precede their effects, whatever the nature of the specific cause or specific effect; action at a distance is the exception rather than the rule. In other words, a general associative system may have evolved in response to some strikingly invariant aspects of all environments: a single, general system is sufficient to detect contingencies between events, regardless of the nature of those events. We may be biased towards learning about some things rather than others, but the mechanisms underlying such biases, if innate, may simply be sensory or perceptual, or subtle effects on attention, rather

---

Box 10.4 Conditioning as the perception of causal relations

Laboratory studies of Pavlovian and instrumental conditioning in animals have a long history and a worse reputation, conjuring up images of dogs helplessly drooling at the sound of the dinner bell, or rats trundling their way through mazes or pressing levers in Skinner boxes on various schedules of reinforcement. But the laws of conditioning reveal an associative learning process nicely tuned to detecting real causal relationships, which thus allows animals to predict, and sometimes control, the occurrence of those events of consequence to themselves that psychologists call reinforcers (Dickinson, 1980; Mackintosh, 1983; Rescorla, 1988). Just as causes usually immediately precede their effects and do not act at a distance, so conditioning depends on the temporal and spatial contiguity of conditional stimulus, or response, and reinforcer. If the occurrence of an event, A, is sometimes, but not always, followed by another event, X, then although A may be a contributing cause of X, it cannot be a sufficient cause. But if you can find no other event better correlated with the occurrence of X, A is the only cause you know about. If, on the other hand, another event, B, occurs alongside A, but only on those occasions when X follows, then B is clearly the cause of X and A's occurrence is probably a chance coincidence. In the absence of B, animals will show conditioning to A when it occasionally signals the occurrence of a reinforcer, X, but the addition of B will 'overshadow' conditioning to A. Conditioning thus occurs selectively to better predictors of reinforcement at the expense of worse predictors, thereby allowing animals to attribute the occurrence of a reinforcer to its most probable cause.

---

than complete, encapsulated modules. Thus we may be predisposed to looking at other people's faces rather than their feet, but the system that learns the significance of facial expressions, that a smile of welcome usually promises good things and an angry frown bad things, may be exactly the same as that which learns that the colour and texture of a fruit signifies when it is ripe to eat, that cats purr when contented while dogs bark when excited or threatening, or (fond parental wish) that saying 'please' and 'thank you' is more likely to get you what you want than an abrupt demand and no acknowledgement. It may even be the same system as that which learns that certain ways of trying to solve certain kinds of problem lead to successful solutions with both immediate and longer-term pay-offs, while other attempted solutions get one nowhere. And because the world of young children is full of things they are allowed to do, and even fuller of those they are not allowed to do, it would not be beyond the power of a general associative system to learn a rather general permission schema, which could be applied to new problems involving permissions and obligations.

Beyond IQ?

Are there differences in ability unrelated to IQ or experience?

It is time to return to the questions from which we started earlier in this chapter. How far do IQ tests succeed in measuring the various components of human intelligence? What is the nature of this intelligence they are trying to measure? Some authorities, such as Ceci (1990) and Gardner (1993) have given an uncompromising answer to these questions, arguing that IQ tests have failed, because they have been based on a false premise. People do not differ in any set of general-purpose cognitive abilities in the first place. There is only a set of independent cognitive modules, each specialized, either innately or as a result of experience, for a particular purpose. Is this a fair or necessary reading of the evidence?

From the observation that our knowledge of the world is confined to particular domains, and that our ability to solve problems depends on their domain, it simply does not necessarily follow that our knowledge and problem-solving abilities are the product of domain-specific modules. By chance, or bowing to parental pressure, or as a result of an interest sparked by particular friends or teachers, a young girl may take up chess as a hobby, rather than ballet, horses, or computers. In due course, she becomes very good at chess and, in spite of a no more than average IQ, easily defeats less skilled players with much higher IQ scores. She will also show much better memory for the positions of a dozen or more pieces on the board—provided they were positions that might be reached during the course of a normal game. This does not mean that the human mind contains a chess-playing module (or anything even remotely like it), and that she was blessed with a powerful version of it. She has learned a great deal more about chess than unskilled players, and this has included more powerful and economical ways of encoding the position of pieces on the board. But there is good evidence that her working-memory system is just as susceptible as that of the non-expert to interference (Robbins *et al.*, 1996). In other words, there is no reason to believe that her expertise depended on any particularly efficient hardware. Practice really can make pretty perfect. It can certainly be more important than IQ, and more important than one of the more important component mechanisms underlying IQ.

Differences in skill or expertise in a particular domain may be quite independent of IQ. But if they are a consequence of differences in amount of experience or practice, this independence proves rather little. There is, as a matter of fact, good evidence that differences in IQ are correlated with differences in the speed at which people acquire moderately complex skills, and the efficiency of their performance at early stages of practice (Ackerman, 1988). That the advantage of a high IQ tends to disappear with continued practice, as Ackerman also found, simply confirms one of the assumptions of Sternberg's 'triarchic' theory, namely that intelligence is engaged in, and thus best measured by, the solution of novel problems (Sternberg, 1985). And it also suggests that most people can become reasonably skilled at many tasks if they devote enough time to them.

The finding that there was no correlation between differences in IQ and differences in practical competence in any domain would be critical, therefore, only if we could be assured that these differences in competence were not associated with large differences in experience of the domain in question. The business managers studied by Sternberg *et al.* (1995) had greater tacit knowledge of business than students, and their solutions to various simulated problems were judged superior by experts. Even though differences in tacit knowledge do not appear to be correlated with IQ scores, this still fails to address the critical question. However, the further observation that successful managers showed evidence of superior tacit knowledge than their less successful contemporaries, even when years of experience were taken into account, is much more important. It does suggest that there may be differences in practical intelligence or competence that are independent both of IQ and of amount of experience. A determined defender of IQ might argue that years of experience as a business manager can be no more than a crude measure of the amount of time spent thinking about one's work and pondering the problems it raises. That is possibly true: in the last analysis it may always be possible to appeal to differences in interest or motivation to account for differences in expertise. But it is worth considering one final example.

In 'A day at the races', Ceci and Liker (1986) reported on the achievements of 30 devotees of harness racing (where the rider sits in a small two-wheeled cart pulled by the horse rather than riding the horse as in flat racing or steeplechasing). They initially tested over 100 men, all of whom had bought a copy of *Early form*, a paper that contains the relevant past statistics of the runners in the following day's race. Only moderately serious punters will take the trouble to buy something whose sole purpose is to give one time to start calculating probable odds of favourites. Of these 100 men they selected a group of 30 who displayed greatest knowledge about harness racing, and then asked these 30 men to predict, on the basis of information provided by *Early form*, the favourite, and also the first, second, and third favourites, in 10 of tomorrow's races. They chose this as their dependent variable since it is, in fact, important for serious gamblers to be able to predict such odds, in order to decide whether it will be worth their while to bet on a particular horse. Fourteen of the 30 men were astonishingly good at this, predicting the favourite with an accuracy of 93 per cent, and the first three favourites in correct order in 53 per cent of races. The remaining 16 were notably less skilled, with accuracies of 55 per cent and 8 per cent, respectively. Ceci and Liker then gave a variety of further tests to all 30 men, involving handicapping real races and hypothetical races, at all of which the 14 'experts' were substantially better than the 16 less expert men. Finally, by detailed analysis of their performance, Ceci and Liker were able to show that the experts were using some seven different variables which they allowed to interact in complex ways to solve their tasks. These variables included: a horse's lifetime's earnings; speed in previous races; jockey; details of prior races including the opposition; the amount of time spent on the outside trying to pass other carts; speed at different points in the race; and nature of the track. The critical difference between the two groups of 14 and 16 men, however, was in the complexity of the interactions between these variables that the experts employed. Whether a horse has won his last race is, after all, less important than against whom he has won, and on what course; actual speed can only be calculated by taking into account the proportion of time the horse was forced to pass other carts on the outside. And so on. It was the ability to allow for interactions such as these that seemed to be the secret of the 14 experts' success.

By any normal standards, of course, all 30 men were experts; they were all exceptionally knowledgeable about harness racing; they had been to the races at least twice a week for, on average, the past 16 years; even the non-experts were well above chance in their predictions (Ceci and Liker estimated the odds against predicting the first three favourites in each of 10 races as something like 40 000 : 1). But why were they not as good as the 14 experts? Were they perhaps less intelligent? No. The average IQ of the 14 experts was 100.8 (range 81–125), and of the 16 non-experts 99.3 (range 80–130). There was, moreover, no correlation between IQ and success in Ceci and Liker's handicapping tasks, nor between IQ and the extent to which the interactive model provided a good account of each individual's performance. Whatever it was that distinguished the two groups, apart from their success, it was not measured IQ (or educational or occupational level on which again, the two groups were closely matched).

It is hardly surprising that someone who goes to the races every day should end up knowing a lot more about racing than the rest of us. But both groups had done this: indeed the non-experts had spent marginally more years going regularly to the races than had the experts. They were initially selected from a larger group of over 100 committed racegoers on the basis of their superior knowledge about harness racing. It is, of course, possible that the 14 experts had, in some sense, acquired more relevant information during their years spent going to the races than had the 16 non-experts. But if so, the difference is between one group who knew a great deal more about harness racing than the rest of us would ever want to know, and a second group who knew *even* more.

Ceci and Liker's study would appear to confirm the results of Sternberg's study of business managers in two important ways. Their experts' skill was not simply a function of the opportunity for unusually prolonged practice. The non-experts had equally prolonged opportunity. Secondly, the experts' skill seems to have involved some cognitively complex operations. It was not, for example, just a matter of memorizing dates as calendar calculators do. The process of allowing for higher-order interactions between numerous variables sounds like the sort of intelligent problem-solving activity that IQ scores are supposed to reflect: it cannot be put on one side—as musical or artistic talent, which we could reasonably allow to be independent of general intelligence.

There remain some unanswered, and probably unanswerable, questions. The strong inference one might want to draw from the study is that, since experts and non-experts had equal opportunity to develop the relevant skills, the experts must have been more intelligent, in ways not measured by an IQ score, to have done so more effectively. That inference may not be justified. Perhaps the difference was one of motivation or actual time spent studying form books at home and trying to beat the system. Perhaps the experts gambled more, and so needed to win more than the non-experts. It is usually possible to appeal to unmeasured and uncontrolled factors in any natural or quasi-natural experiment. Nevertheless, Ceci and Liker's study remains highly suggestive and I should be inclined to take its results more or less at face value.

What, then, is their explanation? No one, presumably, is going to suggest that humans possess a horse race handicapping module and that the 14 experts were fortunate enough to have a more efficient one. Nor is there any need to appeal to such a fanciful idea, for a consideration of the nature of the task suggests a plausible alternative. Ceci and Liker's expert racegoers had become exceptionally skilled at predicting the value of an outcome, a horse's starting odds, from the value of a number of independent variables (past races, jockey, etc.) and their interactions. The detection of such contingencies is precisely the role I assigned to the general-purpose associative system described by modern conditioning theory. It is also exactly the task people are required to perform in experiments on 'implicit learning'.

Implicit learning as a source of tacit knowledge and expertise

In a typical laboratory experiment on implicit learning, people are shown a sequence of events, for example a series of lights being illuminated on a screen, or a series of apparently random letters of the alphabet (Berry and Dienes, 1993; Reber, 1993). The sequence of events is not, in fact, random, but the sequential dependencies between them are so complex, and the events usually occur so rapidly, that there is little chance that people will be able to work out all the rules underlying the sequences. Nevertheless, they clearly learn a great deal about them. In the artificial grammar learning task developed by Reber (1967), people are asked to study a set of apparently arbitrary letter strings that are actually generated by the Markov process illustrated in Fig. 10.3. They are then told that there was a 'grammar' or set of rules that generated the strings they had been studying and are asked to judge whether new letter strings are or are not 'grammatical' (see Fig. 10.3 for further explanation). Although usually unable to articulate the rules of the grammar, people perform significantly above chance on this final test. In other experiments, a sequence of stimuli appear, in rapid succession, in different positions on a screen in front of the subject, and their task is to respond as rapidly as possible to the appropriate response key below each position. In a control condition, the sequence of stimuli is entirely random, but in an experimental condition it is, at least in principle, predictable. In one version of the task, a particular 16-trial sequence of positions is repeated over and over again (Willingham *et al.*, 1993). In another, the position of the sixth stimulus in each block of six trials is predicted, in a complex way, by the positions of the second and fourth stimuli (Cleeremans and McClelland, 1991). Reaction times are generally speeded up when it is possible to predict the occurrence of the stimulus one is required to respond to. Evidence that subjects have learned something about the trial sequences in these experiments is provided by the observation that they respond faster in experimental (predictable) than in control (random) conditions. Implicit learning tasks can even be made a bit more realistic: people can be asked to 'manage' an imaginary factory and take decisions about purchasing policy or employee relations, whose outcomes are dependent on the interaction of a large number of variables (Berry and Broadbent, 1984).

In all these cases, people's performance indicates quite clearly that they have learned something about the task they were set. But their knowledge is usually no more than fragmentary, and they are poor at articulating it. They are certainly unlikely to draw a picture of the Markov process illustrated in Fig. 10.3 in Reber's artificial grammar task. According to Reber, their learning is implicit, rather than explicit, with implicit learning being defined as:

> The acquisition of knowledge that takes place largely independently of conscious attempts to learn and largely in the absence of explicit knowledge of what was acquired. (Reber, 1993, p. 5)

Reber's definition of implicit learning may remind the reader of Sternberg's account of tacit knowledge. Wagner and Sternberg defined tacit knowledge as knowledge that is

> not openly expressed or stated . . . informal rather than formal, and . . . usually . . . not directly taught . . . We do not wish to imply that such knowledge is completely inaccessible to conscious awareness, unspeakable, or even unteachable, but merely that it usually is not taught directly to most of us . . . Much tacit knowledge may be disorganized and relatively inaccessible, making it potentially ill suited for direct instruction. (Wagner and Sternberg, 1986, p. 54)

Two quite independent research traditions have homed in on a very similar set of ideas.

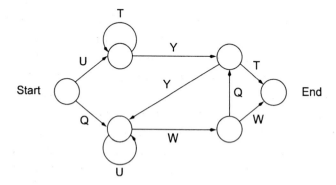

Fig. 10.3 A Markov artificial grammar which generates strings of letters. To generate a string, start from the circle marked Start, and follow any arrow to another circle until you reach the circle marked End. Each arrow has an associated letter and the string generated is determined by the path taken. The loops at some circles allow you to repeat the same letter more than once. Examples of 'grammatical' strings would be: UYT, QWQT, QUUWW. An 'ungrammatical' string would be QYQW.

Wagner and Sternberg's tacit knowledge, which they assume to underlie practical intelligence or competence, seems plausibly regarded as a product of the implicit learning system studied in some highly contrived laboratory experiments. But how can we characterize implicit learning more precisely?

Reber initially described implicit learning as the unconscious acquisition of knowledge about complex, abstract rules. The idea seemed to be that the participants in an artificial grammar learning experiment really had internalized the set of rules corresponding to the Markov process illustrated in Fig. 10.3, and since they certainly could not articulate these rules, their knowledge must be unconscious (see Reber, 1993). This interpretation has led to prolonged dispute, it being argued, for example, that sufficiently careful probing of participants' explicit understanding usually reveals fragmentary knowledge of certain brief sequences that would often have been sufficient to explain their performance on test (Perruchet, 1994; Shanks *et al.*, 1994). Fortunately this dispute need not concern us; for our purposes it is unimportant whether or not implicit learning is wholly unconscious. There are other, more interesting ways of characterizing the difference between implicit and explicit learning.

Laboratory studies of implicit learning require people to detect complex contingencies between rapidly occurring sequences of events. This, as we have already noted, is precisely the function of the general-purpose associative system postulated by modern conditioning theory. So a plausible characterization of the distinction between implicit and explicit learning, and one now advanced by Reber (1993) himself, is that implicit learning is the product of a basic associative system, while explicit learning is the product of a cognitive system which generates and tests hypotheses, detects other kinds of relationships between events, infers rules, and decides between alternative conclusions on the basis of the evidence (see McLaren *et al.*, 1994; Shanks, 1994).

If this distinction is a valid one, it seems clear that IQ tests are more likely to measure the operations of the explicit system than those of the implicit, associative system. There is, indeed, good evidence for this. In a study of 20 American college students, Reber *et al.* (1991) found no correlation between IQ scores (on a shortened form of the WAIS) and performance on an implicit learning (artificial grammar) task, although they found a highly significant correlation between IQ and performance on an explicit letter-series-completion task. A much larger study of over 400 14-year-old schoolchildren (Feldman *et al.*, 1995) also found a negligible correlation, of 0.05, between earlier WISC IQ scores and performance on an implicit sequence learning task—although such explicit knowledge about the sequences as the children did acquire was related to their IQ scores. A study of Cambridge sixth-form (senior high school) schoolchildren also found a negligible correlation between IQ and performance on an implicit, artificial grammar learning task (Mackintosh and Bennett, 1998). But here there was an important additional finding: the children's educational attainment (GCSE exam grades) were modestly correlated not only with their IQ scores, but also with their performance on the implicit learning task. Thus IQ and implicit learning ability apparently measured *independent* aspects of educational attainment.

We are now in a position to draw a number of threads together into a reasonably plausible set of hypotheses. The associative learning system studied in laboratory experiments on implicit learning in people and conditioning in animals, and modelled by standard connectionist networks (Shanks, 1994), is a general-purpose system that furnishes us with much of our knowledge of the structure of the world in which we live. It was responsible for Ceci and Liker's gamblers' ability to detect the complex relationship between a horse's past history and its likely odds in tomorrow's race. It enabled Sternberg's business managers to learn that some solutions to a problem yield more desirable outcomes than others. It was partly responsible for our schoolchildren's knowledge of the material that appeared in their GCSE exams. It probably contributes to experts' mastery of any particular domain.

It may also help to explain variations in performance. Although Reber (1993) has suggested that implicit learning ability, being 'evolutionary old', may show little variation in the general population (see Reber *et al.*, 1991), other studies have found substantial variation in performance on artificial grammar or sequence reaction time tasks (Feldman *et al.*, 1995; Mackintosh and Bennett, 1998), and significant correlations between implicit learning scores and other types of procedural performance. It remains to be seen whether variations in implicit learning ability would explain such differences in performance as that seen by Ceci and Liker between their 14 expert and 16 non-expert handicappers.

The demonstration that experts in any domain are very much more knowledgeable and skilful than those less expert, without necessarily differing in IQ, has always been open to the relatively uninteresting interpretation that the difference between experts and non-experts is simply a matter of the amount of time they have devoted to acquiring the relevant knowledge and skills. But perhaps there is also a difference in the efficiency with which people acquire such knowledge and skills, and such differences can be measured by performance on implicit learning tasks. If that is so, then since we also know that implicit learning ability is independent of IQ, we have an additional explanation of differences in expertise. There is no reason to question that differences in IQ have a significant effect on the acquisition of skill at early stages of practice. There is even less reason to doubt that experience and practice are essential for high levels of expertise. But it is possible that variations in implicit learning ability account for an important part of the remaining variance in the tacit knowledge, practical competence, or expertise that contributes to the efficient performance of a complex job.

Finally, it is worth relating this argument to one advanced earlier in the context of black–white differences in IQ (Chapter 5). There is good reason to believe that blacks' practical competence may be seriously underestimated by their IQ scores, and the explanation offered there was that blacks and whites did not differ in 'learning ability'. It should be clear that the learning ability being referred to is implicit learning ability, and is probably better measured by performance on artificial grammar or sequence reaction time tasks than by any explicit test of learning or memory—even rote learning or simple digit span, where the black–white difference is vanishingly small. This general argument has found few adherents, for the not very good reason that a version of it has been advanced by Jensen (1973). But Jensen himself has done little to enhance its popularity when he argues that the distinctly modest correlation between IQ and measures of rote learning or memorization proves that IQ must be measuring a complex, abstract problem-solving ability, and thus really is a measure of what we understand by intelligence, precisely because it is not measuring 'mere' rote learning (Jensen, 1980). The force of Jensen's argument here depends partly on the assumption that rote learning—for example of nonsense syllables in the experimental psychologist's laboratory—really is of no further interest or importance. But that assumption, when applied to implicit, associative learning, is false. It is easy to deride rote learning as 'mere', and associative learning as a paradigm of an unintelligent process— if only because it is probably similar to the process underlying simple conditioning in animals. But associative learning theory has provided a powerful explanation of the way intelligent people (college students) learn a variety of tasks—including judging contingencies between events, diagnosing the relationship between symptoms and diseases, and classifying variable instances of two or more categories into their appropriate classes (Shanks, 1994). Outside the psychological laboratory, it seems possible that the same process underlies the acquisition of much knowledge and a variety of skills that enter into our everyday life. If this is true, IQ tests measure only *part* of the general cognitive processes determining success in the outside world.

Social intelligence

Are there other aspects of intelligence not measured by IQ tests? Almost certainly— provided that 'other aspects of intelligence' are defined in a sufficiently liberal manner. Rather than enumerate all the possibilities, let us conclude with a brief discussion of one particular candidate—social, personal, or emotional intelligence. This should be sufficient to illustrate the kinds of argument that have been advanced in support of proposals for a particular intelligence, as well as some of the problems attendant on such proposals.

The idea that one could distinguish social from other aspects of intelligence has a history dating back at least as far as the early days of IQ testing (see Sternberg, 1985). Common sense or everyday experience are both consistent with the idea that we spend much of our time engaged in social interactions with others, and that some people seem more successful than others in such interactions. Certainly, one of the aspects of an intelligent person's behaviour emphasized by many of the respondents in Sternberg *et al.*'s (1981) study (see Chapter 1) was a factor the authors labelled 'social competence'. Gardner (1993) has talked of both interpersonal, i.e. social intelligence, and intrapersonal intelligence, which perhaps corresponds more closely to the concept of <u>emotional intelligence</u> advanced by Mayer and Salovey (1993). Goleman (1996) has popularized the concept of emotional intelligence, at the same time as blurring the already somewhat unclear distinction between Gardner's interpersonal and intrapersonal intelligences.

There is another, important strand to the concept of social intelligence—that provided by research on non-human primates. Why, asked Humphrey (1976), should apes and monkeys apparently be so much more intelligent than other mammals? It is not as if their daily lives are fraught with practical difficulties; for most of them, their food supply is reasonably plentiful and their predators few. Why do they need to be so intelligent? Humphrey's answer was that their intelligence is social rather than practical. Most primates live in quite large social groups, and their intelligence evolved to cope with the demands of social life, the need to learn one's place in a social hierarchy, how to interact with one's social superiors and inferiors, how to co-operate with others, and how, sometimes, to outwit them. Premack and Woodruff (1978) went one step further by attributing, at least to chimpanzees, the possession of a 'theory of mind' which, they proposed, underlay the chimpanzee's ability to understand, control, or predict the behaviour of others. The idea has been taken up by numerous developmental psychologists, some of whom have argued that we possess a domain-specific 'theory of mind module', that allows the developing child to understand that other people have hopes, fears, beliefs, and wishes; and the absence or imperfect development of which in autistic children is responsible for their unusual social behaviour (Leslie, 1994; Baron-Cohen, 1995).

The evidence that other primates possess a theory of mind is distinctly sparse, and most primatologists would probably now agree that monkeys at least do not (Seyfarth and Cheney, 1997). Although some continue to argue that at least the great apes do, that too remains a debatable proposition (for different views, see Heyes, 1994; Byrne, 1995). But there can hardly be any serious doubt that, in a loose sense of the term, people have a theory of mind. We routinely use mental predicates to describe and explain the behaviour of others; we attribute desires and beliefs to others and understand that someone else's desires and beliefs may be quite different from our own. The entire enterprise of cognitive psychology, after all, is premised on a theory of mind in this loose sense. But it is quite another thing to say that we possess an innate theory of mind module, which starts to kick in during the second or third year of life, eventually allowing normal children to pass the 'false belief' test (when a 3- or 4-year-old child understands that someone else may not know what he knows—or that someone else's beliefs about the world may be false). The strongest argument for the postulation of domain-specific modules was that the developing child's environment simply does not provide sufficient information to enable a general-purpose intelligence to acquire those competences that all normal children succeed in developing. That does not seem a plausible argument here. Unlike the world of the chimpanzee, the world of the young child is full of people talking about mental states, asking the child what she wants or what she remembers, telling her that something she believed to be true is not true, telling her that they do not know what happened when the toy was broken because they were not there. And so on. There seems ample opportunity for a general-purpose cognitive system, perhaps aided by a few simple mechanisms such as a propensity to look at what a speaker is looking at, to develop a theory of mind, without the need for a full-blown specialist module.

The argument for a distinctly social intelligence, therefore, must look elsewhere for support. How should we go about it? The first step will be to provide some more precise instances of competence with the social domain. That does not seem very difficult. Most people could probably agree on a relatively long list of situations calling for social skills or social intelligence: understanding other people, being sensitive to their feelings, showing an interest in them, responding to their needs, sympathizing with them when they are distressed, putting them at their ease, being the life and soul of the party, showing a suitable level of deference to one's superiors, judging the appropriate level of flattery that the boss likes, being considerate and punctual. And so on. Most people will probably also agree that some of us are better at many of these things than others. So the next step should also not be impossibly difficult: we need to devise tests that measure these skills.

Several such tests have indeed been produced. For example, Guilford and Hoepfner (1971) have tests that require one to select from a set of photographs of faces the two that are displaying the same mental state, or to match the emotion shown in a facial expression with that revealed by a tone of voice. Rosenthal *et al.* (1979) devised the PONS test (profile of non-verbal sensitivity), in which people are shown film clips of brief scenes in which a woman displays various emotional states, and their task is to identify that state. Sternberg and Smith (1985) asked subjects to inspect a series of photographs each containing two people; in one series, their task was to decide whether the couple were friends or strangers, in another, to decide which of two people shown in a work setting was the supervisor and which the supervisee.

Now comes the hard part. Gardner (1993) and Goleman (1996) have both insisted that there is a social or emotional intelligence that is quite independent of the general intelligence measured by standard IQ tests. But neither has produced any serious evidence to support this claim. What would that evidence look like? If people really do differ along a dimension of social intelligence, then the first requirement is that measures of the various social skills outlined above should tend to correlate with one another. It is precisely this positive manifold that in other domains of IQ allows one to talk of verbal ability, spatial ability, reasoning ability, perceptual speed, or even of g itself. In the present case, the evidence for any such positive manifold is distinctly unimpressive. Sternberg and Smith (1985) found no correlation between performance on their tests and on Rosenthal *et al.*'s PONS test, or indeed with any other test of social skills. More remarkably, the correlation between the two parts of their test (photographs of couples and of supervisors) was only 0.09. Similarly, although the PONS test is reasonably reliable, with a test–retest reliability coefficient of 0.69, and although performance on one part of the test correlates reasonably well with other parts, overall performance is only very weakly related to ratings of social skill or competence: the correlations with self-ratings are less than 0.10, those with other people's ratings only marginally higher.

Since these various tests of social skills do not seem to have identified a general dimension of social intelligence, it may seem hardly necessary to address the final question: is social intelligence independent of *g*, or any other aspects of IQ? But one of the few investigations to find any sort of positive manifold in a battery of tests of social skills, also found that these measures correlated quite well with measures of academic intelligence (Ford and Tisak, 1983). Although the correlations between social and academic measures were somewhat lower than those between one social measure and another, the difference was not large (0.26 v. 0.36). This clearly raises the possibility that, in so far as different measures of social competence do agree with one another, this may be because they are related to more general aspects of intelligence. One other observation would be consistent with that. We saw that damage to prefrontal cortex can result in serious deficits in performance on measures of Gf or fluid intelligence. But disorders of emotional intelligence or social competence are another symptom of frontal damage (Chapter 9).

Perhaps the most striking finding from this research is the independence of different tests of social competence. But maybe that should not come as such a great surprise, for on reflection it does seem reasonable to suppose that we are dealing with a wide variety of rather different skills used to cope with the very wide range of demands that social life imposes. Being the life and soul of the party is not the same as being sensitive to other people's feelings, or knowing the right thing to say in an awkward situation. People who are considerate and punctual may not necessarily be good at flattering their superiors. Some of these skills, of course, may be better regarded as aspects of personality or temperament that ought to be kept conceptually distinct from any concept of intelligence or ability—although Mayer and Salovey (1993) argue that this is certainly not the whole story.

Future research may, or may not, produce a stronger call for the concept of social or emotional intelligence independent of other aspects of intelligence measured by IQ tests. Although my discussion of this topic has run the risk of concluding this chapter on a somewhat sceptical or even sour note, it will have served its purpose if it has suggested the sorts of questions that need to be addressed if a good case is to be made out for yet more multiple intelligences.

Summary

Do IQ tests *really* measure intelligence? This is as much a question about the nature of intelligence as one about the nature of IQ tests. One answer would surely be to refer the reader back to the research reviewed in Chapters 8 and 9, which pointed to some of the cognitive components, processes, or operations underlying performance on IQ tests. Are these the sort of processes one would expect to find engaged by a measure of intelligence? Some of them, at least, looked like reasonable candidates.

Studies of the validity, or external correlates, of IQ will never really provide the magic answer some people are looking for. But they will probably have to contribute to that answer. Chapter 2 reviewed some basic evidence of the validity of IQ scores as predictors of educational and occupational success. But, especially in the latter case, not even the most fervent defender of IQ could pretend that these correlations were particularly high. To the extent that the status of a person's job and the success of their performance depends on their ambition, motivation, and personality, no more than modest correlations between IQ and success are to be expected. But there are good reasons for questioning whether, especially at higher levels of achievement, IQ is the only cognitive factor influencing success. There is no real evidence to prove that genius is a product of an exceptionally high IQ (partly because it is not clear how such evidence could ever be obtained), and although Terman's famous longitudinal study revealed some fairly impressive lifetime achievements of a group of high-IQ Californian schoolchildren, there is good evidence that IQ was not the only determinant of their success. Similar conclusions are suggested by studies of successful scientists, architects, and businessmen. In many of these cases, a critical ingredient is simply experience and knowledge: good businessmen are experienced businessmen; good scientists are those who spend all their waking hours thinking about science.

The role of practice in achieving expertise in any domain is by now incontrovertible. Chess players and violinists, so it is estimated, need 10 years of sustained, concentrated practice to achieve any serious eminence in their chosen field. But practice can also enhance a variety of other skills, such as digit span, mental arithmetic, or calendar calculating, and in these cases the evidence suggests that the sheer amount of practice is far more important than IQ in determining the final level of achievement. At the same time, such practice may produce expertise in only a very narrow domain—a digit span of 100, which leaves immediate memory span for letters or words no more than average. Similar domain-specific expertise is evident in the ability of young Brazilian street vendors to perform quite complex feats of mental arithmetic in the context of working out the price of six melons or the amount of change a customer is owed, combined with an inability to solve formally identical problems presented in the standard format of a mental arithmetic test. And perhaps even more strikingly, well-educated university students fail to see how to test the truth of a formal 'if . . . then' statement in Wason's reasoning task, but have no difficulty when the rule is cast in the form of a more familiar statement about permissions or obligations.

Such domain specificity has often been interpreted as evidence for the 'modularity of mind', the idea that we possess domain-specific modules for different types of perceptual input, for recognizing faces or learning our native language, etc., rather than a general-purpose problem-solver. But the two ideas are not mutually exclusive. We may have an innate language acquisition device that allows us to become competent in the grammar of our native language, but also more general-purpose cognitive systems for solving other types of problem. Our knowledge and expertise may be domain-specific, but the means by which we became knowledgeable and expert may be entirely general. Domain-specific expertise, in chess, mental arithmetic, video games, digit span, or calendar calculating, depends on prolonged practice, and can hardly be the result of the possession of innate modules for each of these activities. Nor is the only alternative to the postulation of an indefinite number of domain-specific modules, the equally implausible postulation of a general 'mental logic', which we apply to the solution of any reasoning problem. There are good grounds for rejecting the idea of a mental logic (whether innate or acquired by experience), but the plausible alternative is that we possess general-purpose cognitive systems, which we use to learn the solutions to the particular problems we encounter. We may even learn to generalize those solutions to other similar problems, but not necessarily—what we have learned may often remain confined to the domain with which we had experience.

Differences in expertise and skill are often independent of IQ, and at least in some cases, such as those of Sternberg's successful business managers or Ceci and Liker's racegoers, also appear to be independent of obvious differences in opportunity for practice. If this is true, then the argument that appeals to a general-purpose cognitive system to explain the acquisition of expertise, must find some other general-purpose system, independent of IQ, to do the work required. Wagner and Sternberg have proposed that differences in expertise in a particular job are a consequence of differences in 'tacit knowledge' of the manifold demands of that job. But what explains these differences in tacit knowledge? The concept of tacit knowledge is of knowledge which is informal, poorly articulated, and relatively inaccessible to conscious introspection. It seems closely related to the concept of implicit learning studied by Reber and others in the laboratory, where people show evidence of having learned something about some rather complex sequential dependencies between rapidly occurring events, without being able to articulate the rules underlying those dependencies. And implicit learning, in turn, seems closely related to the concept of associative learning as a system for detecting contingencies between events, as exemplified in studies of simple conditioning. People differ in their performance on implicit learning tasks, and such differences are uncorrelated with differences in their IQ. Implicit or associative learning ability may therefore be the second general-purpose cognitive system that is responsible for the acquisition of practical intelligence or competence in a variety of different domains.

This does not rule out the possibility that there are many other more specialized abilities that underlie differences in people's competence in a variety of different domains. The concept of social intelligence is briefly examined in an attempt to show what would be required to establish the existence of other specific abilities. At present, the case for an independent social intelligence does not look very convincing, and a more plausible reading of the evidence is that differences in people's social competence are better regarded as differences in a whole range of relatively independent skills and aspects of personality.

Epilogue

In his book, *The science and politics of IQ*, Kamin was at pains to emphasize the significance of his title, telling the reader that his book was:

> about the politics of intelligence testing, as well as the science of intelligence testing. To pretend that the two are separable is either naive or dissembling. (Kamin, 1974, p. 2)

It is certainly true that, from early days, much that has been written about IQ testing has been intended to have social and political, as well as scientific, impact. Terman was only too anxious to stress the social and political value of the Stanford–Binet test. And Yerkes thought that the army testing programme provided a unique opportunity to enhance the public status of the fledgling science of psychology, by showing how well IQ could predict at least military competence. The marketing of new IQ tests later became a seriously profitable business, and the success of that marketing depended on claims for the practical utility of the tests. Many of those claims rested on the assertion that an IQ test, taking no longer than an hour to administer, could give a reliable measure of a person's intelligence; that the intelligence so measured was innate and fixed, and was a major determinant of that person's success in all walks of life—of their success in school as a child, of the occupational level they could later aspire to, and of the success with which they would perform their job.

Earlier chapters have commented, in passing, on many of these claims, and in that sense this book too has been about the politics, as well as the science, of IQ. But it should be obvious that my central purpose has been to focus on the science. I do not wish to change that emphasis now, but it may be worth concluding with a few wider comments.

The first of which is this: it has not been only the proponents of IQ tests who have had a social or political axe to grind. So have the tests' critics. And if many of the proponents' claims have been exaggerated, in some cases to the point of dishonesty, much the same can be said of some of the critics' claims. Many of these critics have also, in my judgement, done their cause a serious disservice. Consider: there can be no serious doubt that the heritability of IQ in modern industrialized societies is significantly greater than zero. Critics who insist on denying this conclusion must be casting some doubts on their own scientific credentials—or at least on their ability to read evidence impartially. But they must also be sending out a singularly unfortunate message, namely that they believe that dire political consequences will follow from the demonstration that the heritability of IQ *is* greater than zero. The implication is that their conception of the good society is incompatible with there being genetically influenced differences in people's IQ scores. Do they really believe that? Why? Is it because they have mistakenly identified heritable with immutable, or naively assumed that any environmentally influenced characteristic will readily respond to simple social engineering? Does their reluctance to acknowledge the heritability of IQ extend to other sorts of differences between people—to differences in musical or artistic talent, athletic ability, personality or temperament, personal appearance or attractiveness to the opposite sex? Is the only just society one consisting of clones? If they single out IQ as the one characteristic which cannot be allowed to be in the slightest degree heritable, they are surely investing IQ with even more importance than the most fervent proponents of the tests have ever suggested. They are equating IQ with virtue and merit; they are implying that a high IQ is a necessary prerequisite for any form of success and that a low IQ condemns a person to failure in all walks of life.

Which makes it all the odder that so many critics have also insisted, again in the face of quite good evidence to the contrary, that there is no correlation whatsoever between IQ and anything else of importance. If IQ scores really are unimportant, why should it matter whether they are heritable? Once again, the implication of the critics' claim is that they fear dire social consequences from any demonstration that IQ scores do predict other things of some social significance. Once again, their cause would surely be better served by acknowledging the probable truth of some moderately well-established empirical observations, while questioning some of the more extravagant interpretations that have sometimes been put on those observations.

Thus, a number of proponents of the tests have attempted to estimate the financial benefits that would accrue from the use of IQ tests for job selection. Hunter and Hunter (1984), for example, suggested that the US economy would benefit to the tune of $80 billion a year if applicants for jobs were hired strictly in accordance with their IQ scores. As Wagner (1994) has noted, figures like this ignore two points. First, the pool of talent is not limitless. If a rival organization, with money to burn, is also hiring by IQ score, your organization may end up having to make do with a set of applicants of distinctly lower average IQ. And, at the end of the queue, there will be some unfortunate organization that has only applicants of well below-average IQ to choose from. For this organization, assuming that IQ tests really do predict competence, the universal use of IQ tests to select employees will mean a net loss of utility. Secondly, even if IQ does predict how efficiently employees will perform their job, the simple correlation between IQ and efficiency is not the relevant statistic here. The only way to calculate how much money an organization will save by hiring in accordance with IQ is how much *better* a prediction can be made about an employee's efficiency by adding an IQ test to existing methods of selection.

Arguments about the use of IQ tests in any form of selection, whether for employment or admission to further education, often ignore the fact that the alternative to IQ tests is some other selection procedure. Relatively few employers hire people at random, nor do universities generally admit anyone who applies regardless of their qualifications. It is not that IQ tests are necessarily better than other selection procedures. They may be better in some respects, but worse in others. The point is that the issues that need to be discussed are issues about selection, not about IQ.

Where there are more applicants than posts or places to be filled, how should we go about selecting the successful applicants? On a first come, first served basis? Randomly or by lot? At one time the gods could be trusted to see to it that a lottery selected the right winner. Today, we are inclined to believe that we can, and should therefore try to, do better. We believe, for example, in selection by merit. But what does that mean? There appear to be, broadly speaking, two distinct approaches: we can select on the basis of past accomplishment, or of future potential. In practice, the distinction, like that between tests of achievement and of ability, is less than clear. We usually insist that the accomplishment must somehow be relevant to the position for which we are selecting applicants. Only the most eccentric bankers will select their employees by seeing how well they can sing opera arias. But what is the reason for insisting on the relevance of past accomplishments other than the belief that, if relevant, they will predict future performance? The reason why we require doctors to pass medical exams is because we believe they need to have acquired certain knowledge and skills, in order to practice medicine effectively, and that passing the exam is proof that they have done so.

Selection by merit, whether past or future, will not differ from selection by lot unless the assessment of merit is moderately accurate. If we think that a lottery is unjust, therefore, we should value other selection procedures only to the extent that they are reliable and valid. It follows that if an IQ score adds to the predictive validity of a battery of selection tests, an IQ test should be added to that battery. This is, of course, the standard argument of test theory, but it is not an argument specific to IQ tests. It applies equally to any piece of information used for purposes of selection; if that piece of information increases the validity of the selection procedure, it should be used. But the argument is not necessarily quite as persuasive as is sometimes assumed, for there are several problems that need to be borne in mind. For a start, we must recognize that no selection procedure will be perfectly valid, if only because our criterion measure of success will itself be unreliable and invalid. It is not just that a supervisor's rating or a brief work sample may provide an imperfect measure of how well an employee is performing. An employee's performance may vary along so many different dimensions that it may be unwise to attempt to capture it in a single rating. One middle-manager may run a section of the company that posts higher profits in a given year; another may be responsible for a major reorganization which, although yielding no immediate profit, promises long-term dividends; a third may be more supportive of her staff, who thus show greater loyalty to the company; and a fourth and fifth may excel in yet other aspects of a manager's job. Although this argument should be used with some caution, for it is often an excuse for conservative inertia, prejudice, and muddling along, it is as well to acknowledge that we do not always know exactly what we are looking for in applicants for a job, because we do not always know exactly what constitutes success in that job. Concentration on aspects that are easily measured may lead one to ignore others that turn out to be equally important.

There is, however, a more serious consequence of the inevitable imperfection of any selection procedure. It is a simple matter to show that if a particular test is neither perfectly reliable nor perfectly valid, its use is almost bound to discriminate in favour of some groups at the expense of others. Imagine a particular test given to members of three groups who are applying for a job. Although imperfect, the test is equally reliable and valid for individuals of all three groups, but, as can be seen in the figure, group A has a lower mean score on the test than group B, who score on average below group C. The figure also shows a cut-off score, at group B's mean: applicants with scores above this cut-off are selected, while applicants with scores below the cut-off are rejected. The test selects a higher proportion of group C than of A or B, but that, we might think, is right and proper since the test is equally reliable and valid for all three groups, and a higher proportion of group C meets the criterion for selection.

However, the test is not perfectly reliable or valid. To say this, is to say that a certain proportion of individuals with scores above the cut-off will actually do worse on the job than a certain proportion of people with scores below the cut-off. The first lot were lucky to pass, the second lot unlucky to fail. Such individual cases of injustice are an inevitable consequence of the use of a less than perfectly reliable or valid test, and there is not much that can be done about them. But perhaps we should not be so complacent about the systematic injustice done to members of a particular group. To see why such injustice arises, the figure shows a 'zone of uncertainty' between the two dotted lines on either side of the cut-off score. Let us assume that a certain percentage of applicants within this zone of uncertainty were incorrectly placed: for example, that 25 per cent of those below the cut-off

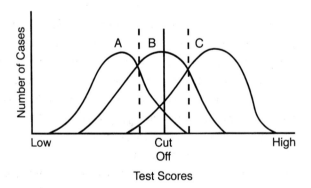

Hypothetical distribution of three groups' scores on a test used for selecting applicants for a job. The cut-off score for selection is shown at the mean of group B's scores. The dotted vertical lines on either side of this cut-off score indicate a 'zone of uncertainty', where the test has a significant probability of misclassifying applicants. See text for further details.

really ought to have been selected, because they would, in fact, perform the job better than 25 per cent of those above the cut-off. For group B as a whole, these errors cancel out: the number of people below the cut-off that were incorrectly rejected is exactly the same as the number of those above the cut-off that were incorrectly accepted. For group C, however, the number of incorrect acceptances is far greater than the number of incorrect rejections, while for group A the number of incorrect rejections is far greater than the number of incorrect acceptances. So use of the test has favoured group C and discriminated against group A. There is no need to give real names to these groups to see the social implications of all this.

The discussion of selection in the USA has become obsessed with the issue of group differences, and whether positive discrimination or affirmative action are justified or necessary to counteract them. On the face of it, there is much to be said for the argument that affirmative action or group quotas are unjust because their use implies that people are being treated as members of a group rather than as individuals, and justice requires that people be treated as individuals. Perhaps, in an ideal world, that would be true—although it is not difficult to discern some less lofty motives underlying such arguments, and the figure suggests that the argument may be far too simplistic. Moreover, the fact is that people are inevitably treated as members of groups, especially when group membership is immediately visible, or otherwise easily ascertained. You may be an excellent driver, not only skilled but also sensible and careful, and thus relatively unlikely to be involved in an accident. But if you are male, under the age of 25, and drive an expensive sports car, you will pay heavily for your insurance. And if you are also black and obviously poor, and driving through an inner-city ghetto, you are more likely to be stopped by the police on suspicion that the car is stolen, than you would be if you were white, middle-aged and prosperous looking, and driving through a salubrious suburb. Flynn (1996) has argued persuasively that since individual blacks suffer in so many different ways from being treated as a member of a particular group, a small measure of affirmative action in compensation would hardly come amiss.

Whatever one's views on these undoubtedly problematic issues, the point to remember is that they are not specific to the use of IQ tests. They concern selection in general, not IQ tests in particular. If IQ tests had never been invented, if their use for any purpose whatsoever were to be banned tomorrow, these issues would not go away. We should still have to decide whether our method of selecting one applicant rather than another for a particular job or a place at a particular university was just and fair. We should still need to reconcile fairness to individuals with fairness to groups, and where fairness seemed to conflict with efficiency, we should still have to decide how far to let one win at the expense of the other. The argument often centres round IQ tests, because IQ scores are modestly predictive of success in a variety of settings. But as we have seen, IQ tests are not the only, and not always the best, predictors of success.

In their less guarded moments, Herrnstein and Murray (1994) give the impression that they believe the social consequences of differences in IQ to be of almost boundless significance. They paint, for example, an apocalyptic picture of an American society increasingly segregated by IQ, where a substantial minority of the population is bound, by virtue of its low innate IQ, to live in poverty and squalor, perpetuating a culture of unemployment, crime, drug dependency, and illegitimate births. That there is an 'underclass' in many American cities, the members of which are disproportionately black and who live in this way, is not in dispute. The question is how far this lifestyle is to be attributed to their low IQ. Let us first note a point emphasized by Gould (1997), that the correlations reported by Herrnstein and Murray between IQ (with social background held constant) and such dependent variables as unemployment, criminal behaviour, or teenage pregnancies, are mostly quite modest, rarely more than 0.30, often no more than 0.20. As they acknowledge, 'you cannot predict what a given person will do from his IQ score' (Herrnstein and Murray, 1994, p. 117). Just as there are many other factors that affect how effective people are at their job, so there are many other factors that predict their tendency to engage in a life of crime.

But we should also, and I hope for the last time, remind ourselves that modest correlations do not necessarily imply direct causal connections. If certain forms of generally undesirable social behaviour really were a simple consequence of a low IQ, it would follow that we could eliminate the underclass at a stroke by an intervention that succeeded in raising its members' IQ scores. The obvious reply—that this is a merely fanciful suggestion because we do not know how to raise IQ, is to forget that, even if we cannot do it overnight, the environment of all industrial societies has succeeded in doing it over a rather longer time scale (Chapter 4). The average IQ of Americans, black as well as white, has probably increased by some 15 points since 1945. This dramatic increase in IQ has not been accompanied by any notable decrease in crime or teenage pregnancies.

Many proponents of IQ tests continue to write as though modest correlations between IQ and various indices of social pathology were evidence of a simple causal chain from one to the other. They are even willing to rely on a within-group correlation to prove that a between-group difference in the incidence of a particular pathology is the consequence of a between-group difference in IQ. Thus Gordon (1997) notes that differences in the prevalence of criminal behaviour and HIV infection between blacks and whites in the USA are rather precisely matched by differences in their average IQ scores. Given the 1 SD difference between blacks' and whites' IQ scores, it follows that some 16–17 per cent of whites, but 50 per cent of blacks will have an IQ below 85. Gordon then notes, for example, that in various surveys, 17–18 per cent of white youths had appeared before a juvenile court by the age of 18, and some 15 per cent of white males had been arrested for a serious crime at one time or another. In both cases, the incidence among blacks was just over 50 per cent. In other words, the relative proportion of blacks and whites with an IQ below 85 closely matched the relative proportion of blacks and whites falling foul of the criminal justice system. From which Gordon concludes that the IQ difference between blacks and whites must be responsible for this difference.

A charitable response to this suggestion is that it ignores some equally plausible alternatives. An underclass cut off from mainstream society, where adults have few opportunities for legitimate employment and drugs provide the main lubricant of the economy, where children are brought up by single mothers and attend, and soon drop out from, poor schools, may both tempt adolescents into a life of crime and not do much good for their IQ scores (see Dash (1996) for a graphic account of one such family's life). But the simplest reply to Gordon's argument is to note that the difference in the incidence of criminal behaviour between blacks and whites is far smaller than the difference between males and females. Although there is some evidence that they may be catching up, females still commit far fewer crimes than males. Gordon's thesis thus implies that the sex difference in average IQ, in favour of females, should also be very much larger than that between blacks and whites. The only way to avoid this absurd implication is to appeal to some other factor to explain the sex difference in criminality. And why should one not then appeal to some other factor to explain the black–white difference?

Lubinski and Humphreys (1997) have put forward an even more remarkable suggestion to account for the greater prevalence of babies of low birth weight and infant mortality among US blacks than other American ethnic groups—including American Indians who have a similarly low average IQ and suffer from similar levels of poverty. Lubinski and Humphreys note that blacks obtain significantly lower scores on measures of spatial IQ than other ethnic groups (see Chapter 5), and suggest that this may be the critical causal factor. They might, I suppose, be right, but on the face of it, it is hard to imagine a better example of a correlation that did *not* indicate a straightforward causal connection: how could parents' spatial IQ scores possibly determine whether their baby will die in infancy?

If what Kamin meant was that, as a matter of fact, politics and science have been inextricably entwined in many discussions of IQ, he was surely right. But the interaction between the two has, for the most part, been good for neither. With a few honourable exceptions, political scientists and sociologists have not made particularly valuable contributions to the scientific study of IQ. And very few IQ testers have made a valuable contribution to political science or social policy. But Kamin's thesis was, no doubt, a wider one: that science and politics are in principle inseparable when it comes to a discussion of IQ, and that any statement about IQ is as much a reflection of one's political prejudices as a scientific conclusion. Of course, most scientists have social and political views. And science is not just about the accumulation of factual knowledge. Particularly when it must rely on imperfect, natural experiments, science requires the evaluation and interpretation of evidence. Such evaluation requires judgement, and judgement, as cognitive psychologists should know, can be influenced by prior belief or preconception. So much is obvious. Does it really imply that we should accept only those conclusions about IQ advanced by writers whose political views meet with our approval? Of course not. It means that we should strive all the harder to distinguish between matters of fact and matters of opinion (and not be seduced into believing that there is no distinction between the two); that we should scrutinize other people's theories, and our own, to decide how strongly they are supported by, and how far they go beyond, the available evidence; that we should scrupulously evaluate both the evidence for, and that against, any conclusion we wish to draw. In other words: we should try to do good science.

References

Ackerman, P. L. (1988). Determinants of individual differences during skill acquisition; cognitive abilities and information processing. *Journal of Experimental Psychology: General,* 117, 299–318.

Alderton, D. L., Goldman, S. R., and Pellegrino, J. W. (1985). Individual differences in process outcomes for analogy and classification solution. *Intelligence,* 9, 69–85.

Anastasi, A. (1988). *Psychological testing,* (6th edn). Macmillan, New York.

Anderson, M. (1992). *Intelligence and development: A cognitive theory.* Blackwell, Oxford.

Ankney, C. D. (1992). Sex differences in relative brain size: The mismeasure of woman, too? *Intelligence,* 16, 329–336.

Baddeley, A. D. (1986). *Working memory.* Clarendon Press, Oxford.

Baddeley, A. D. (1996). Exploring the central executive. *Quarterly Journal of Experimental Psychology,* 49A, 5–28.

Baddeley, A. D. (1997). *Human memory: Theory and practice,* (revised edn). Psychology Press, Hove, Sussex.

Baddeley, A. D. and Hitch, G. (1974). Working memory. In *Recent advances in learning and motivation,* (ed. G. A. Bower), Vol. 8. Academic Press, New York.

Baddeley, A. D. and Wilson, B. (1988). Frontal amnesia and the dysexecutive syndrome. *Brain and Cognition,* 7, 212–230.

Baddeley, A. D., Thomson, N., and Buchanan, M. (1975). Word length and the structure of short-term memory. *Journal of Verbal Learning and Verbal Behavior,* 14, 575–589.

Baenninger, M. and Newcombe, N. (1989). The role of experience in spatial test-performance: A meta-analysis. *Sex Roles,* 20, 327–344.

Bajema, C. J. (1963). Estimation of the direction and intensity of natural selection in relation to human intelligence by means of the intrinsic rate of natural increase. *Eugenics Quarterly,* 10, 175–187.

Bajema, C. J. (1968). Relation of fertility to occupational status, IQ, educational attainments, and size of family of origin: A follow-up study of the male Kalamazoo public school population. *Eugenics Quarterly,* 15, 198–203.

Baron-Cohen, S. (1995). *Mind blindness.* MIT Press, Cambridge, Mass.

Barrett, P. T. and Eysenck, H. J. (1992). Brain-evoked potentials and intelligence: the Hendrickson paradigm. *Intelligence,* 16, 361–381.

Bates, T., Stough, C., Mangan, G., and Pellett, O. (1995). Intelligence and complexity of the averaged evoked potential: An attentional theory. *Intelligence,* 20, 27–39.

Bates, T. C. and Eysenck, H. J. (1993a). String length, attention and intelligence: focused attention reverses the string-length–IQ relationship. *Personality and Individual Differences,* 15, 363–371.

Bates, T. C. and Eysenck, H. J. (1993b). Intelligence, inspection time and decision time. *Intelligence,* 17, (4), 523–532.

Baumeister, A. A. and Bacharach, V. R. (1996). A critical analysis of the infant health and development programme. *Intelligence,* 23, 79–104.

Bayley, N. (1969). *The Bayley Scales of Infant Ddevelopment.* Psychological Corporation, New York.

Bayley, N. (1993). *Bayley Scales of Infant Development,* (2nd edn). Psychological Corporation, San Antonio.

Belmont, J. M. and Butterfield, E. C. (1977). The instructional approach to developmental cognitive research. In *Perspectives on the development of memory and cognition,* (ed. R. V. Kail, Jr and J. W. Hagen). Erlbaum, Hillsdale, NJ.

Belmont, L. and Marolla, F. A. (1973). Birth order, family size, and intelligence. *Science,* 182, 1096–1101.

Belmont, L., Stein, Z., and Zybert, P. (1978). Child spacing and birth order: Effect on intellectual ability in two-child families. *Science,* 202, 995–996.

Benbow, C. P. (1988). Sex differences in mathematical reasoning ability in intellectually talented preadolescents: Their nature, effects, and possible causes. *Behavioral and Brain Sciences,* 11, 169–232.

Bennett, H. L. (1983). Remembering drink orders: the memory skills of cocktail waitresses. *Human Learning: Journal of Practical Research and Applications,* 2, 157–170.

Benton, D. and Buts, J. (1990). Vitamin-mineral supplementation and intelligence. *Lancet,* 335, 1158–1160.

Benton, D. and Roberts, G. (1988). Effect of vitamin and mineral supplementation on intelligence of a sample of schoolchildren. *Lancet,* 1, 140–144.

Berry, D. C. and Broadbent, D. E. (1984). On the relationship between task performance and associated verbalisable knowledge. *Quarterly Journal of Experimental Psychology,* 36A, 209–231.

Berry, D. C. and Dienes, Z. (1993). *Implicit learning: Theoretical and empirical issues.* Erlbaum, Hove.

Berry, J. W. (1966). Temne and Eskimo perceptual skills. *International Journal of Psychology,* 1, 207–222.

Binet, A. (1900). Recherches sur la technique de la mensuration de la tête vivante, plus 4 autres mémoires sur la céphalométrie. *L'Année Psychologique,* 7, 314-429.

Binet, A. (1911). Nouvelles recherches sur la mésure du niveau intellectual chez les enfants d'école. *L'Annee Psychologique,* 17, 145–201.

Binet, A. and Simon, T. (1905a). Sur le nécessité d'établir un diagnostique scientifique des états inférieurs de l'intelligence. *Année Psychologique,* 11, 163–190.

Binet, A. and Simon, T. (1905b). Méthodes nouvelles pour le diagnostic du niveau intellectuel des anormaux. *L'Année Psychologique,* 11, 191–244.

Binet, A. and Simon, T. (1911). *A method of measuring the development of the intelligence of young children.* Courier Company, Lincoln, IL.

Birch, H. G., Piñeiro, C., Alcalde, E., Toca, T., and Cravioto, J. (1971). Kwashiorkor in early childhood and intelligence at school age. *Pediatric Research,* 5, 579–584.

Bishop, D. V. M. (1990). *Handedness and developmental disorder.* Lawrence Erlbaum, Hove, Sussex.

Blinkhorn, S. F. (1995). Burt and the early history of factor analysis. In *Cyril Burt: fraud or framed?* (ed. N. J. Mackintosh). Oxford University Press, Oxford.

Blinkhorn, S. F. and Hendrickson, D. E. (1982). Average evoked responses and psychometric intelligence. *Nature,* 195, 596–597.

Block, N. J. and Dworkin, G. (1976). *The IQ controversy.* Pantheon Books, New York.

Bloom, B. S. (1964). *Stability and change in human characteristics.* Wiley, New York.

Boles, D. B. (1980). X-linkage of spatial ability: a critical review. *Child Development,* 51, 623–635.

Bornstein, M. H. and Sigman, M. D. (1986). Continuity in mental development from infancy. *Child Development,* 57, 251–274.

Bors, D. A. and MacLeod, C. M. (1996). Attention, information processing, and IQ. *International Journal of Psychology*, 31, 3452.

Boswell, J. (1988). *The kindness of strangers*. Pantheon Books, New York.

Bouchard, T. J., Jr (1983). Do environmental similarities explain the similarity in intelligence of identical twins reared apart? *Intelligence*, 7, 175–184.

Bouchard, T .J., Jr (1997). IQ similarity in twins reared apart: findings and responses to critics. In *Intelligence: heredity and environment*, (ed. R. J. Sternberg and E. L. Grigorenko). Cambridge University Press, New York.

Bouchard, T. J. Jr. and McGue, M. (1981). Familial studies of intelligence: A review. *Science*, 212, 1055–1059.

Bouchard, T. J. Jr. and Segal, N. L. (1985). Environment and IQ. In *Handbook of intelligence: Theories, measurements and applications*, (ed. B. B. Wolman). Wiley, New York.

Bouchard, T. J. Jr, Lykken, D. T., McGue, M., Segal, N. L., and Tellegen, A. (1990). Sources of human psychological differences: The Minnesota study of twins reared apart. *Science*, 250, 223–228.

Bowles, S. and Gintis, H. (1976). *Schooling in capitalist America: Educational reform and the contradictions of economic life*. Harper and Row, New York.

Bowling, A. C. and Mackenzie, B. D. (1996). The relationship between speed of information processing and cognitive ability. *Personality and Individual Difference*, 20, 775–800.

Brackbill, Y. and Nichols, P. L. (1982). A test of the confluence model of intellectual development. *Developmental Psychology*, 18, 192–198.

Bradley, R. H. Caldwell, B., and Elardo, R. (1977). Home environment, social status, and mental test performance. *Journal of Educational Psychology*, 69, 697-701.

Brand, C. R. and Deary, I. J. (1982). Intelligence and 'inspection time'. In *A model for intelligence*, (ed. H. J. Eysenck). Springer, New York.

Brebner, J. and Cooper, C. (1986). Personality factors and inspection time. *Personality and Individual Differences*, 7, 709–714.

Breslau, N. *et al.* (1994). A gradient relationship between low birth weight and IQ at age 6 years. *Archives of Adolescent Medicine*, 148, 377–383.

Brewer, N. and Smith, G. A. (1984). How normal and retarded individuals monitor and regulate speed and accuracy of responding in serial choice tasks. *Journal of Experimental Psychology: General*, 113, 71–93.

Brigham, C. C. (1923). *A study of American intelligence*. Princeton University Press, Princeton, NJ.

Brinkmann, E. H. (1966). Programmed instruction as a technique for improving spatial visualization. *Journal of Applied Psychology*, 50, 179–184.

Brody, E. B. and Brody, N. (1976). *Intelligence: Nature, determinants and consequences*. Academic Press, New York.

Brody, N. (1992). *Intelligence*, (2nd edn). Academic Press, San Diego, CA.

Broman, S. H., Nichols, P. L., and Kennedy, W. A. (1975). *Preschool IQ: Prenatal and early developmental correlates*. Erlbaum, Hillsdale, NJ.

Broman, S., Nichols, P. L., Shaughnessy, P., and Kennedy, W. (1987). *Retardation in young children: A developmental study of cognitive deficit*. Lawrence Erlbaum, Hillsdale, NJ.

Brown, G. D. A. and Hulme, C. (1995). Modeling item length effects in memory span: no rehearsal needed? *Journal of Memory and Language*, 34, 594–621.

Brown, R. E. (1966). Organ weight in malnutrition with special reference to brain weight. *Developmental Medicine and Child Neurology*, 8, 512–522.

Bryden, M. P. (1982). *Laterality: Functional asymmetry in the intact brain*. Academic Press, New York.

Buffery, A. W. H. and Gray, J. A. (1972). Sex differences in the development of spatial and linguistic skills. In *Gender differences: Their ontogeny and significance*, (ed. C. Ounsted and D. C. Taylor). Williams and Wilkins, Baltimore.

Burke, H. R. (1958). Raven's Progressive Matrices: A review and critical evaluation. *Journal of Genetic Psychology,* 93, 199–228.

Burke, H. R. (1985). Raven's Progressive Matrices (1938): More on norms, reliability and validity. *Journal of Clinical Psychology,* 72, 247–251.

Burks, B. S. (1928). The relative influence of nature and nurture upon mental development: A comparative study of foster parent–foster child resemblance and true parent–true child resemblance. *Yearbook of the National Society for the Study of Education,* 27. Public School Publishing Co., Bloomingdale, IL.

Burleigh, M. (1994). *Death and deliverance: Euthanasia in Germany 1900–1945.* Cambridge University Press, Cambridge.

Buros, O. K. (1935). *Mental Measurements Yearbook.* Gryphon Press, Highland Park, NJ.

Buros, O. K. (1978). *The Eighth Mental Measurements Yearbook.* Gryphon Press, Highland Park, NJ.

Burt, C. L. (1912). The inheritance of mental characters. *Eugenics Review,* 4, 168–200.

Burt, C. L. (1917). The distribution and relations of educational abilities. London County Council.

Burt, C. L. (1921). *Mental and scholastic tests.* King and Son, London.

Burt, C. L. (1943). Ability and income. *British Journal of Educational Psychology,* 13, 83–98.

Burt, C. L. (1949). The structure of the mind. *British Journal of Educational Psychology,* 19, 176–199.

Burt, C. L. (1955). The evidence for the concept of intelligence. *British Journal of Educational Psychology,* 25, 158–177.

Burt, C. L. (1966). The genetic determination of differences in intelligence: a study of monozygotic twins reared together and apart. *British Journal of Psychology,* 57, 137–153.

Burt, C. L. and Moore, R. C. (1912). The mental differences between the sexes. *Journal of Experimental Pedagogy,* 1, 273–284 and 355–388.

Butcher, H. J. (1968). *Human intelligence.* Methuen, London.

Byrne, R. (1995). *The thinking ape: Evolutionary origins of intelligence.* Oxford University Press, Oxford.

Cahan, S. and Cohen, N. (1989). Age versus schooling effects on intelligence development. *Child Development,* 60, 1239–1249.

Campbell, F. A. and Ramey, C. T. (1994). Effects of early intervention on intellectual and academic achievement: A follow-up study of children from low income families. *Child Development,* 65, 684–698.

Campione, J. C., Brown, A. L., and Ferrara, R. A. (1982). Mental retardation and intelligence. In *Handbook of human intelligence,* (ed. R. J. Sternberg).Cambridge University Press, Cambridge.

Cantor, N., Engle, R. W., and Hamilton, G. (1991). Short-term memory, working memory, and verbal abilities—How do they relate? *Intelligence,* 15, 229–246.

Capron, C. and Duyme, M. (1989). Assessment of effects of socioeconomic status on IQ in a full cross-fostering design. *Nature,* 340, 552–553.

Carlson, J. S., Jensen, C. M., and Widaman, K. F. (1983). Reaction time, intelligence and attention. *Intelligence,* 7, 329–344.

Carpenter, P. A. and Just, M. A. (1975). Sentence comprehension: A psycholingusitic processing model of verification. *Psychological Review,* 82, 45–73.

Carpenter, P. A. and Just, M. A. (1986). Spatial ability: An information processing approach to psychometrics. In *Advances in the psychology of human intelligence,* (ed. R. J. Sternberg), vol. 3. Erlbaum, Hillsdale, NJ.

Carpenter, P. A., Just, M. A., and Schell, P. (1990). What one intelligence test measures: A theoretical account of the processing in the Raven Progressive Matrices Test. *Psychological Review,* 97, 404–431.

Carraher, T. N., Carraher, D., and Schliemann, A. D. (1985). Mathematics in the streets and in the schools. *British Journal of Developmental Psychology*, 3, 21–29.

Carroll, J. B. (1993). *Human cognitive abilites.* Cambridge University Press, Cambridge.

Caryl, P. G. (1994). Early event-related potentials correlate with inspection time and intelligence. *Intelligence*, 18, 15–46.

Cattell, J. M. (1890). Mental tests and measurements. *Mind*, 15, 373–381.

Cattell, R. B. (1937). *The fight for our national intelligence.* King and Sons, London.

Cattell, R. B. (1940). A culture-free intelligence test, Part I. *Journal of Educational Psychology*, 31, 161–179.

Cattell, R. B. (1950). *Personality.* McGraw-Hill, New York.

Cattell, R. B. (1971). *Abilities: Their structure, growth and action.* Houghton-Miflin, Boston.

Ceci, S. J. (1990). *On intelligence . . . more or less. A bio-ecological treatise on intellectual development.* Prentice Hall, Englewood Cliffs, NJ.

Ceci, S. J. (1991). How much does schooling influence general intelligence and its cognitive components? A reassessment of the evidence. *Developmental Psychology*, 27, 703–722.

Ceci, S. J. and Liker, J. K. (1986). A day at the races; a study of IQ, expertise and cognitive complexity. *Journal of Experimental Psychology: General*, 115, 255–266.

Ceci, S. J. and Roazzi, A. (1994). The effects of context on cognition: postcards from Brazil. In *Mind in context. Interactionist perspectives on human intelligence*, (ed. R. J. Sternberg and R. K. Wagner). Cambridge University Press, Cambridge.

Chaiken, S. R. (1993). Two models for an inspection time paradigm: Processing distraction and processing speed versus processing speed and asymptotic strength. *Intelligence*, 17, 257–283.

Chaiken, S. R. (1994). The inspection time not studied: Processing speed ability unrelated to psychometric intelligence. *Intelligence*, 19, 295–316.

Chapin, F. S. (1928). A quantitative scale for rating the home and social environment of middle class families in an urban community. *Journal of Educational Psychology*, 19, 99–111.

Charness, N. (1989). Expertise in chess and bridge. In *Complex information processing: The impact of Herbert A. Simon*, (ed. D. Klahr and K. Kotovsky). Erlbaum, Hillsdale, NJ.

Chase, W. G. and Erikson, K. A. (1982). Skill and working memory. In *The psychology of learning and motivation*, (ed. G. H. Bower), vol. 16. Academic Press, New York.

Chase, W. G. and Simon, H. A. (1973). Perception in chess. *Cognitive Psychology*, 4, 55–81.

Cheng, P. and Holyoak, K. J. (1985). Pragmatic reasoning schemas. *Cognitive Psychology*, 17, 391–416.

Chi, M. T. H. (1978). Knowledge structures and memory development. In *Children's thinking: What develops*, (ed. R. S. Siegler). Erlbaum, Hillsdale, NJ.

Child, D. (1990). *The essentials of factor analysis*, (2nd edn). Cassell Educational, London.

Chincotta, D. and Hoosain, R. (1995). Reading rate, articulatory suppression and bilingual digit span. *European Journal of Cognitive Psychology*, 7, 201–211.

Chipuer, H. M., Rovine, M. J., and Plomin, R. (1990). LISREL modeling: Genetic and environmental influences on IQ revisited. *Intelligence*, 14, 11–29.

Chomsky, N. (1972). Psychology and ideology. *Cognition*, 1, 11–46.

Chomsky, N. (1980). *Rules and representations.* Columbia University Press, New York.

Clarke, A. M. and Clarke, A. D. B. (1976). *Early experience: Myth and evidence.* Free Press, New York.

Clarke, A. M., Clarke, A. D. B., and Berg, J. M. (1985). *Mental deficiency: The changing outlook*, (4th edn). Methuen, London.

Cleeremans, A. and McClelland, J. L. (1991). Learning the structure of event sequences. *Journal of Experimental Psychology: General*, 120, 235–253.

Cohen, G. (1989). *Memory in the real world.* Erlbaum, Hove.

Coleman, J. S. (1966). *Equality of educational opportunity*. US Office of Education, Washington, DC.

Connor, J. M., Serbin, L. A., and Schackman, M. (1977). Sex differences in children's responses to training on a visual-spatial test. *Developmental Psychology,* 13, 293–294.

Conrad, R. (1979). *The deaf schoolchild.* Harper and Row, London.

Conway, A. R. A. and Engle, R. W. (1996). Individual differences in working memory capacity: More evidence for a general capacity theory. *Memory,* 4, 577–590.

Cooper, C., Kline, P., and MacLaurin-Jones, L. (1986). Inspection time and primary abilities. *British Journal of Educational Psychology,* 56, 304–308.

Cooper, L. A. (1975). Mental rotation of random two-dimensional shapes. *Cognitive Psychology,* 7, 20–43.

Cooper, L. A. and Podgory, P. (1976). Mental transformations and visual comparison processes: Effects of complexity and similarity. *Journal of Experimental Psychology: Human Perception and Performance,* 2, 503–514.

Cosmides, L. (1989). The logic of social exchange: Has natural selection shaped how humans reason? Studies with the Wason selection task. *Cognition,* 31, 187–276.

Cosmides, L. and Tooby, J. (1994). Origins of domain specificity: The evolution of functional organization. In *Mapping the mind: Domain specificity in cognition and culture,* (ed. L. A. Hirschfeld and S. A. Gelman). Cambridge University Press, Cambridge.

Court, J. H. (1983). Sex differences in performance on Raven's Progressive Matrices: A review. *Alberta Journal of Educational Research,* 29, 54–74.

Court, J. H. and Raven, J. (1995). *Manual for Raven's Progressive Matrices and Vocabulary Scales. Section 7: Research and references.* Oxford Psychologists Press, Oxford.

Cowan, N. (1992). Verbal memory span and the timing of spoken recall. *Journal of Memory and Language,* 31, 668–684.

Cox, G. M. (1926). *Genetic studies of genius,* vol. 2. Stanford University Press, Stanford, CA.

Craik, F. I. M. and Jennings, J. M. (1992). Human memory. In *Handbook of aging and cognition,* (ed. F. I. M. Craik and T. A. Salthouse). Erlbaum, Hillsdale, NJ.

Crombie, I. K., Todman, J., McNeill, G., Florey, C. D., Menzies, I., and Kennedy, R. A. (1990). Effect of vitamin and mineral supplementation on verbal and non-verbal reasoning of school children. *Lancet,* 335, 744–747.

Curtiss, S. (1977). *Genie: A psycholinguistic study of a modern-day 'wild-child'.* Academic Press, New York.

Damasio, A. R. (1994). *Descartes' error. Emotion, reason, and the human brain.* Putnam, New York.

Daneman, M. and Carpenter, P. A. (1980). Individual differences in working memory and reading. *Journal of Verbal Learning and Verbal Behavior,* 19, 450–466.

Daneman, M. and Green, I. (1986). Individual differences in comprehending and producing words in context. *Journal of Memory and Lanugage,* 25, 1–18.

Daneman, M. and Tardif, T. (1987). Working memory and reading skill re-examined. In *Attention and performance XII,* (ed. M. Coltheart). Lawrence Erlbaum Associates, Hove.

Dash, L. (1996). *Rosa Lee.* Basic Books, New York.

Davie, R., Butler, N., and Goldstein, H. (1972). *From birth to seven: A report of the National Child Development Study.* Longman, London.

Deary, I. J. (1993). Inspection time and WAIS-R IQ subtypes: A confirmatory factor analysis study. *Intelligence,* 17, 223–236.

Deary, I. J. (1994). Intelligence and auditory discrimination: separating processing speed and fidelity of stimulus representation. *Intelligence,* 18, 189–213.

Deary, I. J. and Caryl, P. G. (1993). Intelligence, EEG and evoked potentials. In *Biological approaches to the study of human intelligence,* (ed. P. A. Vernon). Ablex, Norwood, NJ.

Deary, I. J. and Stough, C. (1996). Intelligence and inspection time. *American Psychologist,* 51, 599–608.

Deary, I. J., Head, B., and Egan, V. (1989). Auditory inspection time, intelligence and pitch discrimination. *Intelligence,* 13, 135–147.

Deary, I .J., Egan, V., Gibson, G. J., Austin, E. J., Brand, C. R., and Kellaghan, T. (1996). Intelligence and the differentiation hypothesis. *Intelligence,* 23, 105–132.

DeFries, J. C. *et al.* (1979). Familial resemblance for specific cognitive abilities. *Behavior Genetics,* 9, 23–43.

De Groot, A. D. (1951). War and the intelligence of youth. *Journal of Abnormal and Social Psychology,* 46, 596–597.

De Groot, A. D. (1965). *Thought and choice in chess.* Mouton, The Hague.

de Jong, P. F. and Das Smaal, E. A. (1995). Attention and intelligence: The validity of the Star Counting Test. *Journal of Educational Psychology,* 87, 80–92.

Denis, M. (1982). Imagining while reading text: A study of individual differences. *Memory and Cognition,* 10, 540–545.

Detterman, D. K. (1987). What does reaction time tell us about intelligence? In *Speed of information-processing and intelligence,* (ed. P. A. Vernon). Ablex, Norwood, NJ.

Detterman, D. K. and Daniel, M. H. (1989). Correlations of mental tests with each other and with cognitive variables are highest for low-IQ groups. *Intelligence,* 13, 349–359.

Devlin, B., Daniels, M., and Roeder, K. (1997). The heritability of IQ. *Nature,* 388, 468–471.

Dias, R., Robbins, T. W., and Roberts, A. C. (1996). Primate analogue of the Wisconsin Card Sorting Test: Effects of excitotoxic lesions of the prefrontal cortex in the Marmoset. *Behavioral Neuroscience,* 110, 872–886.

Dickinson, A. (1980). *Contemporary animal learning theory.* Cambridge University Press, Cambridge.

Dickstein, L. S. (1978). The effects of figure on syllogistic reasoning. *Memory and Cognition,* 6, 76–83.

Dobbing, J. (1968). Vulnerable periods in developing brains. In *Applied neurochemistry,* (ed. A. N. Davison and J. Dobbing). Blackwell, London and Oxford.

Dumaret, A. and Stewart, J. T. (1985). IQ, scholastic performance and behaviour of sibs raised in contrasting environments. *Journal of Child Psychology and Psychiatry,* 26, 553–580.

Duncan, J., Burgess, P., and Emslie, H. (1995). Fluid intelligence after frontal lobe lesions. *Neuropsychologia,* 33, 261–268.

Duncan, J., Emslie, H., Williams, P., Johnson, R., and Freer, C. (1996). Intelligence and the frontal lobe: The organization of goal-directed behaviour. *Cognitive Psychology,* 30, 257–303.

Duncan, O. D., Featherman, D. L., and Duncan, B. (1972). *Socioeconomic background and achievement.* Seminar Press, New York.

Duncker, K. (1945). On problem solving. *Psychological Monographs,* 58, (whole number 270), 1–113. (Originally published in German in 1935.)

Edwards, J. H. (1957). A critical examination of the reputed primary influence of ABO phenotype on fertility and sex ratio. *British Journal of Preventive and Social Medicine,* 11, 79–89.

Efron, B. (1990). *The decline and fall of hemispheric specialization.* Erlbaum, Hillsdale, NJ.

Egan, V. (1994). Intelligence, inspection time and cognitive strategies. *British Journal of Psychology,* 85, 305–315.

Ekstrom, R. B., French, J. W., and Harman, H. H. (1976). *Kit of factor-referenced cognitive tests.* Educational Testing Service, Princeton, NJ.

Elashoff, J. D. and Snow, R. E. (1971). *'Pygmalion' reconsidered.* Charles A. Jones Publishing, Worthington, Ohio.

El Koussy, A. A. H. (1935). The visual perception of space. *British Journal of Psychology,* 20, (monograph Supplement).

Ellis, N. (1994). Vocabulary acquisition: The implicit ins and outs of explicit cognitive mediation. In *Implicit and explicit learning of languages*, (ed. N. Ellis). Academic Press, London.

Ellis, N. C. and Hennelly, R. A. (1980). A bilingual word-length effect: Implications for intelligence testing and the relative ease of mental calculation in Welsh and English. *British Journal of Psychology*, 71, 43–52.

Ellis, N. R. (1979). *Handbook of mental deficiency, psychological theory and research*, (2nd edn). Erlbaum, Hillsdale, NJ.

Ericsson, K. A., and Charness, N. (1994). Expert performance: Its structure and acquisition. *American Psychologist*, 49, 725–747.

Erlenmeyer-Kimling, L. and Jarvik, L. F. (1963). Genetics and intelligence: A review. *Science*, 142, 1477–1479.

Ertl, J., and Schafer, E. (1969). Brain response correlates of psychometric intelligence. *Nature*, 223, 421–422.

Evans, B. and Waites, B. (1981). *IQ and mental testing: An unnatural science and its social history*. Macmillan, London.

Evans, J. St. B. T., Newstead, S. E., and Byrne, R. M. J. (1993). *Human reasoning: The psychology of deduction*. Erlbaum, Hove.

Eyferth, K. (1961). Leistungen verschiedener Gruppen von Besatzungskindern in Hamburg—Weschler Intelligenztest für kinder (HAWIK). *Archiv für die gesamte Psychologie*, 113, 222–241.

Eysenck, H. J. (1979). *The structure and measurement of intelligence*. Springer Verlag, New York.

Eysenck, H. J. (ed.) (1982). *A model for intelligence*. Springer-Verlag, New York.

Eysenck, H. J. (1986). The theory of intelligence and the psychophysiology of cognition. In *Advances in the psychology of human intelligence*, (ed. R. J. Sternberg), Vol. 3. Erlbaum, Hillsdale, NJ.

Eysenck, H. J. (1995). *Genius: the natural history of creativity*. Cambridge University Press, Cambridge.

Eysenck, H. J. and Schoenthaler, J. J. (1997). Raising IQ level by vitamin and mineral supplementation. In *Intelligence, heredity, and environment*, (ed. R. J. Sternberg and E. Grigorenko). Cambridge University Press, Cambridge.

Farah, M. J., Hammon, K. M., Levine, D. N., and Calvanio, R. (1988). Visual and spatial mental imagery: Dissociable systems of representation. *Cognitive Psychology*, 20, 439–462.

Farber, S. L. (1981). *Identical twins reared apart: A reanalysis*. Basic Books, New York.

Feingold, A. (1988). Cognitive gender differences are disappearing. *American Psychologist*, 43, 95–103.

Feingold, A. (1992). Sex differences in variability in intellectual abilities: A new look at an old controversy. *Review of Educational Research*, 62, 61–84.

Feldman, J., Kerr, B., and Streissguth, A. P. (1995). Correlational analyses of procedural and declarative learning performance. *Intelligence*, 20, 87–114.

Fenson, L., Dale, P. S., Reznick, J. S., Bates, E., Thal, D. J., and Pethnick, S. J. (1994). Variability in early communicative development. *Monographs of the Society for Research in Child Development*, 59, Serial No. 242.

Fletcher, R. (1991). *Science, ideology and the media: The Cyril Burt scandal*. Transaction, New Brunswick, NJ.

Floud, J. and Halsey, A. H. (1957). Intelligence tests, social class and selection for secondary schools. *British Journal of Sociology*, 8, 33–9.

Flynn, J. R. (1980). *Race, IQ and Jensen*. Routledge and Kegan Paul, London.

Flynn, J. R. (1984). The mean IQ of Americans: Massive gains 1932 to 1978. *Psychological Bulletin*, 95, 29–51.

Flynn, J. R. (1987a). Massive IQ gains in 14 nations: What IQ tests really measure. *Psychological Bulletin*, 101, 171–191.

Flynn, J. R. (1987*b*). Race and IQ: Jensen's case refuted. In *Arthur Jensen: Consensus and controversy*, (ed. S. Modgil and C. Modgil). Falmer Press, New York.

Flynn, J. R. (1987*c*). Flynn replies to Nichols. In *Arthur Jensen: Consensus and controversy*, (ed. S. Modgil and C. Modgil). Falmer Press, New York.

Flynn, J. R. (1992). *Asian Americans: Achievement beyond IQ*. Erlbaum, Hillsdale, NJ.

Flynn, J. R. (1993). Skodak and Skeels: The inflated mother-child IQ gap. *Intelligence*, 17, 557–561.

Flynn, J. R. (1996). Group differences: Is the good society impossible? *Journal of Biosocial Science*, 28, 573–585.

Fodor, J. A. (1983). *Modularity of mind*. MIT Press, Cambridge, MA.

Fogarty, G. and Stankov, L. (1988). Abilities involved in performance on competing tasks. *Personality and Inividual Differences*, 9, 35–49.

Ford, M. E. and Tisak, M. S. (1983). A further search for social intelligence. *Journal of Educational Psychology*, 75, 197–206.

Fraser, E. D. (1959). *Home environment and the school*. University of London Press, London.

Frearson, W. M., Barrett, P., and Eysenck, H. J. (1988). Intelligence, reaction time, and the effects of smoking. *Personality and Individual Differences*, 9, 497–519.

Freeman, F. N., Holzinger, K. J., and Mitchell, B. C. (1928). The influence of environment on the intelligence, school achievement, and conduct of foster children. *27th Yearbook of the National Society for the Study of Education*, 27, Part I.

Fulton, M., Thomson, G., Hunter, R., Raab, G., Laxen, D., and Hepburn, W. (1987). Influence of blood lead on the ability and attainment of children in Edinburgh. *Lancet*, 1, 1221–1226.

Galton, F. (1869). *Hereditary genius: An inquiry into its laws and consequences*. Macmillan, London.

Galton, F. (1883). *Inquiries into human faculty, and its development*. Macmillan, London.

Galton, F. (1908). *Memories of my life*. Methuen, London.

Garber, H. L. (1988). *The Milwaukee Project: Preventing mental retardation in children at risk*. American Association on Mental Retardation, Washington, DC.

Garcia, J. (1981). The logic and limits of mental aptitude testing. *American Psychlogist*, 36, 1172–1180.

Gardner, H. (1993). *Frames of mind*, (2nd edn). Basic Books, New York.

Gardner, H. (1997). *Extraordinary minds*. Basic Books, New York.

Garnham, A. and Oakhill, J. (1994). *Thinking and reasoning*. Blackwell, Oxford.

Gathercole, S. E. and Baddeley , A. D. (1990). The role of phonological memory in vocabulary acquisition—A study of young children learning new names. *British Journal of Psychology*, 81, 439–454.

Gathercole, S. E. and Baddeley, A. D. (1993). *Working memory and language*. Erlbaum, Hove.

Gaw, F. (1925). A study of performance tests. *British Journal of Psychology*, 15, 374–392.

Gentner, D. (1989). The mechanisms of analogical reasoning. In *Similarity and analogical reasoning*, (ed. S. Vosniadou and A. Ortony). Cambridge University Press, Cambridge.

Geschwind, N. and Galaburda, A. M. (1987). *Cerebral lateralization: Biological mechanisms, associations and pathology*. MIT Press, Cambridge, MA.

Ghiselli, E. E. (1966). *The validity of occupational aptitude tests*. Wiley, New York.

Giannitrapani, D. (1985). *The electrophysiology of intellectual function*. Karger, Basel.

Gick, M. L. and Holyoak, K. J. (1980). Analogical problem solving. *Cognitive Psychology*, 12, 306–355.

Gick, M. L. and Holyoak, K. J. (1983). Schema induction and analogical transfer. *Cognitive Psychology*, 15, 1–38.

Gilhooly, K. J., Logie, R. H., Wetherick, N. E., and Wynn, V. (1993). Working memory and strategies in syllogistic reasoning tasks. *Memory and Cognition*, 21, 115–124.

Glick, J. (1975). Cognitive development in cross-cultural perspective. In *Review of child development research*, (ed. T. D. Horowitz). University of Chicago Press, Chicago.

Goddard, H. H. (1914). *Feeble-mindedness: Its causes and consequences.* Macmillan, New York.

Goddard, H. H. (1916). *Publication of the Vineland Training School.* No. 11. Vineland, NJ.

Goddard, H. H. (1917). Mental tests and the immigrant. *Journal of Delinquency, 2,* 243–277.

Goldberg, R. A., Schwartz, S., and Stewart, M. (1977). Individual differences in cognitive processes. *Journal of Educational Psychology, 69,* 9–14.

Goleman, D. (1996). *Emotional intelligence.* Bloomsbury, London.

Gordon, H. (1923). *Mental and scholastic tests among retarded children.* Board of Education pamphlet No. 44, London.

Gordon, H. W. and Kravetz, S. (1991). The influence of gender, handedness, and performance level on specialized cognitive functioning. *Brain and Cognition, 15,* 37–61.

Gordon, R. A. (1997). Everyday life as an intelligence test: Effects of intelligence and intelligence context. *Intelligence, 24,* 203–320.

Goswami, U. C. (1992). *Analogical reasoning in children.* Erlbaum, Hove.

Gottesman, I. I. (1991). *Schizophrenia genesis.* Freeman, New York.

Gould, S. J. (1986). *The flamingo's smile.* Penguin Books, London.

Gould, S. J. (1997). *The mismeasure of man,* (2nd edn). Penguin Books, London.

Gray, J. L. (1936). *The nation's intelligence.* Watts, London.

Guilford, J. P. (1967). *The nature of human intelligence.* McGraw-Hill, New York.

Guilford, J. P. (1982). Cognitive psychology's ambiguities: Some suggested remedies. *Psychological Review, 89,* 48–59.

Guilford, J. P. and Hoepfner, R. (1971). *The analysis of intelligence.* McGraw Hill, New York.

Gustafsson, J.-E. (1988). Hierarchical models of individual differences in cognitive abilities. In *Advances in the psychology of human intelligence,* (ed. R. J. Sternberg), Vol. 4. Erlbaum, Hillsdale, NJ.

Gutkin, T. B. and Reynolds, C. R. (1981). Factorial similarity of the WISC-R for White and Black children from the standardization sample. *Journal of Educational Psychology, 73,* 227–231.

Hahn, W. K. (1987). Cerebral lateralization of function: From infancy through childhood. *Psychological Bulletin, 101,* 376–392.

Haier, R. J., Robinson, D. L., Braden, W., and Williams, D. (1983). Electric potentials of the cerebral cortex and psychometric intelligence. *Personality and Individual Differences, 4,* 591–599.

Hall, V. C. and Kaye, D. B. (1980). Early patterns of cognitive development. *Monographs of the Society for Research in Child Development,* Serial no. 184.

Halpern, D. E. (1992). *Sex differences in cognitive abilities,* (2nd edn). Lawrence Erlbaum, Hillsdale, NJ.

Hampson, E. (1990). Variations in sex-related cognitive abilities across the menstrual cycle. *Brain and Cognition, 14,* 26–43.

Hanley, J. R., Young. A. W., and Pearson, N. A. (1991). Impairment of the visuo-spatial scratch pad. *Quarterly Journal of Experimental Psychology, 43A,* 101–125.

Harman, H. H. (1976). *Modern factor analysis,* (2nd edn). University of Chicago Press, Chicago.

Harnqvist, K. (1968). Relative changes in intelligence from 3–18. I. Background and methodology. *Scandinavian Journal of Psychology, 9,* 50–64.

Harrell, T. W. and Harrell, M. S. (1945). Army General Classification Test scores for civilian occupations. *Educational and Psychological Measurement, 5,* 229–239.

Harshman, R. A., Hampson, E., and Berenbaum, S. A. (1983). Individual differences in cognitive abilites and brain organization, Part I: Sex and handedness differences in ability. *Canadian Journal of Psychology, 37,* 144–192.

Hartigan, J. and Wigdor, A. K. (1989). Fairness in employment testing: validity generalization, minority issues, and the General Aptitude Test Battery. National Academy Press, Washington, DC.

Hearnshaw, L. S. (1979). *Cyril Burt: psychologist.* Hodder and Stoughton, London.

Heath, A. F. (1981). *Social mobility*. Fontana, London.

Hebb, D. O. (1949). *The organization of behavior: A neuropsychological theory*. John Wiley, New York.

Hebb, D. O. and Penfield, W. (1940). Human behavior after extensive removal from the frontal lobes. *Archives of Neurology and Psychiatry*, 44, 421–438.

Hedges, L.V. and Nowell, A. (1995). Sex differences in mental test scores, variability, and numbers of high scoring individuals. *Science*, 269, 41–45.

Hendrickson, A. E (1982). The biological basis of intelligence. Part I: Theory. In *A model for intelligence*, (ed. H. J. Eysenck). Springer-Verlag, New York.

Hendrickson, A. E. and Hendrickson, D. E. (1980). The biological basis for individual differences in intelligence. *Personality and Individual Differences*, 1, 3–33.

Hendrickson, D. E. (1982). The biological basis of intelligence. Part II: Measurement. In *A model for intelligence*, (ed. H. J. Eysenck). Springer-Verlag, New York.

Hermelin, B. and O'Connor, N. (1978). The idiot savant: flawed genius or clever Hans? *Psychological Medicine*, 13, 479–481.

Herrnstein, R. J. (1973). *IQ in the meritocracy*. Atlantic-Little Brown, Boston.

Herrnstein, R. J. and Murray, C. (1994). *The bell curve: Intelligence and class structure in American life*. Free Press, New York.

Hertzig, M. E., Birch, H. G., Richardson, S. A., and Tizard, J. (1972). Intellectual levels of schoolchildren severely malnourished during the first two years of life. *Paediatrics*, 49, 814–824.

Heyes, C. M. (1994). Social cognition in primates. In *Animal learning and cognition*, (ed. N. J. Mackintosh). Academic Press, London.

Hick, W. E. (1952). On the rate of gain of information. *Quarterly Journal of Experimental Psychology*, 4, 11–26.

Hier, D. B. and Crowley, W. F., Jr (1982). Spatial ability in androgen-deficient men. *The New England Journal of Medicine*, 306, 1202–1205.

Higgins, J. V., Reed, E. W., and Reed, S. C. (1962). Intelligence and family size: A paradox resolved. *Eugenics Quarterly*, 9, 84–90.

Hines, M. (1982). Prenatal gonadal hormones and sex differences in human behavior. *Psychological Bulletin*, 92, 56–80.

Hirschfeld, L. A. and Gelman, S. A. (ed.) (1994). *Mapping the mind: Domain specificity in cognition and culture*. Cambridge University Press, Cambridge.

Hitch, G. J. (1978). The role of short-term working memory in mental arithmetic. *Cognitive Psychology*, 10, 302–323.

Holyoak, K .J. (1984). Analogical thinking and human intelligence. In *Advances in the psychology of human intelligence*, (ed. R. J. Sternberg), Vol. 2. Erlbaum, Hillsdale, NJ.

Horn, J. (1985). Remodeling old models of intelligence. In *Handbook of intelligence*, (ed. B. B. Wolman). Wiley, New York.

Horn, J. L. and Donaldson, G. (1976). On the myth of intellectual decline in adulthood. *American Psychologist*, 31, 701–719.

Horn, J. L. and Knapp, J. R. (1973). On the subjective character of the empirical base of Guilford's structure-of-intellect model. *Psychological Bulletin*, 80, 33–43.

Horn, J. M., Loehlin, J. C., and Willerman, L. (1979). Intellectual resemblance among adoptive and biological relatives: the Texas adoption project. *Behavior Genetics*, 9, 177–207.

Horn, J. M., Loehlin, J. C., and Willerman, L. (1982). Aspects of the inheritance of intellectual abilities. *Behaviour Genetics*, 12, 479–516.

Horn, W. F. and Packard, T. (1985). Early identification of learning problems: a meta-analysis. *Journal of Educational Psychology*, 77, 597–607.

Howe, M. J. A. (1989). *Fragments of genius: The strange feats of idiots savants*. Routledge, London.

Howe, M. J. A. and Smith, J. (1988). Calendar calculating in 'idiots savants': how do they do it? *British Journal of Psychology*, 79, 371–386.

Hull, C. L. (1928). *Aptitude testing*. World Book Co., New York.

Hulme, C., Thomson, N., Muir, C., and Lawrence, A. (1984). Speech rate and the development of short-term memory span. *Journal of Experimental Child Psychology*, 38, 241–253.

Humphrey, N. K. (1976). The social function of intellect. In *Growing points in ethology*, (ed. P. P. G. Bateson and R. A. Hinde). Cambridge University Press, Cambridge.

Hunt, E. (1978). Mechanics of verbal ability. *Psychological Review*, 85, 109–130.

Hunt, E. (1985). Verbal ability. In *Human abilities: An information-processing approach*, (ed. R. J. Sternberg). Freeman, New York.

Hunt, E. (1987). The next word on verbal ability. In *Speed of information-processing and intelligence*, (ed. P. A. Vernon). Ablex, Norwood, NJ.

Hunt, E., Lunneborg, C. L., and Lewis, J. (1975). What does it mean to be high verbal? *Cognitive Psychology*, 7, 194–227.

Hunter, J. E. (1986). Cognitive ability, cognitive aptitudes, job knowledge, and job performance. *Journal of Vocational Behavior*, 29, 340–362.

Hunter, J. E. and Hunter, R. F. (1984). Validity and utility of alternative predictors of a job performance. *Psychological Bulletin*, 96, 72–98.

Hunter, J. E., Schmidt, F. L., and Rauschenberger, J. (1984). Methodological, statistical, and ethical issues in the study of bias in psychological tests. In *Perspectives on bias in mental testing*, (ed. C. R. Reynolds and R. T. Brown). Plenum, New York.

Husén, T. (1959). *Psychological twin research*. Almqvist and Wiksell, Stockholm.

Husén, T. (1960). Abilities of twins. *Scandinavian Journal of Psychology*, 1, 125-135.

Hyde, J. S. (1981). How large are cognitive gender differences? *American Psychologist*, 36, 892–901.

Hyde, J. S. and Linn, M. C. (1988). Gender differences in verbal ability: A meta-analysis. *Psychological Bulletin*, 104, 153–169.

Hyde, J. S., Fennema, E., and Lamon, S. J. (1990). Gender differences in mathematics performance: A meta-analysis. *Psychological Bulletin*, 107, 139–155.

Irwin, R. J. (1984). Inspection time and its relation to intelligence. *Intelligence*, 8, 47–65.

Jacklin, C. N., Wilcox, K. T., and Maccoby, E. E. (1988). Neonatal sex-steroid hormones and intellectual abilities of six year old boys and girls. *Developmental Psychobiology*, 21, 567–574.

Jackson, M. (1980). Further evidence for a relationship between memory access and reading ability. *Journal of Verbal Learning and Verbal Behavior*, 19, 683–694.

Jencks, C. (1972). *Inequality: A reassessment of the effect of family and schooling in America*. Basic Books, New York.

Jencks, C. (1979). *Who gets ahead? The determinants of economic success in America*. Basic Books, New York.

Jencks, C. (1992). *Rethinking social policy: Race, poverty, and the underclass*. Harvard University Press, Cambridge, MA.

Jensen, A. R. (1969). How much can we boost IQ and scholastic achievement? *Harvard Educational Review*, 39, 1–123.

Jensen, A. R. (1973). *Educability and group differences*. Methuen, London.

Jensen, A. R. (1980). *Bias in mental testing*. Methuen, London.

Jensen, A. R. (1981). *Straight talk about mental tests*. Methuen, London.

Jensen, A. R. (1982). The chronometry of intelligence. In *Advances in the psychology of human intelligence*, (ed. R. J. Sternberg), Vol. 1. Erlbaum, Hillsdale, NJ.

Jensen, A. R. (1985). The nature of the black–white difference on various psychometric tests: Spearman's hypothesis. *Behavioral and Brain Sciences*, 8, 193–219.

Jensen, A. R. (1987*a*). Differential psychology: Towards consensus. In *Arthur Jensen: consensus and controversy*, (ed. S. Modgil and C. Modgil). The Falmer Press, New York.

Jensen, A. R. (1987*b*). Individual differences in the Hick paradigm. In *Speed of information-processing and intelligence*, (ed. P. A. Vernon). Ablex, Northwood, NJ.

Jensen, A. R. (1989). Raising IQ without increasing *g*? A review of the Milwaukee Project: Preventing mental retardation in children at risk. *Developmental Review*, 9, 234–258.

Jensen, A. R. (1990). Speed of information processing in a calculating prodigy. *Intelligence*, 14, 259–274.

Jensen, A. R. (1997) The puzzle of nongenetic variance. In *Intelligence, heredity and environment*, (ed. R. J. Sternberg and E. Grigorenko). Cambridge University Press, Cambridge.

Jensen, A. R. and Figueroa, R. A. (1975). Forward and backward digit-span interaction with race and IQ: Predictions from Jensen's theory. *Journal of Educational Psychology*, 67, 882–893.

Jensen, A. R. and Reynolds, C. R. (1983). Sex differences on the WISC-R. *Personality and Individual Differences*, 4, 223–226.

Jensen, A. R. and Sinha, S. N. (1993). Physical correlates of human intelligence. In *Biological approaches to the study of human intelligence*, (ed. P. A. Vernon). Ablex, Norwood, NJ.

Jensen, A. R. and Whang, P. A. (1993). Reaction times and intelligence: A comparison of Chinese–American and Anglo-American children. *Journal of Biosocial Science*, 25, 397–410.

Johnson, M. H. and Morton, J. (1991). *Biology and cognitive development*. Blackwell, Oxford.

Johnson-Laird, P. N. (1983). *Mental models*. Cambridge University Press, Cambridge.

Johnson-Laird, P. N. and Byrne, R. M. J. (1991). *Deduction*. Erlbaum, Hove.

Jones, S. (1996). *In the blood: God, genes and destiny*. Harper Collins, London:

Jonides, J., Smith, E. E., Koeppe, R. A., Awh, E., Minoshima, S., and Mintun, M. A. (1993). Spatial working memory in humans as revealed by PET. *Nature*, 363, 623–625.

Joynson, R. B. (1989). *The Burt affair*. Routledge, London.

Juel-Nielsen, N. (1980). *Individual and environment: Monozygotic twins reared apart*. (Revised edition of 1965 Monograph.) International Universities Press, New York.

Jurden, F. H. (1995). Individual differences in working memory and complex cognition. *Journal of Educational Psychology*, 87, 93–102.

Just, M. A. and Carpenter, P. A. (1992). A capacity theory of comprehension: individual differences in working memory. *Psychological Review*, 99, 122–149.

Kail, R. (1991). Developmental change in speed of processing during childhood and adolescence. *Psychological Bulletin*, 109, 490–501.

Kail, R., Carter, P., and Pellegrino, J. W. (1979). The locus of sex differences in spatial ability. *Perception and Psychophysics*, 26, 182–186.

Kamin, L. J. (1974). *The science and politics of IQ*. Erlbaum, Potomac, MD.

Kamin, L. J. (1981). *Intelligence: The battle for the mind*. (H. J. Eysenck versus Leon Kamin). Macmillan, London.

Karier, C. J. (1972). Testing for order and control in the corporate liberal state. *Educational Theory*, 22, 154–180.

Kaufman, A. S. and Doppelt, J. E. (1976). Analysis of WISC-R standardization data in terms of the stratification data. *Child Development*, 47, 165–171.

Keane, M. (1987). On retrieving analogues when solving problems. *Quarterly Journal of Experimental Psychology*, 39A, 29–41.

Keil, F. (1984). Mechanisms in cognitive development and the structure of knowledge. In *Mechanisms in Cognitive Development*, (ed. R. J. Sternberg). W.H. Freeman, New York.

Kevles, D. J. (1985). *In the name of eugenics: Genetics and the uses of human heredity*. Knopf, New York.

Kimura, D. and Hampson, E. (1992). Neural and hormonal mechanisms mediating sex differences in cognition. In *Biological approaches to human intelligence*, (ed. P. A. Vernon). Ablex, Norwood, NJ.

Klemp, G. O. and McClelland, D. C. (1986). What characterizes intelligent functioning among senior managers? In *Practical intelligence: nature and origins of competence in the everyday world*, (ed. R. J. Sternberg and R. K. Wagner). Cambridge University Press, Cambridge.

Kline, P. (1991). *Intelligence: The psychometric view*. Routledge, London.

Kline, P. (1993). *Personality: The psychometric view*. Routledge, London.

Kosslyn, S. M. (1983). *Ghosts in the mind's machine: Creating and using images in the brain*. Norton, New York.

Kranzler, J. H. and Jensen, A. R. (1989). Inspection time and intelligence: A meta-analysis. *Intelligence, 13*, 329–347.

Kranzler, J. H. and Jensen, A. R. (1991). The nature of psychometric g: Unitary process or a number of independent processes? *Intelligence, 15*, 397–422.

Krashen, S. D. (1989). We acquire vocabulary and spelling by reading: Additional evidence for the input hypothesis. *The Modern Language Journal, 73*, 440–464.

Kyllonen, P. C. and Christal, R. E. (1990). Reasoning ability is (little more than) working memory capacity?! *Intelligence, 14*, (4), 389–433.

Landsdown, R. and Yule, W. (eds) (1986). *The lead debate: The environment, toxicology, and child health*. Croom Helm, London.

Langsford, P. B., Mackenzie, B. D., and Maher, D. P. (1994). Auditory inspection time, sustained attention, and the fundamentality of mental speed. *Personality and Individual Differences, 16*, 487–497.

Lansman, M., Donaldson, G., Hunt, E., and Yantis, S. (1982). Ability factors and cognitive processes. *Intelligence, 6*, 347–386.

Larson, G. E. and Alderton, D. L. (1990). Reaction time variability and intelligence: 'Worst performance' analysis of individual differences. *Intelligence, 14*, 309–325.

Larson, G. E. and Saccuzzo, D. P. (1989). Cognitive correlates of general intelligence: toward a process theory of g. *Intelligence, 13*, 5–31.

Larson, G. E., Merritt, C. R., and Williams, S. E. (1988). Information processing and intelligence: Some implications of task complexity. *Intelligence, 12*, 131–147.

Lave, J., Murtaugh, M., and de la Roche, O. (1984). The dialectic of arithmetic in grocery shopping. In *Everyday cognition: Its development in social context*, (ed. B. Rogoff and J. Lave). Harvard University Press, Cambridge, MA.

Lavin, D. E. (1965). *The prediction of academic performance: A theoretical analysis and review of research*. Russell Sage Foundation, New York.

Lawrence, E. M. (1931). An investigation into the relation between intelligence and inheritance. *British Journal of Psychology*, (Monograph Supplement), **16**, 1–80.

Lazar, I. and Darlington, R. (1982). Lasting effects of early education: A report from the consortium for longitudinal studies. *Monographs of the Society for Research in Child Development, 47*.

Leahy, A. (1935). Nature–nurture and intelligence. *Genetic Psychology Monographs, 17*, 236–308.

Leather, C. V. and Henry, L. A. (1994). Working memory span and phonological awareness tasks as predictors of early reading ability. *Journal of Experimental Child Psychology, 58*, 88–111.

Legree, P. J., Pifer, M. E., and Grafton, F. C. (1996). Correlations among cognitive abilities are lower for higher ability groups. *Intelligence, 23*, 45–57.

Leslie, A. M. (1994). ToMM, ToBY, and Agency: Core architecture and domain specificity. In *Mapping the mind: Domain specificity in cognition and culture*, (ed. L. A. Hirschfeld and S. A. Gelman). Cambridge University Press, Cambridge.

Levy, J. (1976). Cerebral lateralization and spatial ability. *Behavior Genetics, 6*, 171–188.

Levy, P. (1992). Inspection time and its relation to intelligence: issues of measurement and meaning. *Personality and Individual Differences, 13*, (9), 987–1002.

Lewis, E. O. (1933). Types of mental deficiency and their social significance. *Journal of Mental Science,* 79, 293–304.

Lewontin, R. C. (1975). Genetic aspects of intelligence. *Annual Review of Genetics,* 9, 387–405.

Linn, M. C. and Peterson, A. C. (1985). Emergence and characterization of sex differences in spatial ability: A meta-analysis. *Child Development,* 56, 1479–1498.

Linn, R. L. (1973). Fair test use in selection. *Review of Education Research,* 43, 139–161.

Locurto, C. (1991a). Sense and Nonsense about IQ: The case for uniqueness. Praeger, New York.

Locurto, C. (1991b). Beyond IQ in preschool programs? *Intelligence,* 15, 295–312.

Loehlin, J. C. (1989). Partitioning environmental and genetic contributions to behavioral development. *American Psychologist,* 44, 1285–1292.

Loehlin, J. C. (1992). *Genes and environment in personality development.* Sage, Newbury Park, CA.

Loehlin, J. C. and Nichols, R. C. (1976). *Heredity, environment and personality: A study of 850 sets of twins.* University of Texas Press, Austin, TX.

Loehlin, J. C., Lindzey, G., and Spuhler, J. M. (1975). *Race differences in intelligence.* Freeman, San Francisco.

Loehlin, J. C., Horn, J. M., and Willerman, L. (1989). Modeling IQ change: Evidence from the Texas adoption project. *Child Development,* 60, 993–1004.

Logie, R. H. (1995). *Visuo-spatial working memory.* Erlbaum, Hove.

Logie, R. H. and Marchetti, C. (1991). Visuo-spatial working memory: Visual, spatial or central executive? In *Mental images in human cognition,* (ed. R. H. Logie and M. Denis). North Holland Press, Amsterdam.

Logie, R. H., Gilhooly, K. J., and Wynn, V. (1994). Counting on working memory in arithmetic problem solving. *Memory and Cognition,* 22, 395–410.

Lohman, D. F. (1988). Spatial abilities as traits, processes, and knowledge. In *Advances in the psychology of human intelligence,* (ed. R. J. Sternberg), Vol. 4. Lawrence Erlbaum, Hillsdale, NJ.

Longstreth, L. E., Davis, B., Carter, L., Flint, D., Owen, J., Rickert, M., and Taylor, E. (1981). Separation of home intellectual environment and maternal IQ as determinants of child's IQ. *Developmental Psychology,* 17, 532–541.

Lubinski, D. and Humphreys, L. G. (1990). A broadly based analysis of mathematical giftedness. *Intelligence,* 14, 327–355.

Lubinski, D. and Humphreys, L. G. (1997). Incorporating general intelligence into epidemiology and the social sciences. *Intelligence,* 24, 159–201.

Luria, A. R. (1966). *Higher cortical functions in man.* Tavistock Publications, London.

Luria, A. R. (1976). *Cognitive development, its cultural and social foundations.* Harvard University Press, Cambridge, MA.

Lynn, R. (1978). Ethnic and racial differences in intelligence: International comparisons. In *Human variation: The biopsychology of age, race, and sex,* (ed. R. T. Osborne, C. E. Noble, and N. Weyl). Academic Press, New York.

Lynn, R. (1982). IQ in Japan and the United States shows a growing disparity. *Nature,* 297, 222–223.

Lynn, R. (1990). The role of nutrition in secular increases in intelligence. *Personality and Individual Differences,* 3, 273–285.

Lynn, R. (1991). Race differences in intelligence: a global perspective. *Mankind Quarterly,* 31, 255–296.

Lynn, R. (1992). Does Spearman's g decline at high-IQ levels? Some evidence from Scotland. *Journal of Genetic Psychology,* 153, 229–230.

Lynn, R. (1994a). Some reinterpretations of the Minnesota transracial adoption study. *Intelligence,* 19, 21–27.

Lynn, R. (1994b). Sex differences in intelligence and brain size: A paradox resolved. *Personality and Individual Differences,* 17, (2), 257–271.

Lynn, R. (1996a). *Dysgenics: Genetic deterioration in modern populations*. Praeger, Westport, CT.

Lynn, R. (1996b). Racial and ethnic differences in intelligence in the United States on the Differential Ability Scale. *Personality and Individual Differences*, 20, 271–273.

Lynn, R. (1997). Geographical variation in intelligence. In *The Scientific study of human nature: Tribute to H. J. Eysenck at eighty*, (ed. H. Nyborg). Erlbaum, Hillsdale, NJ.

Lynn, R. and Hampson, S. (1986a). The rise of national intelligence: evidence from Britain, Japan and the USA. *Personality and Individual Differences*, 7, 23–32.

Lynn, R. and Hampson, S. (1986b). The structure of Japanese abilities: An analysis in terms of the hierarchical model of intelligence. *Current Psychological Research and Reviews*, 41, 309–322.

Lynn, R. and Pagliari, C. (1994). The intelligence of American children is still rising. *Journal of Biosocial Science*, 26, 65–67.

Lynn, R., Hampson, S. L., and Howden, V. (1988a). The intelligence of Scottish children, 1932–1986. *Studies in Education*, 6, 19–25.

Lynn, R., Pagliari, C., and Chann, J. (1988b). Intelligence in Hong Kong measured for Spearman's g and the neurospatial and verbal primaries. *Intelligence*, 12, 423–433.

McCall, R. B. (1977). Childhood IQ's as predictors of adult educational and occupational status. *Science*, 197, 482–483.

McCall, R. B. and Carriger, M. S. (1993). A meta-analysis of infant habituation and recognition memory performance as predictors of later IQ. *Child Development*, 64, 57–79.

McCarthy, R. A. and Warrington, E. K. (1990). *Cognitive neuropsychology*. Academic Press, London.

McCartney, M., Harris, O., and Bernieri, F. (1990). Growing up and growing apart: A developmental meta-analysis of twin studies. *Psychological Bulletin*, 107, 226–237.

McClelland, D. C. (1973). Testing for competence rather than for 'intelligence'. *American Psychologist*, 28, 1–14.

Maccoby, E. E. and Jacklin, C. N. (1974). *The psychology of sex differences*. Stanford University Press, Stanford, CA.

McGeorge, P., Crawford, J. R., and Kelly, S. W. (1996). The relationship between WAIS-R abilities and speed of processing in a word identification task. *Intelligence*, 23, 175–190.

McGlone, J. (1980). Sex differences in brain asymmetry: A critical survey. *Behavioral and Brain Sciences*, 3, 215–264.

McGue, M. and Bouchard, T.J., Jr (1989). Genetic and environmental determinant of information processing and special mental abilities: A twin analysis. In *Advances in the psychology of human intelligence*, (ed. R. J. Sternberg), Vol. 5. Erlbaum, Hillsdale, NJ.

McGue, M., Bouchard, T. J., Jr, Iacono, W. G., and Lykken, D. T. (1993). Behavioral genetics of cognitive ability: A life-span perspective. In *Nature, nurture and psychology*, (ed. R. Plomin and G. E. McClearn). American Psychological Association, Washington, DC.

Mackenzie, B. and Bingham, E. (1985). IQ, inspection time, and response strategies in a university population. *Australian Journal of Psychology*, 37, 257–268.

MacKinnon, D. W. (1962). The nature and nurture of creative talent. *American Psychologist*, 17, 484–495.

Mackintosh, N. J. (1983). *Conditioning and associative learning*. Oxford University Press, Oxford.

Mackintosh, N. J. (ed.) (1995). *Cyril Burt: Fraud or framed?* Oxford University Press, Oxford.

Mackintosh, N. J. (1996). Sex differences and IQ. *Journal of Biosocial Science*, 28, 559–571.

Mackintosh, N. J. and Bennett, E. S. (1998). IQ, implicit learning and educational attainment, (in preparation).

Mackintosh, N. J. and Mascie-Taylor, C. G. N. (1986). The IQ question. In *Personality, cognition and values*, (ed. C. Bagley and G. K. Verma). Macmillan, London.

McLaren, I. P. L., Green, R. E. A., and Mackintosh, N. J. (1994). Animal learning and the implicit/

explicit distinction. In *Implicit and explicit learning of languages*, (ed. N. C. Ellis). Academic Press, London.

MacLeod, C. M., Hunt, E. B., and Mathews, N. N. (1978). Individual differences in the verification of sentence–picture relationships. *Journal of Verbal Learning and Verbal Behavior*, 17, 493–507.

McLoughlin, C. S. and Koh, T. H. (1982). Testing intelligence: A decision suitable for the psychologist. *Bulletin of the British Psychological Society*, 35, 308–311.

McMichael, A. J., Baghurst, P. A., Wigg, N. R., Vimpani, G. V., Robertson, E. F., and Roberts, R. J. (1988). Port Pirie cohort study: Environmental exposure to lead and children's abilities at the age of four years. *New England Journal of Medicine*, 319, 468–475.

Mahaffey, K. R., Annest, J. L., Roberts, J., and Murphy, R. S. (1982). National estimates of blood lead levels: United States, 1976–1980. *New England Journal of Medicine*, 307, 573–579.

Manktelow, K. I. and Over, D. E. (1990). Deontic thought and the selection task. In *Lines of thinking: Reflections on the psychology of thinking*, (ed. K. Gilhooly, M. Keane, R. Logie and G. Erdos), Vol. 1. John Wiley and Sons, Chichester.

Manning, W. H. and Jackson, R. (1984). College entrance examinations: Objective selection or gatekeeping for the economically privileged. In *Perspectives on bias in mental testing*, (ed. C. R. Reynolds and R. T. Brown). Plenum, New York.

Marjoribanks, K. (1972). Ethnic and environmental influences on mental abilities. *American Journal of Sociology*, 78, 323–337.

Martin, M. (1978). Memory span as a measure of individual differences in memory capacity. *Memory and Cognition*, 6, 194–198.

Martin, R. C. (1993). Short-term memory and sentence processing: Evidence from neuropsychology. *Memory and Cognition*, 21, 176–183.

Mascie-Taylor, C. G. N. (1984). Biosocial correlates of IQ. In *The biology of human intelligence*, (C. J. Turner and H. B. Miles). Proceedings of the 20th Annual Symposium of the Eugenics Society, London.

Mascie-Taylor, C. G. N. and Gibson, J. B. (1978). Social mobility and IQ components. *Journal of Biosocial Science*, 10, 263–76.

Masters, M. S. and Sanders, B. (1993). Is the gender difference in mental rotation disappearing? *Behavior Genetics*, 23, 337–341.

Mayer, J. D. and Salovey, P. (1993). The intelligence of emotional intelligence. *Intelligence*, 17, 433–442.

Medawar, P. B. (1982). *Pluto's Republic.* Oxford University Press, Oxford.

Mehta, Z. and Newcombe, F. (1991). A role for the left hemisphere in spatial processing. *Cortex*, 27, 153–167.

Mercer, J. R. (1973). *Labeling the retarded.* University of California Press, Berkeley, CA.

Mercer, J. R. (1984). What is a racially and culturally nondiscriminatory test? A sociological and pluralistic perspective. In *Perspectives on bias in mental testing*, (ed. C. R. Reynolds and R. T. Brown). Plenum, New York.

Mercer, J. R. and Lewis, J. F. (1978). *System of multicultural pluralistic assessment.* Psychological Corporation, New York.

Merkel, J. (1885). Die zeitlichen Verhaltnisse der Willensthatigkeit. *Philosophische Studien*, 2, 73–127.

Meyers, C. E., Nihira, K., and Zetlin, A. (1979). The measurement of adaptive behavior. In *The handbook of mental deficiency, psychological theory and research*, (2nd edn), (ed. N. Ellis). Erlbaum, Hillsdale, NJ.

Michael, J. S. (1988). A new look at Morton's craniological research. *Current Anthropology*, 29, 349–354.

Miles, T. R. (1957). Contributions to intelligence testing and the theory of intelligence: I. On defining intelligence. *British Journal of Educational Psychology*, 27, 153–165.

Miller, G. W. (1970). Factors in school achievement and social class. *Journal of Educational Psychology*, 61, 260–269.

Miller, L. T. and Vernon, P. A. (1992). The general factor in short-term memory, intelligence and reaction time. *Intelligence*, 16, 5–29.

Mishkin, M. (1964). Perseveration of central sets after frontal lesions in monkeys. In *The frontal granular cortex and behaviour*, (ed. J. M. Warren and K. Akert). McGraw-Hill, New York.

Mishkin, M. and Manning, F. J. (1978). Non-spatial memory after selective prefrontal lesions in monkeys. *Brain Research*, 143, 313–323.

Moore, E. G. J. (1986). Family socialization and the IQ test performance of traditionally and transracially adopted black children. *Developmental Psychology*, 22, 317–326.

Morley, R. (1996). The influence of early diet on later development. *Journal of Biosocial Science*, 28, 481–487.

Morris, R. G., Ahmed, S., Syed, G. M., and Toone, B. K. (1993). Neural correlates of planning ability: frontal lobe activation during the Tower of London test. *Neuropsychologia*, 13, 67–78.

Nagoshi, C. T. and Johnson, R. A. (1987). Cognitive ability profiles of Caucasian vs. Japanese subjects in the Hawaii Family Study of Cognition. *Personality and Individual Differences*, 8, 581–583.

Needleman, H. C. *et al.* (1979). Deficits in psychological and classroom performance of children with elevated dentine lead levels. *New England Journal of Medicine*, 300, 689–695.

Needleman, H. C., Geiger, S. K., and Frank, R. (1985). Lead and IQ scores: a reanalysis. *Science*, 227, 701–703.

Neisser, U. (1976). General, academic, and artificial intelligence. In *The nature of intelligence*, (ed. L. Resnick). Erlbaum, Hillsdale, NJ.

Neisser, U. (1996). Intelligence: Knowns and unknowns. *American Psychologist*, 51, 77–101.

Netley, C. and Rovet, J. (1982). Verbal deficits in children with 47, XXY and 47, XXX karyotypes: A disruptive and experimental study. *Brain and Language*, 17, 58–72.

Nettelbeck, T. (1987). Inspection time and intelligence. In *Speed of information processing and intelligence*, (ed. P. A. Vernon). Ablex, Norwood, NJ.

Nettelbeck, T. and Kirby, N. H. (1983). Measures of timed performance and intelligence. *Intelligence*, 7, 39–52.

Nettelbeck, T. and Lalley, M. (1976). Inspection time and measured intelligence. *British Journal of Psychology*, 67, 17–22.

Nettelbeck, T., Edwards, C., and Vreugdenhil, A. (1986). Inspection time and IQ: Evidence for a mental speed-ability association. *Personality and Individual Differences*, 7, 633–641.

Neubauer, A. C. and Bucik, V. (1996). The mental speed–IQ relationship: Unitary or modular. *Intelligence*, 22, 23–48.

Neubauer, A. C. and Freudenthaler, H. H. (1994). Reaction-times in a sentence picture verification test and intelligence: Individual strategies and effects of extended practice. *Intelligence*, 19, 193–218.

Newman, H. H., Freeman, F. N., and Holzinger, K. H. (1937). *Twins: A study of heredity and environment*. University of Chicago Press, Chicago.

Nichols, R. C. (1987). Racial differences in intelligence. In *Arthur Jensen: Consensus and controversy*, (ed. S. Modgil and C. Modgil). Falmer Press, New York.

Nicolson, R. (1981). The relatioship between memory span and processing speed. In *Intelligence and learning*, (ed. M. Friedman, J. P. Das, and N. O'Connor). Plenum Press, New York.

Norman, D. A. and Shallice, T. (1986). Attention to action: Willed and automatic control of behaviour. In *Consciousness and self-regulation. Advances in research and theory*, (ed. R. J. Davidson, G. E. Schwarts, and D. Shapiro), Vol. 4. Plenum Press, New York.

Oden, M. H. (1968). The fulfillment of promise: 40 year follow-up of the Terman gifted group. *Genetic Psychology Monographs*, 77, 3–93.

Owen, A. M. (1997). The functional organization of working memory processes within human lateral frontal cortex: The contribution of functional neuroimaging. *European Journal of Neuroscience*, 9, 1329–1339.

Page, E. B., and Grandon, G. M. (1981). Massive intervention and child intelligence: The Milwaukee Project in critical perspective. *Journal of Special Education*, 15, 239–256.

Parkin, A. J. (1997). *Memory and amnesia*, (2nd edn). Blackwell, Oxford.

Pasamanick, B. and Knobloch, H. (1966). Retrospective studies of the epidemiology of reproductive casualty, old and new. *Merrill-Palmer Quarterly*, 12, 7–26.

Pedersen, N. L., Plomin, R., Nesselroade, J. R., and McClearn, G. E. (1992). A quantitative genetic analysis of cognitive abilities during the second half of the life span. *Psychological Science*, 3, 346–353.

Pellegrino, J. W. (1986). Deductive reasoning ability. In *Human abilities: An information-processing approach*, (ed. R. J. Sternberg). W.H. Freeman, New York.

Penrose, L. S. (1948). The supposed threat of declining intelligence. *American Journal of Mental Deficiency*, 58, 114–118.

Penrose, L. S. and Raven, J. C. (1936). A new series of perceptual tests: Preliminary communication. *British Journal of Medical Psychology*, 16, 97–104.

Perruchet, P. (1994). Learning from complex rule-governed environments: On the proper functions of nonconscious and conscious processes. In *Attention and performance*, (ed. C. Umilta and M. Moscovitch), Vol. XV. MIT Press, Cambridge, MA:.

Petrides, M. (1995). Functional organization of the human frontal cortex for mnemonic processing. *Annals of the New York Academy of Sciences*, 769, 85–96.

Petrides, M., Alivisatos, B., Evans, A. C., and Meyer, E. (1993). Functional activation of the human frontal-cortex during the performance of verbal working memory tasks. *Proceedings of the National Academy of the United States of America*, 90, 878–882.

Petrill, A. A. and Thompson, L. A. (1993). The phenotypic and genetic relationships among measures of cognitive ability, temperament and scholastic achievement. *Behavior Genetics*, 23, 511–518.

Phillip, E. E. (1973). Discussion. In *Law and ethics of A.I.D. and embryo transfer*, (ed. G. E. W. Wolstenholme and D. W. Fitzsimons), Ciba Symposium. Elsevier, North Holland.

Phillips, K. and Fulker, D. W. (1989). Quantitative genetic analysis of longitudinal trends in adoption designs with application to IQ in the Colorado Adoption Project. *Behavior Genetics*, 19, 621–658.

Piaget, J. and Inhelder, B. (1969). *The psychology of the child*. Basic Books, New York.

Pinker, S. (1994). *The language instinct: The new science of language and mind*. Allen Lane, London.

Plomin, R. (1994). *Genetics and experience: The interplay between nature and nurture*. Sage, Thousand Oaks, CA.

Plomin, R. (1997). Identifying genes for cognitive abilities and disabilities. In *Intelligence, heredity and environment*, (ed. R. J. Sternberg and E. Grigorenko). Cambridge University Press, Cambridge.

Plomin, R. and Loehlin, J. C. (1989). Direct and indirect IQ heritability estimates. *Behavior Genetics*, 19, 331–342.

Plomin, R., McClearn, G. E., Pedersen, N. L., Nesselroade, J. R., and Bergeman, C. S. (1988). Genetic influence on childhood family environment perceived retrospectively from the last half of the life span. *Developmental Psychology*, 24, 738–745.

Poltrock, S. E. and Agnoli, F. (1986). Are spatial visualization ability and visual imagery ability equivalent? In *Advances in the psychology of human intelligence*, (ed. R. J. Sternberg), Vol. 3. Erlbaum, Hillsdale, NJ.

Premack, D. and Woodruff, G. (1978). Does the chimpanzee have a theory of mind? *Behavioral and Brain Sciences*, 4, 515–526.

Pylyshyn, Z. W. (1973). What the mind's eye tells the mind's brain: A critique of mental imagery. *Psychological Bulletin*, 80, 1–24.

Pylyshyn, Z. W. (1981). Psychological explanations and knowledge-dependent processes. *Cognition*, 10, 267–274.

Rabbitt, P. (1993). Does it all go together when it goes? The Nineteenth Bartlett Memorial Lecture. *Quarterly Journal of Experimental Psychology: Human Experimental Psychology*, 46A, 385–434.

Ramey, C. T. (1992). (Carolina Abecedarian Project) High-risk children and IQ: Altering intergenerational patterns. *Intelligence*, 16, 239–256.

Raven, J. C. (1938). *Progressive matrices: A perceptual test of intelligence*. H. K. Lewis, London.

Reber, A. S. (1967). Implicit learning of artificial grammars. *Journal of Verbal Learning and Verbal Behavior*, 6, 317–327.

Reber, A. S. (1993). *Implicit learning and tacit knowledge: An essay on the cognitive unconscious*. Oxford University Press, Oxford.

Reber, A. S., Walkenfeld, F. F., and Hernstadt, R. (1991). Implicit and explicit learning: Individual differences and IQ. *Journal of Experimental Psychology: Learning, Memory and Cognition*, 17, 888–896.

Record, R. G., McKeown, T., and Edwards, J. H. (1970). An investigation of the differences in measured intelligence between twins and single births. *Annals of Human Genetics*, 34, 11–20.

Ree, M. J. and Earles, J. A. (1992). Intelligence is the best predictor of job performance. *Current Directions in Psychological Science*, 1, 86–89.

Renner, J. M. and Rosenzweig, M.R. (1987). *Enriched and impoverished environments: Effects on brain and behavior*. Springer-Verlag, New York.

Reschly, D. and Jipson, F. (1976). Ethnicity, geographical locale, age, sex, and urban rural residence as variables in the prevalence of mind retardation. *American Journal of Mental Deficiency*, 81, 154–161.

Reschly, D. J. and Sabers, D. L. (1979). An examination of bias in predicting MAT scores from WISC-R scores for four ethnic-racial groups. *Journal of Educational Measurement*, 16, 1–9.

Rescorla, R. A. (1988). Pavlovian conditioning: It's not what you think it is. *American Psychologist*, 43, 151–160.

Resnick, S. M., Berenbaum, S. A., Gottesman, I. I., and Bouchard, T. J., Jr (1986). Early hormonal influences on cognitive functioning in congenital adrenal hyperplasia. *Developmental Psychology*, 22, 191–198.

Retherford, R. D. and Sewell, W. H. (1988). Intelligence and family size reconsidered. *Social Biology*, 35, 1–40.

Retherford, R. D. and Sewell, W. H. (1991). Birth order and intelligence: further tests of the confluence model. *American Sociological Review*, 56, 141–158.

Reynolds, C. R., Chastain, R. L., Kaufman, A. S., and McLean, J. E. (1987). Demographic characteristics and IQ among adults: Analysis of the WAIS-R standardisation sample as a function of the stratification variables. *Journal of School Psychology*, 25, 323–342.

Rhodes, L., Dustman, R., and Beck, E. (1969). The visual evoked response: A comparison of bright and dull children. *Electroencephalography and Clinical Neurophysiology*, 27, 364–372.

Richardson, K. (1991). *Understanding intelligence*. Open University Press, Milton Keynes.

Robbins, T. W. *et al.* (1996). Working memory in chess. *Memory and Cognition*, 24, 83–93.

Roberts, R. D., Beh, H. C., and Stankov, L. (1988). Hick's law, competing-task performance, and intelligence. *Intelligence*, 12, 111–130.

Robinson, D. L., Haier, R. J., Braden, W., and Krengel, M. (1984). Psychometric intelligence and visual evoked potentials: A replication. *Personality and Individual Differences*, 5, 487–489.

Robitscher, J. (1973). *Eugenic sterilization*. Charles C. Thomas, Springfield, IL.

Rodgers, J. L. and Rowe, D. C. (1985). Does contiguity breed similarity? A within-family analysis of nonshared sources of IQ differences between siblings. *Developmental Psychology*, 21, 743–746.

Roe, A. (1953). A psychological study of eminent psychologists and anthropologists, and a comparison with biological and physical scientists. *Psychological Monographs: General and Applied*, 67, No. 353.

Rose, A. A., and Feldman, J. F. (1995). The prediction of IQ and specific cognitive abilities at 11 years from infancy measures. *Developmental Psychology*, 31, 685–696.

Rose, S., Kamin, L. J., and Lewontin, R. C. (1984). *Not in our genes*. Penguin Books, London.

Rosenthal, R. (1994). Interpersonal expectancy effects: A 30-year perspective. *Current Directions in Psychological Science*, 3, 176–179.

Rosenthal, R. and Jacobson, L. (1968). *Pygmalion in the classroom*. Holt, Rinehart, and Winston, New York.

Rosenthal, R., Hall, J. A., Di Matteo, M. R., Rogers, P. L., and Archer, D. (1979). *Sensitivity to nonverbal communication: The PONS Test*. Johns Hopkins Press, Baltimore.

Roth, E. (1964). Die Geschwindigkeit der Verarbeitung von Information und ihr Zusammenhang mit Intelligenz. *Zeitschrift für Experimentelle und Angewandte Psychologie*, 11, 616–622.

Rovet, J. and Netley, C. (1982). Processing deficits in Turner's Syndrome. *Developmental Psychology*, 18, 77–94.

Rugg, M. D. and Coles, M. G. H. (1995). *Electrophysiology of mind: Event-related brain potentials and cognition*. Oxford University Press, Oxford.

Rush, D., Stein, Z., and Susser, M. (1980). *Diet in pregnancy: A randomized controlled trial of nutritional supplements*. Liss, New York.

Rushton, J. P. (1992). Cranial capacity related to sex, rank and race in a stratified random sample of 6,325 U.S. military personnel. *Intelligence*, 16, 401–413.

Rushton, J. P. (1995). *Race, evolution and behavior: A life history perspective*. Transaction Publishing, New Brunswick, NJ.

Rushton, J. P. and Ankney, C. D. (1996). Brain size and cognitive ability: correlations with age, sex, social class and race. *Psychonomic Bulletin and Review*, 3, 21–36.

Russell, J. (1996). *Agency: Its role in mental development*. Erlbaum (UK) Taylor and Francis, Hove.

Rutter, M., Tizard, J., and Whitmore, K. (1970). *Education, health and behaviour*. Longman, London.

Saccuzzo, D. P., Larson, G. E., and Rimland, B. (1986). Visual, auditory and reaction time approaches to the measurement of speed of information processing and individual differences in intelligence. *Personality and Individual Differences*, 7, 659–667.

Salthouse, T. A. (1991). Mediation of adult age differences in cognition by reductions in working memory and speed of processing. *Psychological Science*, 2, 179–183.

Salthouse, T. A. (1993). Influence of working memory on adult age differences in matrix reasoning. *British Journal of Psychology*, 84, 171–199.

Samelson, F. (1975). On the science and politics of IQ. *Social Research*, 42, 467–488.

Samelson, F. (1979). Putting psychology on the map: Ideology and intelligence testing. In *Psychology in social context*, (ed. A. Buss). Wiley, New York.

Sarason, S. B. and Doris, J. (1979). *Educational handicap, public policy, and social history*. Free Press, New York.

Sausanne, G. (1979). On the relationship between psychometric and anthropometric traits. *American Journal of Physical Anthropology*, 51, 421–423.

Scarr, S. (1992). Developmental theories for the 1990s: Development and individual differences. *Child Development*, 63, 1–19.

Scarr, S. (1997). Behavior—genetic and socialization theories of intelligence: Truce and reconciliation. In *Intelligence: Heredity and environment*, (ed. R. J. Sternberg and E. Grigorenko). Cambridge University Press, New York.

Scarr, S. and Carter-Salzman, L. (1982). Genetics and intelligence. In *Handbook of human intelligence*, (ed. R. J. Sternberg). Cambridge University Press, Cambridge.

Scarr, S. and McCartney, K. (1983). How people make their own environments: a theory of genotype → environment effects. *Developmental Psychology*, 54, 424–435.

Scarr, S. and Weinberg, R. A. (1976). I.Q. test performance of black children adopted by white families. *American Psychologist*, 31, 726–739.

Scarr, S. and Weinberg, R. A. (1977). Intellectual similarities within families of both adopted and biological children. *Intelligence*, 1, 170–191.

Scarr, S. and Weinberg, R. A. (1978). The influence of 'family background' on intellectual attainment. *American Sociological Review*, 43, 674–692.

Scarr, S. and Weinberg, R. A. (1983). The Minnesota adoption studies: Genetic differences and malleability. *Child Development*, 54, 260–267.

Scarr, S., Weinberg, R. A., and Waldman, I. D. (1993). IQ correlations in transracial adoptive families. *Intelligence*, 17, 541–555.

Schaie, K. W. (1990). The optimization of cognitive functioning in old age: Predictions based on cohort-sequential and longitudinal data. In *Successful aging: Perspectives from the behavioural sciences*, (ed. P. M. Baltes and M. M. Baltes). Cambridge University Press, Cambridge.

Schaie, K. W. (1996). *Intellectual development in adulthood: The Seattle Longitudinal Study*. Cambridge University Press, Cambridge.

Schaie, K. W. and Hertzog, C. (1983). Fourteen-year cohort-sequential analyses of adult intellectual development. *Developmental Psychology*, 19, 531–543.

Schama, S. (1989). *Citizens*. Knopf, New York.

Schmidt, F. L., Ones, D. S., and Hunter, J. E. (1992). Personnel selection. *Annual Review of Psychology*, 43, 627–670.

Schneider, W., Körkel, J., and Weinert, F. E. (1990). Expert knowledge, general abilities and text processing. In *Interactions among aptitudes, strategies and knowledge in cognitive performance*, (ed. W. Schneider and F. E. Weinert). Springer-Verlag, New York.

Schoenthaler, S. J., Amos, S. P., Eysenck, H. J., Peritz, E., and Yudkin, J. (1991). Controlled trial of vitamin-mineral supplementation: Effects on intelligence and performance.*Personality and Individual Differences*, 12, 351–362.

Schweinhart, L. J. and Weikart, D. P. (1980). Young children grow up: The effects of the Perry Preschool Program on youths through age 15. *Monograph of the High/Scope Educational Research Foundation*, No. 7.

Scottish Council for Research in Education (1949). *The trend of Scottish intelligence*. London University Press.

Scribner, S. (1986). Thinking in action: some characteristics of practical thought. In *Practical intelligence: Nature and origins of competence in the everyday world* (ed. R. J. Sternberg and R. K. Wagner). Cambridge University Press.

Seashore, H. G., Wesman, A. G., and Doppelt, J. E. (1950). The standardization of the Weschler Intelligence Scale for Children. *Journal of Consulting Psychology*, 14, 99–110.

Seyfarth, R. M. and Cheney, D. L. (1997). Behavioral mechanisms underlying vocal communication in nonhuman primates. *Animal Learning and Behavior*, 25, 249–267.

Shagass, C., Roemer, R. A., Straumanis, J. J., and Josiassen, R. C. (1981). Intelligence as a factor in evoked potential studies in psychopathology. Comparison of low and high IQ subjects. *Biological Psychiatry*, 11, 1007–1029.

Shah, P. and Miyake, A. (1996). The separability of working memory resources for spatial thinking and language processing: An individual differences approach. *Journal of Experimental Psychology: General*, 125, 4–27.

Shallice, T. (1988). *From neuropsychology to mental structure*. Cambridge University Press, Cambridge.

Shanks, D. R. (1994). *Human associative learning*. Cambridge University Press, Cambridge.

Shanks, D. R., Green, R. E. A., and Kolodny, J. A. (1994). A critical examination of the evidence for unconscious (implicit) learning. In *Attention and performance,* (ed. C. Umilta and M. Moscovitch), Vol. XV. MIT Press, Cambridge, MA.

Sharma, R. (1971). Unpublished Ph.D. thesis. University of London, London.

Shaywitz, B. A. *et al.* (1995). Sex differences in the functional organisation of the brain for language. *Nature,* 373, 607–609.

Shepard, R. N. (1978). The mental image. *The American Psychologist,* 33, 125–127.

Shepard, R. N. and Metzler, J. (1971). Mental rotation of three dimensional objects. *Science,* 171, 701–703.

Shields, J. (1962). *Monozygotic twins brought up apart and brought up together.* Oxford University Press, Oxford.

Shields, J. (1978). MZ twins: their use and abuse. In *Twin research: Psychology and methodology,* (ed. W. Nance), Liss, New York.

Shuey, A. M. (1958). *The testing of negro intelligence.* J. P. Bell, Lynchberg, VA.

Shuey, A. M. (1966). *The testing of negro intelligence,* (2nd edn). Social Science Press, New York.

Shute, V. J., Pellegrino, J. W., Hubert, L., and Reynolds, R. W. (1983). The relationship between androgen levels and human spatial abilities. *Bulletin of the Psychonomic Society,* 21, 465–468.

Sigman, M., Neumann, C., Jansen, A. A. J., and Bwibo, N. (1989). Cognitive abilities of Kenyan children in relation to nutrition, family characteristics, and education. *Child Development,* 60, 1463–1474.

Silverstein, A. B. (1982). Factor structure of the Wechsler Adult Intelligence Scale-Revised. *Journal of Consulting and Clinical Psychology,* 50, 661–664.

Skodak, M. and Skeels, H. M. (1949). A final follow-up study of one hundred adopted children. *Journal of Genetic Psychology,* 75, 85–125.

Skuse, D. (1984). Extreme deprivation in early childhood—II. Theoretical issues and a comparative review. *Journal of Child Psychology and Psychiatry,* 31, 893–903.

Smith, E. E., Jonides, J., Koeppe, R. A., Awh, E., Schumacher, E.H., and Minoshima, S. (1995). Spatial versus object working-memory—PET investigations. *Journal of Cognitive Neuroscience,* 7, 337–356.

Smith, I. M. (1964). *Spatial ability: Its educational and social significance.* University of London Press, London

Smyth, M. M. and Pendleton, L. R. (1989). Working memory for movements. *Quarterly Journal of Experimental Psychology,* 41A, 235–250.

Smyth, M. M. and Scholey, K. A. (1992). Determining spatial span: The role of movement time and articulation rate. *Quarterly Journal of Experimental Psychology,* 45A, 479–501.

Smyth, M. M. and Scholey, K. A. (1994). Interference in immediate spatial memory. *Memory and Cognition,* 22, 1–13.

Smyth, M. M. and Scholey, K. A. (1996). Serial order in spatial immediate memory. *Quarterly Journal of Experimental Psychology: Human Experimental Psychology,* 49A, 159–177.

Snow, R. E. (1995). Pygmalion and intelligence. *Current Directions in Psychological Science,* 4, 169–171.

Snow, R. E. and Yalow, E. (1982). Education and intelligence. In *Handbook of human intelligence,* (ed. R. J. Sternberg). Cambridge University Press, Cambridge.

Snow, R. E., Kyllonen, P. C., and Marshalek, B. (1984). The topography of ability and learning correlations. In *Advances in the psychology of human intelligence,* (ed. R. J. Sternberg), Vol. 2. Erlbaum, Hillsdale, NJ.

Snyderman, M. and Herrnstein, R. J. (1983). Intelligence tests and the Immigration Act of 1924. *American Psychologist,* 38, 986–995.

Snyderman, M. and Rothman, S. (1988). *The IQ controversy: The media and public policy.* Transaction Publishers, New Brunswick, NJ.

Sommer, R. and Sommer, B. A. (1983). Mystery in Milwaukee: Early intervention, IQ, and psychology textbooks. *American Psychologist*, 38, 982–985.

Sowell, T. (1978). *Essays and data on American ethnic groups*. The Urban Institute, Washington, DC.

Sowell, T. (1981). *Ethnic America: A history*. Basic Books, New York.

Spearman, C. (1904). General intelligence, objectively determined and measured. *American Journal of Psychology*, 15, 201–293.

Spearman, C. (1927). *The abilities of man*. Macmillan, London.

Spearman, C. and Jones, L. L. (1950). *Human ability*. Macmillan, London.

Spilsbury, G. A. (1992). Complexity as a reflection of the dimensionality of a task. *Intelligence*, 16, 31–45.

Spitz, H. H. (1986). *The raising of intelligence: A selected history of attempts to raise retarded intelligence*. Lawrence Erlbaum Associates, Hillsdale, NJ.

Spitz, H. H. (1992). Does the Carolina Abecedarian early intervention project prevent sociocultural mental retardation? *Intelligence*, 16, 225–237.

Spitz, H. H. (1993). When prophecy fails: On Ramey's response to Spitz's critique of the Abecedarian Project. *Intelligence*, 17, 17–23.

Stafford, R. E. (1961). Sex differences in spatial visualization as evidence of sex-linked inheritance. *Perceptual and Motor Skills*, 13, 428.

Stage, C. (1988). Gender differences in test results. *Scandinavian Journal of Educational Research*, 32, 101–111.

Stanford, W. B. and Luce, J. V. (1974). *The quest for Ulysses*. Phaidon Press, London.

Stankov, L. and Crawford, J. D. (1993). Ingredients of complexity in fluid intelligence. *Learning and Individual Differences*, 5, 73–111.

Staszewski, J. J. (1990). Exceptional memory: The influence of practice and knowledge on the development of elaborative encoding strategies. In *Interactions among aptitudes, strategies, and knowledge in cognitive performance*, (ed. W. Schneider and F. E. Weinert). Springer-Verlag, New York.

Stein, Z., Susser, M., Saenger, G., and Marolla, F. (1972). Nutrition and mental performance. *Science*, 178, 708–713.

Stelzl, I., Merz, F., Ehlers, T., and Remer, H. (1995). The effect of schooling on the development of fluid and crystallized intelligence: A quasi-experimental study. *Intelligence*, 21, 279–296.

Stern, W. (1912). *Die Psychologische Methoden der Intelligenzprüfung*. Barth, Leipzig.

Sternberg, R. J. (1977). *Intelligence, information processing and analogical reasoning: The componential analysis of human abilities*. Erlbaum, Hillsdale, NJ.

Sternberg, R. J. (1985). *Beyond IQ: A triarchic theory of intelligence*. Cambridge University Press, New York.

Sternberg, R. J. (1990). *Metaphors of mind: Conceptions of the nature of intelligence*. Cambridge University Press, New York.

Sternberg, R .J. and Gardner, M. K. (1983). Unities in inductive reasoning. *Journal of Experimental Psychology: General*, 112, 80–116.

Sternberg, R. J. and Powell, J. S. (1983). Comprehending verbal comprehension. *American Psychologist*, 38, 878–893.

Sternberg, R. J. and Rifkin, B. (1979). The development of analogical reasoning processes. *Journal of Experimental Child Psychology*, 27, 195–232.

Sternberg, R. J. and Smith, C. (1985). Social intelligence and decoding skills in nonverbal communication. *Social Cognition*, 3, 168–192.

Sternberg, R. J. and Weil, E. M. (1980). An aptitude-strategy interaction in linear syllogistic reasoning. *Journal of Educational Psychology*, 72, 226–234.

Sternberg, R. J., Conway, B. E., Ketron, J. L., and Bernstein, M. (1981). People's conceptions of intelligence. *Journal of Personality and Social Psychology,* 41, 37–55.

Sternberg, R. J.,Wagner, R. K., Williams, W. M., and Horvath, J. A. (1995). Testing common sense. *American Psychologist,* 50, 912–926.

Sternberg, S. (1975). Memory scanning: new findings and current controversies. *Quarterly Journal of Experimental Psychology,* 17, 1–32.

Stone, B. J. (1992). Prediction of achievement by Asian–American and White children. *Journal of School Psychology,* 30, 91–99.

Stough, C. K. K., Nettelbeck, T., and Cooper, C. J. (1990). Evoked brain potentials, string length and intelligence. *Personality and Individual Differences,* 11, 401–406.

Streissguth, A. P., Barr, H. M., Sampson, P. D., Darby, B. L., and Martin, O. C. (1990). IQ at age 4 in relation to maternal alcohol use and smoking during pregnancy. *Developmental Psychology,* 25, 3–11.

Streufert, S. and Streufert, S. C. (1978). *Behavior in the complex environment.* Winston and Sons, Washington, DC.

Streufert, S. and Swezey, R. W. (1986). *Complexity, managers, and organizations.* Academic Press, Orlando.

Stumpf, H. and Eliot, J. (1995). Gender related differences in spatial ability and the *K* factor of general spatial ability in a population of academically talented students. *Personality and Individual Differences,*19, 33–45.

Sundet, J. M., Tambs, K., Magnus, P., and Berg, K. (1988). On the question of secular trends in the heritability of intelligence test scores: A study of Norwegian twins. *Intelligence,* 12, 47–59.

Sutherland, G. (1984). *Ability, merit and measurement.* Clarendon Press, Oxford.

Taylor, H. F. (1980). The IQ game: A methodological inquiry into the heredity–environment controversy. Rutgers University Press, New Brunswick, NJ.

Teasdale, T. W. and Owen, D. R. (1984). Heredity and familial environment in intelligence and educational level—a sibling study. *Nature,* 309, 620–622.

Teasdale, T. W. and Owen, D. R. (1989). Continuing secular increases in intelligence and a stable prevalence of high intelligence levels. *Intelligence,* 13, 255–262.

Teichner, W. H. and Krebs, M. J. (1974). Laws of visual choice reaction time. *Psychological Review,* 81, 75–98.

Terman, L. M. (1916). *The measurement of intelligence.* Houghton Mifflin, Boston, MA.

Terman, L. M. (1932). An autobiography. In *A history of psychology in autobiography,* (ed. C. Murchison), Vol. 2. Clark University Press, Worcester, MA.

Terman, L. M. and Merrill, M. A. (1937). *Measuring intelligence.* Houghton Mifflin, Boston.

Terman, L. M. and Oden, M. H. (1947). *The gifted child grows up. Genetic studies of genius, IV.* Stanford University Press, Stanford, CA.

Terman, L .M. and Oden, M. H. (1959). *The gifted group at mid-life. Genetic studies of genius, V.* Stanford University Press, Stanford, CA.

Teuber, H. L. (1964). The riddle of frontal lobe function in man. In *The frontal granular cortex and behavior,* (ed. J. M. Warren and K. Albert). McGraw-Hill, New York.

Thomas, H., Jamison, W., and Hummel, D. D. (1973). Observation is insufficient for discovering that the surface of still water is invariantly horizontal. *Science,* 181, 173–174.

Thompson, L. A., Detterman, D. K., and Plomin, R. (1991). Associations between cognitive abilities and scholastic achievement: Genetic overlap but environmental differences. *Psychological Science,* 2, 158–165.

Thompson, L. A., Dettermann, D. K., and Plomin, R. (1993). Differences in heritability across groups differing in ability, revisited. *Behavior Genetics,* 23, 331–336.

Thomson, G. H. (1916). A hierarchy without a general factor. *British Journal of Psychology,* 8, 271–281.

Thomson, G. H. (1921). The Northumberland Mental Tests. *British Journal of Psychology*, 12, 201–222.

Thomson, G. H. (1939). *The factorial analysis of human ability*. University of London Press, London.

Thorndike, E. L. (1925). *The measurement of intelligence*. Teachers College, Columbia University, New York.

Thorndike, R. L. (1987). Stability of factor loadings. *Personality and Individual Differences*, 8, 585–586.

Thurstone, L. L. (1931). Multiple factor analysis. *Psychological Review*, 38, 406–427.

Thurstone, L. L. (1938). *Primary mental abilities*. University of Chicago Press, Chicago.

Thurstone, L. L. (1940). *The vectors of mind*. University of Chicago Press, Chicago.

Thurstone, L. L. (1947). *Multiple factor analysis*. University of Chicago Press, Chicago.

Thurstone, L. L. and Thurstone, T. G. (1941). *Factorial studies of intelligence*. University of Chicago Press, Chicago.

Till, N. (1992). *Mozart and the enlightenment*. Faber and Faber, London.

Tizard, B. (1974). IQ and race. *Nature*, 247, 316.

Tresch, M. C., Sinnamon, H. M., and Seamon, J. C. (1993). Double dissociation of spatial and object visual memory: Evidence from selective interference in intact human subjects. *Neuropsychologia*, 31, 211–219.

Tuddenham, R. D. (1948). Soldier intelligence in World Wars I and II. *American Psychologist*, 3, 54–56.

Ungerleider, L. G. and Mishkin, M. (1982). Two cortical visual systems. In *Analysis of visual behavior*, (ed. D. J. Ingle, M. A. Goodale, and R. J. W. Mansfield). MIT Press, Cambrige, Mass.

Valenstein, E. S. (1973). *Brain control*. Wiley, New York.

VanCourt, M. and Bean, F. D. (1985). Intelligence and fertility in the United States: 1912–1982. *Intelligence*, 9, 23–32.

Van Daalen-Kapteijns, M. M. and Elshout-Mohr, M. (1981). The acquisition of word meanings as a cognitive learning process. *Journal of Verbal Learning and Verbal Behaviour*, 20, 386–399.

Van Valen, L. (1974). Brain size and intelligence in man. *American Journal of Physical Anthropology*, 40, 417–424.

Van Wieringen, J. C. (1978). Secular growth changes. In *Human growth*, (ed. F. Falkner and J. M. Tanner), Vol. 2. Plenum Press, New York.

Vernon, P. A. (1981). Level I and Level II: A review. *Educational Psychologist*, 16, 45–64.

Vernon, P. A. (1987). Level I and Level II revisited. In *Arthur Jensen: Consensus and controversy*, (ed. S. M. Modgil and C. Modgil). Falmer Press, Philadelphia, PA.

Vernon, P. A. and Jensen, A. R. (1984). Individual and group differences in intelligence and speed of information processing. *Personality and Individual Differences*, 5, 911–923.

Vernon, P. A. and Weese, S. E. (1993). Predicting intelligence with multiple speed of information-processing tests. *Personality and Individual Differences*, 14, 413–419.

Vernon, P. A., Nador, S., and Kantor, L. (1985). Group differences in intelligence and speed of information-processing. *Intelligence*, 9, 137–148.

Vernon, P. E. (1947). Research on personnel selection in the Royal Navy and the British Army. *American Psychologist*, 2, 35–51.

Vernon, P. E. (1950). *The structure of human abilities*. Methuen, London.

Vernon, P. E. (1957). *Secondary School selection. A British psychological inquiry*. Methuen, London.

Vernon, P. E. (1969). *Intelligence and cultural environment*. Methuen, London.

Vernon, P. E. (1982). *The abilities and achievements of Orientals in North America*. Academic Press, New York.

Vickers, D. (1979). *Decision processes in visual perception*. Academic Press, London.

Vincent, K. R. (1991). Black/white IQ differences: Does age make the difference? *Journal of Clinical Psychology,* 47, 266–270.

Vining, D. R. (1986). Social versus reproductive success: The central theoretical problem of human sociobiology. *Behavioral and Brain Sciences,* 9, 167–216.

Vining, D. R. (1995). On the possibility of the reemergence of a dysgenic trend with respect to intelligence in American fertility differentials: An update. *Personality and Individual Differences,* 19, 259–263.

Vogel, F., Kruger, J., Schalt, E., Schnobel, R., and Hassling. L. (1987). No consistent relationships between oscillations and latencies of visual evoked EEG potentials and measures of mental performance. *Human Neurobiology,* 6, 173–182.

Voyer, D., Voyer, S., and Bryden, M. P. (1995). Magnitude of sex differences in spatial ability: A meta-analysis and consideration of critical variables. *Psychological Bulletin,* 117, 250–270.

Wagner, R. K. (1994). Context counts: The case of cognitive-ability testing for job selection. In *Mind in context: Interactionist perspectives on human intelligence,* (ed. R. J. Sternberg and R. K. Wagner). Cambridge University Press, Cambridge.

Wagner, R. K. and Sternberg, R. J. (1986). Tacit knowledge and intelligence in the everyday world. In *Practical intelligence: Nature and origins of competence in the everyday world,* (ed. R. J. Sternberg and R. K. Wagner). Cambridge University Press, Cambridge.

Walker, C. H. (1987). Relative importance of domain knowledge and overall aptitude on acquisition of domain-related information. *Cognition and Instruction,* 4, 25–42.

Waller, J. H. (1971). Achievement and social mobility: Relationships among IQ score, education and occupation in two generations. *Social Biology,* 18, 252–259.

Warren, N. (1973). Malnutrition and mental development. *Psychological Bulletin,* 80, 324–328.

Wason, P. (1968). Reasoning about a rule. *Quarterly Journal of Experimental Psychology,* 20, 273–281.

Watkins, M. J., Peynircioglu, Z. F., and Brems, D. J. (1984). Pictorial rehearsal. *Memory and Cognition,* 12, 553–557.

Wechsler, D. (1944). *Measurement of adult intelligence,* (3rd edn). Williams and Wilkins, Baltimore.

Wechsler, D. (1958). *The measurement and appraisal of adult intelligence,* (4th edn). Williams and Wilkins, Baltimore.

Weinberg, R. A., Scarr, S., and Waldman, I. D. (1992). The Minnesota transracial adoption study: A follow-up of IQ test performance at adolescence. *Intelligence,* 16, 117–135.

West, A. M., Mascie-Taylor, C. G. N., and Mackintosh, N. J. (1992). Cognitive and educational attainment in different ethnic groups. *Journal of Biosocial Science,* 24, 539–554.

Weyl, N. (1969). Some comparative performance indexes of American ethnic minorities. *Mankind Quarterly,* 9, 106–119.

White, K. R. (1982). The relation between socioeconomic status and academic achievement. *Psychological Bulletin,* 91, 461–481.

Widaman, K. F. and Carlson, J. S. (1989). Procedural effects on performance in the Hick paradigm: Bias in reaction time and movement time parameters. *Intelligence,* 13, 63–85.

Willerman, L., Horn, J. M., and Loehlin, J. C. (1977). The aptitude-achievement test distinction: a study of unrelated children reared together. *Behavior Genetics,* 7, 465–470.

Willingham, D. B., Greeley, T., and Bardone, A. M. (1993). Dissociation in a serial response time task using a recognition measure: Comment on Perruchet and Amorin (1992). *Journal of Experimental Psychology: Learning Memory and Cognition,* 19, 1424–1430.

Wilson, R. S. (1983). The Louisville Twin Study: Developmental synchronies in behavior. *Child Development,* 54, 298–316.

Wilson, F. A. W., O Scalhaide, S. P., and Goldman-Rakic, P. S. (1993). Dissociation of object and spatial processing domains in primate prefrontal cortex. *Science,* 260, 1955–1958.

Wissler, C. (1901). The correlation of mental and physical tests. *Psychological Review Monograph Supplement*, 3, no. 6.

Wolf, R. M. (1965). The measurement of environments. In *Proceedings of the 1964 Invited Conference on Testing Problems*, (ed. C. W. Harris). Educational Testing Service, Princeton, NJ.

Woodrow, H. (1940). Interrelations of measures of learning. *Journal of Psychology*, 10, 49–73.

Yoakum, L. S. and Yerkes, R. M. (1920). *Army mental tests*. Holt, New York.

Zajonc, R. B. (1983). Validating the confluence model. *Psychological Bulletin*, 93, 457–480.

Zajonc, R. B. and Markus, G. B. (1975). Birth order and intellectual development. *Psychological Review*, 82, 74–88.

Zajonc, R. B., Markus, G. B., Berbaum, M. L., Bargh, J. A., and Moreland, R. L. (1991). One justified criticism plus three flawed analyses equals two unwarranted conclusions—a reply. *American Sociological Review*, 56, 159–165.

Zhang, Y., Caryl, P. G., and Deary, I. J. (1989). Evoked potential correlates of inspection time. *Personality and Individual Differences*, **10**, 379–384.

Zigler, E. and Muenchow, S. (1992). *Head start: The inside story of America's most successful educational experiment*. Basic Books, New York.

Author index

Subject index